Lecture Notes in Computer Science　9864

Commenced Publication in 1973
Founding and Former Series Editors:
Gerhard Goos, Juris Hartmanis, and Jan van Leeuwen

Wenfeng Li · Shawkat Ali
Gabriel Lodewijks · Giancarlo Fortino
Giuseppe Di Fatta · Zhouping Yin
Mukaddim Pathan · Antonio Guerrieri
Qiang Wang (Eds.)

Internet and Distributed Computing Systems

9th International Conference, IDCS 2016
Wuhan, China, September 28–30, 2016
Proceedings

 Springer

Editors
Wenfeng Li
Wuhan University of Technology
Wuhan
China

Shawkat Ali
Central Queensland University
North Rockhampton, QLD
Australia

Gabriel Lodewijks
Delft University of Technology
Delft
The Netherlands

Giancarlo Fortino
University of Calabria
Rende (CS)
Italy

Giuseppe Di Fatta
University of Reading
Reading
UK

Zhouping Yin
Huazhong University of Science
  and Technology
Wuhan
China

Mukaddim Pathan
CSIRO ICT
Acton
Australia

Antonio Guerrieri
ICAR-CNR
Rende (CS)
Italy

Qiang Wang
Wuhan University of Technology
Wuhan
China

ISSN 0302-9743   ISSN 1611-3349   (electronic)
Lecture Notes in Computer Science
ISBN 978-3-319-45939-4   ISBN 978-3-319-45940-0   (eBook)
DOI 10.1007/978-3-319-45940-0

Library of Congress Control Number: 2016950411

LNCS Sublibrary: SL3 – Information Systems and Applications, incl. Internet/Web, and HCI

Preface

IDCS 2016 was the 9th annual event of the conference series dedicated to the Internet and distributed computing systems and was held in Wuhan, China. The previous eight successful conferences included IDCS 2008 in Khulna, Bangladesh; IDCS 2009 in Jeju Island, South Korea; IDCS 2010 and IDCS 2011 in Melbourne, Australia; IDCS 2012 in Wu Yi Shan, China; IDCS 2013 in Hangzhou, China; IDCS 2014 in Calabria, Italy; and IDCS 2015 in Windsor, UK.

The Internet, including widespread use of mobile and wireless devices, has grown as a ubiquitous infrastructure to support the fast development of diversified services. The advent of the Internet of Things, cyberphysical systems, and big data is creating a new technology revolution, i.e., the next generation of internet and Industry 4.0. The integration of the digital world with the physical environment makes our world more intelligent and efficient. Large-scale networked intelligent systems require higher cooperation and interoperation of heterogeneous IoT platforms.

IDCS 2016 received innovative papers on emerging models, paradigms, technologies, and novel applications related to Internet-based distributed systems, including the Internet of Things, cyber-physical systems, wireless sensor networks, next-generation collaborative systems, extreme-scale networked systems, and cloud-based big data systems. The audience included researchers, PhD students, and practitioners that have a general interest in the different aspects of the Internet and distributed computing systems with a more specific focus on practical and theoretical aspects of the cyber-physical systems built with the integration of computer networks, distributed systems, wireless sensor technology, and network applications for complex real-life problems.

IDCS 2016 received a large number of submissions from 13 different countries: 30 regular papers and 18 short papers were accepted after a careful review and selection process. The selected contributions covered cutting-edge aspects of cloud computing and the Internet of Things, sensor networks, parallel and distributed computing, advanced networking, smart cities and smart buildings, big data, and social networks, and smart logistics technology and methods.

The conference also featured six keynote presentations: "Towards Multi-layer Interoperability of IoT Platforms: the INTER-IoT approach" was given by Prof. Giancarlo Fortino, DIMES-University of Calabria, Italy; "An Application of the IoT in Belt Conveyor Systems" was given by Prof. Gabriel Lodewijks, Delft University of Technology, The Netherlands; "IoT and Big Data in Intelligent Buildings" was given by Prof. Weiming Shen, National Research Council Canada, Canada; "Security and Privacy in Social Networks" was given by Prof. Yang Xiang, Centre for Cyber Security Research, Deakin University, Australia; "Developments and Prospects of Intelligent Water Transport in China" was given by Prof. Xinping Yan, Wuhan University of Technology, China; and "Semantic Web Technology for Industrial Internet of Things" was given by Prof. Hai-Bin Yu, Shenyang Institute of Automation, Chinese Academy of Sciences, China.

The conference was held at the Chutian Guangdong International Hotel in Wuhan. The conference venue is immersed in the natural landscape of Donghu Lake and the historic site of the national museum, Hubei Museum.

IDCS 2016 set up a career forum for PhD and master students to provide them with the opportunity to present their project work and discuss how to develop a novelty research topic. A workshop "Smart Transportation and Logistics" proposed by Prof. Xiaoli Jiang, Delft University of Technology, The Netherlands, was accepted by the conference and 11 papers were accepted for this session.

We would like to thank Wuhan University of Technology, the Science and Technology Council of Wuhan, and University of Calabria for providing financial support to the conference and grants to PhD students from overseas countries, and for offering 2 rewards, one for the best paper and one for the best PhD student paper.

The successful organization of IDCS 2016 was possible thanks to the dedication and hard work of a number of individuals. In particular, we would like to thank Antonio Guerrieri and Qiang Wang (Publications Chair) for their commendable work for the conference publicity and proceedings. We also express our gratitude to the students at the Logistics and Robotics Lab of Wuhan University of Technology, who provided their voluntary support during the conference.

September 2016

Wenfeng Li
Shawkat Ali
Gabriel Lodewijks
Giancarlo Fortino
Giuseppe Di Fatta
Zhouping Yin
Mukaddim Pathan
Antonio Guerrieri
Qiang Wang

Organization

Honorary Conference Chairs

Youlun Xiong	Huazhong University of Science and Technology, China
Desheng Jiang	Wuhan University of Technology, China
John Gray	University of Manchester, UK

General Chair

Wenfeng Li	Wuhan University of Technology, China

Conference Chairs

Shawkat Ali	University of Fiji, Fiji
Gabriel Lodewijks	Delft University of Technology, The Netherlands
Giancarlo Fortino	University of Calabria, Italy
Giuseppe Di Fatta	University of Reading, UK
Zhouping Yin	Huazhong University of Science and Technology, China
Mukaddim Pathan	Telstra Corporation Limited, Australia

Technical Program Chairs

Deming Liu	Huazhong University of Science and Technology, China
Fazhi He	Wuhan University, China
Chaozhong Wu	Wuhan University of Technology, China
Shengwu Xiong	Wuhan University of Technology, China

PhD Workshop Chair

Mengchu Zhou	New Jersey Institute of Technology, USA

Publicity and Industry Chair

Christian Vecchiola	IBM Research and Development, Australia

Publications Chairs

Antonio Guerrieri	ICAR-CNR, Italy
Qiang Wang	Wuhan University of Technology, China

Steering Committee - IDCS Series

Jemal Abawajy	Deakin University, Australia
Rajkumar Buyya	University of Melbourne, Australia
Giancarlo Fortino	University of Calabria, Italy
Dimitrios Georgakopolous	RMIT University, Australia
Mukaddim Pathan	Telstra Corporation Limited, Australia
Yang Xiang	Deakin University, Australia

Program Committee

Shawkat Ali	University of Fiji, Fiji
Gianluca Aloi	University of Calabria, Italy
Rajkumar Buyya	The University of Melbourne, Australia
Mert Bal	Miami University, USA
Jingjing Cao	Wuhan University of Technology, China
Xiaojiang Chen	Northwest University, China
Min Chen	Huazhong University of Science and Technology, China
Massimo Cossentino	National Research Council, Italy
Zhicheng Dai	Huazhong Normal University, China
Marcos Dias De Assuncao	Inria Avalon, LIP, ENS de Lyon, France
Claudio De Farias	PPGI-IM/NCE-UFRJ, Brazil
Jerker Delsing	Lulea University of Technology, Sweden
Giuseppe Di Fatta	University of Reading, UK
Sisi Duan	Oak Ridge National Laboratory, USA
Declan Delaney	University College Dublin, Dublin
Giancarlo Fortino	University of Calabria, Italy
Xiuwen Fu	Wuhan University of Technology, China
Joaquin Garcia-Alfaro	Télécom SudParis, France
Antonio Guerrieri	ICAR-CNR, Italy
Maria Ganzha	University of Gdańsk, Poland
Luca Geretti	University of Udine - DIEGM, Italy
Chryssis Georgiou	University of Cyprus, Cyprus
Raffaele Gravina	University of Calabria, Italy
John Gray	University of Manchester, UK
Bin Guo	Télécom SudParis, France
Dimitrios Georgakopoulos	University of Thessaly, Greece
Mohammad Mehedi Hassan	King Saud University, Saudi Arabia
Fazhi He	Wuhan University, China

Xiaoya Hu	Huazhong University of Science and Technology, China
Jaehoon Paul Jeong	Sungkyunkwan University, South Korea
Desheng Jiang	Wuhan University of Technology, China
Xiaoli Jiang	Delft University of Technology, The Netherlands
Ram Krishnan	University of Texas, USA
Dimitrios Katsaros	RMIT University, Australia
Qi Kang	Tongji University, China
Wenfeng Li	Wuhan University of Technology, China
Bin Li	Fujian University of Technology, Fuzhou, China
Xiaolei Liang	Wuhan University of Science and Technology, China
Valeria Loscri	Inria Lille-Nord Europe, France
Antonio Liotta	Eindhoven University of Technology, The Netherlands
Dengming Liu	Huazhong University of Science and Technology, China
Bin Lei	Wuhan University of Science and Technology, China
Gabriel Lodewijks	Delft University of Technology, The Netherlands
Jie Mei	Wuhan University of Technology, China
Kashif Munir	UOHB, Saudi Arabia
Carlo Mastroianni	ICAR-CNR, Italy
Mustafa Mat Deris	UTHM, Malaysia
Marco Netto	IBM Research, Brazil
Enrico Natalizio	Université de Technologie de Compiègne, France
Andrea Omicini	Alma Mater Studiorum–Università di Bologna, Italy
Sergio Ochoa	Universidad de Chile, Chile
George Pallis	University of Cyprus, Cyprus
Mukaddim Pathan	Telstra Corporation Limited, Australia
Marcin Paprzycki	IBS PAN and WSM, Poland
Pasquale Pace	University of Calabria, Italy
Ting Qu	Guangdong University of Technology, China
Wilma Russo	University of Calabria, Italy
Ramesh Sitaraman	University of Massachusetts, Amherst, USA
Giandomenico Spezzano	CNR-ICAR and University of Calabria, Italy
Jingtao Sun	National Institute of Informatics, Japan
Riaz Ahmed Shaikh	King Abdul Aziz University, Saudi Arabia
Corrado Santoro	University of Catania, Italy
Claudio Savaglio	Università della Calabri, Italy
Weiming Shen	National Research Council, Canada
Wenan Tan	Shanghai Second Polytechnic University, China
Parimala Thulasiram	University of Manitoba, Canada
Giorgio Terracina	Università della Calabria, Italy
Paolo Trunfio	DEIS, University of Calabria, Italy
Rainer Unland	University of Duisburg-Essen, ICB, Germany
Athanasios Vasilakos	NTUA, Greece
Andrea Vinci	ICAR-CNR, Italy
Chaozhong Wu	Wuhan University of Technology, China

Contents

Distributed Computing and Big Data

Distributed Scheduling and Optimization

Internet of Things and Applications

Smart Networked Transportation and Logistics

Wireless Sensing and Controlling Networks

Body Sensor Networks and Wearable Devices

Continuous Gesture Recognition Based on Hidden Markov Model

Meng Yu[(✉)], Gang Chen, Zilong Huang, Qiang Wang, and Yuan Chen

School of Logistics Engineering, Wuhan University of Technology,
Wuhan 430063, Hubei, China
ymmona@126.com

Abstract. Gesture is a compelling interactive mode, which makes interaction become more active than before. With the development of acceleration sensor, it has played an important role in gesture recognition of human-computer interaction. This paper represents a gesture recognition based on accelerometer, which is modeled by Hidden Markov Model (HMM). For "continuous" gesture recognition, it is a vital problem of how to obtain real valid data in a series of raw gesture data accurately and efficiently. To solve this, we proposed a new gesture detection method based on energy entropy and combined with threshold. Gesture data is analyzed in energy distribution of frequency domain by Short Time Fourier Transform (STFT), which can calculate energy entropy that reflects signal energy distribution. Then an appropriate threshold is set up to determine the start and end of gesture. Through experiments, the proposed method can be proved that it works well in detecting valid gesture data while recognition time and the computation load can be reduced in the case of guaranteeing recognition precision.

Keywords: Gesture recognition · HMM · Energy entropy · STFT

1 Introduction

Gesture recognition has become one of the important research fields of human-computer interaction. The essence of it is that human's hand is used as a computer input device by judging the meaning of user's gesture without any other intermediate media.

Users can interact with surrounding equipment by using simple custom gestures. However, it is necessary to collect data before defining a kind of gesture. At present, there are three types of methods to obtain gesture data: the method based on computer vision, the method based on data glove and the method based on acceleration sensor. The method based on computer vision has been researched for a relatively long time. It is an ideal approach not only in terms of the success rate of recognition but also the complexity of recognition algorithm, but it has an obvious drawback which requires high outside conditions such as good light and background conditions for obtaining gesture images. Although the images can reach high recognition rate by using the method based on data glove, because of the high prices of equipment, this method cannot be used widely. By contrast, the method based on acceleration sensor is not subject to these

© Springer International Publishing AG 2016
W. Li et al. (Eds.): IDCS 2016, LNCS 9864, pp. 3–11, 2016.
DOI: 10.1007/978-3-319-45940-0_1

restrictions and users can operate the device by one single hand. Therefore, this method can be adopted widely.

With the development of micro-electromechanical technology, the performance of the acceleration sensor has got a qualitative leap and related theory and realization technology has been also constantly improved. Although the research of gesture recognition technology based on the acceleration sensor has just started, the mobile devices (mobile phone, pad and so forth) with built-in acceleration sensor has been becoming increasingly popular, this technology develops rapidly and is not just in the lab for research.

Wang et al. [1] integrated the acceleration sensor, antenna and the processor in a pen and used it for handwriting and gesture recognition. They used neural networks to training data, and the final recognition rate reaches 98 %. Lu et al. [2] designed a wheelchair that controlled by gestures and transmits data by Bluetooth. They used the discrete Hidden Markov Model to establish the gesture data modeling, and the final recognition rate was about 95 %. Joselli et al. [3] collected gesture data by using the phone's built-in sensor and built a gesture recognition framework based on mobile phones. They used Hidden Markov Model for gesture classification recognition, with the final recognition rate at 90 %. Schlömer et al. [4] used the Wii controller for data acquisition and processing, and achieved the purpose of controlling browsing TV pictures. They used Hidden Markov Model for gesture recognition, with the final recognition rate at 90 %. Yamagishi et al. [5] used a kind of ring that integrates sensor and Bluetooth for data collection and transmission, which aimed to control computer by gestures and judge the beginning and end of gestures by adopting touch sensor. They used the DTW (dynamic time warping) algorithm for classification recognition, and the final recognition rate is approximately 90 %. Zhou et al. [6] used Virtus advanced acceleration sensors for acceleration data collection, and extract gesture information in the method based on threshold. Finally, they used the Hidden Markov Model for gesture recognition, with the rate of recognition at 93 % and response time at around 0.2 s. Lu et al. [7] established gesture modeling with the acceleration signal and surface electromyogram signal and processed data in C++ program. They used the DTW for gesture recognition, the average recognition rate was about 93 % and response time is less than 0.3 s.

This paper puts forward a kind of gesture recognition scheme based on acceleration sensor. The scheme adopts the MPU6050 acceleration sensor for collecting gestures acceleration signal. After the gesture data being preprocessed such as smoothing filtering and automatic detection, these data are extracted into the characteristic parameters of gestures and the discrete Hidden Markov Model for gesture recognition is constructed.

2   The Basic Procedures of Gesture Recognition System

The processes of gesture recognition system based on acceleration can be divided into six parts: gesture data acquisition, data preprocessing, feature extraction, gesture modeling, gesture classification and recognition. The pipeline of gesture recognition is shown in Fig. 1.

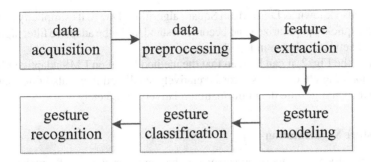

Fig. 1. Pipeline of gesture recognition

In order to meet the system real time and accuracy requirements, considering the calculation complexity, the amount of input data cannot be too large and redundant information should be removed as much as possible. So in procedure of the whole system, this paper focuses on data preprocessing and gesture segmentation.

2.1 Gesture Data Preprocessing

Due to inevitably produce shake caused by users' movement and the influence of the acceleration sensor itself precision, data collected by sensors tend to have a lot of noise. Because of that, it increases the difficulty of the subsequent gesture data feature extraction and also reduces accordingly gesture recognition accuracy at the same time. As a result of that, it needs to filter and reduce the noise of gesture data.

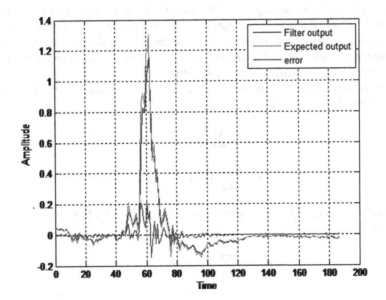

Fig. 2. Error analysis

LMS is also known as Least Mean Square algorithm. Due to its simplicity and practicality, it is quickly popularized and becomes a standard in the adaptive filter algorithm. The filtering effect is shown in Fig. 2.

Through the Fig. 2, it can be seen that the method based on LMS adaptive filter has a good smoothing effect and its error is relatively small and it can also filter out noise and keep the valid gesture data information relatively completely.

2.2 Gesture Segmentation

When the preprocessed data stream arrives to the computer, it passes through a segmentation module which identifies the beginning and the end of gestures. In this paper, we proposed a new gesture detection method based on energy entropy combined with threshold. The analysis of the method is described as follow.

The system adopts Short Time Fourier Transform (STFT) to obtain the feature of gesture data in the time domain and frequency domain.

Defined gesture data sequence (n) in the data segment at time n as follows:

$$x_n(m) = x(m)w(n - m) \tag{1}$$

Where $w(n)$ is a window function. The discrete Fourier transform of formula above can be described as:

$$STFT(n, \omega) = \sum_m x(m)w(n - m)e^{(-jm\omega)} = \sum_m x_n(m)e^{(-jm\omega)} \tag{2}$$

Gesture data is analyzed by STFT as shown in Fig. 3, where energy level of gesture is distinguished by color.

Data fluctuations are mainly caused by the hand jitter when it keeps static. Energy is relatively weak and relatively uniformly distributed in each band. However, dynamic gesture data is caused by movement in low frequency, so that energy of gesture is distributed in low band and it changes with time. Therefore, we can quantitative analysis of the gesture data by calculating entropy energy.

Given energy distribution on m bands E_1, E_2, $\cdots$ E_m, The total energy E is the sum of the individual components. It can be described as follows:

$$E = \sum_{j=1}^{m} E_j \tag{3}$$

$$E_j = \sum_k \left| D_j(k) \right|^2 \tag{4}$$

Where D_j is energy spectra value of gesture. Given $P_j = E_j/E$, Energy Entropy can be described as follows:

$$H = -\sum_j P_j \log_2 P_j \tag{5}$$

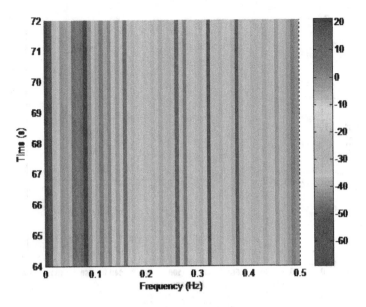

(a) Static data of gesture

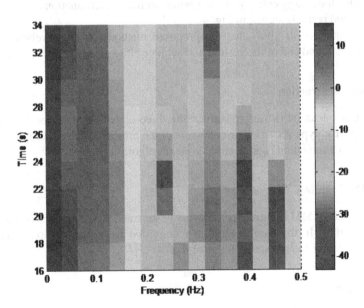

(b) Movement of gesture

Fig. 3. Gesture data analyzed by STFT

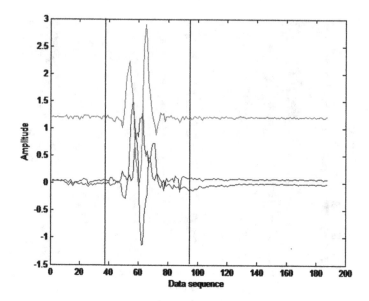

Fig. 4. Gesture segmentation

Calculated the energy entropy of one gesture with the determination threshold value is set to 2.0 and result is shown in Fig. 4.

Experimental results show that the proposed method can effectively distinguish between the start and end of the gesture and achieve effective detection of gesture data.

2.3 Feature Extraction

The vector quantization is used to convert the three-dimensional sensor data into one dimensional prototype vectors. The collection of the prototype vectors is called a codebook. Vector quantization is done using k-means algorithm.

2.4 HMM Training

In our system the HMM is initialized for every gesture and then optimized by the Baum-Welch algorithm. In the case of gesture recognition from acceleration signals, the number of states in each model is set to be five.

2.5 Recognition

In the recognition phase we use the Bayes classification to decide the output gesture.

Given the trained HMM model, $\lambda = \{\lambda_1, \lambda_2, \cdots, \lambda_n\}$, under the known observation sequence O, we obtain:

$$P = \max\left(P\left(\lambda_j|O\right)\right) j = 1, 2 \ldots, n \tag{6}$$

Where P is the percentage of the output gesture and $P(\lambda_j|O)$ is defined as:

$$P(\lambda_j|O) = \frac{P(O|\lambda_j)P(\lambda_j)}{\sum_{i=1}^{N} P(O,\lambda_j)} = \frac{P(O|\lambda_j)P(\lambda_j)}{\sum_{i=1}^{N} P(O|\lambda_j)P(\lambda_j)} \qquad (7)$$

3 Experiments

In order to verify the effectiveness of the proposed solution of accelerometer-based gesture recognition, this paper design a gesture recognition system based on PC which configuration is 4G memory with Intel i3 processor. Then recognition rate of six gestures was verified.

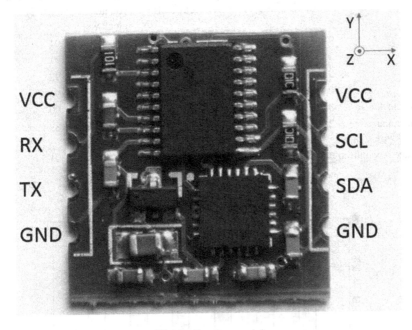

Fig. 5. Sensing model

MPU6050 module we used is shown in Fig. 5 and is essentially MEMS 3-axes acceleration sensing chip integrated with Micro Control Unit (MCU) and Bluetooth wireless data chips.

In order to test the accuracy of the recognition, a series of gestures have been created. In our experiments, we defined six gestures as shown in Fig. 6.

All gestures were repeated one hundred times by 6 members, which provided a six hundred examples overall. The recognition results can be seen on Table 1.

These results show a high fidelity recognition rate of the proposed solution with an average recognition rate of 91 % and 94 % for right gesture.

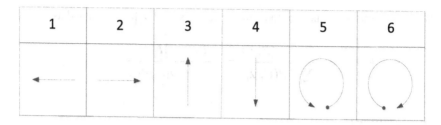

1	2	3	4	5	6

Fig. 6. The gesture database used in tests

Table 1. Recognition rate

Gesture	Up	Down	Left	Right	Circle clockwise	Circle counter clockwise	Recognition rate(%)
Up	91	2	1	1	3	2	91
Down	3	91	0	1	2	3	91
Left	0	0	92	1	4	3	92
Right	0	0	2	94	1	3	94
Circle clockwise	3	2	1	2	90	2	90
Circle counter clockwise	2	4	3	1	1	89	89
Average recognition rate							91.17

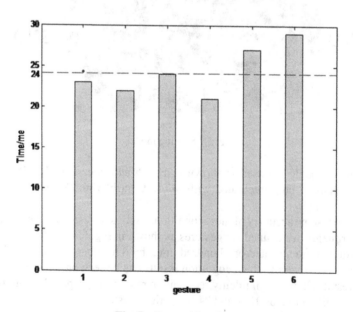

Fig. 7. Recognition time

The recognition time of six gestures in the test is shown as Fig. 7. The results show that the Circle Counter Clockwise gesture has the highest recognition time of 29 ms and the right gesture has the lowest recognition rate of 21 ms, while the solution has an average recognition time of 24 ms. It can meet real-time requirements.

Cai et al. [8] use DTW algorithm to classify seven kinds of gestures, reaching an average recognition rate of 90 % with recognition time of 50 ms. It shows that the proposed solution is effective and practical.

4   Conclusions

In this paper, we utilize the acceleration data to recognize the hand gestures. On the algorithm of hand gesture recognition, we propose a real-time gesture segment method based on the energy entropy which can segment the gesture sequences out of the sensing data automatically. And then we utilize the trained HMM and Bayes method to judge the gestures online. The experiments show that the gesture data processing used in this paper can effectively detect gestures, and reach a good recognition rate and real-time, which is suitable for real-time interactive wearable device.

Acknowledgments.   This research is supported by Program of International S&T Cooperation, "Smart Personal Mobility System for Human Disabilities in Future Smart Cities (2015DFG12210)" and 2015 Major Programs of Henan Province, "Research and Application of Key Technology for Smart Passengers Service Platform Based on Things of Internet (151100211400)".

References

1. Wang, J.S., Chuang, F.C.: An accelerometer-based digital pen with a trajectory recognition algorithm for handwritten digit and gesture recognition. IEEE Trans. Ind. Electron. **59**(7), 2998–3007 (2013)
2. Lu, T.: A motion control method of intelligent wheelchair based on hand gesture recognition. In: Industrial Electronics and Applications, pp. 957–962 (2013)
3. Joselli, M., Clua, E.: gRmobile: a framework for touch and accelerometer gesture recognition for mobile games. In: VIII Brazilian Symposium on Games and Digital Entertainment, pp. 141–150 (2009)
4. Schlömer, T., Poppinga, B., Henze, N., et al.: Gesture recognition with a Wii controller. In: Proceedings of Tei, pp. 11–14 (2008)
5. Yamagishi, K., Jing, L., Cheng, Z.: A system for controlling personal computers by hand gestures using a wireless sensor device. In: IEEE International Symposium on Independent Computing, pp. 1–7 (2014)
6. Zhou, S., Shan, Q., Fei, F., et al.: Gesture recognition for interactive controllers using MEMS motion sensors. In: International Conference on Nano/Micro Engineered and Molecular Systems, pp. 935–940 (2009)
7. Lu, Z., Chen, X., Li, Q., et al.: A hand gesture recognition framework and wearable gesture-based interaction prototype for mobile devices. IEEE Trans. Hum. Mach. Syst. **44**(2), 293–299 (2014)
8. Cai, X., Guo, T., Wu, X., et al.: Gesture recognition method based on wireless data glove with sensors. Sens. Lett. **13**(2), 134–137 (2015)

A New Modeling Method
of Photoplethysmography Signal
Based on Lognormal Basis

Yun Luo[1], Wenfeng Li[1(✉)], Wenbi Rao[2(✉)], Xiuwen Fu[1], Lin Yang[1],
and Yu Zhang[1]

[1] School of Logistics Engineering, Wuhan University of Technology,
Wuhan, People's Republic of China
504200297@qq.com,
{liwf,XiuwenFu,lyang,sanli}@whut.edu.cn
[2] School of Computer Science and Technology,
Wuhan University of Technology, Wuhan, People's Republic of China
wbrao@whut.edu.cn

Abstract. Human photoplethysmography (PPG) signal carries abundant physio-logical and pathological information of cardiovascular system, which can be used to monitor cardiovascular health in the daily life. The existing modeling methods are mainly based on Gaussian basis, which fail to conform to the long-tail features of PPG pulse waveforms. And other several existing methods based on Lognormal basis don't work well in daily monitoring. In this paper, we proposed a new modeling method based on the long-tail Lognormal basis. Fitting calculations get an adaptive time domain by introducing the mode of the corresponding Lognormal basis and are implemented by the proposed successive-fitting solution. The simulations have proved that the proposed method has a good fitting accuracy and efficiency and is suitable for daily monitoring of cardiovascular health in body sensor networks (BSNs). Besides that, a closer relation between the cardiovascular health and the vector parameters of the Lognormal basis also can be expected.

Keywords: PPG · Lognormal basis · Modeling · Daily monitoring

1 Introduction

PPG signal contains lots of human physiological and pathological information. Analyzing the PPG signal is an important method to diagnosis cardiovascular health in BSNs [1–3]. Until now, PPG signal has been widely used for monitoring cardiovascular health in the daily life [4–7]. As shown in Fig. 1, a PPG pulse waveform can divided into two branches and usually contains three waves. The first wave is the main wave. The tidal wave is in the middle of the main wave and the dicrotic notch. The dichotic wave is behind the dicrotic notch. Peaks of the three waves carry rich physiological and pathological information of the cardiovascular system.

PPG pulse waveforms have obvious long-tail features. The existing modeling methods are mainly based on Gaussian basis [8–10], which fail to conform to the

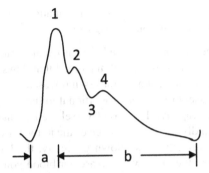

1. main wave, 2. tidal wave, 3. dicrotic notch, 4. dicrotic wave
a. ascending branch, b. descending branch

Fig. 1. PPG signal

long-tail features of PPG pulse waveforms. And other several existing methods based on Lognormal basis don't work well in daily monitoring [11–13]. In [8], the researchers used a six Gaussian bases model to fitting the PPG signal, the method has a high fitting accuracy, but the efficiency is not suitable for daily monitoring of cardiovascular health. [9] used a three Gaussian bases model. [10] proposed a successive fitting method to detect the secondary peak, but didn't give a modeling solution for the PPG signal. [11] used a single fitting model with five Lognormal bases, and get a good goodness of fit after iteration process, but the efficiency is not suitable for daily monitoring. [12] used a single fitting model with four Lognormal bases. [13] used a successive fitting model with four Lognormal bases, but the time domain of each fitting calculation is fixed, which can't adjust to different periods of PPG signals independently, so the accuracy is limited and the effect is not very good used in daily monitoring. In this paper, we proposed a successive-fitting solution based on the long-tail Lognormal basis, and introduced the mode of the corresponding Lognormal basis to get an adaptive time domain of the fitting calculations.

The structure of this paper is organized as follows. The background of this paper is briefly introduced in Sect. 1. In Sect. 2, the method of Lognormal basis modeling is depicted. The simulation results are illustrated in Sect. 3. The conclusions are drawn in Sect. 4.

2 Method of Lognormal Basis Modeling

2.1 Physiological Mechanism of PPG Pulse Waveforms

Initial waves are generated in the proximal aorta due to the left ventricular systolic and diastolic activities. Initial waves propagate along the arterial tree and corresponding reflected waves are created by the vascular resistance during the propagation. Therefore, the obtained PPG signal not only carry the information of left ventricular ejection and the aortic valve closure, but also resistance information (e.g., arterial wall elasticity, peripheral vascular resistance and blood viscosity).

(a) Initial Waves. In the early stage of the left ventricular contraction, the left ventricle squeezes blood into the aorta. At this point, the blood that flows into the proximal aorta is much more than the outflow, which makes intravascular blood volume increases rapidly. As the blood vessel pressure is proportional to the blood volume, the pressure of the blood vessel rises rapidly. The blood vessel wall is under more pressure than normal, so it expands rapidly. In the later stage of the left ventricular contraction, as the left ventricular ejection velocity slows down gradually, the blood that flows into the proximal aorta is less than the outflow, intravascular blood volume and the pressure of the blood vessel gradually decrease, thus making blood vessel wall recoil.

The PPG pulse waveform that caused by the left ventricular contraction is called the main wave. In the diastolic period, the left ventricular pressure is decreasing. This phenomenon would cause the proximal aorta blood flow to the left ventricle. At the meanwhile, blood continues to flow out from the proximal aorta, thus causing the accelerated decrease of the intravascular volume and pressure, and the recoiling of blood vessel wall. After a short time, aortic valve is closed, the blood that flow to the left ventricle would crash against the aortic valve and flow back again to the proximal aorta. At the same time, due to the inertia, the blood that from the adjacent vascular segment continues to flow to the proximal aorta. Two strands of blood promote the brief increase of the proximal aorta's blood volume and pressure, and the expansion of the blood vessel wall. The PPG pulse waveform that caused by the closure of the aortic valve is called the dicrotic wave.

(b) Reflected Waves. After the PPG pulse waveform is formed in the proximal aorta, it propagates along the arterial tree. And reflected waves are generated under the influence of aortic physiological factors (e.g., arterial wall elasticity, peripheral vascular resistance and blood viscosity). This makes a part of blood flow back to the aorta, increasing the intravascular blood volume and the blood vessel pressure, and thus expanding the blood vessel wall. The reflected wave of the main wave is called the tidal wave, and the reflected wave of the dicrotic wave is called the trailing wave.

2.2 Model of PPG Pulse Waveforms

(a) Segmentation of PPG Pulse Waveforms. The main wave of a PPG pulse waveform is created by left ventricular contraction. The tidal wave is the reflected wave of the main wave. The dicrotic notch is caused by the flowing back of the blood to the left ventricle in the proximal aorta. The dicrotic wave is caused by the closure of the aortic valve. And the reflected wave of the dicrotic wave is called the trailing wave. So a PPG pulse waveform is composed by the main wave W_1, the tidal wave W_2, the dicrotic wave W_3 and the tail wave W_4. Assume the start time of W_1, W_2, W_3, W_4 are

t_1, t_2, t_3, t_4 respectively. The start time and end time of PPG signal are t_{str}, t_{end} respectively. Then the fitting PPG signal W can be expressed as:

$$W = \begin{cases} W_1, & t_1 = t_{str}, t_1 \leq t < t_2 \\ W_1 + W_2, & t_2 \leq t < t_3 \\ W_1 + W_2 + W_3, & t_3 \leq t < t_4 \\ W_1 + W_2 + W_3 + W_4, & t_4 \leq t \leq t_{end} \end{cases} \tag{1}$$

The fitting PPG signal can be expressed in the time domain as:

$$W(t) = \begin{cases} W_1(t - t_1), & t_1 = t_{str}, t_1 \leq t < t_2 \\ W_1(t - t_1) + W_2(t - t_2), & t_2 \leq t < t_3 \\ W_1(t - t_1) + W_2(t - t_2) + W_3(t - t_3), & t_3 \leq t < t_4 \\ W_1(t - t_1) + W_2(t - t_2) + W_3(t - t_3) + W_4(t - t_4), & t_4 \leq t \leq t_{end} \end{cases}$$
$$t_1 = t_{str} = t_1 < t_2 < t_3 < t_4 < t_{end} \tag{2}$$

(b) Lognormal Basis. PPG pulse waveform is characterized as long-tail. To improve the fitting accuracy, here Lognormal basis is used to fit the PPG signal. The finite Lognormal basis $W_i(t)$ is defined as:

$$W_i(t) = \frac{\alpha_i}{t - t_i} exp\left(\frac{(ln(t - t_i) - \beta_i)^2}{\gamma_i}\right), \quad \gamma_i < 0, i = 1, 2, 3, 4 \tag{3}$$

Then the Lognormal basis parameters can be defined as $L_i = \{t_i, \alpha_i, \beta_i, \gamma_i\}$. Adding the end time, a PPG pulse waveform's parameters can be expressed as $L = \{t_1, \alpha_1, \beta_1, \gamma_1, t_2, \alpha_2, \beta_2, \gamma_2, t_3, \alpha_3, \beta_3, \gamma_3, t_4, \alpha_4, \beta_4, \gamma_4, t_{end}\}$. Namely a PPG pulse waveform can be represented by a feature vector of 17 parameters.

2.3 Successive-Fitting Solution

The fitting efficiency is determined by the number of the fitting function's parameters. In this paper, we present a solution that uses a successive-fitting with single function instead of a single-fitting with multiple functions. The successive-fitting solution include the main wave fitting, the tidal wave fitting, the dicrotic wave fitting and the tail wave fitting. The whole fitting process is shown in Fig. 2.

(a) Main Wave Fitting. W_D denotes a period of the original PPG signal. The start and end time of W_D are t_{str} and t_{end}. The main peak of W_D is denoted as t_{p1}. t_{sd1} denotes the left zero crossing point around t_{p1}. Considering that the time domain of the existing fitting calculations lacks adaptive adjustment, we introduce M_1 which represents the mode of W_1. M_1 and its rang are expressed in Eq. (5). The start time of W_1 denoted as t_1 equals the start time of W_D denoted as t_{str}. The optimal Lognormal basis representation is obtained by minimizing the mean squared error (MSE_1) between W_1 and W_D.

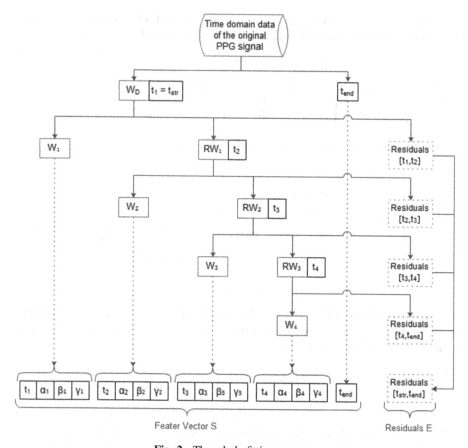

Fig. 2. The whole fitting process

$$t_1 = t_{str} \tag{4}$$

$$M_1 = exp(\beta_1 + \gamma_1/2), \quad t_{sd1} \leq M_1 \leq t_{p1}$$
$$\Rightarrow \ln(t_{sd1}) - \gamma_1/2 \leq \beta_1 \leq \ln(t_{p1}) - \gamma_1/2 \tag{5}$$

$$MSE_1 = \frac{1}{M_1} \sum_{t=t_1}^{t_1+M_1} (W_1(t) - W_D(t))^2, \quad t_1 \leq t \leq t_1 + M_1 \tag{6}$$

(b) Tidal Wave Fitting. RW_1 denotes the residual wave of W_D after the main wave fitting. The first peak of RW_1 is denoted as t_{p2}. t_{sd2} denotes the left zero crossing point around t_{p2}. M_2 represents the mode of W_2. M_2 and its rang are expressed in Eq. (9). The time domain of Eq. (6) is between t_1 and $(t_1 + M_1)$. So the start time of W_2 denoted as t_2 equals $(t_1 + M_1)$. The optimal Lognormal basis representation is obtained by minimizing the mean squared error (MSE_2) between W_2 and RW_1.

$$RW_1 = W_D - W_1 \tag{7}$$

$$t_2 = t_1 + M_1 \tag{8}$$

$$M_2 = exp(\beta_2 + \gamma_2/2), \quad t_{sd2} \leq M_2 \leq t_{p2}$$
$$\Rightarrow \ln(t_{sd2}) - \gamma_2/2 \leq \beta_2 \leq \ln(t_{p2}) - \gamma_2/2 \tag{9}$$

$$MSE_2 = \frac{1}{M_2} \sum_{t=t_2}^{t_2+M_2} (W_2(t) - RW_1(t))^2, \quad t_2 \leq t \leq t_2 + M_2 \tag{10}$$

(c) **Dicrotic Wave Fitting.** RW_2 denotes the residual wave of RW_1 after the tidal wave fitting. The first peak of RW_2 is denoted as t_{p3}. t_{sd3} denotes the left zero crossing point around t_{p3}. M_3 represents the mode of W_3. M_3 and its rang are expressed in Eq. (13). The time domain of Eq. (10) is between t_2 and $(t_2 + M_2)$, so the start time of W_2 denoted as t_3 equals $(t_2 + M_2)$. The optimal Lognormal basis representation is obtained by minimizing the mean squared error (MSE_3) between W_3 and RW_2.

$$RW_2 = RW_1 - W_2 \tag{11}$$

$$t_3 = t_2 + M_2 \tag{12}$$

$$M_3 = exp(\beta_3 + \gamma_3/2), \quad t_{sd3} \leq M_3 < t_{p3}$$
$$\Rightarrow \ln(t_{sd3}) - \gamma_3/2 \leq \beta_3 < \ln(t_{p3}) - \gamma_3/2 \tag{13}$$

$$MSE_3 = \frac{1}{M_3} \sum_{t=t_3}^{t_3+M_3} (W_3(t) - RW_2(t))^2, \quad t_3 \leq t \leq t_3 + M_3 \tag{14}$$

(d) **Tail Wave Fitting.** RW_3 denotes the residual wave of RW_2 after the dicrotic wave fitting. The time domain of Eq. (14) is between t_3 and $(t_3 + M_3)$, so the start time of W_4 denoted as t_4 equals $(t_3 + M_3)$. The end time of the fitting calculation here equals the end time of W_D denoted as t_{end}. The optimal Lognormal basis representation is obtained by minimizing the mean squared error (MSE_4) between W_4 and RW_3.

$$RW_3 = RW_2 - W_3 \tag{15}$$

$$t_4 = t_3 + M_3 \tag{16}$$

$$MSE_4 = \frac{1}{t_{end} - t_4} \sum_{t=t_4}^{t_{end}} (W_4(t) - RW_3(t))^2, \quad t_4 \leq t \leq t_{end} \tag{17}$$

3   Simulation Results

The MIMIC II (Multiparameter Intelligent Monitoring in Intensive Care) Databases contain clinical signals and vital signs time series obtained from hospital medical information systems. The signals in the MIMIC II Databases are multiparameter recordings, which are obtained from both a bedside monitor and the medical records of the patient [14].

In this paper, a hundred individual records are extracted for simulations. The successive-fitting results are shown in Fig. 3.

As illustrated in Fig. 3, the four fitting processes all have a good fitting accuracy. The overall fitting result is shown in Fig. 4.

Table 1 shows the comparison results between the existing modeling methods and the proposed method. As showed in Table 1, the Lognormal methods has a much higher fitting accuracy than the Gaussian methods, this is because of the consistent long-tail feature between the Lognormal basis and the PPG pulse waveforms. And the number of the successive methods' per-fitting parameters is far less than the single methods'. So, for these Lognormal methods, although the single fitting method is a little bit better than the proposed method in fitting accuracy, it performed poorly in

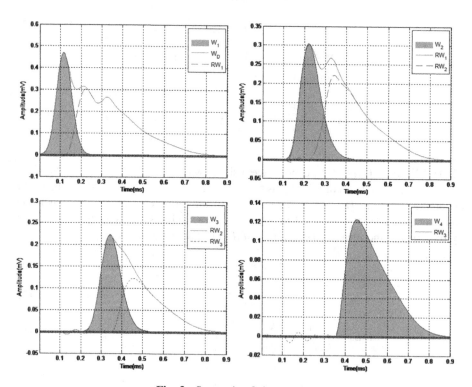

Fig. 3. Successive-fitting results

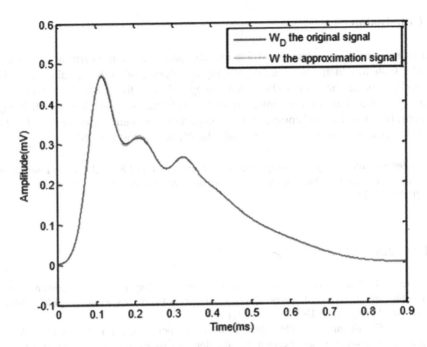

Fig. 4. Overall fitting result

Table 1. Fitting accuracy of serveral different models of PPG signal

Bases type	Gaussian	Gaussian	Gaussian	Lognormal	Lognormal	Lognormal
Bases no.	2	3	4	4	4	4
Fitting type	Single				Successive	
					Fixed time domain	Adaptive time domain
Parameters no. per fitting	6	9	12	16	4	4
Average MSE	0.2073	0.1792	0.1508	0.0165	0.0192	0.0171

terms of fitting efficiency. And for the successive lognormal methods, as showed in Table 1, the proposed method has better performance on fitting accuracy than the one with fixed time domain. The results have proved that the proposed method can meet the requirements of both accuracy and efficiency for daily monitoring of cardiovascular health.

4   Conclusion

PPG signal carries abundant physiological and pathological information of cardio-vascular system, which can be used for daily monitoring of cardiovascular health in BSNs. The simulation results show that, compared with the existing methods, the modeling method based on the long-tail Lognormal basis not only has a high fitting accuracy, but also has good computational complexity, thus being more suitable for the real time application to daily cardiovascular health monitor in the BSNs.

Acknowledgement. This paper is supported in part by the National Natural Science Foundation of China (61571336), the International science & technology cooperation project (No. 2015DFG12210).

References

1. Fortino, G., Giannantonio, R., Gravina, R., et al.: Enabling effective programming and flexible management of efficient body sensor network applications. IEEE Trans. Human-Machine Syst. **43**(1), 115–133 (2013)
2. Fortino, G., Giampà, V.: PPG-based methods for non invasive and continuous blood pressure measurement: an overview and development issues in body sensor networks. In: IEEE International Workshop on Medical Measurements and Applications Proceedings, pp. 10–13 (2010)
3. Chen, W., Lei, S., Guo, L., Chen, Y., Pan, M.: Study on conditioning and feature extraction algorithm of photoplethysmography signal for physiological parameters detection. In: Proceedings of the Image and Signal Processing, pp. 15–17 (2011)
4. Allen, J.: Photoplethysmography and its application in clinical physiological measurement. Physiol. Meas. **28**(3), 1–39 (2007)
5. Kyriacou, P.A., Powell, S., Langford, R.M., Jones, D.P.: Investigation of oesophageal photoplethysmographic signals and blood oxygen saturation measurements in cardiothoracic surgery patients. Physiol. Meas. **23**(8), 533–545 (2002)
6. Johansson, A.: Neural network for photoplethysmographic respiratory rate monitoring. Med. Biol. Eng. Comput. **41**(5), 242–248 (2003)
7. Binns, S.H., Sisson, D.D., Buoscio, D.A., Schaeffer, D.J.: Doppler ultrasonographic, oscillometric sphygmomanometric, and photoplethysmographic techniques for noninvasive blood-pressure measurement in anesthetized cats. J. Vet. Intern. Med. **9**(6), 405–414 (1995)
8. Li, D., Zhao, H., Li, S., Zheng, H.: A new representation of photoplethysmography signal. In: Cai, Z., Wang, C., Cheng, S., Wang, H., Gao, H. (eds.) WASA 2014. LNCS, vol. 8491, pp. 279–289. Springer, Heidelberg (2014)
9. Martin-Martinez, D., Casaseca-de-la-Higuera, P., Martin-Fernandez, M., et al.: Stochastic modeling of the PPG signal: a synthesis-by-analysis approach with applications. IEEE Trans. Biomed. Eng. **60**(9), 2432–2441 (2013)
10. He, X., Goubran, R.A., Liu, X.P.: Secondary peak detection of PPG signal for continuous cuffless arterial blood pressure measurement. IEEE Trans. Instrum. Measur. **63**(6), 1431–1439 (2014)
11. Huotari, M., Vehkaoja, A., Määttä, K., et al.: Photoplethysmography and its detailed pulse waveform analysis for arterial stiffness. J. Struct. Mech. **44**(4), 345–362 (2011)

12. Kostamovaara, J.: Arterial stiffness estimation based photoplethysmographic pulse wave analysis. In: Proceedings of the Spie, pp. 73–76 (2010)
13. Zhao, H., Dou, S.C., Li, D.Z., et al.: Mathematical modeling of pulse wave based on lognormal function. J. Northeast. Univ. Nat. Sci. **37**(2), 169–173 (2016)
14. Database of MIMIC II (2016). http://physionet.org/mimic2/mimic2&underscore;waveform&underscore;overview.shtml

A Neuro-Fuzzy System for Classifying Fatigue Degree of Wheelchair User

Xinyun Hu[1(✉)], Raffaele Gravina[2], Wenfeng Li[1], and Giancarlo Fortino[2]

[1] School of Logistics Engineering, Wuhan University of Technology, Wuhan, China
{huxinyun, liwf}@whut.edu.cn
[2] Department of Informatics, Modeling, Electronics and Systems,
University of Calabria, Rende, Italy
rgravina@dimes.unical.it, g.fortino@unical.it

Abstract. With the increase of disabled people, the functionalities of smart wheelchair as a mobility-assisted equipment are being more and more enriched and extended. However, fatigue detection for wheelchair users is still not explored widely. This paper proposes a complete system and approach to classify fatigue degree for manual wheelchair users. In our system, physiological and kinetic data are collected in terms of sEMG, ECG, and acceleration signals. The necessary features are then extracted from the signals and integrated with self-rating method to train a neuro-fuzzy classifier. Finally, four degrees of this fatigue status can be distinguished by our system; this can provide further fatigue prediction and alertness in case of musculoskeletal disorders (MSD) caused by underlying fatigue.

Keywords: Fatigue classification · Smart wheelchair · Neuro-fuzzy classification · SEMG · ECG

1 Introduction

At present, with the worldwide population aging trend and the increase of disabled people, demand of mobility-assisted equipment like wheelchairs is increasing enormously. According to the latest report of world health organization [1], there are more than 1 billion persons around the world suffering from different degrees of disability and handicap. Specifically, nearly 20 % of them are undergoing serious difficulties because of lack of body functionality. It directly leads that the traditional electronic wheelchair has been insufficient to meet the requirements of persons with handicaps.

Even though a wide variety of multi-functional wheelchairs with different functionalities [2] are available, there are still some fundamental needs to be explored. Compared to healthy people, due to the declining of physical function, the elderly usually is not much sensitive to perceive the underlying physical fatigue. The undetected cumulative fatigue for wheelchair users - often irreversible - can cause musculoskeletal disorsers (MSD) [3] like spinal cord injury, stroke, paralysis, etc. Therefore, classification and prediction of fatigue, as a reference for wheelchair user, is significantly meaningful to prevent the development of such injuries.

© Springer International Publishing AG 2016
W. Li et al. (Eds.): IDCS 2016, LNCS 9864, pp. 22–33, 2016.
DOI: 10.1007/978-3-319-45940-0_3

Fatigue detection during dynamic states is being studied pervasively in sports among healthy people. Lots of wearable devices have been invented to detect fatigue and avoid the injuries caused by exercise [4]. However, the fatigue research for wheelchair user is constricted to the particular muscle signal detection and analysis, which might not essentially solve the injury problems caused by fatigue. In other words, the physical fatigue for wheelchair user does not simply mean the tiredness of a specific muscle, since physiological signal is just one source of weariness information. Although there are a few works concentrating on classifying and predicting fatigue from both physiological and kinetic point of view [5], the literature on fatigue analysis in wheelchair using multi-sensor information is still limited. For the algorithm of fatigue classification, although there exists many theoretical methods such as artificial neural network (ANN), Bayesian classifier, fuzzy logic (FL) classifier, Hidden Markov Model (HMM) classifier [6], the accuracy of fatigue classification is still not satisfying.

The objective of this study is to classify the wheelchair user fatigue using both physiological and kinetic signals, so to effectively detect fatigue from a Body Sensor Network (BSN) [19] worn by the user. Fatigue is directly measured with sEMG signal, as well indirectly taking also into account ECG and acceleration signals. At the same time, specific signal features linked to tiredness are selected, which are used as fatigue indexes. Finally, an ANN-based classifier is chosen in our system, which is found having relatively high classification accuracy in comparison with the existing methods by Kaiser et al. [7]. The relationships between fatigue, biological signals, and kinetic signal are not easily determined due to the existence of uncertainty. However, this problem can be solved by the neuro-fuzzy classification method proposed by Nauck et al. [8] which is qualified as an effective method to categorize biological signal.

In this paper, we present a neuro-fuzzy approach to classify wheelchair user fatigue using both physiological signals (sEMG, ECG) and kinetic signals (acceleration). Section 2 describes the related work in terms of the functionalities of current smart wheelchairs and the fatigue analysis in dynamic state. Section 3 mainly illustrates the hardware and the classification method including the preprocessing, feature extraction, as well as the neuro-fuzzy classification system. Section 4 describes implementation process and shows the preliminary results from sEMG and ECG signal point of view. Finally, the contribution of our study is highlighted, in the meanwhile, several ideas are given to further research in Sect. 5.

2 Background and Related Work

2.1 The Overview of the Functionalities of Current Smart Wheelchair

To facilitate impaired people' independence, many scientific works devoted to make the electric wheelchair "smarter" have been published recently. Those works aim at enriching wheelchair functionalities in terms of health informatics [9], assistive robotics [10], human computer interface [11] and emotion and behavior recognition [12]. Health informatics concerns the monitoring of various kinds of health parameters, such as heartbeat, respiration rate, blood pressure, etc., to acquire physical and psychological states avoiding emergency situations. Assistive robotics is another significant source for upgrading the smart wheelchair concentrating on extending its features in terms of navigation, obstacle detection, safety maintenance, etc. Besides that, a wide range of human computer interfaces are accessible nowadays, as people lack the fundamental ability (e.g. paralysis, stroke) to control traditional manual wheelchair. Facial movement, eye movement, and sEMG signals are used extensively for controlling the electric wheelchair. At last, emotion [13] and behavior recognition is being recently utilized to help take care of disabled and elderly people in the wheelchair, so that the burden of caregivers is significantly relieved.

2.2 Fatigue Detection and Classification in Dynamic State

Fatigue can be defined as a decrease in physical movement performance due to internal and external forces [14]. The aggregation of underlying fatigue during dynamic state usually causes serious injuries that are often irreversible. Therefore, the best way to avoid the injuries is to detect fatigue, classify fatigue degree and predict it, rather than asking for medical assistance.

Several literature works focus on fatigue analysis in athletics field. Manero et al. [4] designed a pair of jogging leggings with embroidered sEMG electrodes, which is capable of recording muscle activity data of quadriceps group, thus avoiding Running Related Injuries (RRI). With the purpose of classification of the exhaustion state for athletes, Eskofier et al. [15] utilized heart rate variability (HRV) features and two biomechanical features to distinguish the runner's fatigue state with an accuracy of 88.3 %.

Besides, similarly to the quadriceps group for a runner, the deltoid group, brachii group and upper trapezius are considered the most active muscle during propulsion for a manual wheelchair user. Many researchers use sEMG signal to analyze those muscles. sEMG activity of 7 muscles have been recorded and verified to be relevant to the fatigue by Masuda et al. [16], as the manual wheelchair users use two different propulsion speeds. M. Pilarski et al. [5] used both physiological data and kinetic data to anticipate the time remaining until muscle fatigue, and kinematic data like acceleration has been adopted to analyze wheelchair user' fatigue by Nagamine K [17]. Regarding the classification of fatigue, Al-Mulla et al. [18] use elbow angle data to define the boundaries (Non-Fatigue, Transition-to-Fatigue and Fatigue) of the sEMG signal. Eskofier et al. [15] use Support Vector Machine and Linear Discriminant Analysis to categorize 21 features of muscle fatigue.

3 Proposed Method

3.1 Smart Wheelchair

This work is based on the smart wheelchair - a BSN-based [19] mobile healthcare system for wheelchair user [20], developed by Robotics Laboratory at Wuhan University of Technology. The overall system is able to perform four main functionalities: wheelchair overturn detection, body posture recognition, physiological signals monitoring and location tracking. To detect and classify the fatigue, we have further improved the smart wheelchair from a hardware point of view.

The fatigue measurement system shown in Fig. 1 is composed of three kinds of sensors and one computation device.

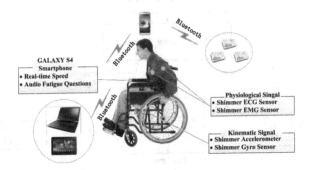

Fig. 1. Diagram of hardware deployment

First, we choose seven upper limb muscles (Deltoid posterior, Middle deltoid, Deltoid anterior, Triceps brachii, Biceps brachii, Pectorailis major and Upper trapezius) as target muscles. Seven pairs of electrodes of Shimmer sEMG sensors are attached on the belly of target muscles of wheelchair user with bipolar configuration, which is the most universe placement way of electrodes recommended by J. Hermens [21]. In addition, a Shimmer ECG sensor is used to monitor the ECG signal. A chest strap is utilized to fix the ECG sensor on the human body.

Secondly, we mount an accelerometer under the seatrest to collect the acceleration signals, because it is beneficial to get kinetic information during wheelchair user's movements.

Finally, we use a Samsung GALAXY S4 smartphone, running the SPINE framework [22, 23], that can play audio files with predefined fatigue questions and record the corresponding answer. In addition, DigiHUD Speedometer and MultiShimmerSync (google application) are installed in the smartphone to monitor the real-time speed of wheelchair and collect sensor data. The phone is placed on the rack fixed on the wheelchair handrest.

The overall process of signal collection and fatigue classification is shown in Fig. 2. At the beginning of the process, three types of information are collected in terms of sEMG, HRV and acceleration. Both the physiological and kinetic signals are then preprocessed on the Shimmer node. Then, we use Bluetooth to transmit the biological and biomechanics data to the smartphone for further calibration, which is easily done by the shimmer sensors. Furthermore, with acting as a gateway, the smartphone stores, packages and transmit the data in wireless way to the data service for classification, which is based on a neuro-fuzzy classification system. Through the matching of the trained database, we can get the real-time recognition of fatigue degree. The database has been trained in advance with self-rating method. From the ratings in Tab.1, four kinds of fatigue degree and three types of status are shown. Furthermore, the warning system would be developed for alerting and predicting the underlying fatigue, which is efficiency and effective to avoid the second injury caused by fatigue.

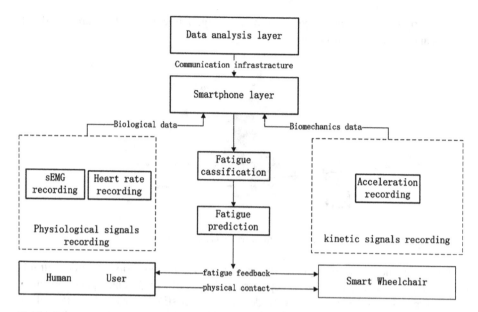

Fig. 2. Diagram of the proposed wheelchair with its various signal recordings and communication flow

3.2 Signal Processing for Fatigue

Preprocessing of sEMG and ECG signals. With the purpose of acquiring more useful sEMG signals, the present system includes a signal preprocessing script written in MATLAB. Each sEMG signal is sampled at 1024 Hz. Then, we apply a second order Butterworth high-pass filter with a cut-off frequency of 20 Hz to remove the baseline noise and the movement artifact noise [24]. Figure 3 shows the sEMG signal before and after filtering by our designed filter. We choose the biceps brachii as a target muscle to validate the effectiveness of the designed filter. sEMG signal is collected over 8 s in two different situations. The left two diagrams illustrate the comparison of the raw sEMG signal and the filtered one when the muscle is totally relieved, while the right ones present

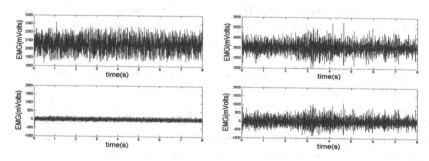

Fig. 3. The comparation of raw sEMG signal and filtered one when muscle is totally relieved (left) and the comparation of raw sEMG signal and filtered one when generating force (right)

the same comparison when it is generating force. After filtering, the difference of sEMG signal between the two situations is easily observed.

For the ECG signal, we focus on HRV feature corresponding to the variation of RR-interval. Therefore, a Shimmer sensor node equipped with the dedicated ECG expansion module is used to record the ECG signal with 100 Hz sampling frequency. Then, to remove both the interference and baseline drift, and to extract effective features of ECG signal as fatigue indexes [25] (as discussed in Sect. 2.2.B), a low-pass filter with a 50 cut-off frequency and a smoothing filter are adopted [26].

Features Extraction. Feature extraction from sEMG signals is a complex task, since sEMG signal is controlled by the nervous system and depends on the anatomical and physiological properties of the muscles. On the other hand, it is significant and effective for the classification of muscle fatigue. Basically, there are a wide variety of approaches proposed in literature [27] to perform muscle fatigue analysis, which can be divided in (i) amplitude-based parameters analysis, (ii) spectral analysis, (iii) time-frequency based parameters analysis and (iv) non-deterministic parameters. In amplitude-based analysis, the averaged rectified value (ARV) is widely studied by reference to detect the muscle fatigue. With the increase of muscle fatigue degree, ARV is correspondingly rising, because more muscle fibers are recruited. Regarding the time-frequency based parameters, instantaneous mean frequency (IMNF) is widely studied with the changes of muscle fatigue degree. In our proposed system, the ARV and IMNF features are selected to analyze muscle fatigue. The computation formulas are shown respectively below:

$$\text{ARV} = \frac{1}{n} \sum_n |x_n| \tag{1}$$

$$Fmean_t = \frac{\int_0^\infty f \cdot PSD(f) \cdot df}{\int_0^\infty PSD(f) \cdot df} \tag{2}$$

where x_n is the value of sEMG signal, and n is the number of sample. $Fmean_t$ denotes the mean power frequency at the time t, while $PSD(f)$ is the power spectrum density at frequency f.

With the purpose of acquiring the HRV features related to fatigue, five parameters of the ECG signal have been deeply analyzed [28]. In the frequency-domain analysis, first of all, power spectral density (PSD) of the RR series is calculated. Then, total power (TP), low frequency power (LP), high frequency power (HP) and low/high frequency power (LF/HF) are analyzed as basic indexes of fatigue, while the standard deviation of RR_i (SDNN) is studied widely in the time domain. Since there is not well established consensus on the relationship between fatigue and HRV features, suitable feature selection is very important for fatigue classification. Basically, LP and LF/HF are rising with the fatigue increasing. In the time domain, SDNN is positively correlated to fatigue degree.

In our study, LF and SDNN of ECG signal are utilized to monitor fatigue degree. The calculation formulas are shown respectively below:

$$\overline{RR_i} = \frac{1}{N}\sum_{i=1}^{N} RR_i \qquad (3)$$

$$SDNN = \sqrt{\frac{1}{N-1}\sum_{i=1}^{N}(RR_i - \overline{RR})^2} \qquad (4)$$

$$LF = \int_{f_1}^{f_2} PSD(f)df \qquad (5)$$

where N stands for the sample number of RR interval. $\overline{RR_i}$ means the mean value of RR_i. The definition of low frequency power is the area under the PSD function in the frequency (0.04–0.15 Hz). Therefore, f_2 equals to 0.15 Hz, while f_1 equals to 0.04 Hz.

3.3   Fatigue Classification Based on NEFCLASS

A neuro-fuzzy classification approach (NEFCLASS) for data classification was first proposed by Nauck [8]. Since the relationship between sEMG, ECG, acceleration signal feature and fatigue cannot be quantified directly, the fuzzy set, which is used to represent some form of uncertainty, can describe it effectively. In addition, fuzzy logic can integrate human decision-making capability in the form of IF-THEN rules. All the relationship between feature inputs and fatigue (or non-fatigue) can be fuzzed into a value that lies in [0, 1], which is expressed by the membership function show in Fig. 4. Then, the integration of IF-THEN rules and those fuzzy sets can determine the output. All the membership function and IF-THEN rules should be trained and defined by massive samples and acquired knowledge.

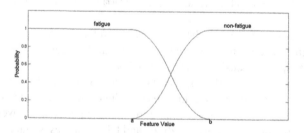

Fig. 4. The S-shaped membership function

Figure 5 illustrates the neuro-fuzzy classification structure. X_i denotes the feature of sEMG, HRV, and acceleration signal. S-shape membership functions using Eq. (3) are used and given appropriate names (low and high) respectively.

$$f(x;a,b) = \begin{cases} 0, x \le a \\ 2\left(\dfrac{x-a}{b-a}\right)^2, a \le x \le \dfrac{a+b}{2} \\ 1-2\left(\dfrac{x-b}{b-a}\right)^2, \dfrac{a+b}{2} \le x \le b \\ 1, x \ge b \end{cases} \tag{6}$$

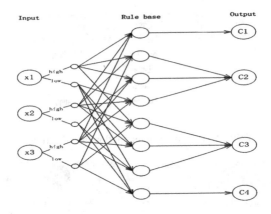

Fig. 5. The structure of a neuro-fuzzy classification system

Values a and b are critical points to separate fatigue status. Each input X_i has its own probability in different fuzzy set. More precisely, (i) the value X_i less than a totally belongs to fatigue fuzzy set; (ii) the value X_i between a and b has its own possibility in fatigue set and non-fatigue set respectively; (iii) the value X_i more than b is completely subject to non-fatigue set.

Rule base is determined by self-rating of subjects and training samples is described in Table 2. The output C_i, which corresponds to fatigue degree, in this table is the reasonable assumption of category results.

4   Experiments

4.1   Experiment Procedures

In our experiments, we recruited twenty volunteers (10 males, 10 females, mean age 25 ± 5 years, mean weight 60 ± 15 kg) without any history of upper-limb injury or any neuromuscular disorder to execute the designed exercise. The participants are required to propel our wheelchair and keep a 1.6 m/s speed on a flat concrete track until they are not able to maintain the fixed speed. The current speed can be checked easily by the DigiHUD Speedometer on the smartphone. According to the description of hardware in Sect. 3.1, we recorded sEMG, ECG and acceleration signals using the freely available MultiShimmerSync application. In the meanwhile, participants used self-rating description in Table 1 to record their fatigue degree during each exercise. The participant is instructed to answer the questions about their subjective fatigue level with a self-rated degree in Table 1. We also define '*extremely* tired' as fatigue status, while '*little* tired' and '*rather* tired' are transition states, and '*not tired at all*' is non-fatigue status. Then, the collected data are analyzed in Matlab. The designed scripts were used for preprocessing, feature extraction and training parameters of neuro-fuzzy system classification.

Table 1. Wheelchair user self rating transcription

Spoken Answer	Meaning	Status
0	Not at all	Non-fatigue
1	Little	Transition
2	Rather	Transition
3	Extremely	Fatigue

Table 2. Rule bases integrated with self-rating

Rule	Input (if)			Output (then)
	x1	x2	x3	Self-rating
1	high	high	high	Extremely
2	high	high	low	Rather
3	high	low	high	Rather
4	low	high	high	Rather
5	high	low	low	Little
6	low	high	low	Little
7	low	low	high	Little
8	low	low	low	Not at all

4.2 Preliminary Results

We let subject A follow the experiment protocol for 1 min. The upper diagram of Fig. 6 shows the original collected sEMG signal, while the middle one shows the filtering sEMG signal. The last one presents the change of ARV value, which shows an increase in time domain with the increase of fatigue degree.

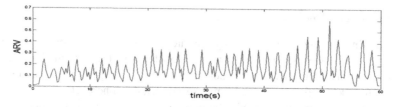

Fig. 6. The diagram of the relationship between ARV and fatigue degree

In the meanwhile, we choose 0.25 s as time interval to calculate the IMNF value which presents a noticeable decrease with the rising of fatigue degree in Fig. 7.

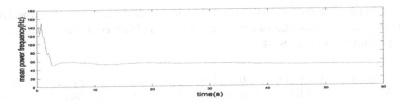

Fig. 7. The diagram of the relationship between IMNF and fatigue degree

Subject A was asked to follow the experiment procedure described in Sect. 4.1 for 100 s so as to record the ECG signal. We used Kubios software [29] to calculate the LF and SDNN value of ECG signal with a 30 s window and 80 % overlap. Although the beginning of the diagram (Fig. 8) shows a slight decrease because of the warm-up activity, the whole trend is an increase. Therefore, it is in accordance with the assumption in relationship between ECG signal feature and fatigue status.

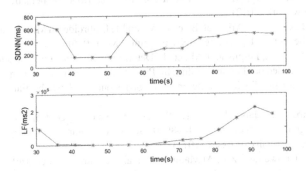

Fig. 8. The diagram of the relationship between SDNN, LF and fatigue degree

5 Conclusions

Targeting manual wheelchair users, a method and a full operating prototype system of fatigue degree classification has been proposed in this paper, as well as the result of relationship between sEMG signal, ECG signal and fatigue status. In our system, the two main sources of physiological and kinetic data (sEMG, HRV and acceleration signal) are collected and analyzed by Shimmer sensors. Afterwards, the necessary features are extracted from the signals and integrated with self-rating method to train the neuro-fuzzy classification classifier in service center. Finally, four degrees of fatigue status can be distinguished, which can provide further fatigue prediction and alertness by the smartphone interface in case of musculoskeletal disorders (MSD) caused by underlying fatigue.

Future research will be devoted to investigate the relationship between acceleration feature and fatigue status. By applying multi-sensor data fusion, we will use those kinetic and physiological feature data to train the proposed neuro-fuzzy classifier so that the optimization parameters are then determined to classify the fatigue degree of wheelchair user. Furthermore, the comparison among the existed classifiers for analyzing fatigue will be performed in future work.

Acknowledgement. The research is financially supported by China-Italy S&T Cooperation project "Smart Personal Mobility Systems for Human Disabilities in Future Smart Cities" (China-side Project ID: 2015DFG12210, Italy-side Project ID: CN13MO7). And also Wuhan University of Technology Graduate Student Innovation Research Project (Project ID: 2015-JL-016).

References

1. World health statistics 2015: World Health Organization 2015. http://www.who.int/gho/publications/world_health_statistics/2015/en/
2. Simpson, R.C.: Smart wheelchairs: a literature review. J. Rehabil. Res. Development **42**(4), 423 (2005)
3. Ma, R., Chablat, D., Bennis, F., Ma, L.: Human muscle fatigue model in dynamic motions. In: Lenarcic, J., Husty, M. (eds.) Latest Advances in Robot Kinematics, pp. 349–356. Springer, New York (2012)
4. Manero, R.B., Grewal, J., Michael, B., et al.: Wearable Embroidered Muscle Activity Sensing Device for the Human Upper Leg. arXiv preprint arXiv (2016)
5. Pilarski, P.M., Qi, L., Ferguson, P.M., et al.: Determining the time until muscle fatigue using temporally extended prediction learning. In: Proceedings of the 18th International Functional Electrical Stimulation Society Conference (IFESS), Donostia-San Sebastian, Spain, 7–8 June 2013
6. Rechy-Ramirez, E.J., Janet, E., Hu, H.: Stages for developing control systems using EMG and EEG signals: a survey, pp. 1744–8050. School of Computer Science and Electronic Engineering, University of Essex (2011)
7. Kaiser, M.S., Chowdhury, Z.I., Al Mamun, S., et al.: A neuro-fuzzy control system based on feature extraction of surface electromyogram signal for solar-powered wheelchair. Cogn. Comput. 1–9 (2016)
8. Nauck, D., Kruse, R.: NEFCLASSmdash; a neuro-fuzzy approach for the classification of data. In: Proceedings of the 1995 ACM Symposium on Applied Computing, pp. 461–465 (1995)
9. Postolache, O., Freire, J., Girao, P., et al.: Smart sensor architecture for vital signs and motor activity monitoring of wheelchair users. In: Proceedings of the 2012 IEEE 6th International Conference Sensing Technology (ICST), pp. 167–172 (2012)
10. Dryvendra, D., Ramalingam, M., Chinnavan, E., et al.: A better engineering design: low cost assistance kit for manual wheelchair users with enhanced obstacle detection. J. Eng. Technol. Sci. **47**(4), 389–405 (2015)
11. Wallam, F., Asif, M.: Dynamic finger movement tracking and voicecommands based smart wheelchair. Int. J. Comput. Electr. Eng. **3**(4), 497 (2011)
12. Dzemydienė, D., Bielskis, A.A., Andziulis, A., et al.: Recognition of human emotions in reasoning algorithms of wheelchair type robots. Informatica **21**(4), 521–532 (2010)
13. Gravina, R., Fortino, G.: Automatic methods for the detection of accelerative cardiac defense response. IEEE Trans. Affect. Comput. 1949–3045 (2016)
14. Ji, Q., Lan, P., Looney, C.: A probabilistic framework for modeling and real-time monitoring human fatigue. IEEE Trans. Syst. Man Cybern. Part A Syst. Hum. **36**(5), 862–875 (2006)

15. Eskofier, B., Kugler, P., Melzer, D., et al.: Embedded classification of the perceived fatigue state of runners: Towards a body sensor network for assessing the fatigue state during running. In: Proceedings of the 2012 IEEE 9th International Conference Wearable and Implantable Body Sensor Networks (BSN), pp. 113–117 (2012)

16. Masuda, K., Masuda, T., Sadoyama, T., et al.: Changes in surface EMG parameters during static and dynamic fatiguing contractions. J. Electromyogr. Kinesiol. **9**(1), 39–46 (1999)

17. Nagamine, K., Iwasawa, Y., Matsuo, Y., et al.: An estimation of wheelchair user's muscle fatigue by accelerometers on smart devices. In: Proceedings of the 2015 ACM International Joint Conference on Pervasive and Ubiquitous Computing and Proceedings of the 2015 ACM International Symposium on Wearable Computers, pp. 57–60. ACM (2015)

18. Al-Mulla, M.R., Sepulveda, F., Colley, M.: sEMG techniques to detect and predict localised muscle fatigue. INTECH Open Access Publisher, Osaka (2012)

19. Alexandros, P., Nikolaos, B.: A survey on wearable sensor-based systems for health monitoring and prognosis. IEEE Trans. Syst. Man Cybern. Part C (Appl. Rev.) **40**(1), 1–12 (2010)

20. Yang, L., Ge, Y., Li, W., et al.: A home mobile healthcare system for wheelchair users. In: Proceedings of the 2014 IEEE 18th International Conference Computer Supported Cooperative Work in Design (CSCWD), pp. 609–614 (2014)

21. Hermens, H.J., Freriks, B., Disselhorst-Klug, C., et al.: Development of recommendations for SEMG sensors and sensor placement procedures. J. Electromyogr. Kinesiol. **10**(5), 361–374 (2000)

22. Fortino, G., Giannantonio, R., Gravina, R., Kuryloski, P., Jafari, R.: Enabling effective programming and flexible management of efficient body sensor network applications. IEEE Trans. Hum. Mach. Syst. **43**(1), 115–133 (2013)

23. Fortino, G., Galzarano, S., Gravina, R., Li, W.: A framework for collaborative computing and multi-sensor data fusion in body sensor networks. Inf. Fus. J. **22**, 50–70 (2015)

24. De Luca, C.J., Gilmore, L.D., Kuznetsov, M., et al.: Filtering the surface EMG signal: movement artifact and baseline noise contamination. J. Biomech. **43**(8), 1573–1579 (2010)

25. Andreoli, A., Gravina, R., Giannantonio, R., Pierleoni, P., Fortino, G.: SPINE-HRV: a BSN-based toolkit for heart rate variability analysis in the time-domain. In: Lay-Ekuakille, A., Mukhopadhyay, S.C. (eds.) Wearable and Autonomous Biomedical Devices and Systems for Smart Environment. LNEE, vol. 75, pp. 369–389. Springer, Heidelberg (2010)

26. Covello, R., Fortino, G., Gravina, R., et al.: Novel method and real-time system for detecting the Cardiac Defense Response based on the ECG. In: 2013 IEEE International Symposium on Medical Measurements and Applications Proceedings (MeMeA), pp. 53–57 (2013)

27. González-Izal, M., Malanda, A., Gorostiaga, E., et al.: Electromyographic models to assess muscle fatigue. J. Electromyogr. Kinesiol. **22**(4), 501–512 (2012)

28. Tran, Y., Wijesuriya, N., Tarvainen, M., et al.: The relationship between spectral changes in heart rate variability and fatigue. J. Psychophysiol. **23**(3), 143–151 (2009)

29. Tarvainen, M.P., Niskanen, J.P., Lipponen, J.A., et al.: Kubios HRV–heart rate variability analysis software. Comput. Meth. Program. Biomed. **113**(1), 210–220 (2014)

Detecting Novel Class for Sensor-Based Activity Recognition Using Reject Rule

Chuhaolun Deng, Wenjing Yuan, Zhiwen Tao, and Jingjing Cao[✉]

School of Logistics Engineering, Wuhan University of Technology, Wuhan, 430077, China
{ChuhaolunDeng,Krystal_Yuan,zwtao0222}@163.com,
bettycao@whut.edu.cn

Abstract. Many researches have shown that data streams are continuous and changeable which make them hard to be classified accurately. The major difficulty in data classification is concept evolution, namely, novel class detection. Learn++ group methods are normally employed for stream data, however, these methods hardly handle the novel class detection problem. Therefore, in this paper, we introduce an approach that combines Learn++.NSE with reject option and our research findings can be used in activity recognition whose data streams are collected by body-worn sensors. In our experiment, the proposed approach shows better performance than Learn++.NSE algorithm.

Keywords: Activity recognition · Learn++.NSE · Novel class detection · Reject rule · Soft output

1 Introduction

Activity recognition is normally utilized for analyzing and classifying people's activities accurately. In other words, it can tell people whether the candidates are working, sitting, or sleeping, and even more complex human behaviors [1, 7]. Monitoring human movements using wireless body sensor networks (BSNs) has enormous potential for changing people's daily lives, which can advance a series of human-based application domains including caring people's health and security, real-time observation and so on [1, 22, 23].

There are two kinds of activity recognition, one is offline recognition and the other is online. As for the former, classification works in a stationary environment, which contains many static and constant samples, and it is recognized by classifying some of the identified data. In this case, video-based activity recognition could be accomplished [7], and it is of high accuracy for activity recognition. But there are some shortages including inconvenience and lack of privacy protection. In this approach, we focus on the sensor-based activity recognition, which are more portable than video-based activity recognition. In contrast, the latter deals with the environment that is always changing. For instance, a set of data streams are constantly sending to the system and sometimes class evolution occurs. Thus, the classification system should be updated according to previous datasets or classifiers in real-time and adapt to the newly coming samples, i.e., the offline aims at all existing samples while the online deals with recent samples.

© Springer International Publishing AG 2016
W. Li et al. (Eds.): IDCS 2016, LNCS 9864, pp. 34–44, 2016.
DOI: 10.1007/978-3-319-45940-0_4

As to the online activity recognition, data needing to be processed are not static, unique characteristics and uncertain length cause that it is difficult to capture and recognize these newly coming data streams [1]. Furthermore, concept drift and concept evolution (novel class detection) should be considered seriously. The former refers to the phenomenon that the statistical characteristics of the target variable change over time, which results in continuous decrease in the prediction accuracy. The latter is the result of class evolution in data streams. For example, supposing the bipartition includes standing and sitting, but recent data refer to lying, so the "lying" is a novel class. However, the literatures of concept evolution are not many at present, so we propose an approach in which the incremental learning plays an important role.

Learn++.NSE is an incremental learning algorithm in nonstationary environments, which has been confirmed that tracking a variety of concept drift environments shows great performance. It was employed in our approach, but as far as we know, Learn++.NSE hardly deals with the situation where a novel class occurs. For this problem, we propose an approach based on reject rule to deal with novel class detection, which showed better performance when combined with Learn++.NSE. As we know, in some situations, especially in activity recognition, the cost of error is greater than the cost of non-classification, such as detecting the "fall" activity of old people is more significant than identifying it as existing activities, so we have worked out a reject rule to reject uncertain data, and treat uncertain data as novel class sample. The contribution of our paper can be detailed as follows:

(1) Learn++.NSE training phase takes advantage of the weight assignment to add or delete class, however, this method, cannot identify the new class accurately in online activity recognition scene. In this work, we emphasize on utilizing reject rule to construct novel class detection mechanism to relieve the problem.

(2) Learn++.NSE testing phase ignores novel class detection, while this paper can easily obtain the similar novel class detection method in testing phase according to the novel class detection method in training phase.

2   Related Work

Currently BSNs are mainly employed to monitor single individual only, but actually, they can also concentrate on cooperation groups of individuals [24]. Learn++.NSE was presented by Polikar along with his colleagues in 2011, and it is considered as the key point we need to adapt to the changing data streams and overcome other challenges [6]. As other members of the Learn++ family, the algorithm learns incrementally, namely, for each batch of data, it trains one new classifier and combines these classifiers by using a dynamically weighted majority voting, without previously seen data. Determining the voting weights, which is the novelty of the algorithm, due to the time-adjusted accuracy of classifiers [3]. Learn++.NSE works in concept drift in nonstationary environments, and it has been confirmed that tracking a variety of concept drift environments shows great performance. Then the classifier will be updated by computing error, redistributing weight according to a set of data streams and the recent samples, followed by abolishing the classification which has high error or cannot adapt to the newly coming data by given a zero weight. As for weighted majority voting mechanism, each classifier has different influence in the combined strong learner and, the bad classifiers have little efficiency but the great ones play a major part in ensemble classification [6].

Learn++.NSE employed in activity recognition may solve the concept evolution problem [6]. However, as for novel class detection, the result is not satisfying, especially for classifier whose structure of each training class is fixed, such as ELM (Extreme Machine Learning) [10]. Further, the entire classification results will be affected if the classification is changed, so, it did not work well in many applications. When a new class sample comes, the system cannot recognize it, and this sample is still classified into previous classes, ignoring the new class. In other words, this part may not match our system well so it should be optimized in some ways.

There are some methods proposed for novel class detection in data streams, which referred to many common classification algorithms and analyzed their advantages and disadvantages respectively [12, 13, 17, 18]. There is no doubt that it is necessary to detect the novel class that cannot be seen but does exist in continuous data streams and distinguish it from others effectively. To maintain the space covered by the existing (known) class characteristics, newly coming data designated as "insiders" means the same as an existing class while "outsiders" are related to unknown classes, which depend on whether it is located inside or outside the covered space [12].

When a set of data are not found in any existing classes, i.e., all existing classes can't match it. In the case of uncertainty, the error caused by misclassify will reduce the efficiency of the system, since the cost of the error is greater than that of non-classification, thus we should reject the data [11, 20, 21]. The external scheme of reject rule is based on the result of the whole classification system but ignores the internal structure. Assuming a threshold t_e to discriminate each classifier based on their reliability appraised by *Hamming distance*. Our paper will emphasize on embedding the external scheme of reject rule into Learn++.NSE to detect novel class (Fig. 1).

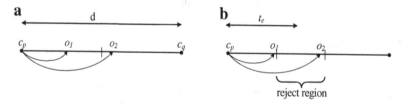

Fig. 1. An example of reject option for external scheme [11]

The paper is made up of several parts as follows: in Sect. 3, we thoroughly analyze the composition of our approach. In Sect. 4, an experiment using opportunity activity recognition data set is conducted, followed by the conclusions and future work in Sect. 5.

3   Proposed Approach

In this section, we will continue to introduce the approach in detail. Figure 2 shows our modified algorithm by combining Learn++.NSE and reject option together.

Input: Training data $D^{(t)} = \{x_i \in X \,; y_i \in \Omega\}$ where $i = 1,2,\ldots, m^{(t)}$

Supervised learning algorithm **BaseClassifier**

Sigmoid parameters a (slope) & b (inflection point)

Do for $t = 1,2,\ldots$

If $t = 1$, **Initialize** $D^{(1)}(i) = w^{(t)}(i) = 1/m^{(1)}, \; \forall i$

Go to step 4. **Endif**

1. Compute error of the existing ensemble on new data

$$E^{(t)} = \sum_{j=1}^{m(t)} 1/m^{(t)} \cdot [\, H^{(t-1)}(x_i) \neq y_i\,] \qquad (1)$$

2. Update and normalize instance weights

$$w^{(t)}(i) = 1/m^{(t)} \cdot \begin{cases} E(t) & H(t-1)(xi)=yi \\ 1 & \text{otherwise} \end{cases} \qquad (2)$$

$$D^{(t)}(i) = w^{(t)}(i) \Big/ \sum_{j=1}^{m(t)} w^{(t)}(j) \qquad (3)$$

3. Call **BaseClassifier** with $D^{(t)}$ to obtain h_t

4. Call reject option on $D^{(t)}$ to obtain $\theta_1^{(t)}$ and $\theta_2^{(t)}$

5. Evaluate all existing classifiers on new data $D^{(t)}$ and obtain pseudo error

$$\varepsilon_k^{(t)} = \sum_{j=1}^{m(t)} D^{(t)}(i) \cdot [\, h_k(x_i) \neq y_i\,] \qquad (4)$$

If $\varepsilon_{k=t}^{(t)} > 1/2$, generate a new h_k

If $\varepsilon_{k<t}^{(t)} > 1/2$, set $\varepsilon t = 1/2$

$$\beta_k^{(t)} = \varepsilon_k^{(t)} / (1 - \varepsilon_k^{(t)}) \qquad (5)$$

6. Compute the weighted average of all normalized errors for k^{th} classifier h_k: For $a,b \in R$

$$\omega_k^{(t)} = 1 / (\, 1 + \exp(-a\,(\,t - k - b\,))) \qquad (6)$$

$$\boldsymbol{\omega}_k^{(t)} = \omega_k^{(t)} \Big/ \sum_{j=0}^{t-k} \omega_k^{(t)} \qquad (7)$$

$$\bar{\beta}_k^{(t)} = \sum_{j=0}^{t-k} \omega_k^{(t-j)} \beta_k^{(t-j)}, \; k = 1,2,\ldots, t \qquad (8)$$

7. Calculate voting weight and normalized

$$W_k^{(t)} = \log 1 / \bar{\beta}_k^{(t)} \qquad (9)$$

$$norm(W_k^{(t)}) = \frac{W_k^{(t)} - \min\{W_*^{(t)}\}}{\max\{W_*^{(t)}\} - \min\{W_*^{(t)}\}} \qquad (10)$$

8. Compute ensemble decision

$$H^{(t)}(x) = \arg\max_{c \in \Omega} \sum_{k=1}^{t} W_k^{(t)} [\, h_k(x_i) = c\,] \qquad (11)$$

End for

Output: Return final hypothesis $H^{(t)}(x)$

Fig. 2. Improved Learn++.NSE algorithm

Specifically, suppose we utilize base classifier with soft output, such as ELM, and the parameters $a = 0.5$ defines the slope and $b = 10$ defines the halfway crossing point of the sigmoid to compute the final voting weight of the eventual classifier in Learn++.NSE., which will be used later, we input training dataset $D^{(t)}$ where t is time index and m means the number of the datasets. When $t = 1$, for all value i, initializing penalty distribution $D^{(t)}$ equals to instance specific error weights of the first batch of data, $w^{(t)}$ as $1/m$. Then, call the base classifier with $D^{(1)}$ so that we can get the first hypothesis h_1. In step 1, compute the error E^t of existing ensemble classifier on newly coming data to evaluate the performance. According to the comparison between two results obtained respectively from the classifier and reality, if it is classified correctly, updating instance weights as E^t, otherwise the instance weights would be 1. Normalizing instance weights and calculating penalty distribution in step 2. Then we can get a new hypothesis h_k coming from $D^{(t)}$ in step 3. Followed by step 4, applying the reject rule to detect novel class. Next, current data classified by the new hypothesis and all the existing hypothesis are evaluated on current data to calculate the error ε. The new hypothesis which obtains an error more than 1/2 should be replaced by another creative one, while every ε of the rest would be saturated to 1/2 if the error is greater than 1/2. Thus, we can obtain the normalized error β according to each ε in step 5. In order to emphasize each classifier's recent performance, we use a sigmoidal weighting function in step 6, in which the parameters a and b are used to compute the final voting weight and normalize it, where a defines the slope while b defines the halfway crossing point of the sigmoid. Weighted errors $\bar{\beta}$ obtained from sigmoidal weights combined normalized classifier errors. In step 7, calculating classifier voting weights W and normalize it. The $\max\{W(t) \; *\}$ is the greatest value in the tth feature and the $\min\{W(t) \; *\}$ is the smallest, so that W obtain a value in the range of [0, 1]. Finally the final hypothesis $H^{(t)}$ are obtained in step 8.

In the case of hard decoding, it can revise binary errors induced in the hard decision process, and the reliability can be evaluated only by examining the Hamming distance between the codewords and the binary output vector. The greater the distance is, the greater the error will be, but the magnitude of the soft outputs are completely ignored, which represents an indicator of the reliability of the decision coming from the dichotomizer. Therefore, there is a common strategy that considering the real-valued output of a dichotomizer normalized in the interval $[-1, 1]$, then collecting the results into a real-valued output vector. For the soft decoding in external scheme, the reject option can empolder the loss function associated with the employed dichotomizer. The reliability of the decision could be evaluated by examining the loss distance related to the decision. A loss value assumed should be normalized in the range [0, 1].

At the training phase, in this paper, we utilize base classifier with soft output as the base classifier, such as ELM. When new data comes, the classifier will output a column vector $v^{(t)}$. For example, there are 3 classes initially, then vector $v_1 = [1, -1, -1]^T$ said the first class, $v_2 = [-1, -1, 1]^T$ said second class and $v_3 = [-1, -1, 1]^T$ said third class. However, as a matter of fact, the output vector can not achieve such a stable value, but real numbers in interval. Meanwhile, the novel class is not visible but does exist will also affect the result. Therefore, for each dataset, we calculate the loss func tion (L_2 in this paper) between classifier's output vector $v^{(t)}$ and v_i ($i = 1, 2, 3$) respectively, then take the maximum value as $R^{(t)}$. When $t = 1$, $R^{(1)}$ as the first threshold $\theta_1^{(1)}$ of reject rule, for future data, $\theta_1^{(t)}$ is the mean of all current existing $R^{(t)}$.

When the error existed between the output vector $v^{(t)}$ and the three kinds of classes, there are two possibilities, one is the deviation of the classifier and the data itself. The other possibility is that the new class is produced. The output vector cannot be divided into any classes, needs to be classified into new class so it should be rejected. Thus, $\theta_1^{(t)}$ cannot be used as the only threshold in reject rule which also need to rely on another threshold $\theta_2^{(t)}$. For the training data, we know the correct classification of each set of data in advance, and it will be compared with the output of the classifier, if misclassified, $\theta_2^{(t)} = 1$, otherwise $\theta_2^{(t)} = 0$. When $\theta_2^{(t)} = 1$ and $R^{(t)} > \theta_1^{(t-1)}$ are satisfied at the same time, we believe that the data meet reject rule, namely, the dataset will be rejected.

In this case, we avoid the use of fixed threshold in each set of data. The two thresholds in different data is dynamic change so that can better match each dataset and make the result more accuracy.

In the testing phase, we don't know the actual class of the test data. So only consider a threshold $\theta_1^{(t)}$, namely when $R^{(t)} > \theta_1^{(t-1)}$, the data should be rejected and can be assumed to have occurred the concept evolution. We use it as a method of novel class detection (Fig. 3).

Therefore, our reject rule algorithm can be expressed as follows:

For $t = 1, 2, \ldots$ **Do**

1. calculate the loss function from classifier's output vector
$$R^{(t)} = max\,[L_2\,(v^{(t)}, v_i\,)] \qquad (1)$$
2. obtain the first threshold from each dataset
$$\theta_1^{(t)} = (1/t)\sum\nolimits_{j=1}^{t} R^{(t)} \qquad (2)$$
3. obtain the second threshold
$$\theta_2^{(t)} = \begin{cases} 1 & \text{misclassified} \\ 0 & \text{correct} \end{cases} \qquad (3)$$
4. decide the reject option
   If $\theta_2^{(t)} = 1\ \&\ R^{(t)} > \theta_1^{(t-1)}$ \qquad (4)
   Do *reject*
   # class = *# class* + 1
   Endif
End

Fig. 3. Reject rule based novel class detection algorithm description

4 Experiment

4.1 Dataset

In this experiment, we adopted an opportunity activity recognition data set from UCI machine learning repository, and the descriptions of these datasets could be found in [19]. We chose the data comes from body-worn sensors which include 11 3D acceleration sensors mounted on the upper body, hip and leg (column 1 to column 33). And 7 inertial measurement units, five are on the upper body and others are mounted on the user's shoes (column 34 to 130). The inertial measurement units provide readings of: 3D acceleration, 3D rate of turn, 3D magnetic field, and orientation of the sensor with respect to a world coordinating system in quaternions.

4.2 Experimental Setup

Learn++.NSE in [3] is used as the basic weighted ensemble approach which works in nonstationary environments while creating a reject rule for the reject option aims to deal with concept evolution in data stream which may change continuously [11]. We use ELM as the base classifier instead of CART and SVM because of its fast learning speed and good generalization performance. In sigmoidal weighting function, we use the two parameters ($a = 0.5$ and $b = 10$). The initial number of classes are 3. The feature set size = 130 for body-worn sensors while the $m = 1000$ means the number of data in each training dataset $D^{(t)}$ and testing dataset $Dt^{(p)}$. In our experiment, $t = 20$ in the training dataset and it occurs the fourth class when t equals to 11, 13, 15, 17 and 19. Likewise in the testing dataset where $p = 14$ and concept evolution happened when p equals to 5, 7, 9, 11 and 13.

4.3 Experimental Result

Summary results of our experiments are shown in Tables 1 and 2. The first two rows refer to the average test accuracy for testing data only has existing class, without or with novel class detection (NCD), while the following two rows show the result including novel class. T is the number of batch data used for training phase, namely, the number of classifier. The testing data are tested singly, and the process is not time-ordered, since the data of training phase are processed by Learn++.NSE, the previous data will affect later data while training. The best results of two tables are in bold.

Table 1. Performance of 10 samples containing novel class in each dataset.

# *novelCls* = 10	T = 8	T = 12	T = 16	T = 20
exAveTestAcc	0.7860 ± 0.0317	0.7869 ± 0.0242	0.7891 ± 0.0217	0.7923 ± 0.0153
exAveTestAccNc	**0.8234 ± 0.0039**	**0.8229 ± 0.0082**	**0.8258 ± 0.0055**	**0.8260 ± 0.0065**
ncAveTestAcc	0.7850 ± 0.0338	0.7873 ± 0.0230	0.7908 ± 0.0205	0.7932 ± 0.0177
ncAveTestAccNc	0.8256 ± 0.0046	0.8250 ± 0.0074	0.8274 ± 0.0063	0.8284 ± 0.0070

As for Table 1, when the number of samples containing novel class is small (i.e. #novelCls = 10, accounting for 1 % of the total test samples), no matter the test sample contains a new class or not, the effect of adding NCD mechanism is similar. The result will not be affected by the number of classifiers to a large extent.

Table 2. Performance of 100 samples containing novel class in each dataset.

# novelCls = 100	T = 8	T = 12	T = 16	T = 20
exAveTestAcc	0.7864 ± 0.0243	0.7854 ± 0.0277	0.7878 ± 0.0230	0.7916 ± 0.0182
exAveTestAccNc	**0.8219 ± 0.0045**	**0.8253 ± 0.0074**	**0.8238 ± 0.0050**	**0.8209 ± 0.0070**
ncAveTestAcc	0.7981 ± 0.0253	0.7949 ± 0.0278	0.7878 ± 0.0265	0.8012 ± 0.0315
ncAveTestAccNc	0.7982 ± 0.0176	0.8114 ± 0.0263	0.8086 ± 0.0230	0.8126 ± 0.0222

Similarly, as for Table 2, when the number of samples containing novel class is slightly large (i.e. #novelCls = 100, accounting for 10 % of the total test samples), the result of the test will be affected by the novel class of samples, but the performance is still better than the algorithm without NCD mechanism. In particular, when $T = 8$, that is, the novel class has never appeared in training sample, the testing results with the NCD is not obvious. However, when the novel class appears in the training sample, the performance of algorithm with NCD is enhanced. On the other hand, the new algorithm will improve the performance of the algorithm in the case of no novel class.

Generally speaking, no matter how many samples contain novel class, the accuracy of the algorithm with NCD has been greatly improved in the experiment. The current algorithm will be affected when the novel class occurs frequently, but in general, alleviate the adverse effects of the new class significantly.

In addition, we demonstrate two typical results of the experiment with 10 samples containing novel class (Figs. 4 and 5). From Fig. 4 we can see that the classifier in the Learn++.NSE will be affected by all existing classifiers. So, when there appears a new

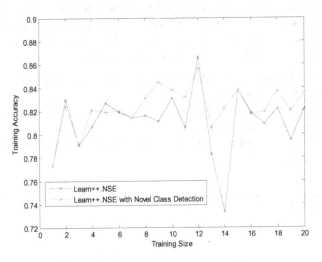

Fig. 4. Training accuracy comparison between Learn++.NSE and our approach

class, the accuracy of training may be lower as shown in the 13th and the 14th classifier. Figure 5 also indicates that the improved algorithm shows better performance than Learn++.NSE in most cases, while the testing data without new classes may perform not so well, such as the third dataset. In usual cases, the proposed algorithm is better than Learn++.NSE for the data which include a new class.

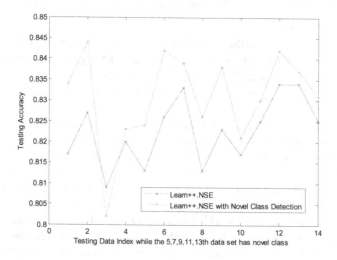

Fig. 5. Testing accuracy comparison between Learn++.NSE and our approach

5   Conclusions and Future Work

In this paper we described how to deal with concept evolution in non-stationary environments. In our proposed approach, we combine Learn++.NSE with reject rule which shows better accuracy than single Learn++.NSE algorithm in novel class detection. No matter how many samples containing new class are there, the proposed approach showed great performance as well as alleviating the adverse effects of the new class significantly.

There are also some parts could be explored as follows:

(1) How to ensure the accuracy of the classification when a large amount of data should be classified to the new class.
(2) Only a new class is considered in our experiment. More attention should be paid to multiple new classes in future work.
(3) We may also find out a method which is able to increase or delete classes according to novel class detected.

Acknowledgments. This work was supported by the National Natural Science Foundation of China (Grant No: 61502360)

References

1. Abdallah, Z.S., Gaber, M.M., Srinivasan, B., et al.: Adaptive mobile activity recognition system with evolving data streams. Neurocomputing **150**, 304–317 (2015)
2. Polikar R., Udpa L., Udpa S., et al.: Learn++: an incremental learning algorithm for multilayer perceptrons. In: Proceedings of 25th. IEEE International Conference on Acoustics, Speech and Signal Processing, vol. 6, pp. 3414–3417 (2000)
3. Ditzler G., Polikar R., Chawla N.: An incremental learning algorithm for non-stationary environments and class imbalance. In: 2010 20th International Conference on Pattern Recognition (ICPR), pp. 2997–3000. IEEE (2010)
4. Ditzler, G., Muhlbaier, M.D., Polikar, R.: Incremental Learning of New Classes in Unbalanced Datasets: Learn++.UDNC. In: Gayar, N., Kittler, J., Roli, F. (eds.) MCS 2010. LNCS, vol. 5997, pp. 33–42. Springer, Heidelberg (2010)
5. Muhlbaier M., Topalis A., Polikar R.: Incremental learning from unbalanced data. In: Proceedings of 2004 IEEE International Joint Conference on Neural Networks, vol. 2, pp. 1057–1062. IEEE (2004)
6. Elwell, R., Polikar, R.: Incremental learning of concept drift in nonstationary environments. IEEE Trans. Neural Netw. **22**(10), 1517–1531 (2011)
7. Hongeng, S., Nevatia, R., Bremond, F.: Video-based event recognition: activity representation and probabilistic recognition methods. Comput. Vis. Image Underst. **96**(2), 129–162 (2004)
8. Fahad L.G., Tahir S.F., Rajarajan M. Feature selection and data balancing for activity recognition in smart homes. In: 2015 IEEE International Conference on Communications (ICC), pp. 512–517. IEEE (2015)
9. Kwapisz, J.R., Weiss, G.M., Moore, S.A.: Activity recognition using cell phone accelerometers. ACM SigKDD Explor. Newslett. **12**(2), 74–82 (2011)
10. Huang, G.B.: What are extreme learning machines? filling the gap between Frank Rosenblatt's dream and John von Neumann's puzzle. Cogn. Comput. **7**(3), 263–278 (2015)
11. Simeone, P., Marrocco, C., Tortorella, F.: Design of reject rules for ECOC classification systems. Pattern Recogn. **45**(2), 863–875 (2012)
12. Bouguelia M.R., Belaïd Y., Belaïd A.: Efficient active novel class detection for data stream classification. In: ICPR-International Conference on Pattern Recognition, pp. 2826–2831. IEEE (2014)
13. ZareMoodi, P., Beigy, H., Siahroudi, S.K.: Novel class detection in data streams using local patterns and neighborhood graph. Neurocomputing **158**, 234–245 (2015)
14. Masud, M.M., Chen, Q., Khan, L., et al.: Classification and adaptive novel class detection of feature-evolving data streams. IEEE Trans. Knowl. Data Eng. **25**(7), 1484–1497 (2013)
15. Farid, D.M., Zhang, L., Hossain, A., et al.: An adaptive ensemble classifier for mining concept drifting data streams. Expert Syst. Appl. **40**(15), 5895–5906 (2013)
16. Al-Khateeb T., Masud M. M., Khan L., et al.: Stream classification with recurring and novel class detection using class-based ensemble. In: 2012 IEEE 12th International Conference on Data Mining (ICDM), pp. 31–40. IEEE (2012)
17. Masud M.M., Al-Khateeb T.M., Khan L., et al.: Detecting recurring and novel classes in concept-drifting data streams. In: 2011 IEEE 11th International Conference on Data Mining (ICDM), pp. 1176–1181. IEEE (2011)
18. Masud, M.M., Gao, J., Khan, L., et al.: Classification and novel class detection in concept-drifting data streams under time constraints. IEEE Trans. Know. Data Eng. **23**(6), 859–874 (2011)

19. Roggen D., Calatroni A., Rossi M., et al.: Collecting complex activity datasets in highly rich networked sensor environments. In: 2010 Seventh International Conference on Networked Sensing Systems (INSS), pp. 233–240. IEEE (2010)
20. Bartlett, P.L., Wegkamp, M.H.: Classification with a reject option using a hinge loss. J. Mach. Learn. Res. **9**, 1823–1840 (2008)
21. Pillai, I., Fumera, G., Roli, F.: Multi-label classification with a reject option. Pattern Recogn. **46**(8), 2256–2266 (2013)
22. Fortino, G., Giannantonio, R., Gravina, R., et al.: Enabling effective programming and flexible management of efficient body sensor network applications. IEEE Trans. Hum. Mach. Syst. **43**(1), 115–133 (2013)
23. Ghasemzadeh, H., Panuccio, P., Trovato, S., et al.: Power-aware activity monitoring using distributed wearable sensors. IEEE Trans. Hum. Mach. Syst. **44**(4), 537–544 (2014)
24. Fortino, G., Galzarano, S., Gravina, R., et al.: A framework for collaborative computing and multi-sensor data fusion in body sensor networks. Inf. Fusion **22**, 50–70 (2015)

SwimSense: Monitoring Swimming Motion Using Body Sensor Networks

Jiaxin Wang[1(✉)], Zhelong Wang[1], Fengshan Gao[2], and Ming Guo[1]

[1] School of Control Science and Engineering, Dalian University of Technology,
Dalian 116024, Liaoning, China
wangjx19890828@mail.dlut.edu.cn
[2] Department of Physical Education, Dalian University of Technology,
Dalian, China
swimclub@dlut.edu.cn

Abstract. In order to effectively improve training quality of the swimmers, the activity monitoring technology based on body sensor networks (BSN) may be qualified for this task. In this paper, a monitoring system (SwimSense) for human swimming training locomotion based on BSN is established. SwimSense includes six measurement nodes, which can monitor the swimming strokes of several swimmers synchronously. The receiving node is connected with personal computer (PC) through USB cable, which allows the collected motion data can be transmitted to PC through wireless radio frequency communication, and the collected data can be used to motion analysis. The preliminary monitoring system mainly has two functions, at the first place, different swimming strokes may be recognized by using the monitoring system, and the selective classifier is Hidden Markov Model, and then according to the results of classification and the characters of different swimming strokes, phase segmentation of each swimming stroke is executed by using Support Vector Machine for the detailed research in the future.

Keywords: Body sensor networks · Motion recognition · Phase segmentation · Swimming

1 Introduction

In recent years, as the raising of social material level, more and more people are interested in physical training, especially for some obese people. Many sports have been favored by people, such as playing tennis, playing badminton and running, etc. For swimming, it is one of the most favorite sports, and it has much more unimaginable benefits, for example, swimming training has contributed to improve the cardiovascular system and the lung capacity, it also has raise the blood circulation of body, and it helps the body to improve the adaptability of temperature variation. More importantly, it can contribute to lose weight for obese people. It was because of this, swimming is enjoyed by more and more people. Meanwhile, a growing number of scholars have devoted themselves to the study of swimming.

© Springer International Publishing AG 2016
W. Li et al. (Eds.): IDCS 2016, LNCS 9864, pp. 45–55, 2016.
DOI: 10.1007/978-3-319-45940-0_5

Traditionally, the study of swimming is mainly based on video mode like Image and video camera. Smith et al. [16] gave a detailed comments of the proposed psychological tools used in the evaluation of swimmers by using the video camera. Ceseracciu et al. [1] proposed a video system to analyze the arm movements during front crawl swimming, and the authors recruited 5 sprint swimmers to execute front crawl swimming. Dubois et al. [5] presented a novel method to improve automatic segmentation performance of limb phases for swimming for stroke correction by using the image analysis techniques. However, it has a lot of disadvantages in this mode [11], such as high cost, inconvenient carrying and limited scope, etc.

In recent ten years, micro-electro-mechanical system (MEMS) has made significant progress. The technology of body sensor networks (BSN)[6–8] emerges as the times require, and its main function is to monitor the behavior of the human body by using a wide variety of sensors. The purpose of this is because using BSN is able to overcome some shortcomings existing in video mode mentioned above.

There also have many researches of swimming training based on BSN in literatures. Ohgi et al. [14] designed a new device including two ADXL250s to measure the wrist acceleration of freestyle swimming, and the swimmers came from Japanese top level colleges, the authors just used the DLT method to calculate the hand path during underwater stroke. In 2002, Ohgi et al. [13] also developed a data processing apparatus including acceleration data and angular velocity data to analyze underwater stroke activity in swimming, and the apparatus was attached to the wrist joint of one subject. In order to overcome the shortcomings of the traditional model, Lee et al. [10] did the research that an inertial system was valid to measure temporal motion of a freestyle stroke, and the authors employed six subjects to participate in the experiment, At last, a comparison is performed among the 2D video capture, a 3D infrared camera system and inertial sensor system. Dadashi et al. [3] put forward a new method to detect an automatic approach of automatically segmenting sequence events of breaststroke swimming, two inertial sensor nodes placed on the right arm and the right leg of one body were used, also the detection method the authors chose was Hidden Markov Model (HMM). Topalovic [17] designed an online monitoring system of swimming training by using a 3D accelerometer, 10 swimmers were invited to test the effectiveness of this system.

In this paper, a preliminary monitoring system based on BSN is proposed, the system is able to achieve two capabilities. One is that three different swimming strokes including front crawl (FC), breaststroke (BS) and back crawl (BC) may be distinguished by using HMM. After that, the phase segmentation is done for each swimming stroke. In this way, we can obtain the accurate detection of swimming event, which is useful for the precise calculation of the swimming stroke parameters in our future researches.

The rest of this paper is organized as follows: Sect. 2 introduces the hardware platform and describes the algorithms framework for recognizing swimming stroke styles and segmenting the stroke phases; Experimental methods are introduced and the results are showed in Sect. 3; Sect. 4 concludes the overall research.

2 System Overview and Algorithms

2.1 Hardware Platform

Swimming monitoring system (SwimSense) proposed in this paper includes a wireless receiving node, six measurement nodes and a personal computer (PC) as shown in Fig. 1. The receiving node is connected with PC through USB cable which is mainly to control measurement nodes for data collection and transmission, and the communication with inertial measurement nodes is 2.4 GHz wireless by RF transceiver. The sensor chips in each measurement node are a single-axis analog gyroscope, a dual-axis analog gyroscope and a 3-axis accelerometer.

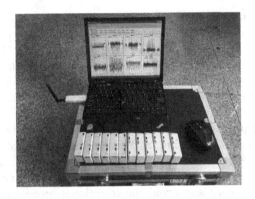

Fig. 1. The profile of swimming monitoring system (SwimSense).

The sensor performance specification is summarized in Table 1. Each inertial measurement node contains an ARM microprocessor and a flash memory which can save the raw data offline when the subject swim in the swimming pool. Each measurement node is powered by a 1200 mAh lithium polymer battery, which enables the measurement node work more than 6 h. The highest sampling rate of the data collection system is 200 Hz (the sampling rate of 50 Hz is used by our system in the following experiment), which can be selected by the receiving node. The collected raw motion data are processed offline using the software of the system which is written by C# and MATLAB 2012a.

Table 1. Specification of sensor performance

Sensor type	Full scale	Sensitivity	Bandwidth
Accelerometer	±6 g	330 mV/g	550 Hz
Gyroscope	±500°/s	0.5 mV/°/s	140 Hz

2.2 Algorithm Framework

Stroke Recognition. The first step of the designed system is used to recognize three swimming strokes, which are front crawl (FC), breaststroke (BS) and back crawl (BC), respectively. In this paper, the classifier we chose is Hidden Markov Model (HMM). HMMs is a probability statistical model, and it is able to recognize activity sequence. The function of HMM is mainly to establish one or more of Markov chains by using hidden states. Now in many recognition fileds [12, 18], the model has been widely used to many applications, because a much higher recognition accuracy rate may be achieved, especially for some complex activities.

Phase Segmentation. Swimming stroke can be described by intervals, periods motion phases, which may exist different phase segmentation plans according to the different study goals, such as gait phase detection [19]. Here, we consider motion phase segmentation as a pattern recognition process, however, its goal is to identify specific motion state based on the basic types of known movement. From the point of view of time, phase segmentation is used to recognize instant human movement. In this research, segmenting motion phase automatically is a supervised learning process, and the Support Vector Machine (SVM) [2] classifier is used as the recognition algorithm. SVM is a novel learning algorithm for small sample, and it is different from other classification algorithms (like naive Bayes, decision tree and neural network) based on statistical theory, SVM does not use the probability theory and avoid the traditional process from induction to deduction, which is very useful to simplify the problems of classification. SVM is given priority although they do not provide a set of rules understandable to humans.

Algorithm Procedure. Biomechanical variables (e.g., stroke count and rate) can be calculated from stroke phase, and many motion analysis algorithms need to detect the human motion phase, such as zero velocity update algorithm (ZUPT) in pedestrian navigation [19] or gait analysis [15]. Hence, it is meaningful to get the stroke phases for monitoring the performance of the swimmer,

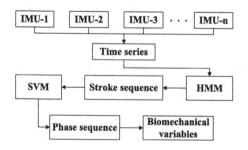

Fig. 2. The algorithm framework of swimming monitoring system.

and stroke styles and phases can also be regarded as biomechanical variables. In order to automatically achieve the phase segmentation plans of different stroke styles using off-line algorithms after each swimming exercise, HMM classifier first recognizes the stroke sequence in time series, and then SVM classifier segments the time series of different stroke styles based on the results of recognized stroke sequence. The overall framework of the proposed system is shown in Fig. 2.

3   Experimental Validation and Results

3.1   Data Collection Protocol

One subject is employed to participate in the swimming experiment. He needs to execute three competitive swimming styles including front crawl (FC), breast-stroke (BS) and back crawl (BC) separately. Six inertial sensors measurement nodes are attached to left wrist and right wrist (node 5 and node 15), shins (node 17 and node 18), chest (node 11) and abdomen (node 14) respectively, which are shown in Fig. 3. This study analyzes the motion pattern of swimming stroke in three competitive swimming based on motion data of different body parts. The raw data of IMU is shown in Fig. 4.

Fig. 3. Six sensor nodes attached to one subject.

3.2   Stroke Recognition

For our monitoring system, the first function is that our system is able to classify three swimming strokes including front crawl (FC), breaststroke (BS) and back crawl (BC). According to the theory of pattern recognition, some works like preconditioning, feature extraction and feature selection need to be carried

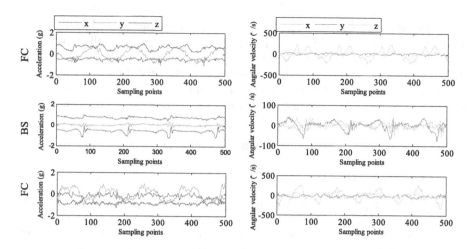

Fig. 4. Acceleration signals and angular velocity signals from the sensor node attached to the left wrist. The first column represents acceleration signals, and the second column represents the angular velocity signals. Rows represent classes of three swimming strokes, and from top to bottom, they are front crawl (FC), breaststroke (BS) and back crawl (BC), respectively.

out before swimming strokes recognition. In the stage of preconditioning. The sliding window we chose is equal to 2 s according to the sampling frequency and characteristics of swimming strokes. In the paper, five features including time-domain features and frequency-domain features are chosen, and time-domain features are mean, variance, kurtosis and correlation coefficient, the frequency-domain feature is energy. At last, the feature dimension is equal to 180 (5 features × 6 sensors × 6 axes), and we may obtain 108 samples in total after preconditioning and feature extraction. In the stage of feature selection, the feature selection method named robust linear discriminant analysis [9] is used to reduce the dimension of features.

In the process of recognition, the classification algorithm we chose is HMM, and Table 2 gives the final classification result of three swimming strokes. From the table we can see that the three swimming strokes may be distinguished completely, which explains that our monitoring system is very efficient in the process of swimming strokes.

Table 2. The confusion matrix of three strokes classification result by using HMM

	BC	BS	FC
BC	24	0	0
BS	0	42	0
FC	0	0	42

3.3   Phase Segmentation

The fundamental prerequisite of biomechanical analysis is the phase analysis using inertial sensors in swimming [4]. Through the stroke recognition process, monitoring system can achieve accurate recognition of stroke styles, e.g., front crawl (FC), breaststroke (BS) and back crawl (BC), (see Sect. 3.2). According to the stroke sequence results of HMM algorithm, phase segmentation algorithm (SVM classifier) can select time series raw data of different body parts for segmenting the stroke phase of different stroke styles. Here, different phase segmentation plans are validated based on complex kinematic events in different styles of swimming strokes (front crawl, breaststroke and back crawl).

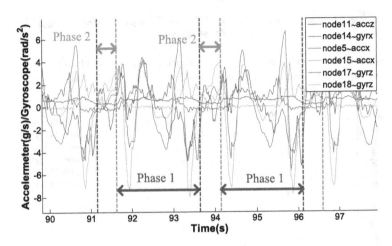

Fig. 5. The stroke of front crawl is divided into non-breathing (blue line) and breathing (green line) based on breathing motion of the upper trunk. (Color figure online)

Front Crawl Phase. According to breathing motion of the upper trunk in front crawl, the stroke phases are divided into non-breathing phase (phase 1) and breathing phase (phase 2). Raw data contains Z-axis accelerometer on chest (node 11), X-axis angular velocity on abdomen (node 14), X-axis accelerometer on left and right wrists (node 5 and node 15), and Z-axis angular velocity on left and right shins (node 17 and node 18) as shown in Fig. 5. The segmentation effect of front crawl phases is shown in Fig. 6, and the artificial labels are obtained according to the video recordings.

Breaststroke Phase. According to motor pattern of the limbs in breaststroke [3], the stroke phases are divided into three phases: the period from the beginning of Hand back-sweep to Leg flexion (phase 1), the period from the beginning of Leg flexion to Leg extension (phase 2) and the period from the beginning of Leg extension to Hand back-sweep (phase 3). Raw data contains X-axis accelerometer on chest (node 11), Y-axis angular velocity on abdomen (node 14), Z-axis angular

52   J. Wang et al.

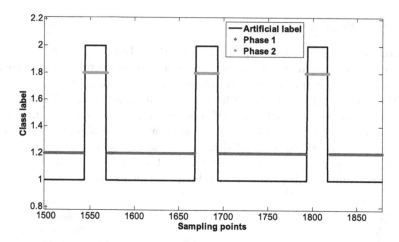

Fig. 6. System can provide the result of monitoring front crawl phase: Non-breathing phase (blue line) and Breathing phase (green line). (Color figure online)

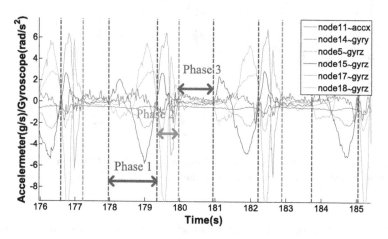

Fig. 7. The stroke of breaststroke is divided into arm non-glide (phase 1), leg propulsion (phase 2) and stable glide (phase 3) based on arm and leg alternating motor pattern.

velocity on left and right wrists (node 5 and node 15), and Z-axis angular velocity on left and right shins (node 17 and node 18), which is shown in Fig. 7. The segmentation effect of breaststroke phases is shown in Fig. 8.

Back Crawl Phase. According to alternating recovery motion of left and right arms in back crawl, the stroke phases are divided into left hand recovery (phase 1) and right hand recovery (phase 2). Each recovery motion period begins with one hand out of the water and ends up with the another out of the water. Raw data contains X-axis angular velocity on chest (node 11), Y-axis accelerometer and

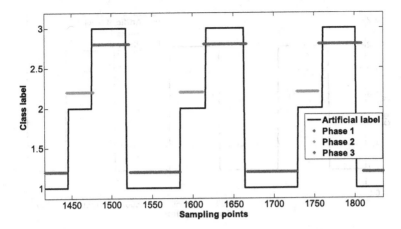

Fig. 8. System can provide the result of monitoring breaststroke phase: Arm non-glide phase (blue line), Leg propulsion phase (green line) and Stable glide phase (red line) (Color figure online)

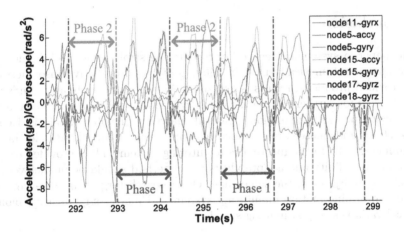

Fig. 9. The stroke of back crawl is divided into left hand recovery (blue line) and right hand recovery (green line) based on alternating recovery motion of left and right arms. (Color figure online)

Y-axis angular velocity on left and right wrists (node 5 and node 15), Z-axis angular velocity on left and right shins (node 17 and node 18). As shown in Fig. 9, the duration between phase 1 and phase 2 is very close comparing to the segmentation plans of front crawl and breaststroke. The segmentation effect of back crawl phases is shown in Fig. 10, and it is easy to judge the performance of the phase segmentation according to the artificial labels.

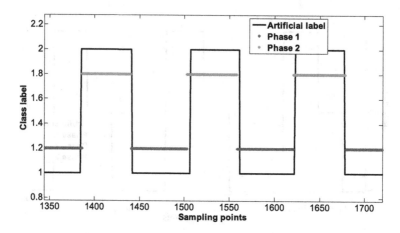

Fig. 10. System can provide the result of monitoring back crawl phase: Left hand recovery phase (blue line) and Right hand recovery phase (green line). (Color figure online)

4   Conclusion

In this paper, a systematic method of recognizing stroke styles and segmenting stroke phases automatically in swimming sport based on body sensor network that provided promising results is proposed. A monitoring system (SwimSense) is established for further calculating more swimming stroke parameters, and the fundamental prerequisite of biomechanical analysis is the phase analysis. Hence, stroke styles and phases are regraded as prime biomechanical variables in our preliminary study. In the future, the monitoring system will be provided to athletes and the validity and adaptability of the method should be further verified for different subjects at the same time. Our research targets are to eventually provide an on-line motion monitoring system and more comprehensive biomechanical variables, e.g. swimming speed.

Acknowledgments. This work was supported by National Natural Science Foundation of China under Grant No. 61473058, Fundamental Research Funds for the Central Universities (DUT15ZD114), and National Natural Science Foundation of China under Grant No. 61174027.

References

1. Ceseracciu, E., Sawacha, Z., Fantozzi, S., Cortesi, M., Gatta, G., Corazza, S., Cobelli, C.: Markerless analysis of front crawl swimming. J. Biomech. **44**(12), 2236–2242 (2011)
2. Cortes, C., Vapnik, V.: Support-vector networks. Mach. Learn. **20**(3), 273–297 (1995)

3. Dadashi, F., Arami, A., Crettenand, F., Millet, G.P., Komar, J., Seifert, L., Aminian, K.: A hidden Markov model of the breaststroke swimming temporal phases using wearable inertial measurement units. In: 2013 IEEE International Conference on Body Sensor Networks, pp. 1–6 (2013)
4. de Magalhaes, F.A., Vannozzi, G., Gatta, G., Fantozzi, S.: Wearable inertial sensors in swimming motion analysis: a systematic review. J. Sports Sci. **33**(7), 732–745 (2015)
5. Dubois, R.P., Thiel, D.V., James, D.A.: Using image processing for biomechanics measures in swimming. Procedia Eng. **34**, 807–812 (2012)
6. Fortino, G., Galzarano, S., Gravina, R., Li, W.: A framework for collaborative computing and multi-sensor data fusion in body sensor networks. Inf. Fusion **22**, 50–70 (2015)
7. Fortino, G., Giannantonio, R., Gravina, R., Kuryloski, P., Jafari, R.: Enabling effective programming and flexible management of efficient body sensor network applications. IEEE Trans. Human-Machine Syst. **43**(1), 115–133 (2013)
8. Galzarano, S., Giannantonio, R., Liotta, A., Fortino, G.: A task-oriented framework for networked wearable computing. IEEE Trans. Autom. Sci. Eng. **13**(2), 621–638 (2016)
9. Guo, M., Wang, Z.: A feature extraction method for human action recognition using body-worn inertial sensors. In: 2015 IEEE 19th International Conference on Computer Supported Cooperative Work in Design (CSCWD), pp. 576–581 (2015)
10. Lee, J.B., Burkett, B.J., Thiel, D.V., James, D.A.: Inertial sensor, 3D and 2D assessment of stroke phases in freestyle swimming. Procedia Eng. **13**, 148–153 (2011)
11. Chen, L., Hoey, J., Nugent, C., Cook, D.J., Yu, Z.: Sensor-based activity recognition. IEEE Trans. Syst. Man, Cybern. Part C (Appl. Rev.) **42**(6), 790–808 (2012)
12. Lin, J.C., Wu, C.H., Wei, W.L.: Error weighted semi-coupled hidden Markov model for audio-visual emotion recognition. IEEE Trans. Multimedia **14**(1), 142–156 (2012)
13. Ohgi, Y.: Microcomputer-based acceleration sensor device for sports biomechanics. In: Proceedings of IEEE Sensors Conference, pp. 699–704 (2002)
14. Ohgi, Y., Yasumura, M., Ichikawa, H., Miyaji, C.: Analysis of stroke technique using acceleration sensor IC in freestyle swimming. Eng. Sport **250**, 503–511 (2000)
15. Qiu, S., Wang, Z., Zhao, H., Hu, H.: Using distributed wearable sensors to measure and evaluate human lower limb motions. IEEE Trans. Instrum. Measur. **65**(4), 1–12 (2016)
16. Smith, D.J., Norris, S.R., Hogg, J.M.: Performance evaluation of swimmers: scientific tools. Sports Med. (Auckland, N.Z.) **32**(9), 539–554 (2002)
17. Topalovic, M., Eyers, S., Exadaktylos, V., Olbrecht, J., Berckmans, D., Aerts, J.-M.: Online monitoring of swimmer training using a 3D accelerometer identifying swimming and swimming style. In: Proceedings of the 2nd International Congress on Sports Sciences Research and Technology Support, pp. 111–115 (2014)
18. Trabelsi, D., Mohammed, S., Chamroukhi, F., Oukhellou, L., Amirat, Y.: An unsupervised approach for automatic activity recognition based on hidden Markov model regression. IEEE Trans. Autom. Sci. Eng. **10**(3), 829–835 (2013)
19. Wang, Z.L., Zhao, H.Y., Qiu, S., Gao, Q.: Stance phase detection for ZUPT-aided foot-mounted pedestrian navigation system. IEEE/ASME Trans. Mechatron. **20**(6), 3170–3181 (2015)

Cloud Computing and Networking

SDNFV-Based Routing Service Composition Model

Chao Bu[1], Xingwei Wang[1,2(✉)], Lianbo Ma[1], and Min Huang[3]

[1] School of Software, Northeastern University, Shenyang, China
bc_0722@126.com, wangxw@mail.neu.edu.cn, malb@sia.cn
[2] School of Computer Science and Engineering, Northeastern University,
Shenyang, China
[3] School of Information Science and Engineering, Northeastern University,
Shenyang, China
mhuang@mail.neu.edu.cn

Abstract. With the rapid development of Internet, varieties of new types of applications are emerging out. Accordingly, the user communication demands for diversified applications exhibit more and more complex characteristics. The conventional approach to deal with this issue for Internet Service Provider (ISP) is continuous purchasing of new physical network equipment, which inevitably causes high technical costs and operating expense. Fortunately, the paradigms of decoupling control plane from data plane in Software Defined Networking (SDN) and decoupling functional services from underlying physical equipment in Network Function Virtualization (NFV) bring significant insights to deal with this challenging issue. Accordingly, with appropriately reusing diversified software-based routing functions and then adaptively selecting them to compose customized routing services, a novel SDNFV (i.e., SDN and NFV) based routing service composition model is proposed. In addition, considering continuously generated information by large-scale network communication activities, we combine machine learning with the proposed model. According to the user feedbacks for the provided services, the appropriate routing function selection and service composition is trained and optimized by the method of multi-layer feed-forward neural network. Simulation results verify the feasibility of the proposed model.

Keywords: Software defined networking · Network function virtualization · Routing service · Machine learning · Multi-layer feed-forward neural network

1 Introduction

The Internet technology and network scale are continuously developing and expanding, which brings constantly emerging new types of applications. The user communication demands for these types of applications are becoming more and more diversified and personalized. Traditionally, ISP purchases and develops new physical network equipment to satisfy the user frequently changing demands, which always leads to high technical costs and operating expense [1]. It is obviously unsustainable for ISP. In addition, current operating equipment may be eliminated without being fully utilized, which

W. Li et al. (Eds.): IDCS 2016, LNCS 9864, pp. 59–71, 2016.
DOI: 10.1007/978-3-319-45940-0_6

causes serious resource waste. Therefore, we consider dealing with the problem based on the software-based method instead of the traditional hardware-based method. We propose reusing various routing functions (packet scheduling, bandwidth allocation, traffic shaping, transcoding, error control, etc.), and adaptively selecting and composing appropriate ones into customized routing services for different types of applications with the user service experience optimized.

With allocating diverse routing functions in a multi-grained approach considered, to achieve flexibility, programmability and global superiority for composing routing services, the networking paradigms of Software Define Networking (SDN) [2] and Network Function Virtualization (NFV) [3] bring great inspiration to this paper. From the perspective of routing, SDN decouples control plane from data plane, its logically centralized control plane can configure routing under a global view, and promote routing service management and innovation. NFV decouples software-based functional services from hardware-based network equipment. In this approach, the software-based routing functions are modularized and interface-standardized, which promotes diverse routing functions to be individually improved, migrated, reused, and assembled in the form of service chain [4]. Therefore, we propose the SDNFV-based routing service composition model.

Currently, various routing functions bring great convenience to compose diversified and personalized routing services for different types of applications. However, the routing function selection and service composition are becoming more and more complicated. In addition, the user communication demands are more fine-grained (response time, video clarity, fault-recovery ability, etc.), which needs that ISP has to take each demand of the user into account to select appropriate routing functions to compose services, to optimize the user satisfaction degrees for the provided services. However, the relationships between the user demands and the appropriate routing functions are non-linear, which means that it is hard to map several fixed routing functions just according to the user several demands. Considering the current increasing information generated by the user continuous network communication activities through applications, we propose the idea of combining machine learning with routing service composition. We leverage the method of multi-layer feed-forward neural network to learn and train routing function selection and service composition according to different demands from the users and their corresponding feedbacks for the provided services.

In some related researches such as [5–7], the idea of service chain is proposed to promote function selection and service composition, to achieve the purpose of reusing exiting functions. And some researches such as [8–10], also combine the idea of function composition with entire service design and development, to achieve rapidly providing diverse services. However, the above researches did not consider the adaptive evolvability of the services composed by multiple functions, and did not support optimizing the function selection and service composition according to each round feedback information. In addition, the researches above just mainly focus on network services without taking routing services into account. In this paper, our proposed routing service composition model presents the corresponding solutions to these challenges, it also continuously optimize routing function selection and service composition from the perspective of improving the user service experiences.

2 Routing Service Composition Model

Based on the decoupling of control plane and data plane in SDN, and decoupling of software-based functions and hardware-based equipment in NFV, we propose routing service composition model from the perspective of network routing. The system framework of the proposed model consists of two layers (i.e., control layer and physical layer), and its details are shown in Fig. 1.

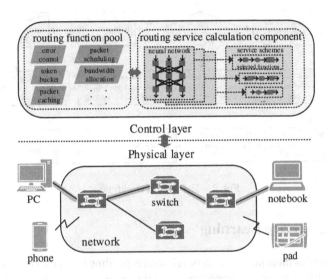

Fig. 1. The system framework

The control layer is the routing service control center that presents network traffics and abstracts network views. It is in charge of routing function selection and service composition. The routing function pool (RFP) in this layer contains diverse routing functions (routing corresponded protocols and algorithms) that are modularly designed with standardized interfaces. Thus, the functions can be reused, extended and combined together into routing services. The routing service calculation component (RSCC) is used to generate schemes for selecting functions and composing services by leveraging the method of multi-layer feed-forward neural network. Thus, according to the user demands and feedbacks for the routing services each round, the corresponding routing functions selection and service composition is adjusted and optimized for each type of applications. In addition, the routing service composition schemes (RSCSs) are generated by this component, and distributed to the involved switches.

The physical layer is in charge of forwarding packets according to the distributed RSCSs. This layer consists of switches, links and diverse network terminals (computer, pad, mobile phone, etc.). The switch is NFV-enabled, and can be embedded into required routing functions by the RFP. It allocates functions and composes services to deal with and forward packets according to the matched RSCSs. In addition, it transfers the information of the user demands and feedbacks to the control layer. The information is learned by the RSCC, and used to adjust the corresponding neural networks. In this approach, the RSCSs are continuously optimized, then, the updated RSCSs are distributed to switches.

When ISP receives the application request for routing service, the detail workflow of providing service is described as shown in Fig. 2.

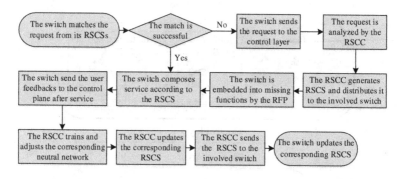

Fig. 2. The system workflow

3   Routing Service Learning

The RSCC contains multiple neural networks corresponding to the user different demand situations for different types of applications. In this paper, we take the user fine-grained communication demands for applications into account, such as video clarity, response time, fault-recovery ability mentioned above and so on. We take each of the user demands as one neuron in the input layer. For example, the video clarity is usually divided into four levels as 360P, 480P, 720P and 1080P currently. We map the four levels to interval [0, 1], which means 0.25, 0.5, 0.75 and 1 represent 360P 480P, 720P and 1080P respectively. If the user video clarity demand is 720P, we take 0.75 as the input of the clarity neuron in the input layer of neural network. Then, the input information is calculated and processed by the hidden layer and the output layer, the routing functions selection results are obtained and the corresponding RSCS is generated. After each service, the user service feedbacks are sent to the RSCC, the corresponding neural network is trained and adjusted according to the feedbacks. In this approach, each neural network and the corresponding RSCS are optimized continuously based on large-scale users' network activity information (e.g. sending communication demands, obtaining routing services, returning service feedbacks).

We assume a multi-layer feed-forward neural network with n neurons in the input layer, q neurons in the hidden layer and m neurons in the output layer as shown in Fig. 3. We define several sets for elements of the neural network as follows.

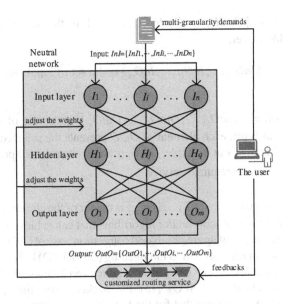

Fig. 3. The training neural network for routing service

Definition 1. $InI = \{InI_1, \ldots, InI_i, \ldots, InI_n\}$ is the set of inputs for neurons in the input layer, each element of InI presents one of the user demands.

Definition 2. $I = \{I_1, \ldots, I_i, \ldots, I_n\}$ is the set of neurons in the input layer, each neuron of I receives the corresponding element of InI.

Definition 3. $H = \{H_1, \ldots, H_j, \ldots, H_q\}$ is the set of neurons in the hidden layer.

Definition 4. $O = \{O_1, \ldots, O_l, \ldots, O_m\}$ is the set of neurons in the output layer, each element of O presents one certain routing function in the RFP and serves as this function's ID.

Definition 5. $IH = \{IH_{11}, \ldots, IH_{ij}, \ldots, IH_{nq}\}$ is the set of weights between the neurons in the input layer and the neurons in the hidden layer. For example, IH_{ij} presents the weight between the i-th neuron in the input layer and the j-th neuron in the hidden layer.

Definition 6. $HO = \{HO_{11}, \ldots, HO_{jl}, \ldots, HO_{qm}\}$ is the set of weights between the neurons in the hidden layer and the neurons in the output layer. For example, HO_{jl} presents the weight between the j-th neuron in the hidden layer and the l-th neuron in output the layer.

Definition 7. $InH = \{InH_1, \ldots, InH_j, \ldots, InH_q\}$ is the set of inputs for the neurons in the hidden layer.

Definition 8. $OutH = \{OutH_1, \ldots, OutH_j, \ldots, OutH_q\}$ is the set of outputs of the neurons in the hidden layer.

Definition 9. $InO = \{InO_1, \ldots, InO_l, \ldots, InO_m\}$ is the set of inputs for the neurons in the output layer.

Definition 10. $OutO = \{OutO_1, \ldots, OutO_l, \ldots, OutO_m\}$ is the set of outputs of the neurons in the output layer, each element of $OutO$ presents the selected probability of its corresponding function. For example, $OutO_l$ presents the selected probability of the function O_l to compose the required service.

Definition 11. $OC = \{OC_1, \ldots, OC_k, \ldots, OC_p\}$ is the set of the classes of routing functions. There are multiple protocols and/or algorithms that can achieve a same purpose. For example, the algorithms of aggregate-based congestion control (ACC) [11], network border [12], stateless fair rate estimation fair queuing (CSFREFQ) [13] and approximate fairness through partial finish time (AFpFT) [14], they can be classified into a class of Core Stateless Fair Queuing (CSFQ) [15] for packet scheduling purpose. Thus, $O_l \in OC_k, OC_k \subset O$. We can infer that for the functions in a same class, no more than one of them can be selected for a required service.

According to the InI and IH defined above, the InH_j can be calculated as follow.

$$InH_j = \sum_{i=1}^{n} InI_i \times IH_{ij} \tag{1}$$

Similarly, the InO_l can be calculated as follow.

$$InO_l = \sum_{j=1}^{q} OutH_j \times HO_{jl} \tag{2}$$

We choose the typical Sigmoid function f as the neuronal activation function for the neurons in the hidden layer and the output layer. The f is shown as follow.

$$f(x) = \frac{1}{1 + e^{-x}} \tag{3}$$

Here, x represents the input of each neuron in the hidden layer and the output layer.

Therefore, we can infer that each element of $OutH$ and $OutO$ belongs to the interval $[0, 1]$. $OutH_j$ and $OutO_l$ can be calculated as follows.

$$OutH_j = f(InH_j) \tag{4}$$

$$OutO_l = f(InO_l) \tag{5}$$

$OutO_l$ presents the selected probability of the function O_l. We assume T as the threshold value for selecting the function. If $OutO_l \geq T$, O_l is allowed to be selected as one function component for the required service; otherwise $OutO_l < T$, O_l is not allowed to be selected as one function component for the service. In addition, according to the definition 11, no more than one function of a class can be selected for a service. We can infer that for the functions in OC_k, the selected function O_l' must satisfy Eq. (6).

$$\begin{cases} O_l' \in OC_k \\ O_l \in OC_k \\ OutO_l' \geq T \\ OutO_l' \geq \forall OutO_l \end{cases} \tag{6}$$

Here, we can infer that if $\forall OutO_l < T$, no function in OC_k can be selected for the service.

In this approach, the functions are selected to compose the required routing service according to Eqs. (5) and (6). We define $SO = \{SO_1, \dots, SO_g, \dots, SO_r\}$, each element of this set presents one selected function, here, $SO \subset O$.

The user actual satisfaction degree for the provided service is defined as ASD. We assume the user expected satisfaction degree for the service is defined as ESD. The error between ASD and ESD is define as E.

$$E = |ASD - ESD| \tag{7}$$

In this paper, we propose the method of error back propagation based on rewards and punishments to train and optimize the neural network. When $ASD \geq ESD$, the corresponding weights are rewarded. The bigger ASD is than ESD, the greater the reward is. When $ASD < ESD$, the corresponding weights are punished. The smaller ASD is than ESD, the greater the punishment is.

We take the weights between the hidden layer and the output layer as examples. For HO_{jl}, its adjustment method is shown as follow.

$$HO_{jl} \leftarrow HO_{jl} + \Delta HO_{jl} \tag{8}$$

When $ASD \geq ESD$, which means that the actual provided routing service is better than the user expected one. According to the perceptron method, learning-rate is given as $\alpha \in [0, 1]$, the ΔHO_{jl} is calculated as follow.

$$\Delta HO_{jl} = \begin{cases} a \times E \times OutH_j, & SO \cap OC_k \neq \emptyset, O_l \in OC_k, O_l \in SO \\ a \times \varepsilon \times OutH_j, & SO \cap OC_k \neq \emptyset, O_l \in OC_k, O_l \notin SO \\ -a \times E \times OutH_j, & SO \cap OC_k = \emptyset, O_l \in OC_k \end{cases} \tag{9}$$

Here, $0 < \varepsilon \ll |\Delta e|$. Under the situation of $ASD \geq ESD$, if one function in OC_k is selected, it means this type of function is necessary for the required service. The weights connected to the functions in OC_k are rewarded. The weight connected to the selected function obtain the biggest reward, the weights connected to the others functions in OC_k are rewarded with little increments. However, if none of OC_k is selected, it means this type of function is not necessary for the required service. The weights connected to the functions in OC_k are reduced.

When $ASD < ESD$, which means that the actual provided routing service is worse than the user expected one, the ΔHO_{jl} is calculated as follow to replace Eq. (9).

$$\Delta HO_{jl} = \begin{cases} a \times E \times OutH_j, & SO \cap OC_k = \emptyset, O_l \in OC_k \\ -a \times E \times OutH_j, & SO \cap OC_k \neq \emptyset, O_l \in OC_k, O_l \in SO \\ -a \times \varepsilon \times OutH_j, & SO \cap OC_k \neq \emptyset, O_l \in OC_k, O_l \notin SO \end{cases} \tag{10}$$

Under the situation of $ASD < ESD$, some demands are not satisfied by the provided service, it means some necessary functions may not be selected to compose the service. If none of OC_k is selected, the weights connected to the functions in OC_k are increased, because the purpose of this type of functions may be important for satisfying the user demands. If one function of OC_k is selected, the weights connected to the functions in OC_k are punished, because this type of functions may bring bad performance for the service. However, the weights connected to unselected functions in OC_k are just reduced with little decrements.

In the multilayer neural network, neurons in the hidden layer are not visible, their output errors cannot be measured directly. Therefore we adjust the weights between the input layer and the hidden layer according to the error of the output layer shown as follows.

$$IH_{ij} \leftarrow IH_{ij} + \Delta IH_{ij} \tag{11}$$

$$\Delta IH_{ij} = \begin{cases} a \times E \times InI_i, & ASD \geq ESD \\ -a \times E \times InI_i, & ASD < ESD \end{cases} \tag{12}$$

With the user continuously communication activities in the network, the corresponding neural networks are trained and adjusted according to the user feedbacks for the provided services. In this approach, the routing function selection and service composition is progressively optimized, and the user service experience is also gradually improved.

4   The Simulation Experiments

4.1   The Simulation Setup

The proposed SDNFV-based routing service composition model (NRSC) is simulated under the Linux platform (Intel core i5 3.3 GHz, 16 GB DDR3 RAM). We simulate the control plane based on the Floodlight [16] architecture, it is in charge of calculating routing services and generating service composition schemes. The switch is simulated based on OpenFlowClick [17], it is a kind of software-based switch by leveraging the Click Modular Router [18]. The Click Modular Router is extendable, programmable, and assembled by a series of packet processing modules called elements that can be flexibly selected and embedded. And the OpenFlowClick element allows the controller to install service composition schemes into switches to guide packet processing. We choose the applications of video streaming type in the simulation due to more than 86 % of global Internet traffics being this type currently [19], and the initial data of training neural network is from EPFL-PoliMI video quality assessment database [20]. We take QoS as the simulation example, and select multiple algorithms that can achieve functions of admission control, bandwidth allocation, packet scheduling, error control, traffic shaping and cache handling as the selectable functional components on the communication paths of applications.

In addition, we use two real networks, i.e., CERNET [21] and INTERNET2 [22] shown in Fig. 4, as the simulation network topologies. For comparison purpose, we also simulate the typical Integrated Service mechanism (ISM) to compare with the proposed NRSC.

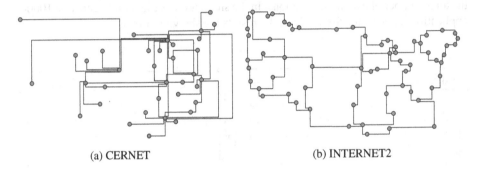

(a) CERNET   (b) INTERNET2

Fig. 4. The network topologies

4.2 The Simulation Results

4.2.1 The User QoS Satisfaction Degree

We first compare the user QoS satisfaction degrees (UQSDs) for the routing services provided by NRSC and ISM. The UQSD presents the probability of the provided services satisfying the user demands. We take parameters of bandwidth, loss rate, delay, and jitter into account, to compare the service according to these parameter actual values. Here, the relative importance of each parameter is set as bandwidth: 11.1 %; loss rate: 58.9 %; delay: 14.9 %; jitter: 15.1 % according to [23]. The results are shown in Fig. 5.

The UQSD of NRSC is higher than that of ISM. The UQSD of ISM is decreasing obviously with the network load becoming heavy (i.e., 10^2 flows, 10^3 flows, 10^4 flows, 10^5 flows, 10^6 flows). This is because ISM is incapable to adjust its service provision schemes adaptively according to the changing network load. However, the routing service composition schemes of NRSC are adaptively generated according to the user demands. They can be continuously adjusted and optimized based on the feedbacks from the user under different network statuses.

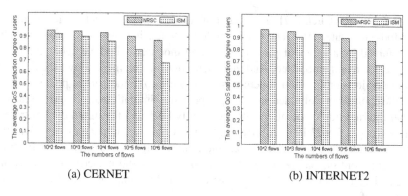

(a) CERNET   (b) INTERNET2

Fig. 5. UQSD

4.2.2   The Function Utilizing Ratio

We compare the function utilizing ratios (FURs) for composing services under NRSC and ISM. The FUR is ratio of the number of functions selected to compose services to the total number of candidate functions. In the simulation, we randomly generate 10000 application requests for the services, the results are shown in Fig. 6.

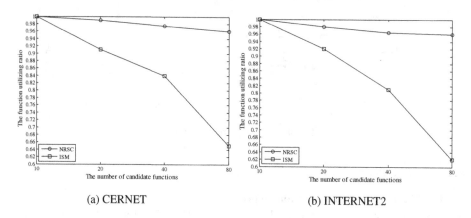

(a) CERNET   (b) INTERNET2

Fig. 6. FUR

The FUR of NRSC is much higher and more stable than that of ISM, especially when the number of candidate function is increasing rapidly. This is because ISM just composes services according to its configured schemes. It cannot adaptively generate new schemes to compose services. However, NRSC is guided by the user feedbacks, it can make fully use of the candidate functions by adaptively trying possible and feasible service composition schemes to compose diversified services to satisfy the user different demands.

4.2.3 The Routing Service Setup Time

We also compare the routing service setup time (RSST) under NRSC and ISM, and use relative values (set the biggest value as 1 and others are their ratios to it). The results are shown in Fig. 7.

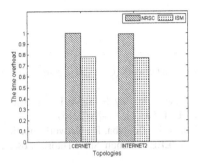
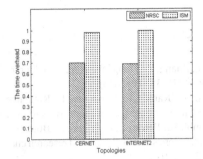

(a) The RSST for the new request   (b) The RSST according to the established scheme

Fig. 7. RSST

When the request cannot be matched to one of the established service composition schemes (that is, this request is a new type request that has not been provided service before), the time overhead of NRSC is higher than ISM. This is because the control layer should calculate a new service composition scheme for this type of requests, and the corresponding functions should be embedded into the switch. However, for the successfully matched schemes, the RSST of NRSC is much lower than that of ISM as shown in Fig. 7(b).

5 Conclusion

In this paper, based on the networking ideas of SDN and NFV, the routing service composition model is proposed. It composes diversified and customized routing services by selecting appropriate routing functions, to satisfy the user different communication demands for different types of applications. In addition, the idea of machine learning is combined with the proposed model by leveraging the multi-layer feed-forward neural network, to train and adjust the service composition schemes according to the user feedbacks. In this approach, the routing function selection and service composition are optimized continuously along with the user communication activities through applications.

In order to improve the practicability of our work, we plan to do prototype implementation of the proposed NRSC to further verify its effectiveness and enhance its performance. In this paper, NRSC is mainly devised to compose services by selecting appropriate routing functions. Furthermore, based on NRSC, we consider taking routing resources into account to compose services by allocating resources and selecting functions together in our feature research.

Acknowledgments. This work is supported by the National Natural Science Foundation of China under Grant No. 61572123, the National Science Foundation for Distinguished Young Scholars of China under Grant No. 61225012 and No. 71325002, and the Liaoning BaiQianWan Talents Program under Grant No. 2013921068.

References

1. Wu, J., Zhang, Z., Hong, Y., Wen, Y.: Cloud radio access network (C-RAN): a primer. IEEE Netw. **29**(1), 35–41 (2015)
2. Kreutz, D., Ramos, F., Verissimo, P., Rothenberg, C., Azodolmolky, S., Steve, U.: Software-defined networking: a comprehensive survey. Proc. IEEE **103**(1), 14–76 (2015)
3. Mijumbi, R., Serrat, J., Gorricho, J., Bouten, N., Turck, F., Boutaba, R.: Network function virtualization: state-of-the-art and research challenges. IEEE Commun. Surv. Tutorials **18**(1), 236–262 (2016)
4. Ding, W., Wen, W., Wang, J., Chen, B.: OpenSCaaS: an open service chain as a service platform toward the integration of SDN and NFV. IEEE Netw. **29**(3), 30–35 (2015)
5. Wang, P., Lan, J., Zhang, X., Hu, Y., Chen, S.: Dynamic function composition for network service chain: model and optimization. Comput. Netw. **92**, 408–418 (2015)
6. Federica, P., Mehmet, U., Barbara, M.: Context-aware service composition and delivery in NGSONs over SDN. IEEE Commun. Mag. **52**(8), 97–105 (2014)
7. Chen, G., Chen, H., Hu, H., Wang, Z., Lan, J.: Enabling network function combination via service chain instantiation. Comput. Netw. **92**, 396–407 (2015)
8. Jon, M., Jokin, G., Nerea, T., Eduardo, J.: Toward an SDN-enabled NFV architecture. IEEE Commun. Mag. **53**(4), 187–193 (2015)
9. Ran, Y., Yang, E., Shi, Y., Chen, S.: A NaaS-enabled framework for service composition in software defined networking environment. In: 2014 IEEE Globecom Workshops (GC Wkshps), pp. 188–193 (2014)
10. Gamez, N., Haddad, J., Fuentes, L.: SPL-TQSSS: a software product line approach for stateful service selection. IEEE International Conference on Web Services, pp. 73–80 (2015)
11. Mahajan, R., Bellovin, S., Floyd, S., Ioannidis, J., Paxson, V., Shenker, S.: Controlling high bandwidth aggregates in the network. ACM SIGCOMM Comput. Commun. Rev. **32**(3), 62–73 (2002)
12. Albuquerque, C., Vickers, B., Suda, T.: Network border patrol: preventing congestion collapse and promoting fairness in the internet. IEEE/ACM Trans. Netw. **12**(1), 173–186 (2004)
13. Li, J., Lin, Y., Yang, C.: Core-stateless fair rate estimation fair queuing. Int. J. Commun Syst **19**(6), 679–697 (2006)
14. Eshete, A., Jiang, Y.: Approximate fairness through limited flow list. In: International Teletraffic Congress, pp. 198–295 (2011)
15. Abbas, G., Halim, Z., Abbas, Z.: Fairness-driven queue management: a survey and taxonomy. IEEE Commun. Surv. Tutorials **18**(1), 324–367 (2016)
16. Project Floodlight (2016). http://www.projectfloodlight.org/projects/
17. OpenFlowClick (2016). http://archive.openflow.org/wk/index.php/OpenFlowClick
18. Eddie, K.: The Click modular router. ACM Trans. Comput. Syst. **18**(3), 263–297 (2000)
19. Yin, H., Jiang, Y., Lin, C., Luo, Y., Liu, Y.: Big data: transforming the design philosophy of future internet. IEEE Netw. **28**(4), 14–19 (2014)
20. EPFL-PoliMI (2016). http://vqa.como.polimi.it

21. CERNET (2016). http://www.topology-zoo.org/
22. INTERNET2 (2016). http://www.internet2.edu/
23. Kim, H., Dong, G., Kim, H., Cho, K., Choi, S.: QoE assessment model for video streaming service using QoS parameters in wired-wireless network. In: International Advanced Communication Technology, pp. 459–464 (2012)

Service Model Design and Application of Product Design and Component Procurement for Small and Medium Sized Concrete Mixer Manufacturers Based on Cloud Manufacturing

Guofu Luo, Xianglong Yang[✉], and Jun Ma

Mechanical and Electrical Engineering Institute, Zhengzhou University of Light Industry, Zhengzhou, People's Republic of China
hnyxld@126.com, 1047354948@qq.com, majunfirst@sohu.com

Abstract. In China, there are many Small and Medium Sized Concrete Mixer Manufacturers generally face with the following problems: small scale, lacking money, product market homogenization competition and so on. The passage aims to apply the features of cloud manufacturing service to the Small and Medium Sized Concrete Mixer Manufacturers, which will help solve the problems of scarce design ability and backward component procurement management mode appearing in these kinds of manufacturers. Besides, the passage mainly focuses on a life cycle of product design and component procurement in Concrete Mixer Manufacturers and builds a model of product design and component procurement service. Through researching on the Cloud manufacturing service platform for Small and Medium Sized Concrete Mixer Manufacturers and building cloud manufacturing service platform system, as well as combining them with some instances, the passage will introduce the function structure, service mode and working flow of cloud manufacturing service platform. Cloud manufacturing service platform focus on product design and components procurement links of concrete mixer manufacturing life cycle and build product design and parts procurement service model. Through Researching on the Cloud manufacturing service platform architecture of small and medium sized concrete mixer manufacturing enterprise and building cloud manufacturing service platform system as well as combining them with an instance, the function structure, service mode and working flow of cloud manufacturing service platform are introduced.

Keywords: Cloud manufacturing · Service model · Concrete mixer · Product design · Parts purchasing

1 Introduction

With the help of network and cloud manufacturing service platform, cloud manufacturing can centrally manage a variety of manufacturing resources and capacity through a combination of cloud computing, networking, big data, knowledge services and other

© Springer International Publishing AG 2016
W. Li et al. (Eds.): IDCS 2016, LNCS 9864, pp. 72–80, 2016.
DOI: 10.1007/978-3-319-45940-0_7

emerging technologies. Based on that, cloud manufacturing can achieve the sharing of manufacturing resources and manufacturing capacity in the form of service. So cloud manufacturing has created a new mode of networked manufacturing that can provide service for all types of manufacturing activities in the whole life cycle of product manufacturing [1–3].

At present, Small and Medium Sized Concrete Mixer Manufacturing Enterprises (SMCMME) of China generally exist the following problems: small-scale enterprises, low capability of industrial chain integration, low capability of designing new product single production structure, which seriously affect the development of enterprises and restrict the market competitiveness of enterprises. Therefore, to improve the enterprise's R&D capability and management level, it is necessary to propose an advanced manufacturing mode. The new mode could not only improve enterprises' ability to resist market risk, but also promote manufacturing industry shift from "productive manufacturing" to "service-oriented manufacturing". Cloud manufacturing, basing on the core mind that Manufacturing is service, can effectively integrate resources of concrete mixer industry chain and optimize manufacturing resource allocation of industrial chain. Accordingly, cloud manufacturing could point out the direction for the future development of manufacturing industry in China. For cloud manufacturing, many experts and scholars have studied the concept, key technology and application model. In 2009, an academician called Bohu Li and his team were not only firstly formalize the concept of Cloud manufacturing in the world, but also discussed specific content of cloud manufacturing and analyzed differences between cloud manufacturing and the existing network manufacturing mode in the literature [4], and the literature putted forward the key technologies for implementing about cloud manufacturing with the help of an application prototype of CMfg, i.e., COSLMSCP; Combining the advantages of cloud manufacturing services platform for Small and Medium Sized Manufacturing Enterprises, the literature [5] studied key standard techniques and system architecture of platform, their research idea and content were discussed in same time; On the basis of the previous studies on the concept of cloud manufacturing, the literature [6] putted forward the issues of service mode and key technology that were faced in the application process of mechanical processing and other specific industries.

Following the philosophy that manufacturing is service, this paper researched on the content of cloud manufacturing service by combining the characteristics of SMCMME. Based on that, the service models for product design and parts procurement were constructed. In addition, architecture and system of cloud manufacturing service platform were built by using an example. This paper also explored functional structure, service model and work-flow of cloud manufacturing services platform so that service could be throughout product life cycle.

2 Cloud Manufacturing Service for Concrete Mixer

The core concept of cloud manufacturing is that manufacturing is service, namely providing all aspects of manufacturing services throughout the product life cycle. The service model of cloud manufacturing has multi-to-one nuclear structure as well as multi-to-multi network structure [7], as shown in Fig. 1. In terms of SMCMME,

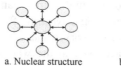

a. Nuclear structure   b. Network structure

Fig. 1. The service model of cloud manufacturing service platform

enterprises collaboration is mainly based on the network structure on the platform, which embodies the idea that centralized resource are distracted service. To the service form of network structure, enterprises are not only service requesters but also service providers. They are less dependent on each other, so they have strong ability to resist market risks.

In terms of SMCMME, the industrial chain of network structure includes the following services: demonstration, design, components procurement, manufacturing, sales and business management activities, etc. But design and parts procurement are the key links of the whole life cycle according to actual situation of SMCMME.

2.1   Design Service Link

R&D period of products is the beginning of the product manufacturing process, and it is not only the longest stage in the production life cycle of concrete mixer but also the most important factors that can influence product performance and market competitiveness. SMCMME are mostly short of design capacity, they usually make micro-innovations about the function of concrete mixer by the design mode of imitate, manufacturing, and improve.

Cloud manufacturing service platform for SMCMME uses database technology to establish design unit information database libraries and parts design scheme selection libraries. Different types of virtualized design resources, including modeling software and simulation software, are stored in the platform server by using resource virtualization technology. Design organization can call the above design resources. Through collaborative design function, manufacturing enterprises can on-line view the progress of the product design in real time and put forward amendments to design organization, which can improve the design efficiency of product and cut the design cost. As shown in Fig. 2, Design services link of concrete mixer is divided into three parts: overall product design, detailed design of parts and components, mechani- cal structure simulation. Because concrete mixer is made up of hundreds of components, the use of existing component models and design techniques can greatly shorten the design time and cost as well as improve design efficiency.

2.2   Parts Procurement Services Link

Take JZ320 hydraulic automatic track mixer for example, concrete mixer is made up of hundreds of components, as shown in Table 1. In the course of procurement, factors that affect procurement performance include quality、cost、supplier. Due to insufficient

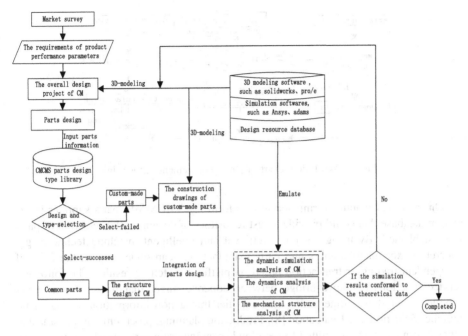

Fig. 2. Work-flow chart of design service

funds, the market anti-risk ability of SMCMME is poor. Whether the specific situat- tion of parts procurement is appropriate, which will affect production costs and production planning, such as parts' varieties, specifications, quality and delivery time; if parts inventory is inappropriate, it will affect the mobility of funds. Therefore, under the premise to ensure the quality of the parts, it is the most importance that SMCMME buy from appropriate parts suppliers at appropriate time on the right price.

Table 1. Parts purchasing list of JZ320 hydraulic automatic rail type mixer

Procurement methods	Classification	Name
Home-maded parts	Mechanical structure	U-sliding steel wall, Movable body, Rotatable telescopic bracket, Balance leg, etc.
Outsourcing parts	Electric control system	Electric system control box, motors Controller, etc.
	Hydraulic control system	Hydraulic cylinder, Hydraulic pump, Hydraulic tubing, etc.
	Mechanical structure	Mixing drum, Pulley, Drawstring, Tyre, etc.

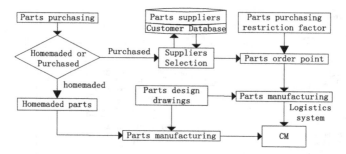

Fig. 3. Work-flow chart of parts procurement service link

On the cloud manufacturing service platform for SMCMME, parts supplier information database that could provide a vast repository of design model selection of parts was established. By using resources retrieval and intelligent matching technolo- gy, concrete mixer manufacturers and parts manufacturers can trade parts in the form of independent trading or transaction based on platform matching results. The following service functions put up a bridge between concrete mixer manufacturers and parts suppliers, including online-trade parts, supplier transaction information management, Supplier Selection and Evaluation [8]. Production planning, procureme- nt of parts and other information are submitted to the cloud manufacturing services platform so as to make the decision for production time, parts purchasing quantity, production planning and other information. Then the platform will select the appropriate ordering policy to ensure the appropriate ordering point and carry on the parts purchasing service based on the above restriction factor, as far as possible to reduce the order cost of the enterprise. The work-flow of parts procurement service link is shown in Fig. 3.

3   Cloud Manufacturing Service Platform Architecture for Small and Medium Sized Concrete Mixer Manufacturing Enterprises

According to the service characteristics of the whole life cycle of SMCMME, the cloud manufacturing service platform, based on resource sharing and on-demand cus- tomization, is established. During the whole life cycle, the cloud manufacturing service platform has three participants: concrete mixer cloud manufacturing resource demand (CMCMD), concrete mixer cloud manufacturing resources provided the suppliers (CMCMS), concrete mixer cloud manufacturing platform manager (CMCMM). Three participants have different functions and play different roles in the whole service process. CMCMD publish service resource requirements on the platform so as to find the best cooperation partner; CMCMM is mainly responsible for resource management and application rules that include the platform construction, maintenance and opera- tion, safety, etc., which could put up a bridge of cooperation between resources sup- pliers and resources demand; CMCMS provide a variety of software and hardware

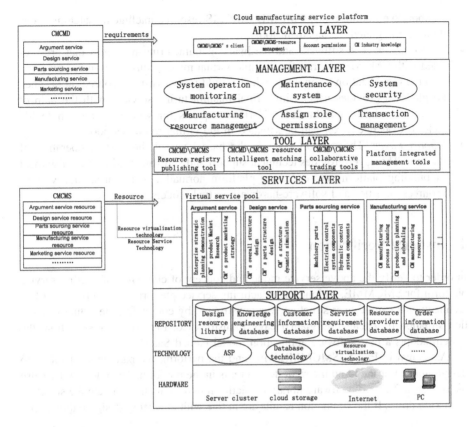

Fig. 4. Cloud manufacturing service platform architecture of SMCMME

manufacturing resources and release to the platform data center. The platform is divided into 5 layers, as shown in Fig. 4:

- *Application Layer*: This layer is a human-computer interaction layer between users and platform. Users can make the following operations: registering enterprise account information, publishing service information for demand and other operations. In addition, transaction progress of the platform could be intuitively exploded to users by the form of graphic or dialog interaction.
- *Management Layer*: This layer is mainly responsible for maintenance and supervision of the platform, so it is the core layer of the platform. Manufacturing management layer can not only reasonably allocate the process and responsibilities of the transaction, but also make a reasonable plan to use the manufacturing resource of platform efficiently.
- *Tool Layer*: This layer provides a range of support tools to deal with the customer requirement. In order torealize management functions of cloud manufacturing services platform, the tool layer provides a range of technical supports, including CMCMD \ CMCMS resource registry publishing tools, CMCMD\ CMCMS

collaborative trading tools, CMCMD\CMCMS resource intelligent matching tools, platform integrated management tools.

- *Service Layer*: The software and hardware manufacturing resources that are provided with CMCMS are transformed into virtual manufacturing resources by using resource virtualization technology, which would form a virtual resources pool. Then the platform provides users with virtual manufacturing services with the help of service virtualization technology. Various requests for service of the whole life cycle of Concrete mixer can be satisfied in the virtual resources pool.
- *Support Layer*: The support layer is the base layer of the normal operation of platform. This layer provides technical support and software-hardware environment for building platform and operating platform normally, so it can storage various resources statistics and software-hardware virtual models.

4   Instance Verification

In order to verify the above service mode and concept of cloud manufacturing service platform for SMCMME, a cloud manufacturing service platform system based on B\S architecture for multi-user structure was constructed by combining the actual production situation of Zhengzhou giant Heavy Industries Co. Ltd. In this dissertation, the system adopts a new software application model named SaaS.

As shown in Fig. 5, SMCMME will send the performance parameter of mixer to design units after they find the right design units in the platform. Then design units use the design software of software library of platform to design and simulate the structure of mixing drum. If the simulation results are in line with the theory design requirement,

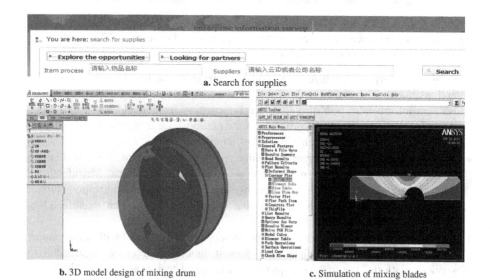

a. Search for supplies

b. 3D model design of mixing drum   **c.** Simulation of mixing blades

Fig. 5. Design service of mixing drum based on cooperative interaction

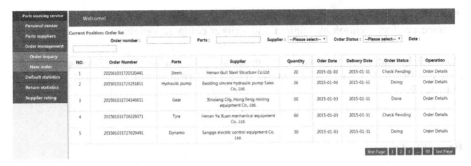

Fig. 6. Parts procurement service interface

design units send the design drawings to parts manufacturers so as to manufacture sample. In the collaborative design and simulation based on cloud manufacturing, multiple units can timely view the execution progress the design task and feedback design units to improve the design efficiency of mixing drum.

Figure 6 is the function module of Parts procurement services. If SMCMME purchase parts by the mode of independent transaction, they can select the appropriate parts suppliers through the module of Service Resource Classification or the window of Parts Procurement Services. If the parts and components are traded through the window of Parts procurement services, parts supplier library can be viewed in the window of Parts Sourcing Services, and we can view the orders information that include the parts name, supplier, the number of parts, production planning, order status and other information by clicking Order Management. Meanwhile, we can master the real-time order transaction status and view the progress, amounts, buyer and other information in the window of Order Details. Clicking Default Statistics or Return Statistics to view the abortive order transactions, which could help enterprises to change the parts procurement plan in a timely manner and avoid resulting in unnecessary losses for default, return and other violations. SMCMME can perform credit scoring for parts supplier though the module of Supplier Rating, which can provide credit reference for other parts purchasing activities.

5 Conclusion

In view of problems existing in the SMCMME in China, this paper has built cloud manufacturing service platform architecture and system model for SMCMME by combining the service features of cloud manufacturing. Focusing on analyzing the design services link and the parts procurement services link of the platform, this paper putted forward the service mode and work-flow so as to solve these problems that the design ability of SMCMME is insufficient and the parts procurement management mode of SMCMME is backward, as well as introducing the whole operation process of the system. In addition, the service mode of parts purchasing was introduced by an example. Cloud manufacturing service platform could greatly improve the enterprise's ability to consolidate upstream and downstream industry chain, which would help improve the transformation and upgrading of the production model of SMCMME and enhance product technology content and market competitiveness.

Acknowledgment. This work has been supported by Innovation Plan of Science and Technology in Henan Province (164200510004), funded by Department of Science and Technology of Henan Province.

References

1. Zhang, L., Luo, Y.L., Tao, F.: Cloud manufacturing: a new manufacturing paradigm. Enterp. Inf. Syst. **8**(2), 1–21 (2014)
2. Li, B.H., Zhang, L., Ren, L.: Further discussion on cloud manufacturing. Comput. Integr. Manuf. Syst. **17**(3), 449–457 (2011)
3. Li, B.H.: Introduction to cloud manufacturing. ZTE Technol. J. **16**(4), 5–8 (2010)
4. Li, B.H., Zhang, L.: Cloud manufacturing: a new service-oriented networked manufacturing model. Comput. Integr. Manuf. Syst. **16**(1), 1–7 (2010)
5. Yin, C.: Common key technology of cloud manufacturing service platform for small and medium enterprise. Comput. Integr. Manuf. Syst. **17**(3), 495–503 (2011)
6. Guo, L.: Research on cloud manufacturing service platform key technology for machining. Thesis of degree in Doctor of Engineering, Chongqing University, October 2014
7. Li, B.Y.: Research on multi-alliance enterprises swarm for collaborative technology base on cloud service platform. Thesis of degree in Doctor of Engineering, Southwest Jiao-tong University, May 2015
8. Cheng, S.Y.: Research on the resource and service management mode and its prototype development for cloud manufacturing. Thesis of degree in Master of Engineering, Zhejiang University, March 2013

A Novel Access Control Model for Cloud Computing

Rajat Saxena$^{(\boxtimes)}$ and Somnath Dey

Cloud Computing Lab, Department of Computer Science and Engineering,
Indian Institute of Technology Indore, Indore, India
{rajat.saxena,somnathd}@iiti.ac.in

Abstract. Cloud Computing is the fast growing and the dominant field of Information Technology (IT) industry. It proposes on demand and cost effective services such as Software as a Service (SaaS), Platform as a Service (PaaS) and Infrastructure as a Service (IaaS). Many security challenges are drawn from these services in cloud environment such as abuse of cloud services, data security, malicious insider and cyber-attacks. Although various access control policies and models such as Mandatory Access Control (MAC) and Role Based Access Control (RBAC) are existing, but these are not suitable for Cloud access control requirements.

In this paper, we analyze and identify different important gaps of the conventional access control schemes based on the their demerits and cloud access requirements. We also propose a Combinatorial Batch Codes Based Access Control (CBCBAC) model, which fulfill all the cloud access control requirements.

Our approach ensures the secure and efficient sharing of resources among various non-trusted tenants and also has the capacity to support different access permission to the same user for using multiple services securely. We also implement a prototype of our work which depicts the effective access control in the cloud environment.

Keywords: Cloud computing · Collaborative simulation · Combinatorial Batch Codes (CBC) · Mandatory Access Control (MAC) · Role Based Access Control (RBAC) · Access control models · Task-Role Based Access Control

1 Introduction

Cloud computing [1] is defined as services and applications that are enforced on a distributed network using virtual resources and accessed by common networking standards and Internet protocols. In cloud, resources [2] are not only virtually and limitless, the implementation details of the physical systems on which software runs are abstracted from the user as well.

In cloud data [3] is stored and operated in multi-tenant systems, which are distributed and shared by unrelated users within a large area. In addition, maintenance of security audit logs may be difficult or impossible for a user that has

© Springer International Publishing AG 2016
W. Li et al. (Eds.): IDCS 2016, LNCS 9864, pp. 81–94, 2016.
DOI: 10.1007/978-3-319-45940-0_8

limited resources. Thus, cloud service providers must devote proper security measures and resources to maintain privacy and data integrity. The customer also must ensure that the provider has taken the proper security measures to protect their information.

In a cloud environment [4], the users might have limited CPU, battery power and communication resources. So, effective access control is one of the basic security issues in the Cloud environment. Many access control models are existing for different scope, organizations, communities and environments, but each model has many drawbacks and limitations.

Organization. The rest of the paper is organized as follows: In the Sect. 2, we describe literature survey on access control with the current state of art works, identifying limitations of these models and a proposal of an efficient access control method. In the Sect. 3, we describe our Combinatorial Batch Codes Based Access Control (CBCBAC) model based on requirement observation. In Sect. 4 we describe implementation phases and performance analysis of our approach. In Sect. 5, we provide security analysis of our scheme. Finally, we conclude in Sect. 6.

2 Literature Survey

Some basic access control methods are followed:

1. **Mandatory Access Control (MAC) Model:** In this model [5], a central authority is responsible for taking access decisions regarding a subject which requests for accessing objects. For secure access MAC model assigns an access class to each subject and object. An access class provides a security level to secure information flow between subject and object with dominance relationship. Although we have Bell and lapadula [6] and Biba [7] as two distinct variants and improvement of this model and provides protection against indirect information flow and leakage, but both this variant have a guarantee of complete secrecy of information.
2. **Discretionary Access Control (DAC) Model:** In this model [8], owner of the objects have the authority and the ability to restrict access to their objects or membership in certain groups or information in the objects based on user identities. DAC model is implemented either via identity based access control or Access Control Matrix/Access Control List (ACL). DAC model is generally less secure than the MAC model, so it used in low level protected systems.
3. **Role Based Access Control (RBAC) Model:** In this model [9], "a subject's responsibility is more important than whom the subject is", so a subject can have more than one role or be a member of multiple groups. Thus, this model is more realistic way to control access of resources in organizations. But it has the following drawbacks:
   - Choosing the right roles for representation of a system is not an easy task and may occur a worse situation when subjects dividing into categories based upon roles.

- Classification by subject into a number of categories makes mandatory for each subject to have a role in order to access the system.
- This model does not provide any kind of sensitivity to the information.
- This model does not delegation principle which is applicable in case of absences of employees.
- In this model relationships define according to identities not just roles.
- This model does not support dynamic activation of access rights for certain tasks assigned to the staff.

4. **Task-Role Based Access Control (T-RBAC) Model:** This model [10] is based on Role Based Access Control model and assigns permissions to the tasks instead of roles. So, the user is assigned roles and this role is assigned tasks that have permissions. It uses a workflow authorization model for synchronizing workflow with authorization flow. Thus, this model uses tasks to support active access control and roles to support passive access control.

5. **Attribute Based Access Control (ABAC) Model:** This model [11] is based on a set of attributes associated with a requester or resource to be accessed in order to make decisions. This attribute may or may not be related with each other. After defining attributes, each attribute is considered as a discrete value and values of all attributes are compared against a set of values by a policy decision point to deny or grant access. This model may be either Policy Based Access Control (PBAC) or Claims Based Access Control (CBAC). Thus, for accessing the system, subject just only needs to authenticate with the system and then it provides its attributes. It is a crucial decision in cloud computing that how many and what kind of attributes should be used for making decisions.

6. **Risk-Based Access Control (RBAC) Model:** This model [12] handles different kinds of risk levels and used operational need principal for adoption of access decision. It has a dynamic security policy which changes according to risk levels. The model implementation is difficult for cloud computing because of the high amount of analysis is required for assessment of risk levels.

7. **Adaptive Access Control Model:** This model [13] is based on contextual information such as time and security information. In it authors build a trust relationship between Cloud Service Providers (CSP's) and its consumers with role based access control system. A trust management system is maintained, which update and change trust level after each transaction. In this scheme, it is assumed that An Authority Authorization Centre (AAC) is maintained by each cloud which calculate and modified trust level based upon the users behaviour. This model has suffered from potential single point of attack and policy information failure.

8. **Cloud Optimized Risk Based Access Control (co-RBAC) Model:** This model [14] inherits the features of distributing environment, merge distributed authentication services together and have the ability of issuing certificate same as Certificate Authorities (CA). In this model hierarchical cache have been embedded to improve overall efficiency of access control

system. Dependency on CA for issuing certificate might cause efficiency and scalability problems because for each access time new certificate is needed.

9. **Task-Role Based Access Control Method:** In this method [15], Access activation or deactivation of permission depends on current task or process state. This scheme uses workflow authorization with synchronization workflow. Thus, tasks support active access control and roles support passive access control. It is implemented with Amazon Elastic Compute Cloud (Amazon EC2). But it suffered from heterogeneity problem, thus no clear indication of semantic and separation problem between the roles and tasks is handled.

10. **Ontology Using Role Based Access Control (O-RBAC) Model:** This model [16] provides the appropriate policy with an exact role for every tenant. Every subject can have multiple roles in multiple sessions. Thus, a role hierarchy is based on domain ontology and can be transferred between various ontological domains. This model has to ensure granting access decisions in a reasonable time and according to system requirements.

11. **Attribute Role-Based Access Control (ARBAC) Model:** This model [17] is a combination of Attribute Based Access Control and Role Based Access Control. It is implemented using eucalyptus open source cloud infrastructure. The main objective of this model is protecting data privacy. But the model does not provide clear explanation or evidence how it is protected. The role of component privacy manager and how they will combine RBAC and ABAC is not clearly depicted.

These conventional access control methods are very prohibitive, time consuming and error prone for novice users. We observed following limitations on conventional access control methods.

1. Cloud environment is complex and sophisticated because of dynamic nature of the cloud resources.
2. Data location is hidden from cloud users and may be in different countries that have different regulations for the same data. They may not trust with each other and may cause Service Level Agreement (SLA) issues.
3. Conventional models would be suffering from lack of flexibility in scalability and attribute management.
4. Cloud computing has heterogeneity and variety of services.
5. Diversity in access control policies and interfaces can cause improper interoperability.
6. High frequency delegation of large number of users, different classification, high dynamic performance and mobility features.
7. Different access permissions to a same cloud user, and giving him/her ability to use multiple services with regard to authentication and login time.
8. Multi tenancy, virtualization, sharing of resources and credential transformation are crucial aspects of cloud environment.

To keep these limitations in mind, we proposed a novel Combinatorial Batch Codes Based Access Control (CBCBAC) model, which have many levels of security depending upon the trust hierarchy. It supports many sensitive levels of information to implement restriction on reading and modification of information on cloud. Our approach verifies and guarantees that the cloud service provider could not learn about any data content stored in the cloud server during the efficient access control. Specifically, our contribution in this work can be summarized as the following three aspects:

1. We motivate the access control of data in cloud computing, and provide a new access control scheme with Combinatorial Batch Codes (CBC).
2. To the best of our knowledge, our scheme is the first to support scalable and efficient access control with CBC in the cloud computing.
3. We analyze the security and performance of our proposed scheme with current state-of-the-art.

3   The Proposed Scheme

In this section, we present our access control scheme for cloud services with antecedent research goals in mind. First, we establish notation related to our scheme, then we explain the details about CBC. There after we describe our scheme with CBC. Thereafter, we discuss algorithms that subsequently represent our scheme.

3.1   Notation and Preliminaries

1. h : The maximum height of the hierarchy.
2. id : Identity tuple (id_1 .....id_τ), where $1 \leq \tau \leq h$.
3. PP : Public Parameters.
4. κ : Security Parameter.
5. Msk : Master Key.
6. $E_{id}(\bullet)$ and $D_{id}(\bullet)$: denote the encryption and decryption algorithms.
7. M : Message.
8. C : Cipher-text.
9. G and G_T : Cyclic and multiplicative group of prime order p.
10. g : Random Number Generator.
11. u and v : Prime numbers $\in G$ and G_T, respectively.
12. e : Bilinear map.
13. pk : Public Key.
14. sk : Private Key.
15. $\mathcal{C}$: Combinatorial Batch Codes.
16. n : Number of file blocks.
17. m : Number of Cloud servers.
18. N : Total storage over m servers.
19. k : Selected number of elements.
20. t : Number of file blocks that at most read from each server.
21. $\mathcal{F}$: Set of n elements (or file blocks).
22. $\mathcal{S}$: Collection of m subsets of $\mathcal{F}$.

3.2   Combinatorial Batch Codes

Combinatorial Batch Code $\mathcal{C}$ [18] (n, N, k, m, t) is a set system $(\mathcal{F}, \mathcal{S})$, where $\mathcal{F}$ is a set of n elements (called items), $\mathcal{S}$ (called servers) is a collection of m subsets of $\mathcal{F}$ and $N = \sum_{s \in \mathcal{S}} |s|$, such that for each k-subset $\{f_{i_1}, f_{i_2}, ..., f_{i_k}\} \subset \mathcal{F}$ there exists a subset $\mathcal{C}_i \subseteq \mathcal{S}_i$, where $|\mathcal{C}_i| \leqslant t$, i= 1,......, m, such that

$$\{f_{i_1}, f_{i_2}, ..., f_{i_k}\} \subset \bigcup_{i=1}^{m} \mathcal{C}_i \tag{1}$$

If we are fixing t = 1; it means CBC permits only one item to be retrieved from each server. This CBC denotes as an (n, N, k, m)-CBC.

3.3   Combinatorial Batch Codes Based Access Control (CBCBAC) Model

Combinatorial Batch Codes Based Access Control (CBCBAC) model is based on CBC for distribution of access control of Cloud Service Providers (CSP) servers. In CBCBAC model, the generation of the private key can be a computationally intensive task. The identity of an entity must be authenticated before issuing a private key and the private key needs to be transmitted securely to the concerned entity.

CBCBAC model reduces the workload of the PKG by delegating the task of private key generation and hence authentication of identity and secure transmission of private key to its lowest levels. However, only the PKG has a set of public parameters. The identities at different levels do not have any public parameters associated with them. In CBCBAC model, identities are represented as vectors. So for a maximum height h of hierarchy (which is denoted as h-CBCBAC) any identity id is a tuple $(id_1, ..., id_\tau)$, where $1 \leq \tau \leq h$.

Let, $id' = id'_1, ..., id'_j, j \leq \tau$ be another identity tuple. We say id' is a prefix of id if $id'_i = id_i$ for all $1 \leq i \leq j$.

In CBCBAC model, the PKG has a set of public parameters PP and a master key Msk. For all identities at the first level, the private key is generated by the PKG using Msk. For identities at the second level onwards, the private key can be generated by the PKG or by any of the ancestors of that identity. Figure 1 shows the CBCBAC model for the Cloud environment. In this scheme, the private key sk_{id} of id can be generated by an entity whose identity is a prefix of the id and who has obtained the corresponding private key.

Our CBCBAC model $\mathcal{H}$ is specified by following four probabilistic polynomial time (in the security parameter) algorithms:

1. Set-Up : This operation generates the initial security parameters. Here, we use a string of *1* or *0* of length *k* as input and derive the PP and Msk by randomizing the input. The generated master key is known only to the PKG. The PKG also contains the message space M, the cipher-text space C and the identity space I. Figure 2 (a) presents the steps of setup operation.

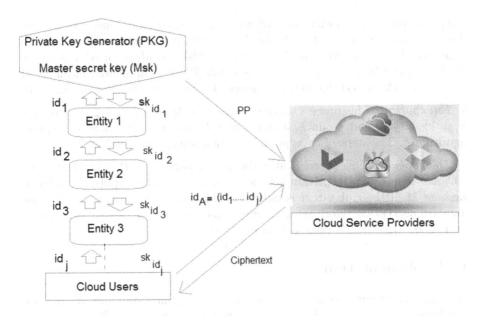

Fig. 1. CBCBAC model for cloud environment

Algorithm 1: Setup operation	Algorithm 3: Encryption operation
Input: $\{0, 1\}^k$	**Input:** PP, id_j and $\mathcal{M}$
Output: Initial Msk, PP	**Output:** C
1. Initial $Msk \xleftarrow{R} \{0,1\}^k$	1. $C \leftarrow E_{id_j}(\mathcal{M})$
2. Initial $PP \xleftarrow{R} \{0,1\}^k$	
(a) Algorithm for **Setup** operation	(c) Algorithm for **Encryption** operation

Algorithm 2: Key generation	Algorithm 4: Decryption operation
Input: $id = (id_1, \cdots, id_j)$, where $j \geq 1$ and $sk(id_{j-1})$ for the identity $(id_1, \cdots, id_{j-1})$	**Input:** PP, id_j C and $sk(id)$
Output: $sk(id)$	**Output:** $\mathcal{M}$, Ψ
1. if j=1 then	1. if Cipher-text is not valid them
2. $sk(id_1) \leftarrow BilinearPair(Msk, id_1)$	2 return Ψ
3. else	3. else
4. $sk(id_j) \leftarrow BilinearPair(sk(id_{j-1}), id_j)$	4. return $\mathcal{M} \leftarrow D_{id_j}(C)$
5. endif	5. endif
6. return $sk(id_j)$	
(b) Algorithm for **Key-gen** operation	(d) Algorithm for **Decryption** operation

Fig. 2. Algorithms for Combinatorial Batch Codes Based Access Control (CBCBAC) model

2. *Key-Generation:* This operation generates the private key $sk(id_j)$ corresponding to the jth identity. This method uses bilinear pairing [9] between identity tuple id $= (id_1, ..., id_j)$, $j \geq 1$ and the private keys $sk(d_{id|j-1})$ for the identities $((id_1, ..., id_{j-1}))$. Bilinear pairing defines a map between two cyclic groups of some prime order and satisfies bi-linearity, non-degeneracy and efficient computability properties [9]. In this algorithm, we define bilinear pairing as BilinearPair(.,.) function. Initially, for $j = 1$, Msk and id_1 are used to generate $sk(id_1)$. By invoking Key-generation algorithm, PKG or an identity at any level can produce the decryption key. Key generation algorithm is given in Fig. 2 (b).

3. Encryption: This process encrypts a message M by a public parameter PP of an identity id and produces a cipher-text C. We use a standard encryption algorithm E. The steps of encryption operation are specified in Fig. 2 (c).

4. Decryption: This process takes the public parameter PP, an identity id, a Cipher-text C and a private key $sk(id)$ as input and compute the original message M. If the cipher-text is not valid, this algorithm produces ψ. We use standard decryption algorithm D corresponding to E in the decryption process. Decryption algorithm is presented in Fig. 2 (d).

4 Implementation

To demonstrate our approach, we implement an application based on Hadoop and MapReduce framework. The experiment has run on two PCs configured with Intel core i7-2600S 2.80 GHz and 16 GB RAM. We have configured Citrix Xen Server 6.2.0 [19] on one PC that is used for file storage. The second PC configured with Cloudera CDH 5.3.0-0 [20]. This is used as a Cloud Service Provider that provides access control of the stored files of cloud users.

The working of CBCBAC model is divided into 5 phases of access control. Fig. 3 describes these phases.

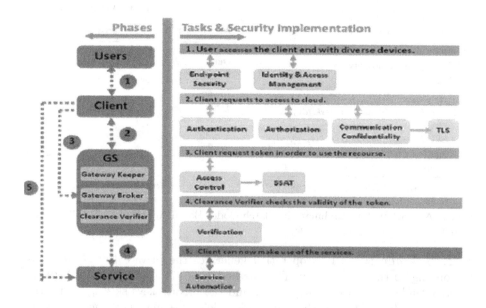

Fig. 3. Phases of access control for cloud environment

1. **Phase 1:** A client program is installed on or downloaded to every endpoint (laptop, cell-phone, etc.) when user accesses the client end. A server or gateway hosts the centralized security program, which verifies logins and sends updates and patches when needed.
2. **Phase 2:** In the second phase, the user contacts the Gate Keeper (GK) service in the Gateway Server (GS) where the communication with the GK (or any other service) uses Transport Layer Security to protect against eavesdropping attacks.
3. **Phase 3:** The GS needs to securely identify their users through authentication and after that, a user must gain authorization for doing certain tasks. With the single sign-on access control token (SSAT), a user logs in once and gain access to all systems without being prompted to log in again in each of them. The Clearance Verifier (CV) checks the validity of the token. If there is no verification in the SSAT, that service should contact the CV.
4. **Phase 4:** This step is a precaution against SSAT forging. If the CV reports back that the Gateway Server did not generate the SSAT, the request is blocked. If the SSAT is examined and proved valid, the CV attaches a verification token to the SSAT.
5. **Phase 5:** Client can now make use of the services.

4.1   Performance Analysis

We measure the performance of our proposed model by computing the efficiency of a user access control that is how efficiently and frequently a user can access data from the cloud service providers. In our scheme, the number of data access can be set flexible according to users requirement. We compute the efficiency on the basis of time of access, encryption and decryption. Efficiency of our scheme is calculated using Eq. 2. Figure 4 shows the performance comparison of our scheme with the different schemes.

$$Efficiency = \frac{Seconds}{Program} = \frac{Instructions}{Program} \times \frac{Clocks}{Instructions} \times \frac{Seconds}{Clocks} \qquad (2)$$

The Advantages of a CBCBAC model are following.

1. It has dynamic performance and mobility features to support remote access to its resources.
2. Cloud based systems need reliable mechanisms for proving users' identities and authenticating them. login time and time of authentication is less to improve performance of the system.
3. A trust relationship between cloud user and cloud service providers is induced to get more attention.
4. The model have scalable in terms of users, enforcement points and policy evaluation.
5. The model have heterogeneous to adopt a vast number of diverse technologies and mechanisms.

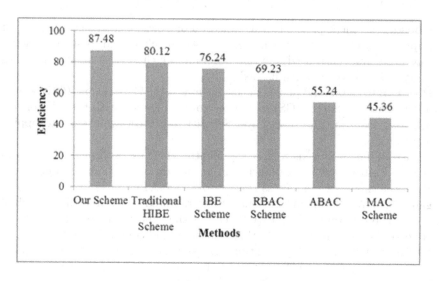

Fig. 4. Efficiency comparison of different methods

6. The model have interoperable among different consumer requirements and resources.
7. It has less computation complexity and response time for providing better Quality of Service (QoS).
8. It must be able to handle the flexibility in virtualization, sharing of resources and attribute management.
9. In case of using multiple cloud, users should be able to assign and ease privileges and transfer their credentials across different layers of clouds.
10. It has auditing and delegation capabilities for policy management to add, delete, change, import, and export of user's file.
11. It has flexibility in configuration, operation and situational awareness for users.
12. It has operating system compatibility and support for passive and active workflows.

5   Security Analysis

In this section we discussed about the standard, soundness requirement of our scheme. In the later part, we test our scheme against Chosen Ciphertext attack.

5.1   Standard Soundness Requirement

Standard soundness requirement of our CBCBAC model is following:

Algorithm 1. Standard soundness requirement of our CBCBAC scheme

---
1: **if** (PP,msk) is output by Set-Up;

   d_{id} is a private key corresponding to the identity tuple id generated by the Key-Generation algorithm;

   and C is the output of the Encryption algorithm for a message M $\epsilon \mathcal{M}$ using id as a public key and PP; **then**

2:    The Decryption algorithm must return M on input d_{id} and C.

3: **end if**

5.2   Test of Our Scheme Against Chosen Ciphertext Attack

At the basic level, the security model of CBCBAC has formalisation of the adversarys inability to distinguish between ciphertexts arising out of two equal length messages M_0 and M_1.

For this, an identity is chosen by the adversary as the target identity, i.e., the goal of the adversary is to compromise the security of the identity it chooses as the target identity. A random bit γ is chosen and challenge the ciphertext is produced by encrypting M_γ under the target identity. The adversary wins if it can predict γ with a probability significantly away from half.

Let our CBCBAC scheme as defined in the previous section is $\mathcal{H}$. The IND-ID-CCA security (Indistinguishability under Adaptive Identity and Adaptive Chosen Ciphertext Attack) for $\mathcal{H}$ is defined in terms of the following game between a challenger and an adversary of the CBCBAC. The adversary is allowed to place two types of oracle queries decryption queries to a decryption oracle $\mathcal{O}_d$ and key extraction queries to a key-extraction oracle $\mathcal{O}_k$.

Figure 5 shows a schematic diagram of the security game defining the security of our CBCBAC scheme.

1. **Set-Up**: The challenger takes as input a security parameter 1^k and runs the Set-Up algorithm of the CBCBAC. It provides $\mathcal{A}$ with the system parameters PP while keeping it the master key Msk.
2. **Phase 1**: Adversary $\mathcal{A}$ makes a finite number of queries where each query is one of the following two types:
   key-extraction query (id): This query is placed to the key-extraction oracle $\mathcal{O}_d$. Questioned on id, $\mathcal{O}_k$ generates a private key d_{id} of id and returns it to A. The Key-Generation algorithm is probabilistic and so if it is queried more than once on the same identity, then it may provide different (but valid) decryption keys.
   decryption query (id,C): This query is placed to the decryption oracle $\mathcal{O}_d$. It returns the resulting plaintext or $\perp$ if the ciphertext cannot be decrypted. $\mathcal{A}$ is allowed to make these queries adaptively, i.e., any query may depend on the previous queries as well as their answers.
3. **Challenge**: When $\mathcal{A}$ decides that Phase 1 is complete, it fixes an identity id^* and two equal length messages M_0, M_1 under the (obvious) constraint that it has not asked for the private key of id^* or any prefix of id^*. The challenger chooses uniformly at random a bit $\gamma \varepsilon 0, 1$ and obtains a ciphertext

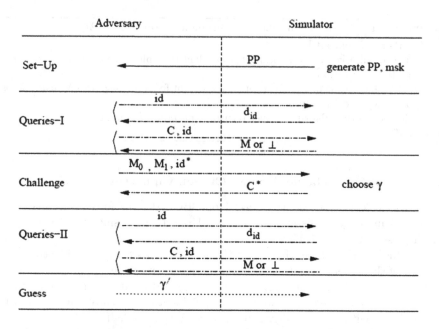

Fig. 5. Work flow of security game for our scheme.

C^* corresponding to γ, i.e., C^* is the output of the Encryption algorithm on input $(\gamma, id^*, \mathrm{PP})$. It returns C^* as the challenge ciphertext to $\mathcal{A}$.

4. **Phase 2**: $\mathcal{A}$ has now issued additional queries just like Phase 1, with the (obvious) restriction that it cannot place a decryption query for the decryption of C^* under id^* or any of its prefixes nor a key-extraction query for the private key of id^* or any prefix of id^*. All other queries are valid and $\mathcal{A}$ can issue these queries adaptively just like Phase 1. The challenger responds as in Phase 1.

5. **Guess**: $\mathcal{A}$ outputs a guess $\gamma_\prime$ of γ. The advantage of the adversary $\mathcal{A}$ in attacking the CBCBAC scheme $\mathcal{H}$ is defined as:

$$Adv_{\mathcal{A}}^{\mathcal{H}} = |Pr[(\gamma = \gamma_\prime)] - 1/2|.$$

Our CBCBAC scheme $\mathcal{H}$ is said to be (t, q_{id}, q_C, ϵ)-secure against adaptive chosen ciphertext attack ((t, q_{id}, q_C,ϵ)-IND-ID-CCA secure) if for any t-time adversary $\mathcal{A}$ that makes at most q_{id} private key queries and at most q_C decryption queries, $Adv_{\mathcal{A}}^{\mathcal{H}}$. In short, we say $\mathcal{H}$ is IND-ID-CCA secure or CCA-secure.

6   Conclusions and Future Work

In this paper, we provide an efficient CBCBAC approach for access control in cloud computing. We survey all the current techniques. We accomplish that none of previous existing techniques practically feasible in cloud context.

We also provide brief security analysis of our scheme. In the near future, we planned to work on implementation and performance analysis of our scheme. This will provide effective and efficient authentication in a cloud environment.

References

1. Saxena, R., Dey, S.: Cloud shield: effective solution for DDoS in cloud. In: Di Fatta, G., Fortino, G., Li, W., Pathan, M., Stahl, F., Guerrieri, A. (eds.) IDCS 2015. LNCS, vol. 9258, pp. 3–10. Springer, Heidelberg (2015). doi:10.1007/978-3-319-23237-9_1
2. Saxena, R., Ruj, S., Sarma, M., Collaborative model for privacy preservation, data integrity verification in cloud computing. In: Proceedings of the Security and Privacy Symposium, IIT Kanpur, Kanpur, India, February 2013
3. Ruj, R., Saxena, R.: Securing cloud data. In: Cloud Computing with e-Science Applications, pp. 41–72, January 2015. doi:10.1201/b18021-4
4. Saxena, R., Dey, S.: Collaborative approach for data integrity verification in cloud computing. In: Martínez Pérez, G., Thampi, S.M., Ko, R., Shu, L. (eds.) Recent Trends in Computer Networks and Distributed Systems Security. Communications in Computer and Information Science, vol. 420, pp. 1–15. Springer, Heidelberg (2014). doi:10.1007/978-3-642-54525-2_1
5. Ausanka-Crues, R.: Methods for access control: advances and limitations, Harvey Mudd College 301
6. LaPadula, L., Bell, D.E., LaPadula, L.J.: Secure computer systems: Mathematical foundations, Draft MTR, The MITRE Corporation 2
7. Biba, K.J.: Integrity considerations for secure computer systems. Technical report, DTIC Document (1977)
8. Lampson, B.W.: Protection. SIGOPS Oper. Syst. Rev. 8(1), 18–24 (1974). doi:10.1145/775265.775268
9. Laurie, B.: Access control (v0. 1) (2009)
10. Oh, S., Park, S.: Task-role-based access control model. Inf. Syst. 28(6), 533–562 (2003)
11. Al-Kahtani, M., Sandhu, R., et al.: A model for attribute-based user-role assignment. In.: 2002 18th Annual Proceedings of Computer Security Applications Conference, pp. 353–362. IEEE (2002)
12. Brucker, A.D., Brügger, L., Kearney, P., Wolff, B.: An approach to modular, testable security models of real-world health-care applications. In: Proceedings of the 16th ACM Symposium on Access Control Models and Technologies, pp. 133–142. ACM (2011)
13. Wang, W., Han, J., Song, M., Wang, X., The design of a trust, role based access control model in cloud computing. In: 2011 6th International Conference on Pervasive Computing and Applications (ICPCA), pp. 330–334. IEEE (2011)
14. Tianyi, Z., Weidong, L., Jiaxing, S.: An efficient role based access control system for cloud computing. In: 2011 IEEE 11th International Conference on Computer and Information Technology (CIT), pp. 97–102. IEEE (2011)
15. Sun, L., Wang, H., Yong, J., Wu, G.: Semantic access control for cloud computing based on e-healthcare. In: 2012 IEEE 16th International Conference on Computer Supported Cooperative Work in Design (CSCWD), pp. 512–518. IEEE (2012)
16. Tsai, W.-T., Shao, Q.: Role-based access-control using reference ontology in clouds. In: 2011 10th International Symposium on Autonomous Decentralized Systems (ISADS), pp. 121–128. IEEE (2011)

17. Mon, E.E., Naing, T.T.: The privacy-aware access control system using attribute- and role-based access control in private cloud. In: 2011 4th IEEE International Conference on Broadband Network and Multimedia Technology (IC-BNMT), pp. 447–451. IEEE (2011)
18. Stinson, D., Wei, R., Paterson, M.B.: Combinatorial batch codes. Adv. Math. Commun. **3**(1), 13–27 (2009)
19. XenServer, Download xenserver 6.2 @ONLINE (2014). http://xenserver.org/open-source-virtualization-download.html
20. Cloudera, Cloudera downloads get started with hadoop @ONLINE (2014). http://www.cloudera.com/content/cloudera/en/downloads.html

Agreement in Epidemic Information Dissemination

Mosab Ayiad, Amogh Katti, and Giuseppe Di Fatta$^{(\boxtimes)}$

Department of Computer Science, University of Reading, Whiteknights,
Reading, Berkshire RG6 6AY, UK
{m.m.ayiad,a.p.katti}@pgr.reading.ac.uk, g.difatta@reading.ac.uk

Abstract. Consensus is one of the fundamental problems in multi-agent systems and distributed computing, in which agents or processing nodes are required to reach global agreement on some data value, decision, action, or synchronisation. In the absence of centralised coordination, achieving global consensus is challenging especially in dynamic and large-scale distributed systems with faulty processes. This paper presents a fully decentralised phase transition protocol to achieve global consensus on the convergence of an underlying information dissemination process. The proposed approach is based on Epidemic protocols, which are a randomised communication and computation paradigm and provide excellent scalability and fault-tolerant properties. The experimental analysis is based on simulations of a large-scale information dissemination process and the results show that global agreement can be achieved without deterministic and global communication patterns, such as those based on centralised coordination.

Keywords: Distributed consensus · Epidemic protocols · Gossip-based protocols · Large-scale distributed computing · Decentralised algorithms

1 Introduction

In distributed computing and multi-agent systems, nodes (processes/agents) are often required to agree on some value or some action. Achieving agreement in large-scale and dynamic distributed systems is a challenging task. Such challenge forms one of the fundamental problems in distributed computing, the so-called *Consensus Problem* [1]. A solution to the consensus problem is often a critical component in many distributed applications, e.g. transactions in distributed databases, leader election, consent on replicas, synchronisation, load balancing.

In a typical formulation of the consensus problem, each participant holds a value and exchanges it with other participants. All participants then decide (*agree*) on a common output which must be one of the held values [2]. The challenge is to achieve and detect agreement among all participants (*Global Consensus*) from only locally available information at each participant when a centralised coordinator is not available.

© Springer International Publishing AG 2016
W. Li et al. (Eds.): IDCS 2016, LNCS 9864, pp. 95–106, 2016.
DOI: 10.1007/978-3-319-45940-0_9

Conceptually, the consensus problem involves the following properties [1]. All non-faulty nodes should eventually decide on some value (*Termination*). The selected value is the same for all non-faulty nodes (*Agreement*). The final decision should be valid, i.e. within the set of proposed and exchanged values (*Validity*). These properties rely on the safety and liveness of the distributed system, where safety implies that the nodes never propose incorrect values and liveness implies that all nodes perform exactly as intended [1].

A basic Epidemic (a.k.a. *Gossip-based*) system consists of a large set of nodes that adopt a randomised communication strategy to implement network services and applications. Epidemic protocols are typically formulated as periodic processes with a fixed cycle length. At each cycle, each node sends its local state to a random peer. During each cycle, a node receives the local state of some other peers and updates the local state. Random pairwise communication provides stochastic guarantees that the nodes in the system ultimately converge to a common state [3]. Two fundamental global operations that can be implemented by means of Epidemic processes are information dissemination (broadcast) and data aggregation. In data aggregation a global synopsis function (*average, count, sum*, etc.) is computed in parallel and consistently at every node.

A typical Epidemic algorithm is formulated by combining the appropriate aggregation function with a particular communication model, e.g. Push-Sum, Push-Pull Averaging, Symmetric Push-Sum [4,5]. Aggregation algorithms may estimate a global value across the neighbours, a group of nodes, or an entire network (*Uniform Gossiping*) [3]. To achieve Uniform Gossiping, an Epidemic membership protocol is adopted to provide a peer sampling service [6].

Interestingly, Epidemic approaches for consensus obtain several advantages over approaches based on deterministic and centralised communication, as they inherited the fault tolerance, scalability, decentralisation and lightweight properties of Epidemic protocols [7]. Moreover, it is found that Epidemic algorithms can support asynchronous applications better, as they exhibit loose coupling and converge in lesser time with acceptable cost [4].

In this paper, we propose a novel Epidemic approach to the consensus problem for information dissemination. For the sake of simplicity and to emphasise the key features of the proposed solution, we adopt a simple Information Dissemination Application (*IDA*) to simulate the underlying information propagation process on which global consensus is required. In *IDA*, each node generates and propagates information in the network. Information items are uniquely identified, though the same item identifier may be generated at several nodes. *IDA* must provide a mechanism to remove duplicates, to ensure propagation of the information to all nodes and to establish a system-wide consensus for each information item.

The rest of the paper is organised as follows. Section 2 defines the model of the distributed system that has been adopted in this work. Section 3 describes *IDA*, the information dissemination application. The *IDA* protocols are presented in Sect. 4. The experimental results of the simulations are described and discussed in Sect. 5. Section 6 discusses some related work. Finally, conclusions and future work are drawn in Sect. 7.

2   Model of the Distributed System

The *impossibility result* [8] (a.k.a. the *FLP result*) refers to the impossibility of detecting consensus in distributed systems of asynchronous and unreliable processes. Achieving consensus is not possible in an asynchronous distributed system with no prior bounds δ and ϕ on, respectively, the communication delay and the relative process speed [2]. The *FLP result* has motivated the identification of the minimal properties of distributed systems that are necessary to solve the consensus problem [9]. Following the work in [2], the proposed solution in this paper is provided for a partial synchrony setting so that upper bounds δ and ϕ are defined but unknown to the nodes. The message exchange is subject to random delays within δ and all processes run at a bounded relative speed ϕ and perform at least one operation in each cycle. The simulations adopt discrete events scheduled with random offsets within fixed time intervals (*cycles*). Within each process, cycles are consecutive and do not overlap. A uniformly distributed synchronisation offset is used for starting each process [5]. Processes perform separate send and receive operations: no complex atomic communication operations are required. As a consequence, interleaved message exchanges exist and message order is neglected. No process lock or exclusive access is present.

The next section introduces the information dissemination application for which global consensus has to be provided.

3   The Information Dissemination Application (IDA)

IDA is adopted to simulate the distributed generation of information items for which propagation and global consensus is required. In this section, we present the conceptual design and practical scenario of *IDA* for the generation and propagation of the information items. In Sect. 4 the proposed protocols for propagation and consensus are described in details.

Information items in *IDA* are assigned unique (sequential) identifiers (ID). At each cycle, a node generates a new item with a given probability. A new item is given the next locally unique ID with no global or centralised coordination. This way, items with a specific ID can be generated simultaneously at different nodes and ID duplication must be resolved.

At each node, an information item is associated with one of three possible states: *Propagation*, *Agreement* and *Commit*. The state diagram is shown in Fig. 1. The same item can be associated with different states at different nodes. The ultimate goal is for each item to reach the final state (*Commit*) at all nodes, which corresponds to global consensus on that item.

Initially, each node is started with an empty information cache C. At each node, an information item is created at each cycle with a given probability. The node at which the item is created is called the *originator*. The item is represented by a tuple, which includes the item ID, the originator ID and the item state. The tuple of a newly generated item is added to the local cache C with initial state *Propagation*. Each tuple also contains some numerical variables that are used

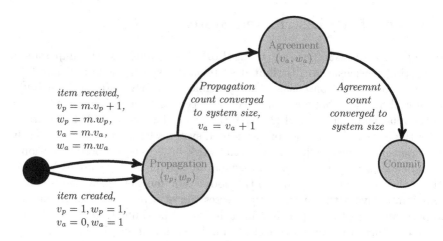

Fig. 1. *IDA* state diagram for an information item

by the consensus protocol and are described in Sect. 4. Each node periodically disseminates the items that are present in its local cache C in the system by sending it to a randomly chosen peer. When a node receives a message with a remote information cache, it updates its local cache by merging the local and remote entries, aggregating identical items and resolving ID duplicates.

Nodes have no explicit or prior knowledge of the system size n. Thereby, each node runs a specific protocol to estimate the current system size. This protocol is detailed in Sect. 4.1.

The proposed consensus protocol is a concatenation of two Epidemic aggregation operations, which are used to estimate the number of nodes in the system which have a particular item in a specific state, respectively, at *Propagation* and *Agreement*. When this estimated count corresponds to the system size within some tolerance, the state of the local copy of the item is updated to the next state (*phase transition*). This protocol is detailed in Sect. 4.2. The action taken at the transition to the *Commit* state depends on the specific application and is out of the scope of this work.

IDA is a simplified and sufficiently general model which may find applications in diverse domains, such as failure detection and consensus, transactions in distributed databases, consent on replicas, etc.

The next section describes the protocols employed for the estimation of the system size and for the two phase transitions.

4   IDA Protocols

In *IDA*, a connected physical topology, routing and transport protocols with no packet loss are assumed. *IDA* employs three protocols: the simple Node Cache Protocol (*NCP*) [5] for membership management; the System Size Estimation Protocol (*SSEP*) for the estimation of the current system size n and the Phase

Transition Protocol (PTP) for determining the state transition of the local copies of information items.

The protocol NCP implements and exports the function $getRandomPeer()$, a peer sampling service with uniform random probability (Uniform Gossiping). In the simulations, we have adopted NCP with a random k-regular overlay topology initialisation. Any other Epidemic Membership Protocols could also be employed and for further details on NCP we refer the reader to [5]. IDA nodes have no knowledge of the system size n. Therefore, each node adopts an Epidemic aggregation protocol, the System Size Estimation Protocol ($SSEP$), to estimate the current system size n. The Phase Transition Protocol (PTP) provides an Epidemic solution to the distributed consensus problem following a three-phase commit protocol approach. The protocols $SSEP$ and PTP are described in the next two sections.

Algorithm 1. System Size Estimation Protocol (SSEP)

---

1 **Initialisation:**
2 $v = 1.0$ *at all nodes,* $w = 1.0$ *at one node and* $w = 0.0$ *at all other nodes*
3 *At each node i: $est = 0.0$* // `size estimation`

---

4 **At each cycle at node i:**
5 $j \leftarrow getRandomPeer()$
6 $v = \frac{v}{2.0}; w = \frac{w}{2.0}$
7 $send(j, v, w, reply = true)$ // Push `message`

---

8 **At event 'receive message m from j' at node i:**
9 **if** $m.reply$ **then**
10 $\quad$ | $\quad$ $v = \frac{v}{2.0}; w = \frac{w}{2.0}$
11 $\quad$ | $\quad$ $send(j, v, w, reply = false)$ // Pull `message`
12 $v = v + m.v; w = w + m.w$
13 **if** $w > 0.0$ **then** $est = \frac{v}{w}$

---

14 **Method** $size() : \mathbb{R}$
15 $\quad$ | $\quad$ **return** est

4.1 The System Size Estimation Protocol (SSEP)

The protocol $SSEP$ implements the Symmetric Push-Sum Protocol for data aggregation [5]. Precisely, it estimates the global function '$count$'. In Algorithm 1, the pair (v, w) is used, where v is the aggregation value and w the aggregation weight. Initially, all node values are set to 1, and weights are set to 0, except for one node that has $w = 1$. At each cycle, a node i halves its pair values (v, w) and sends the pair to a random node (Push). When a node receives a Push message from a remote node j, it halves its local value and weight and sends them to j (PULL). Finally, it combines the local and remote pairs and updates the estimated system size.

SSEP propagates aggregation pairs in the system. The global sum of w will be evenly distributed to all nodes converging to $\frac{1}{n}$, where n is the system size. Similarly, v is aggregated and distributed, and will converge to 1. At each cycle, the local estimation of n can be calculated by $\frac{v}{w}$. Although interleaved messages are present in the system, as long as the mass invariant holds in the system, $\frac{v}{w}$ will quickly converge to n with a relative error as small as desired [3,5]. The estimated system size will hold as long as the system size remains static [5,7]. However, since the protocol is continuously executed, it can also adapt to changes in the system size. Nevertheless, the simulation of dynamic network conditions (e.g., node churn) is out of the scope of this work.

4.2   The Phase Transition Protocol (PTP)

Each *PTP* instance maintains a local cache C of information items. The local cache is initially empty and will be used to store items either created locally or received from other nodes. Each item in C is represented by a tuple, as described in Sect. 3. The tuple contains two aggregation pairs (v, w). One aggregation pair, (v_p, w_p), is used to estimate the number of nodes which have received the item, i.e. the (p)*ropagation* count. The second pair, (v_a, w_a), is used to estimate the (a)*greement* count, that is the number of nodes holding the item at the second phase. The protocol is a cascade of two Epidemic aggregations based on the Symmetric Push-Sum Protocol for the global function '*sum*' [5].

As shown in Algorithm 2, at each cycle, node i halves the two aggregation pairs of each tuple in C. Then, it sends a copy of the local C to a random peer. The protocol *PTP* checks if an agreement is reached for the transition from a phase to the successive. On the event of receiving a message from a peer, the algorithm adds new items, updates the tuple of the items already stored in C and resolves duplicates by keeping either the oldest tuple or keeping the one with the lowest originator ID if the tuples have the same creation time.

At the creation of a new information item at node i, *PTP* selects the next unique identifier (line 4) and inserts a new tuple into C (line 5). *PTP* obtains the estimated system size n from *SSEP* protocol using the function $size()$. For each τ in C, the criterion in line 14 decides upon the transition from *Propagation* to *Agreement*. The aggregation count is compared to the estimated system size with a relative error tolerance (ϵ). The test requires a minimum number of consecutive cycles (MIN) within tolerance to ensure robust transition to the next phase, avoiding early false transitions. The transition to *Commit* is associated with a similar test condition on the *Agreement* count. The transition to *Commit* is shown in lines 18–19. When receiving a message with a remote cache, *PTP* merges local and remote items in lines 25–32. Tuples related to the same information item are aggregated in line 28, duplicate IDs are resolved in line 30 and new items are added to the local cache C in line 32.

Algorithm 2. Phase Transition Protocol (PTP)

---

1 **Require:** $size()$, the SSEP estimation; ϵ, an error tolerance; MIN, a minimum number of consecutive cycles; a local cache of items $C = \{\tau = \langle id, o, t, v_p, w_p, v_a, w_a, state \rangle, ...\}$, where id is the item identifier, o the originator identifier, t the creation time, (v_p, w_p) the propagation pair, (v_a, w_a) the agreement pair and state the item state.

2 **Initialisation:** at each node i: $C \longleftarrow \{\}$

---

3 **At event 'new item generated' at node i:**
4 $id \longleftarrow$ next locally unique identifier
5 $C \longleftarrow C \cup \{\langle id, i, current\_cycle, 1, 1, 0, 1, PROPAGATION \rangle\}$

---

6 **At each cycle at node i:**
7 $j = getRandomPeer()$
8 **foreach** $\tau \in C$ **do**
9 $\quad\lfloor\ \tau = \langle \tau.id, \tau.o, \tau.t, \frac{\tau.v_p}{2}, \frac{\tau.w_p}{2}, \frac{\tau.v_a}{2}, \frac{\tau.w_a}{2}, \tau.state \rangle$
10 $send(j, C, reply = true)$ // Push message
11 **foreach** $\tau \in C$ **do**
12 $\quad$ **switch** $\tau.state$ **do**
13 $\quad\quad$ **case** $PROPAGATION$ **do**
14 $\quad\quad\quad$ **if** $size() > 0.0$ **and** $\left| \frac{size() - \frac{\tau.v_p}{\tau.w_p}}{size()} \right| \leq \epsilon$ for at least MIN cycles **then**
15 $\quad\quad\quad\quad$ $\tau.state = AGREEMENT$
16 $\quad\quad\quad\quad$ $\tau.v_a = \tau.v_a + 1$
17 $\quad\quad$ **case** $AGREEMENT$ **do**
18 $\quad\quad\quad$ **if** $size() > 0.0$ **and** $\left| \frac{size() - \frac{\tau.v_a}{\tau.w_a}}{size()} \right| \leq \epsilon$ for at least MIN cycles **then**
19 $\quad\quad\quad\quad$ $\tau.state = COMMIT$
$\quad\quad\quad\quad$ // and may take some application-specific action.

---

20 **At event 'received m message from j' at node i:**
21 **if** $m.reply$ **then**
22 $\quad$ **foreach** $\tau \in C$ **do**
23 $\quad\quad\lfloor\ \tau = \langle \tau.id, \tau.o, \tau.t, \frac{\tau.v_p}{2}, \frac{\tau.w_p}{2}, \frac{\tau.v_a}{2}, \frac{\tau.w_a}{2}, \tau.state \rangle$
24 $\quad$ $send(j, C, reply = false)$ // Pull message
25 **foreach** $\tau_0 \in m.C$ **do**
26 $\quad$ **if** C **contains** τ_1 **where** $\tau_0.id == \tau_1.id$ **then**
$\quad\quad$ // Resolve duplicate item ID
27 $\quad\quad$ **if** $(\tau_0.t == \tau_1.t$ **and** $\tau_0.o == \tau_1.o)$ **then**
28 $\quad\quad\quad$ $\tau_1 = \langle \tau_1.id, \tau_1.o, \tau_1.t,$
$\quad\quad\quad\quad \tau_1.v_p + \tau_0.v_p, \tau_1.w_p + \tau_0.w_p, \tau_1.v_a + \tau_0.v_a, \tau_1.w_a + \tau_0.w_a, \tau_1.state \rangle$
29 $\quad\quad$ **else if** $(\tau_0.t == \tau_1.t$ **and** $\tau_0.o < \tau_1.o)$ **or** $(\tau_0.t < \tau_1.t)$ **then**
30 $\quad\quad\quad\lfloor\ \tau_1 = \langle \tau_0.id, \tau_0.o, \tau_0.t, \tau_0.v_p + 1, \tau_0.w_p, \tau_0.v_a, \tau_0.w_a, \tau_0.state \rangle$
31 $\quad$ **else**
32 $\quad\quad\lfloor\ C \longleftarrow C \cup \{\langle \tau_0.id, \tau_0.o, \tau_0.t, \tau_0.v_p + 1, \tau_0.w_p, \tau_0.v_a, \tau_0.w_a, \tau_0.state \rangle\}$

---

5   Simulations and Experimental Results

Simulations are carried out using PEERSIM [10], a Java-based discrete-event P2P simulation tool. PEERSIM is flexible, scalable and easy to configure. *SSEP*, *PTP* and *NCP* protocols are implemented in dedicated modules for PEERSIM.

The simulation common settings are as follows. Different random seeds are used in each simulation run to validate performance and enforce randomisation. The system default size is $n = 10000$ nodes and the maximum experiment length is 100 cycles. Membership is managed by *NCP*, which maintains the overlay topology with $k = 10$. The generation of new items in *PTP* is interrupted after the completion of 50 % of the simulation cycles to observe the protocol performance in the residual cycles.

Simulation cycles are time intervals of fixed length, which adopt the cycle structure used in [5]. For experimental purposes, we define Δt, a cycle length that is long enough for all nodes to finish send, receive and aggregate operations, such that $\Delta t = t_1 + t_2 + t_2 + t_3$, where t_1 limits PUSH offsets, t_2 limits transmission delays, and t_3 limits initial synchronisation offsets. In Δt, the portion $t_2 + t_2$ is the maximum communication latency corresponding to the round trip time on the diameter of the network. However, some messages may take very long to arrive ($\delta > \Delta t$) and arrive in later cycles (*Out of Cycle Message*). Out of cycle messages slightly delay the convergence in *SSEP* and *PTP* protocols due to potential loss of aggregation mass. Nevertheless, the aggregation mass is restored when out of cycle messages reach destination.

All protocols are based on the event-driven engine of PEERSIM, where three common events are defined as follows.

1. The ACTIVATE EVENT occurs at every cycle. At the beginning of the simulation, the event is scheduled by a specific initialiser to occur after a random offset within t_3. The event is then scheduled to occur at every Δt. The item generation procedure and the phase transition tests are executed at this event. The cyclic event stops when a maximum number of cycles is reached.
2. The PUSH EVENT is scheduled at a random time $t < t_1$ from the ACTIVATE EVENT. At this event, a node sends a PUSH message to a random peer.
3. The MESSAGE RECEIVE EVENT occurs when a node receives a message from a peer. At this event the incoming message is processed.

The protocol *SSEP* is tested with different system size values (n) and the convergence of the estimated system size is monitored. Figure 2.a shows the percentage of nodes which have locally estimated n within an error tolerance (ϵ); while Fig. 2.b shows the average of the estimated size for all nodes. Figure 2 confirms that 100 % of nodes correctly estimate the system size n after a sufficient number of cycles.

The protocol *PTP* is tested with the generation of a single information item and of multiple items. The diffusion of a single item is shown in Fig. 3, where the percentage of nodes that have achieved a particular phase is illustrated. Additional experiments on single item diffusion are conducted with several values

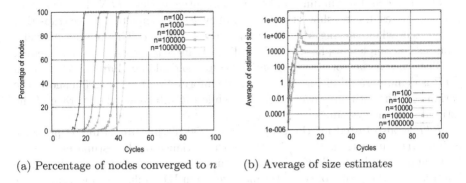

(a) Percentage of nodes converged to n (b) Average of size estimates

Fig. 2. System size estimation in *SSEP* converges to actual system size n ($\epsilon = 0.01$)

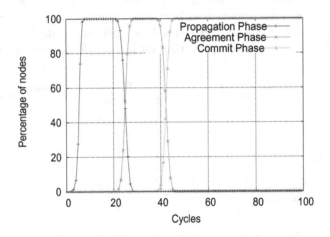

Fig. 3. Percentage of nodes at each phase for a single information item in *PTP* ($n = 10000$, $\epsilon = 0.001$, $MIN = 5$)

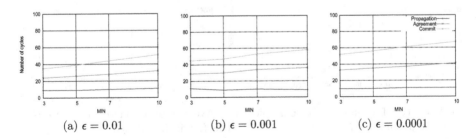

(a) $\epsilon = 0.01$ (b) $\epsilon = 0.001$ (c) $\epsilon = 0.0001$

Fig. 4. Number of cycles to complete a phase transition in *PTP* for a single item varying the minimum number of consecutive cycles MIN and for three values of the error tolerance ϵ ($n = 10000$)

of tolerance ϵ and minimum number of consecutive cycles MIN. Figure 4 summarises the results and shows the number of cycles to complete a phase transition for an item when varying MIN and for a few values of ϵ. The number of cycles required to complete a phase transition linearly increases with both parameters.

The convergence of the *Propagation* count and of the *Agreement* count in PTP is demonstrated in Fig. 5. For a single information item, Fig. 5.a shows the variance of the estimates over all nodes; while Fig. 5.b shows the average of the estimates in the system.

PTP is also tested for the propagation of 50 distinct items in the presence of item ID duplication. Figure 5.c shows the variance of the estimates over all items and all nodes; while Fig. 5.d shows the average of the estimates. It can be inferred that the protocol correctly manages item ID duplicates and that count estimates in the nodes correctly converge to the system size n.

The proposed Epidemic three-phase approach provides a solution to the consensus problem without any centralised coordination. Global agreement and synchronisation can be achieved without global deterministic communication patterns. Moreover, Epidemic protocols have excellent scalability and fault-tolerance, which are important properties for large-scale distributed systems.

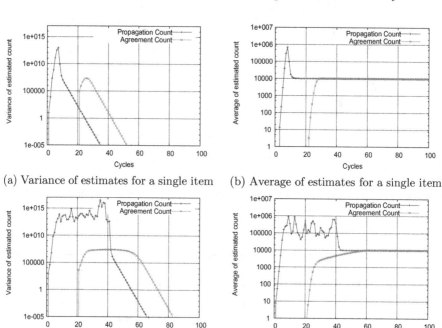

(a) Variance of estimates for a single item

(b) Average of estimates for a single item

(c) Variance of estimates for multiple items (50 distinct items)

(d) Average of estimates for multiple items (50 distinct items)

Fig. 5. Convergence of the *Propagation* and *Agreement* count estimates in PTP ($n = 10000$, $\epsilon = 0.001$, $MIN = 5$)

6   Related Work

Solutions for the consensus problem based on Epidemic approaches have been applied to various applications in distributed systems. The work in [11] proposed general consensus and average consensus algorithms for quantisation of states in randomised networks using the asynchronous Epidemic-based communications of agents. A survey on the consensus problem in multi-agent cooperative control is provided in [12]. The work in [13] uses Epidemic-based ping and time-out mechanism to detect and propagate failures. Correctly operating processes reach consensus when all of them detect the failed ones. In [14], an Epidemic-based aggregation protocol is used to perform a global synchronisation and reduction operation for a fully decentralised K-Means clustering without global communication patterns under node churn and message loss. The work in [15] investigated heuristic methods to detect the convergence of Epidemic aggregation and those methods could be used to build a consensus protocol for data aggregation.

7   Conclusions

This paper presented a phase transition protocol (PTP) to achieve global consensus on the convergence of information dissemination. The proposed solution assumes the minimal properties needed to solve the consensus problem in partially synchronous distributed systems. The solution is based on Epidemic protocols and so it inherits their advantages. A simple application scenario (IDA) of global information dissemination is used to demonstrate the key idea of Epidemic consensus in large-scale distributed systems and could be extended in more complex scenarios, such as data aggregation. In IDA, two main algorithms are introduced, the protocol $SSEP$ to estimate the system size and the protocol PTP to manage phase transitions and achieve global agreement on each information item.

The experimental analysis based on simulations has shown that PTP is able to achieve global consensus on the propagation of information items over a large number of nodes with no centralised coordination, no prior knowledge of system size, and no assumption of the a priori global uniqueness of the item identifiers. However, the solution currently assumes that system size holds during the consensus transition period and that no message loss or churn are present. Future research may address these limitations, introduce optimisations of the performance and communication overhead. A further direction of future investigations is the extension of Epidemic consensus to the data aggregation problem and to dynamic network conditions.

Acknowledgements. The authors Mosab Ayiad and Amogh Katti are supported for their PhD projects, respectively, by the Merit Scholarship Program, Islamic Development Bank, and by the Felix Scholarship.

References

1. Guerraoui, R., Hurfin, M., Mostéfaoui, A., Oliveira, R., Raynal, M., Schiper, A.: Consensus in asynchronous distributed systems: a concise guided tour. In: Krakowiak, S., Shrivastava, S.K. (eds.) BROADCAST 1999. LNCS, vol. 1752, pp. 33–47. Springer, Heidelberg (2000)
2. Dwork, C., Lynch, N., Stockmeyer, L.: Consensus in the presence of partial synchrony. J. ACM **35**(2), 288–323 (1988)
3. Kempe, D., Dobra, A., Gehrke, J.: Gossip-based computation of aggregate information. In: Proceedings of 44th Annual IEEE Symposium on Foundations of Computer Science (2003)
4. Rao, I., Harwood, A., Karunasekera, S.: Impacts of asynchrony on epidemic-style aggregation protocols. In: IEEE 16th International Conference on Parallel and Distributed Systems (ICPADS) (2010)
5. Blasa, F., Cafiero, S., Fortino, G., Di Fatta, G.: Symmetric push-sum protocol for decentralised aggregation. In: The Third International Conference on Advances in P2P Systems Proceedings of AP2PS (2011)
6. Poonpakdee, P., Di Fatta, G.: Expander graph quality optimisation in randomised communication. In: IEEE International Conference on Data Mining Workshop (ICDMW), December 2014
7. Jelasity, M., Montresor, A., Babaoglu, O.: Gossip-based aggregation in large dynamic networks. ACM Trans. Comput. Syst. **23**(3), 219–252 (2005)
8. Fischer, M.J., Lynch, N.A., Paterson, M.S.: Impossibility of distributed consensus with one faulty process. J. ACM **32**(2), 374–382 (1985)
9. Dolev, D., Dwork, C., Stockmeyer, L.: On the minimal synchronism needed for distributed consensus. J. ACM **34**(1), 77–97 (1987)
10. Montresor, A., Jelasity, M.: PeerSim: a scalable P2P simulator. In: IEEE Ninth International Conference on Peer-to-Peer Computing, P2P 2009. IEEE (2009)
11. Cai, K., Ishii, H.: Gossip consensus and averaging algorithms with quantization. In: American Control Conference (ACC) (2010)
12. Ren, W., Beard, R.W., Atkins, E.M.: A survey of consensus problems in multi-agent coordination. In: Proceedings of the 2005 American Control Conference, June 2005
13. Katti, A., Di Fatta, G., Naughton, T., Engelmann, C.: Scalable and fault tolerant failure detection and consensus. In: Proceedings of the 22nd European MPI Users' Group Meeting. EuroMPI 2015. ACM, Bordeaux, France (2015)
14. Di Fatta, G., Blasa, F., Cafiero, S., Fortino, G.: Fault tolerant decentralised K-means clustering for asynchronous large-scale networks. J. Parallel Distrib. Comput. **73**(3), 317–329 (2013)
15. Poonpakdee, P., Orhon, N.G., Di Fatta, G.: Convergence detection in epidemic aggregation. In: an Mey, D., et al. (eds.) Euro-Par 2013. LNCS, vol. 8374, pp. 292–300. Springer, Heidelberg (2014)

Cloud-Based Wheelchair Assist System for Mobility Impaired Individuals

Congcong Ma[1], Wenfeng Li[1(✉)], Jingjing Cao[1],
Raffaele Gravina[2], and Giancarlo Fortino[2]

[1] School of Logistics Engineering, Wuhan University of Technology,
Wuhan, People's Republic of China
{macc,liwf}@whut.edu.cn, bettymoore@126.com
[2] Department of Informatics, Modeling, Electronics and Systems,
University of Calabria, Rende, Italy
rgravina@dimes.unical.it, g.fortino@unical.it

Abstract. This paper proposes a new cloud-based wheelchair assist system to support user mobility of impaired people. The smart wheelchair system is equipped with a pressure sensor cushion and accelerometer for posture detection, GPS for localization purposes, and accelerometer for wheelchair status monitoring. Moreover, impaired people are equipped with a body area network to better support user mobility and independence. Our non-invasive system collects accelerometer, pressure data, and GPS signals to recognize user's daily activities, to track his/her location and to monitor wheelchair status. The proposed system was prototyped using the BodyCloud middleware so as to allow caregivers real-time access to the information generated by the smart wheelchair system. Finally, a case study is proposed to show the effectiveness of the assist system in extracting useful information by using multi-sensor data fusion.

Keywords: Wheelchair assist system · Cloud based · Bodycloud · Multi-sensor data fusion · Body activity · Wheelchair status

1   Introduction

With the increasing number of elder and disabled people, more efficient care services, especially for wheelchair bound individuals, must be delivered. A lot of assistive devices have been proposed so far to facilitate mobility-impaired persons conducting an independent lifestyle. Mobility-assistive equipment and devices such as smart wheelchair are booming to satisfy their requirements. Compared with the traditional wheelchair, smart wheelchair enriches its functionalities in some degree by using different technologies such as Body Area Networks (BANs) [1, 2], Cloud computing [3], heterogeneous sensor data fusion [4], wireless communication, and embedded systems [5].

Current research on smart wheelchairs is mainly focused on physiological and activity monitor in wheelchair [6], human machine interface to control the wheelchair

© Springer International Publishing AG 2016
W. Li et al. (Eds.): IDCS 2016, LNCS 9864, pp. 107–118, 2016.
DOI: 10.1007/978-3-319-45940-0_10

[7], obstacle detection and navigation [8], and wheelchair movement condition estimation. In this paper, we present a Cloud-based Wheelchair Assist System for mobility-impaired individuals. Sensors based on BANs were used to obtain data of the wheelchair user, and a prototype has been developed using the BodyCloud [9] middleware. The caregivers can access the data log of the user, give him/her advices to keep good health and predict some disease risk. In addition, if some dangerous situation such as wheelchair overturns are detected, the system can alarm the caregiver immediately.

The main contribution of the paper is using the BANs and BodyCloud to acquire sensing data and process it in the cloud platform. Furthermore, two case studies of body activity recognition and wheelchair status monitoring have been realized and presented.

The rest of paper is organized as follows. Section 2 discusses related works of the wheelchair system (WHS) and cloud-based health monitoring systems. Section 3 describes our proposed method, the Wheelchair Assist System (WHAS) architecture, and sensors deployment. Section 4 discusses the case study on body activity recognition and wheelchair status monitoring; a description of the BodyCloud-based implementation is also provided. Finally, in Sect. 5 concluding remarks are drawn and interesting future directions are presented.

2 Related Work

In the following, we discuss previous works on body activity recognition, wheelchair status monitoring, and cloud-based health monitoring in WHS.

2.1 Body Activity Recognition in WHS

Several studies propose the use of accelerometers or pressure sensors to monitor wheelchair user activity.

Postolache et al. developed a platform to monitor wheelchair user's physiological stress and physical activity [10]. E-textile electrodes were attached on the wheelchair armrest to monitor the physiological signal and 3D MEMS accelerometer was used to acquire activity data. Yang et al. proposed a wheelchair system that includes accelerometer, wireless heart rate and ECG sensors, wireless pressure detecting cushion, home environment sensing nodes [11]. Activities were recognized and results displayed to both user and caretakers. Hiremath et al. proposed a physical activity monitor system to detect physical activities for wheelchair users [12]. A gyroscope-based wheel rotation monitor was attached on the wheel to capture wheelchair movement, and an accelerometer was worn either on the arm or wrist to track activity data.

Diego et al. proposed a non-invasive way for monitoring long term wheelchair user's pressure changes and tilt usage during daily activities in order to prevent the cause of pressure ulcer [13]. Their proposed method can provide information of tilt usage, pressure changes, wheelchair using occupancy and activity level. Bao et al. utilized a pressure cushion to recognize the sitting posture on wheelchairs [14], density-based clustering methods was proposed to recognize the activity. Fard et al.

used a cushion with 8*8 pressure sensor matrix for continuous monitoring of surface pressure [15], being able to recognize different postures. In a previous work, we used a smart cushion that contains pressure sensors to detect human posture in smart wheelchair [16]. Six kinds of postures were recognized and experimental results showed high classification accuracy.

In contrast with previous literature, here we propose to fuse the accelerometer and pressure sensor data together in order to improve the recognition accuracy and better capturing the transitions among body activities.

2.2 Wheelchair Status Monitoring in WHS

Yang et al. proposed a scalable monitoring system that can automate wheelchair status data logging [17]. An accelerometer was placed under the seat and wheelchair tilt usage data were recorded automatically. Slikke et al. employed a three axis inertial measurement unit to monitor the wheelchair status, in order to prevent overturn [18]. Milenkovi et al. utilized a smartphone with its build-in sensors to capture and record physical activity of manual wheelchair users [19]. An android application can track user's physical activity and determine whether the user hand-propels or push the wheelchair. Sonenblum et al. designed a method with an accelerometer to measure the use of manual wheelchairs [20]. Different types of wheelchair movements such as start, stop and steady state propulsion was recognized. Popp et al. proposed a novel algorithm to detect active propulsion for wheelchair users [21]. Inertial measurement units were used to monitor wheel kinematics and the type of wheelchair propulsion.

In this work, we focused on wheelchair status monitoring using a single tri-axis accelerometer, specifically to monitor the wheelchair overturn.

2.3 Cloud-Based Health Monitoring

Several cloud platforms to support health monitoring systems have been developed. Melillo et al. used cloud computing to develop a platform that can support clinical decision by processing tele-monitored data and providing quick and accurate risk assessment of vascular events and falls [22]. Parane et al. introduced a cloud computing model that can efficiently process the data from healthcare devices and dynamically diagnose the disease [23]. Fortino et al. proposed the BodyCloud middleware that can realize several e-Health services [24].

To our best knowledge, few studies focused on the group of wheelchair users using the cloud computing technology. Skraba et al. provided a speech-controlled cloud-based wheelchair platform for disabled persons [25]. Park et al. developed a customized wheelchair control system taking advantage of cloud-based mobile device [26]. Although significant amount of researches have been carried out in the area of wheelchair systems, there is not a comprehensive project that addresses all aspects. There is rarely data fusion between sensor outputs that provides context information and wheelchair usage status. Conversely, with the technological support of the Body-Cloud middleware, we fused heterogeneous sensor data together to improve body activity and wheelchair status recognition accuracy. BodyCloud [24] is a platform to integrate BSN applications with Cloud PaaS infrastructures. It has been designed to support heterogeneous sensor data stream management, processing and analysis. It obviously supports long-term storage and applications interoperability.

3   Cloud-Based Wheelchair Assist System

3.1   High Level System Architecture

Referred to former research (see Sect. 2), we implemented our Cloud-based WHAS using BANs (Sensing Layer) and BodyCloud (Cloud Platform). Figure 1 presents an overview of our Cloud-based WHAS.

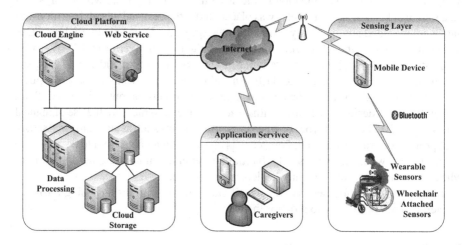

Fig. 1. Cloud-based wheelchair assist system architecture

The system is composed of three main components:

- *Sensing Layer*: Wheelchair-attached sensors and wearable sensors are used to perceive the data; sensing data are collected on the mobile device. The mobile device can also present the result to the caretakers.
- *Cloud Platform*: Raw sensing data and results are transmitted from the mobile device to cloud platform for long term storage. User's data can be evaluated and stored.
- *Application Service*: Applications were developed on both computer and smartphone. The caregiver can monitor user's body condition in real time.

3.2   Sensors Deployment

The WHAS consists of several sensors attached on the chair and worn on the user's body. Figure 2 depicts the sensors deployment of the WHAS.

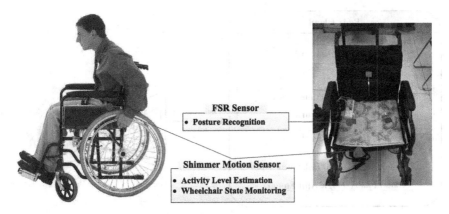

Fig. 2. Components of the smart wheelchair: (a) Sensors worn on user's body; (b) Unobtrusive sensors that attached on the wheelchair.

Shimmer Motion Sensor. Shimmer Motion Sensor [27] offers best data quality with integrated 10 DoF (Degree of Freedom) inertial sensing via accelerometer, gyro, magnetic and altimeter sensors. Shimmers have been widely and effectively used in the field of activity recognition. In this work, we attach a motion sensor on the wheelchair user's waist. By analyzing the accelerometer data, we can estimate the activity level of the wheelchair user. Another motion sensor is placed under the wheelchair seat to monitor the wheelchair status such as wheelchair overturn, dangerous situation due to rugged roads.

FSR Sensor. A seat equipped with three FSR pressure sensors attached to a flat rigid board was used to monitor user's posture transition, in order to alert wheelchair user for preventing pressure ulcer.

3.3   Cloud Infrastructure

The cloud-based WHS is implemented atop the BodyCloud platform [28]. BodyCloud implements a Software-as-a-service (SaaS) approach for real-time storage, online and offline management of human physical signals. BodyCloud provides mechanisms and abstractions to support application services through data collection, processing, and visualization. Applications are defined through specific software abstractions (Group, Modality, Workflow/Node, View). Our BodyCloud-based infrastructure is shown in Fig. 3.

To handle devices with different computation capabilities, we realized a flexible method to dynamically distribute the processing load among the system components. Specifically, three different modes that can be selected upon application launch [29], as shown below:

- *Full Cloud*: the mobile application will only collect the raw data, and send this straight to the cloud. The cloud will then perform all needed processing (i.e. feature extraction and classification).

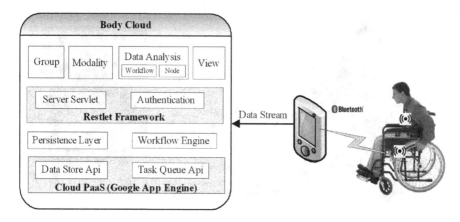

Fig. 3. BodyCloud-based Infrastructure

- *Mix Cloud*: the mobile application will be responsible for raw data collection and feature extraction. These features will then be sent to the cloud for classification.
- *Full Local*: all processing (raw data collection, feature extraction, and feature classification) will be executed on the mobile device. The cloud is therefore used only for long-term storage and graphical visualization of statistics.

The processing control flow of the application services is organized as follows:

- Initial classification model is loaded into a smartphone.
- Sensing data are collected from wearables and sensors attached on wheelchair.
- If Full Cloud mode is selected, raw data are collected by smart device and processed by BodyCloud.
- If Mix Cloud mode is selected, raw data are collected and features are extracted by the smart device, while classification in performed on the cloud.
- If Full Local mode is selected, raw data was collected and features were extracted and classified by smart device.
- High-level information and/or raw sensing data are transmitted to the BodyCloud platform for long term data storage.

4   Case Study and System Implementation

In this section, we describe the recognition algorithm and preliminary results are shown. We collected real sensor data in our lab environment. The experiments involved a sample of 4 participants (3 males and 1 female) with different ages, heights and weights. To simulate a real-life scenario, we asked the participants to perform 4 different activities that are typical for wheelchair users, such as staying stable (sit still on the wheelchair), swing for pressure relief (left-right swing and forward-back swing), twitch on the chair (abnormal state). The activity data were manually labeled during the experiments; each activity was performed for 3 min; between each activity, there subject was asked to rest for 3 min. Finally, two cases of wheelchair overturn were simulated. In the following, we will introduce the proposed activity recognition and wheelchair overturn algorithms.

4.1 Body Activity Recognition

Activity level of long-term wheelchair user can reflect some clues on the health status and mood. Maintaining wrong sitting posture for long periods increases the probability of generating pressure ulcer and wheelchair overturn caused by the unbalanced body weight distribution. Specifically, we attach an accelerometer on the user's waist, while sitting pressure information are gathered using our smart cushion. In our previous research [16], we have already used this cushion to monitor the posture of wheelchair user. Three classifiers, respectively based on Multilayer Perceptron (MLP), Support Vector Machine (SVM) and J48 Decision Tree were compared; 99.5 % posture recognition accuracy has been observed using the J48 classifier. Although high accuracy was obtained, our previous method could only detect static postures, while transition periods cannot be detected. In the present work, we propose the use of a tri-axial accelerometer to solve this problem. More specifically, pressure sensors and accelerometer data are fused together to recognize body activities, including transition periods.

Pressure and acceleration signals are both sampled at a rate of 20 Hz. The accelerometer attached on the waist can be represented as $\{Ax, Ay, Az\}$. The three pressure sensors fixed on the cushion and the backrest are marked as FSR_1 (left side of the cushion), FSR_2 (right side of the cushion), FSR_3 (middle of the backrest), as shown in Fig. 2. Pressure signals are marked as $\{P1, P2, P3\}$. At the time t, raw data can be represented as $R_t = \{Axt, Ayt, Azt, P1t, P2t, P3t\}$.

To distinguish the recognition effect of the sensors, we build three datasets: *Dataset-Acc*, *Dataset-FSR*, and *Dataset-Acc&FSR*.

First, we separated the raw data into windows of 60 samples (i.e. we assume an activity period lasts 3 s), with 50 % overlap. The window size was chosen based on previous results [30]. To reflect the feature of each sample window, we calculate the mean value and standard deviation value. Twelve time domain features are extracted from each frame, as shown in Table 1.

Table 1. Features extracted from pressure and acceleration signals

	Features
Time Domain	MEAN of *Ax, Ay, Az, P1, P2, P3*
	STDEV of *Ax, Ay, Az, P1, P2, P3*

To compare the activity recognition rate with different kinds of sensors, we evaluated three classifiers locally, respectively based on J48, k-Nearest Neighbors (kNN) and Naïve Bayes due to their easier implementation of embedded and mobile environments. Recognition results, summarized in Table 2, show that the joint usage of pressure and accelerometer sensors allows to obtain better performance.

Table 2. Body activity recognition rate with different classifiers

	Dataset-Acc	Dataset-FSR	Dataset-Acc&FSR
J48	94.96 %	94.33 %	**96.85 %**
kNN	94.33 %	96.43 %	95.38 %
Naïve Bayes	94.96 %	90.55 %	95.80 %

In particular, we observe that data fusion of accelerometer and pressure sensor shows better performance with the J48 classifier. For the sake of completeness, in Table 3 we also report the J48 recognition rate for each activity.

Table 3. Activity recognition rate of J48 classifier

Sit Still	Left-right Swing	Forward-back Swing	Twitch on the chair
96.6 %	97.5 %	97.5 %	95.8 %

4.2 Wheelchair Status Monitoring

Wheelchair overturn is an accident that is usually caused by rugged road or the unbalanced weight distribution of posture. Here we discuss the overturn caused by an external force exert to the wheelchair. Since we cannot predict which directions of the force vector are useful, it is impossible to determine a wheelchair overturn only using the variation of one axis. As a consequence, we employ the parameter called Signal Magnitude Vector (SMV) whose computation formula is shown below.

$$SMV = \sqrt{A_x^2 + A_y^2 + A_z^2} \qquad (1)$$

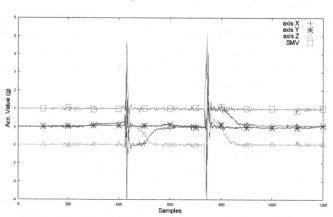

Fig. 4. Wheelchair status monitoring: accelerometer signal for each axis and SMV

We simulated the wheelchair overturn state and also compared the overturn state with stable driven state. As shown in Fig. 4, two obvious peak values, which correspond to the wheelchair overturns, can be observed. When the wheelchair moves stable, accelerometer data from z-axis (vertical axis) fluctuates around -1 g. The horizon plane (x-axis and y-axis) fluctuates around 0 g. SMV values in the range [0.7 g, 1.5 g] can be regarded as a normal state. In case of wheelchair overturn, each axis will have high fluctuation and the SMV will reach a peak value exceeding 2.5 g. We therefore use the empirically-set SMV threshold to 2.5 g to detect wheelchair overturn and issue an alarm to caregivers. When the SMV value is in the range [1.5 g, 2.5 g), our system will detect a dangerous situation. Alarm will be sent to warn the user to avoid dangerous events.

4.3   System Implementation

A case study is carried out to show the capability of our system for real time health monitoring. A web application has been developed atop the BodyCloud platform to provide comprehensive health data. Furthermore, we developed an Android-based application that runs on the smartphone for both caregivers and caretakers.

(a) Body Activity Recognition. The application requires a smart cushion on the seat, one Shimmer node attached to the user's waist, and an Android-based mobile device running the application. This application implements all the modes of operation (see Sect. 3.3). The representation of the input specifications based on BodyCloud is depicted in the following:

- Full Cloud DataFeed: $< bodyMotionNode < accelerometer < x; y; z \gg>$, $< cushionNode < pressure < p1; p2; p3 \gg>$, $< geoLocation >$, $< timestamp>$
- Mix Cloud DataFeed: $< bodyMotionNode < MEAN < acc < x; y; z \gg> >$, $< bodyMotionNode < STDEV < acc < x; y; z \gg> >$, $< cushionNode < MEAN < pressure < p1; p2; p3 \gg> >$, $< cushionNode < STDEV < pressure < p1; p2; p3 \gg$, $< rawReading < acc < x; y; z >$; $pressure < p1; p2; p3 \gg>$, $< geoLocation >$, $< timestamp>$
- Full Local DataFeed: $< bodyActivity >$, $< geoLocation >$, $< timestamp>$

In Fig. 5, a synthetic representation of body activity recognition based on the Body-Cloud workflows is depicted. The underlying BodyCloud middleware has been used to provide remote access to real-time and historical activity information. Views will be displayed on the smartphone.

(b) Wheelchair Status Monitoring. The application requires one Shimmer node under the chair and an Android-based mobile device running the application. This application implements on 2 modes of operation (see Sect. 3.3). The representation of the input specifications based on BodyCloud is depicted below and workflows is depicted in Fig. 6.

- Full Cloud DataFeed: $< chairMotionNode < accelerometer < x; y; z \gg>$, $< geoLocation >$, $< timestamp>$
- Full Local DataFeed: $< fallEvent >$, $< geoLocation >$, $< timestamp>$

Location service was provided for both body activity and wheelchair status monitoring. Commonly, if the wheelchair user is in danger (e.g. in case of twitch, abnormal

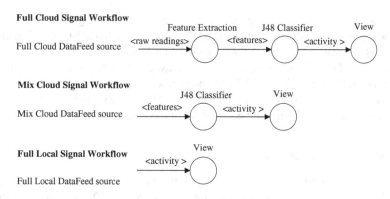

Fig. 5. Graphical representation of the body activity recognition workflow templates.

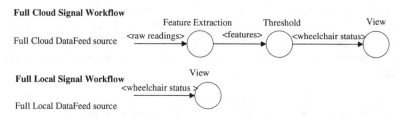

Fig. 6. Graphical representation of the wheelchair status workflow templates.

activity or wheelchair overturn), it is better to know his/her location accurately to provide immediate rescue. When a dangerous situation is detected, user's location is recorded and sent remotely to the cloud platform that informs caregivers so that they can take prompt actions to handle the situation.

5 Conclusion

In this paper, we have proposed a cloud-based WHAS for the mobility impaired individuals. It specifically enables user activity recognition and wheelchair overturn detection. A novel body activity recognition method has been proposed; preliminary results show that it obtains high recognition accuracy. In addition, we have shown how using a single accelerometer it is possible to detect and predict wheelchair overturn efficiently. Applications have been developed to give a friendly interface for both caregiver and caretakers. Raw sensing data and results are transmitted to the cloud platform for long-term storage and analysis. Three BodyCloud-based processing modes have been implemented to show our system ability.

Future research will be devoted to analyze the response delay of our system and additional performance metrics will be measured. Our aim is to provide remote real-time monitoring and 24/7 data access of the mobility-impaired individual status to the care center. We are planning to perform experiments on more subjects, also with the aim of investigating the integration of physiological and physical sensor data to provide users and caregivers more comprehensive health information.

Acknowledgments. The research is financially supported by China-Italy S&T Cooperation project "Smart Personal Mobility Systems for Human Disabilities in Future Smart Cities" (China-side Project ID: 2015DFG12210, Italy-side Project ID: CN13MO7). And also Wuhan University of Technology Graduate Student Innovation Research Project (Project ID: 2015-JL-016).

References

1. Fortino, G., Giannantonio, R., Gravina, R., Kuryloski, P., Jafari, R.: Enabling effective programming and flexible management of efficient body sensor network applications. IEEE Trans. Hum.-Mach. Syst. **43**(1), 115–133 (2013)
2. Gravina, R., Andreoli, A., Salmeri, A., Buondonno, L., Raveendranathan, N., Loseu, V., Giannantonio, R., Seto, E., Fortino, G.: Enabling multiple BSN applications using the SPINE framework. In: Proceedings of International Conference on Body Sensor Networks (BSN 2010), pp. 228–233 (2010)
3. Fortino, G., Fatta, G., Pathan, M., Vasilakos, A.: Cloud-assisted body area networks: state-of-the-art and future challenges. Wirel. Netw. **20**(7), 1925–1938 (2014)
4. Fortino, G., Guerrieri, A., Bellifemine, F., Giannantonio, R.: SPINE2: developing BSN applications on heterogeneous sensor nodes. In: IEEE International Symposium on Industrial Embedded Systems, pp. 128–131 (2009)
5. Fortino, G., Guerrieri, A., Bellifemine, F., Giannantonio, R.: Platform-independent development of collaborative wireless body sensor network applications: SPINE2. In: IEEE International Conference on Systems, Man and Cybernetics, pp. 3144–3150 (2009)
6. Chou, H., Wang, Y., Chang, H.: Design intelligent wheelchair with ECG measurement and wireless transmission function. Technol. Health Care **24**(s1), 345–355 (2015)
7. Srivastava, P., Chatterjee, S., Thakur, R.: Design and development of dual control system applied to smart wheelchair using voice and gesture control. Int. J. Res. Electr. Electron. Eng. **2**(2), 01–09 (2014)
8. Dryvendra, D., Ramalingam, M., Chinnavan, E.: A better engineering design: low cost assistance kit for manual wheelchair users with enhanced obstacle detection. J. Eng. Technol. Sci. **47**(4), 389–405 (2015)
9. Fortino, G., Gravina, R., Guerrieri, A., Fatta, G.: Engineering large-scale body area networks applications. In: Proceedings of the 8th International Conference on Body Area Networks, pp. 363–369 (2013)
10. Postolache, O., Viegas, V., Dias, J.: Toward developing a smart wheelchair for user physiological stress and physical activity monitoring. In: Proceedings of IEEE International Symposium on Medical Measurements and Applications (MeMeA 2014), pp. 1–6 (2014)
11. Yang, L., Ge, Y., Li, W., et al.: A home mobile healthcare system for wheelchair users. In: Proceedings of the 2014 IEEE 18th International Conference on Computer Supported Cooperative Work in Design (CSCWD), pp. 609–614 (2014)

12. Hiremath, S., Intille, S., Kelleher, A., Cooper, R., Ding, D.: Detection of physical activities using a physical activity monitor system for wheelchair users. Med. Eng. Phys. 37(1), 68–76 (2015)
13. Arias, D.E., Pino, E.J., Aqueveque, P., Curtis, D.W.: Daily activity monitoring for prevention of pressure Ulcers in long-term wheelchair users. In: Bravo, J., Hervás, R., Villarreal, V. (eds.) AmIHEALTH 2015. LNCS, vol. 9456, pp. 47–58. Springer, Heidelberg (2015). doi:10.1007/978-3-319-26508-7_5
14. Bao, J., Li, W., Li, J., Ge, Y., Bao, C.: Sitting Posture Recognition based on data fusion on pressure cushion. TELKOMNIKA Indonesian J. Electr. Eng. 11, 1769–1775 (2013)
15. Fard, F., Moghimi, S., Lotfi, R.: Evaluating pressure Ulcer development in wheelchair-bound population using sitting posture identification. Engineering 5, 132–136 (2013)
16. Ma, C., Li, W., Gravina, R., Fortino, G.: Activity recognition and monitoring for smart wheelchair users. In: Proceedings of the 2016 IEEE Computer Supported Cooperative Work in Design (CSCWD) (2016)
17. Yang, T., Hutchinson, S., Rice, L., et al.: Development of a scalable monitoring system for wheelchair tilt-in-space usage. Int. J. Phys. Med. Rehabil. 4, 1–17 (2013)
18. Van, S., Berger, M., Bregman, D., et al.: Wheel skid correction is a prerequisite to reliably measure wheelchair sports kinematics based on inertial sensors. Procedia Eng. 112, 207–212 (2015)
19. Milenkovic, A., Milosevic, M., Jovanov, E.: Smartphones for smart wheelchairs. In: IEEE International Conference on Body Sensor Networks (BSN), pp. 1–6 (2013)
20. Sonenblum, S., Sprigle, S., Caspall, J., et al.: Validation of an accelerometer-based method to measure the use of manual wheelchairs. Med. Eng. Phys. 6, 781–786 (2012)
21. Popp, W., Brogioli, M., Leuenberger, K., et al.: A novel algorithm for detecting active propulsion in wheelchair users following spinal cord injury. Med. Eng. Phys. 38(3), 267–274 (2016)
22. Melillo, P., Orrico, A., Scala, P., et al.: Cloud-based smart health monitoring system for automatic cardiovascular and fall risk assessment in hypertensive patients. J. Med. Syst. 39(10), 1–7 (2015)
23. Parane, K., Patil, N., Poojara, S., et al.: Cloud based intelligent healthcare monitoring system. In: International Conference on Issues and Challenges in Intelligent Computing Techniques, pp. 697–701 (2014)
24. Fortino, G., Parisi, D., Pirrone, V., Fatta, G.: BodyCloud: a SaaS approach for community body sensor networks. Future Gener. Comput. Syst. 35(6), 62–79 (2014)
25. Škraba, A., Stojanović, R., Zupan, A., et al.: Speech-controlled cloud-based wheelchair platform for disabled persons. Microprocess. Microsyst. 39(8), 819–828 (2015)
26. Park, S., Ha, T., Shivajirao, J., et al.: Smart wheelchair control system using cloud-based mobile device. In: International Conference on IT Convergence & Security (ICITCS), pp. 1–3 (2013)
27. Shimmer website (2016). http://www.shimmersensing.com
28. Fortino, G., Gravina, R., Russo, W.: Activity-aaService: cloud-assisted, BSN-based system for physical activity monitoring. In: International Conference on Computer Supported Cooperative Work in Design (CSCWD), pp. 588–593 (2015)
29. Fortino, G., Gravina, R., Li, W., Ma, C.: Using cloud-assisted body area networks to track people physical activity in mobility. In: Proceedings of the 10th International Conference on Body Area Networks (BodyNets 2015), pp. 85–91 (2015)
30. Khan, A., Tufail, A., Khattak, A., et al.: Activity recognition on smartphones via sensor-fusion and kda-based SVMs. Int. J. Distrib. Sens. Netw. 2014, 1–14 (2014)

Distributed Computing and Big Data

Energy Management Policies in Distributed Residential Energy Systems

Sisi Duan[1](✉) and Jingtao Sun[2]

[1] Oak Ridge National Laboratory, Oak Ridge, TN 37831, USA
duans@ornl.gov
[2] National Institute of Informatics, Tokyo 101-8430, Japan
sun@nii.ac.jp

Abstract. In this paper, we study energy management problems in communities with several neighborhood-level Residential Energy Systems (RESs). We consider control problems from both community level and residential level to handle external changes such as restriction on peak demand of the community and the total supply by the electricity grid. We propose three policies to handle the problems at community level. Based on the collected data from RESs such as predicted energy load, the community controller analyzes the policies, distributes the results to the RES, and each RES can then control and schedule its own energy load based on different coordination functions. We utilize a framework to integrate both policy analysis and coordination of functions. With the use of our approach, we show that the policies are useful to resolve the challenges of energy management under external changes.

Keywords: Policy · Energy management · Coordination · Conflicts · Residential energy systems

1 Introduction

According to a recent annual energy outlook report by U.S. Department of Energy [1], the rise of residential energy generation such as solar photovoltaic (PV) capacity in the residential sector grows by an average of about 30 % year from 2013 through 2016. The rising cost of power generation, transmission, and distribution, together with the growth of electricity demand, is expected to produce an 18 % increase in the average retail price of electricity in the following decades. In fact, the deployment of renewable energy such as solar makes it possible to have a self-healing power system [2,3]. Through the use of more economic residential battery storage in the foreseeable future [4], energy management can be more efficient, e.g., power flow can be reserved during daytime to be used in the peak hours so as to reduce the peak demand from the grid. With the development of smart grid, it is desirable to not only manage energy from residential level, but also to integrate existing facilities with grid reliability and resiliency improvements [5] such as preventing power outage and handling power outage.

© Springer International Publishing AG 2016
W. Li et al. (Eds.): IDCS 2016, LNCS 9864, pp. 121–133, 2016.
DOI: 10.1007/978-3-319-45940-0_11

We consider a network of residential energy systems (RESs) that is composed of several communities and each community consists of a small number of neighborhood-level RESs. Each RES is composed of a local energy storage, an inelastic energy load, and (possibly) residential energy generation such as solar PV. In such a network, external changes may occur, e.g., the electricity supply from the grid is limited due to the failure of a power substation or the heavy usage at other communities causes a low supply from the grid. Combined with the everchanging user requirements of different residences, it is important to control the energy load at both community level and residential level.

At the core of our approach is the policy analysis, which is used for the community controller to control the expected energy load of different RESs at the community level based on the external requirements. We propose three policies for the community controller to control the energy loads at RESs with no restriction on the power supply from the grid, with restriction on the total supply, and with restriction on the peak supply, separately. The policies are analyzed based on the predicted renewable energy generation and predicted energy loads of residences at the community controller and distributed to the RESs. Based on the results, each local RES controller can manage its own energy according to the user requirements by changing coordination functions. We employ a framework to integrate the policy analysis and coordination functions. In addition, we also provide a conflict resolution mechanism between policies.

Through the use of the policies and coordination functions, our approach provides an electricity management for each user that is adaptive to external changes. We present two use cases to handle the challenges in the RES network. The first case is to manage the peak demand at the community level in order to prevent power outage. This is achieved by managing the peak demand as a whole at community level and managing the peak demand of each RES locally at RESs. The second case handles a predicted power outage from the grid, where the community controller controls the maximum supply for each RES and RESs can adaptively adjust their local loads. Based on our simulation results, our approach is effective in managing energy loads at RESs to prevent power outage and handle power outage through energy prediction and scheduling.

2   Related Work

Open energy systems and residential energy systems that integrate renewable energy, energy storage, and communication technology have been studied and deployed [2,3]. With the use of communication technology, each residence forms an individual energy system that can support load control. We utilize the model of RES in our study and coordinate functions to adapt to external changes.

Residential energy management has been previously studied [6–11], mainly for the consumers to reduce the electricity costs by shifting electricity purchases according to different pricing model, e.g., real-time pricing, time of use (TOU) pricing, etc. Indeed, from the perspective of consumers, the management of the load can benefit the purchase of electricity. However, in addition to local residential load control, it is also desirable to integrate grid reliability and resiliency, e.g., to prevent power outage. A decentralized control algorithm of residential energy systems was proposed in [12] to balance the load of different residences so as to reduce the peak demand. In addition to the control problem in preventing power outage, we take a step further to use an adaptive framework and analyze through policies to handle various changes in the RES network.

On the other hand, adaptive control of RESs have been previously studied, most of which focus on physical and network layers, e.g., adaptive dynamic routing protocols, or adaptive wireless or low-bandwidth communication links. An adaptive home/building energy management system was studied in [13] to control energy consumption by the convergence of heterogeneous network. Users in their system can freely configure a cooperative network of sensors and home appliances. Their main goal is to adapt to routing changes and ensure that the system operates correctly with heterogeneous equipments. However, they did not consider adaptive changes from the grid or the users for energy management. Coordination adaptation method, as we use for RESs, has been previously been studied. For instance, Bulusu et al. present a coordination-level approach to adapt to fixed environments [14]. Coordination via inter-process communication and synchronization can significantly increase the complexity of adaptation. Our approach, in comparison, separate external requirements at community level from user requirements as policies. Therefore, we can and reduce the complexity of coordinated adaptation and the data can be analyzed more efficiently.

3 RES Network

In this section, we first present the model of the RES network. Then we describe several challenges in energy management in the RES network.

3.1 RES Model

As shown in Fig. 1(a), we consider a network of residential energy systems (RESs) across several communities, where each community consists of a small number of neighborhood-level electricity network of several residences. Each residence has a residential energy system that consists of local energy storage (e.g., battery storage), an inelastic energy load, and possibly one or more residential energy generation (e.g. solar PV generation). The energy load is generated according to the requirements of the users in the residence. Each RES is connected to the electricity grid and can buy and sell electricity. We use a hierarchical controlling model for the RES network, where each RES has a local adaptive controller and each community has a central community controller. The community controllers at different community can coordinate with each other by sending and receiving messages and each community controller can control the energy usage of the community through coordinating functions in each RES.

124 S. Duan and J. Sun

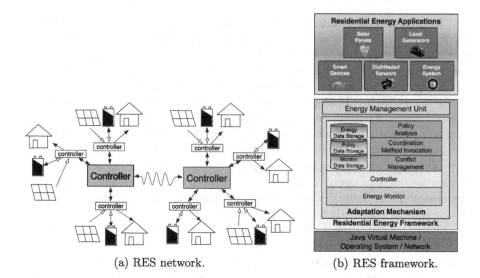

(a) RES network.   (b) RES framework.

Fig. 1. Residential Energy Systems (RESs).

3.2   Challenges

In the presence of changes in the external environment such as the restriction of
the supply from the grid, it is challenging for control in energy management in the
RES network. In this section, we describe two scenarios in energy management
under external changes and their challenges in energy management.

Preventing Power Outage. The most desirable property is to prevent power
outage. Since most residential loads follow similar pattern, i.e., they reach peak in
the morning and during the night, it is desirable to reduce peak demand without
large-scale capital costs. Decentralized control has been previously proposed [12],
where each RES follows certain algorithm to cooperate with each other. However,
there are various changes in the grid and in the RESs, e.g., the capability of the
electricity grid handling peak load may increase or decrease according to the
power generation and user requirements in the whole area, causing a change to
the controlling strategies from the level of the RESs. Therefore, it is desired to
control the energy load at both community level and RES level.

Residential Energy Management Under Power Outage. Modern infrastructure networks are becoming interdependent [15–17] where failures in a network may cause the failures in another network. For instance, if an earthquake
is predicted in the area of nearby power substations, it is highly possible that
the electricity grid can no longer provide enough energy to the residence for a
period of time. However, since each RES may have locally stored electricity and
renewable energy can be generated continuously, with prior electricity storage
and scheduling, RESs can handle the power outage with the best effort.

4   Policy-Based Energy Management

In order to manage energy to handle the challenges described in Sect. 3.2, we propose a policy-based approach, where we build several policies for energy management at a community level. Specifically, we propose three policies in Sect. 4.1 to handle the cases where there is no restriction on energy supply, there is restriction on the total amount of energy supply, and there is a requirement on hourly peak supply from the grid, separately. Based on an analysis of policies, the results are distributed to the RESs in the community and each RES can control and schedule its own energy load based on different coordination functions, as shown in Sect. 4.2. We utilize a framework, as described in Sect. 4.3, to embed the policy analysis and coordination of functions. We also propose solutions to the two scenarios and resolve the challenges based on the proposed policies.

4.1   Policy Analysis

Policies are used to manage the load of each RES at the community level. In this section, we show three policies in our RES framework. Other policies can be added easily for various purposes.

We use a few notations to show the policies. We let n be the number of RESs in the community, $u(j)$ denote the predicted electricity usage for RES j, $g(i)$ represent the predicted electricity generation, and P be the maximum amount of electricity that can be purchased from the grid for the entire community, which is ∞ by default. The value of $u(j)$ and $g(j)$ are measured periodically. Without loss of generality, in the rest of the paper, we consider they are measured every day and represent hourly usage or generation. It can be observed that if $P + \sum_{j=1}^{n} g(j) \geq \sum_{j=1}^{n} u(j)$, there will be no restriction on the electricity usage in the RES network.

M-1: No Restriction. This is the default mode where each RES can schedule their load according to the user requirements. Users can take advantage of the real-time electricity price and schedule their loads according to their preferences.

M-2: Total Energy Restriction. In the case where $P < \sum_{j=1}^{n} (u(j) - g(j))$, some RESs will run under restriction on total electricity usage. For each RES j, if $u(j) > g(j)$, it is allowed to use $\frac{P}{n-t}$, where t is the number of RESs that can manage their loads with no restriction. For any other RES j, if $\frac{P}{n-t} \geq u(j) - g(j)$, $u(j) - g(j)$ is assigned to j, t is increased by one, and the rest users can share the rest electricity. This process continues until there is no user k that satisfies $\frac{P}{n-t} > u(k) - g(k)$, then $\frac{P}{n-t}$ is assigned to each of the rest RESs and the rest users cannot get enough electricity from the grid and must adjust their requirements where some appliances can no longer be scheduled.

M-3: Peak Demand Restriction. In order to reduce the peak demand of the community, the community controller first computes the predicted peak demand, e.g., per hour. If the demand D is higher than a threshold S, it simply assigns $\frac{S}{n-t}$ to each RES, where t is the number of RESs that generate more electricity than their demand. After receiving $\frac{S}{n-t}$, each RES shaves the usage of an amount of energy to other time if the demand is greater than the number.

4.2   Coordination Functions

Each RES receives the analysis results of the policies from community controller and it can schedule its own load locally. Based on different output of the policies, each RES controls its own load through different coordination functions. We propose the following functions in the RESs.

P-1: Prediction of Energy Generation. Assuming a RES has a PV for energy generation, combined with the weather forecast, the energy generation amount can be predicted. This can be a very useful function in residential energy management problems, i.e., for measuring $g(j)$.

P-2: Prediction of Energy Load Profile. Typically each residence has certain electricity usage profile. With certain prediction of events such as upcoming game days, the energy load may change. The prediction of energy load can be effective in preventing power outage, i.e., for measuring $u(j)$.

L-1: Load Management with no Restriction. Each RES has the function to manage their load by scheduling the appliances according to user requirements. This function assumes that there is no restriction on the amount of electricity that can be purchased from the grid.

L-2: Load Management with Restriction. This function schedules the load of appliances by considering that there is a restriction on either the maximum amount of electricity from the grid or the peak demand. Given the restriction, some appliances may not be scheduled or will be scheduled to other off-peak hours. Therefore, it requires that users also set up a priority of their requirements on the appliances that must be used, i.e., if some appliances must be rescheduled, the appliances with no priorities are first considered. There are several algorithms we can use. In this paper, we use a simple algorithm where minimum number of appliances will be affected, i.e., if x Watts are reduced from the predicted total demand, it always reduces the usage of the appliance that requires the maximum load until x Watts are reduced. In addition, in the case where peak demand should be reduced, appliances that can be rescheduled are first moved to other off-peak hours prior to the original scheduled time and then the appliance with the largest demand will not be scheduled.

4.3   Framework

In order to corporate the policies at community controller and coordination functions at RES controllers, we utilize a framework, as shown in Fig. 1(b). Our framework consists of two parts: an *Energy Management Unit* and *Adaptation*

Mechanism, the core of our framework. The former is responsible for collecting all types of data about user information. The latter is responsible for coordinating the invocation of functions to dynamically adapt to different changes through policy analysis. As observed in Fig. 1(b), our framework supports various electronic equipments, e.g., solar panels, local generators, smart devices, various distributed sensors, and energy systems. The data obtained by electronic equipments are aggregated into the *Energy Data Storage*.

We combine the external data[1] with the data of electronic devices in the RES, through which we can provide a predictive analysis for each RES. The core of adaptation mechanism is the *Policy Analysis* and we provide three useful policies to dynamically adapt to the changes in Sect. 4.1. The results of policy analysis are a set of plan tables for the RESs to manage the use of energy, according to different user requirements. In the extreme case, users may need to adjust their requirements for the framework to be resilient to failures. These analysis results are automatically saved into the *Policy Data Storage*.

In our framework, *Controller* has two roles: local RES controller and the community controller. Through communication between them, launching of the coordinating invocations can be decided. *Energy Monitor* monitors the changes in both external and internal of the framework in real-time. When the changes occur, we can change the coordination of the functions in the RESs through *Coordination Method Invocation* mechanism and we include a few coordination functions in Sect. 4.2. The *Conflict Resolution Management* provides a solution to resolve conflicts between internal electronic equipments and the external requirements of the users or applications, which may lead to serious problems.

4.4   Conflict Resolution

As mentioned in Sect. 4.3, conflicts may occur between the adaptation results and local RESs, e.g., some user does not follow the adaptation scheme, electrical appliances malfunction, or the external requirements change. In order to ensure the normal operation of our framework, we provide two kinds of conflict resolution for RES network to resolve both *local conflict* and *global conflict*.

When the electronic appliances malfunction or the users force to use some of them while they are not scheduled by the RES, the RES will not be able to achieve our executable policy's condition according to the output of the policies. In such cases, *local conflict* resolution will be executed. Our Energy Monitor regularly monitors the execution of policies of users. Once the energy monitor catches this conflict, our framework will send a message to controller, the policies will be analyzed by the community controller, and the results will be sent out and executed by RESs.

On the other hand, the conditions of the executable policies may not be satisfied due to the conflict between communities, which will cause *global conflicts* in our RES framework. In this case, the system administrators can use our

---

[1] Currently, our framework only combines the external weather data to show the concept. More data can be combined to improve the accuracy of our analysis.

energy monitor to output the situation of the policy execution, locate the failed communities, and then modify their policies.

4.5   RES Energy Management

Based on above discussion, in this section we briefly introduce the flow of our approach in handling the challenges in Sect. 3.2.

Preventing Power Outage. As shown in Fig. 2, each RES runs either L-1 or L-2 to manage its load. Based on the weather forecast and user requirements, it also predicts energy generation and energy load profile for the next day. For instance, RES A and RES B both run L-1 where the load can be managed with no restriction and users can schedule their load according to the electricity price. The prediction of P-1 and P-2 are sent to the community controller from all the RESs in the same community. The community controller analyzes the results and run the policies. When there is a peak demand greater than the threshold P, the community controller distributes the demand of the users and limits some of them according to the policy, i.e., M-3. In this example, RES A will run L-2 after peak demand management where user A has to reschedule its load according to a restriction, some of the appliances may be scheduled to other time. RES B can continue running L-1 since its predicted load is lower.

Under Predicted Power Outage. When there is a predicted power outage, the workflow is similar with previous case. Namely, each RES still sends its predicted profile through P-1 and P-2 to the community controller. If there is a predicted power outage and the grid can only supply limited amount of energy to the community, the community controller analyzes the total amount of energy in the next day based on the predicted supply from the grid. Based on policy M-2, some RESs may be restricted with the maximum amount of electricity that

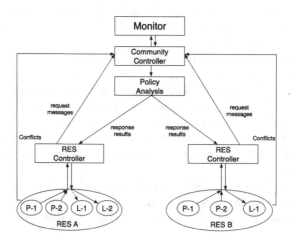

Fig. 2. Flowachart of RES network.

can be purchased from the grid. In this case, the RESs need to run L-2 with a restriction on the total amount of energy in the following day. Although some appliances may not be scheduled to run, users at each RES can still set priorities during the scheduling problem. For instance, it can set a priority to the usage of fridge, i.e., if there is a restriction on the total amount of electricity and some appliances must not be scheduled, other appliances will not be scheduled before fridge is considered. In this way, we both handle predicted power outage and build an adaptive solution according to user requirements.

5   Evaluation

In this section, we show the evaluations of our approach. We write a simulator to implement policies[2] on our framework. The RES controller and the community controller communicate through TCP channel as different servers. In this section, we focus on the effectiveness of our approach in handling external changes. To our best knowledge, most of previous work focus on the energy management at the residence level, which is not the main goal of our paper.

We simulate a community with 8 different residences with various elastic energy load. Each residence may have fridges, Wi-Fi, several lights, computers, smart phone chargers, TVs, hair dryer(s), a rice cooker, thermos, a microwave oven, a washing machine, and vacuum cleaner(s). In this paper, we use different rated powers for the same appliance at the residences to differentiate various brands. In addition, we use a mixed data of renewable energy generation where residences all have different energy generation and RES 5 does not generate renewable energy but it can purchase from the grid and store in its local energy storage. We evaluate the two cases in Sect. 4.5 and demonstrate the effectiveness of our approach to manage energy loads of the RESs.

Preventing Power Outage. We assess the case where the community controller controls the peak demand of the RESs using policy M-3. For simplicity, we ignore the amount of generated energy and assume each RES needs to obtain energy from the grid to show the performance of control on peak demand. As observed in Fig. 3(a) the total predicted demand of the whole community, the peak hours happen during the night between 19 to 22. We set a threshold for 10 kW and each RES needs to reschedule its usage if necessary. As shown in Fig. 3(b) a typical example, RES 4 in general has a high demand and it needs to reduce its demand at time 7, 8, and 20 to 23. We assume that fridge is set to a priority, wifi, lights, and computers can only be turned off instead of being scheduled to another time, and other appliances can be rescheduled. We observe that at most of the peak hours, lights and TVs are suggested to be turned off. The washing machine, rice cooker, thermos, and smart phones are rescheduled.

---

[2] Notice that two or more policies may specify different destinations under the same condition. The current implementation provides two solutions to solve local and global conflicts. However, in our existing implementation, policies are defined without any conflicts between them.

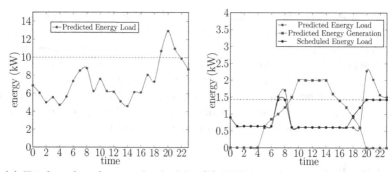

(a) Total predicted energy load of the (b) RES 4 needs to reschedule energy
community.   usage to reduce the peak demand.

Fig. 3. Total predicted energy load of the community, where RESs need to reschedule
their energy usage to reduce the peak demand.

As observed in the figure, the peak demand at the RES is reduced effectively
according to the requirement.

Under Predicted Power Outage. We assess the case for a community to
adapt to low power supply from the grid. We simulate the mode where the
community controller uses the predicted data from the residential controllers to
predict the usage from the grid. When the energy from the grid P is limited due
to some factors such as the failure of a power substation, RESs must be controlled
to reschedule their usage according to M-2. As summarized in Table 1 the total
number of predicted energy load and energy generation, RES 6 generates more
energy than the usage. This indicates that RES 6 can always support itself
regardless of the amount of power from the grid. We limit the maximum amount
of energy from the grid to 45 kW. The community controller runs M-2 and
returns a result of power assignment to the RESs. As observed from the table,
RES 1, 2, 4, 7 can obtain enough energy from the grid due to the low demand.
However, RES 3, 5, and 8 can only obtain 6.43 kW from the grid due to the low
grid supply. Therefore, they need to reschedule their energy usage.

Table 1. Summary of predicted energy load and residential energy generation and
assigned energy (in KW).

RES	1	2	3	4	5	6	7	8
Energy Load	19.29	16.63	22.40	22.05	19.12	20.53	27.28	27.84
Energy Generation	13.02	10.51	14.38	20.85	0.00	21.60	26.20	20.40
Required Energy	6.27	6.12	8.02	1.20	19.12	0.00	1.08	7.44
Assigned Energy	6.27	6.12	6.43	1.20	6.43	0.00	1.08	6.43

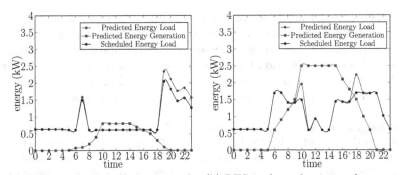

(a) RES 3 where the lights must be turned off for 5.31 hours to reduce the total demand by 1.59kW.

(b) RES 7 where the rice cooker must be turned off for 1.26 hours to reduce the total energy by 1.01kW.

Fig. 4. Predicted energy loads, rescheduled energy loads, and energy generation.

The local controller of user 3, 5, and 8 can schedule their loads according to user requirements, i.e., with priorities on some of the appliances. If we set a priority, for instance on the fridge, it is possible that there is no solution to the usage. As shown in Fig. 4(a), with a priority on the usage of fridge, RES 3 requires 8.02 kW from the grid but is only assigned 6.43 kW. In order to reduce the usage of 1.59 kW, the optimal solution is to turn off the lights for 5.31 h. If there is no restriction, RES 7, as shown in Fig. 4(b), must turn off rice cooker for 1.26 h to reduce the usage by 1.01 kW. In all these cases, the appliances are turned off also to reduce the peak demand. In comparison, since RES 5 cannot generate energy, it is assigned 6.43 kW but requires 19.12 kW. In this case, there is no solution if the fridge cannot be turned off. If there is no priority on the appliances, the optimal solution is that the fridge must be turned off for the whole day and the computers cannot be used for 4.59 h.

Coordination Time. We show in Table 2 the coordination time of executing our defined policies. Each of the costs was the sum of the time interpreting the policies and message transmission to deploy the results. As observed in the table, the time interpreting the policies, in comparison, generates low overhead.

Table 2. Coordination time of policies (in ms).

M-1	M-2	M-3	Avg. Transmission
3.24	6.35	4.70	32.01

6   Conclusion

This paper presents a policy-based energy management approach in distributed residential energy systems. We present several policies for the RESs to adaptively manage their energy loads based on external requirements such as restriction on peak demand and limitation of power supply from the grid. Through the policy analysis at community level, RESs can manage and schedule their loads locally by invoking different coordination functions. We employ a framework to integrate the policy analysis and coordination functions. Based on the evaluation, our approach is effective to prevent power outage and to handle power outage.

Acknowledgment. Sisi Duan is supported by UT-Battelle, LLC under Contract No. DE-AC05-00OR22725 with the U.S. Department of Energy. The United States Government retains and the publisher, by accepting the article for publication, acknowledges that the United States Government retains a non-exclusive, paid-up, irrevocable, worldwide license to publish or reproduce the published form of this manuscript, or allow others to do so, for United States Government purposes. The Department of Energy will provide public access to these results of federally sponsored research in accordance with the DOE Public Access Plan (http://energy.gov/downloads/doe-public-access-plan).

References

1. Eia, U.: Annual energy outlook 2015 with projections to 2040 (2015)
2. Ropp, M., Gonzalez, S., Schaffer, A., Katz, S., Perkinson, J., Bower, W.I., Prestero, M., Casey, L., Moaveni, H., Click, D., et al.: Newblock solar energy grid integration systems: final report of the florida solar energy center team. Technical report, Sandia National Laboratories (2012)
3. Werth, A., Kitamura, N., Tanaka, K.: Conceptual study for open energy systems: distributed energy network using interconnected DC nanogrids. IEEE Trans. Smart Grid **6**(4), 1621–1630 (2015)
4. Shao, S., Jahanbakhsh, F., Agüero, J.R., Xu, L.: Integration of PEVs and PV-DG in power distribution systems using distributed energy storage - dynamic analyses. In: ISGT, pp. 1–6 (2013)
5. Moslehi, K., Kumar, R.: A reliability perspective of the smart grid. IEEE Trans. Smart Grid **1**(1), 57–64 (2010)
6. Erol-Kantarci, M., Mouftah, H.T.: Wireless sensor networks for cost-efficient residential energy management in the smart grid. IEEE Trans. Smart Grid **2**(2), 314–325 (2011)
7. Mohsenian-Rad, A.H., Leon-Garcia, A.: Optimal residential load control with price prediction in real-time electricity pricing environments. IEEE Trans. Smart Grid **1**(2), 120–133 (2010)
8. Pedrasa, M.A.A., Spooner, T.D., MacGill, I.F.: Coordinated scheduling of residential distributed energy resources to optimize smart home energy. IEEE Trans. Smart Grid **1**(2), 134–143 (2010)
9. Molderink, A., Bakker, V., Bosman, M.G.C., Hurink, J.L., Smit, G.J.M.: Management and control of domestic smart grid technology. IEEE Trans. Smart Grid **1**(2), 109–119 (2010)
10. Pipattanasomporn, M., Kuzlu, M., Rahman, S.: An algorithm for intelligent home energy management and demand response analysis. IEEE Trans. Smart Grid **3**(4), 2166–2173 (2012)
11. Werth, A., Kitamura, N., Tanaka, K.: Evaluation of centralized and distributed microgrid topologies and comparison to open energy systems. In: EEEIC, pp. 492–497 (2015)

12. Worthmann, K., Kellett, C.M., Braun, P., Grüne, L., Weller, S.R.: Distributed and decentralized control of residential energy systems incorporating battery storage. IEEE Trans. Smart Grid **6**(4), 1914–1923 (2015)
13. Mineno, H., Kato, Y., Obata, K., Kuriyama, H., Abe, K., Ishikawa, N., Mizuno, T.: Adaptive home/building energy management system using heterogeneous sensor/actuator networks. In: CCNC, pp. 1–5 (2010)
14. Bulusu, N., Estrin, D., Girod, L., Heidemann, J.: Scalable coordination for wireless sensor networks: self-configuring localization systems. In: ISCTA (2001)
15. Johnson, C.W.: Analysing the causes of the Italian and Swiss blackout. In: SCS 28th September 2003 (2007)
16. Cowie, J.H., Ogielsk, A.T., Premore, B., Smith, E.A., Underwood, T.: Impact of the 2003 blackouts on internet communications. Technical report, Renesys Corporation (2003)
17. Ferc, N.: Arizona-southern california outages on 8 September 2011: causes and recommendations. Technical report, Federal Energy Regulatory Commission and the North American Electric Reliability Corporation (2012)

LUTMap: A Dynamic Heuristic Application Mapping Algorithm Based on Lookup Tables

Thomas Canhao Xu$^{(\boxtimes)}$ and Ville Leppänen

Department of Information Technology, University of Turku, 20014 Turku, Finland
{canxu,ville.leppanen}@utu.fi

Abstract. In this paper, we propose and investigate a dynamic heuristic mapping algorithm with lookup table optimizations. Distributed and parallel computing are trends due to the performance requirement of modern applications. Application mapping in a multiprocessor system is therefore critical due to the dynamic and unpredictable nature of the applications. We analyse the communication delay among different tasks in an application. A fundamental algorithm is analysed to optimize the average delay of the mapping region. We discuss and evaluate the effectiveness of the algorithm in terms of average intra-application latency. Results from synthetic applications revealed that average latencies from the mapping regions of the fundamental algorithm have reduced up to 23 % compared with the incremental mapping. By noticing the time overhead of the algorithm due to extra number of search spaces, we introduce a mechanism with lookup tables to speed up the process of searching optimized mapping regions. The lookup table is examined with both size and construction time. Experiments shown that the lookup table is small enough to fit into the cache, and the table can be constructed in milliseconds in most practical cases. The results from real applications show that the average execution time of applications of the proposed algorithm has reduced by 15.2 % compared with the first fit algorithm.

Keywords: Multicore · Network-on-chip · Application mapping · Lookup table

1 Introduction

Distributed and parallel computing are more and more common nowadays. An important reason behind this trend is applications: distributed and parallel applications used to be widely adopted in high-performance and scientific computing, as well as computer servers. Currently the trend is shifted to daily computing, desktop and even mobile applications to utilize the power of distributed and parallel computing extensively. Not only games and real-time audio/video processing, but also signal processing and real-time remote sensing are heavily developed to make use of more processor cores. Commercial desktop and server processors already have more than 20 cores, while it is possible to integrate 10 cores in a mobile processor [17]. The cores are well-utilized by applications: a study shows

© Springer International Publishing AG 2016
W. Li et al. (Eds.): IDCS 2016, LNCS 9864, pp. 134–146, 2016.
DOI: 10.1007/978-3-319-45940-0_12

that even browsers, email clients and video watching applications use as much as 8 cores [11]. It can be predicted that the number of cores in a single chip will still grow in the near future. Mesh interconnect is proposed for massive multi-core processors to alleviate the communication overhead [4]. Processors based on mesh network are manufactured both for research and commercial use [7].

Applications should be mapped to different nodes in the system in order to execute. *Application mapping* consists of finding a mapping region for a given application with several *tasks*. There are usually several constraints and requirements to meet, for example performance, efficiency, temperature and system congestion. The metrics can be affected seriously with different mappings. For instance to reduce thermal hot-spot, tasks in an application should be mapped dispersedly, however system performance may reduce in that case. On the other hand, a congregated mapping can potentially decrease the communication delay among tasks, while certain part of the system can be congested.

Various mapping algorithms have been discussed and studied by previous researches [14,18,22]. For more complex dynamic systems, the mapping algorithm itself should be efficient since finding the optimal solution is usually an NP-hard problem [5,23]. Because of the computation complexity, researchers have focused on heuristic and stochastic algorithms. Chou et al. introduced an incremental mapping algorithm in [3]. The algorithm selects nodes closest to the master node, and then maps the application to the region. A mapping algorithm designed for big data applications is proposed in [21]. The algorithm is optimized for both cache and memory accesses, as well as intra-application communication. To meet the deadline and energy constraints of real-time applications, [2,9] discussed mapping algorithms optimized for such conditions. Instead of contiguous mapping, [6] investigated mixed mapping for mixed-critical concurrent applications, i.e. non-contiguous mapping is applied to increase system throughput while real-time applications are still mapped contiguously for meeting the deadline requirements. A greedy heuristic approximation algorithm is proposed for three-dimensional networks in [23]. Here the authors investigated application mapping in a multi-layer network with limitations of inter-layer connections.

Heuristic algorithms can produce decent mapping results with relatively low time cost, provided that the heuristics are chosen appropriately. On the other hand, multiple results can be evaluated and compared in the algorithm, and quality of the mapping region improves as a result [24]. However the time cost increases linearly as the number of extra searches increases. This can be a problem especially for time critical systems. *Lookup table* has been widely used in computer science to reduce processing time [10]. Applications include arithmetic operations, image processing, cache/memory and even hardware design [8]. A lookup table is a pre-initialized array that replaces the runtime computation with table lookup operations. The additional cost is usually the size and construction time of the table. In this paper, we propose and investigate a novel application mapping algorithm based on lookup table. The algorithm chooses mapping region based on the information stored in the lookup table, and the table is constructed and updated in the background dynamically. We select both synthetic and real applications with different configurations to compare the proposed algorithm with other algorithms.

2   Application Mapping and Communication Delay

The performance of applications is highly affected by communication overhead of different tasks in the application. Figure 1a shows the process of mapping. An application with 5 tasks is being mapped to a 3×3 system in which only 7 nodes are available. Firstly a mapping region is chosen for the given application, e.g. in the figure a 5-node region with cross pattern is selected, and then the tasks are mapped to the region. Obviously the selection of mapping region is crucial in the process. To reduce the possibility of congestion, the region should be as congregate and contiguous as possible. We investigate the metric of *Manhattan Distance* (*MD*), which represents the number of hop counts between two nodes. Apparently the average pairwise *MD* of the nodes in the mapping region determines how congregate the region is. In Fig. 1a, the 5-node region is formed based on a 2×2 square, while assume another 5-node region with a straight continuous line (not shown in the Figure). Both regions are contiguous, however in terms of average pairwise *MD*, the first region is better. Several problems must be addressed in dynamic systems with multiple concurrent applications: first the system is fragmented by different applications, second it might be unworthy to find the optimal result.

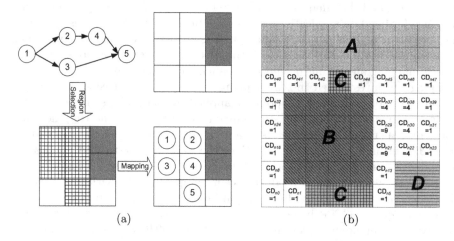

Fig. 1. Procedure of application mapping (a) and examples of mapping four applications (b).

3   The LUTMap Algorithm

In this section, we first define a model for the destination platform. We then propose an algorithm to create the lookup tables dynamically to mitigate the computation overhead of calculating the mapping regions.

3.1   Platform Model

Definition 1. *A multiprocessor system consists of a mesh network $P(X,Y)$ of width X, length Y with $X \times Y$ nodes. Each node n_i is denoted by a coordinate (x,y), where $0 \leq x \leq X - 1$ and $0 \leq y \leq Y - 1$, and $i = y \times X + x$. The Manhattan Distance between n_i and n_j is $MD(n_i, n_j)$.*

Definition 2. *A Task Graph (TG) is a directed acyclic graph, $TG = (N, E)$, where N is the set of nodes and E is the set of directed edges associated with the graph. The amount of traffic (weight of the edge) between nodes n_i and n_j is represented as $w_{i,j}$. $\forall (n_i, n_j) \in E$.*

Definition 3. *An application $A_k(TG_k)$ consists of a list of task nodes N_k, and a list of communication volume between different nodes E_k. To execute the application, it must be mapped to $|N_k|$ nodes. k is the ID of an application.*

Definition 4. *$R_l(A_k)$ is a mapping region in $P(X,Y)$, which consists of a set of $|N_k|$ nodes for $A_k(TG_k)$. Notice that several mapping regions can be evaluated for $A_k(TG_k)$.*

Definition 5. *Average Intra-application Latency ($AIL_{R_l(A_k)}$) is the average latency between internal nodes for an application A_k with a mapping region $R_l(A_k)$. The $AIL_{R_l(A_k)}$ is calculated as:*

$$AIL_{R_l(A_k)} = \frac{\sum\limits_{(n_i,n_j) \in R_l(A_k)} w_{n_i,n_j} \times MD(n_i,n_j)}{|N_k|} \tag{1}$$

Definition 6. *Congregate Degree (CD_{n_i}) is the maximum number of available nodes for n_i in the $x + y+$ (right-up) direction, in a square shape. The CD_{n_i} updates as systems state changes.*

3.2   Region Selection and Mapping

It is obvious that system performance will be affected by different mappings of applications. As an indicator, the AIL shows the average node-node access delay for a mapping decision. This metric can be explained with Fig. 1b. For example, Application C is mapped to nodes n_2, n_3, n_4 and n_{43}, while Application D is mapped to nodes n_6, n_7, n_{14} and n_{15}. To calculate AIL, the average MD between a node and all other nodes in a mapping region is considered. Here we assume $\forall i, j : (n_i, n_j) \in E, w_{i,j} = 1$ for simplicity. Take n_2 in C for instance, $MD(n_2, n_3) = 1$, $MD(n_2, n_4) = 2$ and $MD(n_2, n_{43}) = 6$, hence the average MD for n_2 to other nodes in C is 2.25 ($\frac{9}{4}$). Correspondingly the metric can be calculated for n_3, n_4 and n_{43} as well. At last by multiplying the weight of edges, the average value of them is the AIL_C. Obviously both regions C and D are a possible mapping for a 4-task application, however in terms of AIL, D is preferable compared to C. Lower AIL means lower internal delay of an application, which translates to higher performance and lower power consumption.

To determine the optimal (lowest) AIL for an application, all possible permutations can be enumerated and compared, however the computation complexity can be too high for many systems. Demaine et al. proposed an algorithm that can calculate the optimal value of all pairwise MD of a mesh grid in $\mathcal{O}(n^{7.5})$ [5]. However the algorithm only works in a static empty system. In case of a dynamic system with multiple concurrent applications, the true optimal solution is an $NP\text{-}Hard$ problem [5,12,25]. As a compromise of efficiency and computation complexity, several methods are proposed to achieve sub-optimal results with much lower computation cost, such as simulated annealing, linear programming, heuristic and stochastic algorithms. Here we first explore an algorithm based on the proof of [5], that an optimal mapping region is *convex* and the shape should be *near circular*. Take Fig. 1b for instance, two applications A and B are both with 16 tasks, however AIL_{R_A} is higher than AIL_{R_B} ($AIL_{R_A} = 3.125$, $AIL_{R_B} = 2.5$). Notice that B is not an optimal result in terms of AIL, [5] has given the optimal result with $AIL = 2.484$. It is noteworthy that a circular shape is usually closer to optimal than a square, nonetheless the computation complexity of generating circular shapes is higher than that of squares. We consider an algorithm based on square shape, the *Congregate Degree* is calculated for all the nodes. Figure 1b shows the CDs of all free nodes.

3.3   Fundamental Algorithm

For a given application A_k, the number of tasks $|N_k|$ can be equal, larger or smaller than the CD of a node. As a consequence the free nodes represented by the CD of a node, should be adjusted, or left untouched in case the two numbers are equal. The fundamental algorithm searches for a limited number of mapping regions. R_{max} is defined to control the maximum number of regions in the list of candidate regions (*search space*). Increasing R_{max} takes more time for region evaluation and can possibly generate better results. If $CD_{n_i} > |N_k|$ and the number of tasks can be represented by a square, the smallest square region that is closest to $|N_k|$ is added to the candidate list. Notice that CD_{n_i} represents the highest number of free nodes in a square shape, where smaller squares are evaluated as well in the algorithm. The region is expanded in case the square is smaller than $|N_k|$. The expansion strategy follows the minimum AIL rule, that for all the free nodes, only those closest to the current region are added. Take an 11-task application for instance (Fig. 1b), n_{21} and n_{29} are favourable due to the CDs, two nodes are expanded for both square regions. At last, the candidate regions in the list are compared with AIL. The algorithm always starts with nodes with largest CD. The extra searches will start from free nodes with smaller CDs than the previous one.

The proposed algorithm is firstly evaluated by using synthetic traces. We compare the fundamental algorithm with a different number of search space ($SS*$), the First Fit algorithm (FF), the incremental mapping algorithm in [3] (INC), a greedy mapping algorithm that always chooses nodes nearest to the centre of the mesh network ($PROX/PRO$), the Nearest Neighbour algorithm (NN) and random mapping algorithm ($RAND/RAN$). We use Task Graph

Table 1. Results of different mapping algorithms with different Node Utilizations (NU), the unit of time (μs) represents the average time for each mapping decision. Normalized AIL ($NAIL$) is shown for clarity. System configuration: Core i7 920 2.67 GHz, 8 GB RAM

NU/0.5	SS1	SS2	SS4	SS8	SS16	SS32	FF	INC	PRO	NN	RAN
AIL	77.70	75.02	72.60	71.19	70.44	70.14	111.41	75.24	121.31	92.05	186.82
NAIL	110.79	106.96	103.51	101.51	100.44	100.00	158.85	107.28	172.96	131.24	266.37
Time	71.6	97.5	156.5	273.9	519.9	1011.5	44.9	68.1	46.7	52.0	47.1
NU/0.6	SS1	SS2	SS4	SS8	SS16	SS32	FF	INC	PRO	NN	RAN
AIL	81.00	77.31	73.48	71.68	70.66	70.31	115.68	77.92	133.28	92.62	186.38
NAIL	115.21	109.95	104.51	101.94	100.50	100.00	164.52	110.83	189.55	131.73	265.08
Time	66.0	89.8	140.2	246.6	460.6	886.9	42.6	62.5	44.3	48.7	44.7
NU/0.7	SS1	SS2	SS4	SS8	SS16	SS32	FF	INC	PRO	NN	RAN
AIL	84.61	79.46	74.89	72.42	71.19	70.66	121.18	82.10	143.31	92.44	185.02
NAIL	119.74	112.45	105.98	102.49	100.75	100.00	171.48	116.19	202.80	130.82	261.83
Time	59.9	81.1	125.0	215.0	398.7	759.5	41.0	57.2	41.3	45.8	42.8
NU/0.8	SS1	SS2	SS4	SS8	SS16	SS32	FF	INC	PRO	NN	RAN
AIL	90.82	84.48	77.79	74.49	73.00	72.16	125.05	86.55	154.75	93.41	185.37
NAIL	125.85	117.07	107.80	103.23	101.16	100.00	173.29	119.94	214.45	129.45	256.89
Time	54.2	72.0	108.4	182.5	333.0	628.6	39.3	52.2	39.0	42.9	40.6
NU/0.9	SS1	SS2	SS4	SS8	SS16	SS32	FF	INC	PRO	NN	RAN
AIL	101.20	92.09	83.60	79.24	77.40	75.90	128.04	93.54	164.69	101.68	184.58
NAIL	133.33	121.33	110.14	104.41	101.97	100.00	168.70	123.25	216.99	133.97	243.19
Time	49.3	64.2	94.6	155.9	278.3	523.4	37.6	47.0	37.5	40.6	39.7
NU/1.0	SS1	SS2	SS4	SS8	SS16	SS32	FF	INC	PRO	NN	RAN
AIL	124.83	116.69	107.32	101.73	99.44	98.96	130.20	106.57	176.84	121.40	183.79
NAIL	126.14	117.92	108.45	102.80	100.49	100.00	131.57	107.69	178.70	122.68	185.73
Time	44.4	56.4	79.8	126.7	221.0	408.1	36.4	42.1	36.0	38.3	40.8

Generator [19] to generate 10,000 applications of 1 to 16 tasks with equal possibility. The applications enter and leave the system with first-in-first-out sequence. Provided that the number of free nodes is smaller than the number of tasks of the incoming application, the earliest application will be removed after execution. We investigate systems with different node utilizations. Lower utilized networks have higher number of free nodes and consequently should generate better results. Researchers reported that for modern large-scale systems, the processor utilization can maintain over 80 % [13]. The results are presented in Table 1.

In terms of AIL, the fundamental algorithm achieved improved results with increased number of search space. Higher node utilization leads to higher AIL for all algorithms. $RAND$ provides a baseline for unoptimized mapping, while traditional widely-used algorithms such as FF, NN and $PROX$ did provide better results compared with $RAND$. Unarguably the INC algorithm is superior in all cases than the traditional algorithms. However depending on the system utilization, the results of $SS32$ are 7.28 % to 23.25 % better compared with INC. We notice that different number of search space did have an impact to the quality of the result. For example, the average AIL for all utilizations improved around 19 % by increasing the number of search spaces from 1 to 8. However the improvement is smaller from $SS8$ to $SS32$: the AILs of $SS8$ and $SS16$ under 90 % utilization are 4.41 % and 1.97 % worse than that for $SS32$. The gap is smaller when the utilization is low, and widens gradually as system utilization increases. The time consumed by extra search spaces increases linearly, and in general all algorithms take longer time with lower utilization due to additional free nodes.

3.4 Lookup Table

For a given application, the mapping region should be determined before it can be mapped to the system. Calculating the mapping region usually costs much more time than mapping the application, especially for the proposed algorithm. As aforementioned, the fundamental algorithm sacrifices computation time for better results. The extra time can be a problem for time-critical systems. Therefore we further propose an improved algorithm with lookup table. The table is constructed in the background, and stored in the memory for fast lookup (Fig. 2a). Here we define the table consisting of all the mapping regions which $1 \leq |N| \leq n_{Available}$. Obviously higher number of available nodes means larger table. For each entry in the table, the fundamental algorithm is carried out with certain number of search spaces. Therefore the table contains the information of optimized mapping regions for all possible sizes.

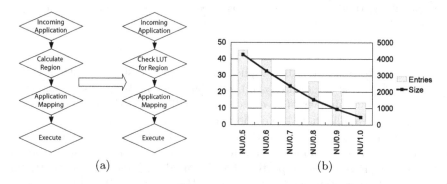

(a)   (b)

Fig. 2. (a), the process of conventional mapping (left) and mapping based on lookup table (right); (b), average number of entries (left Y-axis) of the lookup table with different Node Utilizations ($NU/*$), and the average size of the lookup table shown as bytes (right Y-axis, assuming 32-bit integer).

As aforementioned, there are several key issues for implementing lookup tables. On the one hand, the size of the table should be small enough in order to be efficiently stored in the memory or preferably the cache. Otherwise the time overhead of retrieving the table from the disk could be unworthy. On the other hand, the time spent for constructing the table should be relatively low compared with actual application execution, i.e. if it takes too long time, direct computation might be a better solution. We evaluated both issues by using the same application traces as before, the results are illustrated in Figs. 2b, 3a and b.

As is shown in Fig. 2b, the size of the table is relatively small for the given environment. The table becomes larger as system utilization decreases since there are more available nodes for calculation and storage. For example with 90 % utilization, the average entries of the table are around 20, and the size of the table is about 1 KB. Each entry of the table stores the node information of an optimized mapping region for a certain size, i.e. the table has 10 entries for 10 available nodes, storing information of optimized mapping regions containing 1 to 10 nodes. Notice that even at 50 % utilization, the storage overhead of the table is approximately 4KB, small enough to fit into the cache. The size of the table is linearly related with the number of available nodes.

In terms of table construction time, Fig. 3a shows that the time depends on both the number of search space and system utilization. For high-utilized systems, the construction time is relatively low due to reduced number of available nodes, e.g. all the table construction times for over 80 % utilized systems are below $20ms$ provided that the number of search space is lower than 16. The time increases significantly as system utilization decreases and the number of search space grows due to extra calculation. However as aforementioned the system utilization of large-scale systems is typically over 80 %. Moreover the AIL gap of different number of search spaces is not that high for low utilized systems compared with high utilized systems: for instance in Table 1, the gap of AIL for $SS8$ and $SS32$ is 1.51 % with 50 % utilization, while the gap increases to 4.41 % with 90 % utilization. This implies that a smaller number of search spaces might be more suitable for low utilized system, while a larger number of search spaces is required for highly utilized system.

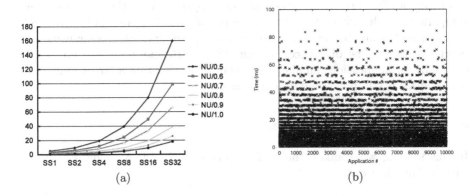

Fig. 3. (a), average construction time (ms, Y-axis) for lookup tables, in terms of different number of Search Spaces ($SS*$) and Node Utilizations ($NU/*$); (b), detailed time spent for each lookup table construction for 10,000 applications.

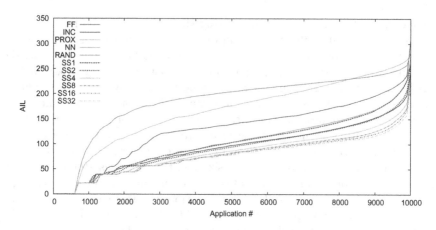

Fig. 4. Comparison of different mapping algorithms with 90 % system utilization. The curves show exact sorted AIL values for 10,000 applications.

Figure 3b illustrates the time cost of each table construction with 90 % utilization and search depth of 32. Notice that the first five data are not shown in the figure (101 to 517 ms due to the system is empty in the beginning, requiring more computation). Overall most tables are constructed within few milliseconds, e.g. 45 % of the lookup tables are calculated under 10 ms, where 75 % are finished below 20 ms. The application execution time is usually much longer than the magnitude of millisecond, especially for large-scale multi-task applications. Therefore the time overhead for calculating the lookup table should be acceptable for most cases. Overall the experiments indicate that the lookup table used here is small enough for the cache and the calculation overhead is practical.

Figure 4 illustrated the detailed AIL results for different algorithms mapping 10,000 applications under 90 % system utilization. Obviously the proposed algorithm produced relatively good and stable results. We notice NN generated comparable results with $SS1$, while the curve of INC is comparable with $SS2$. However higher number of search spaces provide significantly better results in nearly all cases. The differences among $SS8$, $SS16$ and $SS32$ are noticeable especially for applications number over 7000, indicating that a larger number of search space is still preferable in many cases.

4 Application Evaluation

In this section, we evaluate the performance of different mapping algorithms with real applications.

4.1 System Configuration

The experimental environment for applications is based on a full system simulator GEMS/Simics [15,16]. A multiprocessor system with 64 (8×8 mesh) nodes

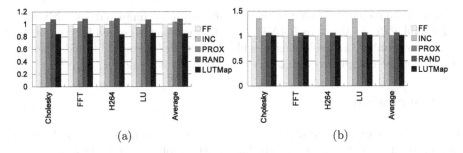

Fig. 5. Normalized application execution time (a) and calculation time of mapping regions (b) for different mapping algorithms.

is simulated, where each node is equipped with a Sun UltraSPARC VIII+ core running at 2 GHz. Several workloads are selected from [1,20], including matrix decomposition (*Cholesky* and *LU*), video coding (*H264*) and *FFT*. All the mapping algorithms are evaluated in the same system state, in which the aforementioned 10,000 applications were executed with the corresponding algorithm with 90 % system utilization. We measure performance metrics in terms of application execution time and time spent for the mapping algorithm. Here the proposed algorithm (*LUTMap* in figures) is set to 32 search spaces, and we only compare results from *FF*, *INC*, *PROX* and *RAND* for simplicity. The normalized results are illustrated in Figs. 5a and b.

4.2 Result Analysis

The experimental results from Fig. 5a show that, in terms of average application execution time, the proposed algorithm *LUTMap* is the best compared with other algorithms. We notice that compared with *INC* and *FF*, on average the four applications run 10.2 % and 15.6 % faster respectively. The two other mapping algorithms perform much worse, the *PROX* is 18.2 % slower for these applications compared with *LUTMap*, while not surprisingly *RAND* is the worst algorithm here. This can be explained from the search depth of the proposed algorithm. While the compactness and continuity of the mapping region are considered in *INC*, it suffered from limited number of search spaces. The essential idea of *INC* is to include the nearest nodes that minimizes average latency of the region without a global view. It is noteworthy that in Table 1 the *NAIL* for *SS*32 has improved 23.3 % over *INC* with 90 % utilization, while the improvement is much less for the four applications. We also note that the improvement of execution time depends on the communication graph of applications, albeit not significant here.

In terms of computation time of the mapping regions, Fig. 5b reveals that the proposed algorithm achieved nearly identical results as *FF* and *PROX*. This is primarily due to the fact that selecting an optimized mapping region in *LUTMap* requires only a table lookup operation and the table is small enough to fit into the memory. Therefore the operation can be completed instantly as is in FF and $PROX$. While in $RAND$ an extra operation is needed for computing a random number, and selecting neighbouring nodes costs additional time for generating the mapping region in INC (on average 35 % slower than FF).

5 Conclusion

We proposed a dynamic application mapping algorithm in this paper. Parallel and distributed processing are trends for modern applications. Systems integrate more and more processor cores to increase the capability of processing multiple applications. However the mapping of applications in such a system is critical for performance and efficiency. We explored the intra-application delay of these systems. A fundamental algorithm is proposed to optimize the delay with improved mapping region selection. The algorithm is proved to be effective in terms of average intra-application delay, however the time cost of calculating additional regions can be a problem. We then investigated a scheme based on lookup tables. The tables are computed dynamically based on the status of the system. Our results show that both the overhead of size and computation time of the lookup table were acceptable for most cases. Experiments were conducted based on real applications with a cycle-accurate simulator. It is shown that checking the lookup table is as fast as other simple mapping algorithms, while the execution time of four applications was improved by 15.6 % compared with the first fit algorithm.

References

1. Bienia, C., Kumar, S., Singh, J.P., Li, K.: The parsec benchmark suite: characterization and architectural implications. In: Proceedings of the 17th International Conference on Parallel Architectures and Compilation Techniques, PACT 2008, pp. 72–81. ACM, New York (2008)
2. Chen, Y.J., Yang, C.L., Chang, Y.S.: An architectural co-synthesis algorithm for energy-aware network-on-chip design. J. Syst. Archit. **55**(5–6), 299–309 (2009)
3. Chou, C.L., Ogras, U., Marculescu, R.: Energy- and performance-aware incremental mapping for networks on chip with multiple voltage levels. IEEE Trans. Comput.-Aided Des. Integr. Circ. Syst. **27**(10), 1866–1879 (2008)
4. Dally, W., Towles, B.: Principles Practices Interconnection Netw. Morgan Kaufmann Publishers Inc., San Francisco (2003)
5. Demaine, E.D., Fekete, S.P., Rote, G., Schweer, N., Schymura, D., Zelke, M.: Integer point sets minimizing average pairwise distance: what is the optimal shape of a town? Comput. Geom. **44**(2), 82–94 (2011). Special issue of selected papers from the 21st Annual Canadian Conference on Computational Geometry
6. Fattah, M., Rahmani, A.M., Xu, T., Kanduri, A., Liljeberg, P., Plosila, J., Tenhunen, H.: Mixed-criticality run-time task mapping for noc-based many-core systems. In: 2014 22nd Euromicro International Conference on Parallel, Distributed and Network-Based Processing (PDP), pp. 458–465, February 2014
7. Fleig, T., Mattes, O., Karl, W.: Evaluation of adaptive memory management techniques on the tilera tile-gx platform. In: 2014 27th International Conference on Architecture of Computing Systems (ARCS), pp. 1–8, February 2014

8. Ghosh, A., Paul, S., Bhunia, S.: Energy-efficient application mapping in FPGA through computation in embedded memory blocks. In: 2012 25th International Conference on VLSI Design (VLSID), pp. 424–429, January 2012

9. Hu, J., Marculescu, R.: Energy-aware communication and task scheduling for network-on-chip architectures under real-time constraints. In: Proceedings of the Conference on Design, Automation and Test in Europe, DATE 2004, vol. 1, p. 10234. IEEE Computer Society, Washington, DC (2004)

10. Hyde, R.: The Art of Assembly Language, 2nd edn. No Starch Press, San Francisco (2010)

11. LaCouvee, D.: Fact or fiction: Android apps only use one CPU core, December 2015. http://www.androidauthority.com/fact-or-fiction-android-apps-only-use-one-cpu-core-610352/

12. Lei, T., Kumar, S.: A two-step genetic algorithm for mapping task graphs to a network on chip architecture. In: 2003 Proceedings of Euromicro Symposium on Digital System Design, pp. 180–187 (2003)

13. Leung, V.J., Sabin, G., Sadayappan, P.: Parallel job scheduling policies to improve fairness: a case study. In: 39th International Conference on Parallel Processing, ICPP. Workshops 2010, San Diego, California, USA, 13–16 September, pp. 346–353 (2010)

14. Leutenegger, S.T., Vernon, M.K.: The performance of multiprogrammed multiprocessor scheduling algorithms. SIGMETRICS Perform. Eval. Rev. 18(1), 226–236 (1990)

15. Magnusson, P., Christensson, M., Eskilson, J., Forsgren, D., Hallberg, G., Hogberg, J., Larsson, F., Moestedt, A., Werner, B.: Simics: a full system simulation platform. Computer 35(2), 50–58 (2002)

16. Martin, M.M., Sorin, D.J., Beckmann, B.M., Marty, M.R., Xu, M., Alameldeen, A.R., Moore, K.E., Hill, M.D., Wood, D.A.: Multifacet's general execution-driven multiprocessor simulator (gems) toolset. Computer Architecture News, September 2005

17. Mediatek: Helio x20, December 2015. http://mediatek-helio.com/x20/

18. de Souza Carvalho, E., Calazans, N., Moraes, F.: Dynamic task mapping for MPSoCS. IEEE Des. Test Comput. 27(5), 26–35 (2010)

19. TGG: Task graph generator, July 2014. http://taskgraphgen.sourceforge.net/

20. Woo, S.C., Ohara, M., Torrie, E., Singh, J.P., Gupta, A.: The splash-2 programs: characterization and methodological considerations. In: Proceedings of the 22nd International Symposium on Computer Architecture, pp. 24–36, June 1995

21. Xu, T., Toivonen, J., Pahikkala, T., Leppanen, V.: BDMap: a heuristic application mapping algorithm for the big data era. In: 2014 IEEE 11th International Conference on Ubiquitous Intelligence and Computing and IEEE 11th International Conference on Autonomic and Trusted Computing, and IEEE 14th International Conference on Scalable Computing and Communications and Its Associated Workshops (UTC-ATC-ScalCom), pp. 821–828, December 2014

22. Xu, T.C., Leppänen, V.: DBFS: dual best-first search mapping algorithm for shared-cache multicore processors. In: Wang, G., Zomaya, A., Martinez Perez, G., Kenli, L. (eds.) ICA3PP 2015. LNCS, vol. 9528, pp. 185–198. Springer, Heidelberg (2015). doi:10.1007/978-3-319-27119-4_13

23. Xu, T.C., Liljeberg, P., Plosila, J., Tenhunen, H.: Exploration of heuristic scheduling algorithms for 3D multicore processors. In: Proceedings of the 15th International Workshop on Software and Compilers for Embedded Systems, SCOPES 2012, pp. 22–31. ACM, New York (2012)

24. Xu, T.C., Leppänen, V.: Cache- and communication-aware application mapping for shared-cache multicore processors. In: Pinho, L.M.P., Karl, W., Cohen, A., Brinkschulte, U. (eds.) ARCS 2015. LNCS, vol. 9017, pp. 55–67. Springer, Heidelberg (2015)
25. Xu, T.C., Liljeberg, P., Tenhunen, H.: A minimal average accessing time scheduler for multicore processors. In: Xiang, Y., Cuzzocrea, A., Hobbs, M., Zhou, W. (eds.) ICA3PP 2011, Part II. LNCS, vol. 7017, pp. 287–299. Springer, Heidelberg (2011)

Distributed Real-Time Database for the Intelligent Community

Xian Zhang[1], Wenbi Rao[1], Xiaosong Zheng[1(✉)], Chunyang Rao[1(✉)], Congcong Ma[2], and Chao Zeng[1]

[1] School of Computer Science and Technology, Wuhan University of Technology, Wuhan, People's Republic of China
zhangxian360@foxmail.com, {wbrao,zxsong}@whut.edu.cn, rcyboom@163.com, 330819585@qq.com
[2] School of Logistics Engineering, Wuhan University of Technology, Wuhan, People's Republic of China
macc@whut.edu.cn

Abstract. As the request of database services about the intelligent community, in this paper, an intense research for the Distributed Real-Time Database (DRTDB) about the intelligent community has been conducted. And then a database service architecture about the intelligent community has been obtained. Besides, the data storage scheme of Main Memory Database (MMDB) and distributed real-time transaction processing technologies have been studied and applied to this intelligent community. The experiments for inserting and querying functions on DRTDB and common database have been done. Finally, the conclusion shows that the technologies of DRTDB and MMDB in this paper can really meet the requirements of intelligent community in the aspect of real-time data access.

Keywords: Intelligent community · Distributed real-time database system · Main memory database · Data storage · Real-time transaction

1 Introduction

Organizations over the world are collecting and storing data at an unprecedented rate. Demands on DRTDB have been increased dramatically because of the growth in Internet use and the explosion of web pages with real-time information in recent years. The MMDB loads data to be handled directly into main memory and manages data in main memory which effectively improve the processing speed [1–3]. So we then apply the technology of MMDB into DRTDB. In this paper, we put forward the design method of the intelligent community oriented distributed real-time database system. Meanwhile, data storage and transaction processing are analyzed and applied to the management of public information platform in intelligent community.

© Springer International Publishing AG 2016
W. Li et al. (Eds.): IDCS 2016, LNCS 9864, pp. 147–154, 2016.
DOI: 10.1007/978-3-319-45940-0_13

2 Architecture

Intelligent community is an emerging Internet of things application [4, 5]. Based on the database technology, the intelligent community is aiming at providing people more convenient and comfortable life environment [6].

In the intelligent community platform, every node of the distributed real-time database generally connects with several monitoring devices and sensors, such as electronic tags, RFID and so on. The data acquisition equipment sends the collected data to the DB servers. DRTDBMS manages all database servers and provides accurate data analysis results. The real-time analysis information can be browsed on the terminal, such as web page, mobile device and so on. The design of database service structure of intelligent community is shown in Fig. 1.

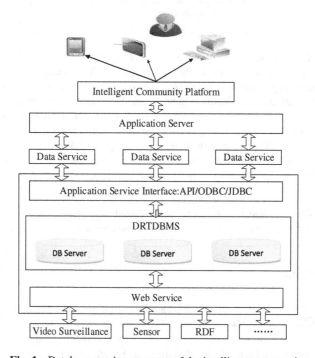

Fig. 1. Database service structure of the intelligent community

The design proposal of the intelligent community oriented DRTDB is as follows: The whole database system includes a DRTDBMS, and each node (DB server) includes a MMDB and DRDB. Data are read and written directly in MMDB which greatly improves the access speed, and each MMDB uses the Primary-Secondary mode and secondary node is the backup. The whole architecture of the intelligent community oriented DRTDB is shown in Fig. 2.

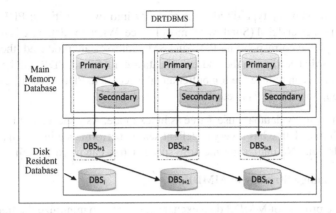

Fig. 2. The whole architecture of the intelligent community oriented DRTDB

This intelligent community platform can be run efficiently, because it not only benefits from its outstanding architecture but also the key technologies of distributed real-time database. In the next section, several key technologies applied here will be discussed.

3   Key Technologies

3.1   MMDB Data Storage Scheme

The frequency of MMDB data access is closely related to the organization of data in memory. In order to reduce the frequency of reading and writing from memory and improve utilization rate of memory and resources to shorten the time of data processing, it's very important to design appropriate data structure of MMDB table data and index. MMDB needs to exchange data between the main memory and the disk, so the question arises: if the exchange is frequent, a lot of time will be wasted which will affect the speed of MMDB [7–9]. Therefore, how to minimize the times of data exchanging is the key problem to improve the performance of MMDB [10].

a)   Data Organization Mode of MMDB

With respect to the data organization mode of MMDB, it includes two kinds of mode: record mode and index mode. Record mode describes the storage mode of data in memory. And we can use it to locate the data's position in memory. Index mode can be used to retrieve data quickly so as to accelerate the query speed.

Record mode mainly includes section type and shadow memory type. These two types are always combined to be used in MMDB.

- The section type is similar with the segmentation paging system. In such type, memory is divided into many blocks and then each block is divided into several sections, and every section stores the address information. The MMDB based on the relational tables such as SQLite, generally uses this type.

- The shadow memory type divides the memory into two partitions: PDB (Primary Database) space and SM (Shadow Memory) space. When the database is performing transactions, the corresponding PDB and SM addresses are produced, then data are read from SM according to the address. If data are not found, PDB will be searched. This approach can reduce the log buffer and the access to PDB. Even after failure of transaction, no rollback is needed.

The main memory database use T tree as index mode. As a special kind of balanced binary search tree, T tree has a very excellent search performance in which a node can store multiple data. No matter in time or in space, T tree can perform well.

b) Data Exchange Strategy of MMDB

During the process of MMDB data exchange, in order to minimize the frequency of data exchange and ensure that data needed for transaction execution are transferred into the main memory, the data exchange subsystem of MMDB must generate an appropriate exchange strategy to perform data exchange between memory and disk. During data exchange, MMDB follows the following rules:

- Data needed for transaction execution have been transferred to memory.
- Reduce the frequency of data exchange.
- Improve the efficiency of data exchange.

Based on the rules discussed above, the data exchange strategies at the time of MMDB initialization and running are designed. Algorithm 1 shows the initial loading algorithm.

Algorithm 1:the initial loading algorithm

INPUT: transaction table called LoadDataSet, and threshold value called fltv
OUTPUT: If succeeding, "success"; else, "fail".
BEGIN
      Traverse LoadDataSet for all of the real-time transaction information;
      All real-time transaction generate list as Tran_List according to priority;
      Get the first element as P from Tran_list;
      If(currently used space in MMDB< fltv)
       Load data for the current transaction into memory;
      Else
       Set load time for the real-time transaction with start time limit which is not loaded;
      Get the next element as P from Tran_list and repeat (4) until P is null;
      If succeeding, return "success"; else, return "fail".
  End

During the time of MMDB initialization, only part of data can be chosen to load into MMDB to meet the deadline of transactions as more as possible. Transaction information and its corresponding dataset information is recorded in table named LoadDataSet. When a transaction is executed, the transaction information will be read from table to judge whether the dataset of the transaction has been loaded. If loaded, MMDB doesn't need to read data from disk during the execution of the transaction.

The steps of transaction dataset loading at runtime are as follows:

- Query the table "LoadDataSet" to check whether there is the transaction information in the table.
- If the transaction information is recorded, whether the dataset of the transaction are in memory is judged. If in memory, it will be executed directly. Otherwise find the data set according to the transaction ID and load it.
- If the transaction information is not recorded, the dataset of the transaction is obtained and loaded into memory. Meanwhile, a new record which describes transaction is added, and its loading dataset is also added into the table "LoadDataSet".

On the basis of the data exchange strategy discussed above, we analyze some important data of the intelligent community platform and conclude: the access frequency of user dictionary in system information is highest, so they need to be loaded permanently in memory as a top priority. Of course, basic information such as project information and data source should be loaded as more as possible. With respect to the collected data, the log and history information, part of which is generally accessed, are very large and frequently updated, so they can be loaded when used and swapped out firstly. The table of data load strategy is shown in Table 1.

Table 1. Data load strategy for some main table in the intelligent community

Data type	Data declaration	Load strategy
Data directory	Role Information	Initial loading, permantly in memory
	System Function	
	Role Privileges	
	Community Information	
	Scene Information	
	Data Acquisition Device Information	
Basic data	Project Information	Load as much as possible, can be swapped out
	Data Source Information	
	Data Source Map	
Management data	Device acquisition Data	Load when used, swapped out firstly
	History Data	
	Log Record	

By the MMDB technology, the data to be handled reside in memory so all transactions can be executed directly in memory. It greatly improves the efficiency of data operation and satisfies the need of the intelligent community platform for big and highly real-time data.

3.2 Distributed Real-Time Transaction Processing

In the intelligent community, information are sensed by the sensor networks and then pushed to the platform. After that, the database system analyzes the collected real-time data and sends them to the interface of the platform to show. Real-time data stream will be handled directly. If not accepted within a certain time, it has been stored in the cache. And over a certain time new real-time data will arrive, so real-time transaction should be used to guarantee that data in the cache are handled timely and efficiently.

In this paper, the background of the intelligent community is developed with Java language. The JTA (Java Transaction API) provides application with the interface to access or update data resource of two or more database servers in a cluster. In addition, it makes the ability of data access stronger combining with the JDBC driver. JTA specifies the interfaces which connect transaction manager with applications and application server. The JTA transaction processing procedure is shown in Fig. 3.

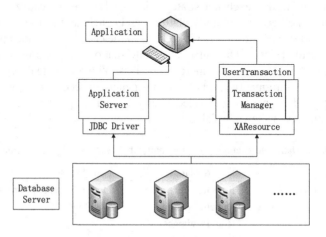

Fig. 3. JTA transaction processing procedure

Application opens a global transaction with the interface "UserTransaction" to associate each thread with transaction processing. Application Server controls and manages the scope of application transaction using the interface "TransactionManager". The interface "XAResource" provides the java mapping based on standard A/Open CAE Specification XA interface to associate entity with the database table of the server.

4   Experiment

4.1   Experimental Environment and Procedure

Experimental platform uses 5 database servers to constitute a distributed database server cluster and also includes an application server, a web service server, a control server, a video server, several data collection devices and clients. 5 database servers are in the same routing environment and unified assigned IP addresses, and each server equips with a memory database and a disk database. 5 database servers can handle data independently and are unified managed by DRTDBS. What's more, we use one of these 5 database servers as a centralized database to do experiment contrast.

We let the platform respectively connect to the distributed real-time database and the centralized database, and then compare the speed of query and insert with same test data. These test data can be collected by the sensors and transmitted to the database in real time. The table named NodeData stores the data collected by the sensors. The table "NodeData" with 63589355 rows of data is selected as a test object. By adjusting the number and data collecting frequency of sensors, the number of data inserted to database can be changed. 100,10000,100000 rows of data are respectively inserted and queried in NodeData, and the time of executing the sql statements in database is recorded.

4.2   Results Analysis

Eventually, Tables 2 and 3 are used to do statistics for the results of the experiment. Table 2 shows that the time of data insert of Centralized Database is nearly 8 times of that of DRTDB when record number is 100. And 5 times for record number 10000, 4 times for record number 100000. Average is 5 times. Also, the time comparison of data query is more obvious with average 11 times.

Table 2. The speed comparison of data insert

Record Number DBServer Type	100	10000	100000
DRTDB	0.003s	0.326s	2.635s
Centralized Database	0.023s	1.632s	10.249s

Table 3. The speed comparison of data query

Record Number DBServer Type	100	10000	100000
DRTDB	<0.001s	0.009s	0.086s
Centralized Database	0.002s	0.166s	1.194s

From Tables 2 and 3, under the environment of distributed real-time database, the speed of reading and writing is faster than that under the environment of Centralized Database. So the applying of data storage technology of distributed real-time memory database can greatly improve the speed of data processing and meet the requirements of real-time data access in the intelligent community.

5   Conclusion

In this paper, the theoretical basis of DRTDB and MMDB are discussed, especially in the aspect of data storage and real-time transaction. The experiment results are analyzed and it is concluded that DRTMDB meets the demand of the intelligent community for database service.

Acknowledgements. This paper is supported in part by the National Natural Science Foundation of China (NO.61571336), the International science & technology cooperation project (NO. 2015DFG12210) and Hubei province science and technology support program (NO.2015B AA120, 2015BCE068).

References

1. Han, Y., Jiang, C., Luo, X.: A study of concurrency control in Web-based distributed real-time database system using extended time Petri nets. In: Proceedings of the International Symposium on Parallel Architectures, Algorithms and Networks, I-SPAN, pp. 67–72 (2004)
2. Lam, K.Y., Kuo, T.W.: Mobile distributed real-time database systems. J. Parall. Distrib. Comput. **69**(10), 866–876 (2001)
3. Komninos, N.: The architecture of intelligent clities: integrating human, collective and artificial intelligence to enhance knowledge and innovation. In: IET International Conference on Intelligent Environments, IET, pp. 13–20 (2006)
4. Cieslicki, D., Schackeler, S., Schwarz, T.: Highly available distributed RAM (HADRAM) for data exchange between power utilities. In: Power Symposium, Naps 2006, North American, pp. 295–302. IEEE (2006)
5. Komninos, N.: Intelligent cities: towards interactive and global innovation environments. Int. J. Innov. Reg. Dev. **1**(4), 62–67 (2009)
6. Paskaleva, K.A.: Enabling the smart city: the progress of city e-governance in Europe. Int. J. Innov. Reg. Dev. **1**(4), 405–422 (2009)
7. Wang, L., Kalbarczyk, Z., Iyer, R K., et al.: Checkpointing of control structures in main memory database systems. In: International Conference on Dependable Systems and Networks, pp. 687–692. IEEE Computer Society (2004)
8. Garciamolina, H., Salem, K.: Main memory database systems: an overview. IEEE Trans. Knowl. Data Eng. **4**(6), 509–516 (1992)
9. Lehman, T.J., Carey, M.J.: A study of index structures for main memory database management systems. In: Proceedings of the 12th International Conference on Very Large Data Bases, pp. 294–303. Morgan Kaufmann Publishers Inc (1986)
10. Lee, J.S., Shin, J.R., Yoo, J.-S.: An efficient distributed concurrency control algorithm using two phase priority. In: Mayr, H.C., Lazanský, J., Quirchmayr, G., Vogel, P. (eds.) DEXA 2001. LNCS, vol. 2113, pp. 933–942. Springer, Heidelberg (2001)

Big Sensor Data: A Survey

Yin Zhang[1(✉)], Wei Li[2], Ping Zhou[2], Jun Yang[2], and Xiaobo Shi[2]

[1] School of Information and Safety Engineering, Zhongnan University of Economics and Law,
Wuhan, China
yin.zhang.cn@ieee.org
[2] School of Computer Science and Technology, Huazhong University of Science and Technology,
Wuhan, China
{weili.epic,pingzhou.cs,junyang.cs,xiaoboshi.cs}@qq.com

Abstract. The big data model has been shown to be very useful for transforming human-generated data and producing value-added business services. On the other hand, much less research has been performed on applying big data models towards machine-generated data such as from large-scale networked sensor systems. This paper surveys the use of big data models towards networked sensor systems and its application towards smart cities and urban informatics. We discuss use-cases for big sensor data research and summarize the common strategies and solutions, identify key techniques and challenges, and discuss a practical framework for handling big sensor data. The paper concludes with a discussion on future trends and research challenges of networked-based sensor systems. The aim of this survey paper is to be useful for researchers and designers to get insights into this emerging area, and motivate the development of practical solutions for application towards smart cities.

Keywords: Big data · Sensor data · Sensor networks

1 Introduction

Big data techniques are targeted towards solving system level problems that cannot be solved by conventional methods and technologies. With the emergence of new networked sensor technologies (e.g. large scale wireless sensor networks, body sensor networks [1–4], Internet/Network/Web/Vehicle-of-Things [5]), the next generation of big data systems will need to deal with machine-generated data from these forms of networked sensor systems [6–9]. This paper is focused on big sensor data systems (a term to conceptualize the application of big data models towards networked sensors) and surveys its applications towards smart cities and urban informatics. This is becoming an important research area [10]. An estimate from IBM is that the volume of machine-generated data sources will increase to 42 % of all data by 2020, up from 11 % in 2005[1]. Much less research has been conducted for big sensor data systems compared with conventional big data systems [11].

---

[1] http://www.ibm.com/big-data/au/en/big-data-and-analytics/operationsmanagement.html.

W. Li et al. (Eds.): IDCS 2016, LNCS 9864, pp. 155–166, 2016.
DOI: 10.1007/978-3-319-45940-0_14

Recently, there has been much research for smart cities. Many smart cities have been established in the world such as in Santander [12], Barcelona [13], and Singapore [14]. In Australia, the state of Tasmania is experimenting with the world's first economy-wide intelligent sensor network technology (Sense-T)[2]. Smart city applications would generate huge amounts of data from a wide variety of data sources ranging from environmental sensors, mobile phones, localization sensors, to data generated by people from social networks. While there is general agreement that the use of these big sensor data would lead to improved services in smart cities, many research challenges remain on how to integrate and utilize these big sensor data. In this survey paper, we take a bottom-up approach and use representative use-cases for big sensor data research, deconstruct the studies to identify key techniques and challenges, and attempt to summarize the common strategies and solutions utilized by different researchers. The use-cases selected for study have been implemented in the real-world.

Figure 1 illustrates the boom of the global data volume. While the amount of large datasets is drastically rising, it also brings about many challenging problems demanding prompt solutions.

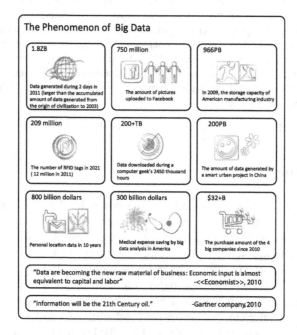

Fig. 1. The continuously increasing big data

---

[2] http://www.sense-t.org.au/.

2 Domains of Big Sensor Data

A definition[3] for big data is given by as "Big data is high-volume, high-velocity, and high-variety information assets that demand cost-effective, innovative forms of information processing for enhanced insight and decision making". An extended definition is that big data systems would involve the five Vs: (1) big volume of data (e.g. involving datasets of terabytes/petabytes), (2) variety of data types, (3) high velocity of data generation and updating, (4) veracity (uncertainty and noise) of acquired data, and (5) big value, as shown in Fig. 2. The first four V's are concerned about data collection, preprocessing, transmission, and storage. The final V focuses on extracting value from the data using statistical and analytical methods.

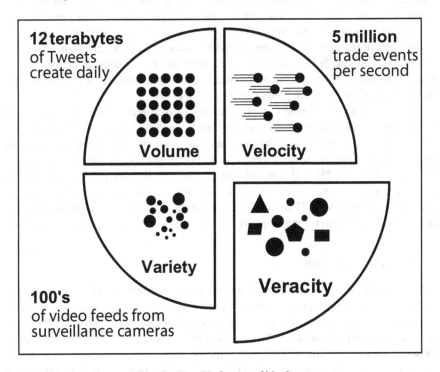

Fig. 2. The 4Vs feature of big data

3 Big Sensor Data Generation and Acquisition

If we take data as a raw material, data generation and data acquisition are an exploitation process, data storage is a storage process, and data analysis is a production process that utilizes the raw material to create new value.

---

[3] http://www.gartner.com/it-glossary/big-data.

3.1 Data Generation

The data collection process consists of three modules: (1) data acquisition, (2) information extraction and cleaning, and (3) data integration, aggregation and representation. The inputs into the data collection process are the raw sensor data values s(x,y,t) harvested from (multiple) sensor farms. The output of the process are the cleaned and aggregated data values s'(x,y,t). The number of output data points would not be more than the number of input data points. The number of output data points may be less than the number of input data points due to data sampling and aggregation. Another characteristic is that the data collection process does not involve utilization of other data sources.

Data generation is the first step of big data. Given Internet data as an example, huge amount of data in terms of searching entries, Internet forum posts, chatting records, and microblog messages, are generated. Those data are closely related to people's daily life, and have similar features of high value and low density [15, 16]. Such Internet data may be valueless individually, but, through the exploitation of accumulated big data, useful information such as habits and hobbies of users can be identified, and it is even possible to forecast users' behaviors and emotional moods [17–20].

Moreover, generated through longitudinal and/or distributed data sources, datasets are more large-scale, highly diverse, and complex. Such data sources include sensors, videos, clickstreams, and/or all other available data sources. At present, main sources of big data are the operation and trading information in enterprises, logistic and sensing information in the IoT [21, 22], human interaction information and position information in the Internet world, and data generated in scientific research, etc. The information far surpasses the capacities of IT architectures and infrastructures of existing enterprises, while its real time requirement also greatly stresses the existing computing capacity [23].

3.2 Big Data Acquisition

As the second phase of the big data system, big data acquisition includes data collection, data transmission, and data pre-processing. During big data acquisition, once we collect the raw data, we shall utilize an efficient transmission mechanism to send it to a proper storage management system to support different analytical applications. The collected datasets may sometimes include much redundant or useless data, which unnecessarily increases storage space and affects the subsequent data analysis. For example, high redundancy is very common among datasets collected by sensors for environment monitoring. Data compression technology can be applied to reduce the redundancy. Therefore, data pre-processing operations are indispensable to ensure efficient data storage and exploitation:

1. **Data Collection**: Data collection is to utilize special data collection techniques to acquire raw data from a specific data generation environment. In addition to the aforementioned three data acquisition methods of main data sources, there are many other data collect methods or systems. For example, in scientific experiments, many special tools can be used to collect experimental data, such as magnetic spectrometers and radio telescopes. We may classify data collection methods from different perspectives. From the perspective of data sources, data collection methods can be

classified into two categories: collection methods recording through data sources and collection methods recording through other auxiliary tools.

Participator sensing is considered as an emerging application scenario for efficient data crowdsourcing from smart device equipped ordinary citizens. Liu et al. in [24–26] presented a novel resource negotiation scheme bridging between dynamic sensing tasks and heterogeneous sensors. Liu et al. in [27–29] proposed a novel framework and subsequent participant selection and incentive mechanism for participatory crowdsourcing including the smart device users, central platform and multiple task publishers. In [30], existing incentive mechanism are extensively surveyed and future research directions are clearly given. Liu et al. [31] extensively analyzed the relationship between energy consumption and smart device user behaviors, and then proposed a novel approach to select the optimal amount of participant while considering possible user rejections. Song et al. [32] introduced an energy consumption index to quantify the average degree of how participants feels disturbed by the energy cost, and proposed a suboptimal approach for participant selection under the multi-task sensing environment. Liu et al. [33] presented a quite novel family-based healthcare monitoring system for long-term chronical disease caring. Event detection systems and energy efficient approaches are given in [34, 35] including both centralized optimal approach and fully distributed suboptimal solutions by participatory sensing. Furthermore, Zhang et al. [36] focused on privacy leakage issues of participatory sensing and presented a participant coordination based architecture and flow to successfully protect user privacy. Finally, Yurur et al. in [37] presented a few posture detections schemes by using the sensor equipped smart devices. Finally, Liu et al. [38] presented a novel concept of quality of service (QoS) index to integrate the multi-dimensional QoS requirements to ensure the degree of QoS satisfactions

2. **Data Transportation**: Upon the completion of raw data collection, data will be transferred to a data storage infrastructure for processing and analysis.. As we known, big data is mainly stored in a data center. The data layout should be adjusted to improve computing efficiency or facilitate hardware maintenance [39]. In other words, internal data transmission may occur in the data center. Therefore, data transmission consists of two phases: Inter-DCN transmissions and Intra-DCN transmissions [40–42].

3. **Data Pre-processing**: Because of the wide variety of data sources, the collected datasets vary with respect to noise, redundancy, and consistency, etc., and it is undoubtedly a waste to store meaningless data. In addition, some analytical methods have serious requirements on data quality. Therefore, in order to enable effective data analysis, we shall pre-process data under many circumstances to integrate the data from different sources, which can not only reduces storage expense, but also improves analysis accuracy.

4 Big Data Storage and Analysis

4.1 Data Storage

The explosive growth of data has more strict requirements on storage and management. In this section, we focus on the storage of big data. Big data storage refers to the storage and management of large-scale datasets while achieving reliability and availability of data accessing. We will review important issues including massive storage systems, distributed storage systems, and big data storage mechanisms. On one hand, the storage infrastructure needs to provide information storage service with reliable storage space; on the other hand, it must provide a powerful access interface for query and analysis of a large amount of data.

Traditionally, as auxiliary equipment of server, data storage device is used to store, manage, look up, and analyze data with structured Relational DataBase Management Systems (RDBMSs). With the sharp growth of data, data storage device is becoming increasingly more important, and many Internet companies pursue big capacity of storage to be competitive. Therefore, there is a compelling need for research on data storage.

4.2 Data Analysis

The analysis of big data mainly involves analytical methods for traditional data and big data, analytical architecture for big data, and software used for mining and analysis of big data. Data analysis is the final and the most important phase in the value chain of big data, with the purpose of extracting useful values, providing suggestions or decisions [43]. Different levels of potential values can be generated through the analysis of datasets in different fields. However, data analysis is a broad area, which frequently changes and is extremely complex. In this section, we introduce the methods, architectures and tools for big data analysis.

Traditional data analysis means to use proper statistical methods to analyze massive data, to concentrate, extract, and refine useful data hidden in a batch of chaotic datasets, and to identify the inherent law of the subject matter, so as to maximize the value of data. Data analysis plays a huge guidance role in making development plans for a country, understanding customer demands for commerce, and predicting market trend for enterprises. Big data analysis can be deemed as the analysis technique for a special kind of data. Therefore, many traditional data analysis methods may still be utilized for big data analysis.

In the dawn of the big data era, people are concerned how to rapidly extract key information from massive data so as to bring values for enterprises and individuals. Although the parallel computing systems or tools, such as MapReduce or Dryad, are useful for big data analysis, they are low levels tools that are hard to learn and use. Therefore, some high-level parallel programming tools or languages are being developed based on these systems. Such high-level languages include Sawzall, Pig, and Hive used for MapReduce, as well as Scope and Dryad LINQ used for Dryad.

5   Big Data Applications

The works in [44–47] used technical sensors embedded in the environment. The work in [44] for Barcelona aimed to expose the daily routines and patterns of people using the city bicycling program. The system collected data on when a bike is picked up or parked. The work in [45] embeds sensor into the city infrastructure. The data collected would be useful for studying the impact of air pollution on respiratory disease, and generating data to inform cycleway development. The work in [46] for Amsterdam used 2400 vehicle detector stations and 60 number plate recognition cameras to decrease the vehicle loss hours. The works in [48–52] used humans as sensors and collect data as people go about their daily routines. The work in [48] used Call Detail Records (CDRs) from a cellular network to characterize the human mobility. The work in [49] collects fine-grained environmental information in the city using data mined from crowdsourced bicycles. The work in [50] used the geolocation from photos on the Flickr social networking website to uncover the movements of tourists in Rome. The work in [51] optimize the 5G small cell networks accounting for the big data from user mobility in urban region. The works in [53, 54] are examples where both technical and human sensors are used. The work in [53] used a combination of GPS data and radio channel measurements from a cellphone network to give the instantaneous position of each mobile element. The work in [54] is for flood risk management in Brazil and used a combination of in-situ water sensors and human participatory sensing to give the water level height.

6   Conclusion, Open Issues, and Outlook

6.1   Data Collection

There are three important challenges for data gathering or collection in big sensor data systems: (1) Other than the 5V's found in conventional big data, big sensor data systems also need to consider an E (energy efficiency) to be fulfilled [55]. This requirement of energy efficiency should be applied at all stages in the big data pipeline whenever there is a non-rechargeable power source to be negotiated [56]. (2) Big sensor data systems will require the collection of data from hundreds of thousands of sensors which could be embedded in "Things" (e.g. garbage cans, street lights, etc.) which could be located and scattered anywhere in the environment. It is prohibitively expensive to implement a sensor relay infrastructure everywhere in the city for data gathering [57]. (3) The third challenge for data collection is to find ways to utilize available sensing infrastructures for new tasks or applications.

6.2   Data Inference

From the paper discussions, we see that a strong emphasis for big sensor data systems is towards using a variety of heterogeneous data sources or historical data to infer missing data or predict future trends in the spatial temporal sensing field. The challenge is to find suitable models and techniques to integrate the various sources of data to solve the big data problem. They used an application from systems biology and showed the diverse data modalities which can be extracted from a single instance of DNA (e.g. the high dimensional expression data, the sparse protein interaction data, the sequence data, the annotation data, and the text mining data). Their approach used the kernel trick where data which has diverse data structures is all transformed into kernel matrices with the same size for combination.

6.3 Value Generation

We find an emphasis towards data-driven research especially using machine learning and complex network techniques. Whereas mathematical models and simulation techniques have been useful for studying the characteristics and behaviors of smaller scale systems, the move to study large-scale systems necessitate the development of new data-driven modeling techniques. Conventional mathematical and simulation models face difficulty in acquiring the correct parameters or in dealing with unpredictable and unknown factors. Amongst, the machine learning approaches, the emergence of deep learning and crossdomain techniques show potential to discover hidden insights and trends in big sensor data systems [58].

6.4 Real-World Applications

Many applications for smart cities (e.g. for earthquake/disaster early warning system, air pollution monitoring) require (near) real-time performance to serve its function [59]. Table 1 presents various typical big sensor data applications. This will drive the

Table 1. Typical Big Sensor data applications

Project	City	Sensors	Data	Analysis	Value
U-Air [60]	Beijing	GPS, environmental sensors, cell phone	Meteorological data, traffic data, human mobility data, Point-of-Interest data, road network data	Neural Network, Conditional Random Field (CRF).	Achieved the inferring of PM10 for entire Beijing in five minutes (near real-time performance) with an accuracy of 82 %.
Sensing city [61]	Christchurch	Environmental Sensors	Air pollution levels, noise levels, water use, traffic flow		Incorporate sensors into building infrastructure
Amsterdam smart city [62]	Amsterdam	2400 vehicle detector stations, 60 number plate recognition cameras	Traffic flow		Traffic flow management to decrease vehicle loss hours by as much as 10 %

"Velocity" characteristic for big sensor data systems. Currently, most (if not all) research on big sensor data systems do not consider this aspect (are performed offline), and research is conducted using historical or past data. In the future, we anticipate the research and development of big sensor data systems where real-time analytics will be performed on large volumes of recently acquired data from multiple sensor farms, and using a number of diverse and historical sources.

References

1. Chen, M., et al.: Body area networks: a survey. Mob. Netw. Appl. **16**(2), 171–193 (2011)
2. Fortino, G., Galzarano, S., Gravina, R., Li, W.: A framework for collaborative computing and multi-sensor data fusion in body sensor networks. Inf. Fusion **22**, 50–70 (2015)
3. Fortino, G., Giannantonio, R., Gravina, R., Kuryloski, P., Jafari, R.: Enabling effective programming and flexible management of efficient body sensor network applications. IEEE Trans. Hum. Mach. Syst. **43**(1), 115–133 (2013)
4. Wan, J., Zou, C., Ullah, S., Lai, C.F., Zhou, M., Wang, X.: Cloud-enabled wireless body area networks for pervasive healthcare. IEEE Netw. **27**(5), 56–61 (2013)
5. Zheng, K., Zheng, Q., Chatzimisios, P., Xiang, W., Zhou, Y.: Heterogeneous vehicular networking: a survey on architecture, challenges, and solutions. IEEE Commun. Surv. Tutor. **17**(4), 2377–2396 (2015)
6. Taleb, T., Ksentini, A.: On alleviating MTC overload in EPS. Ad Hoc Netw. **18**, 24–39 (2014)
7. Lin, K., Xu, T., Song, J., Qian, Y., Sun, Y.: Node scheduling for all-directional intrusion detection in SDR-based 3D WSNs. IEEE Sens. J. (2016). doi:10.1109/JSEN.2016.2558043
8. Lin, K., Chen, M., Deng, J., Hassan, M.M., Fortino, G.: Enhanced fingerprinting and trajectory prediction for IoT localization in smart buildings. IEEE Trans. Autom. Sci. Eng. **13**(3), 1294–1307 (2016)
9. Hossain, M.S.: Cloud-supported cyber-physical localization framework for patients monitoring. IEEE Syst. **PP**, 1–10 (2015). doi:10.1109/JSYST.2015.2470644
10. Zhang, Y.: GroRec: a group-centric intelligent recommender system integrating social, mobile and big data technologies. IEEE Trans. Serv. Comput. (2016). doi:10.1109/TSC.2016.2592520
11. Zheng, K., Yang, Z., Zhang, K., Chatzimisios, P., Yang, K., Xiang, W.: Big data-driven optimization for mobile networks toward 5G. IEEE Netw. **30**(1), 44–51 (2016)
12. Sanchez, L., Muñoz, L., Galache, J.A., Sotres, P., Santana, J.R., Gutierrez, V., et al.: SmartSantander: IoT experimentation over a smart city testbed. Comput. Netw. **61**, 217–238 (2014)
13. Bakici, T., Almirall, E., Wareham, J.: A smart city initiative: the case of Barcelona. J. Knowl. Econ. **4**(2), 135–148 (2013)
14. Kloeckl, K., Senn, O., Ratti, C.: Enabling the real-time city: LIVE Singapore! J. Urban Technol. **19**(2), 89–112 (2012)
15. Lin, K., Wang, W., Wang, X., Ji, W., Wan, J.: Qoe-driven spectrum assignment for 5 g wireless networks using sdr. IEEE Wirel. Commun. **22**(6), 48–55 (2015)
16. Lin, K., Song, J., Luo, J., Ji, W., Hossain, M.S., Ghoneim, A.: GVT: green video transmission in the mobile cloud networks. IEEE Trans. Circ. Syst. Video Technol. (2016). doi:10.1109/TCSVT.2016.2539618

17. Chen, M., Zhang, Y., Li, Y., Mao, S., Leung, V.C.: EMC: emotion-aware mobile cloud computing in 5G. IEEE Netw. **29**(2), 32–38 (2015)
18. Hossain, M.S., Muhammad, G., Alhamid, M.F., Song, B., Al-Mutib, K.: Audio-visual emotion recognition using big data towards 5 g. Mob. Netw. Appl. (2015). doi:10.1007/s11036-016-0685-9
19. Zhou, L.: Specific versus diverse computing in media cloud. IEEE Trans. Circ. Syst. Video Technol. **25**(12), 1888–1899 (2015)
20. Zhou, L., Rodrigues, J.J., Oliveira, L.M.: QoE-driven power scheduling in smart grid: architecture, strategy, and methodology. IEEE Commun. Mag. **50**(5), 136–141 (2012)
21. Chen, M., Wan, J., González, S., Liao, X., Leung, V.C.: A survey of recent developments in home M2 M networks. IEEE Commun. Surv. Tutor. **16**(1), 98–114 (2014)
22. Hossain, M.S., Muhammad, G.: Cloud-assisted industrial internet of things (iiot)–enabled framework for health monitoring. Comput. Netw. **101**, 192–202 (2016)
23. Taleb, T., Ksentini, A., Kobbane, A.: Lightweight mobile core networks for machine type communications. IEEE Access **2**, 1128–1137 (2014)
24. Liu, C.H., Leung, K.K., Bisdikian, C., Branch, J.W.: A new approach to architecture of sensor networks for mission-oriented applications. In: SPIE Defense, Security, and Sensing, International Society for Optics and Photonics, p. 73490L (2009)
25. Liu, C.H., He, T., Lee, K.W., Leung, K.K., Swami, A.: Dynamic control of data ferries under partial observations. In: IEEE WCNC, pp. 1–6 (2010)
26. Liu, C.H., Fan, J., Branch, J.W., Leung, K.K.: Toward qoi and energy-efficiency in internet-of-things sensory environments. IEEE Trans. Emerg. Top. Comput. **2**(4), 473–487 (2014)
27. Liu, C.H., Fan, J., Hui, P., Wu, J., Leung, K.K.: Toward QoI and energy efficiency in participatory crowdsourcing. IEEE Trans. Veh. Technol. **64**(10), 4684–4700 (2015)
28. Liu, C.H., Hui, P., Branch, J.W., Bisdikian, C., Yang, B.: Efficient network management for context-aware participatory sensing. In: Proceedings of the 2011 8th Annual IEEE Communications Society Conference on Sensor, Mesh and Ad Hoc Communications and Networks (Secon), pp. 116–124 (2011)
29. Liu, C.H., Yang, B., Liu, T.: Efficient naming, addressing and profile services in internet-of-things sensory environments. Ad Hoc Netw. **18**, 85–101 (2014)
30. Gao, H., Liu, C.H., Wang, W., Zhao, J., Song, Z., Su, X., et al.: A survey of incentive mechanisms for participatory sensing. IEEE Commun. Surv. Tutor. **17**(2), 918–943 (2015)
31. Liu, C.H., Zhang, B., Su, X., Ma, J., Wang, W., Leung, K.K.: Energy-aware participant selection for smartphone-enabled mobile crowd sensing. IEEE Syst. J. (2015). doi:10.1109/JSYST.2015.2430362
32. Song, Z., Zhang, B., Liu, C.H., Vasilakos, A.V., Ma, J., Wang, W.: QoI-aware energy-efficient participant selection. In: Proceedings of the 2014 Eleventh Annual IEEE International Conference on Sensing, Communication, and Networking (SECON), pp. 248–256 (2014)
33. Liu, C.H., Wen, J., Yu, Q., Yang, B., Wang, W.: HealthKiosk: a family-based connected healthcare system for long-term monitoring. In: Proceedings of 2011 IEEE Conference on Computer Communications Workshops (INFOCOM WKSHPS), pp. 241–246 (2011)
34. Liu, C.H., Zhao, J., Zhang, H., Guo, S., Leung, K.K., Crowcroft, J.: Energy-efficient event detection by participatory sensing under budget constraints. IEEE Syst. J. (2016). doi:10.1109/JSYST.2016.2533538
35. Zhang, B., Song, Z., Liu, C.H., Ma, J., Wang, W.: An event-driven qoi-aware participatory sensing framework with energy and budget constraints. ACM Trans. Intell. Syst. Technol. **6**(3), 42 (2015)
36. Zhang, B., Liu, C.H., Lu, J., Song, Z., Ren, Z., Ma, J., Wang, W.: Privacy-preserving QoI-aware participant coordination for mobile crowdsourcing. Comput. Netw. **101**, 29–41 (2016)

37. Yurur, O., Liu, C.H., Moreno, W.: Unsupervised posture detection by smartphone accelerometer. Electron. Lett. **49**(8), 562–564 (2013)
38. Liu, C.H., Leung, K.K., Gkelias, A.: A generic admission-control methodology for packet networks. IEEE Trans. Wirel. Commun. **13**(2), 604–617 (2014)
39. Chen, M., Zhang, Y., Li, Y., Hassan, M.M., Alamri, A.: AIWAC: affective interaction through wearable computing and cloud technology. IEEE Wirel. Commun. **22**(1), 20–27 (2015)
40. Peng, L.: On the future integrated datacenter networks: designs, operations, and solutions. Opt. Switch. Netw. **19**, 58–65 (2016)
41. Peng, L., Sun, Y., Chen, M., Park, K.: Datacenter-oriented elastic optical networks: architecture, operation, and solutions. TIIS **8**(11), 3955–3966 (2014)
42. Peng, L., Youn, C.H., Tang, W., Qiao, C.: A novel approach to optical switching for intradatacenter networking. J. Lightwave Technol. **30**(2), 252–266 (2012)
43. Zhang, Y., Chen, M., Mao, S., Hu, L., Leung, V.C.: Cap: community activity prediction based on big data analysis. IEEE Netw. **28**(4), 52–57 (2014)
44. Froehlich, J., Neumann, J., Oliver, N.: Measuring the pulse of the city through shared bicycle programs. In: Proceedings of UrbanSense08, pp. 16–20 (2008)
45. Zhang, Y.: iDoctor: personalized and professionalized medical recommendations based on hybrid matrix factorization. Future Gener. Comput. Syst. (2016). doi:10.1016/j.future.2015.12.001
46. Zhang, Y.: Health-CPS: healthcare cyber-physical system assisted by cloud and big data. IEEE Syst. J. (2015). doi:10.1109/JSYST.2015.2460747
47. Yuan, W., Deng, P., Taleb, T., Wan, J., Bi, C.: An unlicensed taxi identification model based on big data analysis. IEEE Trans. Intell. Transp. Syst. **17**(6), 1703–1713 (2016)
48. Becker, R., Cáceres, R., Hanson, K., Isaacman, S., Loh, J.M., Martonosi, M., et al.: Human mobility characterization from cellular network data. Commun. ACM **56**(1), 74–82 (2013)
49. Chen, M., Ma, Y., Song, J., Lai, C.F., Hu, B.: Smart clothing: connecting human with clouds and big data for sustainable health monitoring. Mob. Netw. Appl. (2016). doi:10.1007/s11036-016-0745-1
50. Chen, M., Hao, Y., Qiu, M., Song, J., Wu, D., Humar, I.: Mobility-aware caching and computation offloading in 5 g ultra-dense cellular networks. Sensors **16**(7), 974 (2016)
51. Ge, X., Ye, J., Yang, Y., Li, Q.: User mobility evaluation for 5G small cell networks based on individual mobility model. IEEE J. Sel. Area Commun. **34**(3), 528–541 (2016)
52. Carreño, P., Gutierrez, F.J., Ochoa, S.F., Fortino, G.: Supporting personal security using participatory sensing. Concurr. Comput. Pract. Exp. **27**(10), 2531–2546 (2015)
53. Calabrese, F., Colonna, M., Lovisolo, P., Parata, D., Ratti, C.: Real-time urban monitoring using cell phones: a case study in Rome. IEEE Trans. Intell. Transp. Syst. **12**(1), 141–151 (2011)
54. Chen, M.: NDNC-BAN: supporting rich media healthcare services via named data networking in cloud-assisted wireless body area networks. Inf. Sci. **284**, 142–156 (2014)
55. Chen, M., Mao, S., Liu, Y.: Big data: a survey. Mob. Netw. Appl. **19**(2), 171–209 (2014)
56. Ge, X., Yang, B., Ye, J., Mao, G., Wang, C.X., Han, T.: Spatial spectrum and energy efficiency of random cellular networks. IEEE Trans. Commun. **63**(3), 1019–1030 (2015)
57. Chen, M., Hao, Y., Li, Y., Lai, C.F., Wu, D.: On the computation offloading at ad hoc cloudlet: architecture and service modes. IEEE Commun. Mag. **53**(6), 18–24 (2015)
58. Ji, W., Li, Z., Chen, Y.: Joint source-channel coding and optimization for layered video broadcasting to heterogeneous devices. IEEE Trans. Multimed. **14**(2), 443–455 (2012)
59. Foschini, L., Taleb, T., Corradi, A., Bottazzi, D.: M2M-based metropolitan platform for IMS-enabled road traffic management in IoT. IEEE Commun. Mag. **49**(11), 50–57 (2011)

166   Y. Zhang et al.

60. Zheng, Y., Liu, F., Hsieh, H.P.: U-Air: when urban air quality inference meets big data. In: Proceedings of the 19th ACM SIGKDD International Conference on Knowledge Discovery and Data Mining, pp. 1436–1444 (2013)
61. Sensing City Website (2016). http://sensingcity.org
62. Amsterdam Smart City Website (2016). http://amsterdamsmartcity.com

Predicting Telecommunication Customer Churn Using Data Mining Techniques

Diana AlOmari[✉] and Mohammad Mehedi Hassan

Information Systems Department, King Saud University, Riyadh, Kingdom of Saudi Arabia
Diana.r.alomari@hotmail.com, mmhassan@ksu.edu.sa

Abstract. This paper will illustrate how to use data mining techniques to predict telecommunication customers churn. With a well analysis and interpretation of the data, valuable knowledge and key insights into the customers' needs can be achieved. A sample data based on customer usage was gathered, and different data mining techniques were applied over it. This paper's contribution is to test the capability of a prediction data mining technique, which is the RULES Family algorithm-6 that has never been applied in such a case before. Two pre-stages techniques were applied before the prediction, which are the segmentation "clustering" and the feature selection.

Keywords: Data mining · Predicting customers churn · Decision tree · Neural network · Rules family algorithms

1 Introduction

Nowadays, there is a massive amount of data, which can be analyzed, and with a well analysis and interpretation of this data, this can result in getting valuable knowledge and key insights into customers' needs [1], and one of the biggest storages and most important sources of data are in the telecommunication sector where lots of data are gathered about each customer. Data mining in the telecommunication industry is an enormous field and considered as a continues research field where many studies are still conducted on it to find new techniques, methods, tools to improve the advantage taken from data analysis. Because of that, the focus of this paper is on the customers of the telecommunication sector. Actually, this sector was chosen since the competition in it is very high and generally speaking, business companies struggle to keep their customers rather than attracting new ones since the cost of attracting a new customer is much more than keeping an old one. Data in the telecommunication sector can be customers' demographic data, usage data, network data, etc. So, it is important for these companies to get advantaged of the data they have and analyze it in a way to figure out which customer is going to churn (leave the company to other competitors [2]). To achieve this goal, many different data mining techniques and tools are being used. The importance of such a process is that when customers churn is predicted accurately, that leads to better decisions taken by the telecommunication company as a proactive action to make the customer stay with them and not leaving. Real case data were gathered from Mobily Telecommunication Company, which is a leading telecommunication company in Saudi

© Springer International Publishing AG 2016
W. Li et al. (Eds.): IDCS 2016, LNCS 9864, pp. 167–178, 2016.
DOI: 10.1007/978-3-319-45940-0_15

Arabia, and this data was analyzed using three different data mining techniques, which are decision tree, neural network, and RULE Family algorithm-6. The idea is to compare the accuracy of predicting customers churn through the widely used techniques (Decision tree, neural network) with the RULES Family algorithm-6 which has never been applied in such a case.

Moreover, two pre-prediction techniques were used, which are also considered as data mining techniques. The first one is the segmentation technique "clustering" that was applied over the data set to help understanding the different customers' clusters that we have. The second one is the feature selection technique that was applied to reduce the number of variables that we are testing in the prediction model.

The tools that were used in this experiment were SAS Enterprise Miner 9.3 [3], Excel 2013, and KEEL (Knowledge Extraction based on Evolutionary Learning) which is an open-source software written in Java programming language that can be used for a large number of different data mining and knowledge data discovery tasks. KEEL tool has a simple graphical user interface that can be used to assess the behavior of the algorithms. It contains a huge variety of classical, clustering, preprocessing algorithms and techniques. The main purpose for choosing this software in this thesis is that it contains some RULES family algorithms, which are not available in SAS [4].

2 Data in Telecommunication Field

There is a huge amount of data available about each customer in the telecommunication field, and it has lots of features. Telecommunication data can be divided into main categories which are, customer calls behavior, customer demographic information, customer care information, network operational data, social media data, and general customer information. Customer calls behavior or usage refers to a descriptive information about each call done by the customer. Such data may contains several features, for example, the duration of each call, the frequency of calls per day/week/month, whether the call

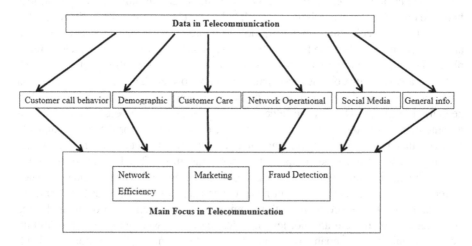

Fig. 1. Data in telecommunication and its usage

was an international or an internal call, roaming or not roaming call, internet usage in terms of "megabytes-gigabytes". All this data is saved at the service provider company and used for applying different analysis tools in order to generate valuable information that can be very useful to the telecommunication company for many purposes. For example, analyzing such data can be used for a marketing purpose in predicting customer churn, targeting specific group of customers, data monetization [16] (Fig. 1).

3   Customer Relationship Management

The term customer relationship management has been used in the last years to refer to the organization's ability to success in the competitive market and improve its perform-ance through identifying, attracting, acquiring and maintaining customers "customer retention". Companies all over the world and in all sectors have to put their efforts to success in this customer relationship management process. Nowadays, for a company to survive in the competitive global environment, they should do an excessive effort toward customers because of the widely opened market where the customer can easily move from one provider (company) to another. Once the company acquired or got the customer, it tries to make him/her as satisfied as possible so the customer doesn't think about moving to another company. When the customer leaves to a competitor, it is called a churn customer. So, companies in different sectors tries to understand their customers' needs and fulfill it so that they don't churn "leave". The issue is that according to many studies, acquiring a new customer costs much more than keeping an old one which referred to as customer retention". Many studies were done to provide guidance on how companies can build a long term relationship with their customers.

4   Literature Review

The idea of this paper was started based on a suggestion by two papers that talked about the RULES Family algorithms and its application into different sectors but not yet in the telecommunication sector [5, 6]. Actually, there are many data mining techniques, tools, and algorithms used for predicting customers churn, but the mostly used ones are the decision tree, neural network [7], classification, and the traditional statically based methods such as the linear regression and logistic regression [7], and many others. In an experiment that was over a public data set and aimed to reduce the customer churn and error rate in the telecommunication industry, authors used the Naïve Bayes' clas-sifier which is based on the Bayesian theorem and the decision tree tool based on C4.5 algorithm. C4.5 is considered as a statistical classifier since it can be used for classifi-cation. The result that they got was 92 % overall accuracy [18]. According to a study which was conducted over 61 journal articles, aiming to analyze the well-known data mining techniques used to build predictive customers churn models in the telecommu-nication field with the pros and cons of them. Authors found that the decision tree tech-nique was used in 26 studies, followed by the neural network and other techniques which mean that the decision tree technique is the most commonly used for predicting churn rate [8]. Whereas the RULES Family Algorithm, which was developed in 1995, is not yet applied in the field of predicting telecommunication customers churn, but it was applied in the banking and healthcare sectors [9]. Moreover, regarding the two pre-prediction techniques, there were other studies who applied either the feature selection or the segmentation but not both. One of these studies was applied over the healthcare sector and it aimed to choose the most suitable cloud-based hospital information system. Two feature selection methods were used in this study, which are the fuzzy Delphi method (FDM) which was used to evaluate the primary indicator and the fuzzy analytical hierarchy process (FAHP) which was used to calculate the weight of these features [10]. However, in this paper, these two techniques were not used because they are not widely used in the case of telecommunication sector. Another similar idea for prediction was also in the healthcare sector, and it was applied to expect the stage of liver fibrosis. Many data mining techniques were used and compared in this study like the decision trees, artificial neural network, K-means neighbor, classification. Additionally, different feature selection methods were explained [11]. As for the segmentation, a study suggested that to do customers churn prediction, there are two ways. One of them is to divide its customers by the profit generated from them and focus retention management only on those customers, or the other option is to mark the entire customer database with respect to the tendency to churn and prioritize the retention effort based on the life time value of customer and churn tendency [12].

5 Basic Idea

The three main ideas that this experiment is based on is shown throw the below steps:

5.1 Feature Selection

a. Different feature selection techniques were applied.
b. Aims to reduce the processing time since we are dealing with less data variables, and hence, improve the overall prediction efficiency.

5.2 Segmentation

a. Apply a clustering algorithm over the data so the customers are divided into groups
b. Aims to increase the prediction accuracy.

5.3 Prediction Model

a. Apply the Rules Family algorithm-6 to predict customer churn and compare its result to other commonly used prediction techniques.
b. Aims to find the capability of the rules family algorithm-6 in predicting customer churn in telecommunication field.

It is important to notice in this section that the segmentation here is considered as unsupervised learning, whereas the prediction step is considered as supervised learning.

The learning technique that the algorithm follows is called supervised learning if the response variable is already known, where the data mining model needs to understand the pattern and values of the explanatory variables that lead to a specific value of the response value. The opposite case is called the unsupervised learning which is considered as a much more challenging where the model has no reference point to learn from and need to figure out the result of a specific pattern.

6 Methodology

There are lots of methodologies that can be followed like the CRISP (Cross-Industry Standard Process for data mining). This widely used methodology was the base for this experiment, which consists of the following steps:

6.1 Understanding the Business Requirements

At this step, it is important to understand the field of business that we are working with, which is the telecommunication sector. Telecommunication companies, like any other companies in the business field, want to keep their customers and don't want to lose them. That is because attracting a new customer cost much more than keeping an old one, and from that point of view, telecommunication companies are putting lots of its capabilities in developing different ways to predict which customer will leave, and by that, telecommunication firms can make a prediction of future behavior of new customers and can develop new strategies before customers start to think about leaving. Thus, it is important to build a very successful and accurate churn analysis model. This experiment was based on data gathered from Mobily Company, which is a telecommunication company in Saudi Arabia. Telecommunication industry in Saudi Arabia is growing at an outstanding rate. In one of the studies over the telecommunication customers in Saudi Arabia, authors aimed to test the effect of different variables, such as the price, brand image, and service quality over the customer loyalty. Authors found that all these variables have a strong relationship with customer decision of moving to another service provider [17]. Many and different facilities and services are continuously being expanded to accommodate the Kingdom's growing market. Three companies are considered as the communication service providers in Saudi Arabia, which are Saudi Telecommunications Company (STC), Mobily, and Zain. They have opened with the same sequence as mentioned before. These companies are in a fierce competition over the mobile network, and Internet services provided to customers in Saudi Arabia, where each one is putting all the efforts to gain and keep customers.

6.2 Identifying Data Source and Data Format

This is the second step in the followed methodology where the data set must be identified. As mentioned before, the collected data was from Mobily Telecommunication Company in Saudi Arabia, and it was based on 10,000 customers. It belongs to prepaid customers with activation date before January 2014. The gathered months are from January 2014 to September 2014 (nine months), with an exclusion of non-voice, corporate, employee, and seasonal customers. The data focus is mainly on the usage details of customers. As for the data format, it was originally in .CSV format, which looks like a general excel file format, and then it was imported into SAS software and turned into SAS file format. Same thing was applied in the KEEL software. As for the available variables, there are 178 variables that are based on the behavioral "usage" data of customers. Main categories are shown in the below table (Table 1).

Table 1. Variables explanation

Variable	Explanation
Customer ID	This variable is an identification of each customer
Churn flag	This variable indicates whether the customer is churn 1, not churn 0.
Customer tenure	This variable indicates how many days the customer has been with the telecommunication company.
Active days	This variable indicates number of days that the customer has used his phone either for a call or internet.
Tariff migration	This variable indicates how many times the customer changed among different tariffs.
Usage variables	Many variables under this category such as number of calls and total minutes of calls "international, roaming, inside KSA, Mobily-to-Mobily, Mobily-to-competitor" plus total usage of data "megabytes" and SMS. All these data were gathered on monthly and weekly basis.

6.3   Data Preparation and Preprocessing

In this phase, the data set is checked and examined to make sure of its completeness, correctness, and make sure that there are no duplicated records. In this experiment, the data was correct with no duplication or missing values. If there were such problems, usually, there are some solutions to overcome these problems. In conclusion, this step aims to prepare the data set so it is ready to be used in the prediction model without any obstacles. So, after this step, data preprocessing is applied through the feature selection. Since there are many variables, it is important to reduce the number of variables, which are under focus and that by applying a feature selection algorithm to help identifying which variables have high influence over the target variable "TARGET_FLAG" which is the churn flag which takes two values, either 1, which means churned, or 0, which means not churned. Two feature selection techniques were used in this experiment, which are the R- square, and sequential R-square. These are the widely used techniques for such purpose.

6.4   Data Exploration

In this step, the data set is examined statistically then the segmentation is applied. The idea of segmentation here means to do clustering of the data set where the customers will be divided based on their behavior "usage." From a data mining point of view, clustering is considered as an unsupervised learning technique where the labels of the groups were not previously defined. Indeed, the unsupervised learning is considered as a more difficult step more that the supervised learning where the data labels were already defined. Clustering analysis is to find groups of objects such that the objects in each group will be similar (or related) to each other and different from the objects in other groups. The clustering technique that was used in this experiment is the centroid technique.

6.5 Building Data Mining Model

At this stage, three different prediction techniques were applied on the same data set to check their capabilities in predicting customers churn. Two techniques are widely used in this field, which are the decision tree and the neural network. The third one is the RULES Family algorithm-6.

6.6 Evaluating the Results

At this stage, we evaluate the accuracy of each one and see which one has the highest accuracy.

7 Experiment

The experiment was started with preparing the data set to be ready for use in the prediction model. There are two main steps at this stage, which are the data partitioning and feature selection.

7.1 Data Partitioning

It is a wisely and significant step to divide the data set into training and validating sets, so that the model will learn from the training set and check its prediction capability from the validating set. The result of data partitioning is as below. It is important to keep each set with the same percentage of churners and non-churners. After this step, it is the time to apply the feature selection (variable selection) step where the most important variables will be specified.

Total data = 10000 customers (Training set = 6969, Validating set = 3031)

The technique used here for partitioning the data set was the stratified technique since the target variable is known.

It's important to mention here that 10 fold-cross validation was applied here to insure the accuracy of the results (Fig. 2).

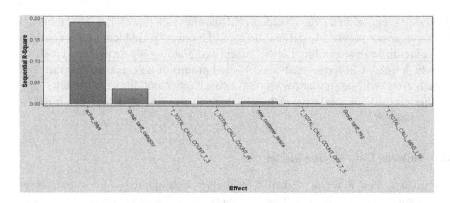

Fig. 2. Sequential R- Square

7.2   Feature Selection

This step was applied through two different techniques, which are the R- square, and sequential R-square. These two techniques were chosen since they gave the best results. The results showed that the main important variables that have a great influence over the target variable "Churn_ Flag".

In the above R-Square figure, each bar represents a variable. While using the SAS software, you can point the arrow to any bar and get an explanation box showing what this variable is.

The idea of applying two different techniques was to make sure of the result that was produced (Fig. 3).

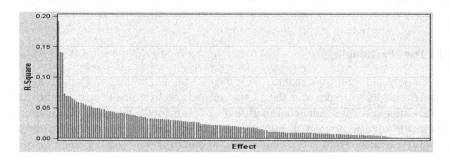

Fig. 3. R-Square

After this preparation and preprocessing stage, the data set was explored using basic statistical analysis and classification.

7.3   Basic Statistical Analysis

When exploring the data set that contains 10,000 customers, we found that 7670 customers with churn flag 0 "Not churn" and 2330 customers with churn flag 1 "Churn."

7.4 Classification

The classification here is called behavioral classification since we are classifying the data set based on the customer behavior "Usage." After classifying the data set using the centroid technique, we got five classes, and as we can see in the below charts, each class has its own characteristics (Table 2).

Table 2. Classes characteristics

Class number	Characteristics
Class # 1	Customers who fall under this class have high values for the variables (international call minutes - usage of the data "the Internet"). This class may represent foreigners who are living in KSA and talking to their families in other countries.
Class # 2	Customers who fall under this class have high values for the variables (SMS - usage of the data "the Internet") This class may represent people who prefer texts.
Class # 3	Customers who fall under this class have high values for all call variables. This class may represent people who might be old people who are not that much into internet "data usage" and talk a lot.
Class # 4	Customers who fall under this class have high values for almost all variables. This class may represent people who heavy users. They can be considered as the high-value customers that the company must take care of since they generate high revenue out of them. They don't have high values in the international calls which may indicate that they are Saudi people.
Class # 5	Customers of this class are average in most of the call variables and data variables. They can be considered as medium value customers.

So the main and most important point behind the classification step is to be able to categorize the customers you have in the data set and understand where each one falls. After that, that will help more in understanding what offers may attract them to stay with you as a service provider.

7.5 Building the Prediction Model

As mentioned before, three data mining techniques were used to predict customers churn, which are:

- **Decision Tree:** The idea of the decision tree can be viewed as a visual representation that is used as a prediction model and an algorithm where the data is classified as a tree that consists of branches and leaves [13]. Decision tree falls under the hierarchical classifiers, Tree classifiers, multistage classification, and the Divide & Conquer strategies. There are many decision tree induction algorithms and here the used one was the ID3. In addition to the decision tree induction algorithms, studies over the years had developed some techniques to assess the accuracy and analyze the decision tree. These techniques are considered as the splitting criteria to assess the splitting accuracy and efficiency of the decision tree. In this experiment, the Entropy algorithm was chosen to identify the variables and cut points that were most predictive of the churn flag. The Entropy result can range from 0–1 where 0 is the best and 1 is the worst. In this experiment, the entropy was specified and set to be maximum up to 0.2.

- **Neural Network:** As the decision tree, neural network is considered as one of the widely used data mining techniques for predicting customers churn. The used technique is the multilayer perception with 3 hidden layers.
- **RULES Family Algorithm-6:** RULE 6 (RULES 6-C) was developed based on RULE 3 plus algorithm aiming to improve the efficiency of dealing with large data sets in a faster manner. It is also characterized by a fast and noise-tolerant search method for extracting IF-THEN rules from instances "examples" [14].

7.6 Evaluating the Results

One of the widely used methods to evaluate the results of prediction is the confusion matrix, which is a matrix used to evaluate the performance of the model in terms of only the model capability of prediction rather than focusing on how fast the model is [15] (Table 3).

Table 3. Decision tree accuracy results

Actual / Predicted	Churn	Not churn
Churn	True Positive 269	False Positive 70
Not churn	False Negative 430	True Negative 2231

Accuracy = (TP+TN) / (TP+TN+FP+FN) = (269+2231)/ (269+2231+70+430) = 2500/3000 = 0.8333 → 83.33 %

RULES Family Algorithm-6: The accuracy result of applying RULES Family Algorithm-6 was given directly by the Keel software without the need to calculate it manually. RULES Family Algorithm gave accuracy equal to 82.47 (Table 4)

Table 4. Neural network accuracy results

Actual / Predicted	Churn	Not churn
Churn	True Positive 347	False Positive 146
Not churn	False Negative 352	True Negative 2155

Accuracy = (TP+TN) / (TP+TN+FP+FN) = (347+2155)/ (347+2155+146+352) = 2502/3000 = 0.834 → 83.4 %

After evaluating all results that we got from the three models, we found that:

- The accuracy of the neural network is the highest one, which makes it the best model in the case of predicting customers churn in the telecommunication sector.
- The second one is the decision tree where the accuracy is very close to the neural network.
- The third place goes to the RULES Family algorithm-6 which gave a good result too, but when compare it to the widely used techniques (Decision tree, neural network), we found that its accuracy less. However, it is considered as a good option and more improvements can be done over it to improve its capability in this field.

8 Conclusion

In conclusion, predicting customers churn using data mining techniques is considered as an ocean of information, methods, and techniques that analysts and experts are still trying to develop and explore day after day, aiming to overcome all difficulties and improving its accuracy. Based on our results of this experiment, which aimed to compare the widely used data mining techniques in predicting telecommunication customers churn; we found that the RULES Family algorithm 6, which has never ever been applied in such case, can predict customers churn and give a reasonable accuracy result, although it gave a lower accuracy result than the neural network and the decision tree, yet the difference was less than 1 %. And by that, the real aim of this paper was reached which is not to prove that the RULES Family algorithm-6 is better or worse than the widely used techniques, but it was to compare it to others and see its capability in such domain.

9 Future Work

More improvements can be applied over the RULES Family Algorithms since it gives promising results. In future, we are working on using the prediction model results and check the segmentation again to figure out from which segments we are having the highest churners. By that the telecommunication company will have a great view of the characteristics of the churners and as a result, they will be able to focus their intention on that group by offering them some offers that matches their usage characteristics. For example, after doing the segmentation, we found that there is a group of customers who do make many international calls, then after doing the prediction, we will come back to the segmentation to check where this churners are "under which group" and let's say that they are under the international calls groups, now that will help the telecommunication company knows which offer to give that group of customers so that they don't leave. "Like giving them few international minutes for free"

Acknowledgements. First of all, we would like to thank our families for supporting us while working on this experiment. Furthermore, many thanks to Mobily Company for giving us the data we worked on, and special thanks to Dr. Ahmed Hashem, General Manager Analytics factory at Mobily Company, for his great cooperation and inspiration.

References

1. Cruickshank, B., Short, E.: Turning big data into valuable analytics. Financial Times (2012)
2. Jayawardhana, P., Perera, D., Kumara, A., et al.: Kanthaka: big data caller detail record (CDR) analyzer for near real time telecom promotions. In: Proceedings of the International Conference on Intelligent Systems, Modelling and Simulation, pp. 534–538. IEEE Computer Society (2013)
3. Chen, Y., Li, B., Ge, X.: Study on predictive model of customer churn of mobile telecommunication company. In: Proceedings of the International Conference on Business Intelligence & Financial Engineering, pp. 114–117. IEEE Computer Society (2011)
4. www.keel.es (2016)
5. Almana, A.M., Aksoy, M.S.: A survey on data mining techniques in customer churn, analysis for telecom industry. Int. J. Eng. Res. Appl. **4**(5), 165–171 (2014)
6. Dahiya, K., Talwar, K.: Customer churn prediction in telecommunication industries using data mining techniques- a review. Int. J. Adv. Res. Comput. Sci. Softw. Eng. **5**(4), 417–433 (2015)
7. Shaaban, E., Helmy, Y., Khedr, A., et al.: A Proposed Churn Prediction Model. IJERA **4**, 693–697 (2012)
8. Hashmi, N., Butt, N.A., Iqbal, M.: Customer churn prediction in telecommunication. a decade review and classification. Int. J. Comput. Sci. Issues (IJCSI) **10**(5), 271–282 (2013)
9. Elgibreen, H., Aksoy, M.S., Aksoy, M.S.: RULES family: where does it stand in Inductive Learning? In: International Conference on Computer Engineering and Applications, pp. 177–186 (2014)
10. Low, C., Chen, Y.H.: Criteria for the evaluation of a cloud-based hospital information system outsourcing provider. J. Med. Syst. **36**(6), 3543–3553 (2012)
11. Hashem, A.M., Rasmy, M.E.M., Wahba, K.M., et al.: Single stage and multistage classification models for the prediction of liver fibrosis degree in patients with chronic hepatitis C infection. Comput. Method. Program. Biomed. **105**(3), 194–209 (2012)
12. Glatz, E., Mavromatidis, S., Ager, B., et al.: Visualizing big network traffic data using frequent pattern mining and hypergraphs. Computing **96**(1), 27–38 (2014)
13. Zhang, X., Gao, F., Huang, H.: Customer-churn research based on customer segmentation. In: Proceedings of the International Conference on Electronic Commerce and Business Intelligence, pp. 443–446 (2009)
14. Elgibreen, H.A., Aksoy, M.S.: RULES – TL: a simple and improved RULES algorithm for incomplete and large data. J. Theor. Appl. Inf. Technol. **47**, 28–40 (2013)
15. Vafeiadis, T., Diamantaras, K.I., Sarigiannidis, G., Chatzisavvas, K.C.: A comparison of machine learning techniques for customer churn prediction. Simul. Model. Practice Theory **55**(1), 1–9 (2015)
16. Weiss, G.M.: Data mining in the telecommunications industry. In: Wang, J. (ed.) Encyclopedia of Data Warehousing and Mining, 2nd edn, pp. 486–491. Montclair State University, New York (2009)
17. Khizindar, T.M., AI-Azzam, A.F.M., Khanfar, I.A.: An empirical study of factors affecting customer loyalty of telecommunication industry in the kingdom of saudi arabia. Br. J. Market. Stud. **3**(5), 98–115 (2015)
18. Churi, A., Divekar, M., Dashpute, S., Kamble, P.: Analysis of customer churn in mobile industry using data mining. Int. J. Emerg. Technol. Adv. Eng. **5**(3), 225–230 (2015)

SLOSELM: Self Labeling Online Sequential Extreme Learning Machine

Zhongtang Zhao[1,2(✉)], Li Liu[1,2], Lingling Li[1,2], and Qian Ma[1,2]

[1] Zhengzhou University of Aeronautics, Zhengzhou, People's Republic of China
{112864041,17116872,498671663,30939260}@qq.com
[2] Collaborative Innovation Center for Aviation Economy Development
of Henan Province, Zhengzhou, People's Republic of China

Abstract. In this paper, to address the transfer learning problem in big data fields, a self labeling online sequential extreme learning machine is presented, which is called SLOSELM. Firstly, an ELM classifier is trained on the labeled training data set of the source domain. Secondly, the unlabeled data set of the target domain is classified by the ELM classifier. In the third step, the high confident samples are selected and the OSELM is employed to update the original ELM classifier. Tested on the real-world daily activity data set, the results show that our algorithm performs well and can achieve 75 % accuracy, which is about 10 % higher than the traditional ELM itself.

Keywords: Extreme learning machine · Activity recognition · Transfer learning · Big data · Pervasive computing

1 Introduction and Related Work

In the traditional supervised learning, it is typically assumed that the unlabeled test data comes from the same distribution as the labeled training data. However, generally the two data sets have different distributions, and in recent years, machine learning researchers have investigated methods to handle mismatch between the training and test domains, with the goal of building a classifier on the labeled data in the old domain(source domain) to perform well on the test data in the new domain(target domain).

To address this problem, many algorithms are presented under the framework of transfer learning, and it is a common scenario in speech processing applications and activity recognition problems. Self-labeling approaches include self-training, co-training, and Maximum Likelihood Linear Regression (MLLR). Self-training is based on the Expectation Maximization(EM) algorithm. The basic EM algorithm [6] aims to maximize the log likelihood $log(p(x|\theta))$ of observed data x. The computation of $p(x|\theta)$ depends on some "hidden" or missing variables z. In the transfer learning setting [7,8], we want to maximize the log likelihood $log(p(x|\theta))$ both on the observations of labeled data $(x_i, y_i) \in L$ and unlabeled data $x_i \in U$, with the labels of L as hidden variables. And the relative importance of the

© Springer International Publishing AG 2016
W. Li et al. (Eds.): IDCS 2016, LNCS 9864, pp. 179–189, 2016.
DOI: 10.1007/978-3-319-45940-0_16

labeled and unlabeled data should be traded off. Co-training [9] is a transfer learning method based on the idea of multi-view learning. Two different classifiers are trained based on different "views" (i.e., feature representations). For each classifier, it is used to label new instances from the unlabeled data set and the confident samples are used as another classifier's training data to train a new one on the next round. This process is repeated till the model converged. MLLR is used for speaker adaptation in speech recognition and was first proposed by [10] and [11]. MLLR adapts a Gaussian mixture HMM to new unlabeled speaker data. It assumes that the Gaussian mixture components in the two domains have the corresponding relationship via linear transformation of means and variances in each Gaussian. Therefore, the model can automatically label the target domain data and the old model can be updated. All the above self labeling approaches need to merge the original training data and the predicted samples to retrain a new model. However, with the training data increasing, the training time will be increased. Therefore, an online sequential learning algorithm is promising.

Sequential learning algorithms have also become popular for feedforward networks. These include resource allocation network(RAN) and its extensions. However, all the sequential learning algorithms process data one by one only and cannot process data chunk by chunk basis. In paper [12], an online sequential extreme learning machine(OSELM) is introduced. OSELM can handle the training data in a sequential manner. At any time, only the newly arrived single or chunk of data(instead of the entire past data) are seen and learned. After the learning procedure, the current chunk of data is discarded immediately. Based on these advantages, OSELM is a promising method and will be employed in our SLOSELM.

In this paper, to address the transfer learning and power efficient problem in big data fields, a self labeling online sequential extreme learning machine is presented, which is abbreviated SLOSELM. First, an ELM classifier is trained on the labeled training data set of the source domain. Second, the unlabeled data set of the target domain is classified by the ELM classifier. In the third step, the high confident samples are selected and the OSELM is employed to update the original ELM classifier.

The rest of the paper is organized as follows. In Sect. 2, SLOSELM is presented in detail. In Sect. 3, experiments on SLOSELM is given. Section 4 concludes the paper.

2   SLOSELM: Self Labeling Online Sequential Extreme Learning Machine

SLOSELM consists of three steps: First, on the labeled samples from source domain, an initial ELM classifier is trained. The ELM model's parameters, such as randomly selected input weight vector α, bias vector b, activated function $G(a, b, x)$ and the number of hidden nodes $\tilde{N}$, the hidden layer output matrix H and the output weight β, are reserved. Second, for a chunk of unlabeled samples from target domain, they are classified by the ELM classifier and from the initial classification results, the high confident samples are chosen out. In the third step, based on the high confident samples, OSELM is employed to update the current ELM model. With the unlabeled samples coming chunk by chunk, step 2 to 3 is repeated.

2.1 ELM: Extreme Learning Machine

Figure 1 shows the network structure of ELM(Extreme Learning Machine), it is a SLFNs(Sigle layer feedforward networks). SLFNs have been studied for several decades. Most of the existing methods for training SLFNs, such as the famous back-propagation algorithm and the Levenberg-Marquardt algorithm, employ gradient methods to optimize the weights in the network. Some existing works also use forward selection or backward elimination approaches to construct network dynamically during the training process. However, neither the gradient based methods nor the grow/prune methods guarantee a global optimal solution. Although various methods, such as the generic and evolutionary algorithms, have been proposed to handle the local minimum problem, they basically introduce high computational cost. One of the most successful algorithms for training SLFNs is the support vector machines (SVMs), which is a maximal margin classifier derived under the framework of structural risk minimization (SRM). The dual problem of SVMs is a quadratic programming and can be solved conveniently. Due to its simplicity and stable generalization performance, SVMs have been widely studied and applied to various domains.ELM is a recent neural network algorithm, which is known to achieve good performance in complex problems as well as reduce the computation time compared with other machine learning algorithms [1–5]. The ELM algorithm does not train the input weights or the biases of neurons, but it acquires the output weights by using the norm least-squares solution and Moore-Penrose in verse of a general linear system [15, 16]. By finding the node giving the maximum output value, we decide the final result.

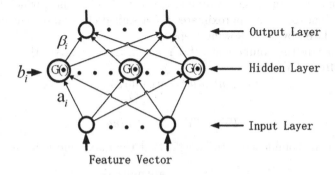

Fig. 1. The network structure of ELM

Algorithm 1. the ELM Algorithm

Require: Given a training set $\aleph = \{(x_i, t_i) | x_i \in R^n, t_i \in R^m, i = 1, 2, \cdots, N\}$,
activation function G(x), and hidden node number $\tilde{N}$.

Ensure:
the weight β.
1: Randomly assign input weight α_i and bias b_i, $i = 1, 2, \cdots, \tilde{N}$.
2: Calculate the hidden layer output matrix H:

$$H = \begin{pmatrix} g(\alpha_1 \cdot x_1 + b_1) & \cdots & g(\alpha_{\tilde{N}} \cdot x_1 + b_{\tilde{N}}) \\ \vdots & \cdots & \vdots \\ g(\alpha_1 \cdot x_N + b_1) & \cdots & g(\alpha_{\tilde{N}} \cdot x_N + b_{\tilde{N}}) \end{pmatrix}_{N \times \tilde{N}}$$

3: Calculate the output weight $\beta = H^\dagger T$, where H is the Moore-Penrose generalized
inverse of matrix H, $T = [t_1, \cdots, t_N]'$.
4: RETURN β

The learning phase for the ELM with a single hidden layer can be summarized
as Algorithm 1.

2.2 Self Labeling the Unlabeled Instances

When the ELM classifier is learned and used to classify a new instance x, the
outputs can be calculated as follows:

$$TY_{1 \times m} = [G(a_1, b_1, x), \cdots, G(a_{\tilde{N}}, b_{\tilde{N}}, x)]_{1 \times \tilde{N}} \cdot \beta_{\tilde{N} \times m}. \tag{1}$$

where m is the number of output nodes, which equals the number of classes in
classification problem, and TY is a vector including m values. Then, the classifier
selects the maximum value of TY and assigns its corresponding index, j, as the
class label of the test instance.

$$j = \arg \min_{j \in [1,m]} TY_j \tag{2}$$

Furthermore, a confidence can be assigned to the instance, which is applied
to show to what extent it approximates the assigned class label. The confidence
can be calculated by the following steps:

(1) To ensure the components of TY are all non-negative, the minimum is
subtracted from TY.

$$MinValue = \arg \min_{TY_j \in TY} TY_j \tag{3}$$

$$TY = TY - MinValue \tag{4}$$

(2) Then the confidence is the weight that the maximum is in the TY.

$$confidence = \frac{\arg \min_{TY_j \in TY} TY_j}{\sum_{TY_j \in TY} TY_j} \tag{5}$$

According to the confidence, the instance can be evaluated. If the confidence is less than a threshold,, the corresponding instance can be seen as a noise and discarded. Otherwise, the instance and its assigned label can be reserved as a sample.

When sufficient enough, the new samples can be used to update the model. We can merge the previous training data and the new samples to rebuild a new classifier. However, in real applications, the training data may arrive chunk-by-chunk, hence, the batch ELM algorithm has to be modified for this case so as to make it online sequential.

2.3   OSELM: Online Sequential Extreme Learning Machine

The ELM described above assumes that all the training data is available for training. However, in real applications, the training data may arrive chunk-by-chunk or one-by-one (a special case of chunk). Therefore, the batch ELM algorithm has to be modified so as to make it online sequential.

Step1: Given a chunk of initial training set:$\aleph_0 = (x_i, t_i)_{i=1}^{N_0}$, assign random input weight a_i and bias b_i, select the activated function G(a,b,x) and hidden node number $\tilde{N}$. the hidden layer output matrix H_0 can be calculated:

$$H_0 = \begin{pmatrix} G(a_1,b_1,x_1) & \cdots & G(a_{\tilde{N}},b_{\tilde{N}},x_1) \\ \vdots & \cdots & \vdots \\ G(a_1,b_1,x_{N_0}) & \cdots & G(a_{\tilde{N}},b_{\tilde{N}},x_{N_0}) \end{pmatrix}_{N_0 \times \tilde{N}} \qquad (6)$$

Then the output weight $\beta_0 = K_0^{-1} H_0^T T_0$, where $K_0 = H_0^T H_0$. And $T_0 = [t_1, t_2, , t_{N_0}]^T$.

Step2: Suppose now that we are given another chunk of data $\aleph_1 = \{(x_i, t_i)\}_{i=N_0+1}^{N_0+N_1}$, then using the a_i, b_i, G, $\tilde{N}$ in Step1, the H_1 can be calculated.

$$H_1 = \begin{pmatrix} G(a_1,b_1,x_{N_0+1}) & \cdots & G(a_{\tilde{N}},b_{\tilde{N}},x_{N_0+1}) \\ \vdots & \cdots & \vdots \\ G(a_1,b_1,x_{N_0+N_1}) & \cdots & G(a_{\tilde{N}},b_{\tilde{N}},x_{N_0+N_1}) \end{pmatrix}_{N_1 \times \tilde{N}} \qquad (7)$$

Further more, we can get the following results:

$$K_1 = \begin{bmatrix} H_0 \\ H_1 \end{bmatrix}^T \begin{bmatrix} H_0 \\ H_1 \end{bmatrix} = [H_0^T H_1^T] \begin{bmatrix} H_0 \\ H_1 \end{bmatrix} = K_0 + H_1^T H \qquad (8)$$

Therefore, the solution is

$$\beta_1 = K_1^{-1} \begin{bmatrix} H_0 \\ H_1 \end{bmatrix}^T \begin{bmatrix} T_0 \\ T_1 \end{bmatrix} = K_1^{-1}(K_1\beta_0 - H_1^T H_1\beta_0 + H_1^T T_1) = \beta_0 + K_1^{-1}H_1^T(T_1 - H_1\beta_0) \qquad (9)$$

As can be seen in Formula 9, β_1 is a function of β_0, K_1, H_1 and T_1, and not a function of the data set $\aleph_0$.

2.4   The Algorithm of SLOSELM

The algorithm of SLOSELM can be described in Algorithm 2.

Algorithm 2. Self Labeling Online Sequential Extreme Learning Machine

---
Require:
    the labeled source domain $D_{src} = \{(x^{(i)}_{src}, t^{(i)}_{src})\}^{N_0}_{i=1}$, where $t^{(i)}_{src}$ is the label of $x^{(i)}_{src}$.
    the unlabeled target domain $D_{tar} = \{(x^{(i)}_{tar}\}^{N_1}_{i=1}$, does not have any labeled samples.
    Only the instance number of D_{tar} is larger than a threshold, η, the self labeling
    algorithm is applied.

Ensure:
    the weight β.
1: Assign random input weight a_i and bias b_i, select the activated function G(a,b,x)
    and hidden node number $\tilde{N}$.
2: calculate $H_0 = \begin{pmatrix} G(a_1, b_1, x_1) & \cdots & G(a_{\tilde{N}}, b_{\tilde{N}}, x_1) \\ \vdots & \cdots & \vdots \\ G(a_1, b_1, x_{N_0}) & \cdots & G(a_{\tilde{N}}, b_{\tilde{N}}, x_{N_0}) \end{pmatrix}_{N_0 \times \tilde{N}}$. Set k=0.
3: **while** $|D_{tar}| > \eta$ **do**
4:    **for** each x in $D_{tar} = \{x^{(i)}_{tar}\}^{N_2}_{i=1}$ **do**
5:      $TY_{1 \times m} = [G(a_1, b_1, x), \cdots, G(a_{\tilde{N}}, b_{\tilde{N}}, x)]_{1 \times \tilde{N}} \cdot \beta_{\tilde{N} \times m}$
6:      $j = \arg \min TY_j$, j is the predicted label of x.
         $\scriptstyle j \in [1,m]$
7:      $MinValue = \arg \min_{TY_j \in TY} TY_j$;
8:      $TY = TY - MinValue$;
9:      $confidence = \arg \min_{TY_j \in TY} TY_j / \sum_{TY_j \in TY} TY_j$
10:     **if** confidence>0.5 **then**
11:       HConfSet=HConfSet+x;
12:       $D_{tar} = D_{tar} - x$;
13:     **end if**
14:    **end for**
15:    k=k+1;
16:    According to high confident data set, HconfSet, calculate
     $H_k = \begin{pmatrix} G(a_1 \cdot x^1_{|HConfSet|} + b_1) & \cdots & G(a_{\tilde{N}} \cdot x^1_{|HConfSet|} + b_{\tilde{N}}) \\ \vdots & \cdots & \vdots \\ G(a_1 \cdot x^N_{|HConfSet|} + b_1) & \cdots & G(a_{\tilde{N}} \cdot x^N_{|HConfSet|} + b_{\tilde{N}}) \end{pmatrix}_{N \times \tilde{N}}$
17:    $K_k = K_{k-1} + H_k^T H_k$
18:    $\beta_k = \beta_{k-1} + K_k^{-1} H_k^T (T_k - H_k \beta_{-1})$
19: **end while**
20: RETURN β

---

3   Experiments

In this section, the SLOSELM was tested on a activity dataset. The data in
that dataset is collected from accelerometer based activity recognition field, in
which the model trained on the data from some specific locations can not well
distinguish the data from other locations.

3.1   Data Collection

In our experiments, Nokia N95 8GB mobile phones are used to collect the accelerometer data. An activity databaset is built from the data collected from these devices. In this database, there are 4 participants and 5 activities. The sliding window with 50 % overlapping method is used to extract the features. The sampling frequency of N95 accelerometer sensor has been reduced to approximately 32 Hz by calling the Nokia Accelerometers plug-in API. Our chosen window size is two seconds and the overlapping time is one second. Thus a complete action can be included in the window. Feature extraction on windows with 50 % overlapping has demonstrated successful in previous work [18].

3.2   Feature Extraction

For triaxial accelerometer, the output voltages can be mapped into acceleration along three axes, a_x, a_y, a_z. As a_x, a_y, a_z are the orthogonal decompositions of real acceleration, the magnitude of synthesized acceleration can be expressed as: $a = \sqrt{a_x^2 + a_y^2 + a_z^2}$, where a is the magnitude of real acceleration, but has no directional information. Therefore, the acceleration magnitude based activity recognition model is orientation independent. Based on the acceleration magnitude series, 17 statistic features [19] are extracted from a sliding window of 256 samples with 50 % overlapping between consecutive windows. These features are mean, standard deviation, energy, mean-crossing rate, maximum value, minimum value, first quartile, second quartile, third quartile, four amplitude statistic features and four shape statistic features of the power spectral density (PSD)[20]. In addition, based on FFT transformation of the acceleration magnitude series, all frequency components from 1 Hz to 128 Hz are extracted and added into the feature vector, totally 145 features. To eliminate the scaling effects among different features, all the features are normalized using the z-score normalization algorithm.

The number of samples of every activity are listed in Table 1.

Table 1. The information of daily activity samples.

Activity Name	Label	Number of Samples
Staying Still	1	4520
Downstairs	2	4293
Walking	3	4327
Running	4	4245
Upstairs	5	4369

3.3   Performance Evaluation

The performance of SLOSELM is evaluated on the data set described above. Three evaluations are conducted in this experiment: cross-validating ELM model on different locations, performance comparison between applying and not applying SLOSELM. All the simulations have been done on the MATLAB2009a environment running on an ordinary PC with 2.6GHz CPU. The source code of ELM and OSELM are download from Professor Huang's page[1]. The sigmoid function is used as the activation function. In the following experiments, 100 is selected as the optimal number of hidden nodes.

Performance Evaluation of ELM: Cross Location Validation. In this section, the experiments aim to test the ELM algorithms's ability to recognize activity data from different locations. Three locations, Hand, Chest Pocket and Trousers Pocket, are presented as A, B and C. The data sets of these locations are represented as $Data_A$, $Data_B$ and $Data_C$, respectively. Each data set is randomly divided into two equal parts, which are represented as $Data_{A1}$ and $Data_{A2}$, $Data_{B1}$ and $Data_{B2}$, and $Data_{C1}$ and $Data_{C2}$.

Without loss of generality, we first assume that A and B are known locations and C is a new one. $Train_{AB}$, which equals $Data_{A1} \bigcup Data_{B1}$, is used to train an ELM model. Then, the ELM model is tested on $Test_{AB}$, which equals $Data_{A2} \bigcup Data_{B2}$, and $Data_C$ respectively. The process is repeated three times and each location is made as the new location in turn. The experiment results are listed in Table 2.

Table 2. ELM recognition results on the known and unknown locations.

TrainData	TestData from known loc	Acc on known loc	TestData from unknown loc	Acc on unknown loc
$Train_{AB}$	$Test_{AB}$	81.07 %	$Data_C$	67.85 %
$Train_{BC}$	$Test_{BC}$	88.41 %	$Data_A$	62.02 %
$Train_{AC}$	$Test_{AC}$	74.53 %	$Data_B$	64.08 %
Mean Accuracy		81.34 %		64.65 %

As can be seen from Table 2, while the test data come from the distribution as training data, the recognition accuracy is high. However, while they come from the different distribution, the accuracy is poor. Therefore, the cross location activity recognition problem should be under the transfer learning framework.

Performance Evaluation of SLOSELM: Cross Location Validation. In this section, the experiments aim to test the SLOSELM algorithms's transfer

---

[1] Source codes and some references of ELM can be found at www.ntu.edu.sg/home/ egbhuang.

learning ability to new locations. $Train_{AB}$ is used as the source domain and $Data_{C1}$ as the target domain. First, an initial ELM model is built on $Train_{AB}$. Second, the ELM model is employed to classify $Data_{C1}$, the confidence of each sample is calculated, and among them, 25 high confident samples are selected to do the online sequential learning. The second step repeats until there are no sufficient samples in $Data_{C1}$.

The performances of the initial model and the new model on the known locations are shown in Table 3.

Table 3. Recognition results on the known locations.

Not Using SLOSELM			Using SLOSELM		
TrainData	TestData	Accuracy	TrainData	TestData	Accuracy
$Train_{AB}$	$Test_{AB}$	81.07 %	$Train_{AB} + HConf_{C1}$	$Test_{AB}$	80.91 %
$Train_{BC}$	$Test_{BC}$	88.41 %	$Train_{BC} + HConf_{A1}$	$Test_{BC}$	87.06 %
$Train_{AC}$	$Test_{AC}$	74.53 %	$Train_{AC} + HConf_{B1}$	$Test_{AC}$	73.98 %

We can see that after model adaptation, the new model almost has the same classification capability as the initial model.

The performances of the initial model and the new model on the new location are shown in Table 4.

Table 4. Recognition results on the unknown locations.

Not Using SLOSELM			Using SLOSELM		
TrainData	TestData	Accuracy	TrainData	TestData	Accuracy
$Train_{AB}$	$Test_{C2}$	67.85 %	$Train_{AB} + HConf_{C1}$	$Test_{C2}$	77.99 %
$Train_{BC}$	$Test_{A2}$	62.02 %	$Train_{BC} + HConf_{A1}$	$Test_{A2}$	73.21 %
$Train_{AC}$	$Test_{B2}$	64.08 %	$Train_{AC} + HConf_{B1}$	$Test_{B2}$	75.82 %

We can see that after model adaptation, accuracy is improved about 11 %.

4   Conclusion and Future Work

In this paper, to address the transfer learning problem, a fast and robust algorithm named as SLOSELM is presented. It can build ELM model on the source domain and transfer the inherent knowledge of the same field to the target domain. And then, it can classify the samples of the target domain and select the high confident samples to online sequentially update the ELM model. Experimental results demonstrate that SLOSELM improves the recognition accuracy obviously without any knowledge of new locations.

In the future, we have the interests in testing our algorithm on different platform, such as iOS, Android and Mobile phone platform, the aim is to construct a universal activity recognition system.

Acknowledgements. This work is supported in part by the National Natural Science Foundation of China (Grant No.U1504609), by the Key Scientific and Technological Project of the Higher Education Institutions of He'nan Province, China (Grant No.15A520003).

References

1. Zong, W., Huang, G., Chen, Y.: Weighted extreme learning machine for imbalance learning. Neurocomputing **101**, 229–242 (2013)
2. Huang, G., Song, S., You, K.: Trends in extreme learning machines: a review. Neural Netw. **61**(1), 32–48 (2015)
3. Huang, Z., Yu, Y., Gu, J., Liu, H.: An efficient method for traffic sign recognition based on extreme learning machine. IEEE Trans. Cybern. (2016)
4. Huang, G.: What are extreme learning machines? filling the gap between Frank Rosenblatt's dream and John von Neumann's puzzle. Cogn. Comput. **7**, 263–278 (2015)
5. Huang, G., Bai, Z., Kasun, L., Vong, C.: Local receptive fields based extreme learning machine. IEEE Comput. Intell. Mag. **10**(2), 18–29 (2015)
6. Dempster, A., Laird, N., Rubin, D.: Maximum likelihood from incomplete data via the em algorithm. J. Roy. Stat. Soc. Ser. B **39**(1), 1–38 (1977)
7. Zhu, Y., Zhong, E., Pan, S., et al.: Predicting user activity level in social networks. In: Proceedings of the 22nd ACM International Conference on Conference on Information & Knowledge Management, pp. 159–168. ACM (2013)
8. Nigam, K., McCallum, A., Thrun, S., Mitchell, T.: Text classification from labeled and unlabeled documents using EM. Mach. Learn. **39**, 103–134 (2000)
9. Blum, A., Mitchell, T.: Combining labeled and unlabeled data with co-training. In: Proceedings of the Eleventh Annual Conference on Computational Learning Theory, COLT 1998, (New York, NY, USA), pp. 92–100. ACM (1998)
10. Leggetter, C., Woodland, P.: Maximum likelihood linear regression for speaker adaptation of continuous density hidden Markov models. Comput. Speech Lang. **9**(2), 171–185 (1995)
11. Digalakis, V., Rtischev, D., Neumeye, L.: Speaker adaptation using constrained estimation of Gaussian mixtures. IEEE Trans. Speech Audio Process. **3**, 357–366 (1995)
12. Liang, N., Huang, G., Saratchandran, P., Sundararajan, N.: fast and accurate online sequential learning algorithm for feedforward networks. IEEE Trans. Neural Netw. **17**, 1411–1423 (2006)
13. Huang, G., Wang, D., Lan, Y.: Extreme learning machines: a survey. Int. J. Mach. Learn. Cybern. **2**(2), 107–122 (2011)
14. Huang, G., Zhu, Q., Siew, C.: Extreme learning machine: theory and applications. Neurocomputing **70**, 489–501 (2006)
15. Feng, G., Huang, G., Lin, Q., Gay, R.: Error minimized extreme learning machine with growth of hidden nodes and incremental learning. IEEE Trans. Neural Netw. **20**(8), 1352–1357 (2009)
16. Huang, G., Ding, X., Zhou, H.: Optimization method based extreme learning machine for classification. Neurocomputing **74**, 155–163 (2010)
17. Roggen, D., Magnenat, S., Waibel, M., Troster, G.: Designing and sharing activity-recognition systems across platforms. IEEE Robot. Autom. Mag. **18**, 83–95 (2011)

18. Bao, L., Intille, S.S.: Activity recognition from user-annotated acceleration data. In: Ferscha, A., Mattern, F. (eds.) PERVASIVE 2004. LNCS, vol. 3001, pp. 1–17. Springer, Heidelberg (2004)
19. Figo, D., Diniz, P., Ferreira, D., Cardoso, J.: Preprocessing techniques for context recognition from accelerometer data. Pers. Ubiquit. Comput. **14**, 645–662 (2010)
20. Wang, X.: High accuracy distributed target detection and classification in sensor networks based on mobile agent framework. Ph.D. thesis, University of Tennessee (2004)

Distributed Scheduling and Optimization

A Modified Genetic Algorithm for Agricultural By-products Logistics Delivery Route Planning Problem

Guofu Luo, Dayuan Wu, Jun Ma[✉], and Xiaoyu Wen

Mechanical and Electrical Engineering Institute, Zhengzhou University of Light Industry,
Zhengzhou, People's Republic of China
luoguofu@zzuli.edu.cn, {wudayuan,68087876}@qq.com,
majunfirst@sohu.com

Abstract. Agricultural by-products collection and delivery route planning is one of the important issues of delivery scheduling optimization for agricultural regional logistics. Aimed at agricultural by-products logistics delivery route planning problem, traditional genetic algorithm was modified by using operator dynamic adjustment methods. The modified Genetic Algorithm (GA) selected different crossover operators, mutation operators and selection pressure with generation growth, which avoided the local optima problem of traditional GA when the chromosome length was long. Compiled script program and tested with Matlab, the modified GA has higher solution accuracy in agricultural logistics model compared with traditional GA.

Keywords: Agricultural by-products · Modified · Logistics · Vehicle Routing Problem · Genetic Algorithm · Dynamic operator

1 Introduction

Agricultural by-products are produced by agricultural production, which include agriculture, forestry, husbandry, fishery, and spinoff products. Tremendous and various agricultural by-products are needed in our daily lives to keep society operating and stable. Therefore, the logistics of agricultural by-products has a great significant. However, the production and retail sites of agricultural by-products are numerous and scattered. The logistics are of low quality, high cost, poor infrastructure, low level of informatization and so on. And the transportation and handling of agricultural by-products are more complex than that of industrial products because one deliver will often have multiple pick-up sites and repeated loading and unloading process [1]. Thus, planning logistics route of agricultural by-products scientifically can effectively avoid the backlog of goods, detour of vehicles, none-load transportation and other negative phenomena [2]. At present, more than 80 % of meat and aquatic products are in a non-cold-chain transportation and marketing state in China, which caused great loss in transport links [3]. And it is necessary to plan the collection and delivery arrangement order based on the physical and biological properties of agricultural by-products. As for delivery of some perishable agricultural by-products, such as lychee, fresh meat and dairy products, routes should be planned scientifically lest the time of non-cold-chain

W. Li et al. (Eds.): IDCS 2016, LNCS 9864, pp. 193–205, 2016.
DOI: 10.1007/978-3-319-45940-0_17

transportation is too long. Therefore, the agricultural by-products delivery vehicle route planning problems are urgent to be solved.

Agricultural by-products delivery vehicle routing problem (VRP) is NP-complete problem [4], which can be solved effectively by GA. GA simulates the process of biological evolution by computer compiling to search and select the optimal solution. It can solve many problems, such as NP-complete problem and multi-objective optimization problem that cannot be solved by mathematical theory. Vitoria P. et al. aimed at multiple deliverymen of beverage transportation and vehicle routing problem with time window (VRPTW), used Tabu Search and Ant Colony Optimization (ACO) to obtain minimum cost route in [5]; Boon E.T. et al. modified GA with local search method, which made GA can discover new areas and refined search results in [6]; Ferani E.Z. et al. optimized VRPTW via hybrid ACO and GA, set fuzzy variables and used local search algorithms in [7]; Sun H.P. et al. ensured population diversity by initializing population with Grefenstette code, and modified GA with edge reconfiguration-simple crossover operator in [8]; Qiu R.Z. et al. established an agricultural products logistics model, and optimized the solution with GIS and Tabu Search in [9]; Yu Y.Y. et al. initialized population with greedy algorithm and modified GA with parameters adaptive adjustment and elite individual retention in [10].

However, the researches above were mostly aiming at less sites models. Traditional GA easily falls into local optima in the case of long chromosomes due to monotonous method of crossover and mutation. Aimed at this problem, traditional GA was modified combined with the characteristics of agricultural by-products logistics in this paper. The modified GA has a strong optimization capacity for long chromosomes population, avoiding premature convergence effectively.

2 Agricultural By-products Logistics Mathematical Modeling Description

In this paper, the research object is agricultural by-products VRP. Fully loaded trucks depart from agricultural by-products depot, and deliver to every retail site. When the remains are insufficient to supply to the next retail site or the next site is too far, trucks can choose to return to the depot and prepare for the next round. Thus, agricultural by-products logistics and deliver problems can be seen as a capacitated vehicle routing problem (CVRP). Furthermore, the relative values of agricultural by-products are low, and it is difficult to realize full cold chain in the whole transportation. Thus perishable grades of agricultural by-products should also be considered to arrange delivery route, prior delivering perishable products.

According to actual agricultural by-products logistics, a four-subscript mathematical model was established: At most M ($m = 1,2,...,M$) trucks depart from agricultural by-products depot, delivering variety of agricultural by-products to I ($i = 1,2,...,I$) retail sites, $i = 0$ representing the depot. Each trucks' maximum load are w_m ($m = 1,2,...,M$), and the amount of input in each retail site is q_i ($i = 1,2,...,I$), and the cost of fuel consumption from i to j is f_{ij}. Each retail is divided into V ($v = 1,2,...,V$) grades according to perishable grades and the types of purchased product. Two variables in this model are as formulas 1 and 2:

$$x_{im} = \begin{cases} 1, & \text{client } i \text{ was dilivered by truck } m \\ 0, & \text{else} \end{cases} \tag{1}$$

$$y_{ijmv} = \begin{cases} 1, & \text{truck } m \text{ visited } j \text{ from } i \text{ delivered } v \\ 0, & \text{else} \end{cases} \tag{2}$$

Restrictions were established according to the descriptions of model and settings of variables:

$$x_{im} = 1 \text{ or } 0, \quad \forall i, m \tag{3}$$

$$y_{ijmv} = 1 \text{ or } 0, \quad \forall i, j, m, v \tag{4}$$

$$\sum_{i=1}^{I} q_i x_{im} \leq w_m, \quad \forall m \tag{5}$$

$$\sum_{m=1}^{M} x_{im} = 1, \quad \forall i \tag{6}$$

$$\sum_{i=1}^{I} y_{ijmv} = x_{im}, \quad \forall i, m \tag{7}$$

$$\sum_{i=1}^{I} y_{ijmv} = x_{jm}, \quad \forall j, m \tag{8}$$

$$\sum_{i,j \in N \times N} y_{ijmv} \leq |N| - 1, N \in \{1, 2, \cdots, I\}, \forall m \tag{9}$$

Formulas 3 and 4 are domains of variables, formula 5 ensuring that every truck meets the load constraints, formula 6 ensuring that each agricultural retail site will be delivered once, formulas 7 and 8 ensuring that each retail site will be delivered one kind of agricultural by-products by one truck, formula 9 being sub-loop elimination operation.

At present, the purpose to plan truck route for agricultural by-products logistics enterprises is to save fuel and to reduce delivery time, and perishable grades of agricultural by-products should also be considered. Thus the objective function can be designed as formula 10.

$$\min S(y) = \sum_{m=1}^{M} \sum_{i=1}^{I} \sum_{j=1}^{I} K_v f_{ij} y_{ijmv} \tag{10}$$

3   Methods of Modified GA

3.1   Modified GA Dynamic Adjustment Operator

The method of modified GA was to divide algorithm into n stages according to the generations, adjust crossover and mutation operator dynamically at each stage, and adjust crossover probabilities and mutation probabilities as well. Different retention choice strategies were used at different stages. Change selection pressure and external environment artificially to make population evolve to the direction which researchers designed. In order to achieve the design goals above, the modified GA took the maximum evolution generation *MaxGen* as the limit criterion, and divided the algorithm into *n* stages according to generation percentage.

The whole modified algorithm was divided into three phases. In prophase phases, search solution extensively to approximate the whole population to the optimal solution, which provided a relative good population for later phases. In metaphase phases, in order to improve genetic diversity of population, it reduced selection pressure, slowed down the population convergence rate, and expanded the search scope. In anaphase phases, due to optimal solution usually hidden in short chromosome segments, it reduced crossover probability, and improved mutation probability.

Different with known optimal solution VRP cases, agricultural logistics delivery enterprises didn't know the optimal solution when receiving orders. Thus the algorithm couldn't set the optimum value as the termination conditions, and the maximum evolution generation *MaxGen* should be set as termination conditions. The modified genetic algorithm process was described in Fig. 1.

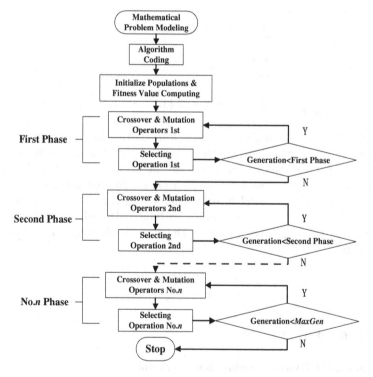

Fig. 1. Modified GA process

Modified method of the algorithm was described in detail as follows.

Step1:   Initialize population, and calculate its fitness value
Step2:   Set probability of crossover *pc*1 and probability of mutation *pm*1, and conduct first phase crossover and mutation operators with initial population
Step3:   Conduct first phase selection operation with population after crossover and mutation, and build a new population
Step4:   If the generation is greater than the first phase limit, enter second phase; If generation smaller than the first phase limit, back to Step3
Step5:   Reset probability of crossover *pc*2 and probability of mutation *pm*2, and conduct first phase crossover and mutation operators with initial population
Step6:   Conduct first phase selection operator with population after crossover and mutation, and build a new population
Step7:   If the generation is greater than the first phase limit, enter second phase. If generation smaller than the first phase limit, back to Step6

.....

Step(m-2):   Reset crossover probability $pc(n)$ and mutation probability $pm(n)$, and conduct No.n phase crossover and mutation operators with population
Step(m-1):   Conduct No.n phase selection operator with population after crossover and mutation, and build a new population
Step(m):   If the generation is greater than *MaxGen*, jump out of evolving functions and output known optimal value. If not, back to Step(m-2)

3.2   Encoded Chromosome and Initialized Population

Chromosome is carrier of genetic information. For a mathematical model in which one truck delivers all retail sites, each retail site with sequence number is a gene. Arrange all the sequence numbers of retail sites into a matrix that has one row and multiple columns without repeat, which constitutes a chromosome and the length *BitLength* is the total amount of retail sites. Every chromosome expresses the sequence of the vehicle visit to each retail site.

Set the population size as *PopSize*. When initializing population, it randomly generates a matrix with *PopSize* rows and *BitLength* columns as initial population.

3.3   Fitness Value Function

Fitness function is an evaluation criterion of individual quality. Construct the fitness value function by total distance of the truck, the smaller the function values are, the better solutions are. Thus the objective function can be written as formula 11.

$$fitness = \sum_{i=1}^{BitLength} \sqrt{\left(x_{i+1} - x_i\right)^2 + \left(y_{i+1} - y_i\right)^2} \qquad (11)$$

3.4   Modified GA Crossover Operators

The function of crossover operator is to exchange segments between each two chromosomes. It can increase diversity of the population.

In prophase phases of modified GA, in order to make the population fast converge to local optimal solution slowly, single point sequential crossover operation was used in the first phase and the second phase to cross parental chromosome with crossover probability $pc = 0.9$. This operator is characterized by a relatively large impact on chromosomes. It is conducive to the emergence of new chromosomes. The specific step is shown as Fig. 2.

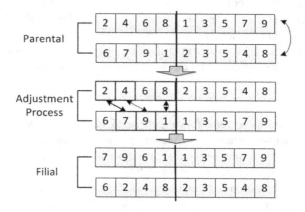

Fig. 2. Single point sequential crossover operator

In anaphase phases, the difference between individuals in population mainly existed in short chromosome segments, and thus double point sequential crossover operator was used as crossover method in the third phase with crossover probability $pc = 0.8$. This operator is characterized by doing crossover operation in a relative short segment, and it has more probability to retain quality gene segments, exploring and discovering new quality chromosomes. The specific step is shown as Fig. 3.

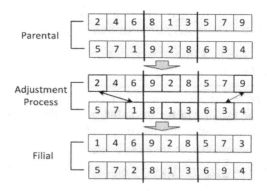

Fig. 3. Double point sequential crossover operator

3.5 Modified GA Mutation Operators

In order to create new chromosomes, mutation operators were designed and encoded in the method. They can generate undiscovered chromosomes that cannot create by cross-over procedures.

Head-tail transposition mutation operator was used in the first phase of modified GA with mutation probability $pm = 0.05$. This operator has a great change in chromosomes structural, and it will have some impact on entire population. The mutation method is shown in Fig. 4.

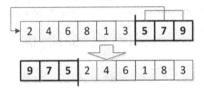

Fig. 4. Head-tail transposition mutation operator

Random interval disorder mutation operator was used in the second phase with $pm = 0.10$. This operator can disrupt and rearrange genes in a random interval. Because the length of the interval is determined randomly, the degree of influence of the operator on the individual is also uncertain, and thus the operator has a stronger global random traversal capability. But the search speed of this operator is slower, so the evolutionary generation of second phase design is relatively more. The mutation method is shown in Fig. 5.

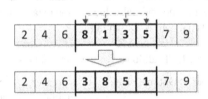

Fig. 5. Random interval disorder mutation operator

Random double point mutation operator was used in the third phase with $pm = 0.15$. In the metaphases and anaphases of GA, population tends to be stable, and adjusting chromosome in partial that can find the optimal solution more accurately. The mutation method is shown in Fig. 6.

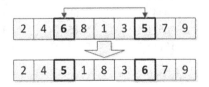

Fig. 6. Random double point mutation operator

3.6   Modified GA Selection Modes

In the first phase of the algorithm, selection method only retained one optimal individual which came from parental and filial population after crossover and mutation, and replaced one individual in parental population randomly.

The main goal of the metaphases was to expand search scope, preventing the population from convergence to local optimal solution. Thus in the second phase, retain one optimal individual from parental and the other from filial population after crossover and mutation, as new population.

In the third phase, retain two optimal individuals from parental and filial population after crossover and mutation, and accelerate the convergence speed of the algorithm to optimal solution.

In these three phases, the methods of extracting individual are roulette.

4   Experiments and Results

In order to verify the performance of the modified algorithm, 100 groups of random coordinate points were taken as a model, located in the 1800×1200 region. It can be assumed that a truck has enough travel distance and goods, delivering all sites from the depot, visiting each site only once, and finally returning to the depot.

Firstly, traditional GA was used to solve the model. Set $PopSize = 500$, $MaxGen = 10000$. Run 10 times in a row. Each optimal value, convergence generation and intersection quantity in optimal path figure are shown in Table 1. Relative optimal solution 14447 was searched in eighth experiment. The optimal value and the mean value of the past generations are shown in Fig. 7, the optimal path is shown in Fig. 8.

Table 1. Traditional GA experimental results

Sequence number	Optimal value	Convergence generation	Intersection quantity
1	14616	6602	9
2	15389	6102	10
3	14971	5835	12
4	16835	5179	8
5	15609	6612	12
6	17358	4893	13
7	15917	6670	13
8	14447	6268	5
9	16571	5485	11
10	15114	5464	12

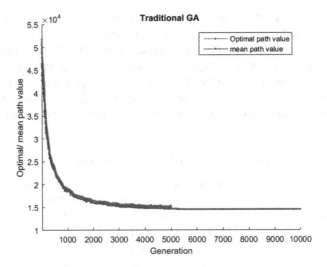

Fig. 7. Traditional GA optimal/mean value

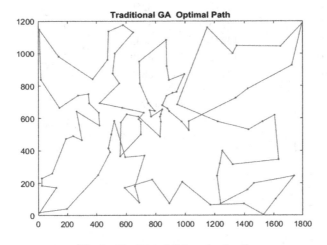

Fig. 8. Traditional GA optimal path

The intersection numbers in optimal path figures give expression to the quality of the results. The less intersection in the figure, the shorter total distance it is generally, the higher quality the result is.

According to Fig. 7, traditional GA searched optimal solution in a single way, so the algorithm was approaching known optimal solution fast at the beginning but reached stable around 2000th generation, and finally converging to the local optimal solution 14447 at 5383th generation. From Fig. 8, it can be seen that the relative optimal path is in a mess and there are 5 intersecting points, which means there must be a better solution for this model.

Then use modified GA based on dynamic operators to solve the model. The modified algorithm was divided into 3 phases, 1 ~ 10 %*MaxGen*, 10 %*MaxGen* ~ 80 %*MaxGen* and 80 %*MaxGen* ~ *MaxGen*. Set *PopSize* = 500, *MaxGen* = 10000. Run the modified program 10 times in a row, and each optimal value, convergence generation and intersection quantity in modified GA optimal path figure are shown in Table 2. Relative optimal solution 12263 was searched in the fifth experiment. The optimal value and mean value of past generations are shown in Fig. 9, and the optimal path is shown in Fig. 10.

Table 2. Modified GA experimental results

Sequence number	Optimal value	Convergence generation	Intersection quantity
1	13141	8437	4
2	12890	9307	4
3	12564	9421	2
4	13005	8196	5
5	12263	9254	1
6	12972	8256	4
7	12726	8721	3
8	13231	8643	6
9	13182	8549	4
10	13435	8876	5

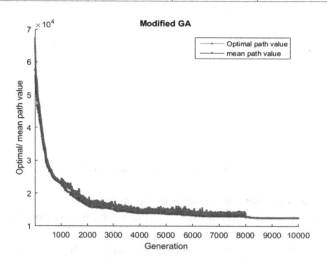

Fig. 9. Modified GA optimal/mean value

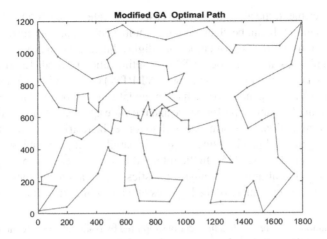

Fig. 10. Modified GA optimal path

It could be seen that the speed of approaching the known best solution was relatively fast in first phase and the optimal value rush at 24000 around. Then the modified algorithm expands the scope of the search population in the second phase, the optimal value approaching the known optimal solution gradually and smoothly. In the third phase, the modified algorithm began to execute local search codes. There were several obvious breakthroughs between 8000th generation and 8300th generation, and finally the approximate optimal solution 12263 was searched in fifth experiment. The optimal path is shown in Fig. 10, and it is an ideal path for there is only one intersecting points.

Comparing Table 1 with Table 2 which shows that traditional GA was difficult to search the relative optimal solution in limited generation and each test result was inaccurate and volatile. The modified GA with dynamic operators could calculate and output an ideal path in the limited generation. The experimental results of modified algorithm were relatively accurate and concentrated and the optimal value floated around 12500.

5   Conclusions and Further Work

The modified GA used dynamic adjustment operators method, which could change search scale and scope dynamically. Compared with traditional GA, it had a significant improvement in the accuracy of search for relative optimal solution of long chain chromosomes model. The experiments showed that the modified GA could break the evolutionary equilibrium effectively, break through local optima, and jump to the global optimal solution by using the dynamic operators. Subsequent researchers can adjust the dynamic operators and continue to improve the algorithm. It can take intersection number into the modified algorithm, once there is a intersecting point, exchange intersecting lines' endpoints and reverse order arrange the relevant chromosome segment, then the result must be a better one. Furthermore, the algorithm can also be advanced by machine learning based on support vector machine, which can adjust and improve parameters of the algorithm automatically [11].

In this experiment, the algorithm of the case is a single vehicle load unlimited path optimization method. It can be changed into a multi-vehicle path optimization method or more restrictions optimization method with slight adjustments, such as vehicle routing problem with pickups and deliveries (VRPPD) optimization method [12] or capacitated vehicle routing problem with time window (CVRPTW) optimization method [13]. The population of GA is independent of each other, and it can be processed in parallel. With the improvement of computer performance and the wide application of cloud computing technology, computational performance will no longer be restricted. It can improve the speed of solving the problem by using large scale parallel computation [14] and distributed computation technology [15]. In the future, the modified GA can be applied in the construction of agricultural by-products logistics information platform, which has important significance to improve the logistics efficiency of agricultural by-products.

Acknowledgments. The research is financially supported by National Key Technology Support Program Project "Research Development and Applied Demonstration of Regional Logistics Information Service Integration Platform for Agricultural By-products" (Project ID: 2014BAH24F03).

References

1. Badia, M.R., Garcia, H.J., Ruiz, G.L., Jimenez, A.T., Villalba, J.I.R., Barreiro, P.: Assessing the dynamic behavior of WSN motes and RFID semi-passive tags for temperature monitoring. Comput. Electron. Agric. **103**, 11–16 (2014)
2. Yong, C.: SLP method based on low-carbon logistics in professional agricultural logistics park layout. In: Proceedings of International Conference on Low-carbon Transportation and Logistics, and Green Buildings, pp. 1063–1068 (2013)
3. Bao, J., Liu, C.: Study on the development of agricultural products cold chain logistics. In: International Conference on Mechatronics, Electronic, Industrial and Control Engineering, pp. 1667–1670 (2014)
4. Jean, F.C., Gilbert, L., Martin, W.P.S., Daniele, V.: Vehicle Routing. In: Barnhart, C., Laporte, G. (eds.) Handbooks in Operations Research and Management Science, vol. 14, pp. 367–428. Elsevier, Amsterdam (2007)
5. Vitoria, P., Reinaldo, M., Marc, R.: Vehicle routing with multiple deliverymen: modeling and heuristic approaches for the VRPTW. Eur. J. Oper. Res. **218**(3), 636–647 (2012)
6. Boon, E.T., Ponnambalam, S.G., Kanagaraj, G.: Differential evolution algorithm with local search for capacitated vehicle routing problem. Int. J. Bio Inspired Comput. **7**(5), 321–342 (2015)
7. Ferani, E.Z., Kuo, R.J., Hu, T.L.: Solving CVRP with time window, fuzzy travel time and demand via a hybrid ant colony optimization and genetic algorithm. In: Proceedings of 2012 IEEE World Congress on Computational Intelligencen (2012)
8. Sun, H.P., Li, J., Guo, W.G.: An improved generic algorithm for solving traveling salesman problems. Math. Pract. Theor. **39**(4), 127–133 (2009)
9. Qiu, R.Z., Zhong, C.E., Xiu, X.H.: Optimization of vehicle routing problem for agriculture products logistics distribution based on the integration technology of GIS and tabu search. Math. Pract. Theor. **41**(10), 145–152 (2011)
10. Yu, Y.Y., Chen, Y., Li, T.Y.: Improved genetic algorithm for solving TSP. Control Decis. **29**(8), 1483–1488 (2014)

11. Simone, S., Roberto, F., Paolo, D.L., Massimo, P., Aurelio, U.: Distributed semi-supervised support vector machines. Neural Netw. Off. J. Int. Neural Netw. Soc. **80**, 43–52 (2016)
12. Yanik, S., Bozkaya, B., Dekervenoael, R.: A new VRPPD model and a hybrid heuristic solution approach for e-tailing. Eur. J. Oper. Res. **236**(3), 879–890 (2014)
13. Selma, K.H., Christian, P., Alice, Y., Mohamed, R.: Heuristics and memetic algorithm for the two-dimensional loading capacitated vehicle routing problem with time windows. Cen. Eur. J. Oper. Res. **21**(2), 307–336 (2013)
14. Boyle, E., Chung, K.-M., Pass, R.: Large-scale Secure computation: multi-party computation for (Parallel) RAM programs. In: Gennaro, R., Robshaw, M. (eds.) CRYPTO 2015. LNCS, vol. 9216, pp. 742–762. Springer, Heidelberg (2015)
15. Juan, A.A., Faulin, J., Jorba, J., Caceres, J., Marques, J.M.: Using parallel and distributed computing for real-time solving of vehicle routing problems with stochastic demands. Ann. Oper. Res. **207**(1), 43–65 (2013)

Multi-objective Optimization of Warehouse System Based on the Genetic Algorithm

Ting Wu$^{(\boxtimes)}$, Hao Wang, and Zhe Yuan

City College of WUST, Wuhan, China
wut0208@163.com, {405598277,779423510}@qq.com

Abstract. As a unit of modern warehouse, the Automated Storage/Retrieval system(AS/RS) plays an important role in modern logistic system. Especially in case of thousands of goods locations, the slotting optimization of warehouse storage system is a crucial step to improve the access efficiency and to reduce the operating costs. With the tiered warehouse as the research subject, this paper firstly analyzed and extracted the key information of related goods location optimization in the warehouse management information system. Then a space optimization model was built, with goods turnover efficiency and stabilities being set as research objectives. By using the MATLAB genetic algorithm toolbox, the multi-objective optimization and simulation of the warehouse system is conducted. Through comparison and analysis of optimization results, the algorithm is finally proved to be applicable.

Keywords: Slotting optimization · Multi-objective optimization · Genetic algorithm · Weight coefficient variation method · Simulation

1 Introduction

With the rapid development of modern logistics technology and great increase of logistics volume, the situation of intensive labor and low efficiency for traditional warehousing industry has been totally changed. The efficiency of modern tiered warehouse is determined by the allocation strategy of warehouse district and goods distribution. A proper layout design of warehouse and reasonable allocation strategy will greatly improve the storage efficiency and reduce the cost, which is a guarantee for the warehouse to achieve modern management and improve its function [1]. The related theory and research methods have become a debated research topic in modern logistics.

In 2010, Gu et al. conceived a random storage policy for the designing of warehouse layout [2]. Larson et al. devised a class-based storage method in designing stage [3]. Lai considered a paper reel layout problem to model the storage assignment problem. The objective is to minimize the transportation cost. In order to solve this N-P hard problem, a simulated annealing method is proposed [4]. Additionally, Sooksaksun et al. [5] developed a particle swarm algorithm for the calss-based storage warehouse optimization. However, these methods are provided to solve the single objective optimization, which could not reflect comprehensive effects of conditions, such as the travel

© Springer International Publishing AG 2016
W. Li et al. (Eds.): IDCS 2016, LNCS 9864, pp. 206–213, 2016.
DOI: 10.1007/978-3-319-45940-0_18

time, distance, cost and safety. Therefore, multi-objective optimization of warehouse system is preferred in this study.

Aiming at the warehouse replenishment problem, Poulos et al. [1] proposed the Pareto-optimal genetic algorithm for warehouse multi-objective optimization, where cost and distances are selected as the objectives. The efficiency of the proposed method has been validated by the daily operations in a real warehouse system. Li et al. [6] also conducted multi-objective optimization for storage assignment, where the gravity center and total time are chosen as the objectives. In order to obtain the optimal solution, the authors developed a genetic algorithm with Pareto-optimization as well as niche technique. In 2012, Sooksaksun [7] proposed a mathematical model that considered both space utilization and labor utilization for multi-objective warehouse design.

Generally, a successful tiered warehouse design should take factors of travel time, cost and quality into consideration. Since the operating cost loss should be reduced during the ordinary warehousing operation process by improving the working efficiency, how to improve the working efficiency while reducing the cost to obtain the maximum profit on the basis of limited resource capacity is the target of this paper. Furthermore, the stabilities at the vertical and horizontal directions are also set as the objective functions of the proposed multi-objective genetic algorithm by considering the safety of the tiered warehouse design.

Since there are three objectives that need to be calculated simultaneously, the challenge for the multi-objective optimization problem is that the objectives are competed and contradictory with each other. In aspect of solving complicated optimization problem, the genetic algorithm presents superior advantages [8, 9]. Therefore, the genetic algorithm is the first choice in this research to solve the multi-objective optimization problem of warehousing system.

For the structure of this paper, Sect. 2 describes the mathematic model of the storage assignment problem. Section 3 introduces the genetic algorithm design for the warehouse layout. Section 4 provides the numerical simulation and case study. And concluding remarks are drawn in Sect. 5.

2 Mathematical Model of Storage Assignment Problem

2.1 Model Description

This section provides a simplified model of the tiered warehouse in the storage center of the third party logistic company A. The model is described as follows: in the warehouse, there are a rows storage racks, and each rack has b columns and c layers. The storage rack that is nearest to the warehouse entry and exit is labeled as first row. The column that is nearest to the exit is labeled as the first column. The bottom of storage rack is denoted as the first layer. The coordinate of arbitrary goods location can be represented by (x, y, z), where x, y and z are numbers of row, column and layer. The ranges for the values of x, y and z are $x = 1, 2 \cdots a$; $y = 1, 2 \cdots b$; $z = 1, 2 \cdots c$ respectively.

When conducting the optimization, the following assumptions should be followed:

- The type of merchandise is assumed to be known. Shapes and volume of various types of goods are supposed to be identical.
- Each location can only hold one type of merchandise.
- The time for cargo access can be ignored so that only sorting and translating times are taken into account.
- The dimensions of all trays on the shelves are supposed to be the equal. But the weights of goods that are stored on the trays can be different.
- The entry and exit modes are both single ports.

2.2 Mathematical Model

Efficiency Analysis of the Warehouse Input-Output. According to the optimization target, the merchandise that present high turnover rate should be placed at the location that is close to the dispatch area in the warehouse. While for the goods that are operated in a low turnover rate, they should be placed in a further area so that to cut down the warehouse input-output time.

Assuming that the coordinate of an arbitrary merchandise is (x, y, z), the output area of the warehouse is set as the origin. V_x and V_y are defined to be the average moving speed of stacker at the x-axis direction and y-axis direction respectively. V_z is the lifting speed at the z-axis direction. Furthermore, V_x is equal to V_y, and both of them are greater than V_z. Then the objective function that is to find the solution to meet the requirement of the highest efficiency is derived as:

$$\min f_1(x, y, z) = \sum_{x=1}^{a} \sum_{y=1}^{b} \sum_{z=1}^{c} \left(\frac{x}{V_x} + \frac{y}{V_y} + \frac{z}{V_z} \right) L_0 P_i \tag{1}$$

where P_i is the turnover rate of the ith type merchandise, and L_0 is the length of unit cell of the goods location.

Stability Analysis of Stacker. The stacker stability is dependent on the gravity center. The lower the gravity center is, the better the stability of the stacker is. Therefore, following the principle that heavy merchandise is allocated at the upper shelf and light merchandise is placed at the bottom can help to reduce the gravity center of the stacker to achieve the purpose of improving its stability. The mass of the merchandise at the coordinate (x, y, z) is defined to be M_{xyz}. In order to meet the requirement that the overall gravity center of all merchandise should be the lowest, the product value of the mass M_{xyz} and the merchandise layer z needs to be minimized. Therefore second objective function of the stability at the vertical direction is shown as:

$$\min f_2(x, y, z) = \frac{\sum_{x=1}^{a} \sum_{y=1}^{b} z L_0 M_{XYZ}}{\sum_{x=1}^{a} \sum_{z=1}^{b} M_{xyz}} \tag{2}$$

In addition to consider the stability in the vertical direction, the weight of merchandise at the two ends of a shelve should be balanced. The balance center in the horizontal direction is located at $\frac{1}{2}b$. Similar to the second objective function of the stability at the vertical direction, the third objective function is derived as:

$$\min f_1(x,y,z) = \sum_{x=1}^{a}\sum_{y=1}^{b}\sum_{z=1}^{c}(\frac{x}{V_x} + \frac{y}{V_y} + \frac{z}{V_z})L_0P_i \tag{3}$$

3   Algorithm Design

3.1   Weight Coefficient Variation Method

In current study, there are several methods to solve multiple objective combinatorial optimization problems using the genetic algorithm, which can be classified into simple weighted sum method, goal programming method, constraint method and weight coefficient variation method. Through the comparison of these methods, the weight coefficient variation method is applied in this paper to decrease the dependence of the optimum solution on priori knowledge [10].

The weight coefficient variation method is specifically described as follows: assuming that there are q objective functions that need minimizing in the multi-objective problems, every objective function $f_i(x)$ $(i = 1, 2, \cdots q)$ is assigned with a weight w_i $(i = 1, 2, \cdots q)$, where w_i denotes the significance of the corresponding objective function $f_i(x)$. Then the multi-objective function can be expressed as:

$$u(f(x)) = w_1f_1(x) + w_2f_2(x) + \cdots w_pf_p(x) = \sum_{i=1}^{p}w_if_i(x) \tag{4}$$

where $w_i \geq 0$ $i = 1, 2, \ldots p$, and $\sum_{i=1}^{p}w_i = 1$.

The stochastic weight w_i can be calculated according to the following equation:

$$w_k = \frac{r_k}{\sum_{i=1}^{p}r_i} \qquad k = 1, 2, \cdots q \tag{5}$$

where r_i is a non-negative random number.

Before the selected individual is crossing, a new set of random weights are generated from the above Eq. (5). And from Eq. (4), fitness value of every individual is also calculated. Then the probability of the ith individual being selected is p_i, which can be defined as:

$$p_i = \frac{(y_i - y_{\min})}{\sum\limits_{i=1}^{q} (y_i - y_{\min})} \qquad (6)$$

In the equation, $y_{\min}$ is the worst individual fitness in the current population. The optimum solution will be provisionally stored and updated in every population when the algorithm has crossover and variation. For the problem that presents q objective functions, there exist q extreme points in the Pareto solution. And every extreme point can make the objective reach the maximal value.

In the genetic algorithm, the initial weight and approach can make the genetic search advance at the direction of the Pareto front and will be adaptively adjusted. Therefore, the well fitted weight vector is not necessary for running the genetic algorithm. Furthermore, once the genetic algorithm is embedded, the disadvantage of the weight and approach in the traditional multi-objective optimization will be remedied by the novel population search and evolution search methods [11, 12].

3.2   Design of the Algorithm

Design of the Coding Method. In this paper, the integer permutation encoding method is selected for coding the mathematical model. The detailed coding method is described as follows:

- A chromosome represents a storage assignment method.
- The number of the genes in the chromosome denotes the number of merchandise. If every chromosome can be divided into N parts, then N can be regarded as the total number of merchandise in every optimized area.
- Every gene on the chromosome denotes a good location, and the position of the gene is the coordinate of the merchandise that represents at the goods allocation.

Determination of the Fitness Function. All of the three objective functions are built to get a global minimum value. From Eq. (1), the value ranges of the three objective functions are $(0, +\infty)$. Therefore, the fitness functions can be determined to be reciprocals of the objective functions. Then the quality of the individual can be evaluated according to the fitness. The smaller the objective function value, the greater the corresponding fitness is. Then the probability of the individual transmitting to the next generation is large with a large fitness value when setting the fitness as evaluation criteria. If the objective function value is approaching to zero, the fitness value will be calculated to be spilled positively. In case of data spilling, all the objective function values should be added to one. Then the modified fitness function is expressed as:

$$F(X, Y, Z) = \frac{1}{\min f(x, y, z) + 1} \qquad (7)$$

And the fitness function corresponding to the objective functions should be modified respectively.

4 Numerical Simulation and Case Study

4.1 Parameter Setting and Data Entry

The A type high cargo area data samples are obtained from a stereoscopic warehouse of the storage center in the third party logistics company A. According to the data exported from the storage information system, the initial merchandise storage scheme is drawn in Table 1, where 15 types of stored merchandise are selected in the optimization process. The rack parameters of the row, column and layer are defined to be 4, 6 and 4.

Table 1. Initial merchandise storage scheme

Goods no.	Turnover	Mass(kg)	Coordinate	Goods no.	Turnover	Mass (kg)	Coordinate
1	0.24	5	(1, 4, 2)	9	0.42	10	(3, 2, 2)
2	0.32	2	(2, 4, 1)	10	0.82	22	(4, 4, 4)
3	0.15	15	(3, 2, 1)	11	0.32	32	(2, 2, 3)
4	0.11	43	(1, 3, 4)	12	0.54	5	(1, 4, 3)
5	0.52	21	(3, 1, 4)	13	0.2	2	(3, 3, 4)
6	0.19	13	(1, 1, 1)	14	0.28	18	(4, 3, 4)
7	0.23	11	(2, 4, 2)	15	0.74	41	(4, 4, 2)
8	0.12	15	(1, 1, 4)				

4.2 Simulation Results

By utilizing the optimization program, obtained solution will convert the chromosome into merchandise coordinates. The detailed merchandise storage information after applying optimization is shown in Table 2.

Table 2. Storage data after optimization

Goods no.	Turnover	Mass (kg)	Coordinate	Goods no.	Turnover	Mass(kg)	Coordinate
1	0.24	5	(1, 2, 2)	9	0.42	10	(3, 2, 1)
2	0.32	2	(1, 2, 1)	10	0.82	22	(1, 3, 1)
3	0.15	15	(1, 4, 1)	11	0.32	32	(2, 2, 1)
4	0.11	43	(1, 1, 1)	12	0.54	5	(2, 1, 2)
5	0.52	21	(3, 1, 1)	13	0.2	2	(1, 1, 2)
6	0.19	13	(3, 1, 2)	14	0.28	18	(4, 1, 1)
7	0.23	11	(2, 3, 1)	15	0.74	41	(2, 1, 1)
8	0.12	15	(1, 1, 3)				

Comparison of the results between the initial and optimized storage scheme is shown in Table 3.

It can be concluded from the comparison results of the three objective function values that the merchandise warehouse entry and exit efficiency, gravity center and

Table 3. Comparison of three objective function values before and after optimization

Comparison data of values	Initial	Optimized	Differences	Ratio(%)
The first objective function	59.51	32.02	27.49	46.19391699
The second objective function	2.9765	1.2156	1.7609	59.16008735
The third objective function	0.7851	0.4365	0.3486	44.40198701

stability of the racks are all greatly improved. The decreased rates are calculated to be 46.19 %, 59.16 % and 44.40 % respectively.

5 Conclusion

In this paper, a novel multi-objective optimization mathematical model has been put forward to study the slotting optimization problem of stereoscopic warehouses. Combining both the weight coefficient variation method and fitness functions, an optimized storage scheme is obtained. The optimized storage scheme can provide a good solution to improve the check-in and check-out efficiency of stereoscopic warehouses. Compared with the traditional storage scheme, the objective function values have been reduced by 46.19 %, 59.16 % and 44.40 % respectively.

References

1. Poulos, P.N., Rigatos, G.G., Tzafestas, S.G., Koukos, A.K.: A pareto-optimal genetic algorithm for warehouse multi-objective optimization. Eng. Appl. Artif. Intell. **6**(14), 737–749 (2001)
2. Gu, J., Goetschalckx, M., McGinnis, L.F.: Research on warehouse design and performance evaluation: a comprehensive review. Eur. J. Oper. Res. **203**(3), 539–549 (2010)
3. Larson, T.N., March, H., Kusiak, A.: A heuristic approach to warehouse layout with class based storage. IIE Trans. **29**(4), 337–348 (1997)
4. Lai, K.K., Xue, J., Zhang, G.: Layout design for a paper reel warehouse: a two-stage heuristic approach. Int. J. Prod. Econ. **75**(3), 231–243 (2002)
5. Sooksaksun, N., Kachitvichyanukul, V.: Particle swarm optimization for warehouse design problem. In: Proceedings of the 11th Conference Asia Pacific Industrial Engineering and Management Systems(APIEMS), Melaka, Malaysia, pp. 1–6 (2010)
6. Li, M., Chen, X., Liu, C.: Pareto and niche genetic algorithm for storage location assignment optimization problem. In: Proceedings of the 3rd International Conference Innovative Computing Information and Control (ICICIC), Dalian, China, pp. 465–468 (2008)
7. Sooksaksun, N.: Pareto-based multi-objective optimization for two-block class-based storage warehouse design. Indus. Eng. Manage. Syst. **11**(4), 331–338 (2012)
8. Cai, H., Aref, A.J.: A genetic algorithm-based multi-objective optimization for hybrid fiber reinforced polymeric deck and cable system of cable-stayed bridges. Struct. Multidisc. Optim. **52**(3), 583–594 (2015)
9. Hirsch, C., Shukla, P.K., Schmeck, H.: Variable preference modeling using multi-objective evolutionary algorithms. In: Takahashi, R.H.C., Deb, K., Wanner, E.F., Greco, S. (eds.) EMO 2011. LNCS, vol. 6576, pp. 91–105. Springer, Heidelberg (2011)

10. Djeffal, F.: Multi-objective genetic algorithms based approach to optimize the electrical performances of the gate stack double gate (GSDG) MOSFET. Microelectron. J. **42**(5), 661–666 (2011)
11. Lins, I.D.: Redundancy allocation problems considering systems with imperfect repairs using multi-objective genetic algorithms and discrete event simulation. Simul. Modell. Pract. Theor. **19**(1), 362–381 (2011)
12. Perez, E.B., Carvalho, M.S.: Optimization of slot-coating processes: minimizing the amplitude of film-thickness oscillation. J. Eng. Math. **71**(71), 97–108 (2011)

A Constraint Programming Based Method for Stockyard Management Problem

Can Wen and Lanbo Zheng$^{(\boxtimes)}$

Wuhan University of Technology, Heping Road 1040, Wuhan, China
{can_wen,lanbozheng}@whut.edu.cn

Abstract. The stockyard management problem in a cargo assembly terminal mainly focuses on finding an efficient allocation of limited resources such as stockyard space, stacking and reclaiming machines to stockpiles such that the waiting time of a vessel fleet at port can be minimized. This highly complex problem involves scheduling with resource constraints in a dynamic environment and is a typical $\mathcal{NP}$-hard problem in general. In this study, we present a constraint programming (CP) based approach to address the problem with utilizing the strength of CP in its flexibility in formulating various complex and nonlinear constraints for industrial applications. In addition, we explore the ability of the CP solver with trying different combinations of constraint propagation and constructive search strategies and report our best findings from an extensive computational study.

Keywords: Stockyard management · Constraint programming · Scheduling · Resource constraint

1 Introduction

In a coal export supply chain, stockyard is usually the place where coal resources from different mines with different characteristics are blended together according to specific recipes required by customers. These blended products are stored on stockyard as "stockpile"s waiting to be loaded on their demand vessels. Stockyard plays a key role in balancing the difference between demand and supply and therefore efficient stockyard management strategies are vital for the efficiency of the whole system. A highly information technology supported system makes a "just-in-time" cargo assembly stockyard management possible where the right resources are to be allocated to the right place at the right time within a comparatively short planning horizon. This strategy helps improve the utilization of terminal resources but involves enormous complexities covering different aspects of coal supply chain management [1]. Based on a real industrial scenario, this problem attracts considerable attention from the optimization groups where various AI and OR techniques are applied to address the complex issues. Gulzynski et al. [4] present a mathematical description together with a combined greedy construction, enumeration and integer programming technique to solve

© Springer International Publishing AG 2016
W. Li et al. (Eds.): IDCS 2016, LNCS 9864, pp. 214–221, 2016.
DOI: 10.1007/978-3-319-45940-0_19

the stockyard management problem. In their approach, an integrated scheduling with the load points and rail parts of the system is also considered. Savelsbergh and Smith [2] use a space-time diagram to geometrically illustrate the resource allocation in a stockyard and they propose a greedy algorithm with partial looka-head and truncated tree search. Belov et al. [3] firstly apply constraint programming to model a real-world cargo assembly problem. With the flexibility of the Minizinc platform, a set of operational assumptions are considered, and a large neighborhood search scheme is designed to evaluate the effects.

Stockyard management problem is a combinatorial problem integrating the properties of packing and resource scheduling problems [2]. Constraint programming, as a powerful technique for solving combinatorial search problems that draws on a wide range of techniques from artificial intelligence, operations research, algorithms, graph theory and elsewhere [5], shows particular modeling and solving strengths in attacking this type of problems. Kilby and Shaw [6] describe in detail the use constraint programming in solving industrial Vehicle Routing Problems. Berger et al. [7] consider a two-dimensional packing problem with allowed rotation deriving from the placement of electronic devices in the electronic system and propose a constraint-based approach to solve it. The result shows that the CP method outperforms the MIP approach. Clautiaux et al. [8] propose a new constraint-based scheduling model and several constraint propagation techniques for solving the 2D orthogonal packing problem. Based on their approach, the space of search tree is smaller and the testing results of some benchmark instances are better than those from previous literatures.

In this paper, we look for an optimal strategy to dynamically allocate stockyard resources including stockyard pads, stacking and reclaiming machines to stockpiles so that the overall departure time of a fleet of vessels with given demands can be minimized. We propose a constraint programming based method and focus on the tractability of the problem by exploring promising combinations of constraint propagation and constructive search techniques provided by a competitive CP solver. The remainder of this paper is organized as follows. In Sect. 2, we give a detailed description of the stockyard management problem, Sect. 3 presents the constraint programming model with interval variables of the particular problem addressed. In the following section, we report computational results with different CP solver settings. We conclude our study in the last section.

2   Stockyard Management Problem

Logistics resources of a cargo assembly terminal generally include dump stations, conveyor belts, stockyard pads, stackers, reclaimers, ship-loaders and berths. Coals are transported from different mines to the stockyard by train. Upon arrival at the stockyard, a train unloads the coal into a dump station and the coal is then transported to the pad by conveyor belts and blended there forming a stockpile by a stacking stream. Once the stockpiles are built and the demanding vessel arrives at the berth, the stockpiles can be loaded onto the vessel in a pre-specified order by the reclaiming and ship-loading systems.

In real scenarios, terminal stockyard is the inventory place of the logistics system. However, due to the restrictions of their geographical locations, stockyard space is least expandable and thus easily becomes a bottleneck of the whole system. Therefore, in this paper, we focus on studying the strategy of allocating stockyard space to coal stockpiles dynamically such that the overall utilization of stockyard space can be maximized. In order to formulate a rigid mathematical model of the problem, we clarify some assumptions. First,, we assume that the incoming trains and outgoing vessels arrive on time, that is, the loading operation of coals to and from stockyard is only constrained by the availability of stockyard space and terminal machines. In general, dump stations, conveyors and stackers are streamed into a stacking streamlines where the capacity determined by stackers. This is the same to reclaiming streams where reclaimers are the bottleneck. Therefore, we consider only stackers and reclaimers instead of all terminal equipments in our resource allocation problem. As for the pads, since in the real scenario investigated, each stockpile is spread across the entire width with the same height, the capacity of a pad can be measured as the length of the pad. Stockyard managers aim at maximizing the throughput over the whole year. However, this objective is influenced by many factors and hard to be evaluated by a mathematical function. Instead, for a given demand within a known planning horizon, we try to minimize the overall loading time of the vessels which is closely related to the original operating goal.

Once a demand specification is received by the terminal, that is the number and sizes of cargoes (stockpiles) to be loaded to a vessel, decisions of where and when to stack and reclaim the stockpiles are to be made. These operations are constrained by some practical regulations. Firstly, any two stockpiles can not occupy the same position in the same time and there must be a 10 m buffering space between two adjacent stockpiles. Secondly, once the stacking or reclaiming of a stockpile starts, it cannot be interrupted until the job is done. Additionally, in this study, a reclaiming procedure for a vessel can only begin when all stockpiles of the vessel have been stacked on the pads. Stockpiles of the same vessel are to be reclaimed in a specific order due to some safety and cost issues. Once a reclaiming job is done, it takes 30 min for a reclaimer to switch to a new job.

3 Notations and Constraint Programming Model

In this section, we first give the notations and then describe in detail the constraint programming model of the stockyard management problem introduced above.

3.1 Notations

Parameter Sets

V	Set of vessels: $V = \{1, \cdots, m\}$
S	Set of stockpiles: $S = \{1, \cdots, n\}$
S(v)	Set of stockpiles of vessel v, given in the order in which they must be reclaimed ($S(v) = \{s_{v_1}, \cdots, s_{v_k}\}$ where k is the number of stockpiles of v, and s_{vi} is the ith stockpile in vs reclaiming order)

Parameters

Len	Length of a pad
len_i	Length of stockpile i on a pad
Tim_i^{stk}	Amount of time to stack stockpile i
Tim_i^{rel}	Amount of time to reclaim stockpile i

3.2 Constraint Programming Model

When building a Constraint Programming (CP) model in solving scheduling problems, *interval variables* which have three attributes denoting "start", "span" and "end" properties of a job are inclined to be used. Compared to integer variables, the interval variables are more naturally to express special constraints such as cumulative constraints which lead to efficient constraint propagations [9]. We define three sets of interval variables l_i, t_i^s and t_i^r to represent respectively the decisions of where to locate and when to stack and reclaim a stockpile i. The CP model is as the following:

$$\text{Minimize} \quad \max\{EndOf(t_i^r)\} \quad \forall i \in S \tag{1}$$

$$EndOf(t_j^r) \le StartOf(t_i^s) \vee EndOf(t_i^r) \le StartOf(t_j^s) \vee EndOf(l_j) + 10 \tag{2}$$
$$\le StartOf(l_i) \vee EndOf(l_i) + 10 \le StartOf(l_j) \quad \forall i, j \in S, \quad i \ne j$$

$$EndBeforeStart(t_i^s, t_i^r) \quad \forall i \in S \tag{3}$$

$$EndBeforeStart(t_{s_{v_i}}^s, t_{s_{v_1}}^r) \quad \forall s_{v_i} \in S(v) \quad v \in V \tag{4}$$

$$EndBeforeStart(t_{s_{v_i}}^r, t_{s_{v_j}}^r) \quad \forall s_{v_i}, s_{v_j} \in S(v) \quad and \quad i < j \tag{5}$$

$$EndOf(t_{s_{v_i}}^r) + 30 \ge StartOf(t_{s_{v_{i+1}}}^r) \quad \forall s_{v_i}, s_{v_{i+1}} \in S(v) \tag{6}$$

$$\sum_{i \in S} pulse(Span(t_i^s, t_i^r), l_i) \le Len \tag{7}$$

$$\sum_{i \in S} pulse(t_i^r, 1) \le 4 \tag{8}$$

$$\sum_{i \in S} pulse(t_i^s, 1) \le 4 \tag{9}$$

$$StartOf(t_i^s) \ge 0, \quad StartOf(l_i) \ge 0 \quad \forall i \in S \tag{10}$$

Function (1) defines the objective of minimizing the overall loading time of vessels. The constraints that any two stockpiles cannot occupy the same place in the same time and any two stockpiles adjacent to each other must keep the buffer distance of 10 m are expressed in (2). In the CP solver we used, *StartOf* and *EndOf* represent respectively the start value and end value of an interval variable, *EndBeforeStart* expresses precedence constraints where the end of the first interval variable is less than or equal to the start of the second interval variable. Specifically, constraint (3) represents that any stockpile cannot be reclaimed until it has been stacked and constraint (4) specifies that reclaiming of a vessel begins after all it demanded stockpiles are stacked. Constraint (5) represents that the reclaiming order of the stockpiles of the same vessel must be followed. The switch time between two consecutive reclaiming jobs is respected as constraint (6). *Pulse* is an elementary function expressing the cumulative usage of a resource represented by an interval variable and *Span* represents the region formed by the minimal *StartOf* to the maximal *EndOf* of a set of interval variables. Constraints (7), (8) and (9) represent the capacity constraints of pad (stockyard space), stackers and reclaimers respectively. Constraint (10) requires that all variables are nonnegative.

4   Computational Study

4.1   Experimental Settings

In this section, we test with different propagation and search strategies provided by ILOG CP optimizer [10] for solving our problem. All experiments are tested on the all-in-one PC with an Intel dual core processor running at 2.50 GHz, with 12 GB of RAM and 64-bit Windows operating system and all programs are written in C++, which is compiled in Visual Studio 2012.

The testing instances derived from a real industrial scenario include information of terminal facilities and demand data. The terminal consists of one pad of 1400 m long, 4 stackers and 4 reclaimers. Demand data includes the number of vessels, and the stockpile information required by each vessel where its length on pad, stacking and reclaiming duration of each stockpile can be inferred. We construct 3 sets of testing instances (8 instances for each set) with the number of vessels scaled from 10 to 40. For each set of the eight instances, the first 4 instances represent the common case in practice where each vessel carries no more than three types of cargoes. The next 2 instances are constructed to test with some extreme cases where most of the vessels carry more than 3 (≤ 6) stockpiles and the last 2 instances mimic vessels carrying large volume cargoes (stockpiles requiring long stacking and reclaiming time). Although simplified somehow to adapt to our study, the testing instances reflect real situation to the largest extend.

As the performance of constraint propagation algorithm and constructive search dominate the efficiency of a CP solver, we conduct a set of experiments to explore the best combined strategy of constraint propagation algorithm and constructive search. The ILOG CP Optimizer provides two constraint propagation algorithms, i.e. the basic propagation and the extended propagation for each type of constraints. Compared to basic propagation, extended propagation spend more time on domain reduction. For the constructive search method, except for the default search in the ILOG CP Optimizer, we propose a preferential search method which first searches for the value of the interval variable representing the stacking time of the first stockpile of each vessel. In our experiments, we test with multiple CP approaches based on different combinations of the discussed propagation and search strategies where, *Basic CP* represents the CP method with default settings, *ExPre*, *ExCum* are the abbreviations of applying extended

Table 1. Results of CP methods with different combination of constraint propagation and search strategies for 10 vessels

Instances	Basic CP			CP with ExPre			CP with ExCum			CP with ExBo			CP with PreSrh			CP with ExPre+PreSrh			CP with ExCum+PreSrh			CP with ExBo+PreSrh		
	Status	Value	Time(s)	Stat	Val	Time	Stat	Val	Time	Stat	Val	Time	Stat	Value	Time	Stat	Val	Time	Stat	Val	Time	Stat	Val	Time
1	Opt	45	2.36	Opt	45	1.46	Opt	45	2.04	Opt	45	2.07	Opt	45	5.99	Opt	45	5.22	Opt	45	4.70	Opt	45	5.07
2	Opt	38	0.28	Opt	38	0.34	Opt	38	0.33	Opt	38	0.34	Opt	38	0.52	Opt	38	0.37	Opt	38	0.35	Opt	38	0.75
3	Opt	35	1.95	Opt	35	1.82	Opt	35	1.60	Opt	35	1.73	opt	35	2.08	Opt	35	1.78	Opt	35	1.71	Opt	35	1.97
4	Opt	45	3.51	Opt	45	3.13	Opt	45	2.70	Opt	45	4.23	Opt	45	3.26	Opt	45	2.74	Opt	45	4.01	Opt	45	6.96
5	Opt	39	10.31	Opt	39	8.32	Opt	39	8.83	Opt	39	10.51	Opt	39	10.33	Opt	39	7.66	Opt	39	5.25	Opt	39	4.77
6	Un	-	600	Un	-	600	Un	-	600	Un	-	600	Opt	45	186.27	F	45	600	Opt	9.76	600	Opt	45	13.59
7	Opt	51	1.08	Opt	51	1.68	Opt	51	1.16	Opt	51	1.75	Opt	51	1.53	Opt	51	1.62	Opt	51	1.45	Opt	51	1.59
8	Opt	49	1.43	Opt	49	2.03	Opt	49	1.83	Opt	49	1.83	Opt	49	2.04	Opt	49	1.90	Opt	49	1.84	Opt	49	2.85

constraint propagation to the precedence and cumulative constraints singly, and *ExBo* applies extended constraint propagation to both of them, *PreSrh* represents the preferential search strategy.

4.2 Computational Results

Table 1 reports the results of the first set of testing instances where the number of vessels is 10 and the time limit is 600 seconds. In the table, each CP approach reported by the solution status, the objective value and the computing time where *Opt*, *F* and *Un* denotes respectively the solution status of optimal, feasible and not find within the time limit.

Observed from Table 1, the two propagation strategies do not distinguish each other, while preferential search has a competitive impact on the result as the 6th instance is solved to optimality. Comparing the results from the three competitive combined propagation and search strategies, we conclude that the combination of Extended Cumulative Constraint propagation and Preferential Search outperforms the other CP approaches considering both running time and solution qualities.

To further explore the ability of the CP approach, we test the most competitive strategy found above with larger data sets which involves 20 and 40 vessels each, and the running time limit is increased to 3600 seconds. The results are reported in Table 2.

From Table 2, for the 20 vessel's case, we can see that the first 4 instances are solved to optimality and feasible solutions can be obtained for the last two instances. However, for instances where most vessels carry more than three cargoes, the system is not even able to find a feasible solution within the time limit. These results provide a useful guide for us in analyzing the real complexity of the stockyard management problem. As for the 40 vessel's case, more effective algorithms are to be designed.

Table 2. Results of the best CP method for larger instances

Instances	20 vessels			Instances	40 vessels		
	Status	Value	Time(s)		Status	Value	Time
1	Opt	71	26.25	1	F	317	3600
2	Opt	70	10.23	2	F	367	3600
3	Opt	83	871.36	3	F	166	3600
4	Opt	78	407.74	4	F	580	3600
5	Un	-	3600	5	Un	-	3600
6	Un	-	3600	6	Un	-	3600
7	F	94	3600	7	F	462	3600
8	F	87	798.23	8	F	174	3600

5   Conclusion

We present a constraint programming based approach to solve a stockyard management problem. Experimental analysis is conducted with testing small to large scale instances deriving from real applications. Our main attention is paid to the capability of constraint programming in solving this particular combined scheduling and packing problem. This is explored through an extensive computational test with various propagation algorithms provided by ILOG CP optimizer. We also present a constructive search algorithm which accelerates the solving process remarkably. Experimental results prove the effectiveness of our approach and provide useful guide for future research.

Acknowledgement. This research is supported by the national natural science foundation of China, no. 71501152.

References

1. Boland, N., Savelsbergh, M.: Optimizing the hunter valley coal chain. In: Gurnani, H., Mehrotra, A., Ray, S. (eds.) Supply Chain Disruptions, pp. 275–302. Springer, New York (2012)
2. Savelsbergh, M., Smith, O.: Cargo assembly planning. Eur. J. Transp. Log. **4**(3), 1–34 (2014)
3. Belov, G., Boland, N., Savelsbergh, M., Stuckey, P.: Local search for a cargo assembly planning problem. In: International Conference on AI and OR Techniques in Constriant Programming for Combinatorial Optimization Problems, pp. 159–175 (2014)
4. Boland, N., Gulczynski, D., Savelsbergh, M.: A stockyard planning problem. EURO J. Transp. Log. **1**(3), 197–236 (2012)
5. Harmelen, F.: Handbook of Knowledge Representation, pp. 759–799. Elsevier, Amsterdam (2008)
6. Kilby, P., Shaw, P.: Vehicle routing, Chap. 23. In: Rossi, F., Van Beek, P., Walsh, T. (eds.) Handbook of Constraint Programming, Foundations of Artificial Intelligence, pp. 801–836. Elsevier Science Inc., New York (2006)
7. Berger, M., Schroder, M., Kfer, K.: A constraint programming approach for the two-dimensional rectangular packing problem with orthogonal orientations. Fraunhofer-Institut fr Techno-und Wirtschaftsmathematik, Fraunhofer (ITWM), pp. 427–432 (2008)
8. Clautiaux, F., Jouglet, A., Carlier, J., Moukrim, A.: A new constraint programming approach for the orthogonal packing problem. Comput. Oper. Res. **35**(3), 944–959 (2008)
9. Laborie, P., Rogerie, J.: Reasoning with conditional time-intervals. In: FLAIRS Conference, pp. 555–560 (2008)
10. Laborie, P.: IBM ILOG CP optimizer for detailed scheduling illustrated on three problems. In: Hoeve, W.-J., Hooker, J.N. (eds.) CPAIOR 2009. LNCS, vol. 5547, pp. 148–162. Springer, Heidelberg (2009)

Business Process Reengineering of Road Passenger Transport Based on Unified Modeling Language Method

Xingxing Li, Yan Chen[⊠], and Wenfeng Li

School of Logistics Engineering, Wuhan University of Technology,
Wuhan, People's Republic of China
554671916@qq.com, chenyan@whut.edu.cn, liwf_cn@126.com

Abstract. Service quality, efficiency and labor costs problems caused by the manual service mode have become the "bottleneck" for the further development of road passenger transport enterprises in China. Issues of business operations, the unreasonable resources disposition, information silo, and so on, have been studied and analyzed in a case study. A business process reengineering model of passenger transport is put forward based on Unified Modeling Language method, considering the application of Internet and information technology. To establish the Use Case diagram and Sequence diagram of Unified Modeling Language method, the function of the passenger business support system and the dynamic interaction between participants are designed, which can achieve information sharing and cooperation. A simulation is made to verify the feasibility and effectiveness of the business process reengineering, which provide a reference for the transformation and upgrading of traditional road passenger transport enterprises.

Keywords: Road passenger transport · Business process reengineering · Unified modeling language model · Simulation

1 Introduction

Road passenger transport is the foundation of the national economy and service industries, which expands the domestic demand and promotes service economic to grow stably in the key areas. In recent years, due to the rapid development of high-speed railway and the growing popularity of private cars, road passenger transport market is being squeezed and powerful impact, as showing a declining trend [1]. The road passenger transport enterprises should change the traditional ideas to improve the situation, and reposition the enterprises' strategic objectives. Implement Business Process Reengineering (acronym BPR) after the research in passenger service mode conversion and reconstruction of the main value chains. BPR emphasizes remodeling design on business process for the purpose of improving the efficiency and quality of service, reducing operational costs [2]. BPR theory was first put forward by the famous American business management guru Michael Hammer, he used the concept of BPR in the book which named "Business Reengineering" with Champy [3] for the first time. With the development of information technology, more and more people combined with

© Springer International Publishing AG 2016
W. Li et al. (Eds.): IDCS 2016, LNCS 9864, pp. 222–230, 2016.
DOI: 10.1007/978-3-319-45940-0_20

information technology and business process. Chiplunkar et al. [4] took into account the driving action of the information technology in the collaborative process of business process reengineering. Jiadong [5] opened up an innovation road of the business processes reengineering from the perspective of information flow. Zangxi [6] pointed out that the Internet thinking brings new requirements on BPR raised in the "Internet era business process reengineering".

The study of BPR by early scholars mainly stay in theoretical research level, the research of practical application in the road passenger transport is less. Development of information technology under the internet background provided an opportunity for the transformation and upgrading of the road passenger transport industry. It can integrate passenger transport resources and improve service efficiency through the application of information technology business process to meet passenger personalized, high-end, diversified demands. The passenger transport business process reengineering model is built by UML method in this paper, in order to achieve information sharing and co-operation among business processes through AnyLogic simulation.

2   Analysis of Traditional Road Passenger Transport Business Process

Road passenger transport business process used to be lead by traditional manual mode. It mainly includes inspecting, scheduling, security checking, ticket selling, ticket checking, settlement and other aspects. And it was done in collaboration by the inspectors, dispatchers, conductors, tellers, settlement clerks, finance officers and others. Due to the business process which is leading by manual service mode has a complex relationship, each passenger transport business is mainly relying on paper documents to transmit and handle information. The main problems are listed as following.

- The people play an important role in the business processes.
- Huge number of paper documents, low utilization of the information system resource, poor information sharing, and cost a long time of each business process.
- Much non value-added business processes, and value-added service is missing.

3   Model of BPR Based on Unified Modeling Language Method

Unified Modeling Language (acronym UML) was first proposed by Booch et al. It can be implemented on different description levels and has become a common standard for object-oriented design [7].

UML is a modeling method appropriate for dynamically changing business requirements, which treats business process as a huge complex object, a combination of these objects in the course of the reorganization of business processes, and ultimately establishes an adaptive organization of passenger-centric, which can perceive changes and trends in passenger demand from the large number of data information. This paper selects Use Case Diagram and Sequence Diagram to build a business process model. They describe the passenger transport business processes from the perspective of static and dynamic interaction.

3.1 Demand Analysis on BPR Model

Complete road passenger transport business processes related to the cases of inspection, maintenance, shift arrangements, vehicle scheduling, distribution of Ticket Number, ticket endorse, ticket refund, security check, ticket checking, settlement, financial reconciliation, it needs special business leaders complete business collaboratively. In the BPR model of information system support, the participants of the internal passenger station business process include 9 categories persons of station agent, inspector, maintenance staff, dispatcher, ticket director, conductor, service staff, tellers and billing treasurer, as shown in Table 1.

Table 1. Business process staff

Business staff category	Business task
Station agent	Manage staffs; Assign permissions
Inspector	check the qualification and security situation of vehicles; mark the results of vehicles inspection
Maintenance staff	Inquiry the results of vehicles inspection; Vehicle maintenance; Update the results of vehicle maintenance
Dispatcher	Inquiry the automatic pre-scheduling tables; Inquiry the scheduling situation of each station; Execute or adjust the scheduling plans
Ticket director	Inquiry and distribute Ticket Number; Aggregate the ticket income
Conductor	Operate ticketing system; Sell tickets
Service staff	Endorse or refund ticket; Adjust the factorage ratio
Tellers	Inquiry timetables; check-in notice; Check tickets information
Billing treasurer	Inquiry ticket income and ticket checked fee; Adjust the settlement ratio; settle the vehicle terminal charge; Electronic signature

3.2 The Establishment of Use Case Diagram

Use Case Diagram including actors, use cases and relationships of three parts, showing actors lead cases execution process through generalization and inheritance relationships.

In the use case diagram, use cases confirmed the corresponding function modules or tasks of the passenger business process management system, and the operation of actors is a prerequisite to start with a use cases. The actors with a same passenger transport information system should have more than one different use cases to accomplish different business tasks. The passenger transport use cases in this paper are named from the perspective of each actor's demand function, and two relationships of Uses and Extends mainly among cases, Use Case Diagram is shown in Fig. 1.

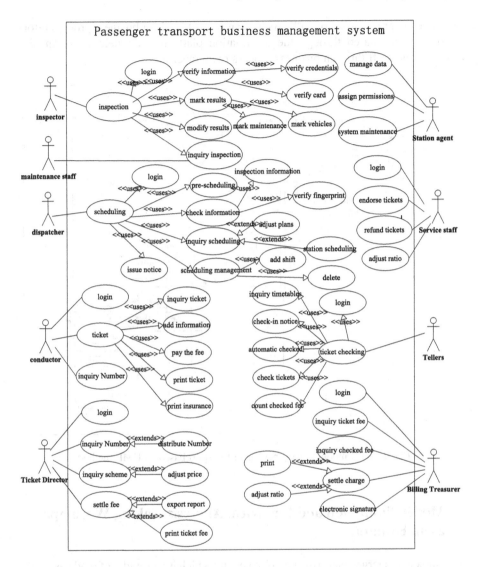

Fig. 1. Use Case Diagram of passenger transport process management system

3.3 The Establishment of Sequence Diagram

In the dynamic model of the passenger transport business process reengineering, it mainly in the establishment of the Sequence Diagram by UML method to describe the interaction process between actors, and it focuses on the sequence of messages to describe how to send and receive messages between actors, as shown in Fig. 2. It shows the information flow transmission of business process sequence from the

Sequence Diagram model of BPR. As we can see, all kinds of business process information can be shared through the information platform after deletion of invalid segments and staff through business process reengineering.

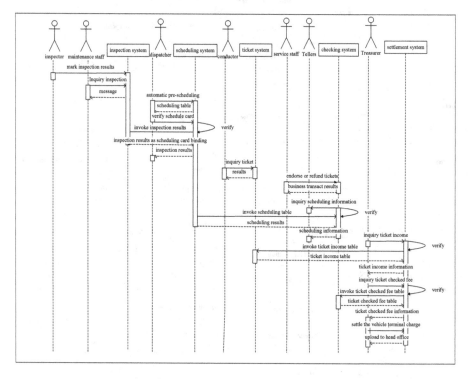

Fig. 2. BPR model of road passenger transport based on UML method

4 Model Simulation and Empirical Analysis-Taking W Company as an Example

W Company is a large enterprise and joint venture which is a provider of road passenger transport and the third party logistics and logistics information technology services. In order to verify the feasibility and effectiveness of passenger business process reengineering model based on UML, this paper simulated the each link of W Company business processes, in order to get the accurate records of each business process operation time, and quantitatively analyze the simulation results between traditional passenger business process and BPR on Anylogic simulation platform.

4.1   Parameter Set in the BPR Model

In order to ensure the validity of simulation results of passenger transport business process reengineering, the simulation model initial conditions should be consistent with the parameters. According to research data acquired from the W, this paper sets the simulation initial time of 0 min and the finish time of 600 min, the average arrival rate of drivers as 0.1 people per minute, the average arrival rate of customers as Poisson(2), the key parameters are as shown in Table 2.

Table 2. Parameters in the BPR model

Parameters	Description	Value	Unit
M	Average daily working hours	600	minute
λ_1	Average arrival rate of drivers	0.1	person/minute
λ_2	Average arrival rate of customers	Poisson(2)	person/minute
λ_3	Average transmission rate of information	3	person/minute
v_1	Average service time of vehicle inspection	triangular(5,8,15)	minute
v_2	Average service time of dispatch	triangular(2,4,5)	minute
v_{31}	Average service time of conductors	triangular(5,6,8)	minute
v_{32}	Average service time of ATVM	triangular(1,2.5,4)	minute
v_{33}	Average service time of Internet ticketing	triangular(5,8,9)	minute
v_4	Average service time of ticket checking	triangular(0.2,0.3,0.4)	minute
v_5	Average service time of settlement	triangular(10,15,20)	minute
$n1$	Number of ticket counters	2	unit
$n2$	Number of ATVM	2	set
$n3$	Number of Internet ticketing website	1	website
$MAXS1$	Services capacity of vehicle inspection	5	person-time
$MAXS2$	Services capacity of dispatch	1	person-time

4.2   Model Validation

Business process reengineering of passenger transport can provide business support for the integration of information technology and customer demand services. In contrast to the simulation model before business process reengineering, it adds the flow of information which generates by source Information module, as shown in Fig. 3.

In the simulation model of BPR, since the larger probability of passengers to select ticket counters and lower efficiency of ticket counters, which in a more time of busy state, so that it has high utilization of the ticket counters. The higher efficiency of the automatic ticketing terminal and less passengers is to select it, so it has low utilization. Under Internet ticketing mode, although the probability of passengers to select is lower than the mode of ticket counters, several passengers can have online transaction at the

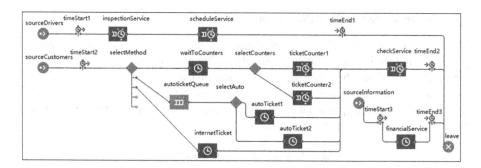

Fig. 3. Simulation model of BPR

same time, therefore the website is occupied more time, there is higher resource utilization, specific utilization data as shown in Fig. 4. Because the efficiency of the ticket counter is lower than ATVM, the average queue length of the ticket counters is much larger than the ATVM, as shown in Fig. 5.

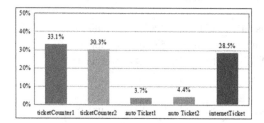

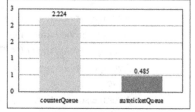

Fig. 4. Utilization of BPR   **Fig. 5.** Average queue length of passengers

Within a period of time (600 min) of the traditional business processes, average time of each driver is 47.804 min, and the average time of each passenger is 21.223 min, as shown in Fig. 6. Within a period time, the average time of each driver is 12.81 min, the average time of each passenger is 7.266 min, and the average time of each billing treasurer is 14.943 min, as shown in Fig. 7.

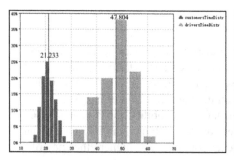

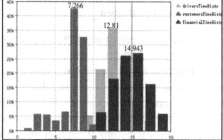

Fig. 6. Total time of traditional business process   **Fig. 7.** Total time of BPR

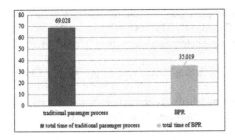
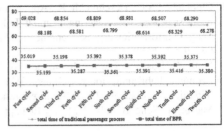

Fig. 8. Total time comparison   **Fig. 9.** Twelve simulation cycle time statistics

The simulation results between traditional business process and BPR shows that the expected value of sojourn time is reducing 34.009 min after BPR, and the efficiency is improved about 49.27 %, as shown in Fig. 8. The expected value of sojourn time after running twelve cycles between traditional business process and business process reengineering are shown in Fig. 9. It can be found in the expected value of sojourn time of two business processes, business process reengineering is always less than the traditional business process, and both them always tend to a stable state of time.

5   Conclusion

This paper builds the BPR model based on UML method, from the perspective of information flow on the impact of business processes coordinated operation for road passenger transport enterprises. The system is achieved through information sharing mechanism to coordinate various business units, thereby reducing the process of filling paper documents and the procedures by multi-level approval. Business process reengineering is not only to increase the level of collaboration and efficiency, but also solves the decentralized management inefficiencies, high labor costs, information cannot be sharing and other issues. The developed model has a value of reference for the transformation and upgrading of passenger transport enterprises. Of course, the study has some shortcomings, such as in the form of limited data and input parameters for the simulation exercise which makes the experimental analysis less reliable in practical terms. However, the results of the simulation may be closer to the real demand on the basis of collecting large amounts of data and information in the future.

Acknowledgement. This work is supported by the project (151100211400) and the project (20152h0158).

References

1. Fu, L.: The research of road passenger transport company operating development under the impact of the traditional high-speed rail. Brand **10**, 209 (2015)
2. Xie, H.: The research on business process & system reengineering in Haier Group. Beijing Jiao tong University (2010)
3. Michael, H., James, C.: Reengineering the corporation: a manifesto for business revolution. Harper Business Publishing, New York (1993)

4. Chiplunkar, S.C., Deschmukh, R.: Application of principles of event related open system to business process reengineering. Comput. Ind. Eng. **3**, 347–374 (2003)
5. Teng, J.: Information process reengineering based on enterprises value chain. Metall. Inf. Rev. **06**, 59–62 (2007)
6. Shui, Z.: Business Process Reengineering in the Internet Era, vol. 4, pp. 49–52. China Economic Publishing House, Beijing (2015)
7. Sébastien, G., Francois, T.: UML for real-time: which native concepts to use. In: Lavagno, L., Martin, G., Selic, B. (eds.) UML for Real, pp. 17–51. Springer, New York (2003)

A Method Based on SNSO for Solving Slot Planning Problem of Container Vessel Bays

Xiaolei Liang[1](✉), Bin Li[2](✉), Wenfeng Li[3], Yu Zhang[3], and Lin Yang[3]

[1] School of Automobile and Traffic Engineering, WUST, Wuhan, China
liangxiaolei@wust.edu.cn
[2] School of Transportation, Fujian University of Technology, Fuzhou, China
whutmse2007_lb@126.com
[3] School of Logistics Engineering, WUT, Wuhan, China
{liwf,sanli,lyang}@whut.edu.cn

Abstract. Stowage planning has an important effect in container shipping and is also a hard combinatorial problem. In order to improve the operation efficiency and reduce the cost, a new optimization method called Social Network-based Swarm Optimization Algorithm (SNSO) is applied to solve the slot planning problem of container vessel bays. As a swarm intelligence optimization algorithm, SNSO is designed with considering population topology, neighborhood and individual behavior comprehensively to improve the swarm search ability. An effective coding and decoding strategy is proposed to optimize the slot planning problem for using SNSO. Finally, fourteen cases of slot planning with different scales are selected to test the proposed algorithm and five swarm intelligence algorithms are selected for comparison in the experiment. The results show that the SNSO has a better performance on solving stowage plan problem in the terms of convergence and accuracy than other selected algorithms.

Keywords: Swarm intelligence · Optimization · Stowage plan · Container terminal

1 Introduction

Container vessel stowage planning is a significant operation in the large-scale container shipping. It aims to ensure the location of each container in a vessel to minimize overstows in middle terminals with consideration of properties of preloaded containers following some basic principles of container stowage and vessel loading requirements, so as to improve the vessel transport and port operation efficiency. A stowage plan is usually produced by terminal and ship companies. Though information technology is well spread in terminal operation system and some initializing computation can finish with computer, the decision of stowage plan is still make manually by stowage coordinators mainly according their experience.

According to practice and related research [1, 2], a stowage planning process generally consists of two planning phases: master planning phase (MPP) and slot planning phase (SPP). In the first phase, the main work is to determine the bay where

© Springer International Publishing AG 2016
W. Li et al. (Eds.): IDCS 2016, LNCS 9864, pp. 231–241, 2016.
DOI: 10.1007/978-3-319-45940-0_21

pre-load containers would be assigned. And in the second phase, each container will be assigned to a specified cell in the vessel with constrains of stability and shifts based. This paper focus on the second phase SSP problem.

SSP problem usually can be classified into two types according to the attribute of discharge terminals on a bay: (1) if all the containers in a specified bay need to be unloaded at the same terminal, it is called single destination slot planning. In this situation, the key element is only the weight of different containers. The aim of this objective is mainly to optimize height of gravity center and transverse moment; (2) while, if the containers have more than one discharge terminals in a bay, it can be described as mixed destination slot planning. Different destinations would cause overstowage and increase the cost of loading/unloading. According to different container loading requirement, if the targeted container need to be loaded at current terminal, we should remove the container over it first, which will cause a cost. Though overstowage is common in container transportation, a reasonable stowage plan can reduce the shift times. We focus on the mixed destination slot planning in this paper.

2   Assumption and Model

2.1   Assumption

In order to represent the slot effectively, a coordinate system of the ship can be shown as Fig. 1 [1]

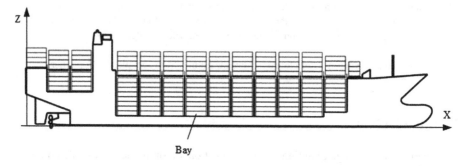

Fig. 1. Structure of a container vessel

The bay, stack and tier are corresponding to the coordinates X, Y and Z axes. That means each slot can be exactly located by (x, y, z). Thus, the coordinates can be constructed as Fig. 2.

The model is constructed under these assumption:

- The quantity of containers and their destination terminal are known;
- The master planning is given and the capacity of the specified bay is enough;
- The structure of the bay is known including tiers and stacks;
- The constraint of hatch cover is simplified and we do not consider its effect.

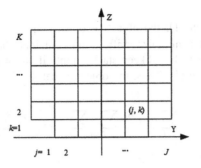

Fig. 2. Structure of a bay

- In real operation, some containers should be located in specified slot. In this work, these containers are not concerned and the type of all containers are the same.

2.2 Model

According to the stowage process, the notation of constants and variables used in the objective model is defined as following:

- Constants

  $I = (1, 2, \ldots, n)$ Containers index set;

  $J = (1, 2, \ldots, m)$ Stacks index set;

  $K_j = (1, 2, \ldots, k)$ Available cell set in stack j;

  $D = (1, 2, \ldots, l)$ Terminal index set;

  $A_{id} = \begin{cases} 1 \\ 0 \end{cases} \forall i \in I, d \in D$ when container i is unloaded in terminal d, $A_{id} = 1$;

  otherwise, $A_{id} = 0$;

- Variables

  $o_i = \begin{cases} 1 \\ 0 \end{cases} \forall i \in I$ when container i is shifting, $o_i = 1$; otherwise, $o_i = 0$;

  $p_{jd} = \begin{cases} 1 \\ 0 \end{cases} \forall j \in J, d \in D$ at least one container in stack j need to be unloaded at

  terminal d, $p_{jd} = 1$; otherwise, $p_{jd} = 0$;

  $e_j = \begin{cases} 1 \\ 0 \end{cases} \forall j \in J$ when stack j is used, $e_j = 1$; otherwise, $e_j = 0$;

  $c_{jki} = \begin{cases} 1 \\ 0 \end{cases} \forall j \in J, k \in K_j, i \in I$ when container i is stowed in cell k, stack j, $c_{jki} = 1$;

  otherwise, $c_{jki} = 0$;

  $\delta_{jkd} = \begin{cases} 1 \\ 0 \end{cases} \forall j \in J, k \in K_j, d \in D$ when container located in cell k, stack j need to be

  unloaded before terminal d, $\delta_{jkd} = 1$; otherwise, $\delta_{jkd} = 0$;

- Objective

  Based on the research [1], the objective of stowage planning optimization here contains three aspects: minimize shift, avoid containers have many different discharge terminals in a stack and keep stacks empty if possible. Different cost can be calculated according to [1]. Thus, the objective can be defined as following:

$$\min 100 \sum_{i \in I} o_i + 20 \sum_{j \in J} \sum_{d \in D - \{1\}} p_{jd} + 10 \sum_{j \in J} e_j \tag{1}$$

s.t. :

$$c_{jki} - c_{j(k+1)i} \geq 0 \quad \forall i \in I, j \in J, k \in K_j \tag{2}$$

$$\sum_{j \in J} \sum_{k \in K_j} c_{jki} = 1 \quad \forall i \in I \tag{3}$$

$$\sum_{i \in I} c_{jki} \leq 1 \quad \forall j \in J, k \in K_j \tag{4}$$

$$\sum_{j \in J} \sum_{k \in K_j} \sum_{i \in I} c_{jki} = |I| \tag{5}$$

$$A_{id} c_{jki} + \delta_{ikd} - o_i \leq 1 \quad \forall j \in J, k \in K_j, d \in D, i \in I \tag{6}$$

$$e_j - c_{jki} \geq 0 \quad \forall i \in I, j \in J, k \in K_j \tag{7}$$

$$p_{jd} - A_{id} c_{jki} \geq 0 \quad \forall j \in J, k \in K_j, d \in D, i \in I \tag{8}$$

The objective (1) is a sum of three weight cost. Constrains (2) means that the cells are enough for each container to be loaded. Equation (3) ensures each container can be located. Each cell just can be used for one container at the same time by (4). Equation (5) stows all the container in the slot. Constrains (6) represents relationship of variables for assigning the overstowage variables o_i for each container. Constrains (7) sets the variable related to the empty stack cost for each stack. Variables related to avoiding avoid containers have many different discharge terminals in a stack.

The above model is a mixed integer program problem which is NPC problem. With the increase of the number of containers, the solution space will become very large, which will be difficult to be solved by conventional method. Thus, several intelligence optimization algorithms or heuristic strategy are applied to solve it. In this paper, we introduce SNSO [3] to optimize the model.

3 Solution Approach

3.1 SNSO Algorithm

Social Network-based Swarm Optimization algorithm (SNSO) is a new swarm intelligence optimization (SIO) algorithm, applied to solve complex optimization problems. Different from some other peer SIO algorithms, SNSO considers the population topology, neighborhood structure and individual learning behavior simultaneously to improve the population search ability. In SNSO, the information sharing among different individuals is based on a social network model, and real individuals are combined with virtual individuals to build a neighborhood. Furthermore, two different position update methods for two types of individuals are defined for enhancing the diversity and search ability of the swarm. In benchmark test, SNSO show a better performance compared with some other swarm intelligence algorithms. Details about the algorithm has been presented in [3].

3.2 Problem Encoding and Decoding

In SNSO, an individual can be represented by a n-dimensional vector $\mathbf{x}_i = (x_{i1}, x_{i2}, x_{i3}, ..., x_{in})$ in continuous space where n denotes the available position in a bay. Due to the slot planning is aim to obtain a reasonable stowage plan, which belong to non-numerical optimization problem in discreet space. Thus how to build a strategy to realize the mapping from an individual in continuous space to a feasible plan in discreet is the key step. Base on real coding strategy, we proposed a new decoding method for mapping an individual to a feasible plan. In the strategy, the index number of each dimension shows the index of containers. Actually, each bay will not be filled completely by containers. Thus some virtual containers are added to fully fill the available positions, which will be deleted after plan making. We sort the elements x_{ij} in $\mathbf{x}_i$ and then obtain a sequence array $\mathbf{s}_i$ (Fig. 1). The load order can be determined by $\mathbf{s}_i$ under the rule that each container should be loaded from the bottom to top. After that, a stowage matrix is obtained but contains some virtual. For each stack, the added containers should be replaced by the real containers over them. Finally, a feasible stowage plan is made (Table 1). Table 2 shows a simple case to show the strategy.

Table 1. Representation of an individual in SNSO

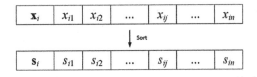

3.3 Procedure

According to the process of SNSO and the decoding strategy above, the process of using SNSO to solve the slot planning problem can be described as following:

Table 2. Encoding strategy

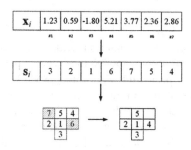

```
Input: No. of the case I; populations size N; maximum
iterations G; fitness function F(x)
Initializing.
   Generate a swarm X=(x₁, x₂ ,…, x_N) randomly;
Main Procedure.
   Loop on k=1,…,G
      ∀x_i,
            Sort the elements in x_i by ascending and get
               the sequence S_i ;
            Decode the S_i to obtain the stowage plan O_i;
            Calculate the fitness f_i=F(O_i) based on the
               function (1);
         Update the global best individual g and the
            history of individual optimal solution p_i;
         Adjust topology, neighborhood and individual
            behavior;
         Update the position of each individual;
   End Loop on k
Output: the best solution g.
```

4   Case Study

4.1   Experiment Setting

In order to test the performance of SNSO in solving slot planning problem, fourteen cases with different scales are designed. Each case is different from others in bay structure, amount of pre-stowage containers and number of discharge ports. The details are shown in Table 3.

Table 3. Cases

Case	Capacity of bay(R × T)	Containers(TEU)	Terminals
Small Scale			
1	4 × 5	15	3
2	4 × 5	15	4
3	4 × 5	18	3
4	4 × 5	18	4
Medium Scale			
5	7 × 8	30	3
6	7 × 8	30	4
7	7 × 8	50	3
8	7 × 8	50	4
Large Scale			
9	11 × 12	60	3
10	11 × 12	60	4
11	11 × 12	60	5
12	11 × 12	100	3
13	11 × 12	100	4
14	11 × 12	100	5

Furthermore, several peer SI algorithms are selected to make a comparison with SNSO, including CLPSO [4], ABC [5], CS [6, 7], BFO [8] and BA [9–11], which are applied in many filed successfully. All the parameters in each algorithm are set as suggested. All the sizes of populations are set as 30 in each algorithm. These algorithms are executed 20 times for each case on same machine with an Intel Core Duo CPU 2.10 GHz, 2G memory and Windows 7 *OS*.

4.2 Result and Discussion

The statics results can be seen in Table 4, including the minimum value (min), maximum value (max), mean value (mean) and standard deviation (SD). It is clear from the result that although SNSO is not the best but close to CS which gets the best

Table 4. Results

Alg.	Max	Min	Mean	SD	Max	Min	Mean	SD
	Case1				*Case2*			
SNSO	150	110	120	10.05	140	110	130	11.52
ABC	130	100	125	8.65	160	130	140	9.99
CS	**130**	**110**	**110**	**8.87**	**140**	**110**	**130**	**10.56**
BFO	190	150	170	15.18	320	180	220	44.43
BA	190	130	150	13.61	320	150	180	39.22
CLPSO	170	110	150	16.82	260	150	180	26.93

(*Continued*)

Table 4. (*Continued*)

Alg.	Max	Min	Mean	SD	Max	Min	Mean	SD
	Case3				*Case4*			
SNSO	170	150	170	4.47	190	170	170	6.16
ABC	**170**	**150**	**160**	**10.26**	170	150	170	10.21
CS	170	150	170	10.05	**170**	**150**	**150**	**9.79**
BFO	450	190	320	90.24	510	150	320	89.32
BA	390	170	210	67.58	530	170	210	96.09
CLPSO	450	150	300	89.94	470	150	190	87.66
	Case5				*Case6*			
SNSO	**130**	**50**	**100**	**24.77**	**140**	**80**	**115**	**21.79**
ABC	170	130	155	12.26	200	150	180	15.01
CS	150	90	125	14.69	180	140	160	9.23
BFO	330	140	210	54.72	380	200	260	50.85
BA	230	120	190	28.19	260	170	200	26.21
CLPSO	290	150	210	37.28	440	180	245	71.19
	Case7				*Case8*			
SNSO	**570**	**310**	**350**	**55.24**	**600**	**380**	**450**	**55.62**
ABC	1430	710	1110	210.55	1780	800	1390	311.23
CS	1390	470	780	228.54	1660	740	1380	290.59
BFO	2990	1590	2410	382.69	3240	1260	2680	534.42
BA	2430	890	1590	447.57	2700	820	1800	464.60
CLPSO	3070	1830	2570	389.13	3560	1940	2730	457.93
	Case9				*Case10*			
SNSO	**210**	**140**	**170**	**25.83**	**210**	**100**	**170**	**26.85**
ABC	290	230	270	16.42	360	240	300	27.13
CS	270	210	250	17.74	320	210	260	30.17
BFO	630	290	400	84.22	640	320	420	82.69
BA	330	210	250	27.13	420	240	280	44.42
CLPSO	590	290	390	84.83	840	270	520	133.55
	Case11				*Case12*			
SNSO	**260**	**130**	**200**	**38.51**	**670**	**490**	**530**	**39.95**
ABC	410	280	350	40.56	3290	1530	2450	483.17
CS	350	250	310	28.00	3030	1950	2610	277.92
BFO	690	310	570	100.19	4930	3390	4080	495.42
BA	430	250	320	44.40	3290	1330	2370	538.03
CLPSO	930	390	680	183.01	6350	4550	5360	515.38
	Case13				*Case14*			
SNSO	**880**	**540**	**680**	**99.77**	**1030**	**670**	**780**	**118.67**
ABC	4260	2260	3590	522.08	4750	3230	3890	461.58
CS	4020	2940	3350	292.47	4510	3350	4000	306.14
BFO	5920	3740	5010	565.19	7010	4510	5740	634.88
BA	5440	2400	3650	800.71	6210	2490	4120	1082.63
CLPSO	7320	4780	6570	640.48	8230	4810	6890	865.13

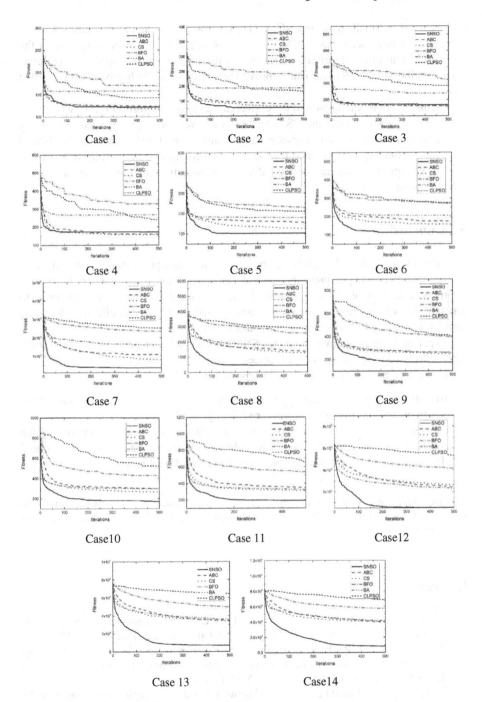

Fig. 3. Median convergence characteristics of different cases

performance in small scale test (Case 1–4). However, with the increase of scale, especially in large scale cases, SNSO shows excellent search ability and obtains the best result than other algorithms. That means the adjustment on topology, neighborhood and individual behavior can improve the optimization ability of SNSO to solve SPP.

Similarly, from comparison of the convergence curves analyses (Fig. 3), we can see that SNSO is close to ABC and CS, which offer a faster convergence speed in the early optimization phase than the rest selected algorithms in small scale cases test. But SNSO offer an outstanding performance than others in medium and large scale tests, which can locate optimal area fast and do deep local search, avoiding falling into local extreme point region.

5 Conclusion

In order to solve the slot planning problem with multiple terminals in container transportation, this paper presents a novel algorithm based on SNSO. It introduces swarm structure topology, neighborhood and individual behavior simultaneously to improve the optimization ability of a swarm. Based on SNSO, an effective decoding strategy is provided to solve the slot planning model.

Experiment results demonstrate that SNSO obtains a better performance than some other selected SI algorithms given fourteen cases.

In the future work, we will focus on the following issues:

1. To solve the stowage planning problem in practice, we need to consider more constrains and do research on master planning problem;
2. The search behavior of a swarm in SNSO should be analyzed for improving the optimization ability in other complex problems and the application of the proposed algorithm to some optimization problems [12, 13] should be pursued.

Acknowledgements. This work was supported in part by National Natural Science Foundation of China (No. 61304210, No.61571336) and Foundation of WUST Fund for Young Teachers (No. 2016xz029).

References

1. Delgado, A., Jensen, R., Janstrup, K., et al.: A constraint programming model for fast optimal stowage of container vessel bays. Eur. J. Oper. Res. **220**(1), 251–261 (2012)
2. Pacino, D., Jensen, R.: Fast slot planning using constraint-based local search. In: Yang, G.-C., Ao, S.-I., Huang, X., Castillo, O. (eds.) IAENG Transaction Engineering Technologies, pp. 49–63. Springer, New York (2013)
3. Liang, X., Li, W., Liu, P.P., et al.: Social network-based swarm optimization algorithm. In: Proceedings of the 2015 IEEE 12th International Conference Networking, Sensing and Control (ICNSC), pp. 360–365 (2015)

4. Liang, J., Qin, A., Suganthan, P.N., et al.: Comprehensive learning particle swarm optimizer for global optimization of multimodal functions. IEEE Trans. Evol. Comput. **10**(3), 281–295 (2006)
5. Karaboga, D., Akay, B.: A comparative study of Artificial Bee Colony algorithm. Appl. Math. Comput. **214**(1), 108–132 (2009)
6. Yang, X., Deb, S.: Engineering optimisation by cuckoo search. Int. J. Math. Model. Numer. Optim. **1**(4), 330–343 (2010)
7. Yang, X., Deb, S.: Cuckoo search via Lévy flights. In: World Congress on Nature & Biologically Inspired Computing, pp. 210–214 (2009)
8. Passino, K.M.: Biomimicry of bacterial foraging for distributed optimization and control. IEEE Control Syst. **22**(3), 52–67 (2002)
9. Mirjalili, S., Mirjalili, S.M., Yang, X.S.: Binary bat algorithm. Neural Comput. Appl. **25**(3–4), 663–681 (2014)
10. Yang, X., Gandomi, A.H.: Bat algorithm: a novel approach for global engineering optimization. Eng. Comput. **29**(5), 464–483 (2012)
11. Yang, X.: A new metaheuristic bat-inspired algorithm. In: González, J.R., Pelta, D.A., Cruz, C., Terrazas, G., Krasnogor, N. (eds.) Nature inspired cooperative strategies for optimization, 65-74. Springer, Berlin (2010)
12. Liang, X., Li, W., Zhang, Y.: A novel swarm intelligence optimization algorithm for solving constrained multimodal transportation planning. J. Shanghai Jiaotong Univ. (Sci.) **49**(8), 1220–1229 (2015)
13. Liang, X., Li, W., Zhang, Y., Zhou, M.: An adaptive particle swarm optimization method based on clustering. Soft. Comput. **19**(2), 431–448 (2015)

Internet of Things and Applications

Design of Distributed Logistics Vehicle Monitoring System with High Load

Shengwu Xiong[1,2], Na Wang[2], Li Kuang[2], Pengfei Duan[1,2(✉)], and Fengjian Yu[2]

[1] Hubei Key Laboratory of Transportation Internet of Things, Wuhan 430070, China
{swxiong,duanpf}@whut.edu.cn
[2] School of Computer Science and Technology, Wuhan University of Technology, Wuhan 430070, China
{1058603760,547207352,974822058}@qq.com

Abstract. There are various types of GPS vehicle terminal protocols and the data transmission is with high concurrency. Since it's of great significance to supervise logistics vehicle for centralized information management, it's imperative to develop a distributed logistics vehicle monitoring system with high load, which is compatible with multi-type terminal protocols. First, this paper formulates a unified communication protocol for the unitive data transmission. Next, a segmentation database is designed to deal with high load. And then three distributed architectures are designed. Through experiments, an optimal one has been selected and implemented by comparing the three architectures.

Keywords: Logistics vehicle monitoring · Distributed forwarding · Communication protocol · Segmentation database

1 Introduction

The logistics vehicle monitoring platform is mainly focused on real-time supervision and management of vehicles. Hu [1] has developed a relatively perfect vehicle monitoring system. But it only supports the single vehicle terminal Austrian, cannot be achieved on various terminals. By reducing the threshold of logistics vehicles monitoring, Sun [2] has put Google maps into the monitoring and made the monitoring services to a wide range. Based on android mobile terminal, Cao [3] has changed the supervision platforms from PC to smart phones, bringing convenience for mobile office. Besides, Ru [4] has applied the BD Navigation into logistics vehicle monitoring, which combines the safety and convenience to the vehicles management. With the help of BD satellite, Huang [5] has achieved superb progress in locating the dangerous goods and extend the usage of BD Navigation satellite system into a wider field. Although the technology of logistics vehicle monitoring has become mature, the main research is still based on a single type of vehicle terminal protocol now, which is difficult to realize the simultaneous supervision of multi-type vehicle terminals [6]. In addition, frequent data transmission of logistics vehicles is likely to put pressure on servers of the monitoring system, while the existing ones cannot solve the problem of high load.

© Springer International Publishing AG 2016
W. Li et al. (Eds.): IDCS 2016, LNCS 9864, pp. 245–253, 2016.
DOI: 10.1007/978-3-319-45940-0_22

In view of above, by involving in five kinds of vehicle terminals, the unified management for various vehicle terminals has developed and a public monitoring system suitable for high load of logistics vehicles has been achieved. Specifically, a unified communication protocol has been designed to facilitate the data transmission in the public system. And then a segmentation database has been designed to deal with high load. Finally, three distributed architectures has been developed, and an optimal one has been selected and implemented by comparing them through experiments.

2   The Unified Communication Protocol

This system is designed to be compatible with five different GPS vehicle terminal protocols. The five protocols are shown in Table 1.

Table 1. Different types of protocol

No.	Name
1	GT08 protocol
2	HQ2.0 protocol
3	Compatible BD protocol
4	JTT808 standard protocol
5	BSJ communication V2.6 protocol

The five protocols have different formats. To integrate them on the same system, it's important to design a unified communication protocol for data transmission. And every protocol needs an adapter to convert itself to the unified format. Thus, the relationship between five protocols and the unified one is shown in Fig. 1.

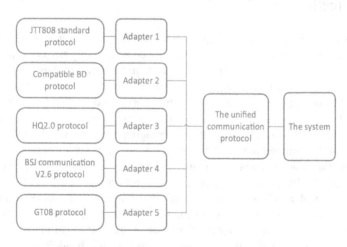

Fig. 1. The relationship between Protocols

In Fig. 1, the five protocols are first converted by adapters, and then they all communicate with the system through the unified protocol. In detail, this paper selected the way of sub package transmission to transmit the data from different terminals. The specific format is shown in Table 2.

Table 2. The format of unified communication protocol

Package number	Description
0	Identification package
1...N	List of specific data packages

In Table 2, the zeroth package is identification package, and the 1...N packages are specific data packages. The platform type, vehicle identifier and terminal protocol type are combined in the identification package to identify the data of system and the vehicle terminal protocol type.

- The first byte of identification package represents the platform type. E.g. 0x01 represents gateway server, 0x02 is communication server etc. It can extend to 255 modules to meet the needs of the existing system.
- The last byte of it represents the terminal protocol type. It can extend to 255 types.
- The vehicle identifier has more than one byte. It mainly used to identify the vehicle unique, and its content is the vehicle terminal SIM card number.

In terms of the specific data packages, every package in the list includes data package type and specific instruction format. The former is shown in Table 3.

Table 3. The data package type

No.	Data package type	Name
1	Route Settings	SETLINECMD_TYPE
2	Driving Data Format	DRIVERECORDDATA_TYPE
3	Location Information	LOCATION_TYPE
4	Response Data Format	GENERAL_REPLAY_TYPE
...	...	...

Every data package type in Table 3, has its own specific instruction format, e.g. the location information shown in Table 4.

Table 4. The specific instruction format of location information

Field name	Type	Description
FlowId	unit	Serial number
Longitude	str	The accuracy is 11 bits
Latitude	str	The accuracy is 11 bits
Speed	double	GPS speed
...	...	...

With the unified communication protocol designed above, it's easier for the public system to be compatible with multi-type terminal protocols.

3 Database Design

In practical, the data of logistics vehicles is relatively huge, and the problem of high load cannot be solved by a single database. Thus, Sharding method [7], which is the process of splitting data up and storing different portions of data on different machines. It can handle more load without large machines [8]. Moreover, it can break through the I/O capacity constraints of single node database server [9].

The Sharding segmentation includes vertical and horizontal. Vertical segmentation is that tables with close logical business are divided into the same database, while horizontal segmentation is to segment tables with huge data into several sub tables [10].

The characteristics of data in system are that basic information of vehicles is generally recorded in sequence with little change, except that GPS data changes continuously resulting in high ratio of data growth. And when in GPS localization, the correction of Baidu map is carried out, so the Baidu correction database is needed.

Combined Sharding method with the above characteristics, this paper designed the suitable database structure for this system, as shown in Fig. 2.

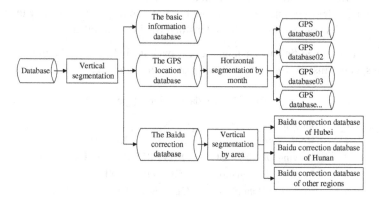

Fig. 2. The sharding database structure

In Fig. 2, based on vertical segmentation, the database is partitioned into three parts: basic information database, GPS location database and Baidu offset database. And then the GPS location database is split by month based on horizontal segmentation; the Baidu offset database is split by region.

4 Design of Distributed Architecture

The main data flow of the monitoring system: one is that different vehicle terminals upload data to the system; the other one is that users operate the system to change the status information of GPS vehicle terminals [11]. So the system is the core.

This paper aims to implement the system module. Due to the requirements of dealing with multi-type GPS vehicle terminals, gateway servers are necessary. Next, web servers are essential to realize the system interaction. Therefore, the first distributed architecture is designed, as shown in Fig. 3.

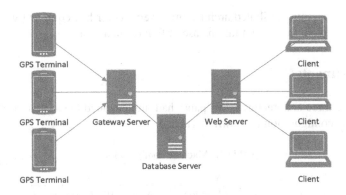

Fig. 3. The first distributed architecture

In Fig. 3, the architecture mainly contains gateway servers, database servers and web servers. It can provide localization and monitoring services for vehicles. And it had been used by Deng [12]. But it generally used for the system with a small number of vehicles, and it's inconvenient in docking with the third party platform.

It needs to consider the access of the third party platform in practical. Actually, the first architecture can dock with gateway servers or others. But it will have a bad impact on the single-function of servers. Therefore, communication servers had been abstracted to deal with it, so developed the second architecture. Compared with the first one, it had added communication servers.

The second one can satisfy the system development. But considering the maintainability, the business processing module had been extracted from gateway servers and web servers to design the third architecture. Advantages are that when added terminal types, it will not affect the business modules; and when business changed, it will not affect the gateway modules. The third one is shown in Fig. 4.

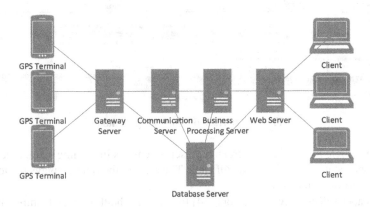

Fig. 4. The third distributed architecture

Finally, the third architecture composed of five parts. Compared with the second one, it had added business processing servers.

Moreover, in any distributed architecture, every server had equipped with a slave component to avoid the system fail in case of failures in any servers.

5   Experiments

Based on the three architectures, this paper had implemented the system respectively. The machine configuration is shown in Table 5.

Table 5. Machine configuration

Type	Value
Server	Windows Server 2008 R2 Enterprise
CPU	Intel(R) Xeon(R) CPU E5620 2.4GHZ
Memory/Hard Disk	16 GB/1.5 TB

The system mainly includes operation, scheduling and monitoring module [13]. Figure 5 shows the example of page rendering in monitoring module.

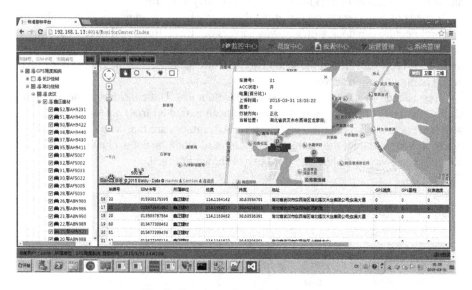

Fig. 5. Interface of monitoring module

In the vehicle list on the left, green represents vehicles in running state; blue represents stopped state; gray represents off state. The map on the right displays the location and state information of vehicles.

This paper selected five indicators [14] to compare the three architectures. Results are shown in Table 6.

Table 6. Comparison results

Architecture	Platform docking	Business expansion	Transmission rate	Development difficulty	Maintainability
First	complex	complex	high	simple	low
Second	simple	complex	medium	complex	medium
Third	simple	simple	medium	complex	high

Considering the advantages of platform docking, business expansion and maintain-ability, the third one is the best. In terms of development difficulty, the more modules, the development cycle will be longer. So the development difficulty of the third architecture is the most. But it will not affect the overall performance of system.

The transmission rate will affect the response time of the whole system. For data transmission, the first architecture needs one layer forwarding, the second needs two, and the third needs three. In order to test the forwarding layer effect on system response time, three architectures are tested with 100,000 data respectively. Results are shown in Fig. 6.

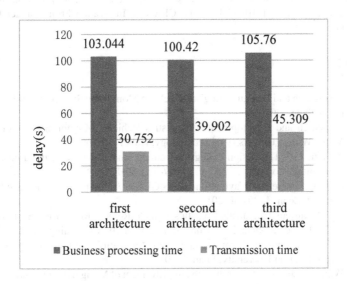

Fig. 6. Comparison of data transmission rate

According to Fig. 6, when dealing with high load, the third one had small increase in transmission time and business processing time. But compared to the first one, it's more convenient in docking with the third party platform. And compared to the second one, it can ensure the maintainability of system. In practical, to satisfy the scalability and maintainability of system, it has to make some sacrifices in performance. So the third one is acceptable in terms of the transmission rate.

What's more, the third one is better than the other two in the former three indicators. So the third architecture had been selected as the optimal one to implement the system.

6   Conclusion

This paper has implemented a distributed monitoring system with loosely coupled and easy extension. It can provide public monitoring and management services for vehicles with multi-type GPS terminals, and it can deal with high load. The key is to enact a unified protocol for data communication within JO modules, and to segment the database by Sharding to meet the demand of high load. There are still some to be improved. Occasionally there will be a memory leak, which will affect the stability of system. This problem will be solved in future research.

Acknowledgements. This work was supported in part by the National High-tech R&D Program of China (863 Program) under Grant No. 2015AA015403, Science & Technology Pillar Program of Hubei Province under Grant No. 2014BAA146, Nature Science Foundation of Hubei Province under Grant No. 2015CFA059 and Hubei Key Laboratory of Transportation Internet of Things under Grant No. 2015III015-B03 and CERNET Innovation Project under Grant No. NGII20151006.

References

1. Hu, K.P.: Research and Design of Logistics Vehicle Monitoring System. Southwest Jiaotong University, Sichuan (2010)
2. Sun, J.: Research and Development of Logistics Vehicles Monitoring System Based on Google Maps. Wuhan University of Technology, Hubei (2010)
3. Cao, G.F., Wu, J.P.: The design of logistic vehicle scheduling platform based on android intelligent terminal. Comput. Sci. Appl. **2**, 147–151 (2012)
4. Ru, C.P.: Design of Beidou Navigation/GPRS/GIS car supervision system based on ARM. Railway Transp. Econ. **3**, 80–84 (2013)
5. Huang, X.: Hazardous Chemicals Logistics Vehicle Remote Monitoring System based on BD2/GPS Dual-mode Applications. Chongqing University, Chongqing (2014)
6. Zhai, B.J.: Study on Car Terminal and GPS Navigation Systems Based on Vehicle Networking. Chang'an University, Shanxi (2014)
7. Liu, Y., Wang, Y., Jin, Y.: Research on the improvement of MongoDB auto-sharding in cloud environment. In: 2012 7th International Conference on Computer Science & Education (ICCSE), pp. 851–854. IEEE (2012)
8. Kristina, C., Michael, D.: MongoDB: The Definitive Guide, p. 135. O'Reilly Media, Sebastopol (2010)
9. Liang, H.: Application and research on sharding technology in MongoDB database. Comput. Technol. Dev. **7**, 15 (2014)
10. IEEE Std 1609. 0-2012. IEEE Draft Guide for Wireless Access in Vehicular Environments (WAVE) - Architecture. IEEE P1609.0/D5[S]. IEEE (2012)
11. Liu, L.: The Research and Implement of Electric Power Enterprise GPS Vehicle Positioning Monitor. Zhongshan University, Guangdong (2011)

12. Deng, C.Q.: The Study of Logistic Whole Process Management System Based on Internet of Thing. Chongqing Jiaotong University, Chongqing (2013)
13. Huang, Q.P., Wang, W.: GPS vehicle orientation, monitoring & control system based on GPRS. Microcomput. Inf. **13**, 277–279 (2007)
14. White, C.E., Bernstein, D., Kornhauser, A.L.: Some map matching algorithms for personal navigation assistants. Transp. Res. Part C: Emerg. Technol. **8**(1), 91–108 (2000)

Design and Implementation of Work-in-Process Management System Based on RFID Technology

Wenchao Yang[1,2(✉)], Guofu Luo[2], and Wenfeng Li[1]

[1] School of Logistics Engineering, Wuhan University of Technology,
Wuhan, People's Republic of China
1030990690@qq.com, liwf@whut.edu.cn
[2] Mechanical and Electrical Engineering Institute, Zhengzhou University of Light Industry,
Zhengzhou, People's Republic of China
1986009@zzuli.edu.cn

Abstract. As to the "rich data but poor information" problem under internet of manufacturing things environment in workshop layer, an RFID-enabled work-in-process management system is presented. The main system function modules and hardware structure are introduced. The bind rules for objects in workshop layer in manufacturing industry under environment of internet of things and RFID tag are studied. Based on XML language, four business event models of smart objects are defined, which are used to realize the tasks in process management system, such as data integration with manufacturing shop layer and business integration with the upper system. A case is given, the result proves that the system has advantages of simple operation, practicability and stability. It can be used to improve production quality and control inventory.

Keywords: Work-in-process · RFID · Information collection · Semantic definition · Data integration

1 Introduction

Due to aggravated global market competition, it has higher requirements for enhancing product quality and reducing production cost & resource consumption, etc. Transparent, intelligent and traceable WIP (work-in-process) management becomes a development trend of manufacturing enterprise. Internet of things technology, especially the maturity of RFID technology plays an important role in facilitating the development of advanced manufacturing management model. Through the application of RFID in manufacturing industry, the information interaction between work-shop and management layers is intensified. As a result, the problem on horizontal "information isolated island" and longitudinal "information fault" in manufacturing industry is tackled. Kohn [1] firstly supports scheduling and process control with RFID data. According to the lack of effective monitoring of manufacturing process in discrete manufacturing industry, effective integration of manufacturing execution system and reliable production management decision software. Qu [2] have proposed RFID-based study on PVI monitoring of discrete manufacturing process to obtain

W. Li et al. (Eds.): IDCS 2016, LNCS 9864, pp. 254–262, 2016.
DOI: 10.1007/978-3-319-45940-0_23

various information occurring to discrete manufacturing process automatically, accurately and in real time. Ni et al. [3] have built a RFID-based vertical distributed application model system framework for automobile production line to solve the problems about the lack & missing of information acquisition data and low artificial operation efficiency during production process. Zhang et al. [4] have proposed a work-in-progress management framework based on smart objects such as radio frequency identification/Auto-ID devices and web service technologies in a ubiquitous manufacturing (UM) environment. Ray [5] and Zhong [6] have studied on RFID-enabled real-time manufacturing execution system (RT-MES). RFID devices are deployed systematically on the shop-floor to track and trace manufacturing objects and collect real-time production data. Jin [7] developed an implementation of the real-time monitoring and management system of 8 channels DVB-C transport stream monitor.

By taking advantage of technical features of RFID, the real-time initiative perception into information of workshop layer could be realized. Effective information of workshop layer could be collected to further optimize manufacturing process, enhance production efficiency, and reduce production cost. Therefore, it is an inevitable tendency to effectively apply advanced technologies including RFID, information acquisition and data processing into WMS (work-in-process management system) to strengthen management of manufacturing workshop layer.

2 Work-in-Process Management System Based on RFID Technology

In this paper, RFID-based WMS is proposed, and the mixed architecture of C\S (client\server) and B/S (browser/server) is adopted. As shown in Fig. 1, C\S architecture is used to integrate the management of RFID file, personnel, quality, production equipment, RFID middleware and data acquisition with business of upper-level system, while B/S architecture is used for traceability of WIP. The system is divided into three layers, namely enterprise layer, WMS layer and manufacturing workshop layer. WMS is integrated with upper-layer enterprise information system; the material, machine tool, forklift and workers of workshop layer are bound with RFID or sensor to obtain their real-time information in so as to realize the comprehensive monitoring of production field. The information is uploaded to the application server via field bus or encrypted WIFI, and then uploaded to the WMS server via industrial ether net so as to realize information integration between WMS and workshop layer.

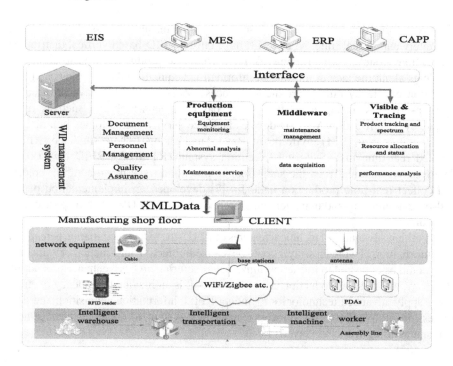

Fig. 1. Architecture of RFID-based WMS

3   System Development

3.1   Division and Binding Rules of Workshop Manufacturing Unit

To realize precise and effective monitoring & control of WIP, it is necessary for the system to collect the real-time data of logistics and information flow of WIP. The perception elements in workshop layer include RFID tag, RFID reader and sensor (like vibration and temperature sensors, etc.).

Firstly, it is necessary to divide manufacturing unit to collect and manage workshop data, as shown in Fig. 2; Secondly, it is necessary to number the machine tool, material, personnel, FRID tag and reader. The numbering rule is based on the following two binding relationship. The relationships among them can be expressed in Fig. 3.

1. As for the binding relationships between reader key equipment and manufacturing procedure, there is a RFID reader in key equipment for each manufacturing unit, so there is one-to-one mapping relationship between key equipment and reader, and there also is one-to-one relationship between key equipment and working position. There might be many devices on one working position.
2. As for the binding relationships among RFID tag, material, worker and production task, there is only one sole RFID tag for each worker, so there is one-to-many corresponding relationship between RFID tag and worker; there is only one sole RFID

tag for every material, so there is one-to-many corresponding relationship between RFID tag and material. Lots of materials are required for a production task, so there is several-for-one relationship between material and production task. As for the relationships among four parts.

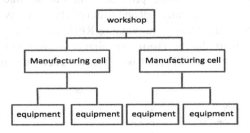

Fig. 2. Division rules of workshop manufacturing unit

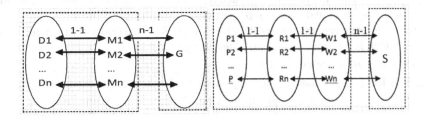

Fig. 3. Binding rules

In Fig. 3, D_n indicates reader n; M_n indicates key equipment n; G indicates working position; 1-1 indicates a one-to-one corresponding mapping relationship between the two parts; n-1 indicates a several-for-one relationship between the two part. P_n indicates worker number n; R_n indicates RFID tag number n; W_n indicates material number n; S indicates production task; 1-1 indicates a one-to-one corresponding mapping relationship between the two parts; n-1 indicates several-for-one relationship between the two parts.

3.2 Building SOs Model

In order to establish corresponding relation between information model and product logistics entity in the information system, the problems including the physical entity encoding and identifying and the corresponding data mapping in management system need to be addressed. As the object tracked and traced by production logistics, traceable unit can be raw materials of product, semi-finished product, item, packing box, pallet, containers and so on. Traceable unit consists of two parts-defining identification information and recording information. The main function of identification information is to ensure the continuity of the tracking and tracing process; the main function of recording information is to achieve the internal and external circulation and tracing. The transformation from tracking and tracing physical entity into tracing information of the different traceable units in the supply chain will realize the visualization and traceability of WIP.

According to above RFID binding principles, the people (like machine operator, workshop supervisor, etc.), machine, tool and materials (such as raw material, WIP and finished product) are bound with corresponding RFID tags. The articles bound with RFID tags are called smart objects. The information of smart objects is defined as a set, and the logistics status of information link node $P_t(S)$ of a certain t time can be described as following:

$$P_t(S) = \left\{ \sum_{j=1}^n M_j(S), \sum_{k=1}^m A_k(S), T, Id(S), L_t(S), U_t(S) \right\}$$

- $\sum_{j=1}^n M_j(S)$ is material parameters, which represents n kinds of main raw material at time t;
- $\sum_{k=1}^m A_k(S)$ is attribute parameter, which represents m kinds of attribute includes the physical properties and chemical properties, etc. at time t;
- T is immediately generated when RFID read-write device to read and write item labels of S, which is the condition or attributes change time;
- $Id(S)$ is electronic tag coding for S;
- $L_t(S)$ is location parameter, which represents the location of the change of state;
- $U_t(S)$ is user operation, the operator ID when the item S information changed.

Through ID number of electronic tag of SOs, information of information flow node at any time could be consulted to obtain pedigree of product information.

3.3 Semantic Packaging of SOs Event

Based on interface standard of EPCIS, the business event of SOs logistics node is described with semantics of XML. According to degree of information polymerization, the event model of SOs is divided into reading event and simple event. The reading event indicates the most primitive event read by the reader, while the simple event indicates the event after filtered and polymerized. The simple event includes:

- Transform events: indicating the event that new articles processed from the old ones;
- Aggregation events: indicating the event that products of higher level realized through packaging;
- Division events: indicating the event that more packs of small level formed after unboxed;
- Move events: indicating the event that the location of product in the enterprise changes.

4 Cases Presentation

4.1 Systematic Deployment of RFID Devices on Shop Floors

IOMOT platform built by Suzhou Boshi Robotics Technology Co., Ltd. is a typical annular flexible automatic production line. It is comprised of some units including loading, image detection, capping, pin, detection, logistics storage, etc.

Firstly, deploy of RFID readers and tags. In workshop, machine, tool and materials are bound with corresponding RFID tags. Physical manufacturing resources attached by RFID tags become smart objects (SOs) which can sense and detect by RFID reader. Their information in different working positions can be read through reader in real time to achieve the purpose of real-time monitoring. Then, deploy communication network. 433 MHz wireless standard is adopted, because the network is easily deployed and the hardware proves relative low power consumption [8].

4.2 Reengineering of the Processes

After the systematical deployment of RFID devices on WIP manufacturing sites. We need reengineer manufacturing processes to realize intelligent manufacturing. Figure 4 flow chart shows the process of manufacturing.

Step1: Target distribution. Distribute process flow card as per the assigned production task and initialize RFID tag.

Step2: Data collection. When the materials affixed with RFID tags circulate between working processes, various events are continuously triggered so that the RFID reader may automatically collect the real-time data of logistics and transmit the data by means of radio communication.

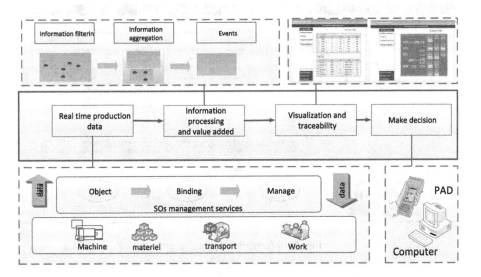

Fig. 4. Reengineering processes

Step3: Data processing. The collected real-time data is analyzed by event processing engine and is transferred into four types of logistics events of high level after pre-processing.

Step4: Visualization and traceability. By combining the logistics events with the process route of materials, logistics status of production targets at different moments is reflected. Therefore, real-time monitoring and tracing towards logistics is realized.

Step5: Decision. The production or upper-layer management personnel can make decision according to order requirement and production state of workshop through chart information of production field released through WMS, like rearrangement for production scheduling, etc.

4.3 Achieved Results

As shown in Figs. 5 and 6, the system optimizes the business process and achieves the visualized management of WIP. There are material information and product attributes in the product database, and EPCIS event database provides logistics information of WIP. The users can fetch RFID tag of commodities by RFID reader or writer, and access the product traceability query platform through the Web Service to obtain product logistics traceability information. The real-time production data obtained by the system plays an important role in optimizing product quality and WIP inventory. Through examples verification, this system has some advantages: simple operation, accurate and immediate information acquisition. With standard interface and information file of XML format, the system is easier to be expanded and integrated, and the system operation is also stable, and with good utility.

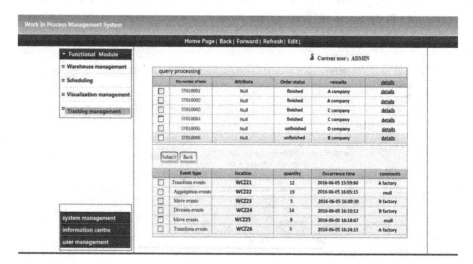

Fig. 5. Information tracing query

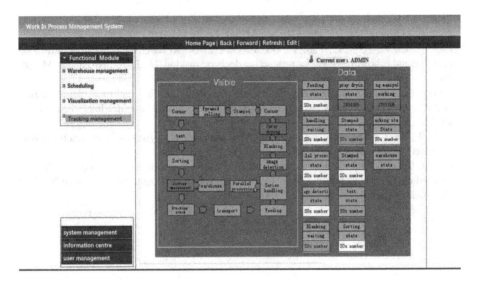

Fig. 6. Real-time monitoring

5 Conclusion

Modern manufacturing technology embraces a developing trend of "efficiency, visualization and greening". It is an in-exorable trend of manufacturing informatization that the internet of things, especially context-aware technologies including RFID, will be applied into workshops in order to realize visualization and traceability of production. The thesis proposes a RFID-based production management system and then explores its critical technologies. Through division of workshop structures and definition on binding rules of RFID, the system models SOs events in different workshops. Besides, the system can also encapsulate semantics of the SOs events, which is beneficial to the collection and integration of real-time information. It is easy to operate and expand, with strong practicability.

Acknowledgment. This work has been supported by Innovation Plan of Science and Technology in Henan Province (164200510004), funded by Department of Science and Technology of Henan Province.

References

1. Wolf, K., Vladmir, B., Jana, L.: Repair-control of enterprise systems using RFID sensory data. IIE Trans. **47**(4), 281–290 (2005)
2. Qu, R., Wang Z.: Journal of Guangxi University. Natural Science Edition, 263–268, February 2011
3. Ni, L., Zhong, H., Duan, C.: Research on RFID application mode in automotive manufacturing production line. Comput. Eng. **12**(4), 224–231 (2013)

4. Zhang, Y.: Real-time work-in-progress management for smart object-enabled ubiquitous shop floor environment. Int. J. Comput. Integr. Manuf. **24**(5), 431–445 (2011)
5. Ray, Y., Li, Z., Pang, L., Pan, Y., Qu, T., George, Q.: RFID-enabled real-time advanced planning and scheduling shell for production decision making. Int. J. Comput. Integr. Manuf. **26**(7), 649–662 (2013)
6. Zhong, R., Dai, Q., Qu, T., Hu, G., Huang, G.: RFID-enabled real-time manufacturing execution system for mass-customization production. Robot. Computer-Integrated Manuf. **29**, 283–292 (2013)
7. Song, J., Jin, L.: The real-time monitoring and management system of 8 channels DVB-C transport stream monitor. Adv. Mater. Res. **4**(5), 605–610 (2013)
8. Dai, Q., Liu, Y.: MES wireless communication networking technology based on 433 Mhz. In: Proceeding of 2nd International Conference on Anti-Counterfeiting, Security and Identification, vol. 12(4), pp. 20–23 (2008)

Improved CTP Routing Protocol Based on Ant Colony Algorithm

Guangyou Yang[1(✉)], Hao Chen[1], and Xiong Gan[2]

[1] Institute of Agricultural Machinery, Hubei University of Technology,
Wuhan, People's Republic of China
pekka@126.com, 535193320@qq.com
[2] School of Mechanical and Electronic Engineering, Wuhan University
of Technology, Wuhan, People's Republic of China
ganxiong001@126.com

Abstract. Aiming at the phenomena of node's load unbalanced with the heavier load the shorter life, poor inter-node link quality with packet loss and bit errors more frequent and packet delay more severe appearing on Agricultural Greenhouse Wireless Sensor Network Monitoring System, a new ant colony algorithm collection tree routing protocol ACA-CTP is submitted, which takes advantage of the characteristics that the ant colony can find the optimal path from the nest to the food source. The algorithm takes three indexes which are ant pheromones, node link quality and packet delay as algorithm optimization factors to improve the path probability selection strategy of Ant Colony Algorithm, combines the improved Ant Colony Algorithm with Collection Tree Protocol and is implemented by using NesC language in TinyOS system. ACA-CTP Routing Protocol selects the optimal routing path between the source and destination nodes to ensure the monitoring data an accurate and real-time transmission to the monitoring platform through the global optimization ability and fast convergence of the improved Ant Colony Algorithm. Simulation results show that ACA-CTP algorithm extends the network lifetime and reduces the packet transmission delay and packet loss rate.

Keywords: Wireless Sensor Network · Ant Colony Algorithm · ACA-CTP routing protocol · Optimal routing path

1 Introduction

Wireless Sensor Network node has the advantages of the small size, the low power consumption and so on, but also the shortcomings of the limited energy and computing power, the limited bandwidth and susceptibility to interference [1, 2]. Therefore, the design of energy-efficient routing protocols is one of the main research contents of WSNs [3].

The merits and efficiency of routing algorithm's path selection mechanism will directly determine the degree of a node's load-balance, the rate of the data collection and transmit-receive, thus affecting the entire network energy consumption and time delay. WSN that develops up to now has a lot of routing protocols such as AODV protocol, LEACH protocol and Flooding protocol, but as CTP routing protocol, these

© Springer International Publishing AG 2016
W. Li et al. (Eds.): IDCS 2016, LNCS 9864, pp. 263–275, 2016.
DOI: 10.1007/978-3-319-45940-0_24

protocols don't consider the node load and transmission delay. A node's overload in the network topology can cause the excessive energy consumption of the node which leads to death of the node, affecting the entire network performance and life cycle. Meanwhile, the overloaded nodes transmission queue is too long to affect the real-time transmission of data [4]. In response to these shortcomings, some domestic and foreign scholars have optimized those routing protocols. The article [5] proposes a balanced aggregation tree routing algorithm LB-CTP, which defines the node balance degree and introduces the mechanism that avoids the busy node accessible. When routing updates, the corresponding nodes select the parent node through LB-CTP routing algorithm to access the network and to share the burden of the busy nodes, which effectively balances the network load.

This paper proposes a new routing algorithm combining Ant Colony Algorithm with CTP routing protocol, named Ant Colony Algorithm Collection Tree Protocol, and implements this algorithm by using NesC language in TinyOS system. The control mechanism of Ant Colony Algorithm is added to the original CTP routing protocol to be the new algorithm ACA-CTP, which adjusts the ratio of the pheromone concentration, inter-node link quality and packet delay time to guide the routing packets to route search with good adaptability and balance of the fast convergence and global search capability. Finally, the performance of CTP routing protocol, AODV routing protocol and ACA-CTP routing protocol is compared by TOSSIM simulation.

2 The Control Mechanism of Ant Colony Algorithm in ACA-CTP Routing Protocol

2.1 The Improved Control Mechanism of Ant Colony Algorithm

In this paper, the inter-node link quality q_{ij} and transmission delay t_{ij} are used to construct the heuristic factor η_{ij} as the evaluation parameters that the QoS network evaluates the routing path [6]. Meanwhile, taking into account the limited computing power of the sensor nodes, the selection probability function, which is a exponentiation formula, is transformed to a multiplication formula to improve the computational efficiency of the algorithm. The improved selection probability function of Ant Colony Algorithm is as follow:

$$
P_{ij}^d(t) = \begin{cases} \dfrac{\alpha \times \tau_{ij}^d(t) - \beta_{ij}(t) + \gamma \times q_{ij}(t)}{\sum\limits_{n \in N_i} \left(\alpha \times \tau_{in}^d(t) - \beta \times t_{in}(t) + \gamma \times q_{ij}(t)\right)} & j \in N_i \\ 0 & j \notin N_i \end{cases} \tag{1}
$$

Wherein, α, β, γ are respectively the adjustable coefficients of the pheromone concentration τ_{ij}, the time delay t_{ij} and link quality q_{ij}. The path selection tendency of the ant colony can be adjusted by choosing the different value of α, β and γ, which means that the shorter the time delay, the better the link quality and the greater the heuristic factor, the greater the probability of the path which the ant colony select. At the same time, the influence and effect of these three parameters on the overall optimization performance and fast convergence are mutual cooperation and closely related, so only the right choice of the ratios of the three parameters can avoid the cases of the premature stagnant and falling into local optimum. Therefore, the relationship among α, β and γ is as follow:

$$\alpha + \beta + \gamma = 1 \tag{2}$$

The pheromone update mechanism of the new Ant Colony Algorithm still remains constantly. By setting the relevant parameters of the pheromone update mechanism and three parameters α, β and γ reasonably, the balance of the convergence speed and global optimization performance of the algorithm, the balance of the network load and the extension of the network life cycle can be all achieved [7, 8].

2.2   The Simulation of the Improved Ant Colony Algorithm

In order to verify the feasibility and universality of the improved Ant Colony Algorithm, the random network topology is established and the Matlab simulation tool is used for its simulation. What the simulation environment is that 200 nodes are randomly generated in the area of 100 × 100 square meters, and then 20 nodes are randomly selected among them. Finally, centered on the 20 nodes selected above, the K-means clustering algorithm is used to cluster the remaining nodes to get 20 center nodes, which are the desired sensor nodes with the communication radius 50 m. The transmission delay, inter-node link quality and pheromone concentration are randomly generated in the random network, and among them, the inter-node link quality takes a random number between 0 and 1, the transmission delay a random number from 0 to 25 and the pheromone concentration from 0 to 10. The algorithm generates the network topology shown in Fig. 1.

As can be seen from Fig. 1, the network model of the improved Ant Colony Algorithm has a uniform distribution of the sensor nodes so that the direct transmission path will not appear if the distance between two nodes is too far away, which makes the network model close to the practical network topology. Node 1 is set to be the data

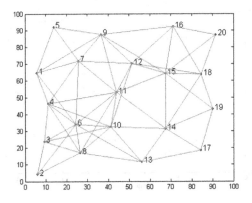

Fig. 1. Network topology

acquisition node and the destination node is Node 20, the iteration time of the algorithm is 20, the number of the dispatch ants is 100 each time, the ratio of the pheromone concentration is 0.4, the ratio of the transmission time delay is 0.4 and the link quality is 0.2, the pheromone evaporation coefficient is 0.8 and the pheromone enhancement factor is 30.

The algorithm generates the optimal path shown in Fig. 2.

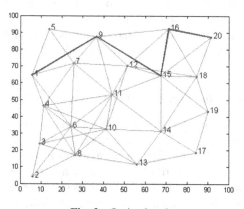

Fig. 2. Optimal path

As shown in Fig. 2, the optimal transmission path chosen by the improved Ant Colony Algorithm is 1-9-15-16-20, and the pheromone concentration, time delay and link quality in Fig. 3 converge when the algorithm iterate at 15 times, which means the improved algorithm feasible.

Simulation tests prove that the improved Ant Colony Algorithm control mechanism of ACA-CTP routing protocol can automatically select the optimal path and maintain the routing path according to the pheromone concentration, time delay and link quality, which lays the theoretical foundation for the realization of ACA-CTP routing protocol.

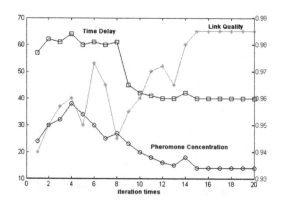

Fig. 3. QoS metric parameters convergence

3   ACA-CTP Routing Protocol

3.1   The Architecture of CTP Routing Protocol

CTP routing protocol is mainly composed of three modules: the link quality estimator, the routing engine and forwarding engine. The link quality estimator, which is located at the bottom, is responsible for an estimated one-hop link quality between the node and its neighbor nodes, and maintains a neighbor table; The routing engine, which is located at the middle layer, uses the information provided by the link quality estimator to select a node with the minimum cost of the transmission from itself to the root node as its parent node, and maintains a routing table; The forwarding engine maintains a send queue which consists of the packets produced by local nodes and the packets produced by other nodes, and send the packet at the head of the send queue at the appropriate time.

3.2   The Realization of ACA-CTP Routing Protocol

ACA-CTP routing protocol, on the basis of CTP routing protocol, introduces three QoS parameters which are the link quality, the time delay and pheromone concentration instead of the single link quality parameter of CTP routing protocol as the new routing selection metrics and the control mechanism of Ant Colony Algorithm to select the optimal path for transmitting data by utilizing its features of routing optimization and fast convergence.

The improvements of ACA-CTP routing protocol on CTP routing protocol are as shown in Fig. 4.

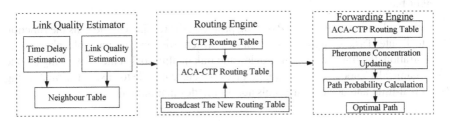

Fig. 4. ACA-CTP routing protocol framework

3.3   The Improvements of the Link Quality Estimator

As shown in Fig. 4, a new metric, the time delay, is introduced into the link quality estimator as a parameter of evaluating the network status, and in order to obtain the transmission time delay between nodes. In TinyOS operating system, the interfaces provided by the timer component TimeSyncC can be directly used to realize FTSP time synchronization algorithm.

3.4   The Improvements of the Routing Engine

New routing table based on the original CTP protocol routing table adds three entries which are the pheromone concentrations, the data transmission time delay and inter-node link quality, and the routing engine transfers the information of the new routing table to the forwarding engine when the link quality estimator calculates the transmission delay and link quality in time to update the routing table periodically. The routing packet format of ACA-CTP routing protocol is shown in Fig. 5.

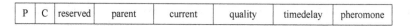

| P | C | reserved | parent | current | quality | timedelay | pheromone |

Fig. 5. ACA-CTP routing packet

The role of each field in ACA-CTP routing packet is as follows:

P: Allowing routing bit, accounting for one bit. P bit allows a node to request routing information from other nodes.
C: Congestion flag bit, accounting for one bit. If a node drops a routing frame, the C bit of the next transmission routing frame must be set.
Reserved: Reservation bit.
Parent: Parent node ID bit, accounting for eight bits.
Current: Current node ID bit, accounting for eight bits.
Quality: Link quality between the current node and the source node, accounting for eight bits.
Time delay: Data transmission time delay between the current node and the source node, accounting for eight bits.
Pheromone: Initial pheromone concentration of the current node, accounting for eight bits.

In the realization of ACA-CTP routing protocol, the routing engine calls the function Update Route Task to update three entries which are the routing table pheromone concentration, the transmission time delay and link quality so that the forwarding engine can dynamically choose the next-hop node of the current node to ensure the monitoring data a real-time and accurate transmission to the destination node.

3.5   The Improvements of the Forwarding Engine

The forwarding engine substitute three QoS parameters from the updated routing table into Eq. (6) to calculate the path transfer probability of the next-hop neighbor nodes of the current node, and then select the maximum transfer probability neighbor node as the parent node of the current node to make the ACA-CTP protocol packet transmit to the destination node along the optimal path. Meanwhile, in order to avoid the node overloading and the forwarding engine falling into the local optimal path, the pheromone volatilize according to the formula (3), and the pheromone concentration dilutes after going through N iterations to ensure the forwarding engine select the optimal path. The working process of ACA-CTP routing protocol is shown as Fig. 6.

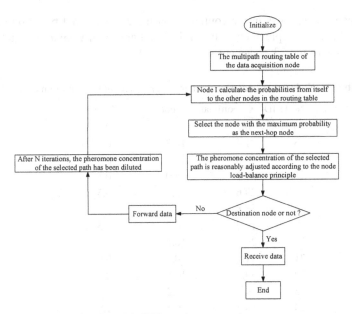

Fig. 6. ACA-CTP routing protocol process

4 ACA-CTP Routing Protocol Simulation

When the simulator TOSSIM is used to test the performance of ACA-CTP routing protocol, unlike the traditional simulation, TOSSIM simulator compile the actual TinyOS program to establish a more realistic simulation environment to analyze the performance of ACA-CTP routing protocol truly.

4.1 Constructing the Simulation Environment

In this paper, an agricultural greenhouse environment is selected as the simulation environment to establish TOSSIM simulation model. The nodes cannot communicate with each other when the simulation just starts. Only when the network topology has been configured, TOSSIM simulation can simulate the network behaviors. When the Java tools from TOSSIM simulator is used to generate the network topology based on the Log-Normal Shadowing Path Loss Model, the network parameters of the agricultural greenhouse environment is extracted and put into a configuration file in which the parameters are shown in Table 1.

Table 1. Network topology parameters configuration

Path loss exponent	Shadowin standard deviation	Close-in reference distance	Close-in reference path loss	Noise floor	White guassian noise
1.551	4 dB	1 m	53 dB	−105 dBm	4 dBm

The nodes coordinates in the configuration file are measured based on the actual position of the nodes deployment at the agricultural greenhouse environmental site, and the coordinates of the 13 nodes are shown in Table 2.

Table 2. Nodes coordinates at the agricultural greenhouse environmental site

Node ID	X coordinate	Y coordinate	Z coordinate
0	0	0	0
3	21.4	10.2	−0.5
4	22.8	14.1	−0.5
5	31.1	4.0	−0.5
6	29.6	0.5	−0.5
8	18.8	2.5	−0.5
9	17.0	10.2	−0.5
20	29.7	16.2	−0.5
21	31.7	10.2	−0.5
22	39.1	14.5	−0.5
23	39.1	16.2	−0.5
24	14.5	−0.5	−1.0
25	25.0	16.2	−0.5

The Java tool is operated to generate two files, namely "link gain.out" and "topology.out". Wherein, "link gain.out" file contains the link gain and noise between any two nodes in the network, and "topology.out" file contains the coordinates of the nodes in the simulation environment.

4.2 Analyzing the Simulation Results

When the simulation environment has been configured, the applications of ACA-CTP routing protocol are written at the application layer of TinyOS protocol stack, and then TOSSIM simulator is operated to achieve the simulation results as shown in Fig. 7.

In Fig. 7, the Ctp Forwarding Engine P of <8> node triggers the send task, which is trying to send a packet in the queue and the queue size is 1 at the moment, and the <8> node is not in a congested state. But then there is no route and do not send the packet, so the Ctp Forwarding Engine P starts retry timer to initiate route requests, and then a routing path is discovered and the packet sent so that the sending queue size is 0. After that, the Ctp Forwarding Engine P receives a packet (head <- [load] <- tail) and then the packet enters the sending queue, so that the queue size is 1. Finally, a routing frame (head <- <- tail) is broadcast and then the simulation is completed. The transfer process of ACA-CTP routing protocol packet can be clearly reflected in Fig. 7, but the performance of ACA-CTP routing protocol could not be directly reflected. Thus, the simulation information of each node at the simulation process is collected to draw ACA-CTP routing protocol network topology as shown in Fig. 8.

The original CTP routing protocol and AODV routing protocol are operated to obtain two network topologies respectively shown in Figs. 9 and 10.

```
DEBUG <8>: CtpForwardingEngineP$0$sendTask$runTask: Trying to send a packet. Que
ue size is 1.
DEBUG <8>: CtpForwardingEngineP$0$sendTask$runTask: no route, don't send, start
retry timer
DEBUG <8>: QueueC$2$Queue$enqueue: size is 0
DEBUG <8>: head <-[bd8adb18] <- tail
DEBUG <8>: QueueC$2$Queue$dequeue: size is 1
DEBUG <8>: head <-<- tail
Completed simulation.
```

Fig. 7. ACA-CTP routing protocol simulation results

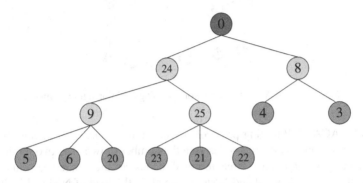

Fig. 8. ACA-CTP routing protocol network topology

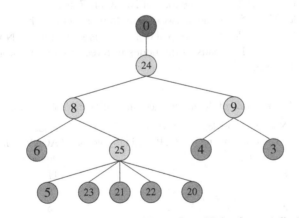

Fig. 9. CTP protocol network topology (Color figure online)

Among them, AODV routing protocol network topology is drawn directly by PC software when the greenhouse wireless monitoring system is being tested in the agricultural greenhouse scene. In the network topology, the red nodes are the aggregation nodes, the yellow nodes are the routing nodes and the green nodes are the terminal nodes.

The above topology diagrams show that the network topologies generated by three routing protocols are all tree network. It can be seen from the comparison of three different network topologies that the nodes at the first layer of the network topology

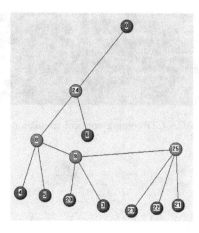

Fig. 10. AODV protocol network topology (Color figure online)

generated by ACA-CTP routing protocol are all routing nodes, of which each has the same number of immediate child nodes with the number of two. The two routing nodes at the second layer all have three terminal nodes as the immediate child nodes. Therefore, the load of Node 9 and Node 25 are all 3, the load of Node 24 is 8 and the load of Node 8 is 2. Similarly, in the network topology generated by CTP routing protocol, the load of Node 24 is 11, the load of Node 8 is 7, the load of Node 9 is 2 and the load of Node 25 is 5. In the network topology generated by AODV routing protocol, the load of Node 24 is 11, the load of Node 8 is 9, the load of Node 9 is 6 and the load of Node 25 is 3. The loads of the nodes in three different network topologies are as shown in Table 3.

Table 3. The loads of the nodes under three different routing protocol

Node ID	Node loads under ACA-CTP routing protocol	Node loads under CTP routing protocol	Node loads under AODV routing protocol
24	8	11	11
8	2	7	9
9	3	2	6
25	3	5	3

In order to compare the merits of the node load-balance performance of three routing protocols, the NLBD, namely Network Load Balance Degree, is introduced as a measurement standard of the network load-balance. The smaller the value of NLBD the more balanced the nodes load in the tree network. If the value of NLBD is zero, the tree network is a balanced aggregation tree. The computational formula of NLBD is as follow:

$$V_{NLBD} = \sqrt{1/n \sum_{i}^{n} (L_i - \bar{L})} \quad i \in [1, n] \tag{3}$$

Wherein, V_{NLBD} is the value of the tree network NLBD, L_i is the value of the node load, $\bar{L}$ is the average value of the node loads and n is the number of the routing nodes

Table 4. NLBD of three different routing protocol

Routing protocol	ACA-CTP	CTP	AODV
NLBD	2.34	3.26	3.03

in the tree network. The formula (3) is used to calculate respectively the NLBD value of the network topologies generated by three different routing protocols and the results obtained are shown in Table 4.

From Table 4, NLBD of ACA-CTP routing protocol is minimum, namely, the performance of balancing the node load which ACA-CTP routing protocol has is the strongest, AODV routing protocol ranks second and CTP routing protocol ranks the end. ACA-CTP routing protocol generates a four-layer aggregation tree, CTP routing pro-

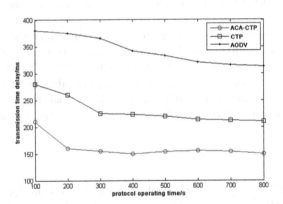

Fig. 11. Comparison of transmission time delay of three routing protocols

tocol a five-layer aggregation tree and AODV routing protocol a six-layer aggregation tree, but the more layers gone through when the terminal node transmit packets to the aggregation node, the longer the cumulative transmission time delay. The variation trend of the transmission time delay of three routing protocols is shown in Fig. 11.

Figure 11 illustrates that ACA-CTP routing protocol has a better real-time performance compared to the other two protocols, and the reason that happens is that due to the introduction of the control mechanism of Ant Colony Algorithm, the convergence speed of ACA-CTP routing protocol is faster than the other two protocols, which leads ACA-CTP routing protocol to be able to seek the optimal path meeting the requirements of QoS constraints in relatively short period of time. But as the routing protocol operating time goes by, the network topology gradually stabilize and so does the transmission time delay, so the difference of the transmission time delay between the three routing protocols gradually shrinks. Packet reception rate is an important indicator of the link quality between nodes, and the variation trend of the packet reception rate of the networks generated by the three routing protocols is shown in Fig. 12.

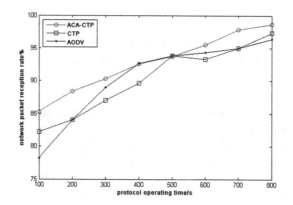

Fig. 12. Comparison of network packet reception rate of three routing protocols

Figure 12 reflects that as the routing protocol operating time goes by, the network topology gradually stabilize, and the network packet reception rate also gradually increases, although the network packet reception rate of ACA-CTP routing protocol is slightly higher than that of the other two routing protocols, the gap between them is not big. So the Qos constraint, link quality, accounts for a small proportion of the three QoS constraints and should not be a decisive factor when selecting the optimal path.

5 Conclusion

In this paper, ACA-CTP routing protocol based on the combination of Ant Colony Algorithm and CTP routing protocol is proposed and has been realized at the network layer and application layer. ACA-CTP routing protocol is verified through TOSSIOM simulator in TinyOS system to balance the load of the nodes in the network preferably, reduce the packet transmission time delay and improve the inter-node link quality, which lays a good foundation for improving the multi-hop data transmission performance of the agricultural greenhouse monitoring system. However, ACA-CTP routing protocol is only simulated in this paper, so the performance of this protocol in practical application remains to be verified.

References

1. Yu, X., Huang, C.: Congestion control algorithm based on ant colony optimization in wireless sensor networks. Appl. Res. Comput. **29**(4), 1525–1528 (2012)
2. Liu, Y., Jiang, X., Nian, X.: Study on congestion control in wireless sensor networks. Appl. Res. Comput. **2**(2), 409–412 (2008)
3. Gnawali, O., Fonseca, R., Jamieson, K.: Collection tree protocol. In: Proceedings of the 7th ACM Conference on Embedded Networked Sensor Systems, pp. 1–14 (2009)
4. Lu, T., Lu, J., Wang, X., Duan, Z.: Design of routing protocol for WSNs based on ant colony algorithm and TinyOS2.x. Appl. Res. Comput. **30**(2), 541–543 (2013)
5. Zhao, C., Wu, Y., Han, H.: Improvement of CTP routing algorithm based on WSN balanced collection tree. Comput. Eng. **38**(14), 62–65 (2012)
6. Lin, G., Ma, Z., Wang, Y.: Ant-based routing algorithm with congestion avoidance. J. Tsinghua Univ. **43**(1), 1–4 (2003)
7. Liu, R., Hu, X.: Ant colony algorithm based on dynamic adjustment of incremental of pheromone. Appl. Res. Comput. **29**(1), 135–137 (2012)
8. Chen, F., Li, R.: Routing cost-based ant colony routing algorithm for wireless sensor networks. J. South China Univ. Technol. **39**(5), 36–43 (2011)

Distributed Cooperative Flocking Control for Multiple Mobile Robots Based on IoT

Qiang Wang[(⊠)], Aosong Li, and Tian Zhu

School of Logistics Engineering, Wuhan University of Technology,
Wuhan 430063, Hubei, People's Republic of China
wangqiang@whut.edu.cn, {550366678,750175066}@qq.com

Abstract. Control of multiple mobile robots raises fundamental and novel problems in controlling the structure of the resulting dynamic graphs, particularly in applications involving the Internet of Things. This paper studies the distributed cooperative control problem of agent groups in the context of multi-agent flocking tasks with second order linear dynamics. A distributed flocking algorithm is proposed which is composed of two parts: motion strategy based on virtual units and stable flocking algorithm with bounded control input. The proposed algorithm handles the movement and reconfiguration of the flock under the environment of Internet of Things (IoT), while maintaining the desired shape for the initial dis-connected network. Experimental results demonstrate the effectiveness of the algorithm as a means to guarantee flocking in a team of robots.

Keywords: Mobile robots · IoT · Flocking algorithm

1 Introduction

Recently, the study of distributed cooperative flocking control for multiple mobile robots has drawn significant interest among researchers in many fields, from ecology to social sciences, statistical physics, and computer graphics, etc. which is mainly due to the fast development and extensive applications of distributed sensor and actuator networks in a variety of engineering areas. The success of distributed cooperative flocking control for multiple mobile robots make the task which single agent cannot complete alone previously can be achieved by multiple mobile robots through information interaction. It has many advantages such as reestablishing cooperative relations through its internal self-organization mechanism when local systems get out of order and having high work efficiency and flexibility.

Flocking is characterized by local interaction, decentralized control and self-organization. During the last decade, there is a large number of literatures focusing on the algorithm and theory of flocking motion control. In 1980s, the "boids" model had been introduced by Reynolds and meanwhile three heuristic rules of separation, cohesion and alignment was proposed as steering forces to create the first computer animation of flocking [1]. A similar model was presented which could achieve the velocity alignment, and the model has many advantages that the movement of the robots can be studied by means of mathematical tools [2]. Based on nearest neighbor

W. Li et al. (Eds.): IDCS 2016, LNCS 9864, pp. 276–286, 2016.
DOI: 10.1007/978-3-319-45940-0_25

rules, the theoretical explanation for the observations of Vicsek's model was proposed by Jadbabaie et al. Tanner et al. considered a flock of autonomous robots moving in the plane and presented a series of local control laws which combined the artificial potential field with the velocity consensus to obtain stable flocking motion in both fixed and switching networks [4]. The study on flocking theory shows that it is feasible to induce the evolution of group behavior, but how to interact with the group to make their behavior drive to the desired goal is a difficult problem. In [5], the authors presented a soft control method: adding a robot to the cluster to intervene in the cluster under the premise of not changing the individual rules and behaviors in order to move the cluster to the desired direction. Moreover, virtual leader algorithm is another kind of group behavior control algorithm, which joins a virtual leader in a group to coordinate the behavior of the group. This algorithm was proposed in [6]. In [7], Olfati Saber presented a kind of clustering algorithm based on pilot feedback under the assumption that scope of action of virtual leaders is overall situation and in constant speed. Su Hou-sheng et al. introduced a method that make sure multiple robots can track virtual leaders in constant velocity under the condition that scope of action of virtual leaders is not an overall situation [8]. In some studies, solutions of cluster problem by means of communication network have been proposed. For example, Liu Fei et al. introduced the current research status of flocking control and focused on how to design the communication mode between robots [9]. Atrianlar et al. designed an adaptive clustering algorithm under the constraint of switched topology and external environment [10]. Wang et al. solve the problems of flocking with both connectivity maintenance and obstacle avoidance for the network of dynamic agents in the case where the initial network is connected [11].

This paper investigates cooperative flocking of multiple mobile robots with double integrator dynamics in the environment of Internet of Things. Distributed cooperative control laws are designed based on velocity consensus protocols combined with artificial potential functions which can guarantee the group interactive network switches only between the connected topologies described by the neighboring graphs. Furthermore, the rigorous proof of the global asymptotic stability is given by means of Lyapunov theory. The rest of the paper is organized as follows. In Sect. 2, the multi-agent flocking problem is formulated as well as preliminaries from graph theory. In Sect. 3, a class of distributed control laws is proposed to simultaneously solve the problem of flocking motion control for cases of initial disconnected interaction topology. The theoretical results and simulation are validated in Sects. 4 and 5, respectively. Finally, conclusions are drawn in Sect. 6.

2 Problem Statement and Preliminaries

2.1 Problem Formulation

Consider a group of robots moving in a two dimensional Euclidean space, each has unit mass dynamics. A continuous-time and second order dynamical model of the system is described by

$$\dot{q}_i(t) = p_i(t)$$
$$m_i\dot{p}_i(t) = u_i(t) \qquad i = 1, 2, \ldots, n \tag{1}$$

where $p_i = (p_{i1}, p_{i2}, \ldots, p_{in})^T \in \Re^2$ is the velocity vector, $q_i = (q_{i1}, q_{i2}, \ldots, q_{in})^T \in \Re^2$ is the position vector of robot, $m_i > 0$ is the mass and there is assumed that $m_1 = m_2 = \ldots = m_n = m > 0$, $u_i = (u_{i1}, u_{i2}, \ldots, u_{in})^T \in \Re^2$ is the control input acting on robot i. In order to achieve the control objective, $u_i \in \Re^2$ should be designed to enable the group to achieve the purpose of desired flocking motion with initially disconnected networks. Furthermore, let $N_i \in \{n_j | (n_i, n_j) \in E(t)\}$ denote all communication neighbors of robot i. And some relative definitions are given as follows.

Definition 1 (Dynamic Graph). The dynamic graph $G(t) = \{V, E(t)\}$ is a time-varying undirected graph of interaction between robots in a group which consists of a set of n vertices $V = \{n_1, n_2, \ldots, n_n\}$, indexed by the robots of the group and an edge set $E(t) = \{(n_i, n_j) | \|x_{ij}(t)\| < R\}$, including unordered pairs of nodes that represent the adjacency relationship between robots, where R is the interaction range of each robot.

Definition 2 (Stable Flock). Consider a system of n mobile robots with dynamics (1). It is called a stable flock when all the robots asymptotically approach the same velocity, collisions between interactive robots are avoided and the final tight configuration of the system can minimize all robot potentials.

2.2 Preliminaries from Algebraic Graph Theory

Suppose all the robots have the same sensing radius R, and the interaction links exist only the distance between the robots is less than R. Thus, when $\|q_{ij}\| = \|q_i - q_j\| \leq R$, robots i and j are able to interact with each other. In order to describe the information flow of the sensing network, the following definitions are given as follows.

Definition 3 (Graph Connectivity). In dynamic interaction graph $G(t)$, if there exists a path between any two vertices, the graph is connected, where a path means a series of distinct vertices which are consecutive and adjacent.

Definition 4 (Graph Laplacian). The graph Laplacian of $G(t)$ is defined by $L(G) = \Delta(t) - A(t)$, in which $A(t) = [a_{ij}(t)]_{N \times N}$ is the adjacency matrix of $G(t)$ defined by $a_{ij}(t) = a_{ji}(t) = 1$ if $(n_i, n_j) \in E(G)$ and 0 otherwise.

3 Distributed Flocking with Initial Disconnected Network

3.1 Distributed Control Strategy Based on IoT

The consensus with initially disconnected robotic network is a problem to be solved immediately for the cooperative control of a group of robots. As shown in Fig. 1(a), the initial robotic network is disconnected. There is no interaction between the fractured robotic networks. The global flocking is not able to be achieved if the related consensus algorithm is applied in the network.

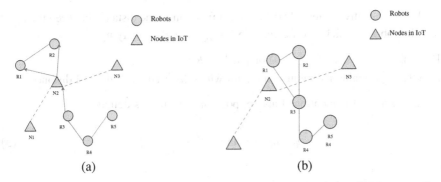

(a)   (b)

Fig. 1. Groups evolution with nodes in IoT

With the development of Internet of Things, a valuable channel will be provided by the ubiquitous wireless communications such as NFC, RFID and ZigBee. The status information of group behavior and group objectives and tasks information can be obtained through collaborative of Things sensing technology. The distribution of the state information, potential field and the evolution goal of swarm robots can be accessed by collaborative awareness technology based on Internet of Things. Thus, the concept of "virtual units" is presented in this paper.

The wireless sensor network can be controlled to produce individual information, and a "virtual units" is formed as a temporary virtual leader. The virtual leader will pilot the robot in each fractured subgroup of robots, and several sub-group of robot will connect finally. Thus, induced information model based on characteristics of wireless sensor networks is built, and a swarm behavior control algorithm is proposed for solving the flocking problem for the multi-robot systems with initially disconnected network. When the entire system has connected topology, the "virtual units" is disappeared, and the neighboring robot will have equal speed and the same direction, leading the rest of the robot to the target position. Finally, the magnitude and direction of the velocity of all robots will tend to converge. The desired distance between the robots can be achieved. As shown in the Fig. 1(b), the node 2 in the IoT is represented as "virtual units" to lead the robot R1, R2 and R3 to connect eventually.

3.2   Flocking Algorithm Using Potential Function

For case where the initial topology is not connected, a control input is presented as follow which combines the potential function of the objectives and tasks with the induced effects of "virtual units".

$$u_i = \alpha_i + \beta_i + \gamma_i + \rho_i + \sigma_i \tag{2}$$

where α_i is used to represent the artificial potential which generate a control component between the robot. It comes from the potential function $\psi(\|q_{ij}\|)$. It used to characterize the function of relative distance of robot and its proximity;

The non-negative potential $\psi(\|q_{ij}\|)$ is a function of the distance between the robot i and the robot j, which is differentiable for $q_{ij} \in (0, R)$, satisfying

(1) $\psi(\|q_{ij}\|) \to \infty$ as $\|q_{ij}\| \to 0$ or $\|q_{ij}\| \to R$.
(2) $\psi(\|q_{ij}\|)$ attains its unique minimum when $\|q_{ij}\|$ equals a desired distance.

According to the mentioned above, potential function is defined as:

$$\psi(\|q_{ij}\|) = \ln\|q_{ij}\|^2 + \frac{d_{ij}}{\|q_{ij}\|^2} \tag{3}$$

where d_{ij} is desired distance

β_i is used to represent the speed convergent control components of the robot i and its neighborhood. γ_i is used to indicate the speed control components to make robot i tends to the desired speed, which depends on external input signal that is the speed of the virtual unit. ρ_i is used to represent a control component of the potential generated by the objectives and tasks. σ_i represents the induction from virtual units.

The virtual units is primarily produced by potential function $\psi(\|q_{ij}\|)$, potential function $\varphi(D)$ of objectives and tasks set D. The mathematical expression is used to represent potential function in multi-robot systems, it can be defined as:

$$\mu_{iv_i} = \begin{cases} f(\psi(\|q_{ij}\|), \varphi(D)), & \delta(i,j)[t] = 0 \\ 0, & \delta(i,j)[t] = 1 \end{cases} \tag{4}$$

where objectives and tasks set $D = \{w_1, w_2, \cdots, w_m\}$, the function of D is defined as:

$$\varphi(q, D) = \frac{d_{v(q_{i,D})}}{1 + d_v(q_{i,D})} = \frac{\prod_{k \in D} d_k(q_i)}{1 + \prod_{k \in D} d_k(q_i)} \tag{5}$$

where $k = 1, 2, \cdots, m$, $d_k(q_i) = \|q_i - w_k\|_2^2$, $d_{v(q_{i,D})} = \prod_{k \in D} d_k(q_i)$, w_k represents the coordinates of the location of the k-th task.

Thus, the specific control algorithm is given as below

$$u_i = -\sum_{j \in N_i} \nabla_{q_i} \psi(q_{ij}) - \sum_{j \in N_t} a_{ij}(p_i - p_j) - m_i(p_i - p_{v_i}) - \nabla \varphi(q_i, D) - \nabla \mu_{iv_i} \tag{6}$$

where p_{v_i} is the speed of the virtual units, μ_{iv_i} represents a potential function of the virtual units.

4 Proof of the Theorem

In the stability analysis, we consider the multiple mobile robots system with the same structure for the sake of simplicity. The physical structure, the performance, mass and damping coefficient of all robots and virtual bodies are considered as the same.

Therefore, $m_1 = m_2 = \cdots = m_n = m$, $p_{v_1} = p_{v_2} = \cdots = p_{v_i} = p_r$. To prove the stability of multiple mobile robots system, an error vector is defined $e_q^i = q_i - p_r t$. Differentiate the formula twice; the following formula can be obtained:

$$\dot{e}_q^i = e_p^i = p_i - p_r$$
$$\dot{e}_p^i = \dot{p}_i = \frac{1}{m} u_i \tag{7}$$

where e_q^i represents the difference vector of the actual speed and the expected speed of the robot i.

According to the description of artificial potentials, $\psi(\|q_{ij}\|) = \psi\left(\left\|e_q^{ij}\right\|\right) = \tilde{\psi}^{ij}$ can be defined, where $e_q^{ij} \triangleq e_q^i - e_q^j$, so $\nabla_{e_q^i} \tilde{\psi}^{ij} = \nabla_{q_i} \psi(\|q_{ij}\|)$ can be introduced. Therefore, the control input of the robot i in error system is as follows:

$$u_i = -\sum_{j \in N_i} \nabla_{e_q^i} \tilde{\psi}^{ij} - \sum_{j \in N_t} a_{ij}\left(e_p^i - e_p^j\right) - me_p^i - \nabla\varphi(q_i, D) - \nabla\mu_{iv_i} \tag{8}$$

According to the control input of (8), all the robots can achieve the velocity alignment and reach the desired configuration as well as maintaining the network connectivity during the whole control process. To prove the hypothesis, it needs to prove that formula (8) is stable, and the same control effect can be produced.

The proof procedure is as follows:

Design a positive semi-definite function

$$J^i = \tilde{\psi}^i + \frac{1}{2} me_p^{iT} e_p^i$$
$$J = \sum_{i=1}^N J^i \tag{9}$$

Function J^i is the energy of the robot i, and the physical meaning of J is the total potential energy and the kinetic energy of all the robots in the error system.

According to the symmetry of $\psi(\|q_{ij}\|)$ and e_q^{ij}, the formula can be introduced as follows:

$$\frac{\partial \tilde{\psi}^{ij}}{\partial e_q^{ij}} = \frac{\partial \tilde{\psi}^{ij}}{\partial e_q^i} = \frac{\partial \tilde{\psi}^{ij}}{\partial e_q^j} \tag{10}$$

The following formula can be deduced:

$$\frac{d}{dt} \tilde{\psi}^i = \sum_{j \in N_i} \left(\nabla_{e_q^i} \tilde{\psi}^{ij}\right)^T e_p^i \tag{11}$$

Differentiate J^i and we can have:

$$\dot{J}^i = \sum_{j \in N_i} \left(\nabla_{e_q^i} \tilde{\psi}^{ij} \right)^T e_p^i + m e_p^{iT} \dot{e}_p^i \tag{12}$$

According to Eq. (7) we can have

$$m\dot{e}_p^i = u_i = -\sum_{j \in N_i} \nabla_{e_q^i} \tilde{\psi}^{ij} - \sum_{j \in N_i} a_{ij} \left(e_p^i - e_p^j \right) - m e_p^i - \nabla \varphi(q_i, D) - \nabla \mu_{iv_i} \tag{13}$$

Through Eqs. (12) and (13) we can have

$$\dot{J}^i = -\sum_{j \in N_i} a_{ij} \left(e_p^{iT} e_p^i - e_p^{iT} e_p^j \right) - m e_p^{iT} e_p^i - \left(\nabla \varphi(q_i, D) + \nabla \mu_{iv_i} \right)^T e_p^i \tag{14}$$

Sum up all $\dot{J}^i$ we can have

$$\dot{J} = -e_p^T [L(t) \otimes I_n] e_p - m e_p^T e_p - \left(\nabla \varphi(q, D) + \nabla \mu \right)^T e_p \tag{15}$$

where $e_p = \left(e_p^1, e_p^2, \cdots, e_p^n \right)$ is the matrix of the speed of all the robots in the error system, and $L(G)$ represents graph Laplacian of system, I_n is n order unit matrix.

According to the knowledge of matrix theory and definition of $L(G)$ matrix, $L(G)$ is the same as I_n, so $L(G)$ is a positive definite matrix, and meanwhile Eigenvalues of $L(G)$ matrix is positive. By the Eqs. (4) and (5) it can be obtained that $\nabla \varphi(q, D) + \nabla \mu$ is constantly non-negative, and because m > 0, we can see $\dot{J} \leq 0$, and only if $e_p^1 = e_p^2 = \cdots = e_p^n = 0$, as $p_1 = p_2 = \cdots = p_n = 0$, $\dot{J} = 0$. By the Lyapunov stability theory shows that the sub-group movement in the case of a multi-robot system with initial disconnected network is stable.

5 Simulation

Using the collaborative sensing technology of Internet of things and the "virtual units" generation mechanism, cooperative control algorithm is proposed to ensure the global connectivity of the robots in the initial disconnected network. In this section, a comparative experiment is shown to verify the effectiveness of the control algorithm. Simulation is based on the development environment of MATLAB platform, and five hollow squares represent five robots. The robots are divided into two groups which not connected. Five robots have the same dynamic performance as the Eq. 1. The velocity of the robots is random, but they must meet the following conditions:

(1) The initial velocity is randomly distributed in the range of [0, 1] m/s, and velocity direction is arbitrary.

(2) The choice of initial position must meet the requirements of the initial discon-nected network topology.

(3) In addition, the assumption that the interaction sensing radius R = 1, expected distance d_{ij} is 1 m, continuous edge delay threshold is 0.7 m.

The simulation test shows the weight information of each robot can be obtained by choosing both robot's ID and the distance between robot's current position and target location as heuristic information. In this simulation, the target position is set as (10 m, 10 m) and it takes up to about 5 s. In order to verify the validity of the control algorithm, two simulation experiments has been done to make a contrast. One group is in the environment with Internet of things, which is shown in Fig. 2. The hollow cycle represents the node in Internet of things, and at some moment, one of nodes forms the "virtual units" to induce aggregation of two sets sub-groups as shown in Fig. 2(b). And then the "virtual units" disappears and reverts to a node as shown in Fig. 2(c).

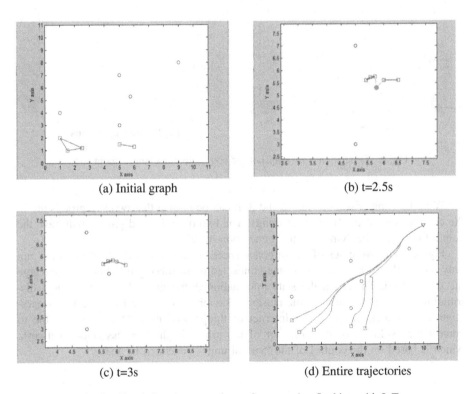

(a) Initial graph

(b) t=2.5s

(c) t=3s

(d) Entire trajectories

Fig. 2. Simulation time snapshots of cooperative flocking with IoT

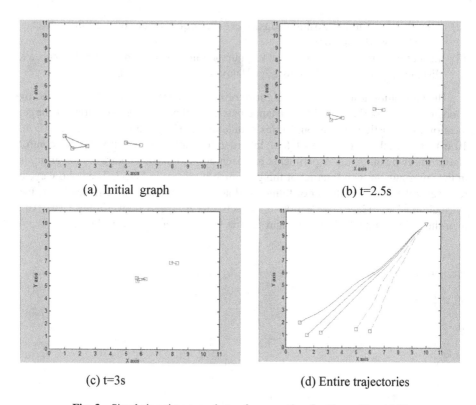

(a) Initial graph   (b) t=2.5s

(c) t=3s   (d) Entire trajectories

Fig. 3. Simulation time snapshots of cooperative flocking without IoT

With the comparison of Figs. 2 and 3, it can be known that two sub-groups are in the environment of the Internet of things. The two disconnected groups will have the connection using the "virtual units" generation mechanism.

Figure 4 are two cases of convergence speed. It shown that the "virtual units" not only induce the formation of two interconnected multi-robot group but also converge the same speed. Therefore, the state information distribution, the potential field distribution, and the evolution of the cluster behavior are obtained by using the cooperative sensing technology of the Internet of things, and meanwhile it is feasible to control the evolution of the behavior of the robots in the wireless sensor network, which is based on the control of the "virtual units" generated by IoT.

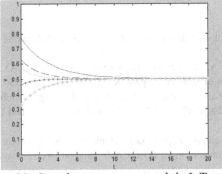

(a) Speed convergence graph in IoT

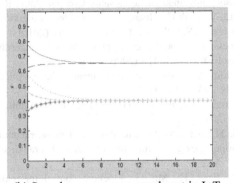

(b) Speed convergence graph not in IoT

Fig. 4. Comparison of speed coverage

6   Conclusion

In this paper, the distributed flocking control of multiple autonomous robots based on IoT is investigated. Several control laws under the environment of IoT are proposed to combine motion control and connectivity control strategies, which aim to enable the robots to asymptotically obtain the stable flocking motion. For the connectedness control, new artificial potentials are designed to make the robots achieve the velocity alignment and reach the desired configuration as well as maintaining the network connectivity during the whole control process. Furthermore, the introduced "virtual unit" algorithm makes all the robots subscribe to the control and function of the "virtual unit", which increases robustness and stability of the system. Future research will focus on simulations and experiments in order to test and verify correctness of theory, and studying the flocking behavior in constraint environments with obstacles.

Acknowledgment. This research was supported by the National Natural Science Foundation of China (No. 61503291)

References

1. Reynolds, C.W.: Flocks, herds, and schools: a distributed behavioral model. Comput. Graph. **21**, 25–34 (1987)
2. Vicsek, T., Czirók, A., Ben-Jacob, E., Cohen, I.I., Shochet, O.: Novel type of phase transition in a system of self-driven particles. Phys. Rev. Lett. **75**(6), 1226–1229 (2006)
3. Tanner, H.G., Jadbabaie, A., Pappas, G.J.: Stable flocking of mobile agents, part I: fixed topology. In: Proceedings. 42nd IEEE Conference on Decision and Control, pp. 2010–2015. IEEE (2010)
4. Tanner, H.G., Jadbabaie, A., Pappas, G.J.: Stable flocking of mobile robots, part II: dynamic topology. In: Proceedings of 42nd IEEE Conference on Decision and Control, Albuquerque, pp. 2016–2021, NM, USA (2003)
5. Liang, X.L., Sun, Q., Yin, Z.H., Wang Y.L., Liu P.N.: Overview of intelligent control methods for large scale unmanned cluster system. Comput. Appl. Res. **32**(1) (2015)
6. Liu, W.X., Chen, J.L., Wan, W.G., Huang, B.: Virtual leader algorithm for flocking motion control. J. Shanghai Univ. (Nat. Sci. Ed.) **16**(4), 349–354 (2010)
7. Olfati-Saber, R.: Flocking for multi-agent dynamic systems: algorithms and theory. IEEE Trans. Autom. Control **51**(3), 401–420 (2006)
8. Su, H., Wang, X., Lin, Z.: Flocking of multi-agents with a virtual leader. IEEE Trans. Autom. Control **54**(2), 293–307 (2009)
9. Liu, F., Ji, Z.J.: The controllability of two order delay discrete multi-robots system. J. Syst. Sci. Complex. **35**(3) (2015)
10. Atrianlar, H., Haeri, M.: Adaptive flocking control of nonlinear multi-agent systems with directed switching topologies and saturation constrains. J. Frankl. Inst. **35**(6), 1545–1561 (2013)
11. Wang, Q., Chen, J., Fang, H., Ma, Q.: Flocking control for multi-agent systems with stream-based obstacle avoidance. Trans. Inst. Meas. Control **36**(3), 391–398 (2013)

Logistics Vehicle Travel Preference of Interest Points Based on Speed and Accessory State

Shengwu Xiong[1,2], Li Kuang[1], Pengfei Duan[1,2(✉)], and Wei Shi[1]

[1] School of Computer Science and Technology, Wuhan University of Technology,
Wuhan, People's Republic of China
{swxiong,duanpf}@whut.edu.cn,
{547207352,986596691}@qq.com
[2] Hubei Key Laboratory of Transportation Internet of Things,
Wuhan, People's Republic of China

Abstract. In a crowded city, directions and speed of vehicles are usually changed arbitrarily. Analyzing travel preferences of vehicle has become a focus of research as it helps to classify region of interest in city and can be used in personalized recommendation and many other areas of application. In this paper, a travel identification method based on vehicle speed and Accessory (ACC) State is proposed. Continuously classifying and merging the trajectory points in GPS data stream, the travel activities of vehicle is extracted. It can provide a basis of data for the research on hot spots and support the research and application of vehicle trajectory data mining in areas of intelligent transportation and logistics.

Keywords: Vehicle speed · ACC state · Travel identification · Hot spots · Logistics vehicle

1 Introduction

It's the main step of vehicle travel identification that converting location information to travel behavior information based on time and space, through a certain stroke recognition algorithm with the original GPS data in sequence received from vehicle terminal. In this way, it can recognize the stop and move stage of vehicles, figure out which sort of location drivers willing to stay, analyze travel preference in deep, as a meaningful research of interest points and other activities about vehicles in logistics field.

At present, travel characteristics research based on GPS trace data has been made certain achievements [1–3]. Recognition algorithm in travel characteristics mainly includes exploring algorithm, clustering algorithm [4, 5] and velocity threshold merging algorithm [6]. The improved clustering algorithm reduces the dependence of prior experience and basic data with wide range of application. Zhou Yonggui [7] mined hot routes within the city by taking into account both R* tree spatial index mechanism and DBSCAN clustering algorithm, making clustering result more accurately and efficiently in the LBSN environment. However, it's not suitable for massive data processing since the amount of data increases and results in a burden of large computation. Xiao Yanli [8] proposed an identification method using the GPS trajectory points with the speed

W. Li et al. (Eds.): IDCS 2016, LNCS 9864, pp. 287–295, 2016.
DOI: 10.1007/978-3-319-45940-0_26

less than a certain threshold. The velocity threshold-merging algorithm has advantages over clustering algorithm in terms of low cost, higher accuracy, faster data update cycle, better research value and practicality, though ignoring the inherent relationship between the vehicle speeds and driving state. In that condition, we can't extract the characteristics of behavior from stop and off stop driving process, limiting the in-depth study and application in temporal and spatial characteristics of vehicle.

In the field of mobile trajectory data mining, Microsoft Asia Research Institute has launched T-Drive [9–11], GeoLife [12, 13], T-Share [14], Urban Computing [15], T-Finder [16] etc. Nevertheless, the vehicle is a constrained moving object, only on a particular route mobile. Vehicle trajectory data has strong spatial-temporal correlation, which means temporal and spatial characteristics of the problem need to be considered in the study.

In the light of the above, this paper proposes the method of travel activity identification based on vehicle speed and accessory (ACC) state based on threshold merging mentioned above in Sect. 1. Section 2 explains the process of our method of travel activities recognition, for research of travel preference around interest points. Collection of 68 logistics vehicles is carried out in Wuhan city. And those several areas logistics vehicle mainly frequented are explored and discussed as interest points in Sect. 3, and Sect. 4 concludes the paper.

2   Materials and Methods

2.1   Data Collection

A vehicle terminal is set to send the GPS data with time segments (30 s) in each logistics vehicle in operation. In this paper, mainly by the interaction between GPS data and vehicle monitoring platform, we obtain the GPS data by real-time acquisition and off-line migration. The real-time information is got through news subscription, and GPS metadata in history is from the WCF service vehicle GPS database of our system. We complete the missing data by off-line migration when subscribing to real-time is abnormal according to the subscription system abnormal log. In the collected GPS database are 68 vehicles containing 140493 parking activities in February 2015.

2.2   Travel and Park Activities

By the heuristic of threshold velocity of the merging algorithm principle, in order to reduce the identification cycle of travel data, the full analysis of the characteristics of GPS terminal trajectory data is made. Thus a stroke recognition algorithm based on the vehicle speed and ACC state is designed for recognition of vehicle GPS data and extraction of parking position.

In the actual traffic scenic, there are two kinds of vehicle stop as we said before, flameout and non-flame residence. In Table 1, we distinguish three types of trajectory points, stationary point, candidate stationary point and moving point by the velocity

Table 1. Types and characteristics of vehicle trajectory data point

	Trajectory point	Velocity	ACC state
1	stationary point	any, normal value: 0	**off**
2	candidate stationary point	$\leq$ threshold	on
3	moving point	$>$ threshold	on

threshold and ACC gear state. The velocity threshold is generally 3–6 km/h. We use it for the vehicle parking position properties analysis as a new method.

There are parking spots that the stationary points of the ACC gear state is off, revealing the vehicle is in flameout state. In the candidate stationary points set, as the vehicle location information is acquired based on time interval, it may be implied real parking position so that it can be treated as a separate class. In Fig. 1, it's a process of travel and park activities recognition with trajectory points based on velocity threshold and ACC state.

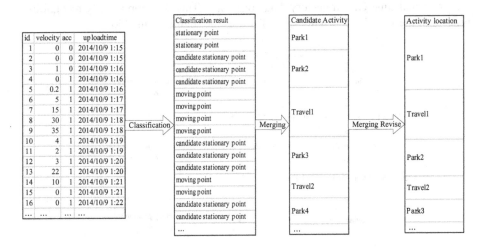

Fig. 1. Recognition process of travel and park activities

2.3 Travel Identification Modeling

We define the travel activities as:

$$PS = \{Park_1, Travel_1, \dots, Park_i, Travel_i, \dots\} \tag{1}$$

In the above formula, PS represents a set of trajectory points in a time sequence, Park is defined as the occurrence of a park activity, Travel is defined as the occurrence of a travel activity. Besides, Park and Travel should alternate in the *PS*. *Park$_i$* means the i_{th} time park activity, and *Travel$_i$* means the i_{th} time travel activity.

$$PT_i^e = TT_i^s \tag{2}$$

$$TT_i^e = PT_{i+1}^s \tag{3}$$

$$PL_i \cdot ps^e = TL_i \cdot ps^s \tag{4}$$

$$TL_i \cdot ps^e = PL_{i+1} \cdot ps^s \tag{5}$$

In the physical sense, the end time of the i_{th} park is the start time of the i_{th} travel, the end time of the i_{th} travel is the start time of the $(i+1)_{th}$ park. Similarly, the location point of the end time of the i_{th} park is as the point as the start time of the i_{th} travel, and the location point of the end time of the i_{th} travel is as the point as the start time of the $(i+1)_{th}$ park. So we use *PL* as location information for research in the next part.

2.4 Recognition Process

In summary, assume that PS is a FIFO (First-In First-Out) sequence, message queue receiving real-time GPS trajectory data constantly. This is a stop activity recognition process of the vehicle shown in Fig. 2. T means the segment time (30 s).

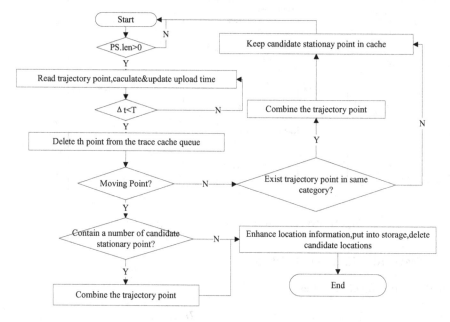

Fig. 2. Identification process of a stop activity in the vehicle trip

3   Results and Analysis

3.1   Classification of Trip Interest Points Based on Baidu POI Database

In this work, we chose the typical urban city-Wuhan encountering different kinds of interest points with 68 logistics vehicle running around. According to attribute classification criteria of interest points, "Standard of urban land classification and planning construction land" (http://www.law110.com/lawserve/guihua/1800004.htm) issued by the state, we divide the interest points into 16 types, such as catering, accommodation, shopping based on the Baidu map POI database CLA category identification and interest point classification criteria of Google Map. What's more, we succeed to figure out 184975 interest points in 187640 for the recognition rate is as high as 98.57 %. Figure 3 is the statistical situation of the interest category in Wuhan. In those points, enterprise, shopping, services and catering, respectively, include 39704, 26443, 20492, 16786 POI points, which accounting for more than 50 %. A large number of enterprises in line with Wuhan indicates it is a traditional industrial city, while shopping, services, catering and entertainment type of points of interest accounted for approximately 40 %, which show that service ability of Wuhan city is good.

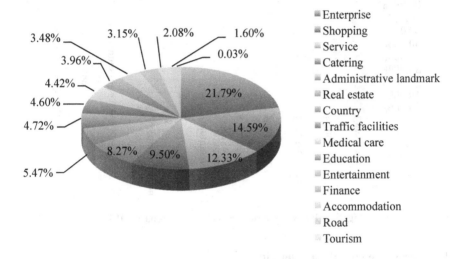

Fig. 3. Proportion of interest points in Wuhan

3.2 Interest Points Recognition of Logistics Vehicle

As shown in Fig. 4, it is a heat map of POI distribution in Wuhan area. In the process of studying the interest point of the vehicle, the way of parking in the event (such as the flameout and non-flame residence) and the length of parking time, and so on, we identify 139220 stop points categories on the collection of 140493 stop activities of 68 logistics vehicles in February 2015 making the recognition rate up to 99.09 %. It can in a certain extent reflect vehicle travel preferences and travel patterns in Fig. 5 that vehicles in monitoring system platform mainly concentrated in the enterprise, education, entertainment and real estate areas and so on.

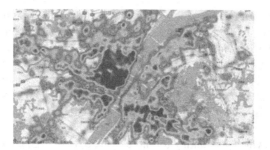

Fig. 4. Heat map distribution of interest points

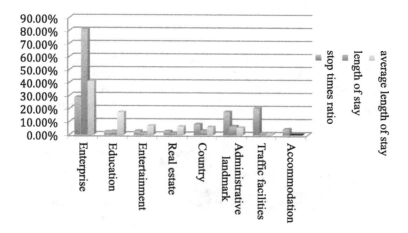

Fig. 5. Main vehicle stop in Wuhan in February 2015

3.3 Average Length of Parking Time

The average length of parking time refers to the ratio of vehicle dwell time at the interest point and residence times. In Fig. 6, obviously, it's over 75 % of the total with type of enterprise, education, entertainment, real estate and country, which means vehicle activities are mainly concentrated in those areas. Through the analysis of park activities data, Jianhu campus in Wuhan University of Technology is one of the highest education activities, the entertainment POI includes the small Forest Farm and Resorts, the real estate mainly includes the city 8090 and the pan Sea International Settlements. For the country, they are Wuhan District of Jiangxia City, Phoenix Road station, China Construction Third Dongxihu Bureau of commodity concrete company. The analysis results are consistent with the actual situation of vehicle operations, showing that the method is feasible and effective for the analysis of vehicle park activity characteristics based on nearest interest points of vehicle park.

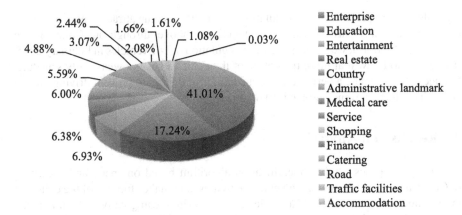

Fig. 6. Average length of parking time around the interest point in Wuhan in February 2015

3.4 Choice for Vehicle Parking at the Interest Points

Table 2 shows 14 kinds of interest points that logistics vehicles choose to park in different period time. Ignoring the impact of road traffic on travel, it reveals that enterprises, country, administrative landmarks and real estate area of interest points are enjoying a higher degree of activity. As the source of GPS data receiving from enterprise logistics vehicles, the concrete transportation closely related to enterprises, administrative landmarks and real estate, indicates the business characteristics of logistics vehicle and high reliability of stroke recognition.

In the process of studying the interest points of the vehicle, the way of staying in the event (such as the flame-out stop, the non flame-out) and the length of stay, and so on,

Table 2. The average length of parking time(s) at interest points in Wuhan in February 2015

	06–10	10–14	14–18	18–22	22–02	02–06
Catering	438	301	695	718	761	1709
Road	868	833	614	268	89	33
Real estate	4107	1314	1930	1811	1493	10211
Service	850	732	566	1486	2893	1190
Shopping	418	435	1348	1534	1065	531
Country	2677	1539	1277	1582	2370	922
Administrative landmark	1775	5501	2929	2444	6027	1235
Traffic facilities	60	376	1255	211	2178	385
Education	5700	5846	4295	3261	12203	12962
Finance	1295	507	92	1266	105	124
Enterprise	21221	3675	4975	6194	9140	3748
Medical care	27	39008	150	253	174	0
Entertainment	2226	1993	2661	1612	3785	1946
Accommodation	0	197	367	19	1494	30

can reflect travel preference and regulation of vehicle, also the attractiveness degree of region of interest. Apart from the work mentioned above, through our Collaborative Supervision Platform, we success to extract regulation of 147 vehicles in February 2015. It's serious to know that more than 50 % of the vehicles share a weak daily schedule. It's necessary to make a periodic task scheduling for drivers to prevent driving fatigue and reduce the occurrence probability of accidents.

4   Results and Analysis

This paper proposes a travel identification algorithm based on speed and accessory (ACC) gear state while analyzing vehicle activities, and makes full use of the collected information about the state of the vehicle. The algorithm can greatly shorten the data update cycle of traditional trajectory stroke recognition and ensure the recognition accuracy. Based on the recognition of the retention activities, we facilitate the research on logistics travel preference around interest points. It's of great significance to the expansion of logistics station in city. And it can reduce additional consumption of vehicle operation and improve efficiency of logistics. Such related data mining applications can be used in not just logistics but vehicle ROI (region of interest) mining and personalized recommendation; intelligent transportation guidance to road service assessment, reflecting capacity of urban road.

Acknowledgments. This work was supported in part by the National High-tech R&D Program of China (863 Program) under Grant No. 2015AA015403, Science & Technology Pillar Program of Hubei Province under Grant No. 2014BAA146, Nature Science Foundation of Hubei Province under Grant No. 2015CFA059, Hubei Key Laboratory of Transportation Internet of Things under Grant No. 2015III015-B03 and CERNET Innovation Project under Grant No. NGII20151006.

References

1. Deng, Z., Ji, M., Chen, W.: Coupling passive GPS tracking and web-based travel surveys. J. Transp. Syst. Eng. Inf. Technol. **10**(2), 178–183 (2009)
2. Stopher, P., FitzGerald, C., Zhang, J.: Search for a global positioning system device to measure personal travel. Transp. Res. Part C **16**, 350–369 (2008)
3. Zhang, B.: Research on the Simplification and Semantic Enhancement of GPS Temporal and Spatial Trajectory Data for Traffic Travel Survey. East China Normal University, Shanghai (2011)
4. Zhou, C., Frankowski, D., Ludford, P., et al.: Discovering personal gazetteers: an interactive clustering approach, pp. 266–273. ACM (2004)
5. Tietbohl, A., Bogorny, V., Kuijpers, B., et al.: A clustering-based approach for discovering interesting places in trajectories. In: SAC, pp. 863–868 (2008)
6. Zhang, J., Qiu, P., Xu, Z.: A method to identify trip based on the mobile phone positioning. J. Wuhan Univ. Technol. (Transp. Sci. Eng.) **37**(5), 934–938 (2013)
7. Zou, Y., Wan, J., Xia, Y.: LBSN user movement trajectory clustering mining method based on road network. Appl. Res. Comput. **08**(8), 102–110 (2013)

8. Xiao, Y., Zhang, Z., Yang, W.: Users' mobility behaviours mining algorithm based on GPS trajectory. Comput. Appl. Softw. **32**(11), 83–87 (2015)
9. Yuan, J., Zheng, Y., Xie, X.: Discovering regions of different functions in a city using human mobility and POIs. In: ACM SIGKDD Conference on Knowledge Discovery and Data Mining, pp. 186–194 (2012)
10. Xue, A., Zhang, R., Zheng, Y., et al.: Destination prediction by sub-trajectory synthesis and privacy protection against such prediction. In: IEEE International Conference on Data Engineering, pp. 254–265 (2013)
11. Yuan, J., Zheng, Y., Xie, X., et al.: T-Drive: enhancing driving directions with taxi drivers' intelligence. IEEE Trans. Knowl. Data Eng. **25**(1), 220–232 (2013)
12. Zheng, Y., Xie, X.: Learning travel recommendations from user-generated GPS traces. ACM Trans. Intell. Syst. Technol. **2**(1), 389–396 (2011)
13. Zheng, V., Zheng, Y., Xie, X., et al.: Collaborative location and activity recommendations with GPS history data. In: Proceeding of the 19th International Conference on World Wide Web (2010)
14. Ma, S., Zheng, Y., Wolfson, O.: T-share: a large-scale dynamic taxi ridesharing service. In: IEEE International Conference on Data Engineering, pp. 410–421 (2013)
15. Liu, Y., Kang, C., Gao, S., et al.: Understanding intra-urban trip patterns from taxi trajectory data. J. Geogr. Syst. **14**(4), 463–483 (2012)
16. Yuan, N., Zheng, Y., Zhang, L., et al.: T-Finder: a recommender system for finding passengers and vacant taxis. IEEE Trans. Knowl. Data Eng. **25**(10), 2390–2403 (2013)

Tools for Ontology Matching—Practical Considerations from INTER-IoT Perspective

Maria Ganzha[1,4], Marcin Paprzycki[1(✉)], Wiesław Pawłowski[2], Paweł Szmeja[1], Katarzyna Wasielewska[1], and Giancarlo Fortino[3]

[1] Systems Research Institute, Polish Academy of Sciences, Warsaw, Poland
{maria.ganzha,marcin.paprzycki,wieslaw.pawlowski,pawel.szmeja,
katarzyna.wasielewska}@ibspan.waw.pl
[2] Faculty of Mathematics, Physics, and Informatics, University of Gdańsk,
Gdańsk, Poland
wieslaw.pawlowski@inf.ug.edu.pl
[3] Dept of Informatics, Modeling, Electronics and Systems,
University of Calabria, Rende, Italy
giancarlo.fortino@unical.it
[4] Warsaw University of Technology, Warsaw, Poland

Abstract. There exists a large body of scientific literature devoted to ontology matching, aligning, mapping translating and merging. With it, comes a long list (90+) of tools that support various aspects of these operations. We have approached such tools from the perspective of the INTER-IoT project, in which one of the goals is to facilitate semantic interoperability of Internet of Things platforms. Thus, we had to answer a question: what is *actually* available when one needs to align/merge ontologies. Here, we summarize our findings.

Keywords: Ontology · Ontology aligning · Ontology merging · Internet of Things

1 Introduction

Today, research concerning ontology alignment, matching, merging, mapping, translating remains popular among researchers. In [21], 694 recent papers from that area have been meticulously selected and evaluated, clearly showing that not only the activity level remains high, but that the interest is growing. Furthermore, in Sect. 4.3 and in Table 5 of [21], a list of approximately 60 tools, deadling with various aspects of ontology mapping, by using different approaches, has been compiled. This suggests that the area is maturing. As a matter of fact, one of the key conclusions, from this paper, was a "positive outlook" for ontology engineering, seen both from the academic and practical perspectives. Moreover, when we have extended our research to tools/platforms found in other sources, such as [10], websites [1,2], as well as resulting from general Web searches, a total of 97 references were gathered.

© Springer International Publishing AG 2016
W. Li et al. (Eds.): IDCS 2016, LNCS 9864, pp. 296–307, 2016.
DOI: 10.1007/978-3-319-45940-0_27

Our interest in ontology engineering comes from the INTER-IoT project [4]. Its goal is to provide novel solutions to the lack of interoperability among Internet of Things (IoT) platforms. While the project, as a whole, is to facilitate interoperability across the hardware-software stack, in the context of this contribution we are interested in the highest layer, semantic, interoperability. The background of our work is provided by two use case scenarios. First, involves joining two eHealth (IoT) platforms. Second, deals with joining an IoT platform from a sea port terminal, supervising container management, with an IoT platform of a logistics company that deals with truck fleet management. In both cases, semantic interoperability involves instantiating a "common ontology". Here, it should be stressed that the actual way, in which the common ontology will be instantiated, is likely to be context and system architecture dependent. Nevertheless, to be able to achieve this goal, we would like to use (if only possible) already existing tools. Hence, we have decided to establish, which of the existing 97 tools can be immediately (or after small modifications) applied to the problem we are facing. The aim of this paper is to summarize results of our investigations.

The main contribution of this work is to go beyond the optimism expressed in [21] and provide a realistic assessment of *tools that are actually available today* (in 2016), their capabilities, and limitations. In this way, unless one of "defunct-tools" is resurrected, only tools listed here (and new ones, created afterwards) need to be considered by practitioners who align/merge ontologies.

To this effect we proceed as follows. In Sect. 2 we provide definitions of key terms used in the paper (and relations between them). We follow, in Sect. 3, with brief summary of the two use case scenarios. These two sections provide the foundation for the analysis of the state-of-the-world of tools for ontology alignment/matching/merging/mapping/translating, A.D. 2016. Here, we first (in Sect. 4) reflected on how someone who needs a specific job done would look at these tools. As a result, by approaching tools from a very pragmatic perspective, 7 tools were selected as worthy further evaluation. In Sect. 5, we present more detailed description of each of them. Next, we present a high-level reflection on the problem of "computing" the common semantics, that we have to address, and for which finding ontology alignments is just the first step (Sect. 6). Section 7, summarizes our key findings.

2   Definitions

Let us start from defining key terms. In the context of semantic interoperability, topics such as ontology alignment, matching, merging and mapping need to be disambiguated. These terms are closely related and sometimes used interchangeably. For each, there are many, sometimes overlapping, definitions. For the purpose of clarity, in the scope of this article, we use the following definitions (see, also, [10]).

Ontology alignment, refers to *finding correspondences between two or more ontologies*. The result of this process is an *alignment*—a set of *correspondences* between entities (atomic alignment) or groups of entities and sub-structures (complex alignment) from different ontologies. A correspondence can be either a predicate about similarity, called a *matching*, or a logical axiom—a *mapping*. Typically used mapping axioms are equivalence and subsumption. In practice, ontology alignment tools often state a degree of confidence for every correspondence in the mapping. An equivalence axiom with a degree of confidence is very close in meaning to a predicate about similarity (a matching). The terms "mapping" and "matching" are often not distinguished in the terminology used by the alignment tools. A set of correspondences can be called "alignment", "matching", or "mapping" practically interchangeably.

Ontology merging is a *process of combining two, or more, ontologies into one*. Consequently, the resulting ontology stores knowledge from all merged ones. Merging often utilizes a set of alignments to create deep interconnections between ontologies and, in the end, merge them into one.

Finally, **ontology translation**, or, more precisely, *semantics translation*, is a *process of changing the underlying semantics of a piece of knowledge*. Given some information described semantically, in terms of a source ontology, it is transformed into information described in terms of a target ontology. Resulting information contains no references to source semantics, instead it has only target semantics. In a good translation, the meaning should be preserved. Semantics translation is an application of ontology alignment. The goal is to enable one-way or two-way "understanding" between software artifacts that implement differing semantics. This is directly applicable to multiple domains such as IoT, bioinformatics and others, because there are competing ontologies that describe the same or very similar area of knowledge. For instance, the IoT ontologies: OpenIoT[1], SAREF[2], and oneM2M[3], have very similar scope. Therefore, it is reasonable to expect that good alignments may be found between them. It is unreasonable, however, to expect each "hybrid IoT" system to implement semantics originating from all of those (and possibly other) ontologies. Therefore, semantics translation is a practical endeavor.

3 INTER-IoT use cases

The context of our work is provided by the two large-scale pilots that are the core of the INTER-IoT project:

– *(e/m)Health* The goal is to facilitate interoperability between two heterogeneous IoT platforms—one for remote use of *non-wearable devices*, and another for devices organized in a *body sensor network*. Both platforms use cloud infrastructure and Bluetooth technology to interact with measuring devices. However, their technologies are different (and thus are not interoperable). On the data and semantics level, one platform exposes JSON web services

---

[1] https://github.com/OpenIotOrg/openiot.

[2] https://sites.google.com/site/smartappliancesproject/ontologies/reference-ontology.

[3] http://www.onem2m.org/technical/onem2m-ontologies.

for third party systems, whereas the other utilizes Google Datastore API. While both platforms gather data with intuitively similar semantic meaning (e.g. temperature, blood pressure) they store them in different formats, and use somewhat different semantics. For example, in one platform temperature is stored in an attribute *Temp* while in the other in an attribute *BodyTemperature*. Integration of the two platforms should result in a comprehensive mHealth system, where querying for patient's "parameters" should provide the physician with measurements gathered by both platforms. It should be noted that the solution should be extendable to include additional platforms with different data formats and semantics (e.g. an ambulance fleet IoT platform, with its own set of on-board measuring devices).

– **Transportation and logistics** The goal is to provide interoperability between at least two IoT platforms in the Port of Valencia (Spain). Platforms that gather sensors data used in container management during loading, unloading and shipment, differ in architecture and technology. However, on the data and semantics level they share some common concepts, e.g. *virtual containers* and *virtual trucks*. At different stages of container management lifecycle, container is controlled and monitored by different systems, e.g. haulier company, container terminal, carrier, consignee. They all store information about containers, but use different data formats and semantics. To be able to exchange information and jointly monitor the situation, common understanding (e.g. of virtual container) is needed. Similarly, when the port haulier company subcontracts shipment services from another company, they want to temporarily consider them as part of their fleet. To exchange data and jointly monitor the flow of transport (e.g. truck position), a common understanding (e.g. of virtual truck) is needed.

In [16], we have discussed semantic representation, currently available in the two areas. The plenitude of models, standards and ontologies (that exist, are in use or under development), as well as semantic and syntactic heterogeneity of data, pose a serious challenge for interoperability. Note, that these (available) models describe only selected aspects of their domains. There is no single comprehensive ontology for (e/m)Health, or for transportation and logistics. Therefore, to adequately semantically represent a domain one needs to deal with multiple ontologies, and consider different data formats and ontology languages used to model parts of the domain. Furthermore, additional ontologies, defining concepts related to various aspects of IoT platforms, also need to be incorporated.

4 Available Research Results and Tools—summary

Let us now look into tools that can be used in our work. Before proceeding, let us stress that, we are interested *only* in "operations performed on ontologies". In other words, we assume that either (which is unlikely) IoT platforms that are to interoperate use ontologies represented in RDF/OWL, or "extraction of semantics" (e.g. from XML, JSON, etc.) has been performed, and RDF/OWL ontologies created as a result. Now, ontology aligning has to take place.

4.1 Criteria for Tool Selection

First, let us stress that we do not approach/classify tools on the basis of the underlying algorithms/methods. This has been already done (see, for instance, [21]). Instead, we propose very pragmatic criteria that are essential when selecting methods for application in real-life use cases:

- availability of the website and the date of the last update—presence on the web site and "recent" date of the last update show vitality of the tool—as a matter of fact, tools that have not been updated for more than 2 years are very suspicious from the point of view of lock-down to a dead-end software,
- number of related publications and date of last publication—larger number of publications indicates that the method is better established (has been reviewed more often), while date of last publication (again) indicates vitality,
- availability of the source code and documentation—crucial for actual use,
- used technology, and I/O data format—indicate what levels of expressiveness can be handled by the method, and what input/output data can be processed; here we also consider the interfaces (GUI and/or command line),
- known academic and commercial utilization—it is very valuable when a method was applied outside of a purely "academic environment",
- scalability—use in the IoT requires tools that are scalable and efficient.

Overall, we are interested in tools that are mature (went though a number of development cycles and resulted in multiple publications), actively maintained and systematically developed, preferably have been applied in real-life scenarios, and bring some promise of scalability.

4.2 Filtering Tools Found in the Literature

We have investigated all methods/tools mentioned in [1,2,21], as well as tools found as a result of internet search, a total of *97*, taking into account criteria from Sect. 4.1. As a result we have reached the following conclusions.

- While numerous tools, implementing ontology matching, appear in the literature, most of them are defunct. We have identified only *nine* that are still alive and more or less correspond to our needs (see, Sect. 5).
- For ∼60% of the tools, we have not found an active website. In many cases, if the website was available, it was very basic and not recently updated.
- We have observed a tendency to present mostly OAEI contest results. While the OAEI initiative is very useful when comparing and evaluating methods, lack of other/follow-up publications shows that the method/tool was developed primarily to participate in the contest.
- Besides few cases, we have not found information about tool's use in projects or commercial applications. Almost all documented use cases came from the OAEI contests.
- Scalability can be deduced only from the results of the OAEI contests. We have not found other results explicitly benchmarking scalability of the methods.

- For $\sim 85\%$ of the tools, we could not find either source code or executables. For the remaining $\sim 15\%$, significant part had no technical documentation, or user manual. Instead, only tools/matching methods were described in publications.
- In $\sim 85\%$ of cases, explicitly stated description of what are the input/output ontologies formats and languages was missing.
- Almost no tool seriously considered situation when the input semantics is not explicitly represented in one of the core ontology languages (RFD/OWL). However, lack of explicit formal RDF/OWL ontology is a typical situation for the ICT systems of today (e.g. use cases of the INTER-IoT project).

5   Working Tools

Let us now look into more details of tools that met our criteria. Note that, in addition to the seven listed below, there are two more "active tools" that could have been listed in this section: YAM++ [9][4] and LODE[5]. However, YAM++ was omitted because there is no source code available (only executables, that cannot be modified, if needed); while LODE is accessible only as a web application (it lacks of a command line interface, or an API).

5.1   LogMap

LogMap [18,22][6] is an open-source tool, developed at the University of Oxford. It can match very large ontologies, such as FMA and SNOMED. Since 2011, LogMap takes part in the OAEI contests, constantly achieving very good results. In 2015, it was the only tool taking part in all OAEI tracks.

LogMap was written in Java, and can be used both from the command-line and via a web-based Ajax interface[7]. The command-line version is available as a stand-alone distribution, as well as in the form of the OAEI packages. As input, the tool accepts any of the OWL API formats, and produces alignments between *classes*, *properties*, and *instances*. As one of very few ontology matching tools, LogMap provides an on-the-fly inconsistency repair capabilities. For consistency checking, it utilizes a method based on propositional Horn-clause satisfiability (Dowling-Gallier algorithm [8]). The source code (last updated in May 2016) is freely available from the *GitHub*. Pre-build packages can be downloaded from the *SourceForge*.

Certain weakness of LogMap lies in the way it computes the candidate mappings/matches. The algorithm finds similarities between concepts, utilizing vocabularies of the input ontologies. Therefore, the result may not be satisfactory if the ontologies are (seriously) lexically disparate, or do not provide enough lexical information.

The website of LodMap lists 11 publications, devoted to various aspects of the tool, with the most recent from 2016.

---

[4] http://www.lirmm.fr/yam-plus-plus/.
[5] http://lode.informatik.uni-mannheim.de/.
[6] https://www.cs.ox.ac.uk/isg/tools/LogMap/.
[7] http://csu6325.cs.ox.ac.uk/.

5.2   COMA

COMA 3.0 [5][8] (previously called GOMA or COMA++) is a framework that supports various matching algorithms and is highly customizable. It is an open source project (code last updated in January 2013) that evolved from the work done at the University of Leipzig. The tool performs matching and merging on XSD (XML Schema), OWL (OWL-Lite), XDR (XML Data Reduced) and relational database schemas. Internally, any supported data format is transformed into a generic model of a directed acyclic graph, which enables processing of schemas and ontologies distributed among multiple namespaces and files. COMA has full GUI support for all its operations.

COMA implements an iterative algorithm based on a collection of matching algorithms (matchers). Selection of matchers, as well as decisions, which matching axioms are correct, is made by the user. Specifically, the user assigns a confidence value to each matching axiom, and can manually create and delete them. Any number of iterations (computing and refining matching axioms) can be performed, each building on the result of previous one. The end result can be saved to a file in a COMA specific format. COMA can use the resulting matching to create, among others, merged ontology, intersection of ontologies, etc. Merging of ontologies and schemas is limited to the, paid, Business Edition of COMA.

Because of its architecture, COMA is a good candidate for a framework for implementation and testing of new matchers. Lack of support for RDF, or more expressive profiles of OWL, are a limiting factor.

5.3   AgreementMaker

AgreementMakerLight [13][9] (AML, a continuation of AgreementMaker and part of the SOMER project) is an automated matching system that acts as an extensible framework that implements many matchers. It is open source and actively updated. Initially, the AgreementMaker was specialized to work with biomedical ontologies but, currently, it can be applied to any ontology in OWL, OBO or SKOS format. It has performed very well in 2014 [11] and 2015 [12] editions of the OAEI competition. It is claimed that the AML can efficiently (i.e. within several minutes) compute alignments on very large ontologies (e.g. WordNet), although it (understandably) requires large amounts of RAM (e.g. 8 GB for ontologies with less than 100 000 classes).

Currently, AML implements 6 matchers that range from simple (label similarity) to complex (so-called, structural matcher), as well as 3 filters (e.g. cardinality filter). Each matcher is configurable, e.g. the string matcher has a choice of four similarity measures. Background knowledge matcher can calculate similarity scores by using an *external* knowledge source, like WordNet. However, it supports matchings between classes and properties, but not individuals. Alignment can be reviewed and each axiom is explained on a graph. Alignment axioms may also be added or removed manually. The results are in the Alignment API [7] format.

---

[8] http://dbs.uni-leipzig.de/Research/coma.html.
[9] http://somer.fc.ul.pt/aml.php.

The AML can work both as a GUI and as a command line application. The possibility to extend the framework with new matchers is very valuable. Unfortunately, the AML does not natively perform ontology merging.

5.4 Alignment API

Alignment API [7][10] is a definition of format (and schema) for storing alignments in RDF, and a set of tools that operate on them. It is designed to be tool-agnostic and to enable storing, exchanging, and sharing alignments. The API itself, outside of simple reference implementations, does not define any matchers, nor does it provide matching or merging services for ontologies or schemas. Instead, it defines a set of standard operations and interfaces for working with alignments. Alignment API specification and tools are actively updated and open source.

An Alignment Server (part of the Alignment API) can store, compare and manage alignments. It can be accessed via pluggable interfaces that currently include: HTTP, SOAP and REST web services and FIPA ACL[11]. The server allows information about the alignment computation process (e.g. program/matcher name, processing time) to be stored in the alignment file. The format is extensible, so any kind of additional information can be added and the schema itself can be extended.

The API defines interfaces for matching algorithms, query translation, finding existing alignments, manipulating alignments, rendering them in a different language, etc. Alignment Server provides a reference implementation of those operations, but for specific problems, own implementations are encouraged.

The official webpage lists close to a hundred tools that are compatible with the Alignment API (including some we list in this article).

5.5 Silk Framework

Silk Framework [23][12] is an open source tool for discovery of links between datasets in the context of the Open Linked Data. It generates links between sources, based on user-provided link specifications. The supported formats include RDF, CSV and XML, with strong focus on RDF. Querying of data is done through a user-specified SPARQL endpoint. Link specifications can be written manually in Silk-LSL (Link Specification Language), or constructed in the Silk Workbench—a Java web application. They can be exported and incorporated into original data sets. Results produced by the Silk can be stored in an Alignment API compatible format.

As opposed to the schema matching systems, Silk discovers and verifies, links between data values and nodes. Support for any SPARQL endpoint means that large amounts of data, spread among SPARQL datasets, can be queried, with full

---

[10] http://alignapi.gforge.inria.fr/.

[11] Jade (http://jade.tilab.com/) Agent Communication Language.

[12] http://silkframework.org/.

interlinking between different graphs and namespaces. Furthermore, Silk allows defining complex data transformations that go well beyond simple `owl:sameAs` links. This can be useful in translation of data between semantics.

Manual input of link specifications means that links cannot be discovered entirely automatically—one needs to specify what kind of linkage pattern (s)he is looking for. In this way, Silk is more of a tool to interlink data, rather than to discover alignments. Note that, Silk does not perform automatic schema matching or ontology merging.

5.6 S-Match

S-Match [17][13] is an open source semantic matching framework that transforms tree-like structures such as catalogs, conceptual models, etc., into lightweight ontologies to then determine the semantic correspondences between them. The project has an up-to-date website with information, including documentation, and tutorials. There are over 20 papers (last from 2011) devoted to various aspects of the project e.g. algorithms implementation.

S-Match is a Java application that can be run from GUI or from command line. The input to the method are text files, in which tree like structures are defined. Using a native input format is one of disadvantages of the tool. Here, input ontologies have to be transformed before running the tool.

The source code is available from *GitHub*(last updated in January 2015). Ready to use pre-build packages (most recent from 2013), can be downloaded from *SourceForge*. S-Match was utilized in 10 documented projects that are referenced on the website.

5.7 OntoBuilder

OntoBuilder[14] project provides an open source set of tools to extract (generate) ontologies from web pages and map ontologies from similar domains, generating an ever-improved single ontology, with which a domain can be queried. OntoBuilder services for schema matching provide several algorithms e.g. similarity flooding, combined algorithm, precedence algorithm, term and value combined algorithm, graph algorithm, value algorithm, term algorithm. The Top K Framework graphical tool allows to view and save best mappings (based on a user-defined threshold). OntoBuilder is written in Java and can be used as a graphical tool, as a jar package, or as a command line tool. The source code and documentation are freely available from the *Bitbucket*repository.

Even though the last publication is from 2010, and last update to the website with downloadable OntoBuilder was done in June 2011, the tool is well documented with 15 publications linked from the website. We suspect that the project is not actively developed (making it the "weakest" of the seven). However, the deliverables produced in the past can provide useful input for our work.

---

[13] http://semanticmatching.org/.
[14] http://iew3.technion.ac.il/OntoBuilder/.

6   From Alignments to Common Semantics

In the project, we need to consider alignments between ontologies from possibly different domains, so that the "content", expressed in semantics of one platform, can be translated to/understood by òther IoT platform(s) (e.g. monitoring virtual container/truck). Moreover, the "common ontology" should provide homogeneous access to heterogeneous data (e.g. patient vital signs originating from different platforms).

At the abstract level, the above situation can be expressed in terms of a *network of ontologies* (cf. [10]), which consists of a set of ontologies, together with a family of pairwise alignments between them. Alignments, which are the essential part of the network of ontologies, can be obtained/developed using tools, which we have discussed so far. Note that the choice of a particular tool, is highly use-case dependent. For some ontologies, alignment might be best computed at the language-level, whereas for others a different approach might be preferable. Therefore, within the INTER-IoT project, we are inclined to use the matching methods in a parametric fashion. It is important to note that tools like the Alignment API (see Sect. 5.4), or the more recent, Distributed Ontology Language (DOL) [19,20], allow for treating alignments as *first-class* citizens. By utilizing them, we can store and perform computations on alignments.

Having obtained the necessary alignments, what we need in the next step, is a systematic way of using them to produce the final *merged ontology*, i.e., the *common semantics* for all involved platforms. An interesting approach, based on concepts from the *category theory* has been proposed in [24], further refined in [6] and implemented as a part of the Heterogeneous Toolset (HETS) [3]. The network of aligned ontologies has to be converted to a *diagram* of ontologies, for which, eventually, HETS computes the merged result. The computation of the final result corresponds to taking the categorical *limit* of the diagram. In case of an ontology format mismatch (e.g. RDF and database schema), tools such as D2RQ (e.g. Openlink Virtuoso) can be used to obtain a common format (discussion of such tools is outside the scope of this paper). Using HETS, one can even maintain the heterogeneous nature of the final ontology, although from the practical point of view it might not be the best approach.

The choice of the ontology merging tool(s), which we shall utilize within the INTER-IoT project is still open, though. HETS is definitely an interesting option, but we still need to investigate the landscape of available solutions.

7   Concluding Remarks

The aim of this paper was to investigate what tools are actually available for someone who needs to align/merge ontologies. The results of investigating 97 possibilities, are somewhat discouraging. Majority of existing research results are purely theoretical, i.e. they end with publication(s), but no tools become available. Large number of tools disappear/stop being maintained within 1–2 years after publication of the last paper. This concerns also tools that have participated in the OEAI competition.

Furthermore, almost no attention is paid to the realistic scenario where ontologies, to be aligned/merged are represented in different formalisms. Recall, that none of the IoT platforms that we are going to deal with, have semantics represented in RDF/OWL. Therefore, translation between JSON/XML demarcated semantics and OWL/RDF will be required. Overall, this indicates a serious chasm between the focus of semantic research (let us deal with the best case scenario of RDF/OWL defined ontologies) and where the needs of the real world are (use of semantic technologies requires, first, extracting and formally representing knowledge existing in real-world ICT systems and, second, building two-way translators). This may also seriously, negatively, affect acceptance and use of semantic technologies, and bringing about the vision of the Semantic Web.

Overall, we have identified seven tools that are alive and can be used for practical applications. They will be considered from the point of view of use case scenarios and potential for generalization outside of the current domain of interest (to support establishing interoperability between *any* IoT platforms). Finally, we aim at implementing interoperable ontologies in agent-based IoT middlewares, similar to these described in [14,15].

Acknowledgments. Research presented in this paper has been partially supported by EU-H2020-ICT grant INTER-IoT 687283.

References

1. 50 ontology mapping and alignment tools. http://www.mkbergman.com/1769/50-ontology-mapping-and-alignment-tools/
2. 50 ontology matching. http://ontologymatching.org/projects.html
3. Heterogenous toolset. http://theo.cs.uni-magdeburg.de/Research/Hets.html
4. INTER-IoT project. http://www.inter-iot-project.eu
5. Aumueller, D., Do, H.H., Massmann, S., Rahm, E.: Schema and ontology matching with COMA++. In: Proceedings of the 2005 ACM SIGMOD International Conference on Management of Data, pp. 906–908. ACM (2005)
6. Codescu, M., Mossakowski, T., Kutz, O.: A categorical approach to ontology alignment. In: Shvaiko, P., Euzenat, J., Mao, M., Jiménez-Ruiz, E., Li, J., Ngonga, A. (eds.) Proceedings of the 9th International Workshop on Ontology Matching Collocated with the 13th International Semantic Web Conference (ISWC 2014), Riva del Garda, Italy, 20 October 2014. CEUR Workshop Proceedings, vol. 1317, pp. 1–12 (2014)
7. David, J., Euzenat, J., Scharffe, F., dos Santos, C.T.: The alignment API 4.0. Semant. Web **2**(1), 3–10 (2011)
8. Dowling, W.F., Gallier, J.H.: Linear-time algorithms for testing the satisfiability of propositional Horn formulae. J. Logic Program. **1**(3), 267–284 (1984)
9. Duyhoa, N., Bellahsene, Z.: Overview of YAM++ − (not) yet another matcher for ontology alignment task. Research report. http://hal-lirmm.ccsd.cnrs.fr/lirmm-01079124
10. Euzenat, J., Shvaiko, P.: Ontology Matching, 2nd edn. Springer, Heidelberg (2013)
11. Faria, D., Martins, C., Nanavaty, A.: AgreementMakerLight results for OAEI 2014. In: ISWC International Workshop on Ontology Matching (OM). CEUR Workshop Proceedings (2014)

12. Faria, D., Martins, C., Nanavaty, A., Oliveira, D., Balasubramani, B.S., Taheri, A., Pesquita, C., Couto, F.M., Cruz, I.F.: AML results for OAEI 2015. In: ISWC International Workshop on Ontology Matching (OM). CEUR Workshop Proceedings (2015)
13. Faria, D., Pesquita, C., Santos, E., Palmonari, M., Cruz, I.F., Couto, F.M.: The AgreementMakerLight ontology matching system. In: Meersman, R., Panetto, H., Dillon, T., Eder, J., Bellahsene, Z., Ritter, N., De Leenheer, P., Dou, D. (eds.) ODBASE 2013. LNCS, vol. 8185, pp. 527–541. Springer, Heidelberg (2013)
14. Fortino, G., Guerrieri, A., Lacopo, M., Lucia, M., Russo, W.: An agent-based middleware for cooperating smart objects. In: Corchado, J.M., Bajo, J., Kozlak, J., Pawlewski, P., Molina, J.M., Julian, V., Silveira, R.A., Unland, R., Giroux, S. (eds.) PAAMS 2013. CCIS, vol. 365, pp. 387–398. Springer, Heidelberg (2013). http://dx.doi.org/10.1007/978-3-642-38061-7_36
15. Fortino, G., Guerrieri, A., Russo, W., Savaglio, C.: Middlewares for smart objects and smart environments: Overview and comparison. In: Internet of Things Based on Smart Objects, Technology, Middleware and Applications, pp. 1–27 (2014). http://dx.doi.org/10.1007/978-3-319-00491-4_1
16. Ganzha, M., Paprzycki, M., Pawłowski, W., Szmeja, P., Wasielewska, K.: Semantic technologies for the IoT–an INTER-IoT perspective. In: Proceedings of the 1st International Workshop on Interoperability, Integration, and Interconnection of IoT Systems (to be published). IEEE Press (2016)
17. Giunchiglia, F., Autayeu, A., Pane, J.: S-Match: an open source framework for matching lightweight ontologies. Semant. Web 3(3), 307–317 (2012)
18. Jiménez-Ruiz, E., Cuenca Grau, B.: LogMap: logic-based and scalable ontology matching. In: Aroyo, L., Welty, C., Alani, H., Taylor, J., Bernstein, A., Kagal, L., Noy, N., Blomqvist, E. (eds.) ISWC 2011, Part I. LNCS, vol. 7031, pp. 273–288. Springer, Heidelberg (2011)
19. Lange, C., Kutz, O., Mossakowski, T., Grüninger, M.: The distributed ontology language (DOL): ontology integration and interoperability applied to mathematical formalization. In: Jeuring, J., Campbell, J.A., Carette, J., Dos Reis, G., Sojka, P., Wenzel, M., Sorge, V. (eds.) CICM 2012. LNCS, vol. 7362, pp. 463–467. Springer, Heidelberg (2012)
20. Mossakowski, T., Codescu, M., Neuhaus, F., Kutz, O.: The distributed ontology, modeling and specification language-DOL. In: Koslow, A., Buchsbaum, A. (eds.) The Road to Universal Logic: Festschrift for the 50th Birthday of Jean-Yves Béziau Volume II. Studies in Universal Logic, pp. 489–520. Springer, Heidelberg (2015)
21. Otero-Cerdeira, L., Rodríguez-Martínez, F.J., Gómez-Rodríguez, A.: Ontology matching: a literature review. Expert Syst. Appl. 42(2), 949–971 (2015)
22. Ruiz, E.J., Grau, B.C., Zhou, Y., Horrocks, I.: Large-scale interactive ontology matching: algorithms and implementation. In: Proceedings of the 20th European Conference on Artificial Intelligence (ECAI), pp. 444–449. IOS Press (2012)
23. Volz, J., Bizer, C., Gaedke, M., Kobilarov, G.: Silk–a link discovery framework for the web of data. In: LDOW, vol. 538 (2009)
24. Zimmermann, A., Krötzsch, M., Euzenat, J., Hitzler, P.: Formalizing ontology alignment and its operations with category theory. In: Bennett, B., Fellbaum, C. (eds.) Proceedings of Formal Ontology in Information Systems, FOIS 2006, Baltimore, Maryland, USA, 9–11 November 2006. Frontiers in Artificial Intelligence and Applications, vol. 150, pp. 277–288. IOS Press (2006)

A Partition Berth Allocation Scheduler Based on Resource Utilization and Load Balancing

Bin Li[1(✉)], Yu Zhang[2], Xiaolei Liang[3], and Lin Yang[2]

[1] School of Transportation, Fujian University of Technology,
Fuzhou, People's Republic of China
mse2007_lb@whut.edu.cn
[2] School of Logistics Engineering, Wuhan University of Technology,
Wuhan, People's Republic of China
{sanli,lyang}@whut.edu.cn
[3] School of Automobile and Traffic Engineering, Wuhan University of Science and Technology,
Wuhan, People's Republic of China
liangxiaolei@whut.edu.cn

Abstract. The systematic solutions to a berth allocation problem (BAP) at container terminals have been scarce owing to their high complexity and strong randomness. This paper extends the past research on modeling of container terminal logistics systems (CTLS) with computational thinking. We introduce and integrate the task scheduling architecture and mechanism in real-time operating system (RTOS) into BAP, and propose a partition berth allocation scheduler based on resource utilization and load balancing. Subsequently, we establish the fundamental principles of scheduler with the computing perspective and decision framework of ARINC 653, which is a design philosophy of RTOS for integrated modular avionics. Finally, the approach is demonstrated by investigating the stress testing of a typical container terminal logistics service case in contrast with the average random berth assignment algorithm based on the comprehensive computational experiments.

Keywords: Berth allocation · Computational logistics · ARINC 653 · Partition scheduling · Resource utilization · Load balancing

1 Introduction

Container terminals are not only the multimodal transportation logistics hubs of the global supply chain, but also the buffer pools for container transfer modes, which both make container terminals play an important role during the whole process of container shipping. At the same time, container terminal logistics systems (CTLS) are provided with the high dynamics, nonlinearity, randomness, coupling, and complexity, so task scheduling and resource allocation (TSRA) at container terminals has been the difficulties and hotspots of operations research and scheduling decision.

Berths are the most important resources in CTLS, and a wide literature launched the studies for berth allocation decision. However, the methodologies to solve TSRA include operational programming, system simulation, intelligent optimization and

W. Li et al. (Eds.): IDCS 2016, LNCS 9864, pp. 308–316, 2016.
DOI: 10.1007/978-3-319-45940-0_28

simulation based optimization primarily. Those register the inadequacies and limitations obviously as container ships become more and more large-scale and the handling technologies at container terminals get increasingly complicated. Thereupon, we tried to propose a berth allocation scheduler by the introduction and integration of the mechanism, policy and algorithm in the real time operating system (RTOS) within the conceptual framework of computational thinking. That is intended to present a new methodology of TSRA for CTLS, which possesses the characteristics of highlighted schedulability, appropriate computational complexity, broad applicability, favorable agility and robustness.

2 Related Works

Most decision makings can be classified as three broad categories: strategic, tactical and operational. As for berth allocation and scheduling (BAS), it can be divided into two categories. One is tactical berth scheduling or berth template problem (BTP), and the other is operational berth scheduling or berth allocation problem (BAP). Most of the existing literatures on berthing decision belong to the latter. Bierwirth summarized the new classification schemes for BAP according to the literatures over past ten years [1, 2]. Imai studied a strategic berth template problem and developed heuristic algorithms to find a better approximate solution [3]. Jin tackled the berthing congestion problem by a schedule template design that is considered simultaneously with another two tactical level decision problems, berth template design and yard template design [4]. Eduardo addressed the tactical berth allocation problem(TBAP) and presented an effective biased random-key genetic algorithm for TBAP [5]. Zhen investigated the tactical-level BAP and proposed a stochastic programming formulation that can cope with arbitrary probability distributions of ships operation time deviation [6]. Legato integrated tactical and operational berth allocation model into a simulation-optimization framework [7]. Wang proposed collaborative mechanisms between container shipping lines and port operators to facilitate port operators to make proper berth allocation decisions [8].

Whether to BTP or BAP, the existing solutions usually are lack of portability, and are typical of high computational complexity as well. Furthermore, they are hard to be applied to the berth allocation under dynamic and uncertain environments. So we proposed the essential conception of computational logistics using computational thinking on the IEEE 54th Annual Conference on Decision and Control (CDC 2015) [9], and its definition is elaborated as follows.

Computational logistics involves the programming, designing, implementation, testing and evaluation of complex logistics systems (CLS), and then includes the planning, controlling, scheduling and decision-making for the related logistics service procedure in the various administrate levels, which forms a unified and quantitative universal approach for design, construction, execution, management and improvement of CLS by the extraction, transformation and application of basic concepts, fundamental principles, decision framework, control mechanism and scheduling algorithms in CS and automatic control theory in accordance with theory of computation and similarity theory.

Now, we present a berth allocation scheduler based on computational logistics, and its fundamental principles and operating mechanism stem from the design philosophy of RTOS. That is synthetic application of hierarchical structure, partition scheduling, processor affinity, resource utilization and load balancing on RTOS.

3   A Hierarchical Partition Schedule Computational Model

3.1   Computational Architecture of Planning and Scheduling

Based on the fundamental principles of computational logistics, computer operating systems are supposed to provide the theoretical basis and feasible measure for TSRA at container terminals. Properly speaking, in consideration of the requirements of fulfilling the sailing schedule strictly, TSRA in CTLS is expected to possess the central characteristics of RTOS. Avionics core processing system (ACPS) is of a hierarchical multitask architecture with strict real time and security guarantee ability that has the potential to provide an essential framework, the related mechanisms and the matching algorithms for TSRA in CTLS.

ARINC 653 is a design philosophy of RTOS for integrated modular avionics (IMA) and makes a definition of ARINC 653 application excutive (APEX), which is obviously superior to the traditional embedded real time operating system (ERTOS) in software architecture and design mechanism for design intention and application scenarios, which is required to be absolutely reliable at all events.

The hierarchy and partition both are at the heart of ARINC 653. The hierarchy is a global and local two-level cooperation scheduling (TCS) mechanism in ARINC 653. The upper level scheduling is partition schedule that is core operating system (COS), and the lower level scheduling is task scheduling that is partitioned operation system (POS). At the same time, the partition includes exactly time partition and space partition in ARINC 653, which both provide a fundamental scheduling framework for periodic jobs and aperiodic tasks.

BAP is a textbook example of space allocation problem with the dynamic constraint conditions in nature. Thereupon, we introduce space partition into BAP. Berth Partition Flexible Scheduler (BPFS) that is the kernel of COS is responsible for interval division, interval management and partition scheduling. The quayside is split up into several berth partitions, and every partition comprises of some berths whose quantity can be dynamic tuning according to service targets and load conditions. Each partition is intended to serve the specially appointed container ships. The dimension of division for partition may be the set of hull forms, ship routings, shipping agent and shipping alliance. That is a good advertisement for processor affinity which is migrated from the domain of computer science to the container terminal logistics.

At the same time, the berth possesses the natural physical isolation for security as long as the safety clearances between container ships are made the full consideration according to the two overall lengths. So berth allocation attaches great importance to resource utilization. Consequently, we import the flexibility into partition schedule. We divide terminal coastline into partitions according to work load and resource configuration. Every partition has the explicit target ships, but the partition can admit other ships once the partition is idle or other partitions are overloaded in contrast with it seriously. The above-mentioned is just the scheduling idea of COS.

In case a calling container ship is designated to a certain partition, the single berth task scheduler (SBTS) that is the major component of POS is going to take job scheduling in hand. Above all, SBTS obtains the real-time job priority (RJP) of calling container ship on the basis of the different class of services and other critical quality attributes, such as ship form, departure time at the latest and so on. The new arrival container ship is inserted into the pending job queue in accordance with RJP that is stationary throughout the stay in port once specified.

The COS and POS constitute the main framework of two-level hierarchical partition scheduling. Thereupon, a hierarchical partition schedule computational model (HPSCM) for BAP is proposed and illustrated by Fig. 1. That proposes a fundamental computational architecture of planning and scheduling for core resources at container terminals, which is not limited to the berth. HPSCM can be customized for different quay side layouts, and is of favorable schedulability, agility, flexibility, robustness and applicability.

3.2   Resources Management and Operational Organization Perspectives

There are some basic viewpoints of computer operating system from the diverse perspectives, such as user environment perspective, virtual machine one, resource management one, and operational organization one. The former two are the comprehension from the exterior, and the latter pair are the essentials of perspective from the interior. Berths are the most important resources of CTLS, and BAP is an issue of resource management and operational organization essentially. Consequently, we integrate the resources management perspective and operational organization one of computer operating system to form a berth allocation computing framework and paradigms within the conceptual framework of computational logistics.

It is worth mentioning that the operational organization of computer operating system focuses on process primarily, which is the cornerstone of TSRA. As a result, we introduce the ideology of process into BAP. If a container ship arrives at terminal, it is just about a job of CTLS. Thereupon a container ship can be abstracted as a job control block (JCB). With the philosophy of computational logistics, each partition is represented as partition control block (PCB) by the lights of abstract mechanism in computer operating system, and each berth is indicated as a berth control block (BCB) similarly. JCB is an abstraction of logistics task, and the PCB and BCB both are the abstraction of berth resources.

The mapping between JCB and PCB/BCB is the nut graph of BAP. HPSCM exactly fulfills the application, binding, release among PCB, BCB and JCB. In fact, HPSCM adopts the scheduler and dispatcher separative structure (SDSS) to fulfill

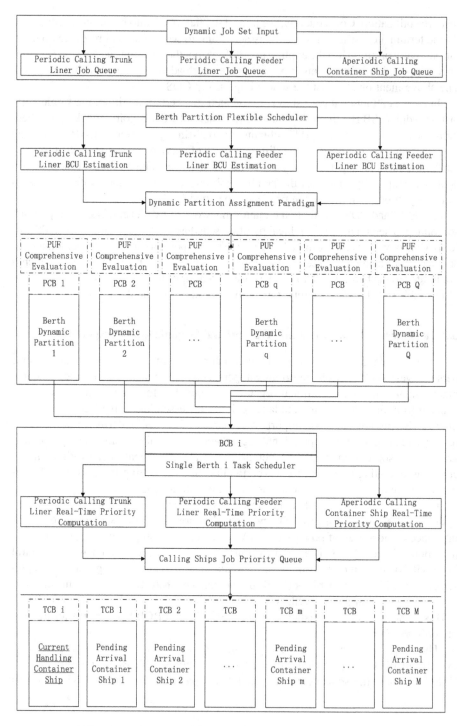

Fig. 1. A hierarchical partition schedule computational model

berth allocation that is showed in Fig. 2. The scheduler that includes partition sched-uler and berth scheduler manage the calling container ship queues for different parti-tions and berths. The dispatcher is responsible for towing an elected container ship to a physical berth to execute loading and unloading containers operation.

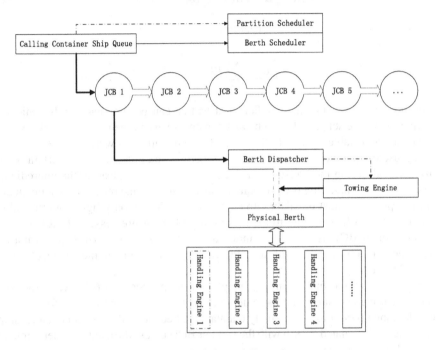

Fig. 2. A berth allocation scheduler and dispatcher separate structure

3.3   Fundamental Principles of Berth Allocation

The central indicators of HPSCM and SDSS are partition utilization factor (PUF) and berth comprehensive utilization (BCU). Moreover, the efficient utilization and load balancing are also the keynotes of berth allocation algorithm (BAA), especially the former. Specifically speaking, the efficient utilization is embodied by two indexes. One is the PUF, and the other is BCU. The latter is the weighted average of the former. PUF and BCU both can give a more comprehensive response to the utilization of core resources.

The traditional berth utilization (TBU) is that the working hours of the wharf berths accounts for the proportion of the calendar time. The working hours of the wharf berth embrace the handling time and a range of auxiliary time. Nevertheless, the proportion between practical handling time and chargeable working hours of berths are distinct for diverse ship forms. The berth activity utilization (BAU) is a more valuable indicator than TBU at least for container terminals.

Therefore, we make a definition of BCU. BCU is composed of two sections. One is the TBU, and the other is BAU. In the matter of single berth, its BCU_i can be defined as follows.

$$BCU_i = c_t TBU + c_a BAU \qquad (1)$$

$$c_t + c_a = 1 \qquad (2)$$

$$PCU_j = \sum_{i=1}^{k} BCU_i \qquad (3)$$

In the equation of (1), the coefficient ct and ca can be stationary or dynamically adaptive. Now, we set ct and ca to be as 0.5 respectively in the prototype of HPSCM, but they are adjustable while CTLS are faced with the different workload.

Because the number of quay crane (QC) loading and unloading on a certain berth is transitional during the logistics service process, and it can lead to the unpredictability of practical handling time for ships. Furthermore, some other random elements of key importance must be taken into consideration. So we only figure out the value of BCU for a berth according to the accomplished departure vessels. That is to say, the indicator of BCU is a dynamic index to a certain ship, moreover, it can not be determined in advance. In addition, PCU_j is just the total of the value of BCU included berths.

Hence, we set the fundamental principles of berth allocation (FPBA) as follows. Firstly, a calling container ship has a default partition according to vessel form unless the task among partitions is extremely unbalanced. Secondly, the bigger container ship is going to be designated a berth with the smaller BCU unless the length of queue among berth is disparity in quantity.

4   Computational Experiments and Performance Evaluation

We select AnyLogic 7.1.2 and SQL Server 2012 to design, implement and execute the simulation experiments and data analysis for expatiate upon the above HPSCM. At the same time, a new container terminal is picked as the scenario in the interpretation of the idea of computational logistics for BAP. The quay side of container terminal contains ten berths, and every berth can admit the largest container ship in service. Each berth is equipped with four quay cranes separately, and the quay crane can migrate between the adjoining berths. The interval between the liner services accords with the Erlang distribution of 4 orders [10]. Two neighboring terminals transfer calling container ships to this terminal in emergency circumstances, which obeys the triangular distribution and normal distribution respectively.

The calling ships are mainly arterial vessels and the large-scale feeder vessels, and their key attributes are same with the description in [9]. We executed the verification, validation, and accreditation (VV&A) first by the average random berth assignment (ARBA) algorithm, and we perform VVA of simulation experiments 100 times using the random seed from 1 to 100. The average result is that there are 3899.70 vessels calling terminal per year and only 4.5 vessels does not finish handling task. Moreover, the container throughput has reached to 10844689.00 TEU that is fully reaching the design capability. So the simulation model has met the actual conditions well. That is supposed to provide a solid foundation for later algorithm analysis and performance evaluation.

We increase the workload by reducing the time interval of liners, and execute the several group experiments with ARBA whose results are showed in Table 1. At the same time, we execute the same simulation experiments with HPSCM, and get the result as are demonstrated in Table 2. Obviously, the performance of the latter is superior to the former greatly. The gap between ARBA and HPSCM is mounting with the load grows rapidly. That indicates that HPSCM possesses the good scheduling performance, which can help CTLS obtain vessels traffic capacity and container throughput.

Table 1. Simulation experimental result with ARBA

Simulation group	Reducing time interval ratio	Average vessel through capacity	Average container throughput	Average demurrage vessels	Average demurrage containers
1	1/2.000	7703.50	21469862.00	18.00	56066.00
2	1/2.250	8718.50	24214767.80	42.90	117141.20
3	1/2.350	9101.13	25293378.38	61.50	175287.75
4	1/2.400	9232.30	25690679.60	103.10	287151.70
5	1/2.450	9363.90	26101454.20	187.70	519220.20
6	1/2.500	9457.60	26316723.30	263.60	756165.50

Table 2. Simulation Experimental Result with HPSCM

Simulation group	Reducing time interval ratio	Average vessel through capacity	Average container throughput	Average demurrage vessels	Average demurrage containers
1	1/2.000	7762.40	21700839.20	12.70	37089.10
2	1/2.250	8729.30	24374742.60	15.70	45615.60
3	1/2.350	9112.88	25389217.50	26.38	75713.75
4	1/2.400	9314.25	25884936.50	38.38	103747.75
5	1/2.450	9450.20	26271804.40	78.20	256510.10
6	1/2.500	9532.70	26403216.20	191.80	639090.90

5   Conclusions

In this paper, we discuss BAP within the conceptual framework of computational logistics, and the idea of scheduler computational model has its roots in RTOS whose task scheduling architecture and mechanisms are introduced and integrated into BAP. Thereupon, we propose a partition berth allocation scheduler based on efficient utilization and load balancing. In fact, it is only just starting. In the future, the scheduling and decision-making modes and tactics in ARINC 653 are introduced into CTLS by the modification and localization, to improve the logistics service efficiency and robustness. In addition, the solution is supposed to be expanded to multimodal container terminals and automated container terminals to indicate the compatibility and creditability.

Acknowledgments. This work was partially supported by the National Natural Science Foundation of China Grant No. 61304210 and 71372202, and the Program for New Century Excellent Talents in the University of Fujian Province, China(No. 2015-54).

References

1. Bierwirth, C., Meisel, F.: A survey of berth allocation and quay crane scheduling problems in container terminals. Eur. J. Oper. Res. **202**(3), 615–627 (2010)
2. Bierwirth, C., Meisel, F.: A follow-up survey of berth allocation and quay crane scheduling problems in container terminals. Eur. J. Oper. Res. **244**(3), 675–689 (2015)
3. Imai, A., Yamakawaa, Y., Huang, K.: The strategic berth template problem. Transp. Res. Part E: Log. Transp. Rev. **72**, 77–100 (2014)
4. Jin, J.G., Lee, D.H., Hu, H.: Tactical berth and yard template design at container transshipment terminals: a column generation based approach. Transp. Res. Part E Log. Transp. Rev. **73**, 168–184 (2015)
5. Lalla-Ruiz, E., González-Velarde, J.L., Melián-Batista, B., Moreno-Vega, J.M.: Biased random key genetic algorithm for the tactical berth allocation problem. Appl. Soft Comput. **22**, 60–76 (2014)
6. Zhen, L.: Tactical berth allocation under uncertainty. Eur. J. Oper. Res. **247**(3), 928–944 (2015)
7. Legato, P., Mazza, R.M., Gulli, D.: Integrating tactical and operational berth allocation decisions via simulation–optimization. Comput. Ind. Eng. **78**, 84–94 (2014)
8. Wang, S.A., Liu, Z.Y., Qu, X.B.: Collaborative mechanisms for berth allocation. Adv. Eng. Inf. **29**(3), 332–338 (2015)
9. Li, B.: Container terminal logistics scheduling and decision-making within the conceptual framework of computational thinking. In: Proceedings of the IEEE 54th Annual Conference on Decision and Control (CDC), pp. 330–337 (2015)
10. Wang, N., Xu, L.J., Song, N.Q., Xu, T.: Distribution function and empirical study of container liner's arrival discipline. J. Dalian Marit. Univ. **39**(4), 107–110 (2013)

Smart Networked Transportation and Logistics

Optimization Model of the Inland Bridge Navigation Hole

Yanfeng Wang[1,2,3], Liwen Huang[1,2], and Yaotian Fan[1,2(✉)]

[1] School of Navigation, Wuhan University of Technology,
Wuhan, People's Republic of China
wyfgy_2002@163.com, wyfgy2002@tom.com,
344060726@qq.com
[2] Hubei Key Laboratory of Inland Shipping Technology,
Wuhan, People's Republic of China
[3] Wuhan Technical College of Communications,
Wuhan, People's Republic of China

Abstract. In order to make full use of the river coast resources and reduce the influence of the inland bridge construction on the shipping and logistics distribution, this paper uses the method combining the dynamic programming and grey theory to establish inland river bridge navigation hole distribution optimization model. Using the Wuhan Zhuankou bridge as an example, according to the Wuhan section of the Yangtze River in 2014 water level value and he bridge area of the underwater terrain features, the model has been verified.

Keywords: Inland river bridge · Shipping · Logistics · Grey theory · Dynamic programming

1 Introduction

With the rapid development of the logistics industry, Logistics along the river, an important part of the logistics industry, has made an increasing significant contribution to the economic growth. Meanwhile, regional layout has become the inevitable trend of logistics advancing. The development level of the logistics industry is directly reflected in the logistics efficiency. Efficiency increasing is an essential support of sustainable development of the logistics industry.

River bridge construction has become one of the major obstacles to the development of the logistics industry along the river. As of 2020, there will be 11 bridges on the Yangtze River in Wuhan. The intensive bridges not only reduce the shipping efficiency and safety, but also affect the regional distribution along the river logistics industry. Therefore, optimizing the navigable bridge holes layout can reduce the impact of the bridge on the navigable environment and effectively improve the impact of the bridge along the river logistics industry.

© Springer International Publishing AG 2016
W. Li et al. (Eds.): IDCS 2016, LNCS 9864, pp. 319–327, 2016.
DOI: 10.1007/978-3-319-45940-0_29

2   Dynamic Model Based on GM

2.1   Grey Correlation Model

Determine the characteristics sequence and factors sequence by grey model. Before analysis the related system by grey correlation, it need find out the characteristics sequence and the corresponding comparison factors sequence of the system. Characteristics sequence is $X_0(t)$, collection of m data: $X_0(t) = \{X_0(1), X_0(2), \ldots, X_0(m)\}$; Factors sequence is $X_i(t)$, which has n sub sequences, and every subsequence is collected m data: $X_i(t) = \{X_i(1), X_i(2), \ldots, X_i(t)\}$.

Grey Model dimension treatment [1]. By means of equalization operators, $X_i(t) = \{X_i(1), X_i(2), \ldots, X_i(m)\}$ is the behavioral sequence of factor X_i, D is equalization sequences operator, $X_iD = \{X_i(1)d, X_i(2)d, \ldots, X_i(m)d\}$, the equalization value of the data is:

$$x_i(k)d = \frac{x_i(k)}{\overline{X}_i}, \quad \overline{X}_i = \frac{1}{n}\sum_{k=1}^{n} x_i(k), k = 1, 2, .., n \tag{1}$$

Correlation degree calculation of grey model. The correlation coefficient between the characteristics sequence and factors sequence at point t is:

$$\xi_{0i}(t) = \frac{\Delta_{\min} + \rho\Delta_{\max}}{\Delta_{0i(t)} + \rho\Delta_{\max}} \tag{2}$$

The correlation degree of system between characteristic sequence and corresponding factors sequence is:

$$\gamma_{0i} = \frac{1}{n}\sum_{t=1}^{n} \xi_{0i}(t) \tag{3}$$

Grey model correlation degree ranking:

$$\Gamma = \begin{vmatrix} \gamma_{11} & \gamma_{12} & \cdots & \gamma_{1q} \\ \gamma_{21} & \gamma_{22} & \cdots & \gamma_{2q} \\ \cdots & \cdots & \cdots & \cdots \\ \gamma_{p1} & \gamma_{p2} & \cdots & \gamma_{pq} \end{vmatrix} \tag{4}$$

According correlation matrix, we can determine the influence between influencing factors and characteristics factors.

2.2   Bridge Layout Dynamic Model Based on GM

According to the analysis of correlation factors, when the water level changes over time, the effective navigable width of bridge will also changes. At the same time under different bridge type scheme, navigable environment impacting of the main associated factors (a. auxiliary navigable hole width; b. auxiliary navigable hole navigating time factor; c. after the completion of the bridge, the auxiliary navigable hole channel width risk factor; d. construction of the bridge, the main navigable hole channel width risk factors) will change.

Therefore, navigable waters bridge optimized scheme should meet: ① It should have a minimal impact on the main navigable hole no matter the bridge is under constructing or completed; ② Water level is a random factor that changes with the time variation, so the optimal scheme of bridge style should make auxiliary navigable hole exert its function more effectively playing.

The optimal scheme of bridge type constrained conditions: ① navigable hole navigable clear width; ② Depth is various in different positions because it is influenced by the bridge area terrain and water level.

Determine correlation factor

Collect four navigation subsequence, and every subsequence is collected m data: $X_i(t) = \{X_i(1), X_i(2), \ldots, X_i(m)\}, (i = 1, 2, 3, 4)$. According to the 2.1 calculation, obtain the four navigation factor correlation matrix.

According to dynamic programming mathematical model, establish the corresponding mathematical model:

- Decision function: $F(t) = At^2 + B + C$;
- State transition equation: $y = Ax + B$, where, y—navigable water level, x—moving bridge pier coordinate values;
- Constraint conditions: $C_1 \leq x \leq C_2$, $n \leq F(t) \leq m$, C_1 and C_2 are displaceable minimum and maximum position of bridge pier, respectively. N and m are the lowest and highest navigable water level of auxiliary navigable hole, respectively.

3 Model Application

In the proposed Wuhan Zhuankou Yangtze River bridge construction scheme (Fig. 1), the 1# navigable hole that locates between 1# and 2# bridge pier. The designed width is 275 m. Due to the influence of water level, the effective navigable clear width of 1# navigable hole varies with the change of water level and the navigable time changes, also.

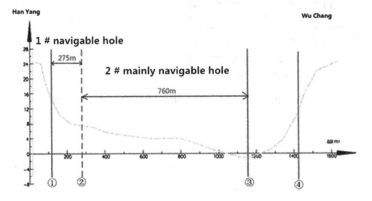

Fig. 1. The proposed Zhuankou bridge floor plan

Therefore, 1# navigable hole as auxiliary navigable hole mainly use for the upstream ship traffic. Upstream ships need sail along the right side to use slow flow in the middle and flood period, especially in the flood period. At this time, 1# navigable hole will be very important. It can guarantee ships two-way navigable all the year round.

3.1 Navigation Factor Grey Correlation Analysis

In the case of 1# Navigable hole of Zhuankou Yangtze River Bridge changed, extracting four factors which have greater impact on navigation, and establishing the mathematical model (Fig. 2).

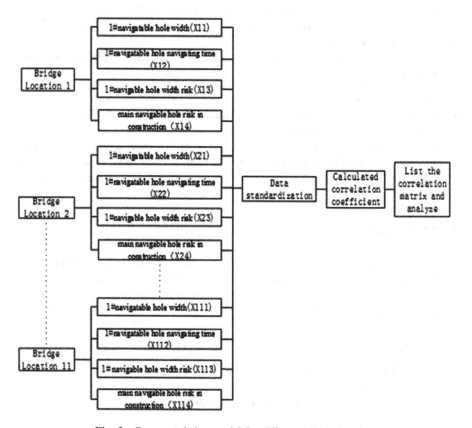

Fig. 2. Grey correlation model for different bridge location

According to grey correlation model, lists the correlation factor matrix (Table 1).

Table 1. Different bridge location correlation factor matrix

Bridge location	X1	X2	X3	X4
Bridge location 1	260 (m)	137 (d)	0.96	1.87
Bridge location 2	265 (m)	141 (d)	0.98	1.85
Bridge location 3	270 (m)	144 (d)	1.00	1.83
Bridge location 4	275 (m)	153 (d)	1.01	1.82
Bridge location 5	280 (m)	157 (d)	1.03	1.80
Bridge location 6	285 (m)	188 (d)	1.05	1.78
Bridge location 7	290 (m)	191 (d)	1.07	1.76
Bridge location 8	295 (m)	192 (d)	1.09	1.74
Bridge location 9	300 (m)	194 (d)	1.11	1.72
Bridge location 10	305 (m)	197 (d)	1.13	1.70
Bridge location 11	310 (m)	201 (d)	1.14	1.69

According to the gray correlation mathematical model, the data of Table 1 will be analyzed. The results are shown in Table 2:

Table 2. Navigation factor correlation matrix

Correlation matrix	X1	X2	X3	X4
X1	1.0000	0.6033	0.8790	0.2395
X2	0.5943	1.0000	0.5904	0.1634
X3	0.8787	0.5989	1.0000	0.2301
X4	0.2395	0.1691	0.2305	1.0000

According to Table 2:

When the biggest difference is minimum, the correlation degree of X2 factor and X1 factor is the highest.

The correlation degree of X4 factor and other factors are the lowest among the four correlation sequences.

3.2 Dynamic Mathematical Model

The three exponential smoothing model is adopted to calculate and analyze the water level of the 2014 data (Fig. 3).

According to the fitting data, get relevant parameter values: a = 14.4825, b = 0.7382, c = −0.0505, mean square error = 1.3385. Therefore, after fitting, the recursive relation function between water level f time series is following: $F(t) = 14.4825 + 0.7382t − 0.0505t^2$, t are time series.

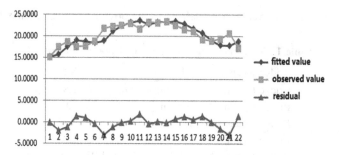

Fig. 3. The water level fitted values, observed values and the residual graph

According to the relationship between width of navigable hole and water level, establish the coordinate values that based on the underwater topographic map 0 point as origin (Table 3).

Table 3. The water level required under different width of 1# navigable hole

1# navigable hole width	2# pier location (abscissa value X)	Minimum required navigable water level (ordinate value Y)
260	375	20.10
265	380	19.57
270	385	19.12
275	390	18.32
280	395	17.72
285	400	17.42
290	405	16.97
295	410	16.67
300	415	16.32
305	420	16.02
310	425	15.67

According to Table 3, fitting the relational functions between #2 bridge pier position and navigable water level, the analysis and calculation results in Table 4 and Fig. 4:

After fitting equation: $y = 53.1182 - 0.088727x$, $(375 \leq x \leq 425)$

Establish dynamic programming mathematical model.

According to dynamic programming mathematical model description, establish the corresponding mathematical model:

- Decision function: $F(t) = 14.4825 + 0.7382t - 0.0505t^2$;
- State transition equation: $y = 53.1182 - 0.088727x$, where, y—navigable water level, x—2# bridge pier coordinate values;
- Constraint conditions: $375 \leq x \leq 425$, $12.184 \leq F(t) \leq 28.584$

Table 4. Equation coefficients and error calculation result

	Equation coefficients	Se	tαSe	t	p	95 % confidence interval	
c1	53.1182	1.7451	3.9478	30.4379	0.0001	49.1704	57.0660
c2	−0.0887	0.0044	0.0099	20.3529	0.0001	−0.0986	−0.0789

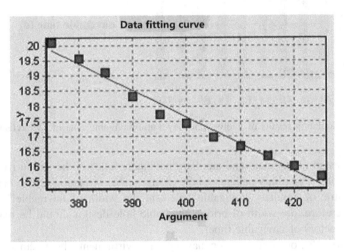

Fig. 4. Fitting of 2# pier location and navigable water level

According to the regression equation of water level in 3.2.1: $F(t) = 14.4825 + 0.7382t - 0.0505t^2$, where t is the time series, and statistics of water level in 2013, for example, under the condition of meet the above navigable water level to calculate, navigable time are shown in Table 5 and Fig. 5:

Table 5. Calculation results of width, water level and navigable time of 1# navigable hole

1# navigable hole navigable water level value (m)	1# navigable hole width (m)	navigable time (day)
15.5	308.9769	214
16	303.3417	209
16.5	297.7064	205
17	292.0711	203
17.5	286.4359	199
18	280.8006	195
18.5	**275.1653**	**188**
19	269.5301	156
19.5	263.8948	153
20	258.2595	149

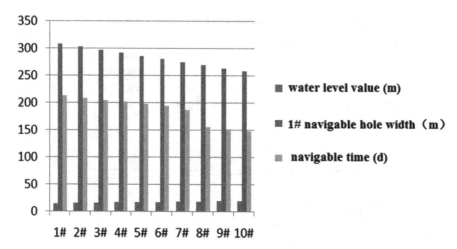

Fig. 5. Calculation results of width, water level and navigable time of 1# navigable hole

In the design of the main and auxiliary navigable holes of the inland river bridge, when the width of auxiliary navigable hole changes, the correlation degree between the navigable time of auxiliary navigable hole and the width of navigable hole is the highest. Therefore, the width of bridge navigable hole design should be mainly considered the factors of navigable time.

In the four factors impacted on navigation environment, the width of auxiliary navigable hole changing has a minimal influence on the navigation environment of construction period.

Proposed Zhuankou Yangtze River bridge as an example, without changing the 1#, 3#, 4# bridge pier locations, 2# bridge piers can be translated 34 m to the south bank, the auxiliary navigable hole increases to 309 m, the width of main navigable hole narrows to 726 m, which can effectively reduce requirements of the auxiliary navigable hole for water level and increase the navigable time from 188 days to 214 days. That is, nearly two-thirds of all the year round can sail, which will reduce the bridge impact on the sailing of upstream ship.

4 Conclusion

Through the above model and case application, we can draw the following conclusions:

- Through analysis of the construction of bridge impacting on the navigation environment, the paper points the factors out, which has a greater influence on the navigation environment in the river bridge area. The grey theory model can deal with fuzziness and different dimension between the bridge impact factors.
- Bridge navigable waters environment is greatly influenced by water level and underwater topography. Therefore, the paper sets up the grey dynamic programming optimization model of bridge hole, and obtains the optimal solution which is based on specific water level and underwater terrain features. In the Zhuankou

Yangtze Bridge case, without excessively increasing the cost of the bridge, the model can optimize the main and auxiliary navigable holes layout and reduce the negative impact of the bridge on the coast of logistics.

References

1. Liu, S., Guo, T., Dang, Y.: Grey Systems Theory and Its Application, pp. 110–116. Science Press, Beijing (1999)
2. Zhang, P.: New algorithm for multidimensional continuing dynamic programming. Control Decis. **26**(8), 1219–1223 (2011)
3. TAN, Z.: Emergency Mechanism and Integration Methods of Risk Assessment for Ship-Bridge Collision in the Yangtze River. Wuhan University of Technology, pp. 86–94 (2011)
4. Huang, C., Hu, S., Gao, D., et al.: Design and realization of assessment system on dynamic risk of ship collision with bridge. China Saf. Sci. J. **23**(4), 120–126 (2013)
5. Wu, Y., Geng, B., Wang, H.: Dynamic finite element numerical simulation of vessel-bridge collision. J. Chongqing Jiaotong Univ. Nat. Sci. **29**(5), 681–684 (2010)
6. Dai, T., Nie, W., Liu, W.: The analysis of ship-bridge collision in main waterway of the Yangtze river. Navig. Chin. **46**(4), 44–47 (2002)
7. Fan, W., Yuan, W.C., Fan, Q.W.: Calculation method of ship collision force on bridge using artificial neural network. J. Zhejiang Univ. Sci. A **9**(5), 614–623 (2008)
8. Sheikh, Y., Shah, M.: Bayesian modeling of dynamic scenes for object detection. IEEE Trans. Pattern Analy. Mach. Intell. **27**(11), 1778–1792 (2005)
9. Duckett, W.: Risk analysis and the acceptable probability of failure. Struct. Eng. **83**(15), 36–44 (2005)
10. Wen, K.L.: The grey system analysis and its application in gas breakdown and VAR compensator finding (Invited Paper). Int. J. Comput. Cogn. **2**(1), 21–44 (2004)
11. Shi, X., Hao, Z.: Fuzzy Control and Its Simulation with MATLAB. Tsinghua University Press, pp. 149–189 (2008)

Key Properties of Connectivity in Vehicle Ad-hoc Network

Jiujun Cheng[1], Pengyu Qin[1(✉)], Mengchu Zhou[2], Zhenhua Huang[1], and Shangce Gao[3]

[1] Key Laboratory of Embedded System and Service Computing of Ministry of Education, Tongji University, Shanghai 201804, China
{chengjj,pengyu_qin,huangzhenhua}@tongji.edu.cn
[2] Department of Electrical and Computer Engineering, New Jersey Institute of Technology, Newark, NJ 07102, USA
mengchu@gmail.com
[3] Faculty of Engineering, University of Toyama, Toyama 930-8555, Japan
gaosc@eng.u-toyama.ac.jp

Abstract. Finding the key properties of connectivity in Vehicle Ad-hoc Network (VANET) is an important challenge because of a wide geographic range, an uneven distribution of vehicles, and low coupling of interconnections. The prior work has mostly concentrated on VANET which are mainly through a WAVE wireless network protocol to implement a hop-by-hop inter-vehicle (V2V) communication. It has a low degree of verisimilitude and lacks formal analysis and theoretical methods to deal with a large-scale open network environment. In this paper, we give some important results on the key properties of connectivity in VANET: (1) The number of edges and nodes obey the Densification Power Law. (2) An entire VANET is not connected. (3) Dense vehicle community contains both vehicles with large degree and small ones. (4) The neighbors' connection of a vehicle with a large degree is sparse. This work should motivate VANET researchers, practitioners, and new comers to know the nature of key properties of connectivity in VANET.

Keywords: Vehicle Ad-hoc Network · Connectivity · TAPASCologne dataset

1 Introduction

At present, vehicles not only become an important part of people's lives, but also user's third important space except for home and office. After solving the family and office network connection problems via WiFi and cellular networks, engineers start to make Internet of Vehicles (IoV) a reality. However, the increase in vehicle usage leads to serious problems like traffic congestion, traffic safety, air pollution and other unexpected issues consequentially. The current way to handle traffic congestion is based on reducing the number of cars per unit area of a road, which cannot alleviate and solve traffic congestion problems effectively because the growing number of cars makes such governmental measures have little effect. On the other hand, it is predicted that VANET could make congestion reduced by about 60 % and short-distance transport efficiency

W. Li et al. (Eds.): IDCS 2016, LNCS 9864, pp. 328–339, 2016.
DOI: 10.1007/978-3-319-45940-0_30

increased by nearly 70 %, such that the capacity of the existing road network is increased by 2–3 times [1]. VANET's main value [2] lies in the processing of information and solving the traffic congestion problem in an effective way. Therefore, it is urgent to study how to use large-scale VANET effectively and solve the connectivity problem so as to provide real-time data for the application layer, distribute time and space resources in a road network, finally solve traffic congestion problems.

At the same time, research on VANET contributes a lot to reducing traffic accident. Accidents have become a global public traffic safety problem. Although road traffic accidents around the world tend to be stable on the whole, the situation is not optimistic yet. Traffic accidents in China are in an upward trend in recent years and the number of traffic fatalities in the past few years was ranked first in the world, which was also under a higher rate of increase. Preventing accidents and reducing traffic fatality rate become an urgent task facing the whole society. According to the experience in Europe, Japan and other developed countries, to reduce traffic fatalities, establishing a VANET system is an important way to reduce traffic deaths. Therefore, if we can solve the VANET connectivity problems such that vehicles can exchange real-time information with each other including vehicle speed, direction of travel, location and so on, their drivers are able to make the appropriate action to avoid traffic accidents.

Commonly we use VANET to refer to IoV networking. Originally, VANET only included V2V communications. Considering the high mobility and shorter WAVE transmission range of vehicles, Road Side Units (RSUs) are used to expand V2V communication range and reduce delays which calls Vehicle-to-Infrastructure/Infrastructure-to-Vehicle (V2I/I2V). However, after the wide area communication technologies such as LTE and WiMAX appeared, infrastructure means not only RSUs, but also base stations. Therefore, there appears a new network architecture, Vehicular Infrastructure-based NETwork (VINET). In this paper, VANET refers to the network of vehicles communicating to vehicle directly or RSUs in order to achieve V2V communication. VINET refers to the network of vehicles communicating with infrastructure, such as RSUs, Wi-Fi AP, LTEeNBs and WiMAX base stations or other communications. VANET received more in-depth study than VINET because: (1) VANET is evaluated from a mobile ad-hoc network that has been researched for many years; (2) Before smart phones were widely used and mobile Internet and fast LTE appeared, VINET is not attractive to researchers. Recently more and more researchers have started to study VINET as well as VANET and VINET hybrid network.

Existing methods have mostly concentrated on VANET, which are mainly through a WAVE wireless network protocol to implement a hop-by-hop inter-vehicle (V2V) communication. It has a low degree of verisimilitude and lacks theories and methods to interconnect vehicles in a large-scale open network environment.

This work models VANET with graphs and its characteristics are studied. They include centrality and community borrowed from complex network analysis. These characteristics provide a theoretical basis for the analysis of large-scale VANET. Dynamics of a large-scale mobility dataset, i.e., TAPASCologne scenario. The main findings are: the number of edges and nodes obey the Densification Power Law; the entire network is not connected; the neighbors' connection of a vehicle with a large degree is sparse. These findings provide a good basis for our research on large-scale heterogeneous VANET's connectivity mechanisms.

The remainder of this paper is organized as follows. Section 2 discusses the related work. In Sect. 3, some definitions of VANET properties are first presented, which include basic network properties, centrality and community structure. Section 4 introduces the dataset we choose, i.e., TAPASCologne which is originated from the Institute of Transportation Systems at the German Aerospace Center (ITS-DLR). Section 5 discusses the model of VANET. Finally, Sect. 6 draws conclusions.

2 Related Work

We mainly summarize the work related to definitions and properties of VANET.

2.1 Researches of VANET

There are many researches to VANET. It is usually defined as the one including the mobile nodes in moving vehicles and static RSUs governed by the commonly-used WAVE protocol or improved 802.11a MAC protocol, such as [3], which provides five different taxonomies of routing protocols. Some researchers also take mobile infrastructure [4] and static nodes into account, e.g. parked vehicles [5]. And [6] investigates a problem for a class of networked nonlinear systems subject to medium access constraint. In [7], based on key indicators such as link healing duration time, number and duration of the communication network and union time from a disconnected network, Viriyasitavat et al. research V2V network connectivity by simulation whose results show that urban areas have a highly dynamic network connection mode. The work [8] abstracts the road scene as a one-dimensional traffic flow at three different channel models so as to analyze respective topological characteristics and compare the neighbor distance, node degrees, number of clusters, continuing time of links and connection quality under different propagation range. The study [9] maps data of Shanghai 4000 taxi collecting from the GPS to a digital map and obtain these taxi trajectories so as to study virtual VANET under the assumption of different communication radius. The results show, when the communication radius is 500 m, it can make the most of the taxi connect to the same network partition and use the cumulative distribution function to analyze the number of neighboring nodes under a different communication radius.

2.2 Properties and Analysis

The work [10] analyzes dynamic changes of VANET connectivity on an urban road with signalized control and investigates the more general k-connected problem. Simulation results show that even if the vehicle is under signalized control, connectivity analysis and simulation results obtained in this paper have a good approximation. The study [11] analyzes the transient topological characteristics and statistic characteristics for VANET based on real and simulated movement trajectory, and considers the impact of market penetration to network connectivity.

Abdrabou and Zhuang [12] use the concept of effective bandwidth theory and practical capacity to compute the maximum distance between two RSUs. Furthermore, it studies how the density of vehicles, transmission range and vehicle's different speeds impact end-to-end packet transmission delay to solve RSU deployment issues. Salvo et al. [13] propose three algorithms to extend the coverage area of VANET RSU, which uses the locations of sender nodes and geometric principles to select the forwarding direction. They gets the best installation configuration for RSU and OBU by analyzing the results. The work [14] designs a new RSU deployment strategies for the file download on VANET, which uses Markov chains to model the connection between vehicles and RSUs and considers a road network as a weighted undirected graph. Then based on edge-first traversal algorithm of graph, it designs an RSU deployment algorithm for file download.

2.3   Summary

Recently, researches into VANET have drawn much public attention and enjoyed an accelerated flush, especially in the area of protocols and communications. However, more effort is required to address their formal modeling and nature.

In this paper, we pay attention to the modeling and analysis methods for the key properties of connectivity. We intend to solve three key questions: (1) what the evolution for VANET graph expresses with time; (2) if the main vehicle can be selected via the centrality measure; and (3) if there is a dense subgraph in VANET's graph.

3   Formal Specification of VANET Properties

Before starting to discuss the overall features of VANET, we need to use right tools to describe networks first. In this paper, we use an undirected graph to describe a VANET network. Undirected graph, $G(t)$, represents the VANET at the time of t. Car set, $V(t) = \{v_i\}$, represents all of the vehicles at t, where $i \in \{1, 2, ..., n\}$ and n represents the number of vertexes in graph. We can use n to describe the number of cars. Link set, $E(t) = \{e_{ij}\}$, represents all the communication links among vehicles at that moment. Link edge $e_{ij}(t)$ exists only if v_i and v_j can communicate with each other at t where $i, j \in \{1, 2, ..., n\}$ and $i \neq j$.

3.1   Basic Network Properties

Definition 1. Degree of vehicle v_i represents the number of other vehicles that can communicate with it at t:

$$d_i(t) = ||\{v_j | \exists e_{ij}(t)\}|| \tag{1}$$

Degree distribution is an important statistic to describe the nature of a network. Vehicle degree distribution $p_t(d)$ at t is defined as the probability that a vehicle's degree is d, which is chosen randomly in VANET at t. Or in other words, it can be equivalently described as the number of vehicles with degree d accounted for the proportion of a total number of vehicles. Degree distribution of many real complex networks follow a power law distribution, whose mathematical expression is $p(k) \sim k^{-\gamma}$, where k means the degree of nodes within 2 to 3.

The curve of a power function in double logarithmic coordinates is a straight decline, such as the distribution of the World Wide Web [15]. Compared with the exponential function, a power function declines slowly, resulting in the presence of a large network of nodes, which are commonly referred as hub nodes.

Definition 2. The density of VANET, $D_G(t)$, represents the ratio of the actual number of links to the largest number of links theoretically at t.

$$D_G(t) = \frac{\|E(t)\|}{n(n-1)} \qquad (2)$$

Definition 3. The average minimum number of links, $h_G(t)$, represents the average minimum number of links if we need any pair of vehicles to communicate with each other in $G(t)$ at t.

$$h_G(t) = \frac{1}{n(n-1)} \sum_{i \neq j \in G} h_{ij}(t) \qquad (3)$$

$h_{ij}(t)$ represents the number of needed hops for the shortest communication link between vehicles i and j at t. The maximum one among the fewest communication link hops between vehicles is called VANET's diameter. The correlation of degrees in VANET describes the relationship between vehicles with large and small degrees. The correlation could be represented by the degree of a vehicle (d) and its average degree ($\overline{d}_{neighbors}$) of its neighboring vehicles. When the VANET correlation is positive, $\overline{d}_{neighbors}$ increases with the growth of d. At the negative situation, $\overline{d}_{neighbors}$ decreases with the growth of d.

3.2   VANET Centrality

Definition 4. Lobby index [16], $L_i(t)$, represents max k which the degree of all adjacent vehicles of v_i are equal to or greater than it:

$$L_i(t) = \max\{k : d_k(t) \geq k\} \qquad (4)$$

Lobby index could be regarded as the generalized form of $d_i(t)$, while it represents the information of all the adjacent vehicles in a communication range. According to [19], a scale-free model's lobby index obeys to the fat-tailed distribution, i.e.

$$P(L(x) \geq k \simeq k^{-\alpha(\alpha+1))} \qquad (5)$$

Where α is index from 0 to 2.

3.3   Community Structure

Empirical studies have shown that many real networks exhibit a common feature: In VANET, there exist a structure whose edges in a group are denser than those between groups. We call this structure as a network community structure. For example, the scientist cooperation network can be divided into several different research groups by the different research topics and methods. Many scholars have proposed the algorithms to identify a network community structure. The traditional methods to identify it include a hierarchical clustering algorithm, spectral analysis method and the one based on the number of edge's betweenness as proposed by Newman [17].

A community of vehicles refers to a dense subnet in VANET which means the number of links within the vehicle group is greater than the number of links between the different car groups. To find it, we can transfer VANET $G(t)$ to a directed graph so as to meet $d_i^{in}(t) = d_i^{out}(t) = d_i(t)$, where $d_i^{in}(t)$ and $d_i^{out}(t)$ are the in-degree and out-degree of u_i at t.

Definition 5. If any subnet $U(t)$ in $G(t)$ belongs to a community, it must satisfy the formula [18]:

$$\sum_{u_i \in U(t)} (d_i^{in}(t))(U(t)) > \sum_{u_i \in U(t)} (d_i^{out}(t))(U(t)) \tag{6}$$

which means degrees in $U(t)$ is greater than the sum degree of all remaining portion towards $G(t)$.

Definition 6. Clustering coefficient [19] $cc_k(t)$ of a vehicle community k in VANET at t is an important parameter to measure the network group level:

$$cc_k(t) = \frac{2\|E_k(t)\|}{\|N_k(t)\|(\|N_k(t)\| - 1)} \tag{7}$$

$\|E_k(t)\|$ is the number of existing links in community k at t. $\|N_k(t)\|$ is the number of vehicles. When there are links between any couple of vehicles, the vehicle community clustering coefficient takes the maximum value of 1. It is the reaction vehicle community at a whole group level. If we need to study the contribution of a single vehicle to the entire community, we can define its local clustering coefficient. If vehicles are linked to vehicle u_i at t and these linked vehicles have $z_i(t)$ links between each other, the local clustering coefficient $lcc_i(t)$ is defined as:

$$lcc_i(t) = \begin{cases} \frac{d_i(t)}{z_i(t)} & z_i(t) > 1 \\ 0 & z_i(t) = 0 \, or \, 1 \end{cases} \tag{8}$$

4   TAPASCologne Dataset

In this paper, the dataset we use is TAPASCologne, which is originated from the Institute of Transportation Systems at the German Aerospace Center (ITS-DLR). It is a combination of a real road topology, accurate micro-movement modeling, real traffic demand and advanced traffic assignment in the region of Cologne, Germany 400 km², including a synthetic track file generated by more than 700,000 trips one day and the data set is the most complete and available mobile vehicle scale model online currently. Then we use the method of Origin/Destination Matrix in TAPASCologne to generate a new dataset. The algorithm is as follows:

First, use matrix O/D to determine the range of map OSM. Then extract and filter data according to the range. The format of data can be recognized by SUMO, a micro mobile emulator. Next step is to input results to SUMO. Matrix O/D is the input to Algorithm Gawron so as to determine the initial distribution of the traffic which is also an input to SUMO. Then, SUMO runs the first vehicle moving simulation and the operation results are fed back to Gawron. SUMO runs the next round according to new information and distribution of the traffic. Finally, repeat this cycle until a traffic assignment can maintain whole transport demand (Fig. 1).

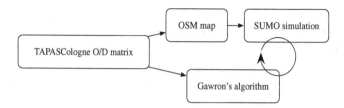

Fig. 1. Generated process of TAPASCologne data set [20]

5 Experiment and Analysis of VANET Properties

5.1 Network Analysis

At first we need to study these changes of snapshots over time between the number of vehicles $V(t)$ and links $E(t)$. Figure 2 shows the number of vehicles and links change over time. Just like other complex networks, the scale of VANET increases as the number of vehicles entering the map area and expanding their wireless antenna transmission range.

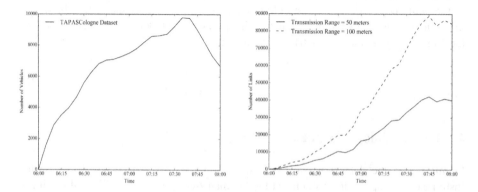

Fig. 2. Number of vehicles/number of links

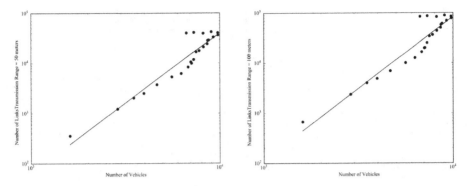

Fig. 3. Relation between number of links and vehicles (transmission range = 50 m/100 m)

Figure 3 describes that the VANET obeys Densification Power Law. After quantitative analysis, we find the numbers of vehicles and links satisfy the following relationship over time:

$$E(t) \propto V(t)^{\alpha} \tag{9}$$

The value of α is not related to the transmission range of a vehicle. This law means that the graph of TAPASCologne VANET is dense. Referring to document [21], $\alpha = 1$ means the average degree is constant over time. The graph is dense when $\alpha = 2$, which tells us that, on the average, the number of links between a vehicle as well as those vehicles connected to it is a constant. This observation has important implications for routing protocol designs. Because in this way, we can estimate the number of network communication links.

5.2   Community Structure Analysis

For dissemination of information services across the entire VANET, we must know if the whole network is connected. In addition, as for the service at sending a message to a specific geographic area (multicast geography and geocast), it is useful to estimate the density of the communication links among the vehicles in this region. Because in this way, we can know the time to operate or avoid flooding.

Figure 4 shows the changes between vehicle count and clustering coefficient of TAPASCologne VANET over time. It can be observed that the number of communities is mainly affected by the transmission range. Specifically, the number of vehicle communities for transmission range of 50 m is double that for 100 m. At the same time, the average clustering coefficient is also affected by the transmission range, i.e., that for transmission range of 50 m is 1.5 times less than that for 100 m.

On the other hand, the number of vehicles for the biggest vehicle community is not impacted by a transmission range. Figure 5 shows the situation on transmission ranges of 100 and 50 m and we can see the percentage of vehicles of the biggest vehicle community in all vehicles, which is exactly the same.

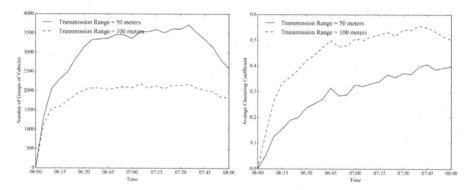

Fig. 4. Number of vehicle groups/average clustering coefficient

In order to study the relationship between vehicle degree and local connectivity, we use local clustering coefficient to quantize the latter, as shown in Fig. 6. The figure shows that the communication range has nothing to do with local connectivity. A dense vehicle community can contain vehicles of both small and large degrees simultaneously. However, for a vehicle with a large degree, its local clustering coefficient is from 0.05 to 0.1, indicating that connections of that vehicle's neighbors is sparse. This is expected, because as for a community with many vehicles, there are not too many links between them. This observation implies that in the non-infrastructure-based VANET and it is difficult to find a 'Faction' with many vehicles. This may result in great trouble for practical applications. For example, in the dissemination protocol, a single broadcast may not reach the effective number of vehicles, while the data cannot be sent to the target vehicle communities in a data distribution protocol.

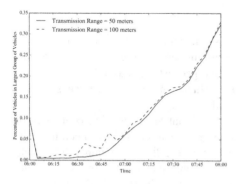

Fig. 5. Percentage of vehicles

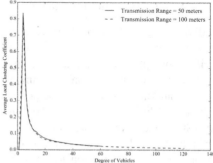

Fig. 6. The relation between degree of in largest group of vehicles and average local clustering coefficient

5.3 Summary

(1) The TAPASCologne VANET includes many communities but the entire network is unconnected:

$$\text{s.t. } hops(v_i, v_j) \sim +\infty. \tag{10}$$

(2) The number of communities is affected by transmission range:

$$\left\| \sum_{\mu_i \in U(t)} (d_i^{in}(t))(U(t)) > \sum_{\mu_i \in U(t)} (d_i^{out}(t))(U(t)) \right\| \sim R > 0 \tag{11}$$

where R represents the transmission range.

(3) The connectivity of vehicle communities is influenced by transmission range:

$$cc_k(t) \propto R. \tag{12}$$

(4) Dense vehicle community contains both vehicles of large and small degrees: If $D_{u1} > D_{u2}$, then $S_{u1} > S_{u2}$ where S_{u1} is the variance of $u1$.

(5) The neighbors' connection with a vehicle of a large degree is sparse:

$$d_i(t) \propto L_i(t)^{-1}. \tag{13}$$

6 Conclusion

This paper uses graph theory to model VANET and analyzes its properties related to a complex network. These properties are then used to do kinetic analysis of the TAPASCologne dataset, the large-scale trajectories of vehicle moment. In the absence of infrastructure, we analyze some basic properties, including the number of vehicles, links, link relationship between vehicles and links, and find vehicles and links obey Densification Power Law. We find that VANET includes many communities. However, the entire network is not connected, implying that some communities cannot communicate with each other. The connectivity of vehicle communities is influenced by a vehicle's transmission range while the number of vehicles in the biggest vehicle community is not impacted by it. In addition, neighbors around a vehicle of high degree are sparsely connected. Our further work is to study how to make a whole network connected.

Acknowledgments. This work was supported in part by NSFC under Grants 61472284, 61272268, 61304039, and by FDCT (Fundo para o Desenvolvimento das Ciencias e da Tecnologia) under Grant 119/2014/A3, and by the Natural Science Foundation Programs of Shanghai under Grant 13ZR1443100, and the Shanghai Rising-Star Program under Grant 15QA1403900, and the Fok Ying-Tong Education Foundation under Grant 142002.

References

1. Kevin, C.L., Uichin L., Mario, G.G.: Routing for vehicular networks (05) (2010)
2. Hedrick, J.K., Tomizuka, M., Varaiya, P.: Control issues in automated highway systems. IEEE Control Syst. Mag. **14**, 21–32 (1994)
3. Cheng, J.J., Cheng, J.L., et al.: Routing in internet of vehicles: a review. IEEE Trans. Intell. Transp. Syst. **16**(5), 2339–2352 (2015)
4. Luo, J., Gu, X., Zhao, T., et al.: A mobile infrastructure based VANET routing protocol in the urban environment. In: International Conference on Communications and Mobile Computing (CMC), pp. 432–437 (2010)
5. Liu, N., Liu, M., Lou, W., et al.: PVA in VANETs: stopped cars are not silent. In: Proceedings IEEE INFOCOM, pp. 431–435 (2011)
6. Zhang, C., Feng, G., et al.: T-S fuzzy-model-based piecewise H-infinity output feedback controller design for networked nonlinear systems with medium access constraint. Fuzzy Sets Syst. **248**, 86–105 (2014)
7. Viriyasitavat, W., Bai, F., Tonguz, O.K.: Dynamics of network connectivity in urban vehicular networks. IEEE J. Sel. Areas Commun. **29**, 515–533 (2011)
8. Akhtar, N., Ozkasap, O., Ergen, S.C.: VANET topology characteristics under realistic mobility and channel models. In: Wireless Communications and Networking Conference (WCNC), pp. 1774–1779. IEEE (2013)
9. Huang, H.-Y., Luo, P.-E., Li, M., et al.: Performance evaluation of SUVnet with real-time traffic data. IEEE Trans. Veh. Technol. **56**, 3381–3396 (2007)
10. Ho, I.-H., Leung, K.K., Polak, J.W.: Connectivity dynamics for vehicular ad-hoc networks in signalized road systems. In: 21st International Teletraffic Congress, 2009. ITC 21 2009, pp. 1–8 (2009)
11. Loulloudes, N., Pallis, G., Dikaiakos, M.D.: The dynamics of vehicular networks in urban environments (2010). arXiv preprint arXiv:1007.4106
12. Abdrabou, A., Zhuang, W.: Probabilistic delay control and road side unit placement for vehicular ad hoc networks with disrupted connectivity. IEEE J. Sel. Areas Commun. **29**, 129–139 (2011)
13. Salvo, P., Cuomo, F., Baiocchi, A., et al.: Road side unit coverage extension for data dissemination in VANETs. In: 2012 9th Annual Conference on Wireless On-Demand Network Systems and Services (WONS), pp. 47–50 (2012)
14. Liu, Y., Niu, J., Ma, J., et al.: File downloading oriented Roadside Units deployment for vehicular networks. J. Syst. Archit. **59**(10, Part B), 938–946 (2013)
15. Huberman, B.A., Adamic, L.A.: Internet: growth dynamics of the world-wide web. Nature **401**(6749), 131 (1999)
16. Korn, A., Schubert, A., Telcs, A.: Lobby index in networks. Physica A **388**(11), 2221–2226 (2009)
17. Newman, M.E.J.: Mixing patterns in networks. Phys. Rev. E **67**(2), 026126 (2003)
18. Fiore, M., Harri, J.: The networking shape of vehicular mobility. In: Proceedings ACM MobiHoc, pp. 261–272 (2008)
19. Katsaros, D., Pallis, G., Stamos, K., Vakali, A., Sidiropoulos, A., Manolopoulos, Y.: CDNs content outsourcing via generalized communities. IEEE TKDE **21**(1), 137–151 (2009)

20. Uppoor, S., Fiore, M.: Large-scale urban vehicular mobility for networking research. In: IEEE Vehicular Networking Conference (VNC), pp. 62–69 (2011)
21. Leskovec, J., Kleinberg, J., Faloutsos, C.: Graphs over time: densification laws, shrinking diameters and possible explanations. In: Proceedings of the Eleventh ACM SIGKDD International Conference on Knowledge Discovery in Data Mining, pp. 177–187. ACM, New York (2005)

An Application of the IoT in Belt Conveyor Systems

Gabriel Lodewijks[1,2(✉)], Wenfeng Li[2], Yusong Pang[1], and Xiaoli Jiang[1]

[1] Delft University of Technology, Delft, The Netherlands
{g.lodewijks,y.pang,x.jiang}@tudelft.nl
[2] Wuhan University of Technology, Wuhan, China
liwf_cn@126.com

Abstract. The Internet of Things and Big data these days means big business. Monitoring Belt Conveyor Systems used to be performed by means of inspectors and off line. These days the developments are towards fully automated inspection systems. The IoT enables that more information from sensor systems becomes available that was not available in the past. Theoretically this means that monitoring Belt Conveyor systems 24/7 should become reality and down-time and unexpected maintenance a thing of the past. All these sensor systems produce a vast amount of information. Big data implies a combination of databases too large and/or too diverse to maintain by regular database management systems. Big data plays an ever-increasing role these days. This paper discusses an application of the IoT in bulk solid handling and transportation systems and the utilization of big data. It discusses recent developments and a case study.

Keywords: IoT · Belt conveyor · Monitoring · Inspection

1 The Internet of Things

In literature the term the "Internet of Things" (IoT), which is multi-disciplinary, is defined in a number of different ways reflecting this multi-disciplinary nature [1–4]. In [5] for example, the IoT is defined as "things or objects, which through addressing schemes interact with each other and cooperate with their neighbors to reach common goals". In [6] the IoT are "interconnecting physical objects with computing and communication capabilities across a wide range of services and technologies". Finally in [7] the IoT is perceived as "Interconnection of sensing and actuating devices providing the ability to share information across platforms through a unified framework... with Cloud computing as the unifying framework". The first definition comes from a networking perspective, the second uses physical attributes as the base for the IoT definition and the third definition emphasizes the use of platforms and the cloud. This paper is party based on [2].

The IoT holds several disciplines and consists of multiple technologies. The technologies are structured in such a way that they form a value chain between a SO and an end-user, see Fig. 1.

© Springer International Publishing AG 2016
W. Li et al. (Eds.): IDCS 2016, LNCS 9864, pp. 340–351, 2016.
DOI: 10.1007/978-3-319-45940-0_31

Fig. 1. Value chain of IoT [2]

Atzori et al. [5] identified three different definitions or visions on the IoT. The IoT can only be useful in application domains where these three visions intersect [7], see Fig. 2. These visions are called:

- 'Internet oriented' vision
- 'Things oriented' vision
- 'Semantic oriented' vision

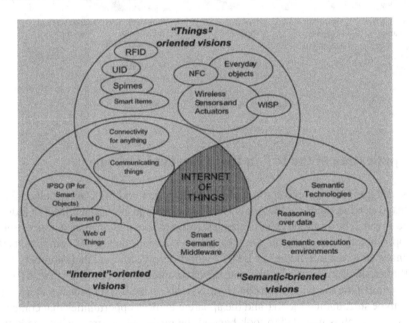

Fig. 2. The IoT as a result of different visions [5]

2 Big Data

Today, an overwhelming amount of data is generated and analyzed by enterprises, Social Media, Multimedia and the IoT [8]. Questions may arise however whether or not this data is useful. Individually it may be considered valueless, but when accumulated data is exploited, useful information can be identified and potential forecasts can be made [9].

The subject of Big Data concerns the need for real-time analysis of enormous datasets and masses of unstructured data, which are gathered in various fields [10]. The data is numerous, it cannot be categorized within standard relational databases and the capturing- and processing processes are executed rapidly. The underlying engine of Big Data is supported by Cloud Computing. With Cloud Computing a much larger scale and more complex algorithms can be employed to meet the, continuously growing, demands of Big Data. However, the rapid evolution of Big Data left little time for the subject to mature in academic literature and there exist little consensus of the fundamental question when data is qualified as Big Data [14]. Still a substantial part of the found literature (multiple authors, cited in [10–12]). The growth of Cloud Computing and Big Data further promote the growth of the IoT [11]. The steps that are used in order to extract information from Big Data fall under the Big Data Value Chain, see Fig. 3.

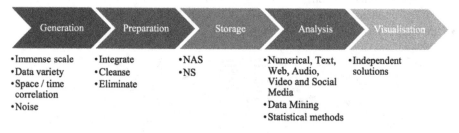

Fig. 3. The big data value chain [2]

3   Application of the IoT in Belt Conveyor Systems

In this paragraph an example of the application of the IoT and Big Data in belt conveyor systems as used in the Bulk Materials Handling and Transportation (BMHT) industry will be given. The example is not intended to be exhaustive or representative for all developments that are going on. On the contrary, the introduction of components that are connected to the Internet in the BMHT world is very slow and their numbers rather low. Rather, this paragraph will illustrate the development of technology that allows the combination of the IoT within belt conveyor systems. In the BMHT industry there seems to be a hype surrounding the IoT and the apparent endless opportunities that come with it. This paragraph is intended to look beyond the hype and illustrate what needs to be done in order to develop a true IoT application for the BMHT.

3.1   Introduction

In the mining industry, large-scale belt conveyors are often the main means for long overland transportation, see Fig. 4.

Fig. 4. Long overland belt conveyor in South Africa (courtesy Conveyor Experts B.V.)

These belt conveyors have many components. Some components are clustered in one location. For example the belt drive system, head pulley and take-up system may all be fairly close to each other at the head of the conveyor. Other components like the tail pulley, the belt loading station and/or brakes may be clustered at the tail of the conveyor. That makes it relatively easy to inspect them and to determine whether or not maintenance or replacement is required to maintain the reliability of the conveyor. Other components like the conveyor belt itself and the idlers are spread-out over the length of the conveyor. For the belt that is not really an issue. Since the belt rotates through the conveyor it suffices to place a conveyor belt monitoring system either at the head or at the tail of the conveyor. Inspection of the idler rolls is a different issue. In current systems an inspector physically has to walk/drive along the system to inspect/monitor the performance of the idler rolls. The question is whether we can ease the monitoring of the idler rolls keeping in mind that there may be 10,000 to 100,000 rolls in one conveyor.

In 2003 the concept of automated maintenance and intelligent monitoring in belt conveyors was introduced [13] and further extended in 2005 [14]. One of the ideas was to provide the idler rolls with wireless sensor technology and see what benefits could be gained by hooking them up to the IoT. This idea, called the smart idler concept, has been first introduced in 2007 in [15]. Since then it has been further developed together with Rulmeca rolls from Italy.

In general the idea seems simple; connect all the idler rolls to the Internet and one has information available 24/7 at any location. This has a couple of advantages: The maintenance department of the company that operates the belt conveyor may be on a different site and can now gain insight into the 'operational health' of the idler rolls 24/7; There is a tendency to lease belt conveying systems instead of owning one. In that case the lessor might want to have insight into the performance/use of the system; If a maintenance contract is in place between an operator of a belt conveyor and a component supplier then the supplier needs information of performance of those components.

However, there are also quite a few questions. The first question was how to assess the technical health of an idler roll. The second question was how to get information on the technical health at the right place, for example at the desk of the maintenance manager. The third question was what should the maintenance manager do with the information, in other words how to interpret the information. A fourth question was what else, or who else, can do something with the gathered information. The next section will provide answers to these and more questions.

3.2   The Technology Behind the Application

In this section the technology behind the smart idler concept will be discussed.

Data Acquisition. In order to assess the technical health of an idler roll it should be realized that in most cases it are the bearings of a roll that malfunction/get stuck so that the roll stops rotating. Before a bearing fails the roll will experience vibrations and the bearings starts to make noise (audible vibrations). In theory it is possible to equip each roll with either an acoustic sensor or an accelerometer to pick up vibrations that indicate potential bearing failure. Both an accelerometer and a microphone measure data as a function of time. In order to translate that data into information, to find the root cause of the failure, it needs to be transformed into a signal in the frequency domain via an Fast Fourier Transformation. This would mean that every sensor node needs to have processing power. This is not feasible. Therefore, the collected data has to be transmitted to a central monitoring unit and processed there. This process means that the central monitoring unit has to 'tune in' with a specific roll and take a measurement based on a certain inspection protocol. The measurement has to be long enough to allow detection of the vibrations in the relevant frequency spectrum. Although it is technically possible to equip each roll with sensors to pick up vibrations, this was deemed too complex and economically not viable.

An alternative way of assessing the 'technical health' of the roll's bearings is by measuring their temperature. Normal operating temperatures range between 20° C and 50° C depending on the ambient temperature. If the temperature of a bearing increases to higher temperatures, ranging from 80° C to 120° C, then that is a clear sign of potential bearing failure. The time between picking up irregularities in bearing behavior and bearing failure using vibration detection sensors is significant larger then when using temperature sensors [16]. However, if the temperature of the bearings can be measured on-line or if the rolls have the ability to notify the central monitoring unit in time in case of temperatures over a certain threshold value then there is still enough time to replace a roll with potential bearing failure before it actually fails.

Each roll is supported by two bearings. However, if one of those bearings fails then the total roll is considered broken and needs replacement. If a bearing is about to fail and its temperature increases then also the temperature of the shaft that supports the bearing will increase. Since both bearings are supported by the same shaft it is sufficient to measure the shaft temperature instead of the temperature of both bearings to assess the condition of the bearings. Therefore, the smart idler concept needs an RFID sensor node for each roll, where the sensor is a thermocouple to measure directly measure the temperature of the shaft, see Fig. 5. The thermocouple data does not need post processing; there is a direct and linear relation between the output voltage of the sensor and the temperature of the shaft. The accuracy of the thermo couple does not have to be very precise. An accuracy of +/- 2 degrees C is deemed sufficient.

Fig. 5. Idler roll equipped with RFID sensor node

Identification and Tracking. Identifying a specific roll is not difficult since each roll is equipped with an RFID sensor node and therefore has a unique number. The biggest challenge is to keep track of which roll is installed where. This asks for a certain discipline during installation of the rolls in terms of administration. On the other hand, identification and tracking can be done automatically by sending a signal for request of identification from the head and the tail of the conveyor to the roll and time the amount of time it takes to get a response. Timing this from the head end and the tail end should give sufficient accuracy on the location of a specific roll.

Communication and Networking. If each roll could measure its own temperature and/ or give a temperature overload warning (temperature too high) then that information still needs to be transmitted to the central monitoring unit and be made available to the Internet. Each roll is equipped with a RFID sensor node that can communicate with the interrogator, see Fig. 6. The above-described nodes have one drawback and that is that the range over which they can communicate with the interrogator is relatively small caused by the internal power limitations. Typically this range is smaller than 10 m. Since the envisioned applications are large scale belt conveyors, see Fig. 6, an alternative way of transmission is required.

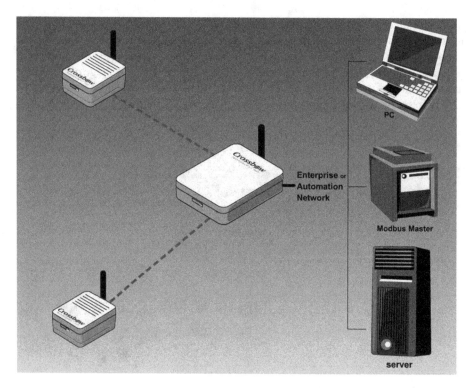

Fig. 6. Nodes, interrogator and systems used in the central monitoring unit (courtesy Crossbow, Inc.)

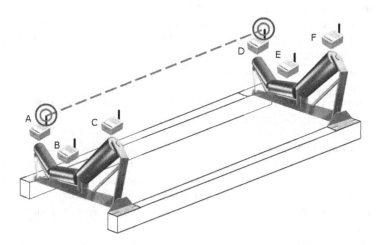

Fig. 7. Direct roll-to-roll communication (in reality the nodes are placed inside the rolls)

Typically the idler pitch varies between the 2.5 and 4.5 m for the carrying belt and between 5 and 10 ms for the return strand. Assume that the temperature of roll A, see

Fig. 7, exceeds its threshold value. At that time the node is activated and starts to transmit its identity (number) and, if required, its temperature. Since the distance between roll A and the interrogator at the central monitoring unit is far more than about 10 m, in fact it may be over 10 km, it needs assistance for the data transmission. Knowing that the system needs to be purely wireless, all nodes need to be able to not only send data but also receive data. In that case direct roll-to-roll communication is possible. The path used for data transmission is not fixed. The network is build up every time a roll starts to transmit data. Examples of data transmission routes are given in the Figs. 8 and 9. The configurations shown in these figures are so-called Hybrid Star (ZigBee) configurations. In principle each roll can participate in the data transmission route. If the node in one of the rolls fails then the network can reconfigure itself. This feature ensures a self-healing LAN network. This concept is shown in Fig. 10.

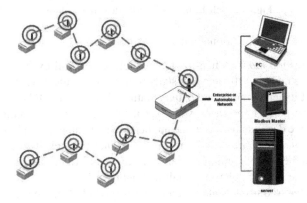

Fig. 8. Communication through the network from nodes through interrogator to automation network

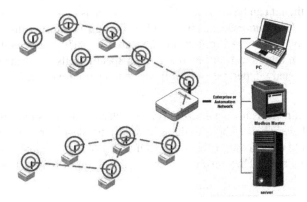

Fig. 9. Alternative data transmission route.

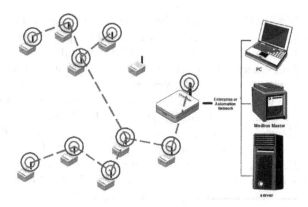

Fig. 10. Self-healing network after node failure

The rolls have three operational modes:

- *Internal activation mode;* when the temperature of the roll exceeds the threshold value then the node is activated and starts to transmit its identity. If required it can also transmit its temperature and battery status. This option will be used initially to determine the correct threshold value for the bearing and roll temperature. The threshold value depends partly on the application and ambient conditions.
- *Central external activation mode;* if a roll does not transmit its identity it can be assumed that the roll temperature is below the threshold value. However, if for whatever reason the node in the roll is malfunctioning or it does not have power then it will not be able to transmit data. Therefore it is possible that the roll temperature is above the threshold value without the node transmitting data. To periodically check whether the nodes are functioning or not the central communication unit can request each node to identify itself and report its temperature and battery status. If a roll does not respond then it can be considered broken and needs replacement [17].
- *Local external activation mode;* if a neighboring roll is transmitting data then the node in the roll is activated to transmit the same data. This mode is used to either support the central request for identification of specific rolls or for the transmission of the identity and temperature of a roll whose temperature exceeded the threshold value.

Currently Rullmeca is testing a set-up where each roll transmits its temperature and rotational speed every half an hour so that a history of the development of the technical health can be build up. This set-up however requires considerably more power and need a more expensive node. They also consider the utilization of routers to ease the data transmission.

Middleware. For the smart idler concept no special middleware was designed from the point of view to support interoperation. Till now middleware software has been developed that allows monitoring all the rolls in the system. The context detection for the system is simple; the temperature of a roll is either below or above a threshold value. Device discovery and management have been discussed above. Basically, a roll can be automatically detected by sending a detection signal from the head and from the tail of the conveyor. Security and privacy are no real issues in the smart idler concepts. It's basically a one-way system from the point of view that the rolls inform the system. The system however does not control the rolls in any way. Privacy is also not an issue in this application since it does not contain any private individuals information. It is envisioned that the middleware will be extended in the future and that a translation from the acquired data, via information, into a maintenance plan will be possible.

Data Storage and Analytics. Depending on what data or information is stored the smart idler concept may lead to Big Data. If every now and then, for example every five minutes, each roll in the system is asked to provide it's temperature then that will lead very fast to a large data base that may need to stored in the cloud. The advantage of having this Big Data is that it will be possible to detect deterioration of rolls over time. This will give insight in the time available between a roll's temperature passing the threshold value and the roll stopping rotating. On the other hand, if only the ID's of those rolls are stored that of which the temperature passed the threshold value, then a small data set will be build up. The latter data can also be deleted as soon as a roll has been replaced. The analytics of the data set is primarily to answer the question at what rate rolls deteriorate. This information is essential for the planning of (preventive) maintenance activities.

Looking at the characteristics of Big Data, the following notes can be made for the smart idler concept:

- Volume
  : the data volume can be very large or relatively small depending on what data is stored (see above).
- Variety
  : data is collected in one format only.
- Velocity
  : data is acquired, sent and analyzed with low data transfer rates (868 MHz) to safe energy.
- Value
  : value is found in structured data.
- Data generation
  : data is generated by the thermocouples in the RFID sensor nodes.
- Data preparation
  : is not necessary. There is a direct correlation between the output of the thermocouple and the roll's temperature.
- Data storage
  : in the Cloud when large amounts of data is stored. May be on a local server when small amounts of data is stored.
- Data analysis
  : Is easy, temperature over the threshold value requires action.
- Data visualization
  : On the screen (for triggering) and in Excel datasheets.

4 Discussion

In the previous paragraphs it has been shown how an IoT application for belt conveyor systems like the smart idler concept can be developed using the characteristics of IoT systems and Big Data. Although the concept has been developed, and still is under further development, it has not yet been implemented in a large-scale belt conveyor. The main reason is the worldwide situation of the mining industry. The smart idler concept has been tested extensively under laboratory conditions in all kind of different configurations and the system works fine. The RFID sensor nodes in the meantime have been further developed to an economical viable concept. However, in practice it is not always easy to convince the procurement department of a mine to invest in technology on forehand. Unexpected downtime of a large-scale belt conveyor may costs up to $300,000. If the idler rolls where the cause of this downtime then this could have been prevented by using the smart idler concept.

The IoT application described in the previous paragraphs only concerned the idler rolls. There are however two other examples of a combination of the IoT and a BMHT system; a belt scraper system [18] and the conveyor belt inspection system [19].

Where the mining industry in general is not seen as a particularly technology intensive industry, it is a capital-intensive industry that justifies the application of advanced technology in order to reduce costs and increase safety. Even when the utilization of Internet connected equipment in the mining industry is very small, the outlook and possible future benefits of systems like the smart idler concept seem to be there. So, where the current role of the IoT in belt conveyor systems is still very small, it may be expected that this will change in the future with a change of tides in the mining industry [20, 21].

References

1. Darrow, B.: Canary in a coal mine, p. 14. Fortune, 1 August 2015
2. Spekreijse, M.D.: IoT and big data in transport systems. Report number 2016. TEL. 7996, Delft University of Technology (2016)
3. Evens, D.: The Internet of Things–how the next evolution of the internet is changing everything. Cisco White Paper, pp. 1–11 (2011)
4. Ashton, K.: That "Internet of Things" thing. RFID J. **22**, 97–114 (2009)
5. Atzori, L., Iera, A., Morabito, G.: The Internet of Things: a survey. Comput. Netw. **54**(15), 2787–2805 (2010)
6. Miorandi, D., Sicari, S., De Pellegrini, F., Chlamtac, I.: Internet of Things: vision, applications and research challenges. Hoc Netw. **10**(7), 1497–1516 (2012)
7. Gubbi, J., Buyya, R., Marusic, S., Palaniswami, M.: Internet of Things (IoT): a vision, architectural elements, and future directions. Future Gener. Comput. Syst. **29**(7), 1645–1660 (2013)
8. Kambatla, K., Kollias, G., Kumar, V., Grama, A.: Trends in big data analytics. J. Parallel Distrib. Comput. **74**(7), 2561–2573 (2014)
9. Chen, M., Mao, S., Liu, Y.: Big data: a survey. Mob. Netw. Appl. **19**(2), 171–209 (2014)
10. Hashem, I.A.T., Yaqoob, I., Badrul Anuar, N., Mokhtar, S., Gani, A., Ullah Khan, S.: The rise of "Big Data" on cloud computing: review and open research issues. Inf. Syst. **47**, 98–115 (2014)
11. Chen, F., Deng, P., Wan, J., Zhang, D., Vasilakos, A.V., Rong, X.: Data mining for the Internet of Things: literature review and challenges. Int. J. Distrib. Sens. Netw. (2015) (i)
12. Gandomi, A., Haider, M.: Beyond the hype: big data concepts, methods, and analytics. Int. J. Inf. Manag. **35**(2), 137–144 (2015)
13. Lodewijks, G.: Strategies of automated maintenance of belt conveyors. In: Proceedings of the BeltCon 12 Conference, Randburg, Republic of South Africa, 23 July–24 July (2003)

14. Lodewijks, G., Ottjes, J.A.: Intelligent belt conveying monitoring & control: theory and applications. In: Proceedings of the BeltCon 13 Conference, Randburg, Republic of South Africa, 3 August – 5 August (2005)
15. Lodewijks, G., Duinkerken, M.B., Lopez de la Cruz, A.M., Veeke, H.P.M.: The application of FRID technology in belt conveyor systems. In: Proceedings of BeltCon 14, Johannesburg, pp. 1–17 (2007)
16. Albers, A.: Acoustic emission analysis. Practicing Oil Analysis Magazine, University of Karlsruhe, Institute of Product Development, Germany (2006)
17. Lodewijks, G., Veeke, H.P.M., Lopéz de la Cruz, A.M.: Reliability of RFID in logistic systems. In: Proceedings of the 2006 IEEE International Conference on Service Operations and Logistics, and Informatics, pp. 971–976 (2006)
18. Lodewijks, G., Versteegh, C.R.J.: Implementing automatic condition monitoring techniques on belt scraper systems. Bulk Solids Handling **26**(4), 252–257 (2006)
19. http://www.veyance.com/bulandingpage.aspx?id=44
20. Fu, X., Li, W., Fortino, G., Pace, P., Aloi, G.: A utility-oriented routing scheme for interest-driven community-based opportunistic networks. J. Univ. Comput. Sci. **20**(13), 1829–1854 (2014)
21. Fortino, G., Bal, M., Li, W., Shen, W.: Collaborative wireless sensor networks: architectures, algorithms and applications. Inf. Fusion **22**, 1–2 (2015)

A Novel Adaptive Negotiation Strategy for Agricultural Supply Chain Centered on Third Party Logistics

Wenjing Guo[1], Wenfeng Li[1(✉)], Weiming Shen[2], Xiaoli Jiang[3],
and Gabriel Lodewijks[3]

[1] School of Logistics Engineering, Wuhan University of Technology,
Wuhan, China
15107170535@163.com, liwf@whut.edu.cn
[2] National Research Council of Canada, Ottawa, Canada
wshen@ieee.org
[3] Delft University of Technology, Delft, The Netherlands
{X.Jiang,g.lodewijks}@tudelft.nl

Abstract. Agricultural supply chain is in general open and dynamic attributed and negotiation is a key strategy to realize collaboration among different entities involved. However, traditional static and offline negotiation strategy may not function well, an agricultural supply chain centered on third party logistics will provide a new collaborative relationship among agricultural materials suppliers, agricultural cooperatives, farmers, agricultural products demanders and third party logistics providers. This paper proposes a novel adaptive negotiation strategy for agricultural supply chain centered on third party logistics. The negotiation strategy consists of an evaluation function in terms of integrity and risk preferences, a concession function in terms of concession preference, time and resources, and a generation function in terms of opponent's behaviors. Afterwards, an procedure was proposed to solve the negotiation strategy. Finally, a simulation experiment was employed to verify the effectiveness of the negotiation strategy.

Keywords: Agricultural supply chain · Third party logistics · Supply chain collaboration · Adaptive negotiation strategy

1 Introduction

Agricultural supply chain centered on third party logistics is a novel supply chain mode proposed in [1]. Under the mode, third party logistics (3PL) providers integrates logistics services and intermediary services. The authors intend to realize the vertical collaboration and horizontal collaboration simultaneously. However, supply chain collaboration tend to be hardly realized among different parties, especially for agricultural supply chain which has instable and dynamic markets. The reason is that all the entities want to maximize their own profit rather than consider the whole cost of supply chain.

Negotiation is a key for supply chain collaboration. Traditional negotiation model focuses on mathematical model building and offline decision making. Recently, lots of research has focused on an agent-based negotiation owing to its real-time, adaptive

W. Li et al. (Eds.): IDCS 2016, LNCS 9864, pp. 352–363, 2016.
DOI: 10.1007/978-3-319-45940-0_32

features. However, due to the interior instability of agricultural supply chain, current agent-based negotiation models will not function well. Therefore, this paper proposed a novel adaptive negotiation strategy for agricultural supply chain centered on third party logistics. The new negotiation strategy is one-to-many and the dynamic market has been considered. What's more, the integrity and opponent's behaviors are also included in an evaluation function and a generation function respectively.

In the negotiation model, third party logistics providers will play a key role. It need to negotiate with agricultural materials providers, agricultural cooperatives and agricultural products demanders respectively. This paper proposed a novel adaptive negotiation strategy for agricultural supply chain centered on third party logistics. The negotiation strategy consists of an evaluation function in terms of integrity and risk preferences, a concession function in terms of concession preference, time and resources, and a generation function in terms of opponent's behaviors. After three phase negotiation, third party logistics providers will get the final partners. The new partnership among them will realize supply chain collaboration under dynamic environments.

The rest of this paper is organized as follows. Section 2 introduces the related research. The novel adaptive negotiation strategy is designed in Sect. 3. Section 4 describes the simulation experiments and analyzes the results. The conclusion and future work are discussed in Sect. 5.

2 Related Research

Supply chain collaboration is a collaborative relationship among all the parties of supply chain in order to save cost, improve quality, decrease risk and increase add-value [2]. These entities keep information sharing and planning coordination based on negotiation and interaction. Wal-Mart, Warner-Lamber, SAP, Manugistics and Benchmarking Partners proposed a collaborative planning, prediction and replenish model (FCPFR). The model requires information sharing among different entities [3]. Manoj Hudnurkar researched the main influence factors of supply chain collaboration. Information sharing was verified as the most important factor [4]. However, in case of agricultural supply chain, information sharing is more difficult to realize than supply chain in other fields. Because farmers tend to be small scale and disperse, and the market demand is always dynamic. What's more, all the parties hope to protect private information when negotiating with opponents. Therefore, an effective and adaptive negotiation model is essential for agricultural supply chain collaboration.

Agent-based automated negotiation can be applied to deal with three topics: negotiation issues, negotiation interaction process and negotiation strategies [5]. Negotiation issues confine the objects of negotiation, such as price, lead time, quantity, quality, et al. The negotiation interaction process regulates the interaction rules among agents for different negotiation issues. Negotiation strategies guide agents' negotiation behaviors, which are introduced by the participants to act in line with the negotiation interaction process for achieving their negotiation issues [6]. Jianye Hao (2014) proposed an adaptive negotiation strategy in bilateral negotiations over multiple items. The strategy provided optimal offer for negotiating partner based on the reinforcement learning based approach [7]. Jiang Zhang, Fenghui Ren, Minjie Zhang (2015) proposed a bayesian-based approach which can help an agent to predict its opponent's preference in bilateral multi-issue negotiation [8]. These papers both proposed an adaptive negotiation strategy. However, none of them consider on specific supply chain. Agricultural supply chain is a unique network which has dynamic demand markets and instable collaboration relationship among different entities. A novel agent-based negotiation model for agricultural supply chain is required. As negotiation issue and negotiation interaction process has been extensively studied in [1], the adaptive negotiation strategy will be focused in this paper.

3   Agent-Based Negotiation Strategy

In the negotiation model, all the negotiation agents need to negotiate on specific negotiation issues, abide by specific negotiation interaction rules and use specific negotiation strategies. Negotiation strategy includes the proposal evaluation function, concession function and generation function. According to the negotiation strategy,

Table 1. Notations of fomulations in the negotiation strategy

Notations	Descriptions
$\{b, s\}$	Buyer agents, seller agents
$P = \{P_1, \ldots, P_i, \ldots, P_M\}$	A set of products
$Q = \{q_1, \ldots, q_i, \ldots, q_M\}$	Quantities of products
I_k	Value of the k-th quantitative negotiation issue
$\hat{I}_k = (m, m_2, m_3)$	Value of the k-th qualitative negotiation issue
$Bid_i = \{P_i, I_1, \ldots, I_j, \ldots, I_K, q_i\}$	The submitted bid of the i-th product
$Pro = \{Bid_1, Bid_2, \ldots\}$	The former proposal submitted by a agent
$Cro = \{Bid_1, Bid_2, \ldots\}$	The latter proposal submitted by opponent agent
V_{min}^k	The minimum utility of the k-th issue
$[min_k^s, max_k^s]$	Value interval of the i-th negotiation issue of buyer agent
$[max_k^b, max_k^b]$	Value interval of the i-th negotiation issue of seller agent
β	Risk preference
$V(I_k)$	Utility function for quantitative negotition issue
$V(\hat{I}_k)$	Utility function for qualitative negotition issue
w_k	The weight of the k-th negotiation issue
$U(Bid_i)$	The utility funtion for Bid_i
$Bid_{s \to b}^t(i)$	The proposal submitted by seller agent in the t-th negotiation round.
$Bid_{b \to s}^t(i)$	The proposal submitted by buyer agent in the t-th negotiation round.
b_k	Discount rate of the k-th negotiation issue
γ	Consession preference
$\alpha_k(t)$	Concession rate of the k-th negotiation issue in the t-th negotiation round
S_j	The cultivated area of agricultural products of the j-th agricultural cooperative
t	Negotiation rounds
T	Negotiation time, $T = 2t$

different negotiation opponents will set different risk preference, concession preference and so on. The notations used in the negotiation strategy are illustrated in Table 1.

3.1 Negotiation Objective

According to the employment relationship between 3PL and agricultural cooperatives, the negotiation issue is price only. The 3PL will buy the agricultural materials and sell the agricultural products. The agricultural cooperatives just need to contribute labor and land.

Based on the buyer-seller relationship between agricultural products demanders and 3PL, a multi-issue negotiation strategy was proposed for the second negotiation phase in this paper, including both price and service quality where price is a quantitative negotiation issue while service quality is a qualitative issue.

The relationship between 3PL and agricultural materials suppliers is buyer-seller. As agricultural materials are produced all year round, agricultural materials suppliers can guarantee the required quantity of agricultural materials of 3PL. Therefore, only price was considered as the negotiation issue in the third negotiation phase.

3.2 Evaluation Function

In the negotiation model, each agent evaluate the proposal submitted by opponent agent by comparing bid's utility. In order to build the utility function among varies issues, all the issues are normalized into a 0–1 scale in this paper. Chunxia Yu proposed a utility function for quantitative negotiation issues on risk prone and risk averse respectively [9]. V_{min}^k is the minimum utility determined by the decision maker for the kth negotiation issue. Equations (1) and (2) show the expressions.
When $0 < \beta \leq 1$,

$$V(I_k) = \begin{cases} V_{min}^k + (1 - V_{min}^k) \times (\frac{I_k - min_k^s}{max_k^s - min_k^s})^{1/\beta} \ Benefit\ agent \\ V_{min}^k + (1 - V_{min}^k) \times (\frac{max_k^b - I_k}{max_k^b - min_k^b})^{1/\beta} \ Cost\ agent \end{cases} \quad (1)$$

When $\beta > 1$,

$$V(I_k) = \begin{cases} exp\left((1 - \frac{I_k - min_k^s}{max_k^s - min_k^s})^{\beta} ln V_{min}^k\right) \ Benefit\ agent \\ exp\left((1 - \frac{max_k^b - I_k}{max_k^b - min_k^b})^{\beta} ln V_{min}^k\right) \ Cost\ agent \end{cases} \quad (2)$$

β represents the risk preference, when $0 < \beta < 1$, the decision maker is a risk lover, which means that the decision maker will risk on the negotiation failure for more profit. Meanwhile, the evaluation function is a concave function, and the second derivative is greater than 0. When $\beta = 1$, the decision maker is a risk neuter, when $\beta > 1$, the decision maker is a risk averter. Meanwhile, the evaluation function is a convex function, and the second derivative is smaller than 0.

Qualitative negotiation issue means that the value of issue is descript by linguistic variables. In this paper, the service quality grades are classified into very good, good, medium, poor and very poor. We use set $(i_0, i_1, \ldots, i_j, \ldots, i_n)$ to express qualitative issue. However, for 3PL and agricultural products demanders, the same notation represents different means. For 3PL, lower grade is better, so $i_0 =$ very good, $i_4 =$ very poor. For agricultural products demanders, higher grade is better, so $i_0 =$ very poor, $i_4 =$ very good. This paper introduce the triangular fuzzy number (TFN) $\hat{I}_k = (m_1, m_2, m_3)$ to normalize the qualitative issue, $m_1 = \frac{i-1}{n}, m_2 = \frac{i}{n}, m_3 = \frac{i+1}{n}$, and $0 \leq m_i \leq 1$ [10]. So, for service grade 'very good', the triangular fuzzy number of 3PL is $(\frac{0}{4}, \frac{0}{4}, \frac{1}{4})$, and agricultural products demander is $(\frac{4-1}{4}, \frac{4}{4}, \frac{4}{4})$ correspondently. The TFNs can be transformed into 0–1 scale based on the graded mean integration representation method as shown in Eq. (3).

$$V \hat{I}_k = \frac{1}{6}(m_1 + 4m_2 + m_3), k = 1, 2, \ldots, K \tag{3}$$

Different decision maker has different weight preference. The utility function of a bid is described as Eq. (4).

$$UBid_i = \sum_k w_k V(I_k) \left(\sum_k w_k = 1 \right), k = 1, 2, \ldots, K \tag{4}$$

This paper proposed the integrity rule during the negotiation process. When the proposal value of an agent is big or less than the maximum or minimum value of the opponent agent, the opponent agent will reject the proposal and believe the agent is not genuine. What's more, we set t_{max} as the maximum negotiation rounds. When $t > t_{max}$, the negotiation is over no matter whether the agreement is reached or not. Equations (5) and (6) illustrate the responding function for different agents.

$$B^s \left(t, Bid_{b \to s}^t(i) \right) = \begin{cases} reject, & t > t_{max} \ or \ I_{b \to s} < min_k^s \\ accept, & U \left(Bid_{b \to s}^t(i) \right) \geq U \left(Bid_{s \to b}^t(i) \right) \quad Cost \\ counteroffer, & U \left(Bid_{b \to s}^t(i) \right) < U \left(Bid_{s \to b}^t(i) \right) \end{cases} \tag{5}$$

$$B^b \left(t, Bid_{s \to b}^t(i) \right) = \begin{cases} reject, & t + 1 > t_{max} \ or \ I_{s \to b} > max_k^b \\ accept, & U(Bid_{s \to b}^t(i)) \geq U(Bid_{b \to s}^{t+1}(i)) \quad Benefit \\ counteroffer, & U(Bid_{s \to b}^t(i)) < U(Bid_{b \to s}^{t+1}(i)) \end{cases} \tag{6}$$

3.3   Concession Function

An adaptive concession function was designed for agricultural supply chain in this paper. As the agricultural products demand market is instable and dynamic, and the number of negotiation opponent agent is unstable as well, this paper introduces a novel concession function in terms of time and resources. Equation (7) shows the concession function. We assumes that when $\alpha(t) > 1$, $\alpha(t) > 1$. When $0 < \gamma < 1$, the concession function is a concave function, then the agent will concede negatively at first, positively after that. When $\gamma > 1$, the concession function is a convex function, then the agent will concede positively at first, negatively after that.

$$\alpha_k(t) = \begin{cases} \left(b_k + (1 - b_k)\left(((t - 1)/t_{\max})^{1/\gamma}\right)\right) \prod_{i=1}^{t} \theta_i & (0 < \gamma \le 1) \\ \\ exp((1 - (t - 1)/t_{\max})^{\gamma} lnb_k) \prod_{i=1}^{t} \theta_i & (\gamma > 1) \end{cases} \tag{7}$$

In the negotiation phase between agricultural cooperatives (AC) and 3PL, resource dependence coefficient $\theta_i = \frac{N^{t-1}}{N^t}$, N^t represents the number of negotiation AC agents in the t-th negotiation round for the 3PL agent. $\theta_i = 1$ for AC agents.

In the negotiation phase between agricultural products demanders (APD) and 3PL, resource dependence coefficient $\theta_i = \frac{N^{t-1}}{N^t}$, N^t represents the number of negotiation APD agents in the t-th negotiation round for the 3PL agent. $\theta_i = \frac{Q^t}{Q^{t-1}}$. Q^t represents the required quantity of agricultural products in the t-th negotiation round for APD agents.

In the negotiation phase between agricultural materials suppliers (AMS) and 3PL, resource dependence coefficient $\theta_i = \frac{N^{t-1}}{N^t}$, N^t represents the number of negotiation AMS agents in the t-th negotiation round for the 3PL agent. $\theta_i = 1$ for AMS agents,.

3.4   Generation Function

The negotiation interaction process has regulated that the offer proposal is successively, and 3PL is the latter proposal all along in [1]. In the negotiation strategy, we builds the generation function in terms ofopponent's behaviors. When the opponent's offer has vast change, the agent will generate a new offer with big change. When the opponent's offer has small change, the agent will generate a new offer with small change.

The generation functions between 3PL agent and AC agents, 3PL agent and APD agents, 3PL agent and AMS agents are showed as Eqs. (8), (9) and (10) respectively.

$$\begin{cases} I_1^s(t) = I_1^s(t - 1) - \alpha^s(t)\left(I_1^s(t - 1) - I_1^b(t - 1)\right) & AC\ agent \\ I_1^b(t) = I_1^b(t - 1) + \alpha^b(t)\left(I_1^s(t) - I_1^b(t - 1)\right) & 3PL\ agent \end{cases} \tag{8}$$

$$\begin{cases} I_k^b(t) = I_k^b(t - 1) + \alpha^b(t)\left(I_k^s(t - 1) - I_k^b(t - 1)\right) & APD\ agents \\ I_k^s(t) = I_k^s(t - 1) - \alpha^s(t)\left(I_k^s(t - 1) - I_k^b(t)\right) & 3PL\ agent \end{cases} \tag{9}$$

$$\begin{cases} I_1^s(t) = I_1^s(t - 1) - \alpha^s(t)\left(I_1^s(t - 1) - I_1^b(t - 1)\right) & AMS\ agents \\ I_1^b(t) = I_1^b(t - 1) + \alpha^b(t)\left(I_1^s(t) - I_1^b(t - 1)\right) & 3PL\ agent \end{cases} \tag{10}$$

3.5 Solving Procedure

- Step 1: 3PL Agent sends invitations to AC Agents, APD Agents and AMS Agents respectively.
- Step 2: Invited AC Agents, APD Agents and AMS Agents submit their initial proposal $\{Bid_1, Bid_2, \ldots\}$ to 3PL Agent.
- Step 3: 3PL Agent sets their risk preference, and evaluate all the bids received from opponent agents according to its utility function and respond function. If the 3PL agent chooses to generate counter proposal, then go step 4. Otherwise, the negotiation is over, and the system transfer the negotiation results to 3PL agent.
- Step 4: 3PL Agent sets their concession rate, and generate counter proposal based on concession function and generation function successively, then submit it to opponent agents.
- Step 5: AC, APD and AMS Agents set their risk preference respectively, and evaluate the counter proposal according to their utility function and respond function. If the agent chooses to generate counter proposal, then go step 6. Otherwise, the negotiation is over, and the system transfer the negotiation results to 3PL agent.
- Step 6: AC Agents, APD Agents and AMS Agents set their concession rate, and generate next round proposal based on concession function and generation function, then submit it to 3PL Agent.

4 Simulation Experiment

As the space limitations and the negotiation between agricultural product demanders and 3PL is the most complex phase, this paper only design the simulation experiment on it. This paper designed 4 supermarkets $\{B_1, B_2, B_3, B_4\}$ for simulation experiment. In order to get the added value, 3PL would like to reach agreements with opponent agents. Therefore, we assumes that the risk preference of 3PL is risk averse, and concession preference is positively at first, negatively after that. Table 2 shows the parameters of 3PL. In the first round, the proposal of 3PL is {Bid1 = (cucumber, 4 yuan per Kg, medium); Bid 2 = (tomato, 4.5 yuan per Kg, medium)}.

In agricultural supply chain, supermarkets is the entities which close to consume markets and decide the demand quantities of agricultural products, then agricultural materials correspondently. In this paper, we set that the risk preference of supermarkets are both risk prone, and concession preference are negatively at first, positively after that. Table 3 shows the parameters of B_1, B_2, B_3, B_4.

As service quality is a qualitative issue, we need to tranform the qualitative languages to triangular fuzzy numbers (TFNs). Table 4 shows the triangular fuzzy numbers of service qualitity for 3PL and APD respectively.

After recieved invitation from 3PL, B_1, B_2 and B_3 accept the invitation in the 1st negotiation round while B_4 accepts the invitation in the 11th negotiation round. Table 5 describes the initial proposal of B_1, B_2, B_3 and B_4.

Table 2. Negotiation parameters of agricultural products for 3PL

Products id	Name	Price interval	Service quality interval	t_{max}	β	γ	b_k
P_1	Cucumber	[3, 4]	[VP, P, M, G, VG]	20	5	4	0.1
P_2	Tomato	[3.5,4.5]	[VP, P, M, G, VG]				
Weight (w_k)		0.6	0.4				

Table 3. Negotiation parameters of agriclutral products of B_1, B_2, B_3, B_4

Supermarkets id	Products id	Price interval	Service quality interval	t_{max}	β	γ	b_k
B_1	P_1	[2.5,4]	[VP,P,M,G,VG]	10	0.4	0.4	1
	P_2	[3,4.5]	[VP,P,M,G,VG]				
	Weight (w_k)	0.3	0.7				
B_2	P_1	[3, 4]	[VP,P,M,G,VG]	20	0.4	0.4	
	P_2	[3.5,4.5]	[VP,P,M,G,VG]				
	Weight (w_k)	0.7	0.3				
B_3	P_1	[3, 4]	[VP,P,M,G,VG]	20	0.6	0.6	
	P_2	[3.5,4.5]	[VP,P,M,G,VG]				
	Weight (w_k)	0.3	0.7				
B_4	P_1	[3, 4]	[VP,P,M,G,VG]	30	0.6	0.6	
	P_2	[3.5,4.5]	[VP,P,M,G,VG]				
	Weight (w_k)	0.7	0.3				

According to the respond function of 3PL, 3PL will reject the proposal from B_1 since the proposal value is less than the minimum value of 3PL. Therefore, at the 1st negotiation round, 3PL only negotiate with B_2 and B_3. With the entry of B_4 in the 11th negotiation round, the resources dependence coefficient of 3PL is $\theta_{11} = 2/3$. In the 8th negotiation round, we assumes that there has a 20 % reduction of the required quantity of B_2 and B_3, so the resources dependence coefficient of B_2 and B_3 is $\theta_8 = 0.8$. Other resources dependence coefficient are both 1 and $V_{min}^k = 0.1$ for all the agents.

Accodring to the parameters and consession functions, we can get the concession rate of 3PL and supermarkets in different negotiation round. Figure 1 shows the concession curve.

Accodring to the parameters and generation functions, the negotiation interaction process between 3PL and B_2, 3PL and B_3, 3PL and B_4 are illustrated in Figs. 2, 3 and 4 respectively.

From Figs. 2, 3 and 4, we can get the the interaction results between 3PL and B_2, 3PL and B_3, 3PL and B_4 respectively. It is clearly that different risk preference will get different utility values, different concession preference will get different concession values. The results verified that our negotiation strategy is useful and effectiveness.

Table 6 illustrates the negotiation interaction results. Comparing B_2 and B_3, we can see that the bigger the risk preference coefficient of supermarkets is, the better the negotiation result is for 3PL. Comparing B_3 and B_4, it is clearly that the later the

Table 4. The triangular fuzzy number for qualitative issues

Linguistics variables	Abbreviation	TFNs of 3PL	TFNs of supermarkets
Very good	VG	(0,0,0.25)	(0.75,1,1)
Good	G	(0.0.25,0.5)	(0.5,0.75,1)
Medium	M	(0.25,0.5,0.75)	(0.25,0.5,0.75)
Poor	P	(0.5,0.75,1)	(0.0.25,0.5)
Very poor	VP	(0.75,1,1)	(0,0,0.25)

Table 5. Initial bids submitted by B_1, B_2, B_3 and B_4

Bid id	Name	Price	Service quality	Supermarkets id
1	P_1	2.5	VG	B_1
2	P_2	3	VG	B_1
3	P_1	3	VG	B_2
4	P_2	3.5	VG	B_2
5	P_1	3	VG	B_3
6	P_2	3.5	VG	B_3
7	P_1	3	VG	B_4
8	P_2	3.5	VG	B_4

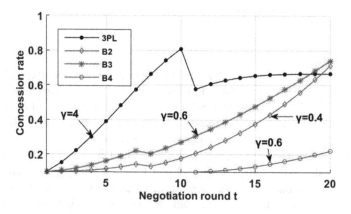

Fig. 1. The concession curve of B_2, B_3, B_4 and 3PL

supermarkets move in negotiation is and the bigger the negotiation deadline of supermarkets is, the worst negotiation result is for 3PL.

From Table 6, we can get the information that, B_3 is the best partner for 3PL, then B_2, B_4 is the worst one. Therefore, when agricultural cooperative partners have efficient cultivate areas, 3PL will accept both of the supermarkets as the agricultural products demander partners. Otherwise, 3PL will give priority to B_3, and give up B_4 if necessary.

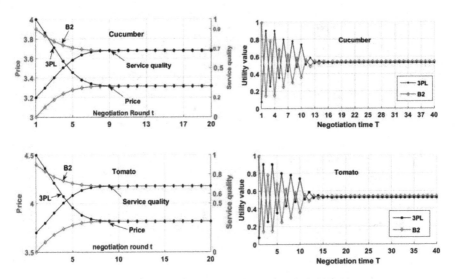

Fig. 2. Negotiation interaction process between 3PL and B_2

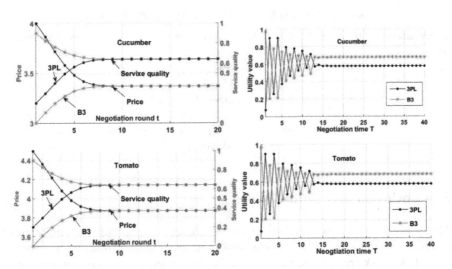

Fig. 3. Negotiation interaction process between 3PL and B_3

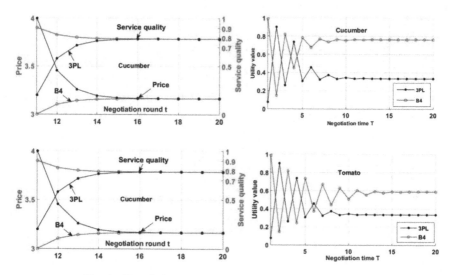

Fig. 4. Negotiation interaction process between 3PL and B_4

Table 6. Negotiation results between 3PL and B_2, B_3 and B_4

Supermarkets id	β	γ	t_{max}	Negotiation results	Final proposal utility
B_2	0.4	0.4	20	{cucumber, 3.315, good; tomato, 3.815, good}	1.048
B_3	0.6	0.6	20	{cucumber, 3.37, good; tomato, 3.87, good}	1.16
B_4	0.6	0.6	30	{cucumber, 3.163, good; tomato, 3.663, good}	0.66

5 Conclusion and Future Work

This paper proposed an adaptive negotiation strategy for agricultural supply chain centered on third party logistics. We introduced an evaluation function in terms of integrity and risk preferences, a concession function in terms of concession preference, time and resources, and a generation function in terms of opponent's behaviors. This paper also proposed a procedure to solve the negotiation strategy. Finally, a simulation experiment is implemented for the negotiation between 3PL and agricultural products demanders.

In the future, further studies will be performed on the final partner choosing model for 3PL based on supply chain cost, and the final collaborative schedule for agricultural supply chain centered on third party logistics.

Acknowledgements. This work is financially supported by the National Science & Technology R&D Program (2014BAH24F03).

References

1. Guo, W., Li, W., Zhong, Y., Lodewijks, G., Shen, W.: Agent-based negotiation framework for agricultural supply chain supported by third party logistics. Computer Supported Cooperative Work in Design (2016)
2. Simatupang, T., Wright, A., Sridharan, R.: Applying the theory of constraints to supply chain collaboration. Supply Chain Manage. **9**(1), 57–70 (2004)
3. James, D., Spier, K.: Revenue sharing and vertical control in the video rental industry. J. Ind. Econ. **49**(3), 223–245 (2001)
4. Hudnurkar, M., Jakhar, S., Rathod, U.: factors affecting collaboration in supply chain: a literature review. Procedia Soc. Behav. Sci. **133**, 189–202 (2014)
5. Faratin, P., Sierra, C., Jennings, N.: Negotiation decision functions for autonomous agents. Robot. Auton. Syst. **24**(3), 159–182 (1998)
6. Louta, M., Roussaki, I., Pechlivanos, L.: An intelligent agent negotiation strategy in the electronic marketplace environment. Eur. J. Oper. Res. **187**(3), 1327–1345 (2008)
7. Hao, J., Song, S., Leung, H., et al.: An efficient and robust negotiating strategy in bilateral negotiations over multiple items. Eng. Appl. Artif. Intell. **34**(9), 45–57 (2014)
8. Zhang, J., Ren, F., Zhang, M.: Bayesian-based preference prediction in bilateral multi-issue negotiation between intelligent agents. Knowl. Based Syst. **84**, 108–120 (2015)
9. Yu, C., Wong, T.: An agent-based negotiation model for supplier selection of multiple products with synergy effect. Expert Syst. Appl. **42**(1), 223–237 (2015)
10. Mikhailov, L.: Fuzzy analytical approach to partnership selection in formation of virtual enterprises. Omega **30**(5), 393–401 (2002)

A Facility Location Problem for the Design of a Collaborative Distribution Network

Xin Tang[1(✉)], Fabien Lehuédé[2], and Olivier Péton[2]

[1] Wuhan University of Technology, 1178, Heping Avenue, Wuhan, China
tangxin@whut.edu.cn
[2] Ecole des Mines de Nantes, Institut de Recherche en Communications
et Cybernétique de Nantes (IRCCyN, UMR CNRS 6597),
4 rue Alfred Kastler, 44300 Nantes, France
{fabien.lehuede,olivier.peton}@mines-nantes.fr

Abstract. This paper deals with the location of intermediate facilities in a two-tiered collaborative distribution network. We consider horizontal collaboration in a geographical cluster of suppliers, with thousands of customers spread over the whole country. The distribution system includes one consolidation facility in the production area and a set of intermediate facilities called regional distribution centers (RDCs). It combines full truckload (FTL) routes between the production area and the RDCs and less-than-truckload (LTL) shipments from the RDCs to each customer. We propose a Mixed Integer Linear Programming formulation for the optimal location of RDCs. This model integrates the two transportation rate structures and enables direct deliveries from the production area to customers when FTL routes are not profitable.

Keywords: Facility location · Collaboration · Distribution · Mixed integer linear programming

1 Introduction

Horizontal collaboration is defined as a business agreement between manufacturers at the same level in the supply chain in order to reach a common objective. This may be achieved by proper manipulation, utilization and sharing of appropriate resources [1]. However, companies that resort to horizontal collaboration are often competitors. They have to overcome many cultural, organizational and technical barriers, including the fear of sharing information, lack of trust, loss of flexibility, loss of their own control or extra cost of new IT tools. Competing companies are often reluctant to share strategic information or resources concerning their core business, while external operations, such as the supply or distribution of goods, are often natural candidates for collaboration.

To increase their competitiveness impacted by market globalization, companies are forced to improve customer service and reduce product cost. In this context, for suppliers who collaborate, pooling the transportation of goods leads to a two-fold cost reduction opportunity. First, gathering together the goods of each collaborator can provide full truckload (FTL) shipments, which are much cheaper than individual less-than-truckload (LTL) shipments. Second, the cost structure of LTL shipments is

W. Li et al. (Eds.): IDCS 2016, LNCS 9864, pp. 364–371, 2016.
DOI: 10.1007/978-3-319-45940-0_33

generally concave, so that economies of scale are observed when several small shipments are consolidated. Moreover, for the customers, joint deliveries instead of separate small-volume deliveries improve the quality of service by packing customer orders together.

The design of collaborative distribution networks falls within the field of supply chain network design. One of the key design issues is facility location, which has received considerable attention from academics and practitioners over the last several decades. In general, facility location problems deal with determining the optimal number, capacity, type, and geographic location of facilities in such a way that the network cost is minimized while customer demand is satisfied. Facility location is often considered over a strategic planning horizon, generally at least several years.

2 Literature Review

2.1 Related Network Design Problems

The model addressed in this paper covers several well-identified problems in the operations research literature.

In the well-known p-median problem, the objective is to locate p facilities so that the weighted average distance between demand nodes and the nearest of the selected facilities is minimized [2]. One extension of the p-median problem to multi-layer logistics or transportation systems is the p-hub location problem [3], which belongs to the broader class of hub location problems [4]. In the p-hub location problem, the goal is to select exactly p candidate locations that are used as cross-docking facilities for the routing of transportation requests. More generally, in hub location problems, the number of hubs is not imposed but each candidate facility has a fixed set-up cost. Hub location problems have traditionally been applied to air transport: it is assumed that all transportation requests must visit at least one hub and that the inter-hub transportation cost is discounted.

When the planning horizon is spread over several time periods, locating a set of facilities becomes a question not only of "where" but also of "when" [5]. The corresponding models are said to be multi-periodic, or dynamic (in contrast to static). The decision variables define which facilities should be opened or closed at each period. This helps in modeling gradual adaptation to economic mutations or organizational changes.

Horizontal collaboration has elicited much literature in recent years but, surprisingly enough, most papers focus on topics other than facility location. Among the main topics studied are the identification and selection of potential partners [6, 7], building of trust within the coalition [8, 9], collaborative information and communication technologies [7, 10] reduction of transportation costs and CO_2 emissions [11, 12], and cost/profit allocation [13, 14].

2.2 Modeling Transportation Costs

One of the main incentives for horizontal collaboration is the cost structure charged by the carriers for LTL shipments. As detailed in Özkaya et al. [15], this cost depends on both tangible and intangible factors. Examples of intangible factors are the degree of competition in the local markets, the desirability of the shipment, and the negotiating power of the shipper.

The combination of FTL and LTL cost structures has been used in papers that optimize transportation in pre-defined networks. Croxton et al. [16] propose a merge-in-transit distribution system with four modes: small package, less-than-truckload, truckload, and air shipment. Lapierre et al. [17] present a compound cost function merging the best use of each category of transport: parcel, LTL or FTL depending on the shipment weight. Krajewska and Kopfer [18] combine four types of costs corresponding to vehicles from their own fleet, vehicles from subcontractors paid on a tour basis, vehicles from subcontractors paid on a daily basis and requests forwarded to independent carrier. The last two categories are roughly similar to FTL and LTL. Lindsey et al. [19] study a more general network in which each shipment can be sent individually (LTL) or possibly consolidated on an FTL route with other shipments.

2.3   Position of Our Problem

As stated above, the combination of FTL and LTL cost structures has been used in papers that optimize transportation in predefined networks. To the best of our knowledge, it has never been considered in the field of facility location.

In this paper, we do not consider any fixed set-up cost for selecting a candidate facility. Thus, we assume that p candidate locations must be selected, but the value of p is not known a priori. Our problem differs from p-hub location for several reasons. First, all product flows have the same origin. So, the RDCs can be viewed as intermediate facilities in a two-tiered distribution network. Second, visiting RDCs is not mandatory; direct shipments can be made from the production zone to customers.

Our mathematical model integrates time periods in the description of the demand but the facility location decision variables are static. In fact, RDCs are cross-docking facilities in which storage is forbidden. Then, time periods correspond to independent shipping campaigns, and one given RDC may receive no material flow for some period. Since there is no set-up cost at RDCs, selecting an RDC that does not receive material flow at every period is not penalized.

3   Problem Settings

3.1   Facilities

The multi-layered distribution network is composed of three types of facilities:

- Production Zone (PZ): composed of a set of suppliers and one Consolidation and Distribution Center (CDC). Suppliers are the collaborating companies. They are the sources of all material flow in the network. The CDC acts as the main collaborative warehouse at the suppliers' gate.
- A set of Regional Distribution Centers (RDCs) which are link points between FTL routes and LTL shipments in the collaborative network.
- A large set of customers who are the destinations of all product flows.

Customer orders are first consolidated at the CDC by so-called supplier routes, and then delivered to the customers, generally through a sequence of two successive transportation segments: FTL routes and LTL shipments. The set of all suppliers and the CDC can be aggregated into a single artificial facility PZ. PZ can be considered a particular Distribution Center (DC) and is the single origin of all FTL routes (we have: DCs = RDCs ∪ PZ).

3.2   FTL Routes and LTL Shipments

Due to shipment consolidation at PZ, FTL routes can be assumed between PZ and each RDC. The use of FTL routes implicitly assumes that enough shipments have been consolidated, making it possible to fill an FTL vehicle. They can be a direct trip from PZ to one RDC or include several RDCs. In the latter case, stopover costs are charged. The cost of an FTL route is assumed constant and known a priori. It is proportional to the distance traveled or hours worked (wages of drivers, fuel, use of truck) and independent of the number of units carried. LTL shipments generally concern the distribution from DCs to final customers.

3.3   Customer Aggregation

When the number of customers is very large, a popular approach is to aggregate all customers from a given area to the centroid of this area. In our case, LTL shippers intrinsically assume aggregation, since shipment costs are given for each geographical area. The territory is partitioned into 95 administrative areas called departments. All customers in the same area have the same LTL shipment cost. They must all be assigned to the same DC during the whole time horizon considered.

A necessary condition for efficiently running collaborative distribution is the synchronization of shipments. When shipments are not performed daily, the activity is split into independent campaigns every week. This results in one or several shipments. During the high season, the delivery pattern corresponds to scenario "Mo Tu /We Th / Fr Sa Su". This means that customer orders received on Mondays and Tuesdays are shipped on Tuesdays evenings and delivered at customers on Wednesday mornings, etc. Thus, 3 shipments leave the production zone weekly on Tuesdays, Thursdays, Sundays. These days are called shipping dates. During the mid-season, the delivery pattern corresponds to scenario "Su Mo Tu We /Th Fr Sa". During the low season, there is only 1 weekly shipping date (on Mondays).

3.4   The Location-Allocation Problem in Collaborative Network Design

We address the strategic-tactical level decisions for a relatively long-term period, typically one year, decomposed into independent shipping dates. The territory is partitioned into departments. All customers from a given department are delivered by the same DC during the whole time horizon. We assume that customer orders can be split into several FTL routes, but partial orders must be consolidated at an RDC and then be shipped at once to the final customers. DCs are cross-docking facilities only, and all products enter and leave these facilities on the same shipping date. Therefore, our study does not consider inventory planning at DCs.

Our study aims to design a collaborative distribution network composed of one production zone (PZ) and several RDCs by determining the optimal number and location of RDCs, the allocation of departments to RDCs, and the number of vehicles on FTL routes for each shipping date. The objective function is to minimize the sum of all transportation costs over the whole time horizon.

4   MILP Formulation

One strong characteristic of the optimization problem considered is that the objective function contains no fixed cost associated with the selection of candidate facilities. Each RDC is operated by a regional LSP in charge of cross-docking operations at the RDC and LTL distribution to customers. LSPs charge a variable cost for each logistic unit processed. This cost is already included in the LTL shipment cost, so that it does not need to appear in our mathematical formulation.

Table 1. Notation used in the mathematical model

Sets	
J	set of DCs
$j_0 \in J$	Production Zone (PZ)
$J^* = J \setminus \{j_0\}$	Set of RDCs
I	Set of customers
D	Set of Departments
$I_d \subset I$	Subset of customers located in department $d \in D$
$D_j \subset D$	Subset of departments that can be served from $j \in J$
W	Set of FTL routes
$W_j \subset W$	Subset of FTL routes visiting $j \in J^*$
$J_w \subset J^*$	Subset of RDCs visited by route $w \in W$
T	Set of shipping dates
Parameters	
p	Number of RDCs to be selected
Q_w	Capacity of the vehicle on the FTL route $w \in W$
q_i^t	Demand of customer i on date t
c_w	Cost of the vehicle on the FTL $w \in W$ which includes stopover cost
c_{ij}^t	Cost of LTL distribution of each of the q_i^t units from distribution center $j \in J$ to customer $i \in I$

The mathematical model uses notations defined in Table 1. Since direct distribution from PZ to customers is authorized, PZ is modeled as a special element of J, denoted j_0. Then, the set of RDCs is denoted by $J^* = J \setminus \{j_0\}$. All departments can be delivered from the PZ. Each FTL route $w \in W$ is operated by a homogeneous fleet of vehicles of capacity Q_w.

Table 2. Variables of the mathematical model

Integer variables	
y_j	1 if RDC $j \in J^*$ is selected, and 0 otherwise
x_{dj}	1 if department $d \in D$ is served by DC $j \in J$, and 0 otherwise
n_w^t	Number of FTL vehicles used on route $w \in W$ on date $t \in T$
Continuous variables	
u_{wj}^t	Number of units on route $w \in W$ unloaded at RDC $j \in J^*$ on date $t \in T$
f_{ij}^t	Number of units shipped from DC $j \in J$ to customer $i \in I$, on date $t \in T$

The model variables are defined in Table 2. The location-allocation problem described can be modeled as follows:

$$\min z = \sum_{t \in T} \sum_{w \in W} c_w n_w^t + \sum_{t \in T} \sum_{i \in I} \sum_{j \in J} c_{ij}^t f_{ij}^t \tag{1}$$

s.t.

$$\sum_{j \in J^*} y_j = p \tag{2}$$

$$\sum_{j \in J} x_{dj} = 1 \qquad \forall d \in D \tag{3}$$

$$\sum_{j \in J} f_{ij}^t = q_i^t \qquad \forall i \in I, \forall t \in T \tag{4}$$

$$f_{ij}^t \leq q_i^t x_{dj} \qquad \forall i \in I_d, \forall d \in D_j, \forall j \in J^*, \forall t \in T \tag{5}$$

$$x_{dj} \leq y_j \qquad \forall d \in D_j, \forall j \in J^* \tag{6}$$

$$n_w^t \leq y_j M_{j,w}^t \qquad \forall w \in W_j, \forall j \in J^*, \forall t \in T \tag{7}$$

$$\sum_{i \in I_d, d \in D_j} f_{ij}^t = \sum_{w \in W_j} u_{wj}^t \qquad \forall j \in J^*, \forall t \in T \tag{8}$$

$$\sum_{j \in J_w} u_{wj}^t \leq Q_w n_w^t \qquad \forall w \in W, \forall t \in T \tag{9}$$

The objective function (1) sums up the cost of FTL routes and the LTL distribution costs. Constraints (2) indicates the number of RDCs to be selected. Constraints (3) are single assignment constraints for each department. Constraints (4) ensure the satisfaction of customer demand. Note that the source $j \in J$ of material flow to customer $i \in I$ can be the RDC assigned to i and/or the production zone. Constraints (5) state that if DC $j \in J$ does not serve department $d \in D_j$, then there is no product flow from j to $i \in I_d$. Constraints (6) state that a department d can only be delivered by an open RDC. Since j_0 is open, this constraint applies only for $j \in J^*$ Constraints (7) state that if an RDC is closed, then the FTL routes visiting this location are not operating. The value of $M_{j,w}^t$ is set at the sum of all customers who can be delivered from $j \in J_w$ on date t, divided by the vehicle capacity:

$$ M_{j,w}^t = \left\lceil \sum_{i \in I_d, d \in D_j, j \in J_w} q_i^t \middle/ Q_w \right\rceil $$

Constraints (8) model flow conservation at an RDC $j \in J^*$. Constraints (9) model vehicle capacity. The natures of decision variables are defined in Table 2.

5   Conclusion

In this paper, we addressed the optimal location of intermediate facilities between a cluster of collaborating suppliers and a large set of customers. We proposed a mixed integer linear programming (MILP) formulation with uncapacitated facilities and no opening fixed cost. The model was enriched with two additional constraints (so called disjunctive constraints and districting constraints that help decision makes to refine their preferences), and then was tested on a real-life case study by using CPLEX 12.6. We didn't detail these constraints and experiments in this version of paper, but they will appear in the extended one.

A first possible extension to this work would be to propose a dynamic facility location model which would enable seasonal opening of RDCs. Another possible extension would be to consider FTL routes visiting several intermediate RDCs.

References

1. Bahinipati, B.K., Kanda, A., Deshmukh, S.G.: Horizontal collaboration in semiconductor manufacturing industry supply chain. an evaluation of collaboration intensity index. Comput. Ind. Eng. 57(3), 880–895 (2009)
2. Daskin, M.S., Maass, K.L.: The p-median problem. In: Laporte, G., Nickel, S., Saldanha da Gama, F. (eds.) Location Science, pp. 21–46. Springer, Berlin, Heidelberg (2015)
3. Campbell, J.F.: Integer programming formulations of discrete hub location problems. Eur. J. Oper. Res. 72(2), 387–405 (1994)
4. Contreras, I.: Hub location problems. In: Laporte, G., Nickel, S., Saldanha da Gama, F. (eds.) Location Science, pp. 311–344. Springer, Berlin, Heidelberg (2015)

5. Nickel, S., Saldanha da Gama, F.: Multi-period facility location. In: Laporte, G., Nickel, S., Saldanha da Gama, F. (eds.) Location Science, pp. 289–310. Springer, Berlin, Heidelberg (2015)
6. Adenso-Díaz, B., Lozano, S., Moreno, P.: Analysis of the synergies of merging multi-company transportation needs. Transportmetrica A Transp. Sci. **10**(6), 533–547 (2013)
7. Cruijssen, F., Cools, M., Dullaert, W.: Horizontal cooperation in logistics: opportunities and impediments. Transp. Res. Part E Log. Transp. Rev. **43**(2), 129–142 (2007)
8. Hingley, M., Lindgreen, A., Grant, D.B., Kane, C.: Using fourth-party logistics management to improve horizontal collaboration among grocery retailers. Supply Chain Manage. Int. J. **16**(5), 316–327 (2011)
9. Leitner, R., Meizer, F., Prochazka, M., Sihn, W.: Structural concepts for horizontal cooperation to increase efficiency in logistics. CIRP J. Manuf. Sci. Technol. **4**(3), 332–337 (2011)
10. Buijs, P., Wortmann, J.H.: Joint operational decision-making in collaborative transportation networks: the role of IT. Supply Chain Manage. Int. J. **19**(2), 200–210 (2014)
11. Pan, S., Ballot, E., Fontane, F.: The reduction of greenhouse gas emissions from freight transport by pooling supply chains. Int. J. Prod. Econ. **143**(1), 86–94 (2013)
12. Pan, S., Ballot, E., Fontane, F., Hakimi, D.: Environmental and economic issues arising from the pooling of SMEs' supply chains: case study of the food industry in western France. Flex. Serv. Manuf. J. **26**(1–2), 92–118 (2014)
13. Audy, J.F., D'Amours, S., Rousseau, L.M.: Cost allocation in the establishment of a collaborative transportation agreement - an application in the furniture industry. J. Oper. Res. Soc. **62**(10), 960–970 (2011)
14. Dai, B., Chen, H.: Profit allocation mechanisms for carrier collaboration in pickup and delivery service. Comput. Ind. Eng. **62**(2), 633–643 (2012)
15. Özkaya, E., Keskinocak, P., Joseph, V.R., Weight, R.: Estimating and benchmarking less-than-truckload market rates. Transp. Res. Part E Log. Transp. Rev. **46**(5), 667–682 (2010)
16. Croxton, K.L., Gendron, B., Magnanti, T.L.: Models and methods for merge-in-transit operations. Transp. Sci. **37**(1), 1–22 (2003)
17. Lapierre, S.D., Ruiz, A.B., Soriano, P.: Designing distribution networks formulations and solution heuristic. Transp. Sci. **38**(2), 174–187 (2004)
18. Krajewska, M.A., Kopfer, H.: Transportation planning in freight forwarding companies: tabu search algorithm for the integrated operational transportation planning problem. Eur. J. Oper. Res. **197**(2), 741–751 (2009)
19. Lindsey, K.A., Erera, A.L., Savelsbergh, M.W.: A pickup and delivery problem using crossdocks and truckload lane rates. EURO J. Transp. Log. **2**(1–2), 5–27 (2013)

Urban Traffic Congestion Based on System Dynamics: Taking Wuhan City as an Example

Kaikai He and Yan Chen[✉]

Wuhan University of Technology, Heping road, Wuhan 1040, China
532154599@qq.com, chenyan@whut.edu.cn

Abstract. With the progress of technology and the rapid development of industry, the urban traffic of China has a tendency to blowout. The growing problem of urban traffic congestion has become an important factor which restricts the further development of urban economy. At present, Chinese urban traffic congestion is widespread, but governance of traffic problems is lagging behind. This paper starts with phenomenon of urban traffic congestion, analyzes the present situation, reasons and effects of urban traffic congestion. Taking Wuhan city as an example, by constructing a causal relationship diagram of urban traffic system, using the principle and method of system dynamics to establish a simulation model for governing the urban traffic congestion, this paper in view of system to comprehensively analyzes the causal relationship between the variables that impact of urban traffic congestion, and puts forward the countermeasures and suggestions which provide a reference for the governance of urban traffic congestion problems to solve the traffic congestion problem in Wuhan.

Keywords: Urban traffic congestion · System dynamics · Simulation

1 Introduction

Urban traffic which is the foundation of social and economic development in the city provides essential conditions for the normal operation of urban living. In China, there is a great development in the scale of the urban road, Smart City and Intelligent Transportation has also made some progress, but overall the intelligence and automation level is still low. With the continuous expansion of city size, large concentration of population in large cities, the excessive development of the number of private cars, the road traffic congestion is becoming more and more serious, which results in the growth in running time, the invalid loss of the energy, the environmental and noise pollution, traffic accidents, the financial loss and a series of problems [1–3].

The problem of urban traffic congestion is the emergence of the rapid development of urban economy. At present, the research of traffic congestion is more and more abundant: Taylor [4] from the perspective of economics, to find the cause of traffic congestion; McKnight [5] believes that controlling the purchase and using of private cars can solve the problem of traffic congestion; Kunsch and Springael [6] are realised by means of fuzzy-reasoning techniques incorporated into the system-dynamics model, this methodological paper presents a planning and control methodology illustrated by a

© Springer International Publishing AG 2016
W. Li et al. (Eds.): IDCS 2016, LNCS 9864, pp. 372–380, 2016.
DOI: 10.1007/978-3-319-45940-0_34

simplified case study on the carbon-tax design in the residential sector. In domestic research, Jiang [7] established a model for congestion formation mechanism based on the theory of system dynamics, and illustrated the misled understanding in conventional road-building policies with the purpose of anti-congestion, and analyzed the implication of the Downs Law under Chinese context; Wang [8], Huapu Lu and Hu Peng analyzed motorized different development policies on the development of city and city traffic system.

There are many factors that affect the urban traffic system. Urban traffic congestion is the result of the interaction of diverse force.

2 Overview of System Dynamics

The system dynamics method was founded in 1950s by Forrester J.W. of the United States of America in MIT. This is based on the feedback control theory and computer simulation technology, which is used for the quantitative research of complex social economic system. There are 3 important components of the system dynamics modeling: the diagram of causal feedback, the flow chart and the equation. Causal feedback diagram describes the causal relationship between the variables; flow chart helps researchers use symbols to express the complex concept of the model; the structure of dynamics model is mainly composed of differential equations, each connection of state variable and the rate equation is a differential equation [9]. By obtaining the analytical formula of the main variable with time, System Dynamics can determine how to implement the optimal control of the system, the development and change of the system state of the target variable can be controlled effectively.

The simulation platform of this paper is VENSIM. The United States Ventana company launched VENSIM that is the widely used system dynamics software. It is a visual modeling software, which can describe the structure of the system dynamics model, simulate the behavior of the system, analyze and optimize the results of the model simulation. VENSIM can provide a simple and flexible way to establish the casual loop, stock and the flow chart and other related models.

3 System Dynamic Analysis and Modeling of Urban Traffic Congestion

Urban traffic system includes the urban population, urban GDP, amount of private car, amount of public traffic, amount of urban freight car, urban motor vehicle travel volume, exhaust emissions, road area of average vehicle and other major variables.

With the continuous development of urban economy, the gradual improvement of the urban infrastructure and increasing opportunities in employment, that results in large number of people swarming into the city, it makes the urban transportation demand growing, the demand that not only reflects in improving of the traffic volume, but also in the continuous increasing of urban logistics volume. On the one hand, as the traffic carrying capacity of a city is limited, the increase in the amount of urban motor vehicles travel will make the car road area smaller and smaller, and cause ultimately the

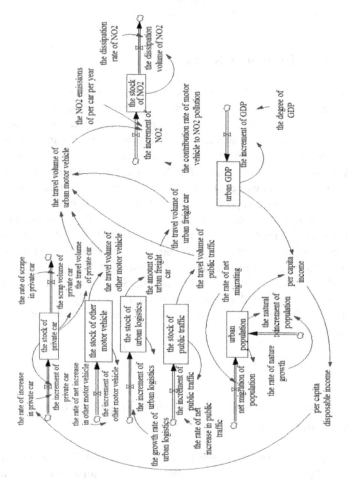

Fig. 1. Flow chart of urban traffic system

phenomenon of traffic congestion. On the other hand, the increasing number of motor vehicles and the increasing of vehicle exhaust emissions is a positive correlation relationship. However, the nature ability that degrades automobile exhaust is limited. Once beyond the capacity of nature, there is going to make automobile exhaust continue to accumulate, which can lead to the city air pollution.

Based on the detailed analysis of the causal relationship about the various factors that affecting the system, using VENSIM that a software for system dynamics to simulate the system model, we can get the stock flow diagram of urban traffic system, as shown in Fig. 1. The urban motor vehicle travel volume are influenced by the stock of private car, the stock of other motor vehicle, urban logistics volume and the stock of public traffic. Public traffic includes buses and operating taxis. The growth rate of private car is related to urban population and urban GDP.

With the increase in the amount of urban motor vehicles, the government's environmental pressure will increase, the different governance blocking policy will be implemented, which will affect the growth rate of private cars. With the improvement of people's awareness of environmental protection, residents will have more choice of public traffic travel mode, which can lead to the growth of urban rail passenger traffic, and directly affect the growth rate of private cars. With the growth of urban GDP, people's consumption psychology will also change, thereby affects the growth rate of private cars. In addition, economic factors and the use of factors will affect the growth rate of private cars in some respect. In order to carry out a detailed analysis of urban traffic congestion, this paper on basis of urban traffic system, puts the ground traffic management factors, policy factors, economic factors, rail transportation, use factors, consumer psychology, consumer satisfaction degree into the original system dynamics model, then gets the improved model, that is the governance system dynamics model of the urban traffic congestion, as shown in Fig. 2. The value of II, the value of R and the per capita of GDP are usually used a judgment basis that predicts whether private cars there into the family, the value of II determines the process of private car getting into the family, so the model using the value of II as the standard. The basic assumption of this model is to predict the simulated data getting rid of the impact of inflation, and the Wuhan government takes long-term support for traffic congestion.

After analyzing and establishing the system dynamics model of the urban traffic system, put the initial parameters, the equation and the table function into the model, and then the model is simulated. Part of the equation of model is shown in Table 1.

4 Model Simulation and Empirical Analysis—Taking Wuhan City as an Example

4.1 Parameter Estimation in Model

Before the simulation of the system dynamics model, the model must be assigned for the constant, the initial value of the state variable, the equation and the function of the table. Referring to the Wuhan Statistical Yearbook-2008, the partial initial parameter settings of the model and the variable settings are shown in Table 2.

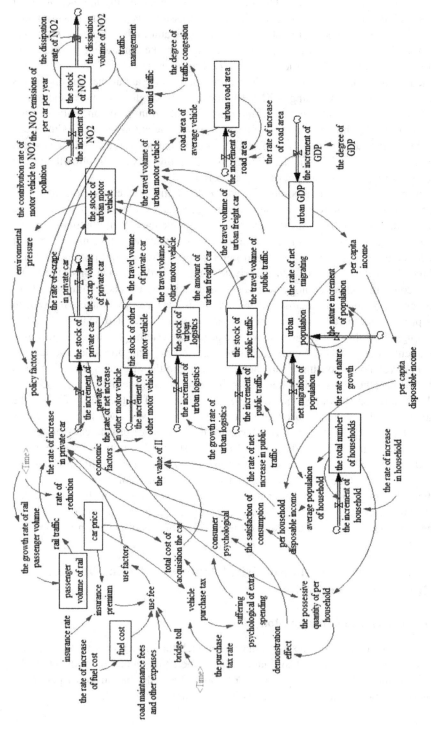

Fig. 2. The system dynamics model of governing urban traffic congestion

Table 1. Part of the equation of the system dynamics model that governing urban traffic congestion

Sequence number	Mathematical expression
(1)	road area of average vehicle = urban road area/the travel volume of urban motor vehicle
(2)	the increment of NO2 = the travel volume of urban motor vehicle*the NO2 emissions of per car per year*the contribution rate of motor vehicle to NO2 pollution
(3)	urban population = INTEG(net migration of population + the nature increment of population, the initial value of urban population)
(4)	the value of II = total cost of acquisition the car/per household disposable income
(5)	the travel volume of urban motor vehicle = the travel volume of public traffic + the travel volume of other motor vehicle + the travel volume of urban freight car + the travel volume of private car
(6)	the rate of increase in private car = economic factors^0.4*ground traffic^0.15*policy factors^0.15*consumer psychological^0.1*use factors^0.1*rail traffic^0.1*the satisfaction of consumption

Table 2. The parameters and initial values of the model that urban traffic system in Wuhan city (2008)

Parameters and initial values of the model	Value	Unit
The stock of private car	272204	car
The stock of public traffic	19113	car
The stock of other motor vehicle	440031	car
Urban population	8.97	ten thousand tons
Urban GDP	411.551	million people
The rate of increase in road area	0.083	million square meters
The dissipation rate of NO2	0.2	–
The scrap of private car	0.06	–
The rate of net migrating	0.002	–
The rate of nature growth	0.00246	–
The purchase tax rate	0.1	–

4.2 Validity Test of the Model

Based on the statistical data of 2008, the urban traffic system of Wuhan city is simulated, and the simulation results of some variables in 2009 compared with the actual historical data statistics, as shown in Table 3.

By comparing the predicted results with the official historical data show that the relative error of the predicted values is less than 10 %. Generally believed that the error range of the system dynamics model in 15 % is reasonable, and the results of the model in the error range. Therefore, the model to describe the behavior and the state of the real

Table 3. The comparison of predicted value and the actual value in 2009

Parameter	Actual value	Analog value	Error
The stock of private car	318195	323923	1.80 %
The stock of public traffic	19378	19916	2.78 %
Urban people	9100000	8993860	−1.17 %
Urban GDP	462.086	477.399	3.31 %

system model is basically consistent, the model is feasible and the urban traffic system dynamics model can more truly reflect the actual system.

4.3   The Simulation of Development Trend

The stock of private car is an important indicator to reflect the degree of the urban traffic congestion. Figure 3 is a comparison chart that the improved model around Wuhan of the stock of private car. As can be seen from the figure, the improved model of private car ownership is far less than the unmodified model in 2020. That is to say, the model can alleviate traffic congestion phenomenon to some extent.

The travel volume of motor vehicle is a visual expression of the model to reflect traffic congestion. As can be seen from Fig. 4, before 2015, the model was less than the improved model for the amount of travel, but in the long term, the improved model can effectively reduce the travel volume of urban motor vehicles.

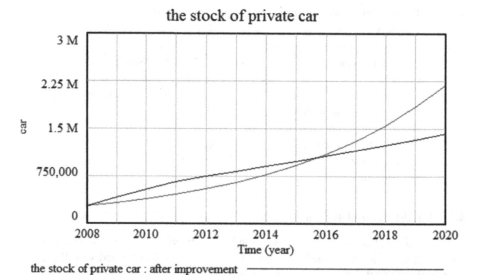

the stock of private car : after improvement ——————————————————
the stock of private car : before improvement ——————————————————

Fig. 3. Comparison of private car ownership in Wuhan before and after improvement

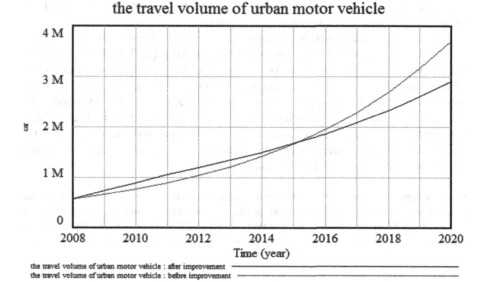

Fig. 4. Comparison of travel volume that urban vehicle before and after improvement

4.4 Countermeasures and Suggestions for the Govern of Traffic Congestion

Through the comparison and analysis of the model's result, we can know that the stock of private car will show a rising trend in the coming period in Wuhan. However, the rapid growth rate is bound to cause the phenomenon of traffic congestion, the model of governing urban traffic congestion can effectively reduce the stock of private car, and it has a certain amount of reality. This article giving the following suggestions, which are based on several main factors that affecting the growth rate of private cars in Wuhan city:

- To strengthen the construction of roads and investments of road infrastructures, reduce the contradictions which are caused by the short of road constructions;
- To develop the high-level and high-capacity public transportation, reducing the stress of roads;
- Adding more restrictions on private cars, for example, increasing bridge tolls and premiums and so on;
- To reasonably control the increasing of fuel charges, strengthen the using and research of energy-saving emission reduction technology.

5   Conclusion

Traffic system is a complex, effected by multiple factors. The main cause of traffic congestion is the traffic imbalance between supply and demand, which is not only reflected in the imbalance between the increase of urban traffic and the supply of urban road infrastructure, but also in the incoordination between the fast growth rate of private cars and increased environmental pollution.

Compared with the previous system dynamics model related to the urban traffic, these factors are considered more comprehensively in this paper. Introducing the urban logistics volume of this variable as well as the population development pattern, characteristics of urban economy, environment to the system model. However, it also has some shortcomings. For example, it's not only simple in aspect of consideration about economy factors, but also unilateral in reflecting the degree of urban traffic congestion by using the travel volume of urban motor vehicle. But this model is able to solve the problem of traffic congestion in city on the whole, it has great academic value and significance in the research of urban traffic congestion.

Acknowledgement. This work is financially support by the Research on the performance appraisal system and its realization and application of transport industry informatization. Sponsored by Chinese Ministry of Transport, 2015–2017 (Project ID: 20151g0127), the Research of "Internet + Passenger transport service" (Project ID: 151100211400).

References

1. Wei, L., Chang, C., Wei, P.: Research on development strategies of china urban public transport. Appl. Mech. Mater. **744–746**, 2086–2089 (2015)
2. Li, T.: Nonlinear dynamics of traffic jams. In: Proceedings of the 2007 IEEE Second International Multi-Symposiums on Computer and Computational Sciences (IMSCCS), pp. 550–555 (2007)
3. Cao, J., Menendez, M.: System dynamics of urban traffic based on its parking-related-states. Transp. Res. Part B Methodol. **81**, 718–736 (2015)
4. Taylor, J.: Urban congestion and pollution-is road pricing the answer. In: Proceedings of the Institution of Civil Engineers-Municipal Engineer, vol. 93 (1992)
5. Mcknight, E.J.: Transportation 2020. Opportunities and challenges. Prof. Eng. **6**(3), 29–31 (1993)
6. Kunsch, P., Springael, J.: Simulation with system dynamics and fuzzy reasoning of a tax policy to reduce CO2, emissions in the residential sector. Euro. J. Oper. Res. **185**(3), 1285–1299 (2008)
7. Jiang, Y.: Reflections on anti-congestion policies in Chinese cities from system dynamics perspective. City Plan. Rev. **35**(11), 73–80 (2011)
8. Wang, J., Lu, H.: System dynamics model of urban transportation system and its application. J. Transp. Syst. Eng. Inf. Technol. **8**(3), 83–89 (2008)
9. Wang, Q.: System Dynamics. Tsinghua University Press, Beijing (1998)

Sensors Deployment in Logistics System by Genetic Invasive Weed Optimization

Yanjun Shi$^{(\boxtimes)}$, Luyang Hou, Xueyan Sun, and Yaohui Pan

School of Mechanical Engineering, Dalian University of Technology,
Dalian 116024, People's Republic of China
syj@dlut.edu.cn, luyang.hou@hotmail.com,
xueyansun@hotmail.com, 1669071862@qq.com

Abstract. Real-time management for the production and manufacturing process of materials is necessary for the flexible manufacturing systems, RFID technique can master the processing situation of material transportation in real-time and thus improve the transportation control as well as the efficiency for the manufacturing system. We herein deploy the RFID readers and tags in the logistics system to manage the production process; and build the deployment mathematical model and the optimization strategies for RFID readers. We also propose a genetic invasive weed optimization (IWOGA) based on the invasive weed optimization (IWO) and genetic algorithm (GA) to optimize the deployment of RFID readers, IWOGA involves a comprehensive evolutionary mechanism therein with the objective of covering all the RFID tags in the whole system using the minimum number of RFID readers with the minimum working frequency. We validate the proposed optimization algorithm in comparison with IWO and GA respectively by a practical numerical example of sensors deployment in logistics system.

Keywords: Logistics system · RFID techniques · RFID reader deployment · Genetic invasive weed optimization

1 Introduction

The application of Internet of Things (IoT) technology has greatly promoted the development of logistics systems in manufacturing systems. As a non-contact automatic identification technology, RFID reader can identify the target objects and gain the data via the coupling transmission characteristics of radio frequency signals and space. It can also identify the objects with a high moving speed and multiple RFID tags simultaneously. The operation of RFID techniques is quick and easy, they can work at low environmental conditions without human interference, etc. [1]. These unique technological advantages make RFID techniques be widely used in numerous fields, such as production management, logistics system, intelligent transportation, etc. For example, the integration of RFID technique and upper software system can control the navigation of transportation truck, and the RFID readers can manage and monitor the tags in logistics system.

© Springer International Publishing AG 2016
W. Li et al. (Eds.): IDCS 2016, LNCS 9864, pp. 381–392, 2016.
DOI: 10.1007/978-3-319-45940-0_35

Han [2] studied the deployment issue of RFID readers in intensive environment to achieve the regional coverage and analyzed several coverage models. The authors improved the particle swarm optimization (PSO) by the mutation operator of genetic algorithm and applied it for solving the coverage problem of several readers. Liu, et al. [3] established an optimization model for RFID system network and proposed a hybrid particle swarm optimization to optimize the RFID reader positions with the goal of covering all the tags in the whole space. Wang and Yang [4] integrated the RFID technology with automated guided vehicle (AGV) system; they realized the transport and extract the information of goods by AGV. This method could improve the flexibility of the manufacturing system. Wang [5] proposed a deployment method for RFID readers based on tabu search (TS).

Cheung et al. [6] proposed an RFID deployment optimizer for the difference between the RFID reader deployment and the actual production environment; it employed a genetic strategy to optimize the RFID layout based on the objective and the data obtained by RFID readers, which was appropriate for the practical dynamic production situation. Huang et al. [7] proposed a systematic solution to deploy the readers in RFID network; they also proposed two simple mechanisms to prevent the conflict of RFID readers. Ray et al. [8] proposed a coupling method for the RFID tags to search the closest reader with an objective of minimizing the energy consumption and built the distributed deployment mathematical model for RFID readers.

In this paper, we establish a mathematical deployment model of RFID readers for the material transportation and delivery in the logistics system of manufacturing system and propose a hybrid genetic invasive weed optimization (IWOGA) algorithm to optimize the location of RFID readers in the logistics system. The objective of this design is to employ the minimum number of readers as well as the minimum working frequency to cover all the tags in the logistics system.

2   Problem Description

2.1   The Working Process of Logistics System

The workflow of material transportation and the production management in a manufacturing system is described as follows:

RFID readers manage and process the read-write operation to the RFID tags that are distributed in the logistics system. The readers are uniformly supervised by the upper application software system, which is interacted with the database system. In this way, the upper computer management systems can realize the real-time tracking and management for the machining process through RFID techniques effectively. All the materials to be processed are transported in the material baskets from one machine to another. The active RFID tags are attached on the material baskets to store the processing information of parts (for instance, the name, number, processing status, etc.) and thus to achieve tracking and management of the parts for its machining process.

When a batch of parts needs to be processed, the industrial trucks transport the materials form the warehouse to the machines, then the trucks unload the materials and execute the other transportation missions. At this time, RFID readers change the processing information on the tags attached on the material basket. After the processing of this batch of parts has finished, these parts will be reloaded in the basket and the management system will assign a truck to transport these parts to the next machine. RFID readers will change the information on this basket again until all the processing work has been accomplished.

It can be seen from above that the machining process of all the parts is managed by the system based on the RFID techniques. RFID readers link the application software system through the wireless communication technology. The diagram of this flow is shown in Fig. 1.

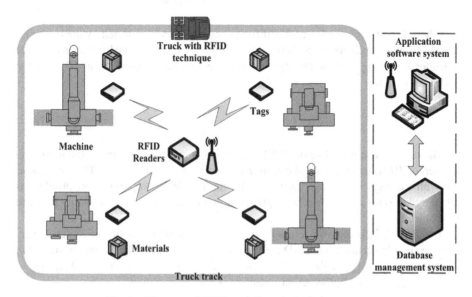

Fig. 1. Diagram of RFID technique in logistics system

This paper aims to set up RFID readers in manufacturing system to cover the RFID tags, the design objective is to minimize the number of RFID readers and the power consumption to reduce the operational costs for the industry. We propose an effective and simple mathematical model to measure the RFID reader deployment and a hybrid algorithm for the deployment of RFID readers, which will be brought out in sequence as follow.

2.2 Deployment Mathematical Model of RFID Readers

The deployment for RFID readers in this paper is to assign n readers to cover m tags that are set in logistics system of two-dimensional space. These RFID tags are attached on the material baskets that are loaded or unloaded near the process machine. We should set the RFID readers to cover all the tags with the minimum working frequency. There are two mainly coverage models, circle and oval coverage model. The circle coverage model is simple and controllable, its main measurement standard is the Euclidean Distance between the readers and tags. We take this model to build our mathematical model for deployment of RFID readers. If the Euclidean Distance is smaller than the effective reading distance of the RFID readers, the tags can be detected by the readers, otherwise cannot.

The circle coverage model is shown in Eq. (1), which means the tags in the detection range of readers can be detected.

$$P(t_i) = \begin{cases} 1 & d_{euc}(c_i, t_j) \leq R_i \\ 0 & d_{euc}(c_i, t_j) > R_i \end{cases} \tag{1}$$

Where $P(t_i)$ represents the probability that the tag j can be detected by the reader i, t means RFID tags and c means RFID readers. $d_{euc}(c_i, t_j)$ represents the Euclidean Distance of reader i and tag j. R_i is the default effective reading distance of RFID reader i. Euclidean Distance is shown as Eq. (2).

$$d_{euc}(c_i, t_j) = \sqrt{(x_i - x_j)^2 + (y_i - y_j)^2} \tag{2}$$

The deployment objective of RFID readers is composed of two parts: the minimum number of RFID readers and the minimum working frequency of RFID readers to cover all the tags in logistics system. This multi-objective optimization problem is transferred into the single-objective optimization problem by setting weighting factor to each objective.

The first optimization objective is to seek the minimum number of RFID readers under the condition that each RFID tag is covered by at least one RFID reader, the set of n readers is $c = \{(x_i, y_i) | i = 1, 2, \cdots, n\}$, the set of m tags is $t = \{(x_j, y_j) | j = 1, 2, \cdots, m\}$. The first optimization objective is shown as bellow.

$$f_1 = \min(n) \tag{3}$$

$$s.t. \quad P(t_i) = 1, \quad i = 1, 2, \cdots, m. \tag{4}$$

The constraint condition ensures the coverage probability of each tags is 1.

The second deployment optimization goal is to minimize the working frequency of all the RFID readers based on the conditions of the first optimization goal. Its working frequency is in direct proportion to the effective reading distance. The farther the readers can cover, the larger the working frequency will be, meanwhile means the energy consumption is higher. We make a quantification between the working frequency M_i and reading distance R_i as $M_i = k * R_i$. Where k is the quantification factor that is numbered as 0.1 in this paper. The purpose is to make the magnitude of the number of required RFID readers close to the sum of working frequencies of all the readers in logistics system. The second deployment optimization goal f_2 is shown in Eq. (5).

$$f_2 = \min \sum_{i=1}^{n} M_i \tag{5}$$

The deployment mathematical model for the RFID readers in the logistics system is shown as Eq. (6).

$$F = w_1 f_1 + w_2 f_2 \tag{6}$$

Where $w_{1(2)}$ represents the weighting of the objective $f_{1(2)}$, and $w_1 + w_2 = 1$. We value the weighting factor as $w_1 = w_2 = 0.5$.

2.3   The Positions of RFID Tags

We herein design a deployment example of RFID readers in logistics system. The nodes (52 in total) coordinates of RFID tags is shown in Table 1.

Table 1. Nodes coordinates of RFID tags

No.	X (mm)	Y (mm)	No.	X (mm)	Y (mm)	No.	X (mm)	Y (mm)
1	7020	3710	18	15130	30370	36	50650	25510
2	8530	8500	19	21500	29540	37	44210	26160
3	14310	8240	20	28420	29200	38	36700	22920
4	20810	9690	21	29000	22870	39	34320	17910
5	27620	7860	22	21670	25670	40	61750	17620
6	29210	3630	23	15810	25080	41	61770	4240
7	29440	17720	24	11090	24930	42	32740	4260
8	27030	15430	25	5920	28560	43	34850	15450
9	19480	13600	26	34630	33050	44	42950	11960
10	14320	13050	27	34300	20780	45	50040	11950
11	9320	13810	28	61710	33110	46	56020	13170
12	7060	17610	29	61600	20840	47	60220	12880
13	3740	20900	30	36900	27910	48	59110	9620
14	29810	20610	31	43070	28270	49	54060	8360
15	31010	33780	32	48520	29700	50	48840	8540
16	3720	33760	33	53770	28970	51	42730	93300
17	10370	29390	34	59730	29530	52	34960	10190
			35	57500	26550			

The nodes of these RFID tags are input in Meter, which is shown in MATLAB coordinate system as Fig. 2 (The red points represent the RFID tags).

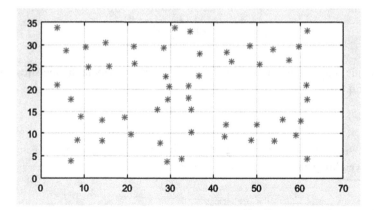

Fig. 2. Nodes of RFID tags in MATLAB coordinate system (Color figure online)

2.4   Deployment Strategy for RFID Readers

We should set the RFID readers to cover the tags after we obtain the coordinate of each tag in the system. The objective is to find the minimum number of readers to cover all the tags. The individuals in iteration are the position set of readers in the logistics system, the encoding form is $c = [x_1, y_1, x_2, y_2, \cdots, x_i, y_i]$, where x_i, y_i is the coordinate of reader $i, i = 1, 2, \cdots, n$. The coordinate set of all tags is $t = \{(x_j, y_j) | j = 1, 2, \cdots, m\}$.

The method to ascertain the number of readers and their effective reading distances, namely the way to calculate the fitness values of individuals is shown as follow.

Step 1:   Initial the population, confirm the parameter n, R_i, R_i^{max}.

Step 2:   Calculate d_{euc} of each RFID tag and each reader according to Eq. (2), the size of distance matrix is $m \times n$.

Step 3:   Build the class set to each reader. Find the reader that has a minimum Euclidean Distance with one tag and attribute this tag in this reader set meeting the condition of Eq. (1). Delete this tag in the tag set. Judge if the tag set is empty, if yes, go to step 6; otherwise go to step 4.

Step 4:   Put the unattributed tags with their Euclidean distances in a sole set. Find the reader that has a minimum Euclidean Distance with these tags and attribute these tags in this reader set if this Euclidean Distance is less than R_i^{max}. Change the effective reading distance of this reader to be enable to cover all the tags in this set, delete this tag in the tag set. Judge if the tag set is empty, if yes, go to step 6; otherwise go to step 5.

Step 5:   If the tag set is still not empty, add one reader to cover the rest tags, go to step 6.

Step 6:   Calculate the fitness values of individuals in this group.

2.5   The Proposed IWOGA

Invasive Weed Optimization (IWO), a new numerical optimal algorithm, which was first proposed by Mehrabian and Lucas in 2006 for solving numerical optimization problems [9]. Its execution process is to simulate the decolonization process of weeds in the nature. IWO has a good adaptability and is easy to program. There are four steps for processing IWO: (1) initial populations; (2) reproduction; (3) spatial distribution; (4) competitive existence.

As to population initialization. We should determine the following parameters of IWO: the number of initial populations M_0, the maximum number of individuals M_{max}, the maximum number of iteration $iter_{max}$. The dimension of the problem dim, the minimum number of seeds s_{min}, the maximum number of seeds s_{max}, the nonlinear index n, the initial step length σ_{init}, the final step length σ_{final}, the current step length σ_{cur}, the maximum and minimum range of solutions x_{max}, x_{min}.

As to reproduction. The number of seeds that the group can produce depends on the fitness values of individuals and the lowest and highest fitness values of all the individuals, which increases linearly with the fitness value from the lowest to the highest. The individuals with low fitness value still have the chance to reproduce though this chance is tiny.

As to spatial distribution. The weeds that are produced by individuals are sowed in the dimension space of dim. The way to generate the seed is to add the value on one solution, which is shown in Eq. (7).

$$\sigma_{cur} = \frac{(iter_{max} - iter)^n}{(iter_{max})^n}(\sigma_{init} - \sigma_{final}) + \sigma_{final} \tag{7}$$

Equation (7) ensures the probability of sowing in the distant region gradually turns small in a non-linear way, which will keep the individuals with the good fitness values and clear the unadapt ones. This mechanism will promote the evolution of the whole group.

As to competitive existence. With the iteration processes on, the whole population will reach its maximum limitation for its rapid propagation. To ensure the elitism and continual evolution of the whole group, IWO sorts the new individuals in sequence according to their fitness values. After that, IWO selects M individuals from the group and clears the rest individuals.

2.6   Genetic Invasive Weed Optimization (IWOGA)

The individuals with the high fitness value will enrich the entire space in iteration, this phenomenon will reduce the diversity of population and may lead the whole group to fall into the local optimum. We improve this defect of the standard IWO by genetic algorithm (GA) and name the new algorithm as Genetic Invasive Weed Optimization (IWOGA). IWOGA includes a comprehensive evolution mechanism to optimize this integrated design problem.

Rather than the rules of generating individuals of the standard IWO, IWOGA adopts the population generation rules based on the integer programming. We use the Eq. (7) to produce the current step; meanwhile, we need to map the real numbers in the iterative process with the integer numbers of equipment. Wherein, we need to convert the real numbers to integer numbers, and then map them to the continuous or non-continuous machine numbers.

We also propose a comprehensive evolutionary mechanism to improve the existing evolutionary strategy. The implementation process is described as: we order each individual by ascending order of their fitness values after acquiring a new population M in a certain generation. Then we save the previous 10 % of M individuals to a new population, crossover the previous 40 % of M, mutate the 40 %–70 % of M, and regenerate the 70 %–100 % M. After these operations, individuals form a new population, and then sort them according to their fitness values. As the population size is larger than M after this mechanism, we keep the population in the size of M and go to the next iteration.

The crossover operation in this mechanism is same as it in genetic algorithm. For the mutation operation, we need to implement mutation to part of population in a certain probability to accelerate convergence and minimize the damage to the good individuals; the individuals can thus be approximate to the optimal solution. The process of mutation operation is to select two random numbers r1 and r2 (where r1 $\sim$ = r2 and r1 < r2) of machines which are no larger than N (N is the number of machines), then exchange the machines in position r1 and r2.

The method to generate the new population w_i is shown in the Eq. (8). It is composed of the parent sequence and the vibration factor, which is $\sigma_{cur} * randn(1, dim)$. The current step σ_{cur} is determined by Eq. (7), in which the $randn$ is subject to lognormal distribution.

$$w_i = f_i + \sigma_{cur} * randn(1, \dim) \tag{8}$$

In summary, this comprehensive evolutionary mechanism employs different strategies for different level of population to ensure the efficiency of the evolution. In this paper, the deployment of RFID readers employs IWOGA for optimization. The flow diagram of IWOGA is shown in Fig. 3.

3   Numerical Example of RFID Readers' Deployment

3.1   Parameter Setting of IWOGA

We set the default effective reading distance R_i of RFID readers as 12 m, the maximum reading distance R_i^{max} as 15 m. The number n of RFID readers as 6. Population initialization is a random number matrix generated in logistics system.

To demonstrate the effectiveness of IWOGA in addressing RFID readers' deployment, we compare IWOGA with two other standard intelligent optimization algorithms. We take genetic algorithm (GA) and invasive weed optimization (IWO) as

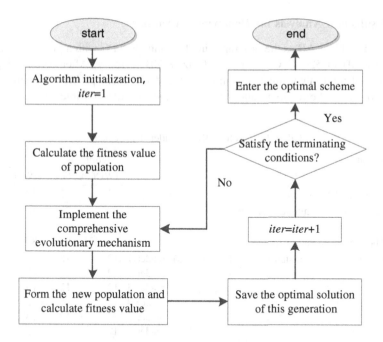

Fig. 3. Flow diagram of IWOGA

a comparison algorithm to prove the superiority of IWOGA on deployment optimization of RFID readers.

For IWOGA and the contrastive algorithms, the necessary parameters are determined as follow: the crossover probability P_c, the mutation probability P_m, the initial step length σ_{init}, the final step length σ_{final}, the number of populations M, the nonlinear index n and the maximum number of iteration $iter_{max}$. The parameter setting of the three algorithms is shown in Table 2 as bellow.

Table 2. Parameter settings of three algorithms

Parameter	Algorithms		
	IWOGA	GA	IWO
M	100	100	100
$iter_{max}$	5000	5000	5000
P_c	0.9	0.9	–
P_m	0.2	0.2	–
$GGAP$	0.9	0.9	–
σ_{init}	1000	–	1000
σ_{final}	0.01	–	0.01
N	3	–	3

3.2 Results and Analysis for Deployment Example

We here take MATLAB as the programming language in a PC with a processor of Intel (R) Core (TM) i5 5200U CPU @ 2.20 GHz, 8 GB memory. After determining the parameters of three algorithms, we optimize the deployment problem by three algorithms and record the relative data of the calculation results in Table 3.

Table 3. Result of RFID reader deployment

Results		Algorithms		
		IWOGA	GA	IWO
Number of RFID tags		52	52	52
The required minimum number of RFID readers		6	7	7
The lowest operating frequency		7.2	8.9	8.8
Effective reading distance of each reader (m)	reader 1	12	12	12
	reader 2	12	12	12
	reader 3	12	12	13
	reader 4	12	15	12
	reader 5	12	12	14
	reader 6	12	12	12
	reader 7	–	14	13
Optimal value of objective function		13.2	15.9	15.8
Calculation time (s)		233.6	304.8	325.6

We can see from the table above that the proposed IWOGA in this paper is better than IWO and GA in solving RFID deployment in logistics system. The result brought out by IWOGA can cover the 52 labels in the entire system by six RFID readers and the minimum effective reading distance of each reader is 12 m, its optimal value is 13.2. When referring to IWO and GA in the deployment of RFID reader, they all require seven readers to cover all the tags; the optimal values are 15.9 and 15.8 respectively. The experimental results proved the superiority of IWOGA that integrates the advantages of GA and IWO in solving the complex engineering optimization problems. Its unique comprehensive evolutionary framework can search the optimal solution effectively with the less time. Table 4 shows the optimal coordinates of the RFID reader deployment by IWOGA.

Figure 4 shows the schematics of the optimal solution by three algorithms in optimizing the deployment of RFID readers in the logistics system. We can visually see from the figure that all the RFID tags can be covered by the RFID readers. The methods by GA and IWO need to increase the operating frequency of some readers to increase the range of coverage and realize the coverage for the entire tags, it will increase the power consumption level undisputedly.

Table 4. Deployment coordinate of RFID reader by IWOGA

Number of readers	Optimal deployment coordinates		Effective reading distance R (m)
	X (m)	Y (m)	
1	33.84	12.97	12
2	15.28	34.74	12
3	54.43	26.30	12
4	37.18	28.77	12
5	54.07	12.94	12
6	12.32	13.27	12

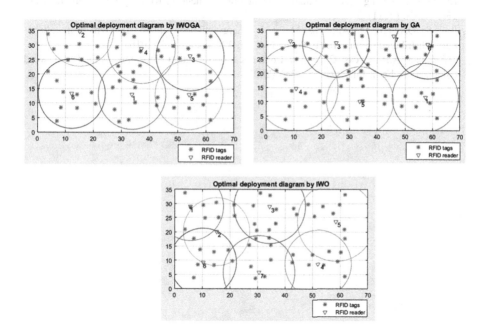

Fig. 4. Optimization results of RFID reader deployment by three algorithms

4 Conclusion

RFID tags and readers are employed in logistics system to manage the production process. The RFID readers are deployed in the system to cover all the RFID tags according to the proposed strategies. The mathematical model of RFID reader deployment is also established. A hybrid optimization algorithm– IWOGA based on the GA and IWO is proposed to optimize the deployment of RFID readers in this system. The comparison with IWO and GA in addressing a practical deployment example shows IWOGA could cover all the tags with the minimum number of RFID readers in the lowest operating frequencies.

References

1. Wang, B.: Review on Internet of Things. J. Electron. Meas. Instrum. **23**(12), 1–7 (2009)
2. Han, F.: RFID System Optimization Deployment Research and Application. Dong Hua University, Master (2013)
3. Liu, K., Ji, Z.: RFID network deployment based on hybrid particle swarm optimization. Appl. Res. Comput. (04), 1326–1328 (2012)
4. Wang, Y., Yang, J.: Integration of RFID and AGV system and its application to the distribution center. Microcomput. Inf. (02), 93–95 (2012)
5. Wang, Y., Yang, J., Zhan, Y., WANPin: RFID networks planning based on tabu search algorithms. Appl. Res. Comput. (06), 2116–2119 (2011)
6. Cheung, B.C.F., Ting, S.L., Tsang, A.H.C., et al.: A methodological approach to optimizing RFID deployment. Inf. Syst. Front. **16**(5), 923–937 (2014)
7. Huang, H.P., Chang, Y.T.: Optimal layout and deployment for RFID systems. Adv. Eng. Inf. **25**(1), 4–10 (2011)
8. Ray, S., Debbabi, M., Allouche, M., et al.: Energy-efficient monitor deployment in collaborative distributed setting. IEEE Trans. Ind. Inf. **12**(1), 112–123 (2016)
9. Mehrabian, A.R., Lucas, C.: A novel numerical optimization algorithm inspired from weed colonization. Ecol. Inf. **1**(4), 355–366 (2006)

Development Strategy of Agriculture Product Logistic in Guizhou Province on the Transportation Network Context

Shanmei Song[1,2(✉)], Meirong Qiu[2], Wenfeng Li[1], and Qiaoxing Li[2]

[1] School of Logistics Engineering, Wuhan University of Technology,
Wuhan 430000, People's Republic of China
Songshanmei@aliyun.com, liwf@whut.edu.cn
[2] School of Management, Guizhou University,
Guiyang 550025, People's Republic of China
{1432798201,317750225}@qq.com

Abstract. Guizhou province is a typical Karst area, and the suitable transportation network is the development breakthrough of logistics. From the transportation perspectives, we adopted grey correlation analysis to do quantitative analysis on the four influence factors, which are total freight volume in Guizhou and the freight volumes of road, railway, water and civil aviation in Guizhou according to the Karst characteristics. On the basis of the analysis results, we draw a conclusion that the main factors to hinder the logistics development of agricultural products are the poor road network environment, the lower infrastructure construction, the old transportation network, the low degree of industry integration and the relative narrow industrial chain. Then we proposed the corresponding countermeasures to promote the healthy and rapid development of agricultural products in Guizhou province.

Keywords: Agricultural products logistics · Complex network transportation · Grey correlation analysis · Karst

1 Introduction

No transportation, then no logistics. The logistics which includes the input logistics, output logistics and the sale logistics must rely on transport to achieve the space transfer of goods. A versatile and smooth line system of transport is an important support condition for the development of modern logistics.

With the implementation of one Belt one Road, Yangtze River Economic Belt and the increased investment of infrastructure, the logistics industry in Guizhou province has been made a great progress because of its unique location advantage and abundant natural resources, and it is now being the logistics node from the logistic end. And, with the promoting of big channel strategy, the integrated network transport pattern of highway, railway and aviation has been initially formed. The development of integrated transportation provides a strong support for the development of logistics economy in Guizhou. However, due to the impact of environment and Karst landform, high transportation cost is still a key problem that hinders the logistics development. Although Guizhou province

W. Li et al. (Eds.): IDCS 2016, LNCS 9864, pp. 393–404, 2016.
DOI: 10.1007/978-3-319-45940-0_36

is an agricultural province, it is affected by the level of economic development and the influence of complex topography, and the agricultural product logistics has a low starting point. Therefore, these factors to analyze on the impact of factors of the various transport modes and agricultural products in Guizhou Province, and aim at reducing transportation costs, and improve the quality of agricultural products, and ensure the healthy and rapid development of agricultural product logistics, together contribute to the realization and the priority of the agriculture modernization in Guizhou.

The development of transportation and logistics is mutual promotion. Ek Bryan et al. (2013) thought the star shaped network with high efficiency, and then made an empirical analysis on subway system in Atlanta [1]; Stefan Hubera (2015) pointed out the major importance of transport logistics which hubs within freight transport, and revealed the integration of transport logistics which hubs lags behind their empirical significance and there are certain restrictions which hamper an adequate integration [2]; Liqing Wen, etc. (2015) built a operation mode of integrated transportation and intelligent logistics coordinated development [3].

In recent years, the research results on the development of agricultural products logistics are quite rich. Chao Chen (2013) pointed out that under the background of urbanization, the logistics development of Chinese agriculture product has the problems of weak infrastructure, high cost of logistics, un-perfect development of the main body of the logistics, and the non-continuous supply chain, low degree of information technology, and so on [4]; Xianliang Shi (2015) believed that the future development of agricultural products logistics park is mainly characterized by the leading multi-industry integration, e-commerce, agriculture-House docking and the last-kilometer intelligence distribution trend [5]; RubénSainz (2013) thought that we should pay more attention to other types of infrastructure such as logistics platforms, not only highways, ports, and airpors [6].

Different scholars used the gray correlation analysis method to study the logistics of agricultural products according to the difference between area and the field of research which induce the difference indicator selection. Zaicheng Shan (2012) selected the dynamic growth rate of some indexes, such as the processing machinery of agricultural products, the rural highway, the highway, the railway operations, the number of agricultural transport vehicles, the farm product warehousing enterprises, and so on, to analyze on products logistics of Chinese agriculture [7]; Liangtao Sun (2014) analyze on the agricultural product logistics in Yunnan from the aspects of agricultural product logistics development in the external environment, demand, infrastructure development, the development of human resources information technology and other selected indicators [8]; Lirong Ma (2014) selected some indicators, such as the logistics of agricultural purchase and processing capacity, logistics capabilities, storage capacity, human resources, information, to analyze the impact of agricultural development [9].

Integrated the results above and on the basis of the perspective of network transportation, we study quantitatively on agricultural products logistics in Guizhou Province by selecting the industrial and economic indexed, and then propose appropriate countermeasures to promote the development strategy based on these results.

2 Grey Correlation Analysis

Grey Correlation Analysis is one of the main contents of grey system theory, and the basic idea is to measure the degree of correlation between the corresponding sequences according to the similarity degree of the geometric shape of the sequences. Its specific analysis steps are as follows:

2.1 To Determine the Reference Sequence and Comparative Sequence

Because of the relative lack of the data of agricultural product flow, an then in order to measure the development of agricultural products logistics in Guizhou province, we selected the amount of freight transport (10000 tons) of Guizhou Province in recent years as a reference sequence Y. And the railway freight volume (10000 tons) Y1, road freight traffic (10000 tons) Y2, the waterway freight volume (10000 tons) Y3, civil aviation throughput (10000 tons) Y4 are the reference sequences, respectively, to measure the correlation of each mode of transport and agricultural products and the related factors of Railway, highway, water transport, civil aviation transportation modes[1].

From the point view of network transportation, we select some comparison sequences from the industrial structure and economic level of urban and rural areas in Guizhou Province. The output values of the first, the second and the third industry (100 million yuan) are selected to measure the impact on the total logistics. The consumption level of urban residents (yuan) reflects the overall economic impact of urban residents. The capita disposable income of urban residents (yuan) is on behalf of the urban residents living standards. Consumption expenditure of urban resident per capita (yuan) measures the consumption of urban residents and represents the impact of agricultural products logistics from the income of urban residents and consumption. The consumption level of rural residents (yuan), the disposable income of rural resident per capita (yuan) and the consumption expenditure of rural residents per capita (yuan) are selected to compare with the income consumption of urban residents. Production of agricultural products (10000 tons) represents the supply of agricultural products and the demand for agricultural products logistics. Transportation, warehousing and postal industry, as well as the fixed assets investment (100 million yuan) are chosen to measure the infrastructure construction of logistics and they are made up the comparison sequence X (i) (i = 1,2,... N), where X(i) means the i'th compared sequence, and N is the sum of comparative sequences (see Table 1).

The agricultural products in this paper mainly include grain, oil, tobacco, fruits, vegetables, etc., and the statistical data of agricultural production (X4) are shown in detail in Table 2, where G refers to grain, O refers to oil, T refers to tobacco, F refers to fruits, V refers to vegetables and S refers to the total of the main agricultural products in Guizhou Province.

---

[1] Note: we do not consider the pipeline transport due to the lack of relevant data.

Table 1. The reference sequence, comparison sequence of agricultural products logistics

Influence factor	Specific indicator	Unit	Code
Agricultural products logistics	Freight volume	10000-ton	Y
Mode of transport	railway freight volume	10000-ton	Y1
	road freight volume	10000-ton	Y2
	waterway freight volume	10000-ton	Y3
	civil aviation throughput	10000-ton	Y4
Industrial structure	The first industry output value	100 million yuan	X1
	The second industry output value	100 million yuan	X2
	The tertiary industry output value	100 million yuan	X3
Living standard of urban residents	Consumption level of urban residents	yuan	X4
	Per capita disposable income of urban residents	yuan	X5
	Per capita consumption expenditure of urban residents	yuan	X6
Living standard of rural residents	Consumption level of rural residents	yuan	X7
	Per capita disposable income of rural residents	yuan	X8
	Per capita consumption expenditure of urban residents	yuan	X9
agricultural products supply	Production of agricultural products	10000-ton	X10
Infrastructure	Infrastructure investment	100 million yuan	X11

Table 2. The output of major agricultural products (unit: million tons)

	2005	2006	2007	2008	2009	2010	2011	2012	2013	2014
G	1152	1038	1101	1158	1168	1112	877	1080	1030	1139
O	84.89	68.24	69.66	68.39	78.68	60.34	78.85	87.38	91.5	98.05
T	34.45	30.71	31.22	37.71	36.92	37.02	32.5	37.31	41.8	35.34
F	95.96	109.19	112.86	114.28	119.74	123.47	128.03	147.7	168	196.38
V	840	875.56	877.34	991.15	1077.8	1202.04	1250.1	1376	1500	1625.6
S	2207.4	2121.7	2191.94	2369.53	2481.4	2535.17	2366.3	2728	2832	3093.9

Data source: The statistical yearbook of Guizhou Province in 2015

The initial data of the relevant factors are shown in Table 3, where Freight volume = railway freight volume + road freight volume + waterway freight volume.

2.2   The Calculation of Relational Degree

(1) The dimensionless. Due to differences of units between the various factors and the large differences in the data, we should make raw data dimensionless in order to allow the comparability between indicators. In general, the technologies include the methods of the standard values, the initial value, the mean of the values, the interval values and others. In this paper, we use the initial value of the process, where each sequence number is divided by the sequence of the first non-zero value and we obtain a new sequence X' below:

$$X'_i = (X'_i(1), X'_i(2), \ldots, X'_i(n)) \tag{1}$$

In which,

$$X'_i(k) = \frac{X_i(k)}{x_i(1)}, i = 1, 2, 3 \ldots N, k = 1, 2, \ldots, n \tag{2}$$

$X_i(k)$ means the ked date of the ith comparison sequence. Take Y for example, the dimensionless in 2014 is 85673 divide by the date in 2005, where is 21771, so the dimensionless is 3.94, in the year of 2014.

(2) Find the sequence of extreme difference, the maximum difference and the minimum difference. Calculated them between the comparison sequence and the reference sequence as follows:

$$\Delta i(k) = |Y'(k) - X'_i(k)|, i = 1, 2, 3, \ldots N \tag{3}$$

And then get

$$M = \text{maxmax } \Delta_i(k), \ m = \text{minmin } \Delta_i(k) \tag{4}$$

(3) Calculate the correlation coefficient and correlation degree. Firstly, let the distinguished coefficient $\varepsilon = 0.5$ ($0 < \varepsilon < 1$), then the correlation coefficient can be obtained:

$$\gamma_{(Y,X_i)} = \frac{m + \in M}{\Delta_i(k) + \in M} i = 1, 2, 3 \ldots N, \ k = 1, 2, \ldots, n \tag{5}$$

And calculate the correlation degree,

$$\gamma_{(Y,X_i)} = \frac{1}{n} \sum_{k=1}^{n} \gamma_{(Y,X_i)}(k), \ i = 1, 2, 3 \ldots, N, \ k = 1, 2, \ldots, n \tag{6}$$

Table 3. The original data of selected indicators in 2005–2014

	2005	2006	2007	2008	2009	2010	2011	2012	2013	2014
Y	21771	24709	26788	33576	34844	40310	44890	52765	72700	85673
Y1	6169	6826	7289	6683	6997	7991	7219	6665	6458	6319
Y2	15082	17284	18834	26156	27031	31409	36684	45000	65100	78017
Y3	520	599	665	737	816	910	987	1100	1142	1337
Y4	3.35	4	4	4.2	5.16	6.17	6.93	7.97	7.76	8.31
X1	368.94	393.17	446.38	547.9	550.27	625.03	726.22	891.91	1029.05	1280.45
X2	826.63	980.78	1148.27	1409	1476.6	1800.06	2194.33	2677.5	3243.7	3857.44
X3	783.49	908.05	1147.25	1377	1252.7	2177.07	2781.29	3282.8	3734.04	4128.5
X4	8623	9491	10551	11749	13000	14707	16783.02	18060	19508	21227
X5	8147.1	9116.61	10678.4	11759	12863	14142.7	16495.01	18701	20667.1	22548.2
X6	6156.3	6848.39	7758.69	8349	9048.3	10058.3	11352.88	12586	13702.9	15254.6
X7	1563	1630	1895	2142	2459	2926	3986.441	4448.4	5383	6620
X8	1877	1984.62	2373.99	2797	3005.4	3471.93	4145.35	4753	5434	6671.22
X9	1552.4	1627.07	1913.5	2166	2422	2852.48	3455.76	3901.7	4740.18	5970.25
X10	2207.4	2121.7	2191.94	2370	2481.4	2535.17	2366.33	2727.5	2831.51	3093.89
X11	144.7	176.4	194	258.2	397.2	518.5	588.9398	756.2	1019.99	1319.9

Data source: The statistical yearbook of Guizhou Province from 2006 to 2015

2.3   Results Analysis

Calculate the correlation degree $\gamma_{(Y,X_i)}$ between the reference sequences Y and the relevant factors of sequence Xi by using Grey Correlation Analysis method. Results are shown in Table 4.

The relationship between the total freight volume and the influencing factors is shown in Fig. 1.

From the data analysis above, we get:

(1) The highest correlation with the total freight volume is the consumption expenditure per capita of rural residents. From Fig. 1, we can see that the indicators related to the living standards of rural residents (X7, X8, X9) are higher than the correlation of urban residents living standards (X4, X5, X6), which shows that the living standard of rural residents has a great influence on the development of logistics. Due to the backward economy and the large gap between urban and rural areas in Guizhou Province, the living standard of rural residents is still an important factor to hinder the development of logistics in the economic level.

(2) The first industry is the most outstanding fact on the industrial structure. Fluctuations in the value of the first industry will lead to the total amount change of freight greatly, which shows that the first industry is still the basis of the logistics development as Guizhou is traditional agriculture area. The large difference of the correlation degree between the output value of the third industry and the gross freight volume reflects their industrial linkage is not strong, and the industry chain is relatively narrow.

(3) About the mode of transport, although the road is the main mode of transport in Guizhou Province, there have higher correlation degree between civil aviation as

Table 4. The sort of the correlation between the otoal freight volume (Y) and influencing factors

Specific indicators	Code	Correlation degree	Sort
Per capita consumption expenditure of urban residents	X9	0.9667	1
Per capita disposable income of rural residents	X8	0.9569	2
The first industry output value	X1	0.9483	3
Consumption level of rural residents	X7	0.9437	4
Per capita disposable income of urban residents	X5	0.9268	5
Civil aviation throughput	X15	0.9176	6
Waterway freight volume	X14	0.9063	7
Consumption level of urban residents	X4	0.9021	8
Per capita consumption expenditure of urban residents	X6	0.8922	9
Road freight volume	X13	0.8870	10
The second industry output value	X2	0.8856	11
The tertiary industry output value	X3	0.8103	12
Railway freight volume	X12	0.7896	13
Production of agricultural products	X10	0.7805	14
Infrastructure investment	X11	0.6925	15

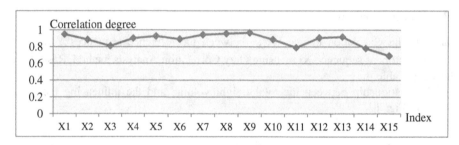

Fig. 1. The total freight volume correlation degree

well as water transport and the total freight, and they indicate that there are some limitations in the future development of the road because they are affected by Karst landform. During the process of one Belt and one Road, the development speed of air and water transportation may be improved.

(4) The size of the output of agricultural products determines the scale of agricultural products logistics. The agricultural product output has smaller impact on the total freight volume, and the agricultural production give a smaller promotion effect on logistics development, which indicates agricultural products logistics is still in its initial stage since Guizhou Province is a traditional agricultural province and it may have a larger development space.

(5) The lower relevance degree of the fixed assets investment in transportation, warehousing and postal services reflects that logistics infrastructure in Guizhou province is still a weak link to hinder the development of logistics.

For a more accurate analysis of the impact of various factors on the different modes of transport, and the influence of different modes of transport on agricultural products logistics, selecting railway freight volume, road freight volume, waterway freight volume and civil aviation throughput as reference sequences, for correlation analysis, and the correlation degree is calculated as Table 5.

The relationship between different transportation modes and the influencing factors are shown in Fig. 2.

(1) Figure 2 shows that the largest correlation with the yield of agricultural products (X10) is the railway freight volume (Y1), and the yield of agricultural products has the most obvious influence on the railway freight volume. Although the highway as the main mode of transport in Guizhou Province, the correlation with the yield of agricultural products is the lowest, and it shows that the railway may be the main transport mode when agricultural product logistics in Guizhou Province is developed. Due to the backwardness of the highway transportation network facilities in Guizhou Province, the road transport is the weak link in the development of agricultural products logistics.

(2) Table 5 shows that the maximum correlation degree is the output of the second industry according to the road transport. In contrast, the first industry association is relatively low. The highway is mainly used for the transportation of manufacture and industry, and the proportion of the first industry, especially agricultural

Table 5. Comparison of correlation analysis between different transportation modes and various influencing factors

	Railway		Highway		Waterway		Civil aviation	
Sort	Code	Degree	Code	Degree	Code	Degree	Code	Degree
1	X10	0.968003	X2	0.926397	X4	0.984666	X4	0.974674
2	X6	0.893791	X7	0.883045	X6	0.982632	X5	0.966813
3	X4	0.889329	X3	0.856087	X5	0.972528	X6	0.966449
4	X5	0.87122	X9	0.850339	X1	0.94193	X1	0.944082
5	X1	0.86316	X8	0.848832	X8	0.930045	X8	0.937545
6	X8	0.848662	X1	0.822063	X9	0.923285	X9	0.934121
7	X9	0.847821	X5	0.812784	X7	0.893531	X7	0.904887
8	X7	0.831609	X4	0.792359	X10	0.860058	X2	0.85831
9	X2	0.797623	X6	0.784783	X2	0.852024	X10	0.857216
10	X3	0.761292	X11	0.690521	X3	0.798787	X3	0.800285
11	X11	0.695469	X10	0.683535	X11	0.708794	X11	0.71101

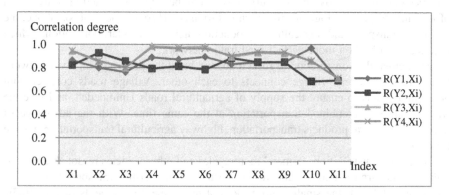

Fig. 2. The correlation degree of different transportation

products, is relatively low. The relationship between water transport and civil aviation is almost coincident, and the consumption level of urban residents is an important factor. The result shows that the water transport and civil aviation transportation have not been well developed in Guizhou province, and the consumption level of urban residents has a great influence on the development of water transport and civil aviation transportation.

(3) Table 5 and Fig. 2 show that the correlation degree of the fixed assets investment of transportation, storage and postal industry is relatively low regardless of the mode of transport, and the growth rate of fixed asset investment is relatively fast in recent years. On the one hand, it shows that the promotion role of transport to current logistics infrastructure is small. On the other hand, it also shows that there is a large development space in the initial stage of agricultural product logistics in Guizhou Province.

3   Measures to Speed up the Development of Agricultural Products Logistics in Guizhou Province

According to the analysis above, the development of agricultural products logistics still exists some problems from the point view of network transport as it is influenced by karst landform, such as the poor highway network environment, backward infrastructure, obsolete network traffic, low degree of industry integration, the relative narrow of industry chain, asymmetric information and other issues. It should take appropriate measures to promote the rapid development of agricultural logistics in Guizhou Province.

3.1   Strengthen the Construction of Infrastructure and Build the Highway Network Interlinked Villages

Because of the special terrain of Karst landform, the infrastructure construction is always an important problem to restrict the development of agricultural product logistics in Guizhou province. It is urgent to strengthen the infrastructure construction of agricultural product logistics in Guizhou Province. Through the analysis above, the highway transport and agricultural production have a smaller correlation, which requires us to build a more perfect road traffic network.

Strengthen the construction of rural road, and build the pattern of highway network that make sure every village connects to each other. Village roads connect with households so as to ensure the supply of agricultural roads Unimpeded, and take the way of rail-road combined transportation at the same time. With the advantage of railway agricultural products transportation, highway agricultural transportation may be promoted.

In terms of distribution, farmers' motorcycles and other vehicles reasonable may be utilized, and farmers may be allowed to participate in logistics transportation. In the mountains of Karst, the small motorcycle tool meets the requirements of road traffic better compared to the truck. For the settlement of distribution center, according to the characteristics of the terrain, distribution center is reasonably planned, and the large public distribution center and the community distribution center are build in the logistics park, which are being three level network system, and then the urban agriculture product logistics in Guizhou Province may be interconnected. From the point view of the cold chain logistics, the rate of cold storage and refrigeration equipment may be strengthened, and the rate of agricultural product damage should be reduced as well. For the information technology, the rate of rural network coverage may be improved, and the farmers' awareness of network service and response to market feedback information should be strengthened in time. In terms of quality, RFID, the bar code and other logistics network technology should be adopted in order to achieve quality traceability in the agricultural product circulation. At last, the information is transparent by using the mobile terminal and other devices to monitor the market.

3.2 Merg into One Belt and One Road, Speed up the Development of Multimodal Transport and Drop-and-Pull Transport

Guizhou Province connects the Eurasian Continental Bridge toward the north through Chengdu, and Chongqing, and connects Guangxi, Guangdong and other regions toward south through the high-speed railway and the highway. Guizhou province should play a full role to the advantages of traffic location, and merge into one Belt and one Road by opening the logistics channel. In the development of the large logistics situation, the fast speed, less loss and low cost requirements should be adapted in some key transport links, which may guide the industrial structure adjustment and give full play to the advantages of road, railway, water transport, aviation and other modes of transport. The multimodal transport may be developed, a comprehensive transport network built, and the biggest advantage of the integrated network of transportation played. At the same time, the Drop-and-pull transport also be vigorously developed in order to reduce the unit costs and improve transport efficiency and turnover rate.

3.3 Extend the Agricultural Industry Chain, and Make the Modern Agriculture "One After Another"

In view of the special features of karst landform in Guizhou Province, Develop the characteristic industry in mountain regions, make agricultural product logistics and combine mountain tourism, open Agricola experience activities, in order to improve consumers' experience degrees. At the same time, through the deep processing of agricultural products, special agricultural products package can be introduced, the brand effect built, and the eco industries developed. The modern agriculture connects with both the second and the third industries, that is to say, the food manufacture of secondary industry and the leisure agriculture of tertiary industry are both linked to the agriculture, and then extended to the industrial chain of modern agriculture, and they promote the three industries to be integrated. It is a driving pole to develop the rural economy in Guizhou Province. It also promotes the industries to be integrated to each other and make agricultural product and logistic to be developed in a certain extent.

3.4 Improve the Goods of Guizhou to Be Sold Outside, Develop the Special Agricultural Product, and Carry Out the Electronic Commerce in Rural Areas

In order to promote the electronic commerce development of agricultural product in Guizhou Province, a series of activities, such as the goods of Guizhou to be sold outside were launched, can open the foreign market of agricultural products in an extent. Along with this good development situation, the way, which may cooperate with the e-commerce platform and rely on tea, tobacco, medicine, fuel, and other characteristics industries, is taken to find the accurate market position and implement the dislocation competition. The schemes of e-commerce platform with distribution and community O2O with distribution and agricultural electricity with logistics are adopted to expand the new circulation pattern, and they can develop the characteristic agriculture product industry and then solve the bought and sold problem of agricultural products. These schemes can continuously develop the agricultural product logistics under the boost of e-commerce.

4 Conclusions

On the point view of the transportation network and by using grey correlation analysis, we quantitatively analyze the influence factors of agricultural product logistics and the transport modes according to the special Karst terrain in Guizhou province. On the basis of the analysis results, we put forward some suggestions to speed up the development of agricultural product logistics in Guizhou province, such as strengthen infrastructure construction, build a diversified road transport network, develop multi-modal transport, expand the industrial chain, and develop agricultural e-commerce and special agricultural products logistics.

Acknowledgement. The paper is supported by the research foundation of talented people in Guizhou University numbered at (2015)018 and the project of Humanities and Social Sciences research Institute of Education Department in Guizhou Province.

References

1. Bryan, E., Caitlin, V., Darren, A.: Efficiency of star-like graphs and the Atlanta subway network. Phys. A **329**, 5481–5489 (2013)
2. Stefan, H., Jens, K., Carina, T.: Consideration of transport logistics hubs in freight transport demand models. Eur. Transp. Res. Rev., 74 (2015)
3. Wen, L.: Study on collaborative development of smart logistics and comprehensive transportation in China. Logistics Technol. **03**, 4–7 (2015)
4. Chen, C., Li, B.: Present situation, problems and countermeasures of China's agricultural products logistics based on urbanization. Res. Agric. Modernization **3**, 328–332 (2013)
5. Shi, X.: The development trend of agricultural products logistics and the counter measures. China Bus. Market **7**, 25–29 (2015)
6. Rubén, S., Jose, B., Susana, V., Samir J.: The Economic impact of logistics infrastructure: the case of PLAZA–the zaragoza logistics platform. Transp. Plann. Technol., **364** (2013)
7. Shan, Z.: Gray correlation analysis of agricultural products logistics and its influence factors. Syst. Eng. **10**, 123–126 (2012)
8. Sun, L.: Study on factors influence agricultural products logistics in yunna based on grey correlation analysis. Logistics Technol. **13**, 64–65 (2014)
9. Ma, L., Ma, D., Zhang, E.: Grey correlation analysis of main influence factors of agricultural logistics for agricultural development – taking Gansu province as an example. Productivity Research, 1, 67–71 + 81 (2014)

The Development Strategies of Logistics in Chongqing City Based on the Complex Traffic Network

Shanmei Song[1,2(✉)], Shuaijun Chen[2], Wenfeng Li[1], and Qiaoxing Li[2]

[1] School of Logistics Engineering, Wuhan University of Technology,
Wuhan 430070, People's Republic of China
songshanmei@aliyun.com, liwf@whut.edu.cn
[2] School of Management, Guizhou University,
Guiyang 550025, People's Republic of China
{862787316,317750225}@qq.com

Abstract. In this paper, we use grey correlation analysis method to make an empirical analysis of the logistics development of Chongqing. According to the time sequence, we respectively determined the Chongqing freight volume and four major characteristics of the transportation mode of freight volume as behavior sequences. Analysis result shows that the Chongqing agriculture is still in an important position, and its output value and the main agricultural production have large correlation with the highway and railway freight volumes, and the living level of urban and rural residents is also the same. Finally, we give some suggestion to structure urban transportation network, strengthen regional cooperation and construct cross-regional transportation network, and so on, which may play a positive role to promote the development of Chongqing logistics. Meanwhile, as one of the Karst areas, the development of Chongqing's experience also provides a good case for the others.

Keywords: Network transportation · Logistics · Grey correlation analysis · Strategy · Chongqing

1 Introduction

Chongqing is the only western municipality which is managed directly by the central government, and it is also the comprehensive reform pilot area as a whole urban and rural development. To develop the agricultural product logistics is vigorously an important content to promote modern agriculture. Integrated with large city and large rural area, Chongqing is a pilot city in our country. It possesses good agricultural industry structure and advantage of agricultural resources. However, the lag of agricultural products logistics has severely restricted the agricultural production, the rural economy development and the income increase of farmers. Therefore, to accelerate the development of modern logistics of agricultural products has an important practical significance for Chongqing.

© Springer International Publishing AG 2016
W. Li et al. (Eds.): IDCS 2016, LNCS 9864, pp. 405–412, 2016.
DOI: 10.1007/978-3-319-45940-0_37

Ma and Yu (2011) said that the efficient logistics of agricultural products can effectively solve the contradiction between demand and supply of agricultural products in different regions, and promote agricultural production, processing and sales. Wang (2009) analyze the present state of agricultural products circulation in Chongqing, and found that over 70 % of the total agricultural products were circulated by all kinds of markets, so the wholesale market at present was still the main operation form for agricultural products in Chongqing city. At the same time, agricultural economic cooperation organization, supermarket chain, agriculture group companies, and the third party logistics enterprise are all beneficial complementarities for the wholesale market.

Grey correlation refers to the uncertain relationship among things or the system factors or the uncertainty relation between the factors and the main behaviors. Grey relational analysis is a measure to analyze discrete sequence correlation between degrees. Its basic idea is according to determine the similar degree of correlation between factor curves. At present, the model structure of grey correlation algorithm is mainly from the following two aspects. One is to construct the correlation degree by reflecting the development between the two sequences or similar order of magnitude, and the other is similarly reflect the development trend of two sequences or curve shape. Then it can mainly describe the degree of proximity of relative change trend between curves (Tian et al. 2008). Shan (2012) used grey correlation to analyze the construction of the logistics of agricultural products in each link and agricultural products logistics value, and concluded that logistics of agricultural products are greatly influenced by agricultural products processing capacity. Eiichi and Thompson (2004) pointed out the transport system is being more and more important research problem for the urban development planning, and they viewed that the main reason includes the urban traffic congestion, environmental impact and energy consumption problem.

The paper is organized as follows. Firstly, we analyze the logistics development in Chongqing by using grey relation analysis. Secondly, we put forward the corresponding policy recommendations, and then summarized the full text in the end.

2 Grey Correlation Analysis

In this paper, we study the correlation degree between the logistics capability and factors related to agricultural production and residents' living standards, and emphatically analyzed the development role of agricultural logistics for Chongqing output. The total production of logistics is an appropriate indicator to measure the level of logistics development, which considers characteristics to easily obtain the data. We take the amount of goods transport and railway transport, road goods transport, water transport freight traffic and civil aviation goods as behavior sequences, and select the data from China statistical yearbook and the China agricultural yearbook during 2005 to 2014. And then we utilized grey correlation analysis method to analyze the above factors by using these data. The variables can be seen in Table 1.

Table 1. Code Variables and Units

Codes	Variables	Units
Y	Cargo transport volume	One hundred million tons
Y1	Railway freight volume	One hundred million tons
Y2	Highway freight volume	One hundred million tons
Y3	Waterway freight volume	Ten thousand tons
Y4	The civil aviation cargo throughput	Ten thousand tons
X11	GDP	One hundred million yuan
X12	The first industrial output value	One hundred million yuan
X13	The second industrial output value	One hundred million yuan
X14	The third industrial output value	One hundred million yuan
X21	Rural residents' consumption level	Yuan
X22	Rural households per capita consumer spending	Yuan
X23	Urban residents consumption level	Yuan
X24	Urban per capita consumer spending	Yuan
X25	Per capita disposable income of urban households	Yuan
X31	Food production	Ten thousand tons
X32	Sugar cane production	Ten thousand tons
X33	Tobacco leaf production	Ten thousand tons
X34	Tea production	Ten thousand tons
X35	Oil production	Ten thousand tons
X36	Vegetable production	Ten thousand tons
X37	Fruit production	Ten thousand tons
X38	Meat production	Ten thousand tons

First of all, we initialized the original data by using the following formula:

$$Y = \frac{X_n}{X_1}, (n = 2, 3, \ldots n.)$$ (1)

Then we use Deng's method to correlate the correlation degree as follows:

$$\gamma(X_0, X_i) = \frac{1}{n} \sum_{k=1}^{n} r(x_0(k), x_i(k))$$ (2)

where the formula is

$$r(x_0(k), x_i(k)) = \frac{\min_i \min_k |x_0(k) - x_i(k)| + \rho \max_i \max_k |x_0(k) - x_i(k)|}{|x_0(k) - x_i(k)| + \rho \max_i \max_k |x_0(k) - x_i(k)|}$$ (3)

And $\rho(\rho \in [0, 1])$ is the distinguishing coefficient, and $\gamma(X_0, X_i)$ represents the relevance and the correlation means better when its value close to 1.

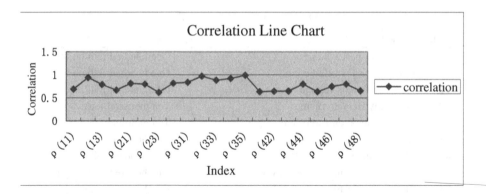

Fig. 1. Correlation line chart

We give their line chart in Fig. 1. According to the results of data analysis, we found that the correlation of highway freight volume (Y2(ρ(12))) is maximum in the mode of transportation. It shows clearly that highway and railway freight volumes are very high from the collected data and the highway freight volume is far higher than the railway traffic because Chongqing is an inland city and it mainly rely on the highway and the railway to transport goods. According to the data analysis of the living standards of urban and rural residents, the correlation degree of per capita disposable income of urban households (X25(ρ(35))) is the highest, and the one of the rural residents' consumption level (X21(ρ(31))) is the lowest.

Apparently, the logistic development in Chongqing mainly depends on the town. The town residents' consumption level is higher, and the product demand is bigger. According to the three industries which are compared with the correlation of total freight volume, the correlation of the third industry output value (X14(ρ(24))) is the largest and the one of the first industry (X12(ρ(22))) followed it. The situation is consistent with state of the economy in Chongqing as the city belongs to the underdeveloped western regions. Its agriculture is still in the important position. On the other hand, as a tourism city, its service industry is relatively rapid. In the main agricultural products in Chongqing, the correlations of tea production (X34(ρ(44))) and the fruit yield (X37(ρ(47))) are in the first and the second position, respectively, so a conclusion is that the sales and transportation of tea and fruit occupy a relatively large proportion in the logistics industry in Chongqing.

In order to clearly visualize their closer ties with the transportation mode, we respectively obtained the correlation and the order by compared each mode as the behavior sequence with railway freight volume, highway freight volume, water transport freight traffic and civil aviation cargo, which is shown in Table 2.

As a whole, the correlations of each index with the highway, railway freight volume are generally high. From the order, the main agricultural production owns the closest relevance with railway freight volume, and it has a great relationship to the volume of agricultural products. In the case of a large number of goods to transport, railway transportation is the first choice. In addition, the correlation degrees of tea and fruit yields, which are compared with other three kinds of freight volume, are higher

Table 2. Sorting by Different Modes of Transportation Character Behavior Sequence

Variable name	Sorting			
	Railway	Highway	Waterway	Civil aviation
GDP	16	10	1	1
The first industrial output value	10	5	11	11
The second industrial output value	17	17	7	3
The third industrial output value	15	9	2	2
Rural residents' consumption level	13	8	4	4
Rural households per capita consumer spending	11	4	6	6
Urban residents consumption level	14	2	3	5
Urban per capita consumer spending	7	3	8	8
Per capita disposable income of urban households	12	1	5	7
Food production	5	16	16	16
Sugar cane production	3	14	15	14
Tobacco leaf production	2	13	14	15
Tea production	8	6	9	10
Oil production	4	15	17	17
Vegetable production	6	11	12	12
Fruit Production	9	7	10	9
Meat Production	1	12	13	13

than other agricultural products, and they are relatively convenient way among a large number of transportation. From the data analysis, the correlations of the first industry and the living level of residents with the highway and railway freight volumes are bigger than that with waterway and civil aviation. Furthermore, the correlation of the second and the third industries with the highway and railway freight traffic is not very high, but the one with the civil aviation is larger than the rest of the other indicators.

According to analysis above, the heavy industry development in Chongqing is relatively slow, and the agriculture and service industries are in very important positions during the current development in Chongqing. The logistics development in Chongqing's main power comes from the urban residents, and to raise the income level of urban residents has a positive role to promote the development of logistic industry in Chongqing. Tea and fruit production has a largest effect on the development of logistics in Chongqing. Compared with other major agricultural outputs, tea production in Chongqing is not very big, but the value of the tea pressure is much higher than the others. To increase tea production and then to improve the quality may play a very important role to promote the development of logistics in Chongqing city. The logistics development in Chongqing, which is as an inland city, still mainly relies on the road and rail transportation. By strengthening highway and railway infrastructure, and improving the water, air and pipeline transportation infrastructures, we can construct a complex and diverse three-dimensional transportation network, then it may has a vital significance to promote the logistics development in Chongqing.

3 The Strategies of Logistics in Chongqing

According to the correlation analysis above, we provide the following suggestions in order to promote the development of logistics industry especially for agricultural products in Chongqing.

3.1 Increased Investment in Logistics Infrastructure and Built an Urban Transportation Network

Chongqing is an inland city and its terrain is exotic as the Karst landform, so it is also known as the mountain city. The logistics infrastructure in Chongqing is undeveloped for other areas, and the growth is limited in the freight turnover and freight volume. Logistics infrastructure restricts the development of logistics industry, and the freight volume and freight turnover growth rely on logistics infrastructure. Then, in order to promote the development of logistics industry in Chongqing, we need to strengthen the input and build the logistics infrastructure. From the previous collection data, the Chongqing logistics freight relies mainly on the highway and railway, and the highway may bear the freight volume far higher than the railway. This situation told us that we should increase the investment on the highway and railway infrastructure construction and may give our efforts to overcome the barriers from the natural environment in Chongqing, such as fried mountain, and to open up the tunnel to increase highway and railway mileages. At the same time, we also should improve the infrastructures such as water transport, air and pipeline transportation channels to create a diverse and comprehensive coverage of the transportation network in order to promote the development of logistics industry in Chongqing, which is the same with Guizhou, Yunnan and the other Karst areas.

3.2 Strengthen Regional Cooperation and Build the Regional Transportation Network in Karst Areas

The six karst regions such as Chongqing and Guizhou, which own the large area, have an lower economic development level related to the eastern regions, then their economic influence is also limited. It may appear with difficulty if only one city bears the logistics center. To combine the current traffic situation with the future development trend in our country, the Karst areas should implement the strategy of logistics center group and form a cross-region transportation network to improve the logistics industry. For example, both Chongqing and Guiyang constitute a Karst logistics center, and radiate and drive the logistics development in Yunnan, Guangxi, Hunan and Sichuan. It requires Chongqing and Guiyang to strengthen cooperation and mutually complement with each other by constructing transportation network. The interconnection between

Karst areas can build the logistics center together and lead to the development of logistics industry in the Karst areas.

3.3 Improve the Science and Technology Content of Agriculture and Deepen its Products Process

To realize the agricultural modernization needs the support of science and technology. Effectively apply the latest technology to agricultural production and improve the production mechanization of agriculture, then the workforce may be liberated and the labor efficiency improved. On the one hand, to improve product yield is also helpful to improve its quality. The improvement of production has a positive effect on the development of logistics in Chongqing, especially in the development of agricultural products logistics. The improvement of agricultural science and technology content also accelerate the development of the logistics industry in Chongqing. For example, to improve the refrigeration technology may accelerate the transportation of perishable foods and damaged products, such as fruit, meat, etc., and then give a good chance to keep fresh. So the loss of fruits can be effectively reduced and the suppliers' income may be improved. At the same time, to deepen the elaborate processing of agricultural products can not only add the product value and reduce the volume of agricultural products but also reduce the loss of agricultural products by comprehensive utilization and effectively increase farmers' income.

3.4 Formulate Relevant Policy and Standardize the Development of Logistics Industry

Government should play positive guiding role by standardizing the development of logistics industry in Chongqing. By integrated the existing laws and regulation of logistics and formulated a forward-looking rules and normative documents, we may have a programmatic document to guide the long-term development of logistics industry in Chongqing. The formulation of logistics law should pay attention to the unity of the content, because the large logistics industry is related with a variety of functional departments. The clear regulatory documents can be used to determine the industrial management departments and promote the coordination with various functional departments, and then the situation that the department documents are contradict with each other may be avoided.

4 Conclusion

By promoted the flow and optimized allocation of resources, the development of logistics industry promotes the extroverted degree of provincial trade and the industry competitiveness, and then develops the regional economy. Under the general background to realize regional economy integration, we must vigorously develop the logistics industry in order to speed up the economic development and alleviate economic gap among provinces, especially between the east and west provinces. From the perspective of empirical analysis and by using grey correlation analysis, we analyzed the main influence factors on agricultural products logistics development in Chongqing city, and then put forward some suggestions to construct the urban transportation network, improve agricultural science and technology, formulate policy law, strengthen regional cooperation, and so on. We hope that the suggestions can rapidly develop the agricultural product logistics in Chongqing city and also provide a reference for the other Karst areas such as Guizhou, Yunnan, etc. The aim is to build the regional transportation network which jointly promotes the development of logistics industry in the Karst areas.

Acknowledgement. The paper is supported by the research foundation of talented people in Guizhou University numbered at (2015)018 and the project of Humanities and Social Sciences research Institute of Education Department in Guizhou Province.

References

Tian, M., Liu, S., Bu, Z.: A research summary of grey correlation algorithm model. Theor. Explor. **01**, 24–27 (2008)

Shan, Z.: Gray correlation degree analysis of logistics of agricultural products and influencing factors. Syst. Eng. **10**, 123–126 (2012)

Yang, J., Wang, H., Yang, C.: Urbanization' influence on the logistics of agricultural products in China. Agric. Technol. Econ. **10**, 63–68 (2011)

Ma, Y., Yu, Y.: Chongqing urban and rural areas as a whole the agricultural products logistics operation mode study. Logistics Technol. **01**, 23–25 (2011)

Wang, Z.: Chongqing Urban and Rural Areas as a Whole the Agricultural Product Logistics System to Build Research. Chongqing Jiao tong university, Chongqing (2009)

Liu, N.: Agricultural industrial structure adjustment and agricultural economic development of the grey correlation analysis —— taking Hei Longjiang province as an example. Anhui Agric. Sci. **14**, 7597–7598 (2010)

Markus, H.: Logistics and freight transport policy in urban areas: a case study of Berlin-Brandenburg/Germany. Eur. Plan. Stud., Abingdon **12**(7), 1035 (2004)

Eiichi, T., Thompson, R.G.: Logistics Systems for Sustainable Cities. Elsevier, Oxford (2004)

The Performance Appraisal
of Port Logistics Informationization

Hongming Chen[1(✉)] and Yan Chen[2]

[1] Management School, Wuhan University of Technology, Wuhan, Hubei,
People's Republic of China
Hongmingchen@live.cn
[2] School of Logistics Engineering, Wuhan University of Technology, Wuhan,
Hubei, People's Republic of China
chenyan@whut.edu.cn

Abstract. China has stepped into the forefront of the world shipping team, which makes the construction of port logistics informationization is imminent. However, there still exist certain defects of comprehensive competition ability in port logistics informationization. In order to make the construction direction more explicit and enhance the comprehensive competition ability, the performance appraisal is obtained as the main topic. Then the evaluation is launched from the development and construction. Through constructing the performance appraisal index system, the input and output variables are defined. Moreover, the DEA efficiency model is introduced to evaluate the performance appraisal based on the 17 A-share listed ports. Furthermore, the efficiency value is calculated and the corresponding references are provided.

Keywords: Port logistics · Informatization · Performance appraisal · Data envelopment analysis

1 Introduction

The development of modern port logistics has promoted the development of port city's economy vigorously. Moreover, the investments of port logistics informatization are increasing because of the economic globalization. Furthermore, the quick response mechanism is provided for the customers through making use of the rapid and efficient port operation. However, the present development situation shows that some problems are still existed as followings. (1) Both the overall construction level and the informatization level are not high, which is difficult to meet the needs of the rapid economic development in China effectively. (2) The informationization construction cannot be targeted according to their own requirements, which can make the input and output reversed easily. Hence, through analyzing the influence factors and construction emphasis of the port logistics informatization in China, the performance appraisal index system is built. Moreover, the performance appraisal is evaluated by econometric model, which not only can provide port logistics informationization performance appraisal with solid theoretical basis, but also provide strong guarantee for strengthening the comprehensive competitiveness of port [1].

© Springer International Publishing AG 2016
W. Li et al. (Eds.): IDCS 2016, LNCS 9864, pp. 413–420, 2016.
DOI: 10.1007/978-3-319-45940-0_38

2 Literature Review

The theory researches of port logistics informationization put forward by the foreign scholars are relatively less compared with applied research. It was first raised by Rushton [2] and Beuthe [3] in 1982. In their discussion, the Informatization Utilization Potential model is introduced to evaluate the performance of the port logistics informationization, and then the information loop estimation model is put forward to study the potential ability of the enterprise. Nikamp [4] argues that performance appraisal is the research purpose of logistics activity based on the analysis of a large number of ports. After that, Gilliam [5] evaluates the port logistics informationization from three aspects: the establishment of strategic direction, the direction of productivity and the customer service evaluation index system. But the key indicators such as capital investment and infrastructure costs didn't mentioned. The performance appraisal methods of the port logistics informationization abroad is referred by the domestic scholars in a certain extent. Yang [6] makes an analysis of the Quanzhou port and in order to make the port development meets the needs of supporting high-speed development. Yan [7] put forward the turning point of the internet of things technology to port management information system's upgrade. All by all, the relevant researches about port logistics informationization performance appraisal are deficient both at home and abroad. Therefore, the research on performance appraisal of port logistics information remains to be deepened.

3 Analysis of the Research Object

3.1 Definition of the Related Content

The academic definition of port logistics informationization is: analyzing, monitoring and controlling the port logistics information by information measures through widely applying of the modern information and management technology. Based on the above analysis, the purpose of controlling logistics, business flow and cash flow can be achieved. In addition, the automation and management decision-making level can be improved efficiently through constructing advanced information infrastructure [8]. Additionally, the costs can be reduced and the service can be raised efficiently.

The information-based performance appraisal is to establish a specific index system referred to the unified standard [9]. Then the methods of mathematical statistics and operations research are applied according to certain procedures. At last, through qualitative and quantitative analysis, to make an objective and fair comprehensive evaluation to the informatization construction level and technology application effect during a certain period process.

Based on the above analysis, the definition of "the performance appraisal of port logistics information" is defined as: first guided by the port logistics informationization development planning. Second a reasonable evaluation index system should be established through discussing the main contents of the construction and application effects. Third the comprehensive evaluation model is employed to evaluate the informationization application effect and the sustainable development ability of informatization construction in this period is proposed objectively, fairly and accurately.

3.2 Construction of the Evaluation Index System

The scientific and reasonable of indexes are directly related to the quality of the performance appraisal. Therefore, the object must be reflected by the index system scientifically and comprehensively. Through the analysis of the research purpose, the corresponding index system construction principles are put forward as follows. ① the principle of government decree. ② the principle of highlight, which also be known as the representative principle. ③ the designing of the index system should meet the principle of combining qualitative and quantitative. It is only through quantitative analysis, the performance can be revealed more intuitively.

When constructing the performance appraisal index system, not only the principles above should be followed, but also combine with the construction goal of the basic enterprise information evaluation indicators classification standard. Through the analysis of port logistics informationization construction comprehensively, the targets are achieved. Besides, all the targets can be referred when constructing the index system. So, based on the above requirements, the performance appraisal index system is constructed in Table 1 [10].

Table 1. The performance evaluation index system of port logistics informationization

First grade index	Second grade index
Informatization construction level	The proportion of information construction investment
	The number of port logistics public information platform
	The construction of electronic data interchange (EDI)
	The number of port passenger transport network ticket system
	The coverage of the port electronic map
	The proportion of computer networking
Informatization application level	The transportation ability of port logistics
	The automation level of logistics informatization
	The management level of port logistics informatization
	The annual growth rate of port logistics informationization
	The net profit growth rate of port logistics informationization
	The visualization level of logistics
	The information level of multimodal transport
	Online service ability
Sustainable development level	The learning ability of employees to information technology
	Information resource guarantee
	Funds safeguard
	Talent guarantee
	Customer satisfaction for port logistics services

4   The Analysis of Evaluation Method

4.1   Evaluation Model Selection

Many methods have been confirmed in evaluating the performance appraisal. And each method has its own applicable range and advantages and disadvantages. Therefore, the performance appraisal method must be chosen according to the background of research object itself. Through comparing all kinds of methods comprehensively, this paper argues that the data envelopment analysis (DEA) method is the most suitable for the performance appraisal [11]. The main reasons are: (1) the DEA model is suitable for small sample analysis. (2) The time sequence data of index can be ignored when the DEA model carried out. Therefore, the application of DEA can reduce research times and enhance the accuracy of research result.

4.2   The Analysis of DEA Model

In order to evaluate the performance of port logistics informationization better, the C^2R model is chosen to do analyze in the paper. The main contents of C^2R model are as in (1) [12].

$$P = \begin{cases} \max \mu Y_{j0} = V_p \\ st. \omega^T X_j - \mu Y_j \geq 0 \\ \omega^T X_0 = 1 \\ \omega \geq 0, \mu \geq 0 \end{cases} \tag{1}$$

In the formula, $\omega^T = (\omega_1, \omega_2, \ldots, \omega_n)$ is the weight of input variable and μ is the weight of input variable. According to formula 1, the linear programming problem is solved. If $V_P = 1$, DEA efficient, if $V_P < 1$, non DEA efficiency. Non DEA efficiency means production below the efficient production frontier. Therefore, it is necessary to do some improvement of the DEA model. The improving method of the model is as follows, as in (2):

$$(D) \begin{cases} \max \alpha = V_D \\ st. \sum_{j=1}^{r} \lambda_j X_j + S^- - X_{j0} = 0 \\ \sum_{j=1}^{r} \lambda_j Y_j - S^+ - \alpha Y_{j0} = 0 \\ \sum_{j=1}^{r} \lambda_j = 1 \\ \lambda_j \geq 0, S^+ \geq 0, S^- \geq 0 (j = 1, 2, \ldots, r) \end{cases} \tag{2}$$

Among them, S is the slack variable. Through solving the problems of the linear planning to get the values of λ, α and S.

The economy significance of α is that on the basis of the basic input elements unchanged, as far as possible to increase the output elements by the same percentage. If the input elements can't be increased, while $\alpha = 1$ and the evaluation unit is effective. Or else, $\alpha > 1$ the evaluation unit is ineffective.

4.3   The Determination of Input and Output Index

Affected by the application signature of the DEA model, corresponding input and output variables are needed to be determined before the evaluation. Referring to the performance appraisal index system in Table 1, the following processing is carried out to the input and output indicators after compared each secondary index comprehensively. Finally, the input indicator is information investment and output indicators are net profit and operating income.

5   Empirical Analysis

When selecting the decision making units (DMU). Firstly, a large number of data collection and analysis are preferred and the port information construction investment is summed up. Secondly, only the number of DMU is more than two times of the input and output indexes can be evaluated by DEA. Therefore, the 17 a-share listed port companies in China are selected as the decision making unit in Table 2.

Before computing the effectiveness a linear relationship must be presented of all indicators' data. Here the SPSS software is used. According to the data processing results, the DEAP software is used to calculate. Then the linear programming equations are constructed. Here we set $V_D = 1$. Then the equations are reconstructed as follows:

$$\min \theta = V_D$$

$$S.T. \begin{cases} 0.518\lambda_1 + 0.461\lambda_2 + 0.412\lambda_3 + 0.041\lambda_4 + 0.016\lambda_5 + 0.159\lambda_6 \\ \quad + 0.052\lambda_7 + 0.012\lambda_8 + 0.028\lambda_9 + 0.092\lambda_{10} + 0.064\lambda_{11} + 0.073\lambda_{12} \\ \quad + 0.028\lambda_{13} + 0.014\lambda_{14} + 0.037\lambda_{15} + 0.017\lambda_{16} + 0.004\lambda_{17} + S_1 = 0.014\theta \\ 295.108\lambda_1 + 165.206\lambda_2 + 154.024\lambda_3 + 51.754\lambda_4 + 18.726\lambda_5 + 88.862\lambda_6 \\ \quad + 37.878\lambda_7 + 2.489\lambda_8 + 30.547\lambda_9 + 43.779\lambda_{10} + 72.612\lambda_{11} + 36.589\lambda_{12} \\ \quad + 18.055\lambda_{13} + 20.661\lambda_{14} + 20.227\lambda_{15} + 12.418\lambda_{16} + 1.582\lambda_{17} - S_2 = 20.661 \\ 78.653\lambda_1 + 27.792\lambda_2 + 16.867\lambda_3 + 12.938\lambda_4 + 6.527\lambda_5 + 5.691\lambda_6 \\ \quad + 5.245\lambda_7 + 5.227\lambda_8 + 4.081\lambda_9 + 3.717\lambda_{10} + 2.878\lambda_{11} + 1.926\lambda_{12} \\ \quad + 1.295\lambda_{13} + 1.254\lambda_{14} + 0.806\lambda_{15} + 0.512\lambda_{16} + 0.223\lambda_{17} - S_3 = 1.254 \end{cases}$$

Table 2. Input and output data of DEA model

DMU code	Name of port	Input (hundred million Yuan)	Output (hundred million Yuan)	
		Information investment	Operating income	Net profit
DMU1	Shanghai port	0.518	295.108	78.653
DMU2	Ningbo port	0.461	165.206	27.792
DMU3	Tianjin port	0. 412	154.024	16.867
DMU4	Tangshan port	0.041	51.574	12.938
DMU5	Shenzhen port	0.016	18.726	6.527
DMU6	Dalian port	0.159	88.862	5.691
DMU7	Yingkou port	0.052	37.878	5.245
DMU8	Yantian port	0.012	2.489	5.227
DMU9	Beibuwan port	0.028	30.547	4.081
DMU10	Rizhao port	0.092	43.779	3.717
DMU11	Xiamen port	0.064	72.612	2.878
DMU12	Wuhu port	0.073	36.589	1.926
DMU13	Jinzhou port	0.028	18.055	1.295
DMU14	Chongqing port	0.014	20.661	1.254
DMU15	Zhuhai port	0.037	20.227	0.806
DMU16	Lianyungang port	0.017	12.418	0.512
DMU17	Nanjing port	0.004	1.582	0.233

Remark: all the data comes from the financial statement of each port in 2015.

The calculation results show that the number of DEA efficient DMU is four: DMU4, DMU5, DMU8 and DMU14. And the technical efficiency value, redundancy and deficiency avulses of other MUSs are shown in Table 3:

Table 3. Value of technical efficiency and redundancy or deficiency

DMU code	Technical efficiency	Redundancy or deficiency of information investment	Redundancy or deficiency of operating income	Redundancy or deficiency of net profit
DMU1	0.460	0.280	0.000	0.000
DMU2	0.267	0.338	0.000	0.000
DMU3	0.265	0.303	0.000	0.000
DMU6	0.380	0.099	0.000	0.000
DMU7	0.529	0.025	0.000	0.000
DMU9	0.788	0.006	0.000	0.000

(*Continued*)

Table 3. (*Continued*)

DMU code	Technical efficiency	Redundancy or deficiency of information investment	Redundancy or deficiency of operating income	Redundancy or deficiency of net profit
DMU10	0.330	0.062	0.000	0.000
DMU11	0.769	0.015	0.000	1.529
DMU12	0.340	0.048	0.000	0.295
DMU13	0.441	0.016	0.000	0.000
DMU15	0.370	0.023	0.000	0.422
DMU16	0.495	0.009	0.000	0.242
DMU17	0.289	0.003	0.000	0.000

The results in Table 3 mean that informatization investment of other ports has a certain degree of redundancy. And there is no insufficient of the ports' revenue and insufficient, which means the development of port logistics information construction has a very important role to port logistics' income. However, the efficiency value of the net profit shows that there are redundancy of the informatization construction investment of Zhuhai port, Xiamen port, Wuhu port and Lianyungang port, while their net output are still inadequate. The phenomenon shows that the construction of port logistics information cannot only blindly focus on information input. Each port should find out the real problems and to solve the problems targeted. Therefore, the results show that the informatization construction investment is not the more the better. To the contrary, the ports should analyze their own situation to avoid insufficient or input redundancy. Then the optimum investment strategy can be achieved.

6 Conclusion

In this paper, the efficiency value is calculated based on the DEA model through constructing the performance appraisal index system of port logistics informatization. Firstly, the function of informationization construction in promoting the development of port logistics has studied. Secondly, the promote function of informationization development to the port logistics development is analyzed objectively. Finally, the 17 a-share listed port companies are chosen to do empirical analysis. The research results not only achieved good effects, but also provide a train of thought for the performance studying of informatization development. The idea could also be referred by other industries in evaluating the performance of informatization construction.

The paper has tried to construct a perfect input and output index framework. While, performance appraisal of port logistics informationization is relatively a new research field. Although many research results have referred in the paper, the research is still limited by the insufficient of the ability and knowledge. Therefore, the improvement need to be explored based on the above results.

Acknowledgement. Research on the performance appraisal system and its realization and application of transport industry informatization. Sponsored by Chinese Ministry of Transport, 2015-2017 (2015364811070).

References

1. Stank, T.P., Keller, S.B., Daugherty, P.J.: Supply chain collaboration and logistics service performance. J. Bus. Log. **22**(12), 29–47 (2001)
2. Rushton, A., Oxley, J., Croucher, P.: The Handbook of Logistics and Distribution Management. Kogan Page Publishers, London (2000)
3. Beuthe, M.: Freight transportation demand elasticity's: a geographic multimodal transpiration network analysis. Transp. Res. Port E **37**, 253–266 (2001)
4. Peter, N.: Comparative modeling European of interregional transport applications to multimodal freight transport. Eur. J. Oper. Res. **155**, 584–602 (2004)
5. Gilliam, K. Review of Transport Economics. Economic Journal (1980) 677–678
6. Ouyang, Z., Ma, J.: The port logistics informationization platform and the J2EE technology frame. Electron. Commer. **11**, 32–36 (2009)
7. Zhang, Y.: Examination of internet things used in port information system construction. Inf. Commun. **07**, 110–111 (2013)
8. Weill, P.: The relationship between investment in information technology and firm performance. Inf. Syst. Res. **4**, 307–333 (1992)
9. Peter, E., Zahir, I.: An exploratory study of information technology evaluation and benefits management practices of SMEs in the construction industry. Inf. Manage. **42**, 227–242 (2004)
10. Cui, Z.: Improving the equipment managing level through the constructing the port information. Sci. Technol. Port **05**, 81–83 (2005)
11. Lotfi, A., Faten, B., Aref, M.: In-vehicle augmented reality traffic information system: a new type of communication between driver and vehicle. Procedia Comput. Sci. **73**, 242–249 (2015)
12. Rasheed, H.: Secure and privacy-aware traffic information as a service in VANET-based clouds. Perv. Mob. Comput. **24**(12), 194–209 (2015)

Synergy Development in New Energy Automobile Industry

Zhang Yan[1,2(✉)]

[1] School of Economics, Wuhan University of Technology,
Wuhan 430070, China
zhangyanwy@whut.edu.cn
[2] School of Foreign Languages, Wuhan University of Technology,
Wuhan 430070, China

Abstract. Based on system synergy theory, this paper establishes the diversification synergy measurement model and empirically analyzes the static and dynamic synergy degrees between Ford's traditional motor industry and its new energy automobile industry. Principal component analysis and regression analysis are employed to analyze the annual statements of Ford from 2010 to 2014. The synergy degree indicate that synergy degrees between its traditional motor business and new energy automobile business keep rising stably, which is a sign of its synergic development.

Keywords: Automotive industry · Synergy development · Multivariate statistical analysis

1 Introduction

Since diversification strategy was first proposed by the American scholar H. Igor Ansoff in 1957, the synergy effects of diversification strategy has long been an important subject which draw much attention of scholars and business executives [1]. At present domestic and foreign scholars have carried out extensive research into diversification and synergy relationship and the correlation between corporation performance and the degree of diversification becomes the subject of major research. Goold and Kabiraj et al. [2, 3] summarize diversification strategy synergy of a corporation as Operating Synergy, Managing Synergy and Financial Synergy and synergy effects is one of the main objectives of corporation advocating diversification. Rumelt [4] believes that obtaining synergy effects, seeking the right type of synergy, establishing an appropriate level of synergy and finding high rewarding synergy opportunities are equally important. Xiang [5] discusses the mechanism for identifying high-rewarding synergy opportunities and creating new synergy manner to achieve synergy effects for corporation diversification strategy and to improve its performance. Based on strategic synergy theory, Shou et al. [6] holds that if a corporation whose main business is closely related to the real estate business enter the real estate industry and successfully realize synergy effects, its main business will be benefited by it. Weijie and Yan [7] fully explore the development laws of corporation strategic synergy by in-depth qualitative and quantitative research on selection of synergy path, dynamic

© Springer International Publishing AG 2016
W. Li et al. (Eds.): IDCS 2016, LNCS 9864, pp. 421–429, 2016.
DOI: 10.1007/978-3-319-45940-0_39

synergy mechanism, synergy performance evaluation and synergy risk control, based on the concept of corporation strategic synergy. Zhou [8] advocates information sharing between diversified businesses and impel potential diversified synergy effects by actively managing different businesses increasing interdependence among its synergy costs.

Therefore, this paper intends to analyze the synergy development of new energy automotive industry, and take Ford's diversified strategy as example by means of the diversified financial synergy effects and adopting principal component analysis.

2 Selection and Definition of Indicators

Indicators for development capacity mainly include: sales growth rate, capital maintenance and increment rate, total asset growth rate, net profit growth rate, per capita net income growth rate etc. Growth rate of per capita net income = (the annual per capita net income -) ÷ last year the per capita net income × 100 %. Capital maintenance and appreciation rate, capital maintenance and appreciation rate = (the owners' equity at the end of the year, net of objective factors ÷ the owner's equity at the beginning of the year) × 100 %. Growth rate of total assets The growth rate of total assets = (total assets at the end of the year − total assets at the beginning of the year)÷total assets at the beginning of the year × 100%. Growth rate of net profit, Growth rate of net profit= (net profit for the current year-net profit for the previous year)÷net profit last year × 100%. Growth rate of per capita net profit, Growth rate of per capita net profit = (per capita net profit for the current year − per capita net profit for the previous year) ÷ per capita net profit for the previous year × 100%.

2.1 Overall Development Index of Definition

(1) The Original Data

Table 1 exhibits specific evaluation indicators of Ford while Table 2 reveals the overall evaluation indexes of Ford's overall development after collection and calculation of original data.

Table 1. Parameters required to evaluate development capacity (in millions)

Year	Total sales	Annual owner's equity	Annual total assets	Annual net profit	Annual percapita net profit
2010	198103.91	8912	7731.22	387.98	3.29
2011	204046.09	10783.52	9833.48	445.54	3.33
2012	206096.55	11969.71	17657.33	1037.22	4.91
2013	208559.58	14243.95	20745.10	1809.92	5.31
2014	212938.75	17235.18	25616.34	2139.65	6.23

Table 2. Capacity index of corporation development

Parameter of indicators	2010	2011	2012	2013	2014
Sales growth rate	0.030	0.010	0.012	0.021	0.020
Capital maintenance and appreciation rate	0.21	0.11	0.19	0.21	0.09
Growth rate of total assets	0.27	0.79	0.39	0.17	0.23
Growth rate of net profit	0.15	0.95	1.33	0.74	0.18
Growth rate of per capita net profit	0.01	0.47	0.08	0.15	0.17

2.2 Standardized Processing of Data

Standardized processing of data includes assimilation and non-dimensionalization of data with the purpose of making the effect of data (indexes) of different nature on evaluation programs assimilated and avoiding external influence of different dimensions on evaluation programs. The normalized original data will be mapped to values changing between the interval [0,1], using the default z-score normalization method in SPSS. This kind of normalization is based on the mean and standard deviation of the original data. Z-score normalization will normalize x (the original value of A) to x'. Z-score standardized method applies to the cases that the maximum and minimum values of A are unknown or beyond the range of outlier data. Results are shown in Table 3.

Table 3. Standardized processing of data

Standardized parameter number	Z1	Z2	Z3	Z4	Z5
1	1.05191	1.0574	1.59764	1.74932	2.06394
2	.57363	−.53431	.15078	.22074	.56030
3	−.76452	−.72411	−.69659	−.68915	−.64935
4	−.54783	−.46315	−.54499	−.51909	−.46738
5	−.58384	−.50878	−.43648	−.41174	−.35272

Statistical indicators of data in Table 3 are shown in Table 4.

Table 4. Descriptive statistics

Indexes	Column	Minimum	Maximum	Mean	Deviation
VAR1	20	.00	7731.22	1644.3330	2150.7987
VAR2	20	.00	9833.48	1946.8635	2688.6283
VAR3	20	.00	17657.33	3395.5950	4874.5814
VAR4	20	.00	20745.10	3947.2040	5727.6769
VAR5	20	.00	25616.34	4350.0780	6699.1447

3 Correlation Analysis

The normalized data are put into SPSS system as input data to analyze the correlation of the original data (indexes), the calculation results of which are shown in Table 6. Judging from the correlation coefficients in Table 5, the correlation between indicators of original data Var1, Var2, Var3 and Var4 is relatively large, indicating that the information represented by these five indicators have greater repeatability. It is advisable to further simplify them using principal component analysis.

Table 5. Correlation matrix

Correlation	Zscore (VAR1)	Zscore (VAR2)	Zscore (VAR3)	Zscore (VAR4)	Zscore (VAR5)
Zscore (VAR1)	1.00	.968	.938	.926	.822
Zscore (VAR2)	.968	1.00	.958	.945	.845
Zscore (VAR3)	.938	.958	1.000	.998	.926
Zscore (VAR4)	.926	.945	.998	1.000	.941
Zscore (VAR5)	.822	.845	.926	.941	1.000

It is apparent that principal component analysis is required to calculate characteristic value of coefficient matrix in Table 5. The analysis results of main components determined by characteristic values are displayed in Table 6. In Table 6, the original indexes ZVar1 and ZVar2 are main components, which can be used as new financial indicators to replace the five selected ones, retaining 98.566 % of the original information still.

Table 6. Total variance decomposition

Component	Total	variance %	Cumulative %	Total	Variance %	Cumulative %
1	4.709	94.178	94.178	4.709	94.178	94.178
2	.219	4.388	98.566	.219	4.388	98.566
3	.044	.873	99.439			
4	.027	.548	99.987			
5	.001	.013	100.000			

4 Comprehensive Development Index of Ford

Table 8 is ingredients matrix (factor loading matrix) obtained by using factor analysis. This matrix is the coefficient of the expression of common factors of each original variable, reflecting the impact of the extraction of the common factors on the original variables. In this paper, two factors extracted covers 98.566 % information contained in the original variables. In Table 7, because the load factor coefficient of each variable is greater than 0.5, common factor 1 is mainly influenced by indicator variables Z1, Z2, Z4 and Z5, while common factor 2 is mainly influenced by indicator variables Z2, Z3 and Z5.

Table 7. Ingredients matrix table

Variable	Composition	
	1	2
Z1	.901	.439
Z2	.923	.667
Z3	.388	.798
Z4	.887	.381
Z5	.643	.931

Table 8. Ingredients score coefficient matrix

Variable	Composition	
	1	2
Z1	.799	−.425
Z2	.801	.321
Z3	−.525	.433
Z4	.733	−.601
Z5	.663	.822

Factor score matrix indicates the relationship between the index variables and extracted common factors. The higher the score is in a common factor, the closer the relationship between the index and the common factor is. Factor score matrix can be calculated out by ingredients matrix and principal components (factors) in Table 8. The corresponding factor scores are composition /root eigenvector, i.e. score matrix as shown in Table 8.

To calculate scores of each principal component of observed data, a linear relationship expression between the principal component scores and the original variables can be established using ingredients score coefficient matrix in Table 9. That is:

$$F1 = 0.799 \times Z1 + 0.801 \times Z2 - 0.525 \times Z3 + 0.733 \times Z4 + 0.663 \times Z5 \quad (1)$$

$$F2 = -0.425 \times Z1 + 0.321 \times Z2 + 0.433 \times Z3 - 0.601 \times Z4 + 0.822 \times Z5 \quad (2)$$

In order to further obtain the comprehensive development index of Ford, we take the cumulative contribution of the Eigen values of two common factors, i.e. 0.98556 as 1, then the weight of two corresponding common factors are 0.94178 /0.98556 and 0.04388/0.98556 respectively. Therefore we can work out Ford's comprehensive development index:

$$Fv = F1 \times 0.94178/0.98556 + F2 \times 0.04388/0.98556 \quad (3)$$

Table 9 exhibits Ford's comprehensive development indicators using the above expressions and the corresponding parameter indexes. By the development indexes,

Table 9. Ford's comprehensive development indexes

Year	2010	2011	2012	2013	2014
Index	0.2453	0.9523	1.2783	1.3569	1.9673

Table 10. Development indexes of ford's new energy automobile business

Year	2010	2011	2012	2013	2014
Index	0.0031	0.2989	0.9877	1.0901	1.8762

Ford Motor Company has achieved rapid business growth from 20010 to 2014 with constantly upgrading business diversification and a significant upward comprehensive development.

The development indexes of new energy automobiles by Ford are calculated in the same way as in calculating Ford's comprehensive development indexes. The results are shown in Table 10. According to the development indexes, Ford's new energy automobile business shows a significant upward trend by the time and diversified automotive business achieved five years of rapid growth.

5 Synergy Development Index of Ford Motor Business and New Energy Automotive Industry

Regression analysis will be introduced to this paper to build the model of the relationship between Ford motor business and new energy automobile business. These two businesses will be dependent and independent variables each time. The fit order and fitting accuracy of the model will be determined by comparison between the correction value and F value of the model. Its equations are as follows:

If Ford motor business is taken as independent variable and the new energy automobile business as the dependent variable, the fitting equation is as follows:

$$Y = 0.298 + 0.756x - 0.612x^2 \ \left(R^2 = 0.525, F = 5.450\right) \qquad (4)$$

If the new energy automobile business is taken as independent variable and Ford motor business as the dependent variable, the fitting equation is as follows:

$$Y = 0.825 + 0.795x \ \left(R^2 = 0.565, F = 3.125\right) \qquad (5)$$

To calculate needed coordinated development values, the development indexes of Ford motor business and new energy automobile business will be fitted into the above two equations respectively to obtain coordinated development value A (required by Ford motor business and diversified business) and coordinated development value B (required by Ford new energy automobile business and diversified business). The values of each coordinate are shown in Table 11.

Table 11. Coordinated development values

Year	2010	2011	2012	2013	2014
A	0.2313	0.4891	0.8712	1.2812	1.6219
B	0.1131	0.5218	0.6712	0.9891	1.1398

6 Diversified Synergy Model

The degree of membership of any element "y" on the set "A" can be described by corresponding membership degree function of real numbers in the interval [0, 1]. Accordingly, synergy model is proposed to describe synergic development between systems:

$$V = \exp\left\{\frac{(Y - Y')^2}{S^2}\right\} \tag{6}$$

In the above formula "v" is for the degree of synergy between the diversified businesses for a corporation, "Y" is for the observed value of actual state of a diversified corporation, "Y'" is for synergy value of operating state of diversified businesses, and "S^2" is for variance of indicator variables of diversified businesses for a diversified corporation.

Because there are static and dynamic synergies between diversified businesses for a corporation, a static synergy model can be in the following form:

$$V_S(i,j) = \frac{\min\{v(i,j), v(j,i)\}}{\max\{v(i,j), v(j,i)\}} \tag{7}$$

In the above formula, "$V_S(i,j)$" is for the static synergy degree between the diversified businesses, "i" and "j" is for a diversified corporation, "$v(i,j)$" is for the synergy degree between coordinated development states of diversified businesses "i" and "j". "$v(j,i)$" is for the synergy degree between coordinated development states of diversified businesses "j" and "i".

As for dynamic synergy degree between diversified businesses for a corporation, it can be expressed as:

$$v_d(t) = \frac{1}{T}\sum_{i=0}^{T-1} v_s(t-i) \quad 0 < v_d(t) \leq 1 \tag{8}$$

In the above formula, $v_s(t-T+1)$, $v_s(t-T+2)$, ..., $v_s(t-1)$ and $v_s(t)$ are degrees of synergy for a corporation during the short period $(t-T) \sim t$. $v(i,j), v(j,i), v_s(i,j)$ and $v_d(i,j)$ are calculated out according to the formulae (6), (7), (8), and Corporate Synergy Degree between Motor Business and New Energy Auto Business are shown in Figs. 1 and 2.

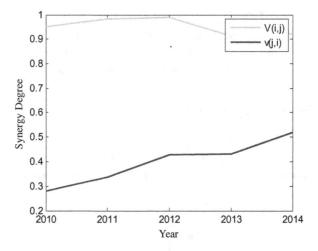

Fig. 1. The synergy degree between coordinated development states of diversified businesses from 2010 to 2014

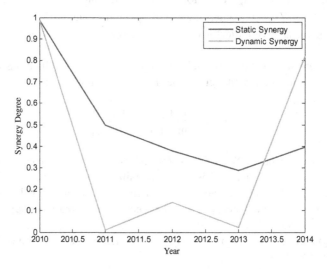

Fig. 2. Synergy curves of ford motor business and new energy auto business from 2010 to 2014

7   Conclusion

This paper proposes a quantitative analysis of synergy effects of automobile corporations advocating diversification strategy, taking Ford Motor Company as the empirical case. We can safely draw the conclusion that synergy development is greatly uncertain between total business and new energy automobile business for auto corporations due to the complexity of diversified corporate businesses. The research results are basically consistent with the facts in terms of synergy development trend from 2010 to 2014 by comparing results of analysis and the actual development of Ford. This is due to the fact that Ford's main automobile business also developed together with the expansion of market share by new energy automobile business. Two kinds of businesses promoted each other and developed side by side. An overall effect was achieved in different aspects of synergic business processes at different stages. By diversified operating synergies and organic collaboration, Ford optimizes its internal resource allocation to maximize the overall synergy effects, making synergy level gradually improved.

References

1. Shen, J.: Synergy effect analysis of the enterprise diversification strategy. Econ. Manage. **23** (2), 49–54 (2009)
2. Goold, M., Luchs, K.: Why diversify? four decades of management thinking. Acad. Manage. Executive **17**(3), 7–25 (1993)
3. Kabiraj, T., Lee, C.C.: Synergy, learning and the changing industrial structure. Int. Econ. J. **18** (3), 365–387 (2004)
4. Rumelt, R.P.: Strategy, Structure and Economic Performance. Harvard University, Cambridge (1974)
5. Lin, X.: Enterprise diversification strategy synergy effect and analysis of its effect on performance. Economist **7**(9), 251–252 (2011)
6. Chen, S., Zeng, D., Yang, Y., Li, C.G.: Diversification strategy synergy effect- a case of study of real estate enterprises. Syst. Eng. **30**(1), 9–14 (2012)
7. Li, W.J., Song, Y.: Synergy of enterprise strategy: theory summary and china practice. Contem. Econ. Manage. **35**(8), 8–15 (2013)
8. Zhou, M.Y.: Synergy, coordination costs and diversification choices. Strat. Manage. **32**(6), 624–639 (2011)

Wireless Sensing
and Controlling Networks

BKR-SIFT: A High-Precise Matching Algorithm

Jiancai Wu[1,2(✉)], Shunyan Wang[1,2], and Wenchi Sun[1,2]

[1] State Key Laboratory of Software Engineering,
Wuhan University, Wuhan, China
{wuxiaofeng,wangsyan,sunwenchi}@whut.edu.cn
[2] School of Computer Science and Technology,
Wuhan University of Technology, Wuhan, China

Abstract. Scaled Invariant Feature Transform (SIFT) is the state-of-the-art local image descriptor for its invariance to image translation, rotation, scaling, and change in illumination. However, its matching precision is not satisfactory in many situations. In this paper, we proposed a more precise matching algorithm—BKR-SIFT. We apply the Best-Bin-First (BBF) algorithm to achieve rough matching firstly. Then, the Kullback-Leibler (KL) divergence similarity score is used as the coarse pruning algorithm. Finally, we apply the Random Sample Consensus (RANSAC) algorithm to refine the matched features furtherly. Experimental results show that our proposed algorithm can reach a higher matching precision with approximately the same time compared to the SIFT.

Keywords: SIFT descriptor · BBF · KL divergence similarity score · RANSAC

1 Introduction

SIFT keypoints are extracted from a series of Difference-of-Gaussian (DOG) images at continuous increasing scales and then they're depicted based on the gradient distributions in the detected regions after which they're normalized to form the 128-dimensional descriptor vectors. Each keypoint contains three properties: scale, orientation and location, all of which make it invariant to image translation, rotation, scaling and change in illumination.

As the development of Computer Vision, SIFT has been applied into more extensive applications, such as object recognition, image registration, robot map perception and navigation and the requirements of the performance precision become higher and higher. As a result, more and more researchers and experts have focused their attention on this hot area and put forward their theories. Alaa E. Abdel-Hakim and Aly A. Farag utilized the color information of the images and proposed CSIFT in [1]. The SIFT descriptor in a color invariant space made it more robust with respect to color and photometrical variations. In [2], a robust image matching technique based on the combination of wavelet transform and Colour-SIFT was presented. In the paper, low frequency and High frequency sub-bands of the image were extracted using wavelet transform after which colour SIFT method was used to extract colour feature

W. Li et al. (Eds.): IDCS 2016, LNCS 9864, pp. 433–445, 2016.
DOI: 10.1007/978-3-319-45940-0_40

descriptors and they claimed that their method got a higher accuracy than the hue-SIFT. In [3], Zhouxin Yang and Takio Kurita broached a scheme to improve the performance of SIFT's descriptor and proposed the BOF-driven SIFT. They established the connection between SIFT and bag of features (BOF) model in descriptor construction and then introduced BOF approaches into SIFT to enhance its robustness. In the paper, they declared that their algorithm consistently outperformed the original SIFT.

2 Related Work

The works mentioned above were all attempted to improve the robustness of the SIFT descriptors. In fact, SIFT has been proven to be the most robust local image descriptor with respect to different geometrical distortions [4]. The descriptor itself is robust enough to be component for various situations. Therefore, our goal is not to improve the descriptor but to refine the matching points in the matching stage. In [5], J. Li and G. Wang proposed an improved SIFT matching algorithm based on geometric similarity. They assumed that there existed a constant similarity ration for correct matches and, based on it, they eliminated false matching points which did not meet this condition. In [6], W. Zhu et al. utilized adaptive threshold and the weighted least square to reduce the outliers and to get a better precision. The most similar theory to our work was proposed in [7]. They applied the principal components analysis (PCA) on two sets of SIFT features of images and used the BBF and the Nearest Neighbor algorithm to find a coarse matching between them in the matching stage. Finally, they used the Kullback-Leibler (KL) divergence similarity score to prune the mismatched features. In the paper, they alleged that their proposed technique could reduce the computational time with approximately the same average precision compared to the conventional SIFT. However, in our studies, we found that their method could cut a lot of computational time indeed, but its accuracy performances are barely satisfactory and we will present its results in the experimental stage.

The rest of the paper is organized as follows: Sect. 3 introduces our algorithm in details and analyzes the reasons why our method can reach a higher accuracy performance. Section 4 presents the experiment results. Finally, we summarize the total works in Sect. 5.

3 The Proposed Algorithm

In our method, we utilize the SIFT algorithm to extract the original features and then we apply the BBF algorithm to obtain the preliminary matched features, which returns the closest neighbor with high probability and provides a significant speedup over exact nearest neighbor search [8]. After that, we adopt the KL-divergence similarity score to prune the mismatches coarsely. Finally, RANSAC algorithm will be used to refine the matched features. As a result, the precision performance has been greatly improved. The main steps of our proposed algorithm are illustrated in the following contents.

A. Keypoint Extraction and Description

In our method, the extraction and description of the features are the same as SIFT algorithm. They consist of four major steps [8]:

1. Scale-space extrema detection using DOG function.
2. Keypoint localization.
3. Orientation assignment based on local image gradient directions.
4. Generating keypoint descriptors.

B. Initial Matching and Coarse Purification

After generating the keypoint descriptors, we apply the BBF algorithm to achieve the initial matching. BBF is an approximate algorithm that uses a modified search ordering for the k-d tree algorithm so that it returns the closest neighbor with high probability and less computational time.

In our implementation, we cut off further search after checking the first 2 nearest-neighbor candidates. Given two set of keypoints $X = \{X_1, X_2, ..., X_n\}$, $Y = \{Y_1, Y_2, ..., Y_m\}$, where $X_i, Y_i \in R^{128}$, X presents the keypoint of the reference image and Y presents the keypoint of the template one. m, n is the number of the keypoints. The descriptors of X_i, Y_j can be depicted as $X_i = \{X_1^i, X_2^i, \cdots, X_{128}^i\}$, $Y_i = \{Y_1^i, Y_2^i, \cdots, Y_{128}^i\}$. The distance of two keypoints can be defined as:

$$d(X_i, Y_j) = \left[\sum_{k=1}^{128} (x_k^i - y_k^i)^2\right]^{1/2} \tag{1}$$

Then the nearest-neighbor candidate of X_i can be accepted as follows:

$$d(X_i, Y_j)/d(X_i, Y_k) < \text{ratio} \tag{2}$$

where Y_j, Y_k represents the nearest neighbor and the second nearest neighbor. The ratio in this paper is 0.7.

Since initial matches have been obtained, we implement the KL-divergence similarity score algorithm on them. The Kullback-Leibler divergence is defined as:

$$D_{kl}(X_i \parallel Y_j) = \sum_{K=1}^{128} x_k^i \ln(\frac{x_k^i}{y_k^i}) \tag{3}$$

KL-divergence is a measure of the difference between two probability distributions X_i and Y_j. If the match is correct, the distribution of the two keypoint will be same or similar. And the more similar they are, the smaller $D_{kl}(X_i \parallel Y_j)$ will be. Thus it can be used as the measure of judging similarity. However it's not symmetric and can not be used as distance measure yet. So we give the symmetric version of it:

$$D_{kl}(X_i, Y_j) = \frac{D_{kl}(X_i \parallel Y_j) + D_{kl}(Y_j \parallel X_i)}{2} \tag{4}$$

Therefore, the symmetric version of KL-divergence can be used as the distance measure of two keypoint vectors [7, 9]. The KL-divergence similarity score is defined as:

$$\text{Score} = \exp = \left(-\frac{D_{kl}(X_i, Y_j)}{2\alpha^2} \right) \tag{5}$$

Before computing the KL-divergence similarity score, each matched keypoint vector is normalized as suggested in [7]. The selection of α is automatic and it will be presented in Sect. 4. Then the KL-divergence similarity score can be used as a measure to pruning the mismatched features.

The selection of α is according to the initial numbers of the matched keypoints. Then, the similarity scores between reference keypoints and the template ones are computed using the equation above. If the score is smaller than a threshold, the matched keypoints will be accepted. The threshold will be presented in Sect. 4.

C. RANSAC Refinement

Although only parts of the mismatches can be discarded by the KL-divergence measure, it's essential since the RANSAC will perform poorly when the percentage of outliers exceeds 50 % [8]. And the KL-divergence measure can keep the matches amount in a proper scope, which will cut down a lot of computational time for RANSAC algorithm. Then, the RANSAC algorithm is implemented on the coarsely purified matches.

In the RANSAC refinement stage, at least 4 matched keypoints should be supplied in order to obtain the correct inliers. We use the least squares method to obtain the least-squares planar homography matrix, which transforms keypoints in the reference images to their corresponding keypoints in the template ones. Then the matrix is used to calculate the transfer error between a keypoint and its correspondence. If the error calculated is smaller than a given threshold, the keypoint will be added into a consensus set. We will obtain some consensus sets in the process and the one contains the most numbers of keypoints will be kept, which is considered the correct one. At the end, the RANSAC algorithm will output the finally matched features.

After two steps of refinement, the accuracy performances of our method are improved significantly.

4 Experimental Results

All of the algorithms in this paper are implemented in C++ on the computer with Intel i7-4700HQ, 2.4 GHZ, 8 G memory. Programming is based on opencv2.4.11 under windows system.

The selection of α in the KL-divergence similarity score measure is automatic based on the initial numbers of matches. Table 1 shows the selection of α.

Another threshold for the KL-divergence similarity score is 0.0075. All the parameters are chosen experimentally.

Table 1. The selection of α

The amount of initial matches (n)	$0 \leq n < 1000$	$1000 \leq n < 3000$	$3000 \leq n$
α	0.09	0.12	0.23

Fig. 1. Images of the dataset

In order to ensure the authenticity, the experimental images are all from the popular Mikolajczyk dataset [11]. This dataset contains eight different groups of images and each group contains 6 images. The images differ in viewpoint, rotation, zoom, illumination and blurriness. Figure 1 shows images of the dataset (the template one of each group).

We adopt the average matching precision (AMP) and average ratio of the matching time (ARMT) to present the accuracy performance and the run time of the algorithm [10]. The AMP and ARMT are calculated as follows:

$$AMP = \frac{\text{the number of correct matched points}}{\text{the number of total matched points}} \tag{6}$$

$$ARMT = \frac{\text{the matching time of one algorithm}}{\text{the matching time of SIFT algorithm}} \tag{7}$$

The result of our proposed algorithm is compared with original SIFT, BSIFT [7], SURF and ASIFT. The fixed 80 % PCA energy level is kept for BSIFT as suggested in [7] and the BBF algorithm is used in the matching stage in ASIFT algorithm which will accelerate it. For each group, images are assigned the number from I1 to I6 (I1 is the template image and the others are reference images) and, for every image, we repeated the experiment 20 times and averaged the results. The number of total matches, correct matches and the accuracy performances of the 5 algorithms are listed in Tables 2, 3, 4, 5, 6, 7, 8 and 9.

In these tables, the rows with gray color show the accuracy performances of the 5 algorithms. It can be easily found that our algorithm has achieved great improvement compared to the original SIFT. We have also noticed that the number of matches, correct matches in our algorithm are close to the number of correct matches in SIFT, which reflects that the most matches discarded by our algorithm are mismatches.

Table 2. The results of bark

bark		I1~I2	I1~I3	I1~I4	I1~I5	I1~I6
SIFT	matches	655	605	818	516	271
	correct matches	430	303	505	257	204
	accuracy	65.65%	50.08%	61.74%	49.81%	75.28%
BKR-SIFT	matches	435	293	406	271	123
	correct matches	385	293	396	228	123
	accuracy	88.51%	100%	97.54%	84.13%	100%
BSIFT	matches	1270	1241	1286	1423	1534
	correct matches	40	0	9	51	13
	accuracy	3.15%	0.00%	0.70%	3.58%	0.85%
SURF	matches	395	250	220	244	121
	correct matches	281	152	114	85	35
	accuracy	71.14%	60.80%	51.82%	34.84%	28.93%
ASIFT	matches	4420	1313	1070	430	233
	correct matches	4199	0	0	0	0
	accuracy	95.00%	0.00%	0.00%	0.00%	0.00%

Table 3. The results of bikes

bikes		I1~I2	I1~I3	I1~I4	I1~I5	I1~I6
SIFT	matches	953	706	427	316	258
	correct matches	866	624	372	253	191
	accuracy	90.87%	88.39%	87.12%	80.06%	74.03%
BKR-SIFT	matches	713	522	332	224	183
	correct matches	710	520	327	219	174
	accuracy	99.58%	99.62%	98.49%	97.77%	95.08%
BSIFT	matches	567	747	1095	1385	1611
	correct matches	2	3	43	64	76
	accuracy	0.35%	0.40%	3.93%	4.62%	4.72%
SURF	matches	1538	1338	1039	867	667
	correct matches	1154	930	580	416	300
	accuracy	75.03%	69.51%	55.82%	47.98%	44.98%
ASIFT	matches	17875	17137	13924	11562	9007
	correct matches	17863	17113	13895	11528	8966
	accuracy	99.93%	99.86%	99.79%	99.71%	99.54%

Table 4. The results of boat

boat		I1~I2	I1~I3	I1~I4	I1~I5	I1~I6
SIFT	matches	2017	1604	586	401	123
	correct matches	1582	839	292	202	44
	accuracy	78.43%	52.31%	49.83%	50.37%	35.77%
BKR-SIFT	matches	1556	754	277	214	43
	correct matches	1412	752	276	185	26
	accuracy	90.75%	99.73%	99.64%	86.45%	60.47%
BSIFT	matches	1786	2101	2495	2486	2818
	correct matches	5	11	17	21	8
	accuracy	0.28%	0.52%	0.68%	0.84%	0.28%
SURF	matches	2699	1987	1734	1703	1206
	correct matches	1348	745	400	195	27
	accuracy	49.94%	37.49%	23.07%	11.45%	2.24%
ASIFT	matches	9500	5101	2664	1944	193
	correct matches	9066	0	1	1	0
	accuracy	95.43%	0	0.04%	0.05%	0

Table 5. The results of graffiti

graffiti		I1~I2	I1~I3	I1~I4	I1~I5	I1~I6
SIFT	matches	1059	388	86	61	20
	correct matches	735	180	28	6	1
	accuracy	69.41%	46.39%	32.56%	9.84%	5%
BKR-SIFT	matches	714	211	36	1	4
	correct matches	648	171	31	0	0
	accuracy	90.76%	81.04%	86.11%	0.00%	0.00%
BSIFT	matches	298	376	486	590	617
	correct matches	4	17	12	0	0
	accuracy	1.34%	4.52%	2.47%	0.00%	0.00%
SURF	matches	1361	1100	835	774	771
	correct matches	699	258	40	12	20
	accuracy	51.36%	23.45%	4.79%	1.55%	2.59%
ASIFT	matches	7651	5158	3693	2068	1073
	correct matches	7531	4719	495	9	2
	accuracy	98.43%	91.49%	13.40%	0.44%	0.19%

Table 6. The results of leuven

leuven		I1~I2	I1~I3	I1~I4	I1~I5	I1~I6
SIFT	matches	1219	994	810	621	482
	correct matches	1175	955	770	582	430
	accuracy	96.39%	96.08%	95.06%	93.72%	89.21%
BKR-SIFT	matches	748	886	758	580	428
	correct matches	746	883	755	580	422
	accuracy	99.73%	99.66%	99.60%	100%	98.60%
BSIFT	matches	450	554	618	699	828
	correct matches	17	15	8	33	27
	accuracy	3.78%	2.71%	1.29%	4.72%	3.26%
SURF	matches	1555	1351	1404	1348	1348
	correct matches	1171	888	712	491	320
	accuracy	75.31%	65.73%	50.71%	36.42%	23.74%
ASIFT	matches	13783	10348	7661	5442	3655
	correct matches	13770	10323	7633	5394	3607
	accuracy	99.91%	99.76%	99.63%	99.12%	98.69%

Table 7. The results of trees

trees		I1~I2	I1~I3	I1~I4	I1~I5	I1~I6
SIFT	matches	1351	1108	415	278	132
	correct matches	1303	1065	380	243	114
	accuracy	96.45%	96.12%	91.57%	87.41%	86.36%
BKR-SIFT	matches	1142	921	346	220	99
	correct matches	1138	921	345	218	98
	accuracy	99.65%	100%	99.71%	99.09%	98.99%
BSIFT	matches	3386	2934	3726	4617	5697
	correct matches	40	46	52	137	200
	accuracy	1.18%	1.57%	1.40%	2.97%	3.51%
SURF	matches	2386	2279	961	1352	2475
	correct matches	1339	1065	518	289	53
	accuracy	56.12%	46.73%	53.90%	21.38%	3.44%
ASIFT	matches	15603	12888	9004	6197	3485
	correct matches	15597	12873	8986	6173	3470
	accuracy	99.96%	99.88%	99.80%	99.61%	99.57%

Table 8. The results of ubc

ubc		I1~I2	I1~I3	I1~I4	I1~I5	I1~I6
SIFT	matches	2703	2043	1119	541	238
	correct matches	2669	1977	1072	506	215
	accuracy	98.74%	96.77%	95.80%	93.53%	90.34%
BKR-SIFT	matches	1541	1339	816	466	208
	correct matches	1501	1339	811	459	206
	accuracy	97.40%	100%	99.39%	98.50%	99.04%
BSIFT	matches	871	1016	1342	1797	2254
	correct matches	3	4	7	14	42
	accuracy	0.34%	0.39%	0.52%	0.78%	1.86%
SURF	matches	2475	2470	1961	2186	1924
	correct matches	2223	1982	1512	1106	594
	accuracy	89.82%	80.24%	77.10%	50.59%	30.87%
ASIFT	matches	30492	28788	25111	17937	11395
	correct matches	30483	28782	25102	17919	11354
	accuracy	99.97%	99.98%	99.96%	99.90%	99.64%

Table 9. The results of wall

wall		I1~I2	I1~I3	I1~I4	I1~I5	I1~I6
SIFT	matches	4988	3548	1553	246	10
	correct matches	4733	3273	1359	220	7
	accuracy	94.89%	92.25%	87.51%	89.43%	70%
BKR - SIFT	matches	1589	1936	1297	217	0
	correct matches	1586	1928	1258	215	0
	accuracy	99.81%	99.59%	96.99%	99.08%	0.00%
BSIFT	matches	1492	1910	2337	2739	3021
	correct matches	20	37	24	28	0
	accuracy	1.34%	1.94%	1.03%	1.02%	0.00%
SURF	matches	2528	1889	1332	431	508
	correct matches	2146	1456	766	201	14
	accuracy	84.89%	77.08%	57.51%	46.64%	2.76%
ASIFT	matches	21622	13374	6442	3579	1365
	correct matches	21619	13372	6441	1135	520
	accuracy	99.99%	99.99%	99.98%	31.71%	38.10%

In Tables 5 ($I1 \sim I5, I1 \sim I6$) and 9 ($I1 \sim I6$), the rotation angles of the images (graffiti I5, graffiti I6, wall I6) are too large so that the number of initial matches is less than 100(in fact only 69, 36, 13 matches respectively) and the percentage of outliers exceeds 50 %. In the case the initial matches is too little, the KL-divergence similarity score pruning stage won't discard too much matches, which results in the failure of the RANSAC purification stage. And we have seen that the accuracy performances of our algorithm in these situations are 0.00 %. It's a deficiency of our algorithm and we will improve it in the future work. When it comes to the BSIFT, we have found that the accuracy performances are barely satisfactory. Although it can accelerate the matching stage, the usage of PCA will lead to the loss in accuracy. From the tables, we can see that in some cases the matches of BSIFT are far more than the other algorithms. This is because the ratio of the nearest neighbor and second nearest neighbor in BSIFT is larger than the other ones as suggested in [7]. The accuracy performances of SURF are not very well. In many cases it could barely reach half of the accuracy compared to our algorithm. But in the cases that exist viewpoint changes, the matching accuracy of it is a little higher than ours, for example in Tables 5 ($I1 \sim I5, I1 \sim I6$) and 9 ($I1 \sim I6$). The accuracy performances of ASIFT are almost as high as ours in most cases. But in the cases that exist zoom and rotation, the performances of it are barely satisfactory. In fact, in Tables 2 ($I1 \sim I3$, $I1 \sim I4$, $I1 \sim I5$, $I1 \sim I6$) and 4 ($I1 \sim I3$, $I1 \sim I6$) the accuracy is 0.00 %, which means the ASIFT algorithm is not robust to the zoom and rotation. In the cases that exist viewpoint changes the matching accuracy of it is also a little higher than ours.

Figure 2 shows the matching accuracy of the SIFT, BKR-SIFT, BSIFT, SURF and ASIFT of the bikes images. In these couples of images, the crossed lines present the mismatches. Figure 2(a) shows the matching accuracy of SIFT. In the image, we can see dozens of mismatches. Figure 2(b) shows the matching accuracy of BKR-SIFT and we could hardly see any mismatches. On the contrary, we could barely find any correct matches in Fig. 2(c) which presents the matching accuracy of BSIFT. Figure 2(d) presents the matching accuracy of SURF and we can see that the result of SURF is not as well as ours. Figure 2(e) presents the matching accuracy of ASIFT and we could barely see any crossed lines, which means there exist little mismatches.

Figure 3(a) $\sim$ (h) show the ARMT of SIFT, BKR-SIFT, BSIFT, SURF and ASIFT of the eight groups of images.

From Fig. 3(a) $\sim$ (h), we can see that the running time of our algorithm is less than SIFT in about half of the situations. In these situations, the detected keypoints of the images are much more than the others but the percentage of correct matches is lower. Therefore, the effect of using BBF algorithm will be significant since the BBF algorithm can accelerate the process of matching. In addition, the KL-d divergence method will discard parts of the mismatches which leaves a small amount of matches for the RANSAC algorithm and makes it run faster. For the other half of the situations, the running time of our algorithm is more than SIFT but in most cases the range of the ratio is from 1 to 1.3. In fact, the average running time of our algorithm is just 1.02 times to the SIFT.

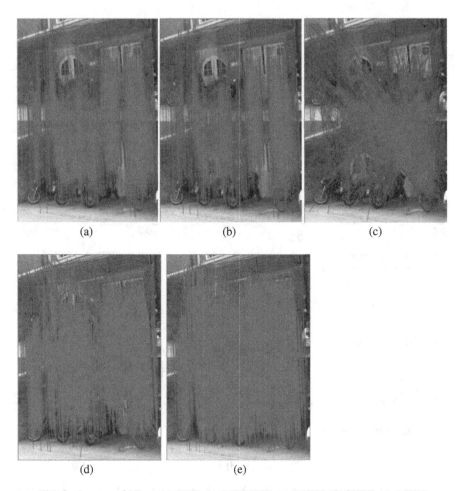

Fig. 2. Images of bikes. (a) SIFT (b) BKR-SIFT (c) BSIFT (d) SURF (e) ASIFT

We can also see that the running time of BSIFT is less than SIFT in most cases. This is because the usage of PCA algorithm will cut down a lot of computational time for BSIFT. Unfortunately, the accuracy performances of BSIFT are too low.

The running time of SURF is about 7 % of the SIFT. This is because the SURF algorithm adopts the faster keypoint detector and descriptor, which greatly frustrates the accuracy performances.

The running time of ASIFT is roughly the same as ours, as well as the accuracy performances. However, the running time of it would be longer if we don't use the BBF algorithm in the matching stage.

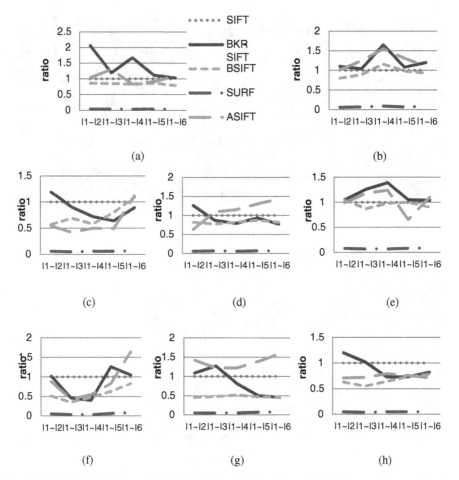

Fig. 3. ARMT of the images. (a) bark (b) bikes (c) boat (d) graffiti (e) leuven (f) trees (g) ubc (h) wall

5 Conclusion

SIFT is the state-of-the-art local image descriptor for its invariance to image distortions but it's not satisfactory in some situations. In this paper, we proposed a BKR-SIFT algorithm and achieved significant accuracy improvement. We use the BBF algorithm to accomplish the initial matching which cut down a lot of computational time. After that, we adopt the KL-divergence similarity score measure to discard parts of the outliers that makes contributions to the later step. Finally, we used the well-known RANSAC algorithm to refine the matches. Experimental results show that the proposed algorithm can effectively eliminate the mismatches with almost the same time as SIFT and therefore reach a high accuracy performance.

Acknowledgments. This research is supported by the Project (SKLSE2012-09-42) of State Key Laboratory of Software Engineering, Wuhan University, Wuhan, China.

References

1. Abdel-Hakim, A.E., Farag, A.A.: CSIFT: a SIFT descriptor with color invariant characteristics. In: 2006 IEEE Computer Society Conference on Computer Vision and Pattern Recognition, pp. 1978–1983 (2006)
2. Kumar, N.A.M., Sathidevi, P.S.: Image match using Wavelet-colour SIFT features. In: 7th IEEE International Conference on Industrial and Information System, pp. 1–6 (2012)
3. Yang, Z., Kurita, T.: Improvements to the descriptor of SIFT by BOF approaches. In: 2013 2nd IAPR Asian Conference on Pattern Recognition, pp. 95–99 (2013)
4. Mikolajczyk, K., Schmid, C.: A performance evaluation of local descriptors. IEEE Trans. Pattern Anal. Mach. Intell. **27**, 1615–1630 (2005)
5. Li, J., Wang, G.: An improved SIFT matching algorithm based on geometric similarity. In: 2015 5th International Conference on Electronics Information and Emergency Communication (ICEIEC), pp. 16–19 (2015)
6. Zhu, W., Jiang, Y., Wang, M., Lai, C.H.: Weighted least squares based improved SIFT matching algorithm. In: 2012 5th International Congress on Image and Signal Processing (CISP), pp. 500–504 (2012)
7. Fotouhi, M., Kasaei, S., Mirsadeghi, S.E., Faez, K.: BSIFT: boosting SIFT using principal component analysis. In: 2014 22nd Iranian Conference on Electrical Engineering (ICEE), pp. 1130–1135 (2014)
8. Lowe, D.G.: Distinctive image features from scale-invariant keypoints. Int. J. Comput. Vis. **60**, 91–110 (2004)
9. Johnson, D.H., Sinanovic, S.: Symmetrizing the Kullback-Leibler distance. IEEE Trans. Inf. Theor. **18**, 96–99 (2003)
10. Xiao, P., Cai, N., Tang, B., Weng, S.W., Wang, H.: Efficient SIFT descriptor via color quantization. In: 2014 IEEE International Conference on Consumer Electronics, pp. 1–3 (2014)
11. Mikolajczyk dataset for images information. http://www.robots.ox.ac.uk/~vgg/research/affine/index.html

Moving Object Detection for Driving Assistance System Based on Improved ORB Feature Matching

Jun Gao[(✉)] and Honghui Zhu[(✉)]

School of Logistics Engineering, Wuhan University of Technology,
Wuhan 430063, China
gaojun407104739@163.com, zhuhonghui@whut.edu.cn

Abstract. In order to overcome the shortcoming of origin feature matching and extract moving objects accurately for real-time driving assistance system. We present a novel moving object detection method based on improved ORB. Firstly, The ORB is used to extract and match feature points. Secondly, we establish an improved Feature Matching Optimization Strategy to remove the mismatched pairs more efficiently. Then differential multiplication and morphology processing are used to accurately segment the moving objects. Finally, a Driving Impact Degree Alarm Mechanism is proposed to give the driver an early warning to take braking measures. Experimental results show that the accuracy of feature matching could be increased to 97 % by our method and the processing speed is fast enough to meet the requirements for real-time driving assistance system. It also has certain advantages in dealing with noise suppression.

Keywords: Differential multiplication · Driving assistance system · Moving object detection · ORB

1 Introduction

Moving objects detection plays a very important role in many vision applications with the purpose of subtracting interesting target area and locating the moving objects from image sequences. It is widely used in vision systems such as traffic control, video surveillance, driver assistance, object recognition, object tracking and behavior understanding. The most challenging part of moving objects detection for driving assistance system is that motion induced by camera moving may dominate the observed motion, which makes existing methods cannot detect the real moving objects from the dynamic background robustly and computationally efficient. In order to continue to use the concept of moving object detection under the static scene. Firstly, we need to calculate the background motion model, compensating background activity for motion estimation. Then we can segment moving objects accurately through post-processing.

The block matching method [1], transform domain matching method [2] and feature points matching method are the common method for motion compensation. Among them, feature matching method has certain advantages in dealing with translation, rotation and scaling changes in image registration. In recent years, many feature matching methods have been proposed. Such as FAST and its variants [3, 4]. It is the method of

© Springer International Publishing AG 2016
W. Li et al. (Eds.): IDCS 2016, LNCS 9864, pp. 446–457, 2016.
DOI: 10.1007/978-3-319-45940-0_41

choice for finding keypoints in real-time systems that match visual features, for example, Parallel Tracking and Mapping. It is efficient and finds reasonable corner keypoints, although it must be augmented with pyramid schemes for scale [5]. Many keypoint detectors include an orientation operator (SIFT and SURF are two prominent examples), but FAST does not. The SIFT keypoint detector and descriptor [6], although over a decade old, have proven remarkably successful in a number of applications using visual features, including object recognition [6] and image stitching [7]. However, it imposes a large computational burden, especially for real-time systems such as visual odometry, or for low-power devices such as cell phones. This has led to an intensive search for replacements with lower computation cost, arguably the best of these is SURF [8]. BRIEF [9] is a recent feature descriptor that uses simple binary tests between pixels in a smoothed image patch. Its performance is similar to SIFT in many respects, including robustness to lighting, blur and perspective distortion. However, it is very sensitive to in-plane rotation. Rublee et al. [10] proposed a very fast binary descriptor based on BRIEF, called ORB (Oriented FAST and Rotated BRIEF) recently, which is rotation invariant and resistant to noise.

However there would be many mismatched pairs appeared by using the origin feature matching method. If lots of mismatched points are introduced to the process of motion estimation, it would affect the accuracy of moving objects detection under driving environment greatly.

In this paper, in order to overcome the shortcoming of origin feature matching and provide accurate silhouette with good spatial and temporal consistency, we present a novel moving object detection method with a real-time performance based on improved ORB. The improvement of our ORB algorithm are mainly as follow: (1) The ORB is used to extract and match feature points. (2) An improved Feature Matching Optimization Strategy is proposed to remove the mismatched pairs more efficiently. (3) Differential multiplication and morphology processing are used to accurately segment the moving objects in the video of Car DVR. (4) A Driving Impact Degree Alarm Mechanism is proposed to give the driver an early warning to take braking measures.

2 ORB Feature Extraction and Matching

ORB is built on the well-known FAST keypoint detector and the BRIEF descriptor. The experiments in papers [10, 11] have shown that ORB is at one or two orders of magnitude faster than SURF and SIFT. Therefore, the ORB is used to solve the problem of feature matching for real-time driving environment between consecutive frames in this paper.

2.1 Oriented FAST

ORB starts by detecting FAST feature points in the image, then adds orientation information for each detected feature points, called Oriented FAST. FAST features are widely used because of their computational properties. However, there are some deficiencies of Fast features: (1) FAST does not produce a measure of cornerness, and it has large responses along edges. (2) FAST features do not have an orientation component. In order to overcome the shortcoming of FAST features, ORB has proposed the following improvement: (1) To make sure that the feature points can adapt to illumination changes, it first sets the threshold low enough to get more than n keypoints, then order them according to the Harris measure, and pick the top n points. (2) In order to allow FAST to be invariant to scale feature, it employs a scale pyramid of the image, and produce FAST features (filtered by Harris) at each level in the pyramid. (3) In order to allow FAST to be invariant to orientation, it uses the intensity centroid which assumes a corner's intensity is offset from its center, and this vector may be used to impute an orientation. With the direction of feature points, we can extract the ORB descriptors according to it.

Rosin defines the moments of a patch as [12]:

$$m_{pg} = \sum_{x,y} x^p y^q I(x, y) \tag{1}$$

and with these moments we may find the centroid:

$$C = (\frac{m_{10}}{m_{00}}, \frac{m_{01}}{m_{00}}) \tag{2}$$

We can construct a vector from the corner's center O, to the centroid $\overrightarrow{OC}$. The orientation of the patch then simply is:

$$\theta = atan2(m_{01}, m_{10}) \tag{3}$$

2.2   Rotated BRIEF

ORB introduces a steered BRIEF descriptor to describe the detected feature points. The BRIEF descriptor is a bit string description of an image patch constructed from a set of binary intensity tests. The feature is defined as a vector of n binary tests. ORB chooses the Gaussian distribution around the center of the patch and a vector length $n = 256$. Since BRIEF compares the value of pixels and it is very sensitive to random noise. So it's important to smooth the image before performing the tests. In ORB implementation, smoothing is achieved using an integral image, where each test point is a 5×5 subwindow of a 31×31 pixel patch, which can suppress the interference of the random noise effectively. BRIEF is non-directional, in order to allow BRIEF to be invariant to in-plane rotation, ORB has proposed the following improvement: For any feature set of n binary tests at location (x_i, y_i), define the $2 \times n$ matrix:

$$S = \begin{pmatrix} x_1 & x_2 & \cdots & x_n \\ y_1 & y_2 & \cdots & y_n \end{pmatrix}$$

Using the patch orientation θ and the corresponding rotation matrix R_θ, then we construct a steered version $S_\theta = R_\theta S$. Then the steered BRIEF operator becomes $g_n(p, \theta) := f_n(p)|(x_i, y_i) \in S_\theta$. Finally ORB uses the greedy search algorithm to select 256 pairs of pixels with low correlation for feature description.

2.3 ORB Feature Matching

Through calculating the hamming distance $D_{S1,S2}$ of feature vector between each feature points in frame 2 and the corresponding feature points in frame 1, we can get the degree of similarity of the two ORB feature descriptors. It also help us to establish the correspondence of feature points between consecutive frames. The larger the value of $D_{S1,S2}$, the lower the degree of similarity of corresponding feature points will be. Otherwise, the higher the degree of similarity of corresponding feature points will be, which means the corresponding feature points between consecutive frames are the feature matching pairs. The performance of ORB feature matching between consecutive frames in the video of Car DVR is demonstrated by Fig. 1.

Fig. 1. The performance of ORB feature matching

3 Improved Feature Matching Optimization Strategy

As shown in Fig. 1, the matching method based on exhaustive search has not considered whether two feature points are belonged to the same area. Therefore, it contains a lot of mismatched pairs. And the more feature points get together, the higher chance of mismatched pairs will be appeared. If lots of mismatched points are introduced in the process of motion estimation, it would affect the accuracy of moving objects detection under driving environment greatly. In order to solve this problem and remove the mismatched pairs effectively. We establish an improved Feature Matching Optimization Strategy for driving assistance system. Firstly, we set a VFR (Vehicle Feasible Region) to remove the useless background information and the matching pairs outside this region as much as possible. Secondly, we proposed an improved BBF (Best Bin First) algorithm based on bidirectional matching to make a preliminary screening for feature matching in the VFR. Finally, the PROSAC (Progressive Sample Consensus) algorithm is used to make a secondary optimization screening. The experiments in Sect. 5 show that our strategy have a faster speed of removing the mismatched pairs than traditional RANSAC algorithm, it's more suitable for real-time moving objects detection.

3.1 Vehicle Feasible Region (VFR)

Video sequences which collected by Car DVR would have a complex background information. In order to reduce the amount of CPU computing and accelerate the real-time processing speed, we should remove the useless background information as much as possible. After analysis the video images for driving environment, we can find that the obstacles are usually concentrated in front of the vehicle and the Vehicle Feasible Region we need to detect is only about 1/3 of the whole images. The VFR for driving environment is generally shaped in triangular, which both sides of the area converge to a point in front and the bottom is slightly wider than the vehicle. Because the visual depth of Car DVR is about 100 m [13]. After amputating the part which exceeds 100 m, the VFR turns into a trapezoidal area which has a narrow top as shown in Fig. 2. By analysis the VFR, we can judge whether the road environment is safe for driving.

Fig. 2. Set the VFR in video sequences

3.2 Feature Matching Optimization: Removing the Mismatched Pairs

(1) An Improved BBF Algorithm. For high-dimensional data, the search efficiency will be poor if we use origin k-d tree algorithm. It's more like an exhaustive search method because most of the nodes will be accessed and compared. BBF is a new variant of the k-d tree search algorithm that makes indexing in higher dimensional spaces practical. The BBF search is an approximate algorithm which finds the nearest neighbour for a large fraction of the queries, and a very close neighbour in the remaining cases. Considering the real-time demand of driving environment, we proposed an improved BBF algorithm to make a preliminary screening for feature matching.

The steps of our improved BBF algorithm can be briefly summarized as follows: (1) For each feature points in frame 2, the KNN(K-Nearest Neighbour) algorithm is used to find the nearest neighbour feature points, and a very close neighbour feature points in the remaining points in frame 1 ($k = 2$). R means the ratio of nearest neighbor distance to next nearest neighbor distance, which represents the quality of feature matching pairs. Set a threshold T_R. If $R < T_R$, then the matching pairs have been found correctly. Set A is used to collect the feature matching pairs we finally get. (2) For each feature points in frame 1, the KNN algorithm is used to find the nearest neighbour feature points, and a very close neighbour feature points in the remaining points in frame 2. Then follow the step (1) to remove the mismatched points. Set B is used to collect the feature matching pairs we finally get. (3) Traverse each element in the set first. If any matching pair in set A, we can find a corresponding matching pair in set B, then we keep this matching pair in set C. Through the bidirectional matching from step (1) and (2), we can get the results of preliminary screening in set C. In this paper, we set $T_R = 0.58$ can guarantee the accuracy of bidirectional matching.

(2) PROSAC Algorithm. PROSAC is an improved RANSAC algorithm, and the robustness and computational efficiency is much better than RANSAC algorithm. The PROSAC algorithm exploits the linear ordering defined on the set of correspondences by a similarity function used in establishing tentative correspondences. Unlike RANSAC, which treats all correspondences equally and draws random samples uniformly from the full set, PROSAC samples are drawn from progressively larger sets of top-ranked correspondences. In this paper, the PROSAC algorithm is used to make a secondary screening after we obtain the feature matching pairs from step (1). The performance of removing the mismatched points in VFR by our proposed optimization strategy is demonstrated by Fig. 3.

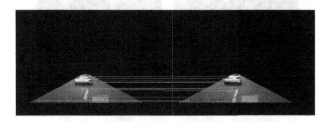

Fig. 3. The performance of removing the mismatched points by our optimization strategy

The steps of PROSAC algorithm can be briefly summarized as follows [14]: (1) Set the initial value $t: = 0$, $n: = m$, $n^*: = N$. (2) Choice of the hypothesis generation set, assume $t: = t + 1$, if $(t = T_n')\&(n < n^*)$, then $n: = n + 1$. (3) Semi-random sample M_t of size m, if $T_n' < t$, then the sample contains $m - 1$ points selected from U_{n-1} at random and u_n, else select m points form u_n at random. (4) Model parameter estimation, compute model parameters p_t from the sample M_t. (5) Model verification, find support (i.e. consistent data points) of the model with parameters p_t, then end the iterative process according to the termination conditions.

4 Moving Object Detection for Driving Assistance System

4.1 Global Motion Estimation

After ORB feature matching, we can find the corresponding relationship of feature points between consecutive frames. The purified matching points are used to calculate the background motion model, compensating background activity. We can obtain the motion compensation by using an affine transformation between consecutive frames. The transformation matrix including translation, rotation and scaling changes caused by camera moving between consecutive frames. The location of feature points in current frame can be found in previous frame through affine transformation. And we can obtain the frame after motion compensating by the following equation [15].

$$\begin{bmatrix} x_k \\ y_k \\ 1 \end{bmatrix} = \begin{bmatrix} m_0 & m_1 & m_2 \\ m_3 & m_4 & m_5 \\ 0 & 0 & 1 \end{bmatrix} \begin{bmatrix} x_{k-1} \\ y_{k-1} \\ 1 \end{bmatrix} \tag{4}$$

The equation means $I_k = M \cdot I_{k-1}$. $(x_{k-1}, y_{k-1})^T$ and $(x_k, y_k)^T$ are the matching pairs between consecutive frames, M means transformation matrix, $(m_0, \ldots, m_5)$ are the motion parameters. The 6-parameter model can be calculated by 3 matching pairs. The performance of motion compensation is demonstrated by Fig. 4.

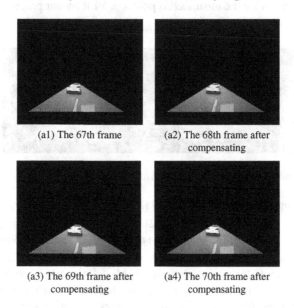

(a1) The 67th frame   (a2) The 68th frame after
                                  compensating

(a3) The 69th frame after   (a4) The 70th frame after
     compensating   compensating

Fig. 4. The performance of motion compensation

4.2 Effective Moving Object Detection

After finding out the motion offset of background between consecutive frames, the image registration processing is taken for the current frame according to the motion offset of the previous frame. Then inter-frame difference is used to remove the background of the frame after image registration. But in practice, due to image noise, illumination changes and the influence of tiny changes in a natural scene. The difference images always contain many false moving objects. In order to suppress the interference of false objects effectively and strengthen the information of moving objects need to be detected, differential multiplication and morphology processing are used to accurately segment the moving objects [16].

The steps can be briefly summarized as follows: (1) Using the first frame I_{k-1} as a reference frame to calculate motion compensating for the subsequent three frames (I_k, I_{k+1}, I_{k+2}). (2) I_{k+1} subtracts I_{k-1} for inter-frame difference, and I_{k+2} subtracts I_k for inter-frame difference respectively. (3) Segment moving objects after Multiplication operation between two subtracted images. (4) The moving objects can be detected effectively after morphology processing in the video of Car DVR. The extracting results of moving object detection is demonstrated by Fig. 5.

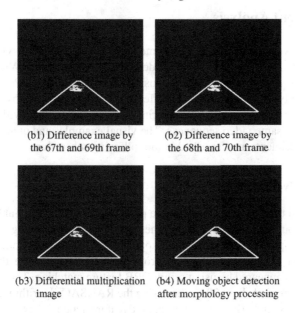

(b1) Difference image by   (b2) Difference image by
the 67th and 69th frame   the 68th and 70th frame

(b3) Differential multiplication (b4) Moving object detection
image   after morphology processing

Fig. 5. Extracting results of moving object detection

4.3   Driving Impact Degree Alarm Mechanism

In the process of actual driving, obstacles would have a influence to safe driving by many factors. In this paper, we propose a Driving Impact Degree Alarm Mechanism for driving assistance system to give the driver an early warning and define a parameter *ID* to calculate Driving Impact Degree in the VFR [13]. We assume that the size of the binary image needs to be detected is $M \times N$, the parameter *ID* can be calculated by the following equation.

$$ID = K_v \sum_{x=1}^{M} \sum_{y=1}^{N} \omega_m GS(x, y) \qquad (5)$$

Among them, ω_m means the influence coefficient of relative distance between the vehicle and the obstacles. There is an inversely proportional relationship between it and relative distance. K_v indicates the influence coefficient of driving speed. There is a proportional relationship between it and driving speed. $GS(x, y)$ is the number of white pixels in the binary image after the processing of moving objects detection.

In a practical application, after getting the value of *ID*, we would set a reasonable threshold *Thr* based on experimental and statistical data. If $ID \geq Thr$, the corresponding alarm measures would be performed to remind the driver to take braking measures.

In this paper, we finally set *Thr* = 2000 through the simulation experiments. It can guarantee the accuracy of early warning.

5 Experiment Analysis

In this section, we experimentally test some results from Car DVR video sequences (640 × 390, 30f/s) with moving objects under driving environment. Without hardware acceleration, the experimental platform using PC machine(Intel Pentium(R) Dual, 2.16 GHz) to analyze the correctness and effectiveness of our method by using OpenCV library debugging in VS2010. Then comparing our proposed method with some existing algorithms on the same video sequences. The visual examples and quantitative evaluations of the experiments are described in the following subsections.

5.1 Quantitative Evaluations

We have defined the following quantitative parameters as shown in Table 1 to analyze the accuracy of our improved algorithm. The performance of removing the mismatched pairs with our improved feature matching optimization strategy is compared with the origin ORB and the ORB+RANSAC. From the table we can see there are many mismatched pairs appeared by using origin ORB feature matching. The matching accuracy has been increased about 20 % after using the RANSAC algorithm, but it still does not perform well enough. By using our improved feature matching optimization strategy, the accuracy of feature matching could be increased to 97 % and the amount of data processing have reduced by about 2/3.

Table 1. Method of matching points purification comparison

Video frames	Matching pairs/True pairs		
	Origin ORB	ORB+RANSAC	Our improved strategy
Frame 75	194/128	103/88	35/34
Frame 347	218/143	134/116	46/45
Frame 1364	157/115	108/92	29/27
Frame 3131	186/121	116/99	33/33
Average matching accuracy	67.5 %	85.6 %	97.0 %

In order to verify the real-time performance of our method, we have also compared the running time of our improved ORB algorithm with the SIFT based and the SUFT based. As shown in Table 2, the result shows that our method can achieve a real-time performance perfectly. Although the complexity of our algorithm has been increased during the process of feature matching optimization, the consuming time of our improved ORB is still about 30 times less than SIFT and 8 times less than SURF. So it's more suitable to detect moving objects for driving assistance system by our method than the SIFT based and the SURF based.

Table 2. Running time comparison

Video frames	Running time		
	SIFT	SURF	Our improved ORB
Frame 75	976 ms	255 ms	32 ms
Frame 347	1093 ms	291 ms	36 ms
Frame 1364	835 ms	233 ms	28 ms
Frame 3131	934 ms	252 ms	31 ms

5.2 Experiment Results

In order to help the driver to get more benefit from our proposal. A visual interface is designed to give the driver an early visual warning and remind the driver to take braking measures. In order to verify the correctness and effectiveness of our method. We have

Table 3. The performance of moving object detection based on our method

Video Frames	Visual Warning	*ID*
		3922
		8765
		1627
		1864
		26

also done some simulation experiments for driving assistance system based on our improved ORB under driving environment. The results are shown in Table 3.

6 Conclusion

In this paper, we present a novel moving object detection method for driving assistance system based on improved ORB. The ORB feature is adopted to compensate for the camera motion. An improved Feature Matching Optimization Strategy is presented to remove the mismatched pairs efficiently in this paper. The experimental results show that the accuracy of feature matching could be increased to 97 % by our method. And the processing speed is fast enough to meet the requirements for real-time driving assistance system. Meanwhile, it has certain advantages in dealing with noise suppression. Next, we will migrate the source codes to an on-board system and test the performance of our method while driving on the road.

References

1. Tsai, J.J., Hang, H.M.: On the design of pattern-based block motion estimation algorithms. IEEE Trans. Circ. Syst. Video Technol. **20**(1), 136–143 (2010)
2. Argyriou, V.: Sub-hexagonal phase correlation for motion estimation. IEEE Trans. Image Process. **20**(1), 110–120 (2011)
3. Rosten, E., Drummond, T.W.: Machine learning for high-speed corner detection. In: Leonardis, A., Bischof, H., Pinz, A. (eds.) ECCV 2006, Part I. LNCS, vol. 3951, pp. 430–443. Springer, Heidelberg (2006)
4. Rosten, E., Porter, R.: Drummond, T: Faster and better: a machine learning approach to corner detection. IEEE Trans. Pattern Anal. Mach. Intell. **32**(1), 105–119 (2010)
5. Klein, G., Murray, D.: Improving the agility of keyframe-based SLAM. In: Forsyth, D., Torr, P., Zisserman, A. (eds.) ECCV 2008, Part II. LNCS, vol. 5303, pp. 802–815. Springer, Heidelberg (2008)
6. Lowe, D.G.: Distinctive image features from scale-invariant keypoints. Int. J. Comput. Vis. **60**(2), 91–110 (2004)
7. Snavely, N., Seitz, S.M., Szeliski, R.: Skeletal graphs for efficient structure from motion. In: IEEE Computer Society Conference on Computer Vision and Pattern Recognition, vol. 1(2) (2008)
8. Bay, H., Tuytelaars, T., Van Gool, L.: SURF: speeded up robust features. In: Leonardis, A., Bischof, H., Pinz, A. (eds.) ECCV 2006, Part I. LNCS, vol. 3951, pp. 404–417. Springer, Heidelberg (2006)
9. Calonder, M., Lepetit, V., Strecha, C., Fua, P.: BRIEF: binary robust independent elementary features. In: Maragos, P., Paragios, N., Daniilidis, K. (eds.) ECCV 2010, Part IV. LNCS, vol. 6314, pp. 778–792. Springer, Heidelberg (2010)
10. Rublee, E., Rabaud, V., Konolige, K., et al.: ORB: an efficient alternative to SIFT or SURF. In: IEEE International Conference on Computer Vision, pp. 2564–2571 (2011)
11. Xie, S.Y., Zhang, W.P., Ying, W., et al.: Fast detecting moving objects in moving background using ORB feature matching. In: 4th IEEE International Conference on Intelligent Control and Information Processing, pp. 304–309 (2013)

12. Rosin, P.L.: Measuring corner properties. Int. J. Comput. Vis. Image Underst. **73**(2), 291–307 (1999)
13. Gao, J., Zhu, H.H., Li, B.: Research of automobile collision avoidance system based on video image processing. Int. J. Appl. Mechan. Mater. **734**, 312–320 (2015)
14. Chum, O., Matas, J.: Matching with PROSAC-progressive sample consensus. In: IEEE Computer Society Conference on Computer Vision and Pattern Recognition, vol. 1, pp. 220–226 (2005)
15. Xue, L.X., Luo, W.H., Wang, Z.C.: Moving object detection algorithm based on ORB feature matching under dynamic scene. Chi. J. Comput. Appl. Softw. **32**(10), 294–297 (2015)
16. Liu, W., Zhao, W.J., Li, C., et al.: Detecting small moving target based on the improved ORB feature matching. Chi. J. Opto-Electron. Eng. **42**(10), 13–20 (2015)

Swarm Robots Formation Control Based on Wireless Sensor Network

Bin Lei$^{(\boxtimes)}$ and Hao Chen

School of Machinery and Automation,
Wuhan University of Science and Technology, Wuhan 430080, Hubei, China
{leibin, chenhao}@wust.edu.cn

Abstract. In this paper, a swarm robots formation control algorithm based on the first-order consensus algorithm was introduced. A modular, low-cost and powerful swarm robots experiment platform which can be used as a mobile wireless sensor network was developed. Simulation and experiment results indicated the effectiveness and applicability of the formation control algorithm.

Keywords: Swarm robots · Consensus · Formation control · WSN

1 Introduction

In recent years, as the applications of robots constantly expanding, the task and the work environment of robot become more complexity, the individual robot is hard to complete it. Because of the properties of robustness, scalability and flexibility, swarm robots that inspired by social insects have gained more and more attentions [1]. A major problem of swarm robots is about formation control which is based on the consensus algorithm. Its main idea is that each robot shares information only with its neighbors while the whole network of robots can coordinate so as to achieve a certain global criterion of common interest and form formation.

Jadbabaie used algebraic graph theory to prove that if the neighbors connected in some way, the running direction of agents will converge [2]. Ren studied the consensus of multi-agent systems under dynamically changing interaction topologies and pointed out that if network topology contains the spanning tree, the system can obtain consensus [3]. Alexander studied the consensus problem of specific wireless sensor networks based on least square method [4]. Andrea studied the consensus problem of two types of multi-agent systems bounded measurement errors [5]. Xi studied the consensus of multi-agent system with state predictor [6]. Sun derived some criteria to reach multi-group consensus for the networks with fixed and witching topology, and discussed the relations between the number of equilibriums and Laplacian matrix [7]. Ni and Cheng using the techniques including algebraic graph theory and Lyapunov theory to analyse the leader-following consensus under fixed and switching topologies [8]. Meng proposed a linear protocol based on the relative state information to solve the global consensus problem for the multi-agent system with input saturation constraints under fixed undirected network topologies and time varying network topologies [9]. Tao studied the global consensus problem for discrete-time multi-agent systems with

W. Li et al. (Eds.): IDCS 2016, LNCS 9864, pp. 458–465, 2016.
DOI: 10.1007/978-3-319-45940-0_42

input saturation constraints under fixed undirected topologies [10]. Ren introduced the consensus based formation control strategies for multi-vehicle systems, and applied variants of the consensus algorithm to tackle formation control problems by appropriately choosing information states on which consensus is reached [11].

In this paper, we introduced a consensus formation control algorithm based on our previous work [12]. To demonstrate the effectiveness and applicability of the algorithm, experiments were carried out by our swarm robots experiment platform-*Colorobot*. Which is a modular, low-cost and powerful platform, and its electronic structure and control principle were also introduced.

2   Prior Knowledge and Consensus Algorithm

2.1   Prior Knowledge

Let $G = \{V, E\}$ be the information interactive network topology graph of swarm robots system, where $V = \{1, 2, 3, \ldots, n\}$ is the set of nodes, $E \subseteq \{(i, j)/i, j \in V\}$ is the set of edges. If G is an undirected graph, the nodes are unordered, then $(i, j) \in V \Leftrightarrow (j, i) \in V$.

Matrix $A(G) = [a_{ij}] \in R^{n \times n}$ is a $n \times n$ matrix, where $a_{ij} = \begin{cases} 1, & \text{if } e_{ji} \in E \\ 0, & \text{else} \end{cases}$, which is the

adjacency matrix of G. Matrix $C(G) = D(G) + A(G) = [c_{ij}] \in R^{n \times n}$ is a $n \times n$ matrix,

$D(G) = [d_{ij}] \in R^{n \times n}$ is a $n \times n$ diagonal matrix, and its diagonal elements $d_{ii} = -\sum_{j=1}^{n} a_{ij}$

is non-positive, $c_{ij} = d_{ij} + a_{ij}$. $C(G)$ is the information interactive network matrix of interactive network graph G (referred to as the interactive network matrix and abbreviated as C). Its declination elements is non-negative real number, and total of row is zero.

2.2   Consensus Algorithm Description

Consensus algorithm and strategies are the rules of interaction among individual robots, which describe the information exchange process between each individual and its neighbors. Establishing the following the first-order system model:

$$\dot{\xi}_i = \varsigma_i, \ i = 1, 2, \ldots, \tag{1}$$

where $\xi_i \in R$ and $\varsigma_i \in R$ represent the status of i-th robot (such as orientation angle, speed and decision-making capacity, etc.) and control input, respectively. The continuous-time consensus algorithm of basic fixed topology can be expressed as follows [3, 12, 13]:

$$\varsigma_i(t) = -\sum_{j=1}^{n} a_{ij}(\xi_i(t) - \xi_j(t)) \tag{2}$$

In matrix form: $\dot{\xi}(t) = C\xi(t)$. And the solution is: $\xi(t) = e^{tC}\xi(0)$

Definition 1: First-order consensus in swarm robots system is said to be achieved if for any initial conditions,

$$\lim_{t\to\infty}\left\|\xi_i(t) - \xi_j(t)\right\| = 0 \ i, j = 1, 2, \ldots, n.$$

Theorem 1: The basic continuous-time consensus algorithm (Eq. 2) can gradually achieve consensus, if and only if the corresponding interactive network graph G has a directed spanning tree [3].

3 Formation Control Based on the Consensus Algorithm

An important application of consensus algorithm is to achieve the swarm robot formation control which refers to controlling the orientation angle, speed and relative distance between individuals of swarm robots to achieve consensus.

A typical mobile robot model, kinematics equations of the first-order system can be expressed as

$$\begin{pmatrix} \dot{x}_i \\ \dot{y}_i \\ \dot{\theta}_i \end{pmatrix} = \begin{pmatrix} v_i^x \\ v_i^y \\ \omega_i \end{pmatrix} = \begin{pmatrix} \cos\theta_i & 0 \\ \sin\theta_i & 0 \\ 0 & 1 \end{pmatrix} \cdot \begin{pmatrix} v_i \\ \omega_i \end{pmatrix}, i = 1, 2, \ldots, n \quad (3)$$

where (x_i, y_i) denotes the location of robot i, and θ_i is the direction angle of robot i. The controlled inputs for robot i are the linear velocity V_i and angular velocity ω_i. Equation (3) can be simplified to a first-order system $\dot{\xi}_i = \varsigma_i$, where the status $\xi_i = [x, y, \theta]^T$, and the control input $\varsigma_i = [v^x, v^y, w]^T$.

Align behavior refers to controlling the direction angles of a group of robots to form consensus. Consensus algorithm of the align behavior is given by [13]:

$$w_i(t) = -\sum_{j=1}^{n} a_{ij}(\theta_i(t) - \theta_j(t)) \quad (4)$$

The matrix form of Eq. (4) is $\dot{\theta}(t) = C\theta(t)$, its solution is $\theta(t) = e^{tC}\theta(0)$. According to Theorem 1, when the interactive graph of swarm robotic system has a directed spanning tree, Eq. (4) can gradually achieve consensus. Which means that the direction angels of the swarm robots gradually aligned finally.

Aggregation and dispersion behavior is used to control the relative distance between a group of robots to achieve consensus. Aggregation and dispersion behavior consensus algorithms are given by [13]:

$$v_i^x(t) = -\sum_{j=1}^{n} a_{ij} k_{ij}^x [|x_i(t) - x_j(t)| - d_x], k_{ij}^x = \frac{x_i(t) - x_j(t)}{|x_i(t) - x_j(t)| + \eta} \quad (5)$$

$$v_i^y(t) = -\sum_{j=1}^{n} a_{ij}k_{ij}^y \big[|y_i(t) - y_j(t)| - d_y\big], k_{ij}^y = \frac{y_i(t) - y_j(t)}{|y_i(t) - y_j(t)| + \eta} \tag{6}$$

where $\sqrt{d_x^2 + d_y^2} > 0$ represents the distance between robots, $0 < \eta < < 1$, which is a very small positive real number. Let $r_i = (x_i, y_i)^\mathrm{T}$ and $r_{ij} = r_i - r_j$, Then, Eqs. (5) and (6) can be rewritten as:

$$v_i(t) = -\sum_{j=1}^{n} a_{ij}k_{ij}(\|r_{ij}\| - d) \tag{7}$$

where, $k_{ij} = \frac{r_i - r_j}{\|r_i - r_j\| + \eta}$.

In summary, combining Eqs. (4) and (7), the first-order formation control algorithm for swarm robots is described as follows:

$$\begin{cases} w_i(t) = -\sum_{j=1}^{n} a_{ij}(\theta_i(t) - \theta_j(t)) \\ v_i(t) = -\sum_{j=1}^{n} a_{ij}k_{ij}(\|r_{ij}\| - d) \end{cases} \tag{8}$$

4 Swarm Robots Experiment Platform

To demonstrate the effectiveness and applicability of the formation control with input constraints, experiments were carried out by our experiment platform-*Colorobot*, which was shown in Fig. 1. The robot has a STM32 flash microcontroller based on a 32-bit ARM Cortex®-M3 core. Seven infrared (IR) proximity sensors are placed around the front of the body to measure how closeness of obstacles or nearby robots. In order to communicate with neighbor robots, each robot has three IR modules, including transmitter and receiver. These IR modules allow the robot to receive messages equally from all directions. Two IR sensors are used to measure angular velocities of the two wheels of the robot, which can provide feedback of the robot's movement to correct errors in path formation algorithm. Bluetooth radio is used to connect with a computer or to communicate with an Android app for remote control of the robot. By using the ZigBee module, swarm robots can build a mobile wireless sensor network for the information interactive network topology, and each robot can be considered as a node.

Fig. 1. Swarm robots experiment platform

5 Simulation and Experiment

5.1 Simulation

As Eq. (8) described, formation refers to controlling the direction angle and relative distance between individuals of swarm robots to achieve consensus. To be better and visually observe the consensus of direction angle and relative distance, the consensus simulation were done. Figure 2 shows the information interactive network graph of the swarm robots experimental platform, which has a directed spanning tree. The network consists of four robots, and each circle in the Fig. 2 denotes an individual robot. Directed line segment means the information transfer direction between robots. Assuming that initial direction angle of robots are $\theta_1(0) = 110°$, $\theta_2(0) = 195°$, $\theta_3(0) = 205°$, $\theta_4(0) = 96°$, respectively. Setting each robot inherent speed is 0.2 m/s, the expected distance between robot 1 and robot 2, robot 2 and robot 3, robot 3 and robot 4 are 0.13 m respectively; the initial position is (1, 0.9), (0.9, 0.95) (0.85, 0.8), (0.75, 0.7), respectively.

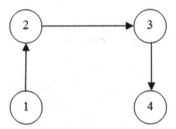

Fig. 2. Information interactive network graph

The interactive matrix of the network is described as:

$$C = \begin{bmatrix} 0 & 0 & 0 & 0 \\ 1 & -1 & 0 & 0 \\ 0 & 1 & -1 & 0 \\ 0 & 0 & 1 & -1 \end{bmatrix}$$

Figure 3(a) illustrates the simulation result of the trajectory of the robots which applied the formation control algorithm Eq. (8). The abscissa denotes the position of the x direction, and the ordinate denotes the position of the y direction. We can found that the robots have different directions and different relative distances at the beginning time, but their direction angles and the relative distance between their neighbors were converged to the same finally. Figure 3(b) shows the evolution of the direction angle. It can be found that with time went on, the direction angle gradually reached consensus. In Fig. 3(c), the distance between robot 1 and robot 2 (d_{1-2}), robot 2 and robot 3 (d_{2-3}), robot 3 and robot 4 (d_{3-4}) were gradually reached to 0.13 m.

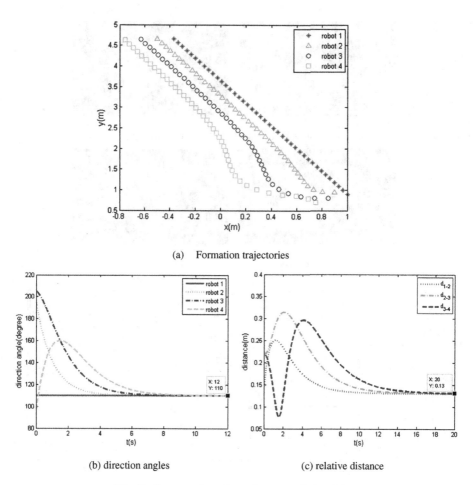

(a) Formation trajectories

(b) direction angles   (c) relative distance

Fig. 3. Swarm robots formation control simulation

5.2 Experiment

In order to further verify the correctness and practicability of the formation control algorithm, the formation experiment was done by the experimental platform. The information interactive network graph and the initial values are the same with the simulation. Figure 4(a), (b), (c) and (d) are the experiment photographs of t = 0 s, t = 2 s, t = 4 s and t = 6 s, respectively. It can be seen that the robots move in the same direction and the distances between neighbors are the same finally. The data of direction angle and relative distance are shown in Fig. 4(e) and (f), respectively. It can be seen that the curves of direction angle and relative distance are approximately overlapped and formed consensus finally.

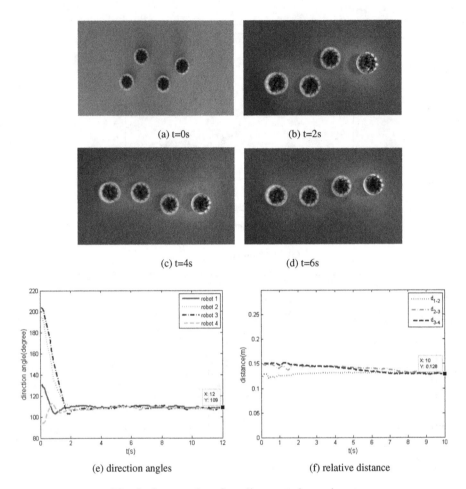

(a) t=0s   (b) t=2s

(c) t=4s   (d) t=6s

(e) direction angles   (f) relative distance

Fig. 4. Swarm robots formation control experiment

6 Conclusions

In this paper, the information interactive network graph and matrix used to represent the information interaction between swarm robots and a formation control algorithm based on the first-order consensus algorithm was proposed. A modular, low-cost and powerful swarm robots platform was developed. The electronic structure and control principle of a swarm robots platform was introduced. MTLAB simulation and swarm robots platform experiment were done, and comparing the results, it can be found that the experiment results were close to the simulation results which verified the effectiveness and practicability of the formation control algorithm.

Acknowledgement. This research is supported by the National Natural Science Foundation of China (No. 61305110), and the Research Project of Hubei Provincial Department of Education (No. Q20121114).

References

1. Rubenstein, M., Ahler, C., Nagpal, R.: Kilobot: a low cost scalable robot system for collective behaviors. Autonom. Robots **17**, 111–113 (2013)
2. Jadbabaie, A., Lin, J., Morse, A.: Coordination of groups of mobile autonomous agents using nearest neighbor rules. IEEE Trans. Autom. Cont. **48**(6), 988–1001 (2003)
3. Ren, W., Beard, R.: Consensus seeking in multi-agent systems under dynamically changing interaction topologies. IEEE Trans. Autom. Cont. **50**(5), 655–661 (2005)
4. Bertrand, A., Moonen, M.: Consensus-based distributed total least squares estimation in ad hoc wireless sensor networks. IEEE Trans. Signal Process. **59**(5), 2320–2330 (2011)
5. Garulli, A., Giannitrapani, A.: Analysis of consensus protocols with bounded measurement errors. Syst. Cont. Lett. **60**(1), 44–52 (2011)
6. Xi, Y.G., Huang, W., Li, X.L.: Consensus of multi-agent system with state predictor. Cont. Decis. **25**(5), 769–772 (2010)
7. Sun, W., Bai, Y., Jia, R., Xiong, R., Chen, J.: Multi-group consensus via pinning control with non-linear heterogeneous agents. In: Proceedings of the 8th Asian Control Conference, pp. 15–18 (2011)
8. Ni, W., Cheng, D.: Leader-following consensus of multi-agent systems under fixed and switching topologies. Syst. Cont. Lett. **59**, 209–217 (2010)
9. Meng, Z., Zhao, Z., Lin, Z.: On global leader-following consensus of identical linear dynamic systems subject to actuator saturation. Syst. Cont. Lett. **62**(2), 132–142 (2013)
10. Yang, T., Meng, Z.Y., Dimarogonas, D.V., Johansson, K.H.: Global consensus for discrete-time multi-agent systems with input saturation constraints. Automatica **50**, 499–506 (2014)
11. Ren, W., Sorensen, N.: Distributed coordination architecture for multi-robot formation control. Robot. Autonom. Syst. **56**(4), 324–333 (2008)
12. Lei, B., Chen H., Zeng, L.C., Gao, Q.J.: Consensus algorithm with input constraint for swarm robots formation control. In: International Conference on Networking, Sensing and Control (ICNSC), pp. 157–162 (2015)

Reliable Data Transmission Method for Hybrid Industrial Network Based on Mobile Object

Ying Duan[1,2], Wenfeng Li[1(✉)], Xiuwen Fu[1], and Lin Yang[1]

[1] School of Logistics Engineering,
Wuhan University of Technology, Wuhan, People's Republic of China
{duanying,liwf,XiuwenFu,lyang}@whut.edu.cn
[2] School of Computer Science, Zhengzhou University of Aeronautics,
Zhengzhou, People's Republic of China

Abstract. Industrial Wireless Sensor Networks (IWSNs) are the core component of the Industrial Internet of Things (IIOT). However, the environmental
noise caused by the physical environment, such as the obstacles in the industrial
scenes will have a significantly negative impact on the performance of IWSNs.
For the wireless links, it will lead to the decrease of the transmission distance,
etc. For the sensor nodes, it will give rise to the failure probability of nodes and
shortening the life cycle. As the common conveyor equipment, Automatic
Guided Vehicle (AGV) is responsible for material delivering in industry. Due to
its flexibility and reliability, reliable maintenance of IWSNs can be guaranteed.
This paper firstly proposed an idea of choosing AGV as mobile object, through
cooperation and networking with IWSNs, to achieve reliable data transmission.
For single or multiple nodes failure, we respectively design Temporary Link and
Mobile Delivering schemes, in order to ensure the reliable data transmission
towards various failure cases.

Keywords: Industrial Wireless Sensor Networks (IWSNs) · Automatic Guided
Vehicle (AGV) · Mobile object · Temporary link · Mobile delivering

1 Introduction

In general, due to the characteristics as large-scale deployment, constrained resources
and wireless communications, wireless sensor networks make itself vulnerable to the
impacts of the surrounding environment [1]. Compared with the general network
application environment, the complexity of the industrial environment increases significantly, and the influence on the performance of the wireless sensor network is also
more evident. Industrial scenarios have the following characteristics [2, 3]: (1) harsh
surrounding environments; (2) various production equipment; (3) more partition of
indoor, it might lead to the rising of node failure probability, the shortening of the life
cycle, and even the entire paralysis of the network. Besides that, it might lead to the
link instability, rising of packet loss and bit error rate. Node failure will have negative
effects on normal industrial production process, such as segmentation of originally
connected network topology, sharp decreasing in the network quality of service [4].

© Springer International Publishing AG 2016
W. Li et al. (Eds.): IDCS 2016, LNCS 9864, pp. 466–476, 2016.
DOI: 10.1007/978-3-319-45540-0_43

However, existing methods of IWSNs often require to introduce additional infras-tructures, thus leading to the extra costs of network maintenance. As a result, the reliability data transmission of IWSNs has become the major bottleneck of wider applications of IWSNs in the industrial scenarios.

In the general production scenarios, as common material handling equipment crossing in various task areas, the existence of AGVs can provide a totally new idea to enhance the reliability of data transmission of IWSNs. Thus, in this paper we attempt to discuss the inner relationship between production organization and invulnerability of IWSNs, and propose two reliable data-transmission methods (i.e., TL and MD) which use mobile objects to replace failure nodes through temporary networking between AGVs and IWSNs.

2 Problem Description

Compared with common WSNs, IWSNs have some unique characteristics [5, 6]: (1) harsh application environment: the industrial environment is always featured with high-humidity, high-noise and high-temperature, which will negatively influence the survivability and stability of IWSNs; (2) strict requirement of real-time data trans-mission: the frequent occurrence of security accidents requires IWSN capable of delivering alarming messages in real time, in order to help the relevant staff make rapid countermeasures; (3) heterogeneous structure: due to the requirements of daily pro-duction tasks, besides static sensor nodes deployed in scenarios, mobile sensor nodes (e.g., AGVs equipped with sensor nodes) common exists, which make IWSNs highly heterogeneous structured; (4) clustering network: since the complete production pro-cess usually involves various working processes and different working process gen-erally corresponds to different working space, production task, production equipment and procedures. Thus, in general production scenario, the deployment of IWSNs is much more complicated than general WSNs and coverage is wider. The star topology for general WSNs cannot be qualified for IWSNs. As clustered structure can be easily extended and maintained, which is widely applied in industrial environments; (5) data redundancy: the density of production equipment makes the sensor nodes deploy densely, which make sensing range of the sensor nodes high-likely overlapped. Due to this, the data converged in sink node is featured with redundancy; (6) data diversity: due to the demands of industrial control, the sensing data of IWSNs usually includes complex data types (e.g., sound and video). These kinds of data have larger message size and need wider link width, thus having higher requirements of transmission reliability.

The industrial area usually includes production area, assembly area, packaging area and controlling area. Each area has specific sensor network for monitoring the daily operation of industrial activity. The sensor network in each area can be seemed as a cluster of the entire IWSN. The sampling data of each cluster will converge in the sink node/base station through multi-hop relay among cluster heads (shown in Fig. 1). Thus, the sensor nodes in IWSN can be categorized into two types: cluster member and cluster head. Cluster member is responsible for sensing the environmental information and relay the data to the cluster head it belongs to. Cluster head is responsible for

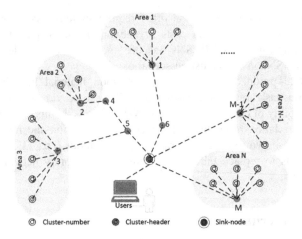

Fig. 1. Topology structure of IWSNs

data converging, inner-cluster data processing and outer-cluster relaying. Besides these tasks, the cluster head also needs to relay messages from other cluster heads. All the collecting data will be delivered to the sink node, which will be used for higher level of industrial service.

As mentioned above, the complexity of industrial environment would affect the operation of IWSNs, thus increasing the failure probability of nodes and links. The typical failure patterns (shown in Table 1) are summarized as below:

(1) The failure of cluster member will not affect the operation of the other sensor nodes in the network. This is because the cluster members are not required to relay message from other clusters and thus its failure will not affect the data-delivery of the remaining nodes;

(2) If cluster head 2 falls into failure, the topology of IWSN will be divided and area 2 will become "Data Island". The sampling data in cluster 2 cannot be transported to the sink node;

(3) If cluster head 4 falls into breakdown, area 2 will become "Data Island". The network topology will be divided;

(4) If cluster head 5 fails, area 2 and area 3 will lost the effective connections with the sink node and thus become Data Island. The failure of cluster head 5 will cause a serious network interruption;

Table 1. The influence of the typical failure node

Failure node	The influence
Cluster number	It can be neglect
Cluster header	Data Island
Sink node	Network paralysis

In generally, the sink node can be provide uninterrupted power. Therefore, in this paper we mainly focus the failure recovery issue of cluster heads (e.g., 2, 4 and 5) rather than cluster members and sink node.

3 Design Schemes

In the current researches, mobile nodes are commonly used to repair the network topology by interconnecting "Data Island". According to the types of mobile nodes, the methods can be categorized into: (1) using mobile node to replace failure node [7, 8], (2) using ferry nodes as message carrier to delivery data [9], (3) using mobile robots [10, 11], (4) using message ferrying [12], (5) using data mules [13], (6) using Mobile Agent to communication [14–16], (7) using wireless mobile objects to receive and relay data [17]. All these solutions require extra infrastructures, which will increase the cost of network maintenance and fail to consider the impacting factors in industrial scenarios. In fact, the common existence of AGVs provides highly-available infrastructures to ensure reliable data transmission in IWSNs. Thus, according to the problem description in Sect. 2, we proposed recovery methods by using AGVs as mobile objects.

In production sites, AGVs will cross various task areas for cargo delivery according to the predefined traces. The AGVs are equipped with sensor nodes and are able to communicate with other sensor nodes when passing by their communication areas. Therefore, besides common delivery tasks, AGVs are also responsible for data collection and relay.

3.1 Temporary Link

When a single cluster fails in the IWSNs, adjacent node of cluster head and its belonging cluster members will not be able to establish a connection for communication, and would cause individual regional isolation, network transmission interruption, or cause more networks interruption, paralysis of the whole sensor network. In this case, we design a temporary link scheme based on the repair of a single failure node.

Temporary link (TL) refers to the use of mobile nodes for temporarily replacing the failure node, and connections of neighbor nodes can be automatically established in network, and then data can be transmitted. Figure 2 is shown as an example, area A is a single cluster region and includes the cluster members, the dotted line in the ellipse is connected with the cluster head node 2, node 4, node 5, and the node sink, the cluster head can communicate between adjacent nodes. When cluster head 4 fails, the cluster head 2 cannot collect data in the region, thus leading to relay breakthrough node 4 to the sink node. Elliptic curve represents the trajectory of the AGV (M), when cluster head 4 fails, AGV communicates with the adjacent nodes of cluster head 4. Temporary link model carries out network connection repair for data transmission.

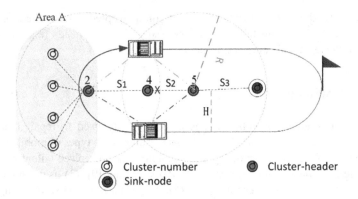

Fig. 2. Scene of TL scheme

3.1.1 Scheme Description

As is shown in Fig. 2, as the data of cluster head node is delivered to the sink node, if cluster head 4 falls into failure, and cluster head 5 is outside the coverage of node 4, internal sensing data of area A cannot be transferred to the sink node, then area A will become the data island. So, we propose a scheme of using AGV as a temporary link, in the practical scenario of AGV vehicle scheduling, its running track might be covered by cluster head 2 and 5. However, this scheme has drawbacks, it is necessary to meet the following conditions to carry out the self-organizing network and data transmission:

Assumption: Let H denote the vertical distance from AGV track to cluster head, R represents the communication coverage radius of cluster head, and V represents the speed of the AGV.

- L1 represents the distance from cluster head 2 to 5:

$$R < L_1 < 2\sqrt{R^2 - H^2}; \tag{1}$$

- L_2 represents the distance of AGV simultaneously networking with cluster head 2 and 5:

$$0 < L_2 < 2\sqrt{R^2 - H^2}; \tag{2}$$

- T_1 represents the time of simultaneously networking:

$$0 < T_1 < \frac{\sqrt{R^2 - H^2}}{V}; \tag{3}$$

Let T2 denote the data delay. Because in industrial scenario, most of the data type are string data, reasonably assume that the wireless link bandwidth is sufficient, and the data transmission has obvious instantaneous characteristics. Therefore, T2 could be ignored, $T_2 \approx 0$.

3.1.2 Advantages and Application Scenarios

The proposed scheme can repair the failure of single cluster head in IWSN and the delay time is short, so that the collected data can be transferred to the sink nodes quickly, and the reliable data transmission of WSNs can be improved. However, if we do not meet the above three basic requirements or confront with multiple node failures, temporary link cannot finish network repair task by a single AGV. In the industrial scenario, multiple node failures are common, such as regional node failure. A typical case is shown in Fig. 2, the cluster head 4 and 5 fail simultaneously, using a single AGV to establish a temporary link, are still unable to establish an effective connection with its original neighbor nodes, and the network is still isolated. Therefore, in Sect. 3.2, we proposed an improved scheme called Mobile Delivering.

3.2 Mobile Delivering

When many cluster heads fails in the IWSNs, multiple neighbor cluster heads are disconnected, thus making cause a large area of network. In this case, we design a ferry node scheme to repair while more than one cluster heads fall into failure.

Mobile Delivering (MD) is referred to the use of mobile nodes to the cluster head within the scope of coverage, automatic networking, establishing connection and data transmission, the mobile node of carrying data movement to the sink node nearby, then directly established connection and data transmission with adjacent cluster head or sink node. As is shown in Fig. 3, area A is single cluster region and include cluster members, the dotted line in the ellipse is connected with the cluster head node 2, node 4, node 5, and the sink node. The cluster heads 4 and 5 fail. Elliptic curve represents the trajectory of the AGV (M). A and B points are the intersection points of the AGV track and the cluster head node 2, C and D points are the intersection points of the AGV track and the sink node. When AGV moves to the region of cluster head 2, the data of cluster head 2 will be received, and then move to the coverage area of the sink node, the data can be transmitted to the sink node. When a large area network is interrupted, Mobile Delivering scheme can repair network connections and establish the data communication. So, this scheme can ensure the reliable data transmission of IWSNs.

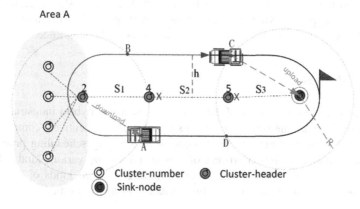

Fig. 3. Scene of MD scheme

3.2.1   Scheme Description

The failure of cluster head node 4 and 5, area A belong to data island, and the data collected by internal node of Area A cannot be transferred to node sink, so the MD scheme is used for reliable data transmission. Because the cluster head 4 does not work, the cluster head node 2 cannot be connected with the cluster head 4, and the data transmission aborts and waits. When the AGV in the trajectory segment AB, cluster head 2 and AGV establish wireless connections and organize into temporary network automatically, the data of cluster head 2 can be transmitted to the AGV; then run AGV in CD track section, sink node and AGV established wireless connection, the data of cluster head 2 transmits to the sink node by AGV.

Assumption: H represents the vertical distance from AGV track to cluster head, R, V represent the communication coverage radius of cluster head and the speed of the AGV, respectively, let S1 denote the distance from cluster head 2 to cluster head 4, S2 represents the distance from cluster head 4 to cluster head 5, S3 represents the distance from cluster head 5 to sink node, connection of AGV and cluster head is established in the current trajectory coincides, L represents the walking distance of AGV in the coverage area of cluster head 2.

Data transmission distance:

$$S = L + \sqrt{R^2 - H^2} + 2H + S_1 + S_2 + S_3 + L - \sqrt{R^2 - H^2}$$
$$= S_1 + S_2 + S_3 + 2H + 2L \tag{4}$$

Assume cluster head 2 as the center, if the AGV turn from its left, then L is positive, else L is negative. From the formula (4), it can be known that the transmission distance of the source node is related to the number of hops from the target node, if i is the hop count, then the formula (5) becomes:

$$S = \sum_{i=1}^{n} S_i + 2H + 2L \tag{5}$$

3.2.2   Advantages and Application Scenarios

Scheme MD can repair the failure of multiple cluster heads in IWSNs, as is shown in Fig. 3. When the node 4 and 5 cannot be connected, a single AGV receives data of cluster head 2 during moving, the communication range of the sink node is arrived through the AGV moving, the data of AGV transmits to the sink node.

4   Case Studies

In order to ensure the reliability of data transmission in the hybrid industrial network environment, we take the production workshop of a pharmaceuticals company as an example, as is shown in Fig. 4. We combine with job shop scheduling process, and analyze the dynamic evolution process of general IWSNs by various kinds of sensor nodes in the industrial environment. After that, we create two kinds of scenarios of node failures and evaluate them according to data transmission time.

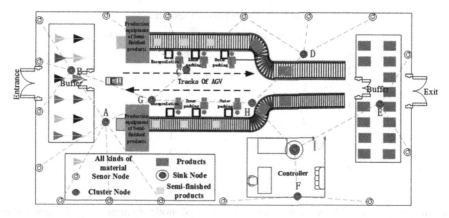

Fig. 4. Structure of the production workshop of a pharmaceuticals company

The workshop consists of two production lines, one material buffer, one product buffer, a control room, an AGV, the variety of sensor nodes and communication equipment. Each production line consists of two semi-finish production equipment and three working procedures (including encapsulation, inner packing and outer packing). Sensor node includes cluster members, cluster heads and the sink node, cluster member points include temperature sensors and humidity sensors, they are deployed around the workshop; cluster head node is located at the top of the workshop; sink nodes are installed in the control room. Table 2 describes the distance among each cluster heads to its neighboring nodes.

Table 2. The distance between the cluster heads

Number	Trajectory of node	Distance(m)
1	B→G	17
2	B→A	15.1
3	A→G	13
4	G→C	14.3
5	G→H	19.1
6	H→D	18
7	H→F	15.4
8	E→F	19.8

The failure of one or more nodes in the shop scheduling process, the network link is interrupted, affecting the data transmission. Therefore, this paper respectively discusses the failure of single node or multiple nodes. In order to simulate the random failure condition, nodes 1 or 2 are randomly failed in the each test, and then analysis and calculate the delay time of data transmission scheme by using TL and MD scheme.

Table 3. Description of test unit

Number	Number of failure node	ID of failure node
1	1	G
2	1	C
3	1	H
4	2	G,C
5	2	A,B
6	2	C,H
7	2	H,D
8	2	G,H

According to Table 3, we configure the cases of node failures, Fig. 5 shows the comparison of the data transmission delay time after the node failure.

Figure 5 shows the failure of a single node, data delay time of TL scheme significantly lower than MD, so the TL scheme outperforms the MD. In the case of multiple failure nodes, the data delay time of TL scheme is closed to infinity, which means that the method cannot be repaired by using this method, so the MD scheme can only be applied. But there also exits some exceptions, as is shown sequence number five in Fig. 5. Because A, B, G and AGV are covered in the same signal range, region A, B of the data can be directly delivered into the G through the AGV. Therefore in this case, the difference between the MD scheme and the TL is not obviously.

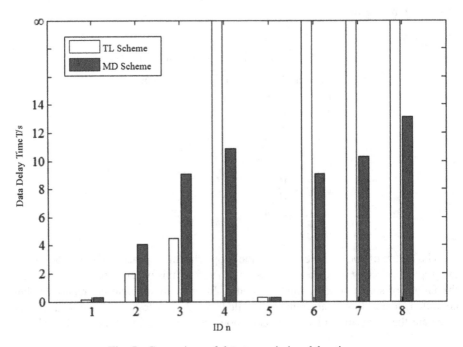

Fig. 5. Comparison of data transmission delay time

5 Conclusion and Future Work

Based on the network reliability data transmission problem in Industrial Internet of Things (IIOT), in this paper, we design Mobile Delivering and temporary link schemes to ensure the connectivity of the network under the condition of a single or multiple failure nodes. Experimental results show that those schemes can improve the reliability of data transmission in the network, and improve the ability of the network to engage into complex tasks under the cases of node failures. However, the influence of AGV trajectory and the production process on the network is not considered in this study. Therefore, the next step is to analyze the node layout of IWSNs and AGV trajectory, optimize the trajectory of the AGV, in order to improve the real-time performance of data transmission in the case of meeting the network reliability. On the other hand, considering the work flow of AGV and residence time, we constructs the network evolution model based on time sequence and ensuring the invulnerability of the network in order to meet the production requirements.

Acknowledgement. This work is supported in part by the National Natural Science Foundation of China (61571336), the National Natural Science Foundation of China (41171341) and the National Key Technology R&D Program (2014BAH24F03).

References

1. Wang, H., Li, Y., Mi, M., Wang, P.: Secure data fusion method based on supervisory mechanism for industrial internet of things. Chin. J. Sci. Instr. **34**(4), 817–824 (2013)
2. Gungor, V., Hancke, G.: Industrial wireless sensor networks: challenges, design, principles, and technical approaches. IEEE Trans. Ind. Electron. **56**(10), 4258–4265 (2009)
3. Al, A., Bertin, H., Dang, T., et al.: Which wireless technology for industrial wireless sensor networks? The development of OCARI technology. IEEE Trans. Ind. Electron. **56**(10), 4266–4278 (2009)
4. Mahmood, M., Seah, W., Welch, I.: Reliability in wireless sensor networks: a survey and challenges ahead. Comput. Netw. **79**, 166–187 (2015)
5. Islam, K., Shen, W., Wang, X.: Wireless sensor network reliability and security in factory automation: a survey. IEEE Trans. Syst. Man Cybern. Part C Appl. Rev. **42**(6), 1243–1256 (2012)
6. Vahdani, B., Tavakkoli-Moghaddam, R., Jolai, F.: Reliable design of a logistics network under uncertainty: a fuzzy possibilistic-queuing model. Appl. Math. Model. **37**(5), 3254–3268 (2013)
7. Wang, L., Wei, R., Lin, Y., et al.: A clique base node scheduling method for wireless sensor networks. J. Netw. Comput. Appl. **33**(4), 383–396 (2010)
8. Fu, X., Li, W., Fortino, G.: Empowering the invulnerability of wireless sensor networks through super wires and super nodes. In: 2013 13th IEEE/ACM International Symposium on Cluster, Cloud and Grid Computing (CCGrid), pp. 561–568. IEEE (2013)
9. Moazzez-Estanjini, R., Wang, J., Paschalidis, I.: Scheduling mobile nodes for cooperative data transport in sensor networks. IEEE/ACM Trans. Netw. **21**(3), 974–989 (2013)
10. Nielsen, I., Dang, Q., Bocewicz, G., et al.: A methodology for implementation of mobile robot in adaptive manufacturing environments. J. Intell. Manuf., 1–18 (2015)

11. Shih, C.-Y., et al.: On the cooperation between mobile robots and wireless sensor networks. In: Koubaa, A., Khelil, A. (eds.) Cooperative Robots and Sensor Networks 2014. SCI, vol. 554, pp. 67–86. Springer, Heidelberg (2014)

12. Zhao, W., et al.: A message ferrying approach for data delivery in sparse mobile ad hoc networks. In: 5th ACM International Symposium on Mobile Ad Hoc Networking and Computing, pp. 187–198 (2004)

13. Matsuura, I., Schut, R., Hirakawa, K.: Data MULEs: modeling a three-tier architecture for sparse sensor networks. In: IEEE SNPA Workshop, pp. 30–41 (2003)

14. Aiello, F., Fortino, G., Guerrieri, A., et al.: Maps: A mobile agent platform for WSNs based on Java sun spots. In: Third International Workshop on Agent Technology for Sensor Networks (2009)

15. Fortino, G., Guerrieri, A., Russo, W., Savaglio, C.: Middlewares for smart objects and smart environments: overview and comparison. In: Fortino, G., Trunfio, P. (eds.) Internet of Things Based on Smart Objects, Technology, Middleware and Applications, pp. 1–27. Springer International Publishing, Switzerland (2014)

16. Fortino, G., Grimaldi, D., Nigro, L.: Multicast control of mobile measurement systems. IEEE Trans. Instrum. Measur. 47(5), 1149–1154 (1998)

17. Saad, W., Han, Z., Başar, T., et al.: Hedonic coalition formation for distributed task allocation among wireless agents. IEEE Trans. Mobile Comput. 10(9), 1327–1344 (2010)

A V-BLAST-Based Cooperative MIMO Transmission Scheme for Heterogeneous Wireless Sensor Networks

Guangyou Yang[1(⊠)], Jun Li[1], and Xiong Gan[2]

[1] Institute of Agricultural Machinery, Hubei University of Technology,
Wuhan, People's Republic of China
pekka@126.com, 1273987282@qq.com
[2] School of Mechanical and Electronic Engineering,
Wuhan University of Technology, Wuhan, People's Republic of China
ganxiong001@126.com

Abstract. The cooperative multiple input multiple output (CMIMO) technique provides an energy-efficient transmission scheme for energy-constrained wireless sensor networks. However, classical CMIMO-based transmission schemes are designed for homogeneous networks, which fail to take full advantage of the heterogeneity among sensor nodes, shortening the network stable time. In this work, an energy-efficient V-BLAST-based cluster-head cooperative MIMO transmission scheme is proposed for heterogeneous wireless sensor network. In order to maximize the network stable time, this work develops energy models to obtain directly the optimal network parameters. Simulation results show that the proposed scheme can improve the energy efficiency and prolong the network stable time in comparison with existing transmission schemes.

Keywords: Heterogeneous wireless sensor networks · CMIMO · V-BLAST · Energy-efficient

1 Introduction

WSNs have been used in variety critical areas, such as intelligent household, industry, agriculture. However, the sensor node is powered by the energy-limited battery, which is difficult to be recharged in most application scenarios, therefore, reducing energy is extremely significant. The CMIMO technique can obtain multiplexing gain and improve energy efficiency by adopting a group of cooperative tiny nodes [1].

In [2], CMIMO communication systems based on alamouti diversity scheme is proposed. A more precise energy model taking into account the overheads of channel training is presented in [3, 4]. In [5], the authors present an V-BLAST-based CMIMO communication system, which have no requirement for cooperation between transmitter side. In [5], the authors present a cluster-based cooperative multiple-input-single-output (MISO) communication scheme and develop the end-to-end energy model to search the optimal network parameters. A V-BLAST-based cluster-heads cooperative transmission scheme (VCHCT) has been presented in [7], VCHCT uses multiple cluster heads for cooperative transmission rather than the single cluster-head or non-cluster-head nodes.

© Springer International Publishing AG 2016
W. Li et al. (Eds.): IDCS 2016, LNCS 9864, pp. 477–486, 2016.
DOI: 10.1007/978-3-319-45940-0_44

Heterogeneous wireless sensor networks are constituted by many micro sensor nodes, which are deployed with different energy and communication characteristics. Energy heterogeneity is ubiquitous in WSNs. However, the classical CMIMO-based transmission schemes ignore the impact of heterogeneity. Based on the CMIMO technique and classical stable election protocol (SEP), we propose an energy-efficient V-BLAST-based cluster-head CMIMO transmission scheme (EVCCM) applied in heterogeneous wireless sensor networks. The simulation results show that our scheme provides longer network stable time than SEP and VCHCT schemes.

2   System Model and Scheme Design

2.1   System Model

To simplify the analysis, we consider the two-level heterogeneous networks that consist of normal and advanced sensor nodes. The initial energy of each normal node is E_0, the advanced nodes own θ times more energy than the normal nodes, the fraction of advanced nodes is m. As shown in Fig. 1, we consider a M × M square monitoring area, including mN advanced nodes and $(1 - m)N$ normal nodes. Similar to [6, 7, 10], we make the following assumptions. The sink node (SN) is equipped with multiple antennas for cooperative receiving and without energy constraint. All nodes are time synchronized and positioned before the operation, and can adjust the transmit power to reach other nodes or SN if needed. The AWGN channel is adopted for short distance communication within a cluster (local communication). The Rayleigh fading channel is adopted for the long-haul communication between cluster-heads and SN. MQAM scheme is used to further improve the energy efficiency. The number of cooperative nodes M_t is equal to the number of receiver antennas M_r. The energy consumption of the selection of cooperative nodes and baseband signal processing blocks is ignored.

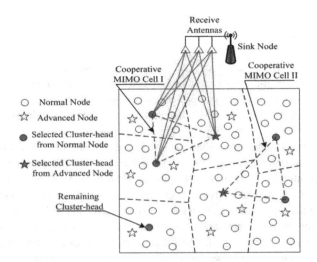

Fig. 1. Cooperative two-level heterogeneous networks

2.2   Scheme Design

Similar to LEACH protocol [10, 11], the operation of EVCCM is divided into rounds, each round includes the following three phases.

Cluster formation phase: All nodes organize themselves into local clusters based on SEP in this phase. First, each node chooses a random number between 0 and 1 separately. If the random number is less than the calculated threshold T(i), then it is selected as a cluster-head, T(i) is defined as:

$$T(i) = \begin{cases} \frac{P_i}{1-P_i(r \bmod \frac{1}{P_i})}, & \text{if } i \in G \\ 0 & \text{otherwise} \end{cases} \qquad (1)$$

Where, P(i) is the average probability of node i to be a cluster-head, r is the current round, G is the set of nodes that still have not become cluster-heads in the most recent rounds (r mod(1/P_i)). Based on the initial energy of node i, SEP protocol sets different weighted probabilities for normal and advanced nodes: if node is the normal node, $P_i = P_{opt}/(1 + m\theta)$. If the node i is the advanced node, $P_i = P_{opt}(1 + \theta)/(1 + m\theta)$. P_{opt} represents the optimal value of P_i, P_{opt} can be computed from $P_{opt} = K_{Copt}/N$ with K_{Copt} denoting the optimal number of cluster-heads. After the nodes have been selected to be cluster-heads, they broadcast the advertisement message to other nodes, then each non-cluster-head node determines the cluster to which it belongs, based on received signal strength. After the formation of the cluster, the cluster-head sets up a TDMA schedule for the cluster members.

CMIMO cell formation phase: This phase is completed according to the modified VCHCT scheme. Each cluster-head transmits a message containing its own ID and location information to the SN, which group cluster-heads into CMIMO cells based on the received message. Similar to LEACH protocol, the proposed scheme is self-organized, and offers no guarantee about the number of cluster-heads to form the CMIMO cell at last [11]. For the remaining cluster-heads, unlike the VCHCT that assume the SN can adapt to form a SIMO system between SN and the remaining cluster-heads, SN in our scheme will require each of them to split its date into M_t parts uniformly and distribute the split data to the M_t cooperative cluster-heads in the nearest CMIMO cell. Once the CMIMO cells form, SN sets up a TDMA schedule for all cluster-heads, and then broadcasts the schedule and cells information.

Data transmission phase: Assume that each cluster member collects L bits data, and transmits the data to its cluster-head by the TDMA schedule in cluster formation phase. After receiving data from all cluster members, the cluster-head fuses data to remove data redundancy. Based on the TDMA schedule and groups information in CMIMO cell formation phase, all cluster-heads transmit their fused data in their time slots. As shown in Fig. 1, the remaining cluster-head splits its fused date into three parts uniformly and distributes the split data to three cooperative cluster-heads in CMIMO cell I to transmit simultaneously their fused data and additional split data to SN. Successively, cluster-heads of CMIMO cell II conduct the simultaneous transmission.

3 Energy Consumption Model

In this section, we analyze the energy system under expected conditions, under which N nodes organize themselves into clusters in each round, each cluster contains a cluster-head and $N/K_c - 1$ member nodes, and K_c cluster-heads form n CMIMO cells ($K_c = nM_t$). As in [11], the total energy consumption E_{total} includes two parts: the energy consumption of local communication E_{local} and energy consumption of long-haul communication E_{long}.

$$E_{total} = E_{local} + E_{long} \qquad (2)$$

To keep the model simple, we include date fusion in local communication. E_{local} and E_{long} can be derived based on energy consumption per bit model between nodes.

3.1 Energy Consumption Model Between Nodes

The total average power consumption between nodes includes two parts [2]: the power consumption of all the power amplifiers P_{PA} and all other circuit blocks P_C. Thus, the energy consumption per bit between nodes is expressed as:

$$E_{bt} = \frac{P_{PA} + P_C}{R_{bt}} \qquad (3)$$

Where, R_{bt} is the bit rate.
P_{PA} can be expressed as:

$$P_{PA} = \begin{cases} (1+\alpha)\bar{E}_b R_{bt} C_{fs} d^2, & d \le d_0 \\ (1+\alpha)\bar{E}_b R_{bt} C_{mp} d^4, & d > d_0 \end{cases} \qquad (4)$$

Where, $\alpha = \xi/\eta - 1$ is the peak-average-ratio (PAR), b is constellation size, η is the drain efficiency of the RF power amplifier, $\bar{E}_b$ is the required energy per bit at the receiver for a certain BER denoted as $\bar{P}_b$, C_{fs} and C_{mp} are constants given by $C_{fs} = \frac{(4\pi)^2 M_l N_f}{G_t G_r \lambda^2}$, $C_{mp} = \frac{M_l N_f}{G_t G_r (h_t h_r)^2}$, M_l is the link margin, N_f is the receiver noise figure, N_0 is the single-sided thermal noise power-spectral-density (PSD) at the room temperature, G_t and G_r are the transmitter and receiver antenna gains respectively, λ is the carrier wavelength, h_t and h_r are separately the heights of transmitter and receiver antenna, d is the transmission distance, d_0 is the transmission distance threshold defined as $d_0 = \sqrt{C_{fs}/C_{mp}}$.

3.2 Energy Consumption Model in Local Communication

For short distance intra-cluster communication, free space model is adopted. The energy consumption per bit for intra-cluster communication is expressed as:

$$E_{bt}^s = (1+\alpha)\bar{E}_b^s C_{fs} d_{toCH}^2 + \frac{P_c^s}{R_{bt}^s} \tag{5}$$

Where, $\bar{E}_b^s$ is the required energy per bit at the receiver for SISO scheme. P_c^s is the circuit power consumption denoted as $P_c^s \approx P_{CT} + P_{CR}$. P_{CT} and P_{CR} are the power consumption for circuit blocks in the transmitter and receiver respectively. R_{bt}^s is the bit rate used in the local transmissions, $R_{bt}^s = bB$ denoted as with B is transmission bandwidth. d_{toCH}^2 is the expected squared distance from the nodes to the cluster head denoted as $d_{toCH}^2 = M^2/(2\pi K_C)$ [11]. For the MQAM modulation scheme reference SISO system, $\bar{E}_b^s$ is expressed as:

$$\bar{E}_b^s = \frac{(2^b - 1)N_0 \left(Q^{-1}\left(\frac{b\bar{P}_b}{4(1-2^{-\frac{b}{2}})} \right) \right)^2}{3b}, \quad (b \bmod 2 = 0) \tag{6}$$

If b is odd, we can obtain $\bar{E}_b^s$ after dropping the term $(1 - 2^{-\frac{b}{2}})$ in (6).

Each member node send L bits data to its cluster-head. Therefore, the transmitting energy consumption of a cluster can be derived as:

$$E_{intra} = L(\frac{N}{K_C} - 1)E_{bt}^s \tag{7}$$

A cluster-head receives L $(N/K_C - 1)$ bits date in each round. Assume E_{DA} is the energy consumption for data fusion per bit, the energy consumption of data fusion is given by:

$$E_{agg} = L(\frac{N}{K_C} - 1)E_{DA} \tag{8}$$

Based on [10], the total bits after fusion can be expressed as:

$$L_{agg} = \frac{(N/K_C - 1)L}{(f_{agg}N/K_C - 2f_{agg} + 1)} \tag{9}$$

Where, f_{agg} is the data fusion factor, Assume the data fusion is perfect, $f_{agg} = 1$.

Local communication contains K_C intra-clusters communication and date aggregation. Hence the energy consumption of local communication can be expressed as:

$$E_{local} = K_C (E_{intra} + E_{agg}) \tag{10}$$

According to (7), (8) and (10), the energy consumption in local communication is given by:

$$E_{local}(K_C, b) = L(N - K_C)[(1+\alpha)\bar{E}_b^s C_{fs} \frac{M^2}{2\pi K_C} + \frac{P_c^s}{B}]$$
$$+ L(N - K_C)E_{DA} \tag{11}$$

3.3 Energy Consumption Model in Long-Haul Communication

The multipath fading model is adopted in the long-haul transmission between CMIMO cells and SN. From (3) and (4), the energy consumption per bit for long-haul communication is expressed as:

$$E_{bt}^m = (1+\alpha)\bar{E}_b^m C_{mp} d_{mtoS}^4 + \frac{P_c^m}{R_{bt}^m} \tag{12}$$

Where, the required average energy per bit for MIMO system $\bar{E}_b^m$ can be calculated based on [5]. d_{mtoS} is the distance of long-haul transmission. SN has no energy constraint, hence the circuit power consumption at the receiver can be omitted. Circuit power consumption for CMIMO transmission can be given by $P_c^m \approx M_t P_{CT}$. The total bit rate of the MIMO system is given by $R_{bt}^m = bBM_t$.

According to (12), energy consumption in long-haul communication can be expressed as:

$$E_{long}(b, M_t, n) = \sum_{k=1}^{n} M_t L_{agg} [(1+\alpha)\bar{E}_b^m C_{mp} d_{mtoS}^4(k) + \frac{P_c^m}{bBM_t}] \tag{13}$$

Where, $d_{mtoS}(k)$ is the distance from the CMIMO cell k to SN. When SN is far away from sensing area, d_{mtoS} is approximately equal to the average distance between cluster-heads and SN $\bar{d}_{CHtoS}$. Hence, the simplified expression of (13) is given by:

$$E_{long}(n, M_t, b) = nM_t L_{agg} [(1+\alpha)\bar{E}_b^m C_{mp} \bar{d}_{CHtoS}^4 + \frac{P_c^m}{bBM_t}] \tag{14}$$

3.4 Total Energy Consumption Model

The total energy consumption model is established to obtain optimum parameters used in system design. According to (2), (11) and (14), total energy consumption per round is derived as:

$$E_{total}(K_C, n, M_t, b) = E_{local}(K_C, b) + E_{long}(n, M_t, b) \tag{15}$$

The total energy consumption above is a function of n, M_t and b. In the case of n = 1, the number of cluster-heads K_C may be less than the given the number of cooperative cluster-heads M_t, hence we consider that n is greater than 1. To simplify the analysis, we consider that M_t is greater than 4 and less than 9. Generally, the constellation size b is less than 14. Thus, the optimization model can be derived as:

$$(n, M_t, b) = \arg\min E_{total}(n, M_t, b)$$
$$s.t. \ \ 2 \leq b \leq 13$$
$$5 \leq M_t \leq 8 \tag{16}$$
$$n = 2, 3, \cdots$$

4 Simulation Results

We perform multiple simulations in MATLAB 2013b to find the optimal network parameters, which will be compared with the estimated parameters obtained by the (16). Meanwhile we evaluate the performance of EVCCM scheme by simulations.

Assume N = 400 nodes are uniformly distributed within a 100 m × 100 m monitoring area, the initial energy of each normal node is E_0 = 100 J. 20 % of the nodes are advanced nodes, which own θ = 1 times more initial energy than the normal node. SN is deployed at (50, 175), L = 4000 bits. The detailed simulation parameters are shown in Table 1.

Table 1. Simulation parameters

η = 0.35	$G_t G_r$ = 5 dB	$\bar{P}_b$ = 0.001
E_{DA} = 5 nJ/bit	M_l = 40 dB	B = 10 kHz
$N_0/2$ = −174 dBm/Hz	N_f = 10 dB	f_c = 2.4 GHz
$h_t = h_r$ = 1 m	P_{CT} = 98.19 mW	P_{CR} = 112.50 mW

We compare our simulation results with the estimated optimal network parameters obtained by the (16). Note that for these simulations, as in [11], we made no restrictions on the distance between the member nodes and their cluster-heads (d_{toCH}) or between cluster-heads and SN (d_{CHtoS}). Figure 2 shows the impacts of the constellation size b on the stability period (R rounds) with M_t = 5, n = 2. We find that the maximum stability period can be achieved when b = 4. It can also be found that the network with b = 6 achieves the best performance after 4500 rounds, but the number of surviving nodes is so small that the whole network becomes unstable and information transfer becomes inaccurate.

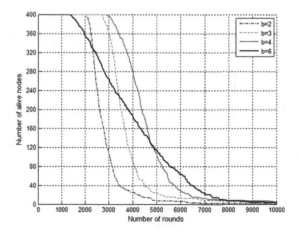

Fig. 2. The impacts of b on R

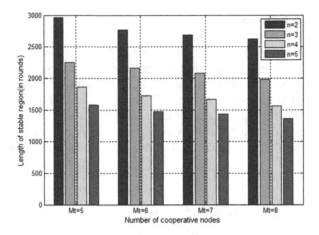

Fig. 3. The impacts of n and M_t on R

Figure 3 shows the impacts of the number of CMIMO cells n and the number of co-operative cluster-heads in a CMIMO cell M_t on the stability period when b = 4. We find that the maximum stability period can be achieved when b = 4, M_t = 5, n = 2, which agrees well with the optimal network parameters obtained by the (16).

Figure 4 shows network lifetime comparison between EVCCM, VCHCT and traditional SEP. The modulation scheme is BPSK for both VCHCT and SEP. We observe that, similar to the results in [7], the stability period of VCHCT seems same as SEP. This is because when the modulation scheme is fixed and the distance of long-haul communication is not too far, the energy saving of MIMO systems is trivial for large scale and high node density wireless sensor networks. It is also shown that the stable time of EVCCM is prolonged about 200 % than SEP and VCHCT.

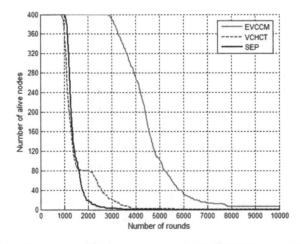

Fig. 4. The network lifetime comparison of SEP, VCHCT and EVCCM

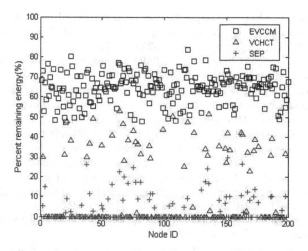

Fig. 5. The remaining energy comparison after1500 rounds of SEP, VCHCT and EVCCM

Figure 5 shows the percentage ratio of the remaining energy to the initial energy for 200 randomly selected nodes after 1500 rounds with three protocols. It is obvious that EVCCM can reduce the energy consumption of networks and balance the energy among different sensor nodes. The remaining energy distribution of nodes is highly asymmetric in VCHCT. It is because VCHCT fails to take full advantages of the extra energy provided by the advanced nodes.

5   Conclusions

This work proposes a novel energy-efficient V-BLAST-based cluster-head cooperative MIMO transmission scheme (EVCCM) applied in heterogeneous wireless sensor network. The proposed scheme makes advanced nodes have the greater probability of participation in remote collaborative communications to balance the energy among different nodes. Besides, a simple joint optimization model is established under expected conditions to estimate directly the optimal network parameters. Simulation results show that EVCCM can prolong the stable time greatly in comparison with SEP and VCHCT.

References

1. Nguyen, D., Krunz, M.: Cooperative MIMO in wireless networks: recent developments and challenges. IEEE Netw. **27**(4), 48–54 (2013)
2. Cui, S., Goldsmith, A., Bahai, A.: Energy-efficiency of MIMO and cooperative MIMO techniques in sensor networks. IEEE J. Sel. Areas Commun. **22**(6), 1089–1098 (2004)
3. Jayaweera, S.: Virtual MIMO-based cooperative communication for energy-constrained wireless sensor networks. IEEE Trans. Wireless Commun. **5**(5), 984–989 (2006)

4. Gai, Y., Zhang, L., Shan, X.: Energy efficiency of cooperative MIMO with data aggregation in wireless sensor networks. In: Proceedings of the IEEE Wireless Communications and Networking Conference (WCNC), pp. 791–796 (2007)
5. Jayaweera, S.: V-BLAST-based virtual MIMO for distributed wireless sensor networks. IEEE Trans. Commun. **55**(10), 1867–1872 (2006)
6. Xu, K., Liu, W., Yang, Z., Cheng, G., Li, Y.: An end-to-end optimized cooperative transmission scheme for virtual MIMO sensor networks. In: Proceedings of the 10th IEEE Singapore International Conference on Communications Systems (ICCS), pp. 1–5 (2006)
7. Ding, J., Liu, D., Zhang, X.: An energy-efficient virtual V-BLAST transmission scheme for cluster-based wireless sensor networks. In: Proceedings of the 2nd IEEE International Conference on Network Infrastructure and Digital Content, pp. 488–493 (2010)
8. Smaragdakis, G., Matta, I., Bestavros, A.: SEP: a stable election protocol for clustered heterogeneous wireless sensor networks. In: Proceeding of 2nd International Workshop on Sensor and Actor Network Protocol and Applications (SANPA), pp. 1–11 (2004)
9. Li, J., Jiang, X., Lu, I.: Energy balance routing algorithm based on virtual MIMO scheme for wireless sensor networks. J. Sens. (2014)
10. Heinzelman, W., Chandrakasan, A., Balakrishnan, H.: An application specific protocol architecture for wireless microsensor networks. IEEE Trans. Wireless Commun. **1**(4), 660–670 (2002)
11. Kong, H.: Energy efficient cooperative LEACH protocol for wireless sensor networks. Communications and networks. J. Commun. Netw. **12**(4), 358–365 (2010)

Analysis of the Intelligent Call System Based on the Emergency Rescue in China

Tianping Zhang$^{(\boxtimes)}$, Lijie Li, Wenfeng Li, and Jie Mei

School of Logistics Engineering, Wuhan University of Technology,
Wuhan, People's Republic of China
ztp_2004@163.com, lijie.li@hotmail.co.uk,
liwf@whut.edu.cn, meijieben@foxmail.com

Abstract. Effective emergency response is crucial when accident happens. It is the core issue of current research on emergency rescue system (ERS) to find out the method to improve the success rate of timely emergency call access. This paper first introduces the present situation of the emergency rescue industry, on basis of which we will analyse the model of the ERS. Then from the viewpoint of improving the success rate of timely emergency call, this paper introduces an intelligent emergency call system model that takes advantages of intelligent network (IN). When emergency accidents occur, the highest level called terminal sometimes cannot timely respond to incoming communication. In this case, continued calling will automatically be transferred to the corresponding other terminals. This strategy improves the adaptability and real-time performance of ERS and the performance of the ERS behaviour control, has very good prospects in the field of emergency rescue.

Keywords: Emergency rescue system · Reliability · Intelligent call forwarding

1 Introduction

Emergency Rescue System's main purpose is to collect the accident site information with the fastest speed, then use the shortest possible time to deal with the accident, reducing the direct and indirect economic losses and casualties caused by the accident to a minimum [1]. How to improve the efficiency of the emergency rescue, enabling ambulance crews accurately arrive at the scene in the first time, preventing accident, minimising accidental injury consequence and maximising social benefits, has been a focus of the current emergency rescue system research [2]. Many developed countries have developed perfect emergency rescue systems. Through detection of accidents, to clarify the whole process of accident, and then to use the advanced architecture, the rescue systems make sure all kinds of rescuers can effectively cooperate, closely linked, to ensure the timeliness and reliability of the rescue. With the development of China's industrialisation and modernisation, urbanisation process is in a steady way. By 2013, the urban population in China had exceeded 700 million. China has 657 cities in total. Therefore, a city's capability of responding to various emergencies is of great importance to national economy and the people's livelihood. With the acceleration of

© Springer International Publishing AG 2016
W. Li et al. (Eds.): IDCS 2016, LNCS 9864, pp. 487–493, 2016.
DOI: 10.1007/978-3-319-45940-0_45

urbanisation process and constant expansion of city size in China, various emergencies due to natural, technological and human factors rise up one by one. Accidents of such kind often cause serious deaths and injuries and huge property losses, becoming serious threats to living quality of urban residents and safety of people's lives and properties. Therefore, cities in China should take all possible and feasible measures to improve their capabilities in responding to various potential emergencies and strengthen their emergency response abilities to assure public security [3]. Emergency rescue system in our country also has limitations in accident detection, the efficiency is not high, rescue related facilities are not complete and each department cannot coordination and so on. These reasons lead to long-term high accident mortality rates in our country, there is a big gap between china and foreign developed countries. Based on the current emergency response situation, this paper focuses on studying automatic call for rescue. This is the accident information acquisition for the emergency rescue system (ERS). The aim of this study is to improve the reliability and efficiency of the ERS [4].

2 Background Research

2.1 The Analysis of Emergency Rescue Industry Form with Its Current Status

The emergency rescue system is shown in Fig. 1, which includes: Abnormal accident information acquisition module [5, 6], Emergency inspection and confirmation, emergency scale classification, Emergency decision analysis expert system, Emergency record database, Accident and emergency rescue, forming emergency handling report. The abnormal accident information acquisition module contains active help and passive

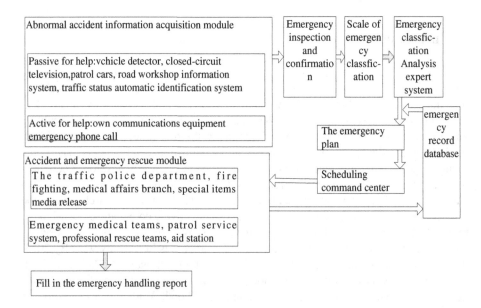

Fig. 1. The emergency rescue system

help. When abnormal accident gathering information is received, the information is put into emergency inspection and confirmation. Scale of emergency classification then enter the decision analysis expert system, expert system combined with the record in the database of emergency data, reference solution is given by expert system for emergency rescue, and then determines the final rescue plan according to the scene of the specific circumstances, scheduling of emergency department for emergency rescue. In the process of emergency scheduling, the unified commanding, coordination of various departments and cooperation with each other should be strengthened, they are together forming efficient emergency rescue system. Rescue resources are divided into internal resources and social resources.

2.2 The Construction of the Emergency Rescue of Developed Countries Abroad

In developed countries, rescue equipment development and emergency rescue system development are carried out at the same time. The popularisation and the correct implementation of traffic accident scene rescue reduce the morbidity and mortality in traffic accident. With the increasing development of science and technology, developed countries are progressing gradually in the traffic accident rescue, first aid network construction, and emergency rescue system, forming a collaborative three-dimensional relief system incorporating land, air, and sea.

2.3 The Domestic Construction of Emergency Rescue

The development of social, economic and cultural prosperity in china has entered an unprecedented rapid development stage. As an economic power, frequency of disasters and emergency accidents, not only causing great losses to the national economy, but also posing a serious threat to people's life safety. The development of China's emergency rescue industry has great development potential, good comprehensive benefits. In recent years, China's emergency rescue industry has gone from nonexistence to existence, gradually forming its shape. Emergency rescue industry involves the industry and services, equipment manufacturing, electronic information, material, medicine, environmental protection, insurance and other fields. In addition, China's society and economy is not harmonious, unstable factors, natural disasters, accidents disasters, public health events and social security incidents frequently happen. Related detection, prevention and treatment of products and services are needed as a guarantee.

2.4 The Urgency to Strengthen the Construction of Domestic Emergency Rescue Industry

Accelerating the construction of domestic emergency rescue industry is the objective requirement to cope with the increasingly frequency of accidents. It is also an important content for cultivating new economic growth point. It is the important base for enhancing national emergency management capability. As shown in Fig. 1, according to the analysis of the emergency rescue system, the premise of rescue must be able to collect accident information timely and effectively, Emergency call phone is the core parts of emergency rescue system for acquisition of the accident information. The function of Emergency call phone is still limited, due to be limitation by a variety factors. Because malfunction of emergency call phone, installation of an emergency call phone even becomes just a decoration, playing no role in the proper emergency action. Some people in trouble simply turned to their own communication equipment for help. But in times of emergency, the person's brain potentially becomes blank. When people are calling, the conversation between the caller and the called terminal falls into a state of chaos. However the caller will choose to continue to call, due to the psychological tension. Carrying communications equipment due to a lack of power will delay the best rescue time, leading to irreparable economic loss and casualty. So functional emergency calls is in urgent need of development to be usable in a variety of emergency rescue situations, as an essential part of emergency rescue system.

3   Analysis of IN Concept Model

3.1   The Advantage of IN

The current communication network is developed in the intelligent and personalised direction. Basic telecommunication services have been unable to meet the needs of people, all kinds of users' demand for telecom business is becoming more and more complicated. So it requires the telecommunication network to provide customers with all kinds of telecom business quickly and flexibly. The traditional method of providing new business is that each provides a kind of new business; all the switches of the Internet have to be increased. IN technology overcomes the shortcoming of the traditional method. The method of exchange which IN adopts is separated from business. Strong adaptability, shorter generated business cycle, at the same time their norms together make the method easier for the manufacturer to implement.

3.2   Introduction of IN Concept Model

IN contains more "artificial intelligence" in the communication network (such as telephone communications network). So IN can provide the business, meeting all types of users' needs at any time. It is a fast, convenient and flexible, economic and effective method with regeneration and implementation of new business. It has a unified theory conceptual model, namely INCM (Intelligent Network Conceptual Model). INCM is a four-plane model, which can be represented as four dimensions. From top to bottom: business layer, the overall function layer, the distribution function layer and the physical layer. Each dimension represents the respective network capacity from different angles, as shown in Fig. 2. The top layer is the business layer, which reflects the capacity of Intelligent Network and gives a clue to the user what kind of business they are doing. Different business operations can have the same properties, or have one or several different business properties. The smallest business unit is the Single Business Property, for example "Call Forwarding", it can be treated as a business property, or a business. The second layer is a global function layer, showing intelligent network platform's open nature. In this layer intelligent network is seen as a whole by constructing. Reusable software function modules of business that can be reused to identify a network of basic capabilities, and then describe how these modules together to achieve business layer determined business and business properties. The third layer is the distribution function layer, showing intelligent network functional entities within the division and its implementation. It defines the functional entities to achieve the functional model with providing message flow between the entities. The fourth layer is the physical layer. The physical layer decides what kind of physical entity to implement to realise the desired functionality in the plane of the distribution functions.

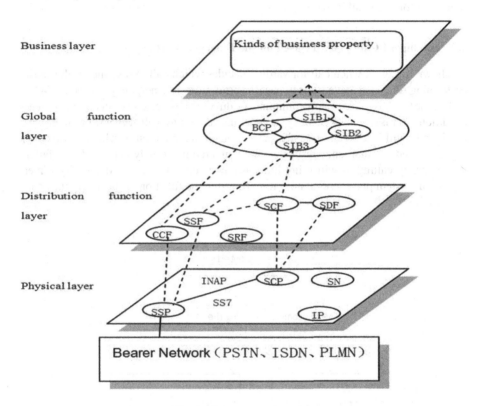

Fig. 2. IN conceptual model

4 The Intelligent Call System Based on the ERS

4.1 The Function of Intelligent Call System Based on the Emergency Rescue

In an emergency situation, how to ensure quality of service (QoS) of users' business, we research on call admission control scheme in multimedia communication network [6–8], and compared to the existing emergency call strategy, designing an emergency rescue call control strategy with intelligent transfer. Then based on the analysis, simulation is carried out by computer. According to the characteristics of business, terminal calls are assigned with different priorities. According to the different priorities and QoS requirements, the user terminal call admission is decided. In order to ensure that the special users communicating smoothly in case of emergency, terminal calls are assigned with different priorities based on intelligent control algorithm. The users of different roles each have their own specific user access permissions through the way of trust negotiation. High prioritised users will access firstly system in case of emergency, low prioritised users will be treated according to high priority users-first principle with different access conditions: refuse to answer, busy, no answer. Using call transfer control strategy timely to redirect call transfer to access, for the sake of avoiding emergency scene environment call interruption.

4.2   Intelligent Call System Based on the Emergency Rescue

As shown in Fig. 3, when call forwarding decides which call to respond, high priority performing role users have priority access permissions in emergency situations. When calling the terminal, if one can't communicate directly, it is because of insufficient access conditions: refuse to answer, busy, no one answer. Using call forwarding timely and continually will lead to call transfer success, avoiding situation in which call for help are suspended. If emergency rescue are not delivered in a timely manner due to failure in emergency calling, it will bring immeasurable economic loss and casualty. Emergency call system plays a regulatory role, fulfilling the function of the emergency calls very well.

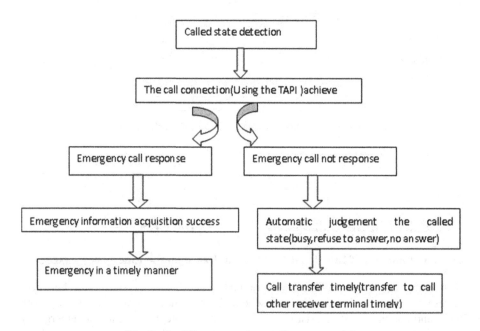

Fig. 3. Intelligent emergency call system model

5   Conclusions

Because of today's society is in a fast developing situation, the existing statistical indicators of emergency rescue are much less collectively accessible which will greatly hampers the fully evaluation of the reliability of emergency rescue system. Though communication infrastructure of our country emergency rescue command system has been implemented, the demand for information management requirements is far larger. The information management system construction arouses more attention. But the information degree of the emergency rescue system is different at every place. There is no uniform standard of information management, information system management level is not high, the level of properly using and sharing information is low. With the development of economy, emergency rescue industry calls for more progress. Construction of information system will be a new hot spot. Therefore, research on information standardisation, promotion of the standardisation of information management has become a research subject in emergency rescue industry in China. Constructing perfect function, effective regulation, timely and effective emergency rescue system corresponds to the need of the development of the society. The emergency telephone call, as an indispensable part of emergency information collection, because of its function being improved, will give birth to a new understanding and use of it among people.

References

1. Duan, W., He, B.: Emergency response system for pollution accidents in chemical industrial parks, China. Int. J. Environ. Res. Public Health **12**(7), 7868–7885 (2015)
2. Zhong, M.: Study in performance analysis of China urban emergency response system based on Petri net. Saf. Sci. **48**(6), 755–762 (2010)
3. Wang, G.: Active in the construction of underground facilities, application of hedge effort to build the mine emergency rescue system for building mode. China Min. Mag. **19**(10), 67–70 (2010)
4. Huang, Y.: Modeling and simulation method of the emergency response systems based on OODA. Knowl. Based Syst. **89**, 527–540 (2015)
5. Sun, Q.: Research on the location model of emergency rescue facilities in the city disaster prevention. Appl. Mech. Mater. **744**, 1745–1748 (2015)
6. Fortino, G., Giannantonio, R., Gravina, R., Kuryloski, P., Jafari, R.: Enabling effective programming and flexible management of efficient body sensor network applications. IEEE Trans. Hum. Mach. Syst. **43**(1), 115–133 (2013)
7. Fortino, G., Fatta, G., Pathan, M., Vasilakos, A.: Cloud-assisted body area networks: state-of-the-art and future challenges. Wireless Netw. **20**(7), 1925–1938 (2014)
8. Fortino, G., Guerrieri, A., Bellifemine, F., Giannantonio, R.: SPINE2: developing BSN applications on heterogeneous sensor nodes. IEEE Int. Symp. Ind. Embed. Syst. 128–131 (2009)
9. Chou, H., Wang, Y., Chang, H.: Design intelligent wheelchair with ECG measurement and wireless transmission function. Technol. Health Care **24**(s1), 345–355 (2015)

Distance Thresholds Analysis for Cooperative Beamforming in WSNs

Xiong Gan[1], Hong Lu[1], and Guangyou Yang[2(✉)]

[1] School of Mechanical and Electronic Engineering, Wuhan University
of Technology, Wuhan, People's Republic of China
ganxiong001@126.com, landzh@whut.edu.cn
[2] Institute of Agricultural Machinery, Hubei University of Technology,
Wuhan, People's Republic of China
pekka@126.com

Abstract. Cooperative beamforming (CBF) scheme may not consume less energy than single-input-single-output (SISO) scheme in wireless sensor networks (WSNs). In order to select an energy efficient transmission scheme from the two schemes, the distance thresholds at which the CBF scheme outperforms the SISO scheme in energy efficiency are investigated, an optimal scheme selection algorithm based on distance thresholds is proposed. Theoretical analysis shows the mathematical expression of distance thresholds. Meanwhile, numerical results validate the effectiveness of our proposed algorithm.

Keywords: Cooperative beamforming · Wireless sensor networks · Distance thresholds

1 Introduction

Sensor nodes are powered by batteries with limited energy, which are laborious or awfully costly to replace or recharge in the majority of the application scenarios. Thus, energy dissipation problem is urgent to be solved in wireless sensor networks (WSNs) [1].

Under the same system requirement, multiple-input-multiple-output (MIMO) system requires less transmit power than single-input-single-output (SISO) system in wireless networks [2]. However, it may be unpractical to deploy multiple antennas for micro sensor node in WSNs. Fortunately, cooperative-multiple-input-multiple-output (CMIMO) scheme based on space-time-block-code (STBC) improves the signal strength at the receiver by forming virtual-antenna-arrays (VAAs), which shows that CMIMO scheme can have more energy efficiency than SISO scheme over certain distance thresholds [3, 4]. In [5], vertical-Bell-labs-layered-space-time (V-BLAST) based CMIMO transmission is proposed and it does not require the local data exchange. However, the number of receive-antennas should be larger than the transmit-antennas. In [6], cooperative beamforming (CBF) based cooperative-multi-input-single-output (CMISO, a variant of CMIMO) transmission is proposed, which shows that CBF scheme has more superiority than STBC scheme in energy efficiency. In [7], the distance threshold for STBC scheme outperforms SISO scheme is

W. Li et al. (Eds.): IDCS 2016, LNCS 9864, pp. 494–502, 2016.
DOI: 10.1007/978-3-319-45940-0_46

presented by numerical results. In [8], CMISO scheme based on STBC with data aggregation is adopted to reduce the energy dissipation in clustered WSNs. However, the distances between source nodes and destination node are considered to be equal in [7, 8], without considering the effect of sensor nodes deployment on the distance thresholds. This paper expands the works in [7, 8], with considering all sensor nodes deployments, the distance thresholds at which CBF scheme outperforms SISO scheme in energy efficiency are given. Based on the energy dissipation model, an optimal scheme selection algorithm is proposed.

The structure of this paper is arranged as follows. Section 2 presents the energy dissipation model. Section 3 proposes the algorithm to select optimal scheme based on distance thresholds. Numerical results and analysis are presented in Sect. 4. Section 5 is the conclusion.

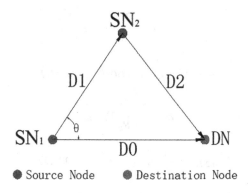

Fig. 1. System model

2   Energy Dissipation Model

Source node SN_1 and source node SN_2 both have L bits data that need to be transmitted to destination node DN. The distance between SN_1 and SN_2 is D1, the distance from DN to SN_1 and SN_2 are D0 and D2, respectively. $< \overline{SN_1 SN_2}$, $\overline{SN_1 DN} > = \theta$, $(0° \leq \theta \leq 180°)$. Figure 1 shows the system model. The Rayleigh fading channel with a square-law path loss is assumed, power control is enabled for sensor nodes. Binary-phase-shift-keying (BPSK) modulation scheme is used for data transmission.

2.1   CBF Scheme

The CMISO transmission scheme based on CBF has two phases. In the first phase, SN_1 and SN_2 use different time slots to exchange their L bits data. In the second phase, SN_1 and SN_2 use cooperative beamforming scheme to encode the data and transmit them to DN. The energy dissipation of CBF scheme E_{CBF} is the sum of the two phases, which is given by

$$E_{CBF} = E_{p1} + E_{p2} \tag{1}$$

Where, E_{p1} and E_{p2} are the energy dissipation in the two phases.

Similar to the energy dissipation model in [3, 4]. E_{p1} and E_{p2} are both consist of two components, circuit energy dissipation and power amplifiers energy dissipation, which is given by

$$E_{p1} = E_{p1,C} + E_{p1,PA} \tag{2}$$

$$E_{p2} = E_{p2,C} + E_{p2,PA} \tag{3}$$

Where, $E_{p1,C}$ and $E_{p2,C}$ are the circuit energy dissipation. $E_{p1,PA}$ and $E_{p2,PA}$ are the power amplifiers energy dissipation.

$$E_{p1,C} = \frac{2L}{R_b} P_{C,SISO} \tag{4}$$

$$E_{p1,PA} = \frac{2L}{R_b} P_{PA,SISO}(\overline{E}_{b\_SISO}, D_1) \tag{5}$$

$$E_{p2,C} = \frac{2L}{R_b} P_{C,CBF} \tag{6}$$

$$E_{p2,PA} = \frac{2L}{R_b} P_{PA,CBF}(\overline{E}_{b,CBF}, D0, D2) \tag{7}$$

The power dissipation $P_{PA,SISO}$ can be represented as [6]

$$P_{PA,SISO}(\overline{E}_{b,SISO}, D) = \frac{\xi}{\eta} \overline{E}_{b,SISO} R_b \frac{(4\pi D)^2}{G_t G_r \lambda^2} M_l N_f \tag{8}$$

Where, ξ is the peak-to-average ratio (PAR), η is the drain efficiency, $\overline{E}_{b,SISO}$ is the required average energy in SISO system, $R_b = bB$ is the bit rate, D is the transmission distance, $G_t G_r$ is the antenna gain, λ is the carrier wavelength, M_l is the link margin and N_f is the receiver noise figure.

$\overline{E}_{b,SISO}$ can be expressed as [4]

$$\overline{E}_{b,SISO} = \frac{N_0}{\left(1 - 2\overline{P}_b\right)^{-2} - 1} \tag{9}$$

Where, N_0 is the single-sided thermal noise power-spectral-density (PSD).

The power dissipation $P_{PA,CBF}$ can be represented as [6]

$$P_{PA,CBF}(\overline{E}_{b,CBF}, D0, D2) = \frac{\xi}{\eta} \frac{\overline{E}_{b,CBF}}{2} R_b \frac{(4\pi)^2((D0)^2 + (D2)^2)}{G_t G_r \lambda^2} M_l N_f \tag{10}$$

Where, $\overline{E}_{b,CBF}$ is the required average energy in cooperative beamforming transmission, which can be expressed as [6]

$$\overline{E}_{b,CBF} = \frac{N_0}{\left(1 - 2\sqrt{P_b/3}\right)^{-2} - 1} \tag{11}$$

2.2 Conventional SISO Scheme

For conventional SISO scheme, SN_1 and SN_2 transmit their L bits data to DN, respectively. The energy dissipation E_{SISO} can be represented as follow.

$$
\begin{aligned}
E_{SISO} &= E_{s1} + E_{s2} \\
&= (E_{s1,C} + E_{s1,PA}) + (E_{s2,C} + E_{s2,PA}) \\
&= (\frac{L}{R_b} P_{C,SISO} + \frac{L}{R_b} P_{PA,SISO}(\overline{E}_{b,SISO}, D0)) + (\frac{L}{R_b} P_{C,SISO} + \frac{L}{R_b} P_{PA,SISO}(\overline{E}_{b,SISO}, D2))
\end{aligned} \tag{12}
$$

Where, E_{s1} and E_{s2} are the energy dissipation from the SN_1 and SN_2 to the DN, respectively. $E_{s1,C}$ and $E_{s2,C}$ are the circuit energy dissipation. $E_{s1,PA}$ and $E_{s2,PA}$ are the power amplifiers energy dissipation.

3 Distance Thresholds Analysis

In this section, the algorithm is presented to select optimal scheme based on distance thresholds. For $(D2)^2 = (D0)^2 + (D1)^2 - 2(D0)(D1)\cos\theta$, we set

$$\frac{L}{R_b} g(D0, D1, \theta) = E_{CBF}(D0, D1, \theta) - E_{SISO}(D0, D1, \theta) \tag{13}$$

So, $g(D0, D1, \theta)$ can be expressed as

$$g(D0, D1, \theta) = (D1)^2 \times R + (D1) \times S(D0, \cos\theta) + T(D0) \tag{14}$$

Where, $R = (\overline{E}_{b,SISO} + \overline{E}_{b,CBF})\frac{\xi}{\eta} R_b \frac{(4\pi)^2}{G_t G_r \lambda^2} M_l N_f$, $S(D0, \cos\theta) = 2\cos\theta(\overline{E}_{b,SISO} - \overline{E}_{b,CBF})\frac{\xi}{\eta} R_b \frac{(4\pi)^2}{G_t G_r \lambda^2} M_l N_f D0$, $T(D0) = 2(\overline{E}_{b,CBF} - \overline{E}_{b,SISO})\frac{\xi}{\eta} R_b \frac{(4\pi)^2}{G_t G_r \lambda^2} M_l N_f (D0)^2 + 4P_{CT} + 2P_{CR}$.

It can be found that, If g(D0, D1, θ) = 0, E_{SISO}(D0, D1, θ) = E_{CBF}(D0, D1, θ), SISO scheme consumes the equal energy as CBF scheme. However, the complexity of CBF scheme is higher than SISO scheme. So, if g(D0, D1, θ) ≥ 0, SISO scheme is selected. Otherwise, CBF scheme is selected. The following Propositions 1, 2 and 3 can be used to select the optimal scheme based on distance thresholds.

Proposition 1. If $D0 \in [0, D0_{TH1}]$ or $(D0 \in [D0_{TH1}, D0_{TH2}]) \cup (\theta \in [0°, 90°])$, g $(D0, D1, \theta) \geq 0$.

Where, $$DO_{TH1} = \sqrt{\frac{(\overline{E}_{b,SISO} + \overline{E}_{b,CBF})(2P_{CT} + P_{CR})}{\frac{1}{2}\cos^2\theta(\overline{E}_{b,SISO} - \overline{E}_{b,CBF})^2\frac{\varsigma}{\eta}R_b\frac{(4\pi)^2}{G_tG_r\lambda^2}M_lN_f + (\overline{E}_{b,SISO}^2 - \overline{E}_{b,CBF}^2)\frac{\varsigma}{\eta}R_b\frac{(4\pi)^2}{G_tG_r\lambda^2}M_lN_f}},$$

$$DO_{TH2} = \sqrt{\frac{(\overline{E}_{b,SISO} + \overline{E}_{b,CBF})(2P_{CT} + P_{CR})}{(\overline{E}_{b,SISO}^2 - \overline{E}_{b,CBF}^2)\frac{\varsigma}{\eta}R_b\frac{(4\pi)^2}{G_tG_r\lambda^2}M_lN_f}}.$$

Proof. $R > 0$, if $D0 \in [0, D0_{TH1}]$, $\Delta = S^2 - 4RT \leq 0$, $g(D0, D1, \theta) \geq 0$. If $D0 \in [$ $D0_{TH1}, D0_{TH2}]) \cup (\theta \in [0°, 90°]$, $\Delta = S^2 - 4RT > 0$, $-S/2R \leq 0$, $g(D0, 0, \theta) \geq 0$, g $(D0, D1, \theta) \geq 0$.

Proposition 2. If $(D0 \in (D0_{TH1}, D0_{TH2})) \cup (\theta \in (90°, 180°])$, when $D1 \in [0, D1_{TH1}] \cup [D1_{TH2}, +\infty)$, $g(D0, D1, \theta) \geq 0$. Whereas, when $D1 \in (D1_{TH1}, D1_{TH2})$, g $(D0, D1, \theta) < 0$.

Where, $$D1_{TH1} = \frac{-S(D0, \cos\theta) - \sqrt{S(D0, \cos\theta)^2 - 4RT(D0)}}{2R}, \quad D1_{TH2} =$$

$$\frac{-S(D0, \cos\theta) + \sqrt{S(D0, \cos\theta)^2 - 4RT(D0)}}{2R}.$$

Proof. $R > 0$, if $(D0 \in (D0_{TH1}, D0_{TH2})) \cup (\theta \in (90°, 180°])$, $\Delta = S^2 - 4RT > 0$, $-S/2R \geq 0$, $g(D0, 0, \theta) \geq 0$. As a result, when $D1 \in [0, D1_{TH1}] \cup [D1_{TH2}, +\infty)$, $g(D0, D1, \theta) \geq 0$. Whereas, when $D1 \in (D1_{TH1}, D1_{TH2})$, $g(D0, D1, \theta) < 0$.

Proposition 3. If $D0 \in [D0_{TH2}, +\infty)$, when $D1 \in [0, D1_{TH3})$, $g(D0, D1, \theta) < 0$. Whereas, when $D1 \in [D1_{TH3}, +\infty)$, $g(D0, D1, \theta) \geq 0$.

Where, $$D1_{TH3} = \frac{-S(D0, \cos\theta) + \sqrt{S(D0, \cos\theta)^2 - 4RT(D0)}}{2R}.$$

Proof. $R > 0$, if $D0 \in [D0_{TH2}, +\infty)$, $\Delta = S^2 - 4RT > 0$, $g(D0, 0, \theta) < 0$. As a result, when $D1 \in [0, D1_{TH3})$, $g(D0, D1, \theta) < 0$. Whereas, when $D1 \in [D1_{TH3}, +\infty)$, $g(D0, D1, \theta) \geq 0$.

By Propositions 1, 2 and 3, the algorithm to select optimal scheme based on distance thresholds is given as follows.

Algorithm: Optimal scheme selection based on distance thresholds

```
Input: D0, D1, θ
Output: Energy efficient transmission scheme
1. Calculate the distance thresholds D0_TH1, D0_TH2, D1_TH1,
D1_TH2 and D1_TH3 according to Proposition 1, Proposition 2
and Proposition 3.
2.     If D0 ∈ [0,D0_TH1] or (D0 ∈ [D0_TH1,D0_TH2]) ∪ (θ ∈ [0°,90°])
3.                Select SISO scheme.
4.     Else if  (D0 ∈ (D0_TH1,D0_TH2)) ∪ (θ ∈ (90°,180°])
5.            If  D1 ∈ [0,D1_TH1] ∪ [D1_TH2,+∞)
6.                Select SISO scheme.
7.          Else
8.                Select CBF scheme.
9.          End
10.  Else
11.          If  D1 ∈ [0,D1_TH3)
12.             Select CBF scheme.
13.          Else
14.                Select SISO scheme.
15.          End
16.  End
```

4 Numerical Results and Analysis

In this section, distance thresholds and the effectiveness of our proposed algorithm are presented. Matlab 2013a is used for numerical results, the system parameters are shown in Table 1, which can be obtained from [3, 4].

In Fig. 2, the distance thresholds $D0_{TH1}$ and $D0_{TH2}$ are plotted against angle value θ under different BER requirements. It can be seen that, for a given BER requirement, $D0_{TH1}$ gets the maximum value when $\theta = 90°$ and $D0_{TH2}$ is a constant value. For a given θ, as BER requirement decreases, $D0_{TH1}$ and $D0_{TH2}$ decrease. For example, when θ is set as $0°$, for BER requirement decreases from 0.0003 to 0.0001, $D0_{TH1}$ decreases from 100.5 m to 57.5 m, $D0_{TH2}$ decreases from 121.9 m to 69.9 m. The reason is that, the lower the BER requirement, the more advantage of CBF transmission scheme, and corresponds to smaller distance thresholds $D0_{TH1}$ and $D0_{TH2}$.

In Fig. 3, the distance thresholds $D1_{TH1}$ and $D1_{TH2}$ are plotted with different D0 under different BER requirements with $\theta = 180°$. It can be seen from Fig. 3 that, for a

Table 1. System parameters

L = 100 bits	ξ = 1(BPSK)	η = 0.35	B = 10 kHz
G_tG_r = 5 dBi	λ = 0.12 m	M_l = 40 dB	N_f = 10 dB
$N_0/2$ = 174 dBm/Hz	R_b = bB	P_{SISO} = 210.6 mw	P_{CBF} = 308.8 mw

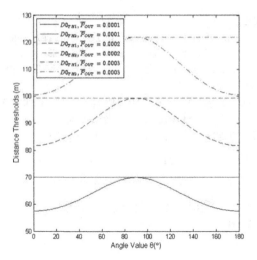

Fig. 2. Distance thresholds $D0_{TH1}$ and $D0_{TH2}$ over angle value θ under different BER requirements

given BER requirement, the larger D0, the smaller $D1_{TH1}$ and the larger $D1_{TH2}$ will be. For example, when $\overline{P}_{OUT} = 0.0002$, for D0 increases from 86 m to 94 m, $D1_{TH1}$ decreases from 37.0 m to 11.7 m and $D1_{TH2}$ increases from 126.9 m to 167.5 m. The reason is that a larger transmission distance D0 corresponds to more advantage of CBF transmission scheme, and corresponds to a larger $[D1_{TH2} - D1_{TH1}]$.

In Fig. 4, the distance threshold $D1_{TH3}$ is plotted under different D0 for different BER requirements with $\theta = 0°$, $\theta = 90°$, $\theta = 180°$. It can be seen from Fig. 4 that, distance threshold $D1_{TH3}$ increases with D0 and θ for a given BER requirement. The reason is that, the advantage of CBF is more obvious in longer transmission distance.

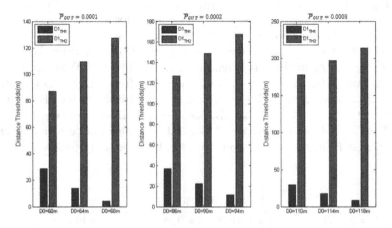

Fig. 3. Distance thresholds $D1_{TH1}$ and $D1_{TH2}$ with different D0 for $\overline{P}_{OUT} = 0.0001$, 0.0002, 0.0003

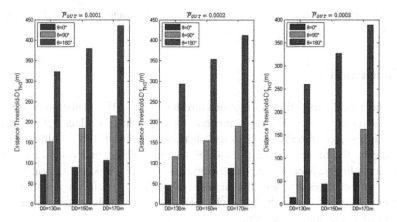

Fig. 4. Distance threshold $D1_{TH3}$ under different $D0$ for different BER requirements with $\theta = 0°$, $\theta = 90°$, $\theta = 180°$

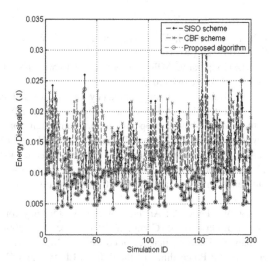

Fig. 5. Energy dissipation comparison among SISO, CBF scheme and proposed algorithm

Meanwhile, for a given $D0$ and θ, distance threshold $D1_{TH3}$ increases as BER requirement decreases. The reason is that, the smaller the BER requirement, the more energy saving in cooperative transmission. The advantage of CBF scheme is more obvious in a smaller BER requirement, and the distance threshold $D1_{TH3}$ increases accordingly.

The energy dissipation of SISO scheme, CBF scheme and proposed algorithm are presented in Fig. 5. In 200 times numerical simulation, BER requirement is set to be 0.0001, $D0$ and $D1$ are randomly selected from 1 m to 100 m, θ is randomly selected from 0° to 180°. The average energy dissipation for SISO, CBF scheme and proposed algorithm are 0.0107 J, 0.0149 J and 0.0099 J, respectively. As can be seen from the

Fig. 5, the proposed algorithm can select an energy efficient scheme from the two schemes.

5 Conclusion

The mathematical expressions of distance thresholds for CBF scheme outperforms the SISO scheme are given. Then, we propose the algorithm to select optimal scheme based on distance thresholds. Numerical results indicate the smaller the BER requirements, the more superiority of CBF scheme will be, and distance thresholds change accordingly. Meanwhile, the effectiveness of our proposed algorithm is validated by numerical results. Note that in this work we only consider a simplified WSNs model under the flat Rayleigh fading channel, a more complex system model can be investigated in our future research.

References

1. Rault, T., Bouabdallah, A., Challal, Y.: Energy efficiency in WSNs: a top-down survey. Comput. Netw. **67**(4), 104–122 (2014)
2. Nguyen, D., Krunz, M.: Cooperative MIMO in wireless networks: recent developments and challenges. IEEE Netw. **27**(4), 48–54 (2013)
3. Cui, S., Goldsmith, A., Bahai, A.: Energy-efficiency of MIMO and cooperative MIMO techniques in sensor networks. IEEE J. Sel. Areas Commun. **22**(6), 1089–1098 (2004)
4. Jayaweera, S.: Virtual MIMO-based cooperative communication for energy-constrained wireless sensor networks. IEEE Trans. Wirel. Commun. **5**(5), 984–989 (2006)
5. Jayaweera, S.: An energy-efficient virtual MIMO architecture based on V-BLAST processing for distributed wireless sensor networks. In: Proceedings of First Annual IEEE Communications Society Conference on Sensor and Ad Hoc Communications and Networks, pp. 299–308 (2004)
6. Fan, J., Yin, Q., Wang, W., Feng, A.: Analysis of energy efficiency for cooperative beamforming in wireless sensor networks. J. Commun. **29**(11), 145–151 (2008)
7. Gai, Y., Zhang, L., Shan, X.: Energy efficiency of cooperative MIMO with data aggregation in wireless sensor networks. In: Proceedings of the 2007 IEEE Wireless Communications and Networking Conference, pp. 791–796 (2007)
8. Gao, Q., Zuo, Y., Zhang, J., Peng, X.: Improving energy efficiency in a wireless sensor network by combining cooperative MIMO with data aggregation. IEEE Trans. Veh. Technol. **59**(8), 3956–3965 (2010)
9. Cui, S., Goldsmith, A., Bahai, A.: Energy-constrained modulation optimization. IEEE Trans. Wirel. Commun. **4**(5), 2349–2360 (2005)

In-Transit Status Perception of Freight Containers Logistics Based on Multi-sensor Information

Qingxia Li, Xiaohua Cao, and Huan Xu[✉]

School of Logistics Engineering, Wuhan University of Technology,
Wuhan, People's Republic of China
983743414@qq.com, 601198999@qq.com, xuhuan0551@163.com

Abstract. Modern logistics requires to percept freight containers in-transit status in real time. However, there is a lack of device which can realize in-transit status perception of freight container logistics, or detect all the essential parameters. This article not only constructs freight container logistics in-transit status perception device architecture based on the Internet of Things technology, but also selects type of Multi-sensor. Then designs interface circuit of perception device from the aspects of logistics routes, container integrity, container internal environment and container door status. Furthermore, this article works out communication protocols combined with Multi-sensor information collection process, develops a Freight Containers Logistics In-Transit Status Perception Device (FCLITSPD). FCLITSPD includes Multi-sensor Module, Positioning Module, Control Module, Communication Module, Status Display and Abnormal Identification Module. Container logistics to achieve by these multi-sensor information visual tracking and security in transit.

Keywords: In-transit status · Freight containers logistics · Status perception · Multi-sensor information

1 Introduction

With the rapid development of globalization, the world's second largest economy, China accounted for a growing share of world trade. Since the reform and opening up of China's import and export trade maintained rapid development, Container transport has been blowout growth [1]. In recent years, special goods, especially perishable goods and dangerous goods traffic is growing [2]. However, due to lack of intelligent monitoring levels and abnormal recognition theory in transit status, China's container logistics accidents, such as the August 10, 2009 in "Hang Lung 518" wheel loader container fall river accident [3]. March 2012 15 "BARELI" container ship ran aground events leading to drowning accidents [4]. In recent years, remote perception and communication technology systems has been developed, but container status detection started late in our country because of container in-transit status detection involves multi-parameter information fusion, heterogeneous networks with complex distal recognition technology, there is no applied to the container logistics in transit status intelligent perception satisfaction program [5]. RFID tag with an electronic seal function, can record door switch

© Springer International Publishing AG 2016
W. Li et al. (Eds.): IDCS 2016, LNCS 9864, pp. 503–512, 2016.
DOI: 10.1007/978-3-319-45940-0_47

frequency and duration of the way of logistics and logistics node implementations door switch reporting, while achieving container automatic identification [6]. Railway freezer stream, usually every 2 h manual thermostat 1 times, especially at night is difficult to ensure the timeliness of the thermostat in transit procedure [7]. The above previous researches used RFID-based container tag and information system for the purpose of detecting containers logistics status, but there was the limit that those researched dealt with multi-sensor information and in-transit status perception. It has a practical signif-icance and urgent necessary for intelligent perception and abnormal identification of Container Logistics in-transit status.

2   In-Transit Status Perception Device Architecture

The freight containers logistics in-transit status perception based on multi-sensor information in this research is depended on IoT, and detects the multi-sensor infor-mation of logistics path and in-transit status(door switch, light intensity, tempera-ture, relative humidity, inclination, velocity and acceleration). Therefore, combined with in-transit container logistics situational awareness needs, this article designs the Freight Containers Logistics In-Transit Status Perception Device (FCLITSPD) archi-tecture [7]. The FCLITSPD consists of Perception Layer, Network Layer and

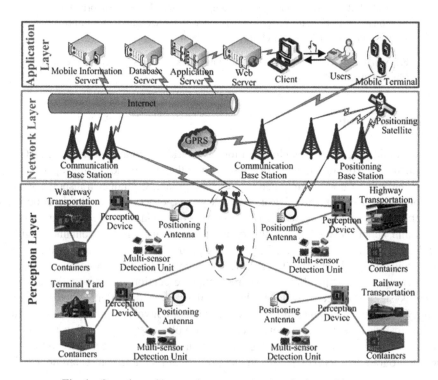

Fig. 1. Overview of in-transit status perception device architecture

Application Layer as its architecture shown in Fig. 1 [8]. Each Function of those layers is shown in detail as follows.

Perception Layer (PL)

- Takes Perception Device (PD) as its main part, which equips not only Multi-sensor Detection Unit (MsDU), but also Positioning Antenna (PA).
- MsDU detects container logistics in-transit status information from different transport mode.
- PA tracks container logistics path and locks its current logistics node.

Network Layer (NL)

- Taken Internet and GPRS as its subjects and as the connecting channel, NL realizes bi-directional communication between PL and AL.
- Transmits information that PL detects to AL, and send AL's commands to PL.
- Achieves the purpose of intelligent perception.

Application Layer (AL)

- Based on Servers and Abnormal Identification Method (AIM), AL visualizes in-transit status information.
- Completes abnormal perception of containers in-transit status simultaneously.
- Early warning according multi-sensor information.

In order to achieve the container in-transit status intelligent perception and realize status abnormal identification based on multi-sensor information, this article designs function block diagram of FCLITSPD shown in Fig. 2, including Multi-sensor Module (MsM), Positioning Module(PM), Control Module (CM), Communication Module (CoM), Status Display and Abnormal Processing Module (SAPM) and Power Module (PoM) [9, 10]. MsM detects container logistics in-transit status parameters, including integrity, environmental and running posture. PM detects status of container logistics path and logistics nodes. CM collects and pre-treats status information, which is detected by MsM and PM. Then CoM sends the container logistics in-transit status information to SAPM. At the same time, CoM receives control commands that are worked out by SAPM; SAPM is used to visualize in-transit status information;

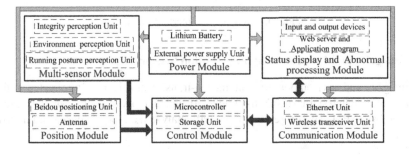

Fig. 2. The function block diagram of FCLITSPD

Meanwhile SAPM displays abnormal result that is percept by abnormal identification method; PM powers each module of FCLITSPD to ensure normal operation.

3 Design of Multi-sensor Interface Circuit

Seen from Fig. 2, FCLITSPD detects various in-transit status, such as door switch, light intensity, temperature, relative humidity, inclination, velocity, acceleration and position. Not only that, multi-sensor information that FCLITSPD detects needs to be transmitted in real time to SAPM. Now that multi-sensor have different interface characteristics, it requires CM possesses a simple interface circuit to achieve the purpose of multi-sensor information detection, meanwhile process and transmit multi-sensor information. Therefore this article chooses microchip technology R&D 8-bit microcontroller PIC18F2525 chip as MCU, with 28 pins and 48K RAM, shown in Fig. 3, interface circuit Fig. 4.

Fig. 3. PIC18F2525 in-kind

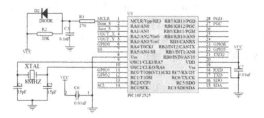

Fig. 4. PIC18F2525 interface circuit

3.1 Integrity and Environmental Perception Sensor

The integrity and environment of container in-transit status is mainly reflected in three aspects, door switch status, inside light intensity and quantity of goods, which is directly provided by SAPM. Therefore, this paper will analyze the type of sensor and interface circuitry.

As is usually, Hall switch is mounted on container door. Under normal circumstances, door is closed, switch dormant; Once door is open, Hall switch outputs microcontroller signal immediately, then the information of door open status is transmitted to SAPM, to achieve door switch status intelligent perception and abnormal identification.

For a long time, integrity of container perception is focused on door switch, light intensity inside container is little used to study container integrity perception. However, it is well known that as sealed container, the light is substantially 0 in-transit, if container is damaged or opened illegally, light intensity inside container will be mutated. Therefore, light inside container is also an important status of integrity.

This article selects light sensor for light intensity detection inside container. When light intensity changes, output of voltage value is dramatic changes, so FCLITSPD uses output voltage value determination light intensity. The integrity & Environmental of the sensor interface circuit shown in Fig. 5.

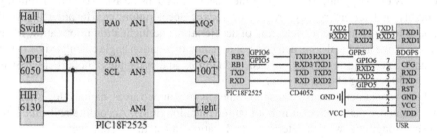

Fig. 5. Diagram of multi-sensor information detection interface circuit

Container in-transit inside the status environment is mainly reflected in three aspects, namely the combustible gas concentration, temperature and relative humidity, following discuss characteristics of three sensor selection.

Because of the diversity of cargo container transport, it requires that sensor can detect a variety of combustible gases with highly sensitivity. MQ-5, with tin oxide (SnO_2) as its core, has high-butane, propane, methane sensitivity and over a wide concentration range with good sensitivity, analog output, and driving circuit is simple, widely applied in industrial combustible gas detection, therefore choose MQ-5 achieve combustible gas detection inside containers.

For the temperature and humidity requirements of goods, especially those dangerous and easy perishable items, in the range of container transportation process more than required, easily lead to damage to the goods or even induced accidents. Choose sensor combination of the basic conditions for article chooses Honeywell digital HIH6130 series HIH6130-021 temperature and humidity sensor temperature and humidity inside the container as a monitoring device. Environmental Perception sensor interface circuit Fig. 5.

3.2   Running Posture and Transport Routes Perception Sensor

The container in transit status running status is mainly reflected in three aspects, namely inclination, speed and acceleration. Speed is detected by PM, inclination and acceleration from the following corresponding 2 aspects.

Due to container logistics remained stable, and the slope of the road up to 10 % (about 5.6°), while container transport vehicles running in the transverse and lateral inclination little change in the way (less than 5.3°), therefore we choose SCA100T-D02 to detect containers inclination when it is smooth running.

SCA100T-D02 works simple, when it is placed horizontally, the default tilt is 0°, this time for zero output; when the sensor is in a certain angle, the sensing element will output the corresponding voltage value based on the detection result, for the analog output. In order to ensure the best characteristics of angle measurement, PIC18F2525 should SCA100T-D02 uses the same power supply voltage, which supply power voltage is 5 V.

When the lateral acceleration is too large, prone to tilting container abnormal, severe cases may even tipping; At the same time, special cargo inside asked container running smoothly, not an emergency braking or sudden acceleration, etc. In order to avoid damage to cargo and better detection of acceleration and inclination information when in motion, we need real-time detection of dynamic inclination angle calculated by using dynamic acceleration. Based on basic conditions and principles, this article selects MPU6050 sensing chip as its core.

Status container in transit transport routes mainly in two areas, namely, logistics and logistics nodes path, reflected in both latitude and longitude. According real-time latitude and longitude, we can determine the location and status of containers.

3.3   Multi-sensor Information Transmission Sensor

This article is designed two kinds of data transmission, respectively, Ethernet and wireless GPRS transmission. When transmission distance is close, Ethernet module realize communication between MCU and abnormal identification center; When in field environment of network, wireless GPRS module achieves microcontroller and abnormal identification center of communication.

3.4   Case Illustration

This article designs a FCLITSPD prototype shown in Fig. 6. FCLITSPD prototype based on multi-sensor, equips PIC18F2525 to detect multi-sensor information and communicate with SAPM through CoM.

Shown as Fig. 7, FCLITSPD prototype detects its inclination characteristic. When container is running smoothly, the inclination max measurement error is −0.12°, relatively error is merely 0.04 at this point, therefore FCLITSPD has excellent characteristic. Anyhow, FCLITSPD measures relevant in-transit status parameters of freight container logistics such as container door switch, light intensity, temperature, relative humidity, inclination, velocity, acceleration and position.

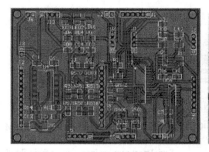

Fig. 6. Outline of FCLITSPD

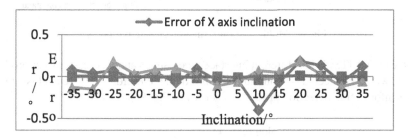

Fig. 7. Outline of FCLITSPD

4   Perception of Multi-sensor Information

As shown in Fig. 7, this article discusses multi-sensor information detection process of FCLITSPD. Now that PM needs 30 s to cold start when FCLITSPD is powered on, firstly initialize microcontroller and start a 30 s timer. When timing out, enable serial port, get ready to receive containers logistics path and node information. At the same time start a 2 s timer, if reception time is over 2 s, containers logistics information collection is failed, failure information will be sent; In the mean time, reset timer and set A/D & MSSP module, then utilize microcontroller ADC module to detect analog information, such as inclination and light intensity; choose I^2C interface & digital I/O to detect digital information, such as door switch, temperature, humidity and acceleration. Finally, send multi-sensor information to SAPM according to communication protocol. Thus SAPM utilizes serial port to send instructions or command to multi-sensor. If instruction is stop detection, then end multi-sensor status perception, waiting for detection command. If there is no stop instruction, restart multi-sensor information detection, start next multi-sensor information detection.

Due to FCLITSPD has different interface types, and it send and receive instructions from SAPM, connected by communication module, therefore next we analysis multi-sensor information detection process, as shown in Fig. 8.

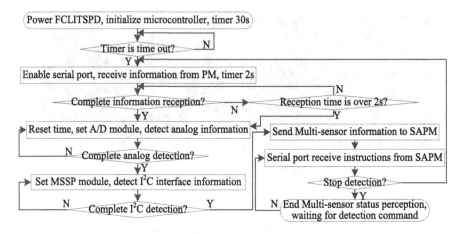

Fig. 8. Multi-sensor information detection process

Due to FCLITSPD has different interface types, sends and receives instructions from SAPM, which connected by communication module, therefore next we analysis multi-sensor information detection process, as shown in Fig. 9.

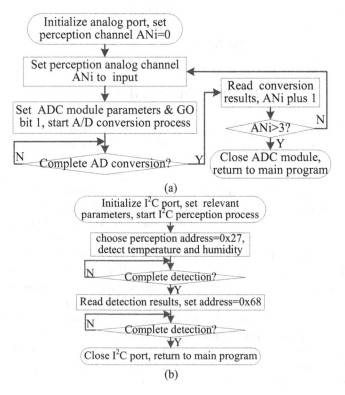

Fig. 9. Analog & I²C information detection process

There are Four kind of analog information need to be detected, so firstly initialize analog port, set perception channel ANi = 0 and set channel ANi be input, then set ADC module parameters, start A/D conversion process. When complete AD conversion, ANi plus 1, restart analog information detection. If ANi > 3, then Close ADC module, return to main program. At the same time, there are two kind of I^2C information need to be perception, so firstly choose address 0x27 to detect temperature and humility. After detection, set address as 0x68 to detect acceleration. If all the I^2C information is detection, close I^2C port, return to main program.

5   Conclusion

In this article we have presented the Freight Containers Logistics In-Transit Status Perception Device (FCLITSPD), an innovative device offering real time multi-sensor information for multimodal transport of container logistics in-transit status by means of continuously detecting on the goods and inside status during transport. Specifically, we focused our attention on in-transit status perception allowing to check the occurrence of as freight containers (e.g., logistics routes, container integrity, container internal environment and container door status), and to realize the visual tracking of freight containers logistics in-transit status.

We have presented an overview of in-transit status perception device architecture, including Perception Layer, Network Layer and Application Layer. FCLITSPD, which is based on IoT, utilizes multi-sensor information, takes advantage of abnormal identification algorithm to accomplish in-transit status perception of freight containers logistics in real time. Internally, multi-sensor interface circuit has been designed from the aspects of container integrity, container internal environment, container door status and logistics path. Further more, this article works out multi-sensor information detection process. Therefore, FCLITSPD is also capable of early-warning when abnormal is identified, while at the same time to ensure the freight container logistics in-transit security.

Acknowledgement. This article is supported by the Science and Technology Support Projects of Hubei Province (No.2014BAA033). The authors will like to express their gratitude to School of Logistics Engineering. The authors greatly acknowledge useful comments and suggestions from the anonymous referees for improving the article. Patents are also derived from the presented work (CN201510459816.5 & ZL201420854059.2).

References

1. Zhong, X.: Analysis of the growth trend of China's port container throughput. Containerization **21**(1), 11–13 (2010)
2. Han, H., Kan, A., Ji, J.: Investigation of monitor-and-control software of marine refrigerated container. In: International Forum on Computer Science-Technology and Applications, pp. 350–353. IEEE (2009)
3. Ke, X.: Exploration and thoughts on railway transport of dangerous goods safety management innovation railway freight, pp. 18 (2015)

4. Wang, H.: Container ship hazardous chemical spills pollution incidents in the marine environment monitoring and emergency - Taking "BARELI" ran a ground accident as an example. Ocean Dev. Manag., 81–87 (2014)
5. Jedermann, R., Pötsch, T., Lloyd, C.: Communication techniques and challenges for wireless food quality monitoring. Philos. Trans. R. Soc. A Math. Phys. Eng. Sci. **372**(2017), 20130304 (2013)
6. Yoon, W.J., Chung, S.H.,Kim, H.P., et al.: Implementation of a 433 MHz active RFID system for U-Port. In: The 9th International Conference on Advanced Communication Technology, pp. 106–109. IEEE (2007)
7. Hou, Y.: railway refrigerated container technology and its application doors, pp. 287–288 (2012)
8. Moon, Y.-S., Jung, J.-W., Choi, S.-P., et al.: Real-time reefer container monitoring system based on IoT. J. Korea Inst. Inf. Commun. Eng. **19**(3), 629–635 (2015)
9. Moon, Y.-S., Choi, S.-P., Lee, E.-K., et al.: Performance evaluation of advanced container security device (ACSD) system based on IoT (Internet of Things). J. Korea Inst. Inf. Commun. Eng. **17**(9), 629–635 (2013)
10. Xiao, X., Li, H., Liu, Y., et al.: Research on safety monitoring and evaluation system of dangerous goods transportation. In: 2011 International Conference on Transportation, Mechanical, and Electrical Engineering (TMEE), pp. 1900–1904 (2011)

A Sliding Window Method for Online Tracking of Spatiotemporal Event Patterns

JunQi Zhang[1]([✉]), ShanWen Zhu[1], Di Zang[1], and MengChu Zhou[1,2]

[1] Key Laboratory of Embedded System and Service Computing,
Ministry of Education, Department of Computer Science and Technology,
Tongji University, Shanghai, China
zhangjunqi@tongji.edu.cn, zhushanwen321@hotmail.com
[2] Department of Electrical and Computer Engineering,
New Jersey Institute of Technology, Newark 07102, USA
zhou@njit.edu

Abstract. Online Tracking of Spatiotemporal Event Patterns (OTSEP) is important in the fields of smart home and Internet of Things (IoT), but difficult to be resolved due to various noises. On account of the strong learning capability in noisy environments, Learning Automaton (LA) has been adopted in the existing literature to notify users once a pattern disappears, and suppress the notification to avoid the distraction from noise if a pattern exists. However, the LA-based models require continuous and identical responses from the environment to jump to another action, which lowers their learning speed especially when the noise level is high. This paper proposes a sliding window method, with which the learning speed is stable in different environments. Experimental results show that the learning accuracy and speed are greatly improved over the existing methods in dynamic and noisy environments.

Keywords: Spatiotemporal event patterns · Sliding window

1 Introduction

Tracking of event patterns is required in many fields. For instance, a smart-home system relies on it to perceive the existence or changes of a user's habit and preference. In [1,2], the event's occurrence is divided into two classes, i.e., "stochastically nonepisodic" and "stochastically episodic". Events in the former happen all the time such as network failures. They follow a known or unknown probability distribution. On the other hand, events in the latter, including earthquake and nuclear explosions, show no pattern and occur in unexpected manners.

Earlier researches focus on the offline mining [3] of the patterns. The studies [4,5] aim at discovering the periodicity of time patterns. However, they fail when the pattern periodicity is beyond a set of predetermined periods. Frequent and Periodic Activities Miner (FPAM) [6,7] can find repetitive patterns without specifying predefined periods.

© Springer International Publishing AG 2016
W. Li et al. (Eds.): IDCS 2016, LNCS 9864, pp. 513–524, 2016.
DOI: 10.1007/978-3-319-45940-0_48

In many cases, pattern appearance and disappearance need to be recognized immediately. Thus, an online learning algorithm is necessary. However, the noisy environment makes it a challenge to track a pattern accurately.

Learning Automaton (LA) [8–10] is a powerful tool that can learn well in a stochastic environment. Due to its online learning mode and robustness, it has been utilized in noisy environments [11,12]. Its procedure can be briefed as follows. At each iteration, an LA sends a chosen action to the stochastic environment. Then it receives a response from the latter. Its state is updated based on this response. It stops when it converges to one action or reaches the maximum iteration count.

Existing literature shows that two LA-based methods can be used to resolve Online Tracking of Spatiotemporal Event Patterns (OTSEP). The first one is Spatiotemporal Pattern Learning Automata (STPLA) [13]. It predefines each potential pattern as a combination of location and time, like { "Mondays at University", "Weekends at Gym"}. To verify each pattern as a hypothesis, a Fixed Structure Stochastic Automaton (FSSA) [14] is adopted to do the hypothesis test. When a pattern disappears, the algorithm is supposed to "notify" the user in time. When a pattern is present, the method should "suppress" the disturbing notification. Therefore "notify" and "suppress" compose the action set of the LA. In [13], the number of states for "notify" is set to be N_1 and that for "suppress" is set to be $N_2 + 1$. If $N_1 = N_2 + 1$, STPLA is of balanced-memory. By tuning N_1 and N_2, STPLA can give "bias" to "notify" or "suppress". Thus STPLA is able to reinforce or weaken the notification probability in general. Experimental results indicate that in both stationary and dynamic environments, STPLA outperforms FPAM [6,7].

STPLA cannot be of both balanced-memory and "bias" toward "notify" or "suppress". Hence, Spatiotemporal Tunable Fixed-Structure Learning Automata (STP-TFSLA) [15] improves it through the replacement of FSSA with Tunable Fixed-Structure Learning Automaton (TFSLA) [16]. By adjusting a new parameter h, it changes the probability of state transition and then indirectly suppresses the notification.

However, the state structure of LA-based methods limits their capability to learn from environments because only continuous and identical response can help the LA escape from the current action. With the increasing noise, their learning speed deteriorates quickly. In addition, the way they tune their bias is not explicit.

This work proposes a new algorithm named as Sliding Window for Online Tracking of Spatiotemporal Event Patterns (SW-OTSEP). By calculating the frequency of a pattern's occurrence in a sliding window, it obtains the estimate of the real probability of a pattern's occurrence. It judges whether a pattern exists by comparing the estimate with a threshold as defined by the user. Its learning speed is quite stable regardless a noise level. Furthermore, by tuning the threshold, it can give bias to "notify" or "suppress" flexibly and explicitly. Experimental results demonstrate that it is as competitive as LA-based methods in stationary environments, and learns more quickly and accurately than them in dynamic environments.

Note that FPAM utilized in [13] is extended with a sliding window instead of the original one [6,7]. It computes the percentage of expected occurrences of an event as the criterion of the acceptance of a pattern and performs worse than STPLA. However, there are two essential differences between it and the sliding window employed in this work. The latter directly computes the frequency of a pattern's occurrence and outperforms both STPLA and STP-TFSLA significantly. Furthermore, its bias toward notification or suppression can be set separately and explicitly, which enables the proposed method to be more robust to noise.

Section 2 analyzes the shortcomings in the existing algorithms. Section 3 presents the proposed SW-OTSEP. Section 4 gives and analyzes the experimental results. Section 5 concludes this paper.

2   The Deficiencies of LA-based Methods

This section analyzes the flaws of the existing LA-based methods, which motivate this work. STP-TFSLA extends STPLA on tunable bias to "suppress" the notification by tuning parameter h. When $h = 0$, STP-TFSLA becomes STPLA. Therefore, only STP-TFSLA is analyzed in this section. In [13,15], both "notify" and "alert" are used to represent the same meaning of reminding a user that the pattern is absent. They are unified in this paper and only "notify" is adopted.

2.1   STP-TFSLA

STP-TFSLA is based on TFSLA and belongs to the FSSA family as represented by

$$< A, B, \Phi, T(\cdot, \cdot), G(\cdot, \cdot) > \tag{1}$$

where $A = \{\alpha_1, \alpha_2, ..., \alpha_r\}$ refers to the action set of an LA. $B = \{\beta_1, \beta_2, ..., \beta_m\}$ is the response set that LA receives from the environment. $\Phi = \{\phi_1, \phi_2, ..., \phi_s\}$ is the internal LA states. $\phi_{t+1} = T(\phi_t, \beta_t)$ is the transition function determining the next state from the current state according to current response as shown in Fig. 1. $G(\phi_t)$ chooses the output action at the current state.

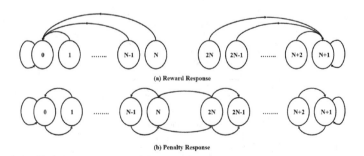

(a) Reward Response

(b) Penalty Response

Fig. 1. State diagram of TFSLA

STP-TFSLA revises T and G in TFSLA to track the spatiotemporal event patterns as follows.

(1) States: $\Phi = \{1, 2, ..., N_1, N_1 + 1, ..., N_1 + N_2 + 1\}$.
(2) Actions: $A = \{Notify,\ Suppress\}$.
(3) Response: $B = \{1, 0\}$ where "1" means reward and "0" means penalty.

Its output function is

$$G = \begin{cases} Notify, & \text{if } \phi_i \in \{1, 2, ..., N_1\} \\ Suppress, & \text{if } \phi_i \in \{N_1 + 1, ..., N_1 + N_2 + 1\}. \end{cases} \quad (2)$$

At instant n, the selected action is $\alpha(n)$ and the response from the environment is $\beta(n)$. Its state transition function is illustrated in Fig. 2 and defined as follows.
if $\beta(n) = 1$

$$\phi(n+1) = \begin{cases} \phi_{k+1}, & \text{if } 1 \le k \le N_1 \\ \phi_{N_1+1}, & \text{if } N_1 + 1 \le k \end{cases} \quad (3)$$

Else if $\beta(n) = 0$ and $r < h$

$$\phi(n+1) = \begin{cases} \phi_{k+1}, & \text{if } 1 \le k \le N_1 \\ \phi_{N_1+1}, & \text{if } N_1 + 1 = k \\ \phi_{k-1}, & \text{if } N_1 + 1 < k \end{cases} \quad (4)$$

Else

$$\phi(n+1) = \begin{cases} \phi_1, & \text{if } 1 \le k \le N_1 \ or\ k = N_1 + N_2 + 1 \\ \phi_{k+1}, & \text{if } N_1 + 1 \le k < N_1 + N_2 + 1 \end{cases} \quad (5)$$

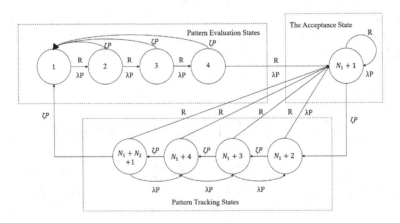

Fig. 2. State transition map and the output function of STP-TFSLA.

Note that r is a random number uniformly sampled from $[0, 1]$. A spatiotemporal event pattern consists of a time primitive and a location primitive. Considering a discrete location primitive set $L = \{l_1, l_2, ..., l_m\}$ and a discrete time primitive set $T = \{t_1, t_2, ..., t_n\}$, the spatiotemporal pattern space can be enumerated. STPLA does not aim at discovering the periodicity of a pattern but judging whether a pattern happens periodically. To do so, STP-TFSLA and STPLA identify each combination as a hypothesis and test each one given a stream of events. The stochastic environment responds to TFSLA with a reward when the event happens and a penalty when it is absent.

STP-TFSLA introduces a parameter h to achieve the bias to "suppress" while maintaining balanced-memory. This parameter can be interpreted as the probability to replace a penalty response with a reward one. It is obvious that a positive h enhances the probability of pattern acceptance. When $h = 0$, STP-TFSLA degenerates to STPLA.

2.2   Flaws of STP-TFSLA

There are three flaws in STP-TFSLA:

(1) The degree of bias cannot be tuned by h explicitly.
(2) The algorithm cannot give bias to "notify".
(3) Its learning speed is limited. State 1 and $N_1 + 1$ are like two black holes that trap LA. Only continuous and identical responses can help LA jump to the states for the other action. For example, given $N_1 = 5$, a stream of responses '111110' enables the action to shift while '111101' cannot.

3   A Sliding Window Method

To overcome the flaws of LA-based methods, this work abandons an LA's structure and introduces a new algorithm named as Sliding Window for Online Tracking of Spatiotemporal Event Patterns, called SW-OTSEP for short. By computing the frequency of an event's occurrence in a sliding window, it gives an estimate of the real probability of an event's occurrence. The estimate at instant n is calculated as:

$$\mu_n = \frac{\sum_{i=n-\omega+1}^{n} X_i}{\omega} \tag{6}$$

where ω is the current size of the sliding window and $1 \leq \omega \leq \omega_{max}$. The result of the observation is:

$$X_i = \begin{cases} 1, & \text{the event happens in the } i\text{th observation} \\ 0, & \text{otherwise} \end{cases} \tag{7}$$

The judgement at instant n is represented by a boolean variable α_n. If the algorithm accepts the pattern, $\alpha_n = 1$. If rejected, $\alpha_n = 0$.

Algorithm 1. SW-OTSEP

1: **BEGIN**
2: Initialize the window size to 1;
3: Initialize α_0 randomly;
4: **while** $n \leq maxIteration$ **do**
5:    **if** $\omega < \omega_{max}$ **then**
6:       $\omega = n$;
7:    **end if**
8:    Calculate μ_n using Eq. (6);
9:    Calculate α_{n+1} using Eq. (9);
10:   **if** $\alpha_{n+1} = 1$ **then**
11:       Accept the pattern hypothesis;
12:       Suppress the notification;
13:   **else**
14:       Reject the pattern hypothesis;
15:       Notify the user;
16:   **end if**
17:   $n = n + 1$
18: **end while**
19: **END**

To tune the bias with more flexibility, two thresholds c_1 and c_2 are introduced. c_1 is used to track the pattern if $\alpha_n = 1$ and c_2 is to judge whether the pattern appears if $\alpha_n = 0$. To summarize:

$$c(\alpha_n) = \begin{cases} c_1, & \alpha_n = 1 \\ c_2, & \alpha_n = 0 \end{cases} \tag{8}$$

Therefore the judgement at instant $n+1$ is:

$$\alpha_{n+1} = \begin{cases} 1, & \mu_n \geq c(\alpha_n) \\ 0, & \mu_n < c(\alpha_n) \end{cases} \tag{9}$$

The procedure is shown in Algorithm 1.

Figures 3, 4 and 5 illustrate this procedure. A window of size 10 is sliding through the event stream, in which the first number is at instant 1. The number "1" represents that the event occurred at the corresponding time while "0" means not. Since each hypothesis is mapped to a specific period, the intervals between every two adjacent numbers are invariant all the time. The estimate is calculated to show the real frequency of the occurrence of an event with a specified period. In Fig. 3, the estimate is 0.8. $c_1 = c_2 = 0.5$. Suppose that the pattern disappears at instant 11, the algorithm needs time to give the correct answer because it has to update the old data in the window. Figure 4 demonstrates the situation that the estimate reaches the critical value of "0.5". All the data in the old environment will be updated starting at instant 20, as shown in Fig. 5. Then the algorithm converges to the new state. It is obvious that the time it costs to

```
1 0 1 1 1 0 1 1 1 1
```

Fig. 3. The event stream of an existing pattern

```
1 0 1 1 1 0 1 1 1 1 0 0 0 0
```

Fig. 4. The event stream of a pattern disappearing after instant 10

```
1 0 1 1 1 0 1 1 1 1 0 0 0 0 0 1 0 0 0 1
```

Fig. 5. The event stream of a pattern disappearing after instant 10

converge to the right action is roughly equal to the window size. It means that this sliding window method learns the variation of a pattern in limited time. This property of our approach can be seen in different noisy environments as shown in the next section.

On the other hand, thresholds c_1 and c_2 control the bias. They represent the degree of accepting a pattern, which is more explicit than parameter h in STP-TFSLA. When c_1 is set to 0.5, the structure is balanced because the acceptance standards for both sides are the same. If c_1 is less than 0.5, it relaxes the demand for a pattern's acceptance and reduces the notification probability. If c_1 is larger than 0.5, it raises the notification probability and tends to deny the existence of a pattern. The difference between c_1 and c_2 is that the former is utilized only under the acceptance of a pattern while the latter works in the opposite situation. Since user can tune two thresholds separately to affect the notification probability in different circumstances, it is evident that the proposed method is more flexible.

4   Experiments

4.1   Experimental Setting

In [13], omission error is defined as that an event is supposed to happen in a regular pattern but does not. Inclusion error is defined as that no event is supposed to take place in no regular pattern but an event occurs. Both are utilized to describe the noise of the environment. Their probabilities are q and p respectively.

The first experiment tests the algorithm performance in stationary environments. The second one investigates the adaptivity of SW-OTSEP in dynamic environments. Furthermore, the significance of window size is inspected.

4.2 Performance After Convergence

This set of experiments tests the performance of STP-TFSLA and SW-OTSEP for 10000 times with 5000 iterations each. The parameters of STP-TFSLA are set according to [15]. For SW-OTSEP, the maximum window size is set to be $\omega_{max} = 40$.

First of all, their performance under the balanced mode is demonstrated in Tables 1 and 2. Both show extraordinary performance in learning accuracy.

Table 1. Notification probability in regular pattern

Algorithms	$q = 0.2$	$q = 0.1$	$q = 0.05$
SW-OTSEP	0.000	0.000	0.000
STP-TFSLA	0.000	0.000	0.000

Table 2. Notification probability in no pattern

Algorithms	$p = 0.2$	$p = 0.1$	$p = 0.05$
SW-OTSEP	1.000	1.000	1.000
STP-TFSLA	1.000	1.000	1.000

The results owing to different c_1 and c_2 are listed in Table 3. To clarify the performance, the parameters are set as $c_1 = c_2$ and the noise is enhanced to $q = 0.4$ and $p = 0.4$. The notification probability increases with the parameters shifting from 0.3 to 0.7 no matter if the pattern exists or not. When the parameters are set larger than 0.5, the algorithm tends to notify the user more. When they are lower than 0.5, the notification is suppressed. The meaning of c_1 and c_2 is comprehensible because it represents the user's estimate of a pattern. They can be set separately to tune the bias more accurately.

Table 3. Notification probability with different c_1 and c_2

Algorithms	c_1	c_2	$q = 0.4$	$p = 0.4$
SW-OTSEP	0.3	0.3	0.000	0.108
	0.4	0.4	0.005	0.518
	0.5	0.5	0.097	0.904
	0.6	0.6	0.482	0.994
	0.7	0.7	0.892	1.000

4.3 Performance in Dynamic Environment

To simulate the spatiotemporal event patterns changing from time to time, our environment switches between the absence and presence of a pattern every

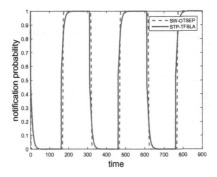

Fig. 6. Comparison between STP-TFSLA and SW-OTSEP under $p = q = 0.05$.

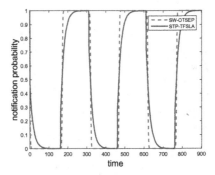

Fig. 7. Comparison between STP-TFSLA and SW-OTSEP under $p = q = 0.1$.

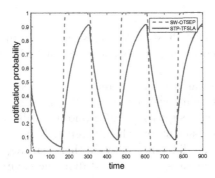

Fig. 8. Comparison between STP-TFSLA and SW-OTSEP under $p = q = 0.2$.

150 iterations. The total iteration count is set to 900 and the experiment is conducted for 10000 times. Both algorithms are tuned unbiased. Figure 6 shows that when the noise from the environment is small, their notification probability converges. The convergence speed of SW-OTSEP is slightly faster than STP-TFSLA's. The result from Fig. 7 is similar to that from Fig. 6. However the

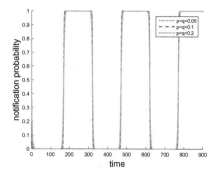

Fig. 9. Learning speed of SW-OTSEP under different noise strength.

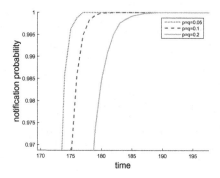

Fig. 10. Learning speed of SW-OTSEP under different noise strength.

convergence speed of STP-TFSLA decreases evidently. In Fig. 8, STP-TFSLA suffers from a strong noisy environment while SW-OTSEP performs almost the same as before.

SW-OTSEP's performance in different environments is demonstrated in Fig. 9. To clarify the stability, we zoom in Fig. 9 to have Fig. 10. The window size is set to 40, and the noise is set to 0.05, 0.1 and 0.2 while $p = q$. In Fig. 9, three curves are quite close to each other. The differences between their learning speed are small while almost no difference between their learning accuracy is observed even in Fig. 10. Its robustness in noisy and dynamic environments is evidently shown.

4.4 Effect of Window Size

In this experiment, we illustrate how the window size affects the learning speed and accuracy. The maximum window size $\omega_{max} = 10, 20, 30$ and 40. A balanced structure $c_1 = c_2 = 0.5$ is utilized. Both p and q are set to be 0.2 and the experiment is conducted in the same dynamic environment given above. Figure 11 shows the results.

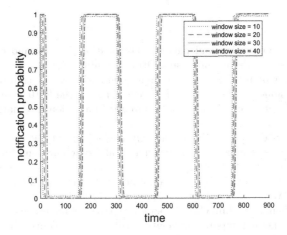

Fig. 11. Comparison between different window sizes under $p = q = 0.2$.

It is clear that a small window size accelerates SW-OTSEP's convergence speed while a large window size converges to a more accurate result. For example, in Fig. 11 the pattern disappears at instant 150. When the window size $\omega = 40$, it converges at instant 190 in average. When $\omega = 10$, it converges at instant 160 in average. The relationship between window size and learning accuracy is also revealed. Comparing the circumstances with $\omega = 20$, 30 and 40, Fig. 11 shows that the differences are almost invisible. Therefore, tuning the window size makes a trade-off between learning speed and accuracy.

5   Conclusions and Future Work

This paper presents a sliding window method for online tracking of spatiotemporal event patterns, which overcomes the flaws of existing LA-based methods. It learns stably in different noisy environments. Meanwhile, it can give bias to either "suppress" or "notify" action more flexibly than the existing ones. Experimental results show that it well outperforms the existing ones in dynamic environments in terms of convergence speed and accuracy.

Future work will focus on optimizing the space and time complexity of the algorithm and discovering the periodicity of spatiotemporal event patterns online.

Acknowledgement. This work is supported by China NSF under Grants No. 61572359, 61272271 and 61332008, US NSF under Grant No. CMMI-1162482, and partly supported by the Fundamental Research Funds for the Central Universities of China (No. 0800219332, 1012015115).

References

1. Bellinger, C.: Simulation and pattern classification for rare and episodic events. Master's thesis, Carleton University, Ottawa, Ontario (2010)
2. Bellinger, C., Oommen, B.J.: On simulating episodic events against a background of noise-like non-episodic events. In: Proceedings of the 2010 Summer Computer Simulation Conference. Society for Computer Simulation International, pp. 452–460 (2010)
3. Ma, S., Hellerstein, J.L.: Mining partially periodic event patterns with unknown periods. In: Proceedings of 17th International Conference on Data Engineering, 2001. IEEE, pp. 205–214 (2001)
4. Youngblood, G.M., Cook, D.J.: Data mining for hierarchical model creation. IEEE Trans. Syst. Man Cybern. Part C **37**(4), 561–572 (2007)
5. Lee, C.H., Chen, M.S., Lin, C.R.: Progressive partition miner: an efficient algorithm for mining general temporal association rules. IEEE Trans. Knowl. Data Eng. **15**(4), 1004–1017 (2003)
6. Rashidi, P., Cook, D.J.: Keeping the intelligent environment resident in the loop. In: 2008 IET 4th International Conference on Intelligent Environments, pp. 1–9. IET, July 2008
7. Rashidi, P., Cook, D.J.: Keeping the resident in the loop adapting the smart home to the user. IEEE Trans. Syst. Man Cybern. Part A Syst. Hum. **39**(5), 949–959 (2009)
8. Thathachar, M.A.L., Oommen, B.J.: Automata Theory and the Modelling of Biological Systems. Academic, New York (1973)
9. Poznyak, A.S., Najim, K.: Learning Automata and Stochastic Optimization. Springer, Berlin (1997)
10. Thathachar, M.A., Sastry, P.S.: Networks of Learning Automata: Techniques for Online Stochastic Optimization. Springer Science & Business Media, New York (2011)
11. Oommen, B.J., Hashem, M.K.: Modeling a student-classroom interaction in a tutorial-like system using learning automata. IEEE Trans. Syst. Man Cybern. Part B Cybern. **40**(1), 29–42 (2010)
12. Huang, D.S., Jiang, W.: A general CPL-AdS methodology for fixing dynamic parameters in dual environments. IEEE Trans. Syst. Man Cybern. Part B Cybern. **42**(5), 1489–1500 (2012)
13. Yazidi, A., Granmo, O.C., Oommen, B.J.: Learning-automaton-based online discovery and tracking of spatiotemporal event patterns. IEEE Trans. Cybern. **43**(3), 1118–1130 (2013)
14. Narendra, K.S., Thathachar, M.A.: Learning Automata: An Introduction. Courier Corporation, North Chelmsford (2012)
15. Jiang, W., Zhao, C.L., Li, S.H., Chen, L.: A new learning automata based approach for online tracking of event patterns. Neurocomputing **137**, 205–211 (2014)
16. Jamalian, A.H., Iraji, R., Sefidpour, A.R., Manzuri-Shalmani, M.T.: Examining the ε-optimality property of a tunable FSSA. In: 6th IEEE International Conference on Cognitive Informatics, Lake Tahoo, CA, pp. 169–177 (2007)

Author Index

Printed in the United States
By Bookmasters